VARIETIES OF SEXUAL EXPERIENCE

Varieties of Sexual Experience

Psychosexuality in Literature

NORMAN KIELL

INTERNATIONAL UNIVERSITIES PRESS, INC.
New York

Library of Congress Cataloging in Publication Data

Kiell, Norman.
     Varieties of sexual experience.

     Includes bibliographies and index.
     1. Sex in literature.   I. Title.
PN56.S5K5   809'.933'53   74-21187
ISBN 0-8236-6725-1

Manufactured in the United States of America

For Hilary and Jon
As They Start Out

CONTENTS

Acknowledgments

I wish to acknowledge my debt to Irene Azarian of International Universities Press for providing the encouragement for my writing this book. I am so indebted to the Ms. Susan Alessi, Betty Klein, Carol Letson, Claire Paroff, and Francine Scheier, all staff members of the Merrick, Long Island, Library, for their graciousness, good humor, and willingness to secure novels and references for me that I am beyond words. It is a genuine pleasure to express my debt to them. And finally, and most of all, I am thankful to my wife, my friend, my sweetheart, Adele.

Merrick, N.Y.
May 30, 1976

Introduction

All of us are travelers in what John Bunyan called the wilderness of this world. In the last two decades we began to travel and explore more openly some of the byways as well as the highways of the sexual wilderness of our lives. Perhaps this book will give some help in understanding the roads we have taken.

I have been concerned with the paths to insight that enrich the scientific approach. The scientist isolates the variables. The artist, on the other hand, glimpses human events in their complex totality.

I have attempted a synthesis of psychosexuality and fiction. While hundreds of articles dot the psychological and literary journals dealing with each of these, nowhere is there a single volume that describes in sustained and systematic fashion the principles of the psychology of sex and illustrates these principles by fictional passages. Inasmuch as fiction borrows from reality, the lines of psychology and literature inevitably and invariably intersect.

Case histories can be terribly dull, and in the hands of most psychiatrists they generally are. Every effort has been bent, in this book, to avoid clinical drabness as well as literary pornography. Psychoanalysis and literature have been closely linked ever since Freud borrowed from Sophocles a name for the most famous of his discoveries: the Oedipus complex. In the early days of psychoanalysis, when Freud was attempting to formulate and corroborate his far-reaching concepts about the nature of man and the actual clinical material at his disposal was still severely limited, he turned respectfully to the analysis of masterworks of art and literature and to the lives of exceptionally

1

creative people. He believed that great works of art and literature contained universal psychological truths. In his interpretation of Jensen's novel *Gradiva,* Freud (1907, pp. 43-44) wrote of the creative writer, "The description of the human mind is indeed the domain which is most his own; he has from time immemorial been the precursor of science, and so too of scientific psychology ... the creative writer cannot evade the psychiatrist nor the psychiatrist the creative writer."

How true. Fictional characters can be understood analytically as if the novels in which they appear were the life histories of real people. The novel is, in a sense, like a theory; its author is attempting to tell us how people "really" behave and to a degree why they behave the way they do. Barchilon and Kovel (1966) have put it well: "The message which the pre-Freudian novels and plays contained waited for ages before it could be decoded and formulated. The post-Freudian writers and artists have listened to psychoanalysis, consciously and unconsciously, and are still speaking loudly. Even though most of them have little to say that is original or creative, they could still offer us some precious clue. But, more important, there are always those few who, unencumbered by some of our scientific requirements, are using their intuitive powers to soar ahead of us and the rest of mankind. As analysts we cannot afford to overlook what these precursors are saying. No matter how difficult this may be, we must guess as best we can at their names and ask: What are the intuitions of the Camuses, Joyces, the Becketts, Millers, Ionescos, the Genets, telling us which we have not yet understood, let alone conceptualized?" (pp. 812-813).

The novelist's creative disposition, arrived at intuitively, frequently matches and surpasses the scientific expertise of the psychiatrist. For example, the discovery of the relationship between literature and his own psychological work was an important element in Robert Coles's growth during his years in the South. Near the end of his book (1972), he reported that the medical and psychiatric tenets he had never before doubted were insufficient to the task before him. "I have learned to draw upon a book like Ellison's *Invisible Man* instead of a book called *The Mark of Oppression,* which offers 'in depth' — of course! —psychiatric case studies of the Negro. I have learned that one does not have to be a political or a social or philosophical 'romantic' to comprehend and appreciate the truth that binds a Faulkner to a Tolstoy, an Agee to a Bernanos, a Simone Weil to an Orwell" (pp. 21-22).

Surely it is not merely by chance that Freud, in his great classical case histories—Dora, Little Hans, the Rat Man, and the Wolf Man—wrote with a vividness, a subtlety, a fluency, and a flair for organization very similar to those of a great novelist, and which won for him the Goethe Prize for Literature. In his *Studies on Hysteria* (Freud and Breuer, 1895, p. 160), he noticed the similarities of his case histories to fiction: "it still strikes me myself as strange that the case histories I write should read like short stories and that, as one might say, they lack the serious stamp of science. I must console myself with the reflection that the nature of the subject is evidently responsible for this, rather than any preference of my own." Nor is it by chance that it was said of William James that, whereas his brother Henry wrote like a psychologist, he, the psychologist, wrote like a novelist (Hofling, 1966).

I have not gone to Roth or Rabelais simply for evidence about sexual life as it exists or has existed. What I have tried to do is state accepted psychological theories about sexual behavior as found in the works of serious scientists, and demonstrate the validity and reliability of their thinking through the work of the creative writer. The rationale for the book, if rationale is needed, is as much psychological as intellectual. So much trash has been written about sex, in the names of both psychology and fiction, that some modifying temperateness may be helpful.

The economy or intensity of many of the literary passages selected to illustrate points of psychological portent may give the reader some intimation of how literature seizes life. These selections represent, naturally, my bias, the scope of my reading—and the latitude of publishers concerning reprint rights. It is hardly to be expected that the choice of all the fictional excerpts will meet with universal approval. For instance, I do not enjoy so-called black humor and, with the exception of a brief sentence or two from Heller's *Catch-22,* nothing from this genre by others, such as Joyce Cary or Donleavy or Vonnegut, will be found here. And after reading some hundreds of novels, looking for appropriate material, I could not always face up to rereading a *Daniel Deronda,* particularly after having read *Desperate Remedies, Pamela, Clarissa,* and books of a similar vein.

There were other problems. As I completed a chapter and was in the midst of writing another, I frequently came across passages from a novel which I thought would fit splendidly in the previously finished chapters. The point to be made is that there are undoubtedly other and perhaps more appropriate excerpts that could be used, and the reader is welcome to make his own substitutions. In the matter of psychological data, I found to my peril that psychology is now so closely linked with social, ethical, religious, and legal issues that, after having completed my chapter on abortion in May 1973, the Supreme Court ruling the next month dated much of what I had to say. I began to rewrite, only to find that a vigorous movement was alive in the land working for a constitutional amendment to wipe out the Court's ruling. I decided not to include the chapter at all, for who knew what the morrow would bring?

In medicine and psychiatry today, new problems and moral questions have arisen that previous generations found unnecessary to consider—simply because they did not exist. Hospital abortion is now regarded as a relatively inexpensive and safe procedure, carrying an infinitesimal mortality rate. This was not always true, but in the modern context it is, and must be dealt with. Social responsibility in the modern usage of the term—responsibility to a community, not just to an individual—is something comparatively new to medicine. The new morality about sex has thrown whole cultures into confusion, looking for guidelines from psychologists and psychiatrists.

We tend to think that sexual behavior is what it morally ought to be. Kinsey's (1948) pioneering work showed it for what it is, but largely in statistical rather than human terms. What makes today's sexual "freedom" so urgent a matter is that it may well be a symptom of people's need to come closer to one another, of their uncertainties, their anxieties, and their fright. As a result of such feelings, some are pulling down the shades and cursing anything new or different; others are, in the best sense, unnerved, puzzled, questioning.

The mammoth sale of self-help sex manuals in recent years may reflect a growing nationwide anxiety about sexual performance and suggests that many people are unsure of themselves in this area of life—and also that they wish to please. It may be a rather wistful readership, including many who do not enjoy themselves sexually, but hope to. Perhaps our native ethos requires that we know what sexual experience other Americans are having, just as it is our duty to know what cars or stereos they buy. Still other sex manual readers might be seeking an external authority that will sanction particular desires: they want to be told that their own tastes are normal. Many are convinced that others are doing brilliantly in bed, that almost everyone is much more talented than they are, until they read the book and realize that the majority of people are not as well off as they. Still others want to be reassured that sex is as shallow and dull as everything else in their lives and that they are not really missing so much. And there are the dedicated narcissists who are so proud of their skill that they must make certain that there is nothing they do not know, while still others use the books as a substitute for sex, as a stand-in for any activity at all.

Hunt's (1974) report on sexual behavior in the 1970's, based on data supplied by the Research Guild, indicates that the United States is experiencing a sexual liberation movement. Since Kinsey's census of American sexual behavior, there have been dramatic increases in the frequency with which most Americans engage in various sexual activities and in the number of persons who include formerly rare or forbidden techniques in their sexual repertoires. The Research Guild's survey studied the sexual attitudes and behavior of 2,026 individuals in twenty-four cities and suburbs, re-examining most of the data amassed by Kinsey and thus providing measurements of change. Some of the key findings indicate that premarital sex has become acceptable and widespread, with the predominant change noted in females, an indication of the virtual abandonment of the double standard. Oral sex is more widely used than heretofore, as is heterosexual anal intercourse, and there is a considerable increase in the variety of coital techniques. Rates of orgasm for females have increased along with frequency of intercourse. Homosexuality has not increased in incidence, although it has in visibility. "The border between the showable and the unshowable, the printable and the unprintable, had practically disappeared.... Even in respectable literary works, descriptions of sex acts ceased to be poetically allusive and indirect. Novels by such writers as Philip Roth and John Updike began to include clinically graphic scenes of masturbation, fellatio, cunnilingus, buggery ... and intercourse of such explicitness that Lady Chatterly seemed second cousin to Heidi..." (Hunt, 1974. p. 197).

Sexual aberrations occur in people with differing psychic structures, and the same sexual act may have a significantly different meaning and function according to the personality. The erotic expression of the sexual deviant is an essential feature of his psychic stability, and much of his life revolves around it. McDougall (1972, p. 371) explained that, "In the long run it is no simple matter to designate what is and what is not perverse. And even so, it is easier to define what we mean by a perversion than what we mean by a pervert. Freud early drew attention to the fact that we are all perverts under the skin, where the pervert-polymorph childish parts of ourselves are hidden. It follows from this that activities which are commonly regarded as perverse — voyeurism, fetishism, exhibitionism, interest in a diversity of possible erotic zones — all might form part of the experience of a normal love relation."

Sex is best understood in the light of, and as a result of, a total life. The individual's sexual life, as reflected in the areas covered in this book — masturbation, coital experiences, homosexuality, group sex, the primal scene, and so on — help shape his personality, and vice versa. While the subjects dealt with in the book do not alone shape one's sexuality, they do represent very special and very important aspects of life. I have tried to deal with a number of aspects of sexuality and literature which have not always had the attention they perhaps merit: olfactory eroticism, anal eroticism, phallic women, the primal scene, drugs and sex, transsexualism and transvestism, among others. Only two chapters refer to acting-out character structures: those dealing with users of the hallucinogens and narcotics. These clinical categories have something in common with sexual deviation and may be different methods of solving the same basic unconscious conflicts, but they lack the specific quality of conscious erotization of defenses.

REFERENCES

Barchilon, J. & Kovel, J. S. (1966), *Huckleberry Finn:* A psychoanalytic study. *Journal of the American Psychoanalytic Association,* 14:775-814.

Coles, R. (1972), *Farewell to the South.* Boston: Little, Brown.

Freud, S. (1907), Delusions and dreams in Jensen's *Gradiva. Standard Edition,* 9:1-95. London: Hogarth Press, 1959.

———— & Breuer, J. (1895), Studies on hysteria. *Standard Edition,* 2:1-305. London: Hogarth Press, 1955.

Hofling, C. K. (1966), The place of great literature in the teaching of psychiatry. *Bulletin of the Menninger Clinic,* 30:368-373.

Hunt, M. (1974), *Sexual Behavior in the 1970's.* Chicago: Playboy Press.

Kinsey, A. C., Pomeroy, W. B. & Martin, C. E. (1948), *Sexual Behavior in the Human Male.* Philadelphia: Saunders.

McDougall, J. (1972), Primal scene and sexual perversion. *International Journal of Psycho-Analysis,* 53:371-384.

CHAPTER ONE

The Primal Scene

The primal scene, witnessed, or thought to be witnessed, by a child, is the dramatic quintessence of all oedipal and castration fears, and can be a shockingly traumatic event.

It is the revival of the primal scene that results in the greatest resistance encountered in psychoanalytic practice. "Horror of the primal scene may be considered more basic than the dread of incest, which itself is largely derived from the former. In the main, it is sadism directed toward the heterosexual parent, viewed by the child as betraying him, which accounts for this horror of the primal scene" (Fairbairn, 1956, p. 113). In the novel, *The Sexton Women* by Richard Neely (1972), John Sexton returns home after an absence of five years to find his father married to a woman twenty years his junior. John hates his father, wants to sleep with his stepmother and does. On arriving home, he reminisces, "I remembered myself as a kid, getting up to go to the bathroom and hearing my mother's voice keening down the hall: 'Tom, please. Easy, Tom. Please, Tom, *please!*' A receptacle, battered but not quite broken. God, how she must have hated him. She had to have hated him. *Had to!*" (p. 47). Later he visits the empty house he had grown up in as a boy. "A sudden revulsion turned me away. I could almost hear his surly voice echoing through the crumbling walls. I didn't want to see my bedroom, and I didn't want to see my brother's. Especially I didn't want to see where my mother had slept with the man who had abused her" (p. 72). John is prompted to attempt to murder his father, first chloroforming him and then burning the house down with his father in it. "I was struck by an odd thought: I had wanted to destroy that house almost as much as I had wanted to destroy my father. It had belonged to him ... and he had corrupted it" (p. 90).

Freud (1916-1917, p. 214) defined the primal scene as "the observation of sexual scenes between adults, especially between parents." Nunberg (1955, p. 256) called it "An experience of very early childhood, be it a traumatic real experience or a fantasy of traumatic intensity. Witnessing parental intercourse, whether in reality or in fantasy, is considered to be the most frequent traumatic primal scene." According to McDougall's (1972, p. 372) elegant definition, it "connotes the child's total store of unconscious knowledge and personal mythology concerning the human sexual relation, particularly that of his parents."

The concept of "primal repression" occupies an uncertain niche in psychoanalytic psychology (Frank and Muslin, 1967). The relation between past and present—between what is forgotten in childhood and what endures and reappears in the adult in the guise of character, symptoms, screen memories, and transferences—continues to occupy a central position in psychoanalytic interest (Frank, 1969). In writing on the development of Freud's concept of primal repression, Frank and Muslin indicated that in 1895-1896, Freud considered the deferred adult neuroses as arising out of early trauma in a more comprehensive way. He proposed in a series of papers (Freud, 1896a, 1896b, 1896c, 1898) that the specific etiology of both hysteria and obsessional neurosis involved incidents of actual sexual stimulation during childhood, the memories of which were revived by sexual excitement following puberty: *"The traumas of childhood operate in a deferred fashion as though they were fresh experiences; but they do so unconsciously"* (Freud, 1896b, p. 167n). Not long afterward, Freud, upon his discovery of normal infantile sexuality and the Oedipus complex which gave new and universal relevance to infantile sexual memories, abandoned the childhood seduction theory. "With the development of topographical concepts and the elaboration of the phenomena of energy transference and the primary and secondary processes, Freud could propose an integrated and comprehensive theory of repression" (Frank and Muslin, 1967, p. 57) brought about by the psychic forces of loathing, shame, and moral and esthetic ideal demands.

According to Freud, primitive infantile processes exert an undue influence on rational behavior; the existence of these processes is largely unknown to the subject; they account for a variety of phenomena, including dreams—what Freud termed "the psychopathology of everyday life," the dynamics of jokes, and neurotic symptomatology; finally, some connection exists between later mental events and processes and those primitive processes which cannot be discerned by ordinary introspection or observation. It was not until 1915 that Freud first used the term "primal repression." "We have reason to assume that there is a *primal repression,* a first phase of repression, which consists in the psychical (ideational) representative of the instinct being denied entrance into the conscious. With this a *fixation* is established; the representative in question persists unaltered from then onwards and the instinct remains attached to it" (Freud, 1915a, p. 148).

Subsequently, Freud (1926) presented primal repression as existing from the time of its onset as an active, defensive, responsive process. Thus the earliest repressions constitute an active process stimulated by an economic factor, i.e., the overwhelming of the ego by excitation. Frank and Muslin's (1967, p. 74) interpretation of Freud's 1926 formulation is that active primal repression cannot begin until the preconscious state exists. Primal repression is associated with the stable establishment of the danger-situation signal-anxiety sequence for any given situation of instinctual overstimulation. Schachtel (1947) stated that childhood amnesia may be due to a formation of the memory functions which makes them unsuitable to accommodate childhood experience, rather than exclusively to a censor repressing objectionable material which, without such repression, could and would be remembered. Eissler (1962) applied the concept of primal repression in its most concrete form: it refers to that within the mental apparatus which has never been conscious.

Freud (1916-1917, p. 71) believed that primal scene fantasies are a phylogenetic possession. "In them the individual reaches beyond his own experience into primeval experience at points where his own experience has been too rudimentary. It seems to me quite possible that all that today is narrated in analysis in the form of fantasy, seduction in childhood, stimulation of sexual excitement upon observation of parental coitus, the threat of castration—or rather, castration itself— was in prehistoric periods of the human family a reality; and that the child in its fantasy simply fills the gaps in its true individual experiences with true prehistoric experiences. We have again and again been led to suspect that more knowledge of the primordial forms of human development is stored up for us in the psychology of the neuroses than in any other field we may explore."

This perhaps can be seen in the work of the Laureate of Nonsense, Edward Lear. As a form of the comic, nonsense was not only an amusement, it surreptitiously served Lear's deep-seated emotional needs. He painted and composed poems that illustrate pregenital sexual impulses, and the bulk of his work contains disguised reproductions of the primal scene. It was through his nonsense that Lear discharged powerful tensions and anxieties. A ten-sentence story for children, accompanied by ten pen-and-ink line drawings, together with other short stories, poems, limericks, and biographical data formed the basis for Barker's (1966) interpretation of the alliterative and invented nonsense words Lear delighted in using. Lear was the twentieth of twenty-one children born to his mother over a twenty-five year period. After an early period of affluence his father was imprisoned for many years for bankruptcy. While the mother brought her husband seasonal delicacies each day, the son was raised by an older sister. The story on which Barker partially built his case is entitled "The Adventures of Mr. Lear, the Polly and the Pusseybite," and reads as follows:

The Polly and the Pusseybite

Mr. Lear goes out a walking with Polly and the Pusseybite. Mr. Lear, feeling tired, and also the Polly and the Pusseybite, sit down on a wall to rest. Mr. Lear, the Polly and the Pusseybite go into a shop to buy a Numbrella, because it began to rain. Mr. Lear, the Polly and the Pusseybite having purchased umbrellas, proceed on their walk. Mr. Lear, the Polly and the Pusseybite arrive at a bridge, which being broken they do not know what to do. Mr. Lear, the Polly and the Pusseybite all tumble promiscuous into the raging river and become quite wet. Mr. Lear, the Polly and the Pusseybite pursue their journey in a benevolent boat. Mr. Lear, the Polly and the Pusseybite incidentally fall over an unexpected cataract, and are all dashed to atoms. The venerable Jebusites fasten the remains of Mr. Lear, the Polly and the Pusseybite together, but fail to reconstruct them perfectly as three individuals. Mr. Lear, and the Polly and the Pusseybite and the two Jebusites and the Jerusalem Artichokes and the Octagonal Oysterclippers all tumble into a deep hole and are never seen or distinguished or heard of never more afterwards [Lear, 1866, pp. 50-54].

The theme of abandonment, desolation, and hoped-for reunion is marked in this and other Lear works, and probably stems from the time the baby Edward was evicted from the parental bedroom to make room for his younger sister, Charlotte. These feelings were reactivated at puberty when his father was jailed. But what is the evidence that Lear witnessed the primal scene, Barker (1966) asks. In the poem, "The Dong with the Luminous Nose," "The Jumblies dancing in circles all night" refers quite probably to the parents in the act of sexual intercourse. "The plaintive pipe of the lively Dong" alludes to Lear's own sexual excitement. When the morning came he was still gazing, still trying to cope with what he had seen, heard, and felt. Yet he was left dumbfounded; what little sense he once possessed, he tells us, had now quite gone out of his head. In rage and desolation he felt obliged thenceforward to repudiate his mother—the bad mother— and to search forever for the good mother, the asexual one. Another hint pointing to an unintegrated primal-scene experience was his recollection of childhood, " 'my imperfect sight in those days . . . formed everything into a horror.' " Why a "horror" instead of, say, a "blur"? Lear's way of putting it strongly suggests that something he had seen was terrifying. Also, there is his statement that " 'I feel woundedly like a spectator all through my life of what goes on amongst those I know' . . . one of Lear's most poignant feelings at the time of the primal-scene experience" (Barker, 1966, pp. 577, 580).

The catastrophe befallen Mr. Lear, the Polly, and the Pusseybite on their stroll, in which their bodies are put back together again but are mismatched, reflects an aspect of the primal scene to which Edward had been exposed. "It poses the specific question of where, in the sexual act, the body of one parent leaves off and that of the other begins; and it betrays Lear's guilt-laden wish to have been a part of what went on in his parents' bed. . . . What is predominantly reflected here . . . is a propensity to distort the body-image . . . not only as a projection of the erotic tumescence of Lear's penis and of the body parts which symbolically represent it, but in a more general way the distortion felt by the whole body in a state of dammed-up libido. From the standpoint of affect, the primal scene was painfully intolerable; in terms of its perceptual and ideational content its fascination was exceeded only by its shocking imcomprehensibility. His eyes, his ears, and his sexual excitement pushed him toward a true assessment of what was going on between his parents. His strong wish to deny his parents' sexuality and his own disturbing erotic sensations, his jealous rage, and his fright, forced him to try to deny its implications. Result — a tormenting and unshakable doubt. The primal-scene experience brought about a sudden and overwhelming flood of sexual excitation, far too intense to be successfully repressed or adequately integrated. Lear was obliged to resort to unstable defenses, and unstable identifications.... As a re-enactment of the primal scene, the nonsense production served two main purposes. In the first place, it was a way of expressing — or reliving — something forbidden, something traumatic, but which nevertheless had a considerable mischievous pleasurable component. This aspect can be thought of as a contribution of the id. Secondly, the nonsense served a defensive function by blunting the original raw affect, and by modifying the ideational content in such a way as to make it unobjectionable, even pleasurable — an ego contribution" (Barker, 1966, pp. 581-583).

"It is not at all impossible," wrote Freud (1916-1917, p. 369), "for a small child, while he is not yet credited with possessing an understanding or a memory, to be a witness of the sexual act between his parents or other grown-up people;... and the possibility cannot be rejected that he will be able to understand and react to the impression *in retrospect.*" It is an occurrence, Freud added, that is continually repeated in the story of a neurotic's childhood, seems hardly ever absent, and is worthy of special attention. During one of his bouts with a depressive reaction in a mental institution, Humbert Humbert in *Lolita* (Nabokov, 1955) was sophisticated enough about psychoanalysis to discover an endless source of robust enjoyment in trifling with the psychiatrists by teasing "them with fake primal scenes" (p. 34). Two swinging couples in John Updike's (1968, pp. 161-162) novel of adultery, *Couples,* develop a pattern of quarrel and reunion, of revulsion and surrender, of fencing with each other deliberately as if with poisoned foils.

"Did you ever see," Harold asked, as they sat around the round grease-stained leather table, "your parents making love?"

"Never. The nearest thing to it, some Sunday mornings the door to their bedroom would be locked."

"Dear Janet," Marion said. "Poor dear Janet. Tiptoeing in her

Sunday-school dress down that long silent hall and pushing, pushing at that locked door."

In *The Married Lovers* by Julius Horwitz (1973), Anne has led an unsatisfying sexual and marital life. Her husband, David, is in a mental hospital following an unsuccessful suicide attempt upon learning of Anne's orgiastic adulteries. The couple find it difficult, if not impossible, to communicate with each other, and in her desperation, Anne sends a series of notes to David in the hospital. One of them reveals her yearning for what she had witnessed earlier with her parents: "I once saw my father on top of my mother and they looked marvelous together with a kind of sheen on their bodies like a race horse and they lapsed into a voluptuous restfulness which I have never forgotten and which I never saw again" (p. 25).

If children do witness sexual intercourse between adults, they almost inevitably regard it "as a sort of ill-treatment or act of subjugation: they view it, that is, in a sadistic sense" (Freud, 1905). This misinterpretation of parental coitus by the child is so universal that Freud called attention to the fact that primal events, if not actually observed, are in all probability produced in fantasy where they are elaborated sadistically. Since the publication of "A Child Is Being Beaten" (Freud, 1919), it has been recognized that beating fantasies are quite prevalent and the latent and manifest content of such fantasies is varied. The infantile wish to be loved by the father was often conceived of by the child as being beaten by him, a view that corresponds to the infantile sexual theory which has as its core the formula: what the father does to his sexual partner, the mother, during coitus is to beat her.

"By interpreting the parental coitus as an act of violence, the child attempts to deny the reality and to reduce to some extent the castration fear . . .; beat and being beaten are familiar experiences to the child and there is nothing mysterious in them. . . . Thus the anxiety is temporarily reduced, through the transformation of the parental love act into a sadomasochistic one, with the father as the sadistic attacker, the mother as the attacked one, and the *child as the innocent by-stander*. Here, possibly, lies the economic gain of the child's sadistic conception of the primal scene and of his beating fantasies modeled on it: the father becomes the guilty and brutal attacker, the mother his degraded partner, and the child in the further sadomasochistic elaboration the innocent victim. . . . At the same time, the beating fantasy represents, on another level, the child's gratification of its oedipal strivings as well as the punishment for them" (Niederland, 1958, pp. 498-499).

Bitter memories of childhood trauma fuel Robbie Gifford's hatred of all authority figures, in Russell Braddon's (1972) *The Thirteenth Trick*. Robbie is a paraplegic, a direct result of having been abused by an alcoholic father and an indifferent mother, when he caught them in sexual intercourse. He recalls to his younger adopted brother Mark the events that took place when he was four years old.

"I was asleep, as all good children of four should be late at night, when suddenly something — I don't know what — woke me. I sat up, terrified, and there, on the big double bed across the other side of that grotty little room, were my dear papa and my sainted mama" — gulping — "naked and writhing and tearing at one another, him forcing her down, holding her spreadeagled with his hands and his knees, and her screaming, her head threshing from side to side."

Now all the colour had gone from his face and his eyes, inward looking, were blind . . . "That's what woke me," Robbie explained. "My mother screaming 'no' and 'stop' and 'bastard' and 'you're too big, you're hurting me,' her head threshing and him pinning her down, spreadeagled, while he humped her — only I didn't realize that's all it was . . . I thought he was killing her. I shouted leave her alone; but he didn't. Didn't even hear me, come to that. And neither did she. So then" — again that shuddering inhalation — "I tried to pull him off her . . . He stopped his humping just long enough to snarl piss off and went straight back to killing her."

With the thumb and little finger of his free hand he pressed at his temples, as if to obliterate the memory inside his skull. "I was petrified. Not for myself. For her. He looked so huge, and pitiless, and I couldn't think what to do . . . so I jumped on his back. He didn't miss a beat. Just bucked me off. I grabbed his hair then: started yanking. And still not missing a beat, he back-handed me on the floor, all the time my mother writhing and moaning and begging him, 'No, Angus, no. *Please,* you're hurting.' So back, battered but undaunted I went. And sank my sharp little teeth into the first thing I saw. Which happened to be his arse. He missed a beat then all right! Reared up, grabbed my neck with one hand, a leg with the other, lifted me over his head, and threw me." Robbie was smiling now: telling a story against himself. "I flew across the room, bounced off the edge of the table, landed on the floor and was just about to start screaming the place down when my mother shouted, 'And bloody stay there.' Which I did, for the simple reason I couldn't move. And I didn't scream because I couldn't feel. I just lay there. While they got at it again" [pp. 127-128].

"Vij," a short story by Nikolai Gogol (1835), is "a colossal creation of the popular imagination," as the author wrote in a footnote. It is primarily a horror story conflated with humorous elements. Absurdity lies at the root of the world Gogol portrays, laughable absurd pretensions and horrifying absurd calamities. It is a realm of pettiness, stupidity, tawdriness, and of irrational mystification where fate is malignant, capricious, amoral, and too nebulous to be opposed, where majesty has no place, grand protagonists are impossible, and men are either bewildered victims or triumphant cheats. It is a world of pathos and ridicule, based on a view of life that, at the antipodes of tragedy, is somehow shattering. The devil is ubiquitous in Gogol's stories, appearing sometimes in human form and sometimes in traditional folklore shape, as in "Vij," one of the great masterpieces in the genre of the demonic. At times, "Vij" presents a frightful vengeance, climaxed by steadily mounting horror, illustrating Gogol's "fear-racked and sado-masochistic fantasies." It tells of a divinity student who, menaced by an old witch, climbs on her back and beats her mercilessly until she dies. Her body thereupon becomes transformed into the corpse of a beautiful young woman. When a vengeful demon, the Vij, appears on the scene to punish the murderer, the latter tries to take refuge within a magic circle of invisibility. Nothing can be hidden from the all-seeing eyes of the Vij, however, and the demon sends a flock of howling monsters to attack the student. Helpless when he is thus exposed to view, the young man collapses and dies of fright. "This fantasy, with its obvious paranoid coloring, may be interpreted as a primal scene in which the son, after destroying his mother through a sadistic attack, takes her place in relation to the father and suffers destruction in his turn. The sexual act is equated with death. The Vij is a persecuting phallic eye..." (Kanzer, 1955, p. 114).

A similar interpretation has been given to *The Bacchae* by Euripides (407 B.C.). The young King Pentheus of the tragedy symbolizes the child who wishes more than anything else to see his parents make love, but who dreads the sight. His spying on the primal scene while hidden in the pine-brake provides him with the gratification of voyeurism; his exposure by Dionysius represents the child discovered watching his parents make love, and his orgiastic death and dismemberment by his mother and the Maenads is the psychic fact of this kind of infantile trauma. "The turning point of the play comes when Pentheus eagerly assents to Dionysius' suggestion that he spy on the Maenads. Overwhelmed, literally flooded by sexual excitement, Pentheus goes to Cithaeron—transformed inwardly by his own irresistible prurience and transformed outwardly by the transvestite robe and wig of the Bacchantes. The boy is led to a scene of Primal Emotion. At last he can see the forbidden games from his position atop the phallic fir tree. Pentheus watches and his excitement surpasses his ability to act. If *Oedipus* taps the fears and desires Freud spoke of, *The Bacchae* taps another, related, and equally compelling set of fears and desires. For every child wishes to penetrate those mysteries his parents enact. To see them, and not to see them; to participate by watching—to 'find out' what it is all about.... Pentheus is exposed, humiliated, tortured, killed, dismembered. The Primal Emotion is the affective energy released by interrupting the Primal Scene: the child discovered watching his parents make love. Such utter destruction as follows—the dismemberment—is the physical fact of *The Bacchae* and the psychic fact of this kind of infantile trauma" (Schechner, 1968, pp. 418-419).

Primitive, crude noises are perceived as a powerful direct contact threat to the archaic mental apparatus (Niederland, 1958). When they are fused later with primal-scene events, they impart to the latter the threatening, uncanny quality of auditory vigilance, instinctual excitement, and deep anxiety that characterizes Edgar Allen Poe's (1843) "The Tell-Tale Heart." The beating of the heart, which the narrator fantasies relates to archaic noise elements of infancy and the primal scene, persisted in Poe's symptoms of being overwhelmed with eerie excitement. The primal scene is infused with anxious excitement accompanied by an intense fear of detection and of punishment and the direct dread of injury and destruction by the parents themselves. It is the omnipotent father the child dreads and whom he imagines, in coitus, attacking his mother. But irrespective of any actual observation, primal fantasies about coital violence are bound to develop in the child's mind. The child preoccupied with primal-scene fantasies cannot escape endowing them with violent connotations which culminate in the sadistic conception of intercourse, and this is undoubtedly to be found in "The Tell-Tale Heart."

True!—nervous—very, very dreadfully nervous I had been and am; but why *will* you say that I am mad? The disease had sharpened my senses—not destroyed—not dulled them. Above all was the sense of hearing acute. I heard all things in the heaven and in the earth. I heard many things in hell. How, then, am I mad? Hearken! and observe how healthily—how calmly I can tell you the whole story.

It is impossible to say how first the idea entered my brain; but once conceived, it haunted me day and night. Object there was none. Passion there was none. I loved the old man. He had never wronged me. He had never given me insult. For his gold I had no desire. I think it was his eye! yes, it was this! He had the eye of a vulture—a pale blue eye, with a film over it. Whenever it fell upon me, my blood ran cold; and so by degrees—very gradually—I made up my mind to take the life of the old man, and thus rid myself of the eye forever.

Now this is the point. You fancy me mad. Madmen know nothing. But you should have seen *me*. You should have seen how wisely I proceeded—with what caution—with what foresight—with what dissimulation I went to work! I was never kinder to the old man than during the whole week before I killed him. And every night, about midnight, I turned the latch of his door and opened it—oh so gently! And then, when I had made an opening sufficient for my head, I put in a dark lantern, all closed, closed, so that no light shone out, and then I thrust in my head. Oh, you would have laughed to see how cunningly I thrust it in! I moved it slowly—very, very slowly, so that I might not disturb the old man's sleep. It took me an hour to place my whole head within the opening so far that I could see him as he lay upon his bed. Ha!—would a madman have been so wise as this? And then, when my head was well in the room, I undid the lantern cautiously—oh, so cautiously—cautiously (for the hinges creaked)—I undid it just so much that a single thin ray fell upon the vulture eye. And this I did for seven long nights—every night just at midnight—but I found the eye always closed; and so it was impossible to do the work; for it was not the old man who vexed me, but his Evil Eye. And every morning, when the day broke, I went boldly into the chamber, and spoke courageously to him, calling him by name in a hearty tone, and inquiring how he had passed the night. So you see he would have been a very profound old man, indeed, to suspect that every night, just at twelve, I looked in upon him while he slept.

Upon the eighth night I was more than usually cautious in opening the door. A watch's minute hand moves more quickly than did mine. Never before that night, had I *felt* the extent of my own powers—of my sagacity. I could scarcely contain my feelings of triumph. To think that there I was, opening the door, little by little, and he not even to dream of my secret deeds or thoughts. I fairly chuckled at the idea; and perhaps he heard me; for he moved on the bed suddenly, as if startled. Now you may think that I drew back— but no. His room was as black as pitch with the thick darkness (for the shutters were close fastened, through fear of robbers), and so I knew that he could not see the opening of the door, and I kept pushing it on steadily, steadily.

I had my head in, and was about to open the lantern, when my thumb slipped upon the tin fastening, and the old man sprang up in bed, crying out—"Who's there?"

I kept quite still and said nothing. For a whole hour I did not move a muscle, and in the mean time I did not hear him lie down. He was still sitting up in bed listening;—just as I have done, night after night, hearkening to the death watches in the wall.

Presently I heard a slight groan, and I knew it was the groan of mortal terror. It was not a groan of pain or of grief—oh, no!—it was the low stifled sound that arises from the bottom of the soul when overcharged with awe. I knew the sound well. Many a night, just at midnight, when all the world slept, it has welled up from my own bosom, deepening, with its dreadful echo, the terrors that distracted me. I say I knew it well. I knew what the old man felt, and pitied him, although I chuckled at heart. I knew that he had been lying .wake ever since the first slight noise, when he had turned in the bed. His fears had been ever since growing upon him. He had been trying to fancy them causeless, but could not. He had been saying to himself—"It is nothing but the wind in the chimney—it is only a mouse crossing the floor," or "it is merely a cricket which has made a single chirp." Yes, he had been trying to comfort himself with these suppositions: but he had found all in vain. *All in vain;* because Death, in approaching him had stalked with his black shadow before him, and enveloped the victim. And it was the mournful influence of the unperceived shadow that caused him to feel—although he neither saw nor heard—to *feel* the presence of my head within the room.

When I had waited a long time, very patiently, without hearing him lie down, I resolved to open a little—a very, very little crevice in the lantern. So I opened it—you cannot imagine how stealthily, stealthily—until, at length a single dim ray, like the thread of the spider, shot out from the crevice and fell upon the vulture eye.

It was open—wide, wide open—and I grew furious as I gazed upon it. I saw it with perfect distinctness—all a dull blue, with a hideous veil over it that chilled the very marrow in my bones; but I could see nothing else of the old man's face or person: for I had directed the ray as if by instinct, precisely upon the damned spot.

And have I not told you that what you mistake for madness is but over acuteness of the senses?—now, I say, there came to my ears a low, dull, quick sound, such as a watch makes when enveloped in cotton. I knew *that* sound well, too. It was the beating of the old man's heart. It increased my fury, as the beating of a drum stimulates the soldier into courage.

But even yet I refrained and kept still. I scarcely breathed. I held the lantern motionless. I tried how steadily I could maintain the ray upon the eye. Meantime the hellish tattoo of the heart increased. It grew quicker and quicker, and louder and louder every instant. The old man's terror *must* have been extreme! It grew louder, I say, louder every moment!—do you mark me well? I have told you that I am nervous: so I am. And now at the dead hour of the night, amid the dreadful silence of that old house, so strange a noise as this excited me to uncontrollable terror. Yet, for some minutes longer I refrained and stood still. But the beating grew louder, louder! I thought the heart must burst. And now a new anxiety seized me—the sound would be heard by a neighbour! The old man's hour had come! With a loud yell, I threw open the lantern and leaped into the room. He shrieked once—once only. In an instant I dragged him to the floor, and pulled the heavy bed over him. I then smiled gaily, to find the deed so far done. But, for many minutes, the heart beat on with a muffled sound. This, however, did not vex me; it would not be heard through the wall. At length it ceased. The old man was dead. I removed the bed and examined the corpse. Yes, he was stone, stone dead. I placed my hand upon the heart and held it there many minutes. There was no pulsation. He was stone dead. His eye would trouble me no more.

If still you think me mad, you will think so no longer when I describe the wise precautions I took for the concealment of the body. The night waned, and I worked hastily, but in silence. First of all I dismembered the corpse. I cut off the head and the arms and the legs.

I then took up three planks from the flooring of the chamber, and deposited all between the scantlings. I then replaced the boards so cleverly, so cunningly, that no human eye—not even *his*—could have detected any thing wrong. There was nothing to wash out—no stain of any kind—no blood-spot whatever. I had been too wary for that. A tub had caught all—ha! ha!

When I had made an end of these labours, it was four o'clock— still dark as midnight. As the bell sounded the hour, there came a knocking at the street door. I went down to open it with a light heart,—for what had I *now* to fear? There entered three men, who introduced themselves, with perfect suavity, as officers of the police. A shriek had been heard by a neighbour during the night; suspicion of foul play had been aroused; information had been lodged at the police office, and they (the officers) had been deputed to search the premises.

I smiled,—for *what* had I to fear? I bade the gentlemen welcome. The shriek, I said, was my own in a dream. The old man, I men- tioned, was absent in the country. I took my visitors all over the house. I bade them search—search *well.* I led them, at length, to *his* chamber. I showed them his treasures, secure, undisturbed. In the enthusiasm of my confidence, I brought chairs into the room, and desired them *here* to rest from their fatigues, while I myself, in the wild audacity of my perfect triumph, placed my own seat upon the very spot beneath which reposed the corpse of the victim.

The officers were satisfied. My *manner* had convinced them. I was singularly at ease. They sat, and while I answered cheerily, they chatted of familiar things. But, erelong, I felt myself getting pale and wished them gone. My head ached, and I fancied a ringing in my ears: but still they sat and still chatted. The ringing became more distinct:—it continued and became more distinct: I talked more freely to get rid of the feeling: but it continued and gained definiteness—until, at length, I found that the noise was *not* within my ears.

No doubt I now grew *very* pale;—but I talked more fluently, and with a heightened voice. Yet the sound increased—and what could I do? It was *a low, dull, quick sound—much such a sound as a watch makes when enveloped in cotton.* I gasped for breath—and yet the officers heard it not. I talked more quickly—more vehemently; but the noise steadily increased. I arose and argued about trifles, in a high key and with violent gesticulations; but the noise steadily increased. Why *would* they not be gone? I paced the floor to and fro with heavy strides, as if excited to fury by the observations of the men—but the noise steadily increased. Oh God! what *could* I do? I foamed—I raved—I swore! I swung the chair upon which I had been sitting, and grated it upon the boards, but the noise arose over all and continually increased. It grew louder—louder—*louder!* And still the men chatted pleasantly, and smiled. Was it possible they heard not? Almighty God!—no, no! They heard!—they suspected!—they *knew!*—they were making a mockery of my horror!—this I thought, and this I think. But any thing was better than this agony! Any thing was more tolerable than this derision! I could bear those hypocritical smiles no longer! I felt that I must scream or die! and now—again!—hark! louder! louder! louder! louder! *louder!*

"Villains!" I shrieked, "dissemble no more! I admit the deed!—tear up the planks! here, here!—it is the beating of his hideous heart!" [pp. 357-362].

Except for symbolic representation, there is a total absence of parental figures in the tales of Poe. This repression acknowledges that to say something about parents is too dangerous and too frightening—"The endless battle between conscience and impulse, the unsleeping enmity of the self and its Imp of the Perverse—these struggles are enacted and re-enacted in Poe's work, but always in disguise" (Hoffman, 1972, p. 226). In the motiveless plot of "The Tell-Tale Heart," the narrator murders an old man for reasons he knows not. He suspects there may be a motive, but it is difficult for him to admit it.

Poe's anxiety about the Evil Eye displays a special form of castration anxiety, as it does with Gogol in "Vij." Scoptophilia may become the object of specific repressions, and in this case may have been prompted by witnessing the primal scene. Extreme cases sometimes occur in shy, inhibited persons who actually do not dare to look at their environment. There are specific consequences that are dreaded by inhibited voyeurs as talion punishment; the evil eye and being turned to stone are examples (Fenichel, 1945, p. 72). Poe's father died or ran away when he was born; his mother died of tuberculosis two years later. Although never formally adopted, he was brought up by a childless Bostonian couple.

The analysis of Poe's work gives clear information regarding the nature of his craving for self-destruction which characterized his entire life. "We cannot have any doubt as to which were the strongest, most traumatic impressions of his early childhood: the sudden drying-up of . . . the milk from his mother's breast, for which the child did not find a substitute, and for which he longed all the more as his existence was affected by hunger and privations. Secondly, the primal scene, after the boy had seen his mother in the embrace of a man (probably the unknown father of the younger sister). Poe's unconscious obviously identified this man with the 'sympathetic friends in Boston' mentioned in the inscription on the picture left him by his mother, together with her miniature. . . . According to the well-known sadistic conception he created the fantasy of the defenseless mother falling into the hands of a brutal, bestial creature and being assaulted and raped. From these impressions of early childhood arise the fundamental motives which run through Poe's works, sometimes conspicuously, sometimes suppressed, disguised, and distorted. . . . The innumerable allusions, sometimes very slightly veiled, to cannibalism and especially to necrophagy thus become understandable, as well as the large part which is played by the teeth and everything related to biting, and the meaning of 'white,' which stands out especially in 'Gordon Pym.' In this tale the warm white stream finally leads him who has advanced where nobody has been before, toward a mysterious apparition (. . . the mother). This fantasy leads on to the return to the womb, a wish-fulfillment which, in the case of Poe, seems to be always combined with horror" (Sachs, 1935, pp. 303-304).

The child fantasies himself still in the womb, and thus in a position to witness the parents' coitus. The evil eye will find him out and thus must be destroyed, and with it the vision of the primal scene and the unconscious oedipal strivings. The destruction is accompanied with terrible threefold vengeance, as Hoffman (1972) suggests, typical of dreams: in "The Tell-Tale Heart" the narrator extinguishes the eye, he smothers the old man to death, and then dismembers him, precisely the fate of Pentheus in the Euripides play. "In its aspect of getting rid of the Evil Eye, this murder is a more intense and violent form of blinding. And the symbolic content of blinding has been self-evident since Oedipus inflicted it upon himself as a partial remission for what the *lex talionis,* more strictly applied, would have required. In striking the Evil Eye of the old man, the young [man] strikes, symbolically, at his sexual power. [As for suffocation] the inability to breathe is an equivalent of impotence. . . . By inflicting this form of death on the old man, the young man is denying his elder's sexual power. And cutting off the hands, the arms, the legs are symbolic castrations" (Hoffman, 1972, p. 231).

"Many children have some fabled ogre," Greenacre (1955) wrote, "often in animal form, or some 'secret,' with which they scare each other and themselves. . . . Psychoanalysis reveals that it is generally some representation of the primal scene, in which the sexual images of the parents are fused into a frightening or awe-inspiring single figure," such as in the case of Mr. Lear, the Polly and the Pusseybite. It is true as well for much of what is developed in the structure and content of many Lewis Carroll stories. In the *Snark,* the "last 'fit' is an acting out of the primal scene with the Baker first standing 'erect and sublime' and then plunging into the chasm between the crags. The *Jabberwock* too seems but another variation of the Snark, but in the hunting of the latter, a whole crew of children participates—i.e., they tell this secret to each other, under the leadership of the Baker, who is rather clearly identified as Charles [Dodgson—Lewis Carroll], and think of this as a frightening exploration. The part of the poem in which the Butcher gives the docile Beaver a lesson in natural history is probably but a thinly disguised picture of a consultation among the little Dodgsons regarding the mysterious life of their awesome parents. It is only the Baker, however, who really knows and suffers ... It appears that the little boy Charles lived too full and exciting a life and was confronted with life's greatest mysteries too emphatically before he could assimilate them" (Greenacre, 1955, pp. 240-242).

In the course of the process of psychoanalysis or intensive psychotherapy the occurrence of the dream having primal-scene content is an expected and usual phenomenon. Much has been written about primal-scene dreams from the standpoint of their content and structure since the early detailed accounts by Freud (1900, 1916-1917, 1918), Róheim (1920), Fenichel (1945), and others. The occurrence of dreams of this nature has long been recognized to represent a form of resistance to the intense anxiety liberated by the developing transference neurosis. Dreams of the primal scene seem to serve defensive functions on several levels. Izner (1959) proposed that primal-scene dream material in analysis and intensive psychotherapy may appear as an attempt at mastery in expressing the infantile wish to be present at the union of the parents in intercourse, and in denying exclusion.

In Lewis Carroll's *The Gardener,* a man—the gardener—appears "sometimes in one guise and sometimes in another, but with its acrobatic, swaying, jigging, snorting rhythm is a typical dream representation of sexual excitement. It is interesting, therefore, to realize that in the very structure of Carroll's stories, these figures all appear as memories which are repeated in dreams. The *Alice* books are presented as dreams, and *Sylvie and Bruno* avowedly represents transitions back and forth between different levels of consciousness, in which the dreaming state plays a prominent part. The gardener's song always comes at the point of a shift from one state to another. The repetitiveness of this excited figure and his constant association with a secret garden, the concern about whether the memory is good in the onlooker and the reciprocal question whether the silly old fellow's brain has been injured—whether his behavior is merrily exciting or a comfort in a state of stress—would lead to the conclusion that there was some actual but repressed memory of the author's which was insistently recurring in hidden forms: that probably in his childhood Charles had been stirred at the sight of an older man, perhaps a gardener, in a state of sexual excitement. Indeed, if one studies the text of *Through the Looking Glass* as it describes Alice's encounter with the White Knight who then sings her the comforting song about the aged, aged man, the fact that this section is a beautiful description of a screen memory becomes apparent" (Greenacre, 1955, p. 230). Carroll's arresting neologisms and portmanteau words and the mysterious frightening creatures he created reveal both primal-scene and birth fantasies. The whole picture is that of an awful fascination with and terror of the sexual life of adults.

The primal scene of the phallic period, the observation of sexual relations between the parents, is superimposed upon an earlier and more basic primal scene at the oral level, in which the infant at the mother's breast was an active participant in an overtly erotic relationship and not an outside observer (Sarlin, 1963). Parental nudity observed by children can produce sexual fantasies and frustrations that might contribute to the formation of neuroses. Oedipal strivings become intensified. Unfulfilled, they arouse tension, frustration, and resentment, which are reflected in neurotic symptoms. In *Brave New World*, Linda, a Beta-minus girl who had worked in the Fertilizing Room in Aldous Huxley's (1932) science-fiction fantasy, had been accidentally left behind in the savage New Mexico reservation by the Director of the Central London Hatchery and Conditioning Centre some twenty years earlier. She had given birth to John and is explaining to a visitor, ". . . John was a great comfort to me. I don't know what I should have done without him. Even though he did get so upset whenever a man . . . Quite a tiny boy, even. Once (but that was when he was bigger) he tried to kill poor Waihusiwa—or was it Popé?—just because I used to have them sometimes" (p. 143).

It was very hot. They had eaten a lot of tortillas and sweet corn. Linda said, "Come and lie down, Baby." They lay down together in the big bed. "Sing," and Linda sang. Sang "Streptocock-Gee to Banbury-T" and "Bye Baby Banting, soon you'll need decanting." Her voice got fainter and fainter . . .

There was a loud noise, and he woke with a start. A man was standing by the bed, enormous, frightening. He was saying something to Linda, and Linda was laughing. She had pulled the blanket up to her chin, but the man pulled it down again. His hair was like two black ropes, and round his arm was a lovely silver bracelet with blue stones in it. He liked the bracelet; but all the same, he was frightened; he hid his face against Linda's body. Linda put her hand on him and he felt safer. In those other words he did not understand so well, she said to the man, "Not with John here." The man looked at him, then again at Linda, and said a few words in a soft voice. Linda said, "No." But the man bent over the bed towards him and his face was huge, terrible; the black ropes of hair touched the blanket. "No," Linda said again, and he felt her hand squeezing him more tightly. "No, no!" But the man took hold of one of his arms, and it hurt. He screamed. The man put up his other hand and lifted him up. Linda was still holding him, still saying "No, no." The man said something short and angry, and suddenly her hands were gone. "Linda, Linda." He kicked and wriggled; but the man carried him across to the door, opened it, put him down on the floor in the middle of the other room, and went away, shutting the door behind him. He got up, he ran to the door. Standing on tiptoe he could just reach the big wooden latch. He lifted it and pushed; but the door wouldn't open. "Linda," he shouted. She didn't answer [pp. 146-147].

The interpretation of the sexual act as cruel and destructive is reflected by the protagonist in *August Is a Wicked Month* by Edna O'Brien (1965, pp. 33-34):

She stared down at the figurations of stone coiled together the way corpses would be and thought of death and how once as a child with her sisters she lay in bed on a Saturday morning thinking of the day of general judgment and rehearsing the two possible alternatives that God would say: "Depart from me ye cursed into everlasting flames which were prepared for the Devil and his angels," or "Come ye, blessed of my father, possesseth the Kingdom prepared for you," and while they rattled off the words she was conscious of her father forcing her mother to submit and drawing the mother's face toward his with his hand under her chin and his thumb and forefinger dug into her, hurting her swallow and his other hand out of sight, doing something under the covers, and her mother resisting and saying "stop," while the children had first an argument and then a bet as to whether God would be up on a rostrum or not.

The minute details recalled by Ellen, the convent-bred, Irish-Catholic girl living in London, who is seeking some kind of love after her lover has rejected her, are testimony to the impact the scene has had upon her.

In *Winter Love* by Han Suyin (1962), Bettina's mother had run off with a man, the first of many. She was five years old at the time, she recalls to her lover, Mara, a married woman:

I remember my mother wiping my shoes with a corner of the window curtain one afternoon, doing it brusquely, all the time her mouth working, talking angrily with a man whose face I couldn't see even in memory; it had worried me, the ragged edge of the curtain dipping toward the floor, and my mother made the tear worse wiping my shoes. Then I was in a cot with bars; at night, awake, wanting to tell my mother about the curtain, and I stood up in my cot to tell her, but I couldn't see her, only the big bed, the blankets, a big humped mass. Another memory, another time; perhaps another hotel room, my mother crying, sitting on the edge of another bed, while I stood, holding something, perhaps a doll, staring at her, and then she lifted her skirt and showed me a big bruise, blue-black on her thigh. That man had done it to her. Or was it another man? I remembered again waking up, looking at blankets, looking at the mounds in the bed, like these low hills in Wales . . . I couldn't see my mother's face at all, nor her hair [pp. 254-255].

Behind the anxieties of the phallic phase and the narcissistic wounds of the primal scene lie deeper terrors concerning separation and identity confusion. To McDougall's (1972) patients, the father was represented as an absence, of itself deeply threatening to identity feeling. "Only the perverse or mythological sexual act permits some illusory recovery of the paternal phallus, albeit in idealized and disguised forms. . . . what has been denied or disavowed has not been recovered in the form of delusions, but is, in a sense, retrieved through a form of *illusion* contained within an act. There is evidence of some breakdown in the capacity to symbolize and to create an inner fantasy world to deal with intolerable reality" (p. 379).

Yukio Mishima, the Japanese novelist and suicide, was much possessed by the vision of the primal scene. In at least two of his novels, it is the primal scene that provides the motivation for the behavior of the anti-heroes. In *The Sailor Who Fell from Grace with the Sea* (1963) and in *The Temple of the Golden Pavilion* (1959), the protagonists, like many other latent homosexuals, played out their revenge on the faithless parents, who, contrary to all they had been led to believe, and contrary especially to what they wanted to believe, had sexual relations together—or with an adult other than the spouse. The strong sexual strivings for possession of the mother and the aggressive tendencies against the father have not, in Mishima's work, been transformed through the workings of the defense mechanisms.

In a number of ways, *The Sailor Who Fell from Grace with the Sea* is similar to a fairy tale: the foolish, unthinking mother vis-à-vis the wicked witch, the evil stepfather, violent forms of death, and cruel killings.

Noboru's widowed mother, Fusako, discovers that the thirteen-year-old boy has secretly left the house at night, whereupon she locks him in his room at bedtime. She forbids him entry to her bedroom.

"Sleep well, dear."

Noboru's mother closed his bedroom door and locked it. What would she do if there were a fire? Let him out first thing—she had promised herself that. But what if the wooden door warped in the heat or paint clogged the keyhole? The window? There was a gravel path below; besides, the second floor of this gangling house was hopelessly high.

It was all his own fault. It would never have happened if he hadn't let the chief persuade him to sneak out of the house that night. There had been endless questions afterward, but he hadn't revealed the chief's name.

They lived at the top of Yado Hill in Yokohama, in a house his father had built. After the war the house had been requisitioned by the Occupation Army and toilets had been installed in each of the upstairs bedrooms: being locked in at night was no great discomfort, but to a thirteen-year-old the humiliation was enormous.

Left alone one morning to watch the house and in need of something to vent his spite on, Noboru began to rummage through his room.

A large chest of drawers was built into the wall adjoining his mother's bedroom. He pulled out all the drawers, and as he was dumping their contents onto the floor he noticed a trickle of light spilling into one of the empty compartments of the chest.

He thrust his head into the space and discovered the source of the light: strong summer sunlight was reflecting off the sea into his mother's empty bedroom. There was plenty of room in the chest. Even a grownup might squeeze in up to his belly if he lay flat. Peering at his mother's bedroom through the peephole, Noboru sensed something new and fresh about it.

The shiny brass beds his father had ordered from New Orleans were set against the wall on the left side just as they had been before his death. A bedspread was smoothed neatly over one of them, and on the white cloth a large letter "K" — Kuroda was the family name. A blue straw sun hat, trailing a long pale-blue ribbon, lay on the bed. On the night table stood a blue electric fan.

Across the room, near the window, there was a dressing table fitted with an oval three-piece mirror. The mirror was not quite closed; the upper edges of the glass glinted through the cracks like splinters of ice. In front of the mirror rose a small city of bottles: eau de Cologne, perfume sprays, lavender toilet water, a Bohemian glass goblet, facets glittering in the light ... a crumpled pair of brown-lace gloves lay withering like cedar leaves.

A couch and two chairs, a floor lamp, and a low, delicate table were arranged directly under the window. An embroidery frame, the beginnings of a pattern needled into the silk, was propped on the couch. The vogue for such things had passed long ago, but his mother loved all kinds of handicraft. The pattern seemed to be the wings of some gaudy bird, a parrot maybe, on a background of silver-gray. A pair of stockings lay in a heap next to the embroidery. The shocking embrace of sheer nylon and the imitation damask of the couch gave the room an air of agitation. She must have noticed a run on her way out and changed in a hurry.

Only dazzling sky and a few fragments of cloud, hard and glossy as enamel in the light bouncing off the water, could be seen through the window.

Noboru couldn't believe he was looking at his mother's bedroom; it might have belonged to a stranger. But there was no doubt that a woman lived there: femininity trembled in every corner, a faint scent lingered in the air.

Then a strange idea assailed him. Did the peephole just happen to be there, an accident? Or — after the war when the soldiers' families had been living together in the house. . . . He had a sudden feeling that another body, larger than his, a blond, hairy body, had once huddled in this dusty space in the wall. The thought soured the close air and he was sickened. Wriggling backwards out of the chest, he ran to the next room. He would never forget the queer sensation he had when, flinging open the door, he burst in.

Drab and familiar, the room bore no resemblance to the mysterious chamber he had seen through the peephole: it was here that he came to whine and to sulk—*it's time you stopped coming into Mother's room so often with that excuse about wanting to watch the ships; you're not a child any more, dear*—here that his mother would put aside her embroidery to help him with his homework while she stifled yawns, or would scold him for not tying his necktie straight, or would check the ledgers she brought home from the shop. . . .

He looked for the peephole. It wasn't easy to find. Cunningly hidden in the ornately carved wainscot, in a spot on the upper border where the rippled pattern overlapped to conceal it—a very small hole.

Noboru stumbled back to his room, gathered the scattered clothing, and stuffed it back into the drawers. When everything was as it had been, he vowed never to do anything that might attract the grownups' attention to the chest.

Shortly after he made this discovery, Noboru began spying on his mother at night, particularly when she had nagged or scolded him. The moment his door was closed he would slip the drawer quietly out of the chest, and then watch in unabating wonder while she prepared for bed. On nights when she was gentle, he never looked.

He discovered that it was her habit, though the nights were not yet uncomfortably hot, to sit completely naked for a few minutes before going to bed. He had a terrible time when she went near the wall mirror, for it hung in a corner of the room he couldn't see.

She was only thirty-three and her slender body, shapely from playing tennis every week, was beautiful. Usually she got right into bed after touching her flesh with perfumed water, but sometimes she would sit at the dressing table and gaze into the mirror at her profile for minutes at a time, eyes hollow as though ravaged by fever, scented fingers rooted between her thighs. On those nights, mistaking the crimson of her bundled nails for blood, Noboru trembled.

Never had he observed a woman's body so closely. Her shoulders, like the shoreline, sloped gently downward. Her neck and arms were lightly tanned, but at her chest, as if an inner lamp were burning, began a zone of warm, fleshy white. Her haughty breasts inclined sharply away from her body; and when she kneaded them with her hands, the rosy nipples danced apart. He saw the trembling belly. And the scar that meant she had borne children. A dusty red book in his father's study had taught him that; he had discovered it on the highest shelf, turned the wrong way, sandwiched between a gardening book and a pocket business manual.

And the zone of black. The angle was bad somehow, and he strained until the corners of his eyes began to ache. He tried all the obscenity he knew, but words alone couldn't penetrate that thicket. His friends were probably right when they called it a pitiful little vacant house. He wondered if that had anything to do with the emptiness of his own world.

At thirteen, Noboru was convinced of his own genius (each of the others in the gang felt the same way) and certain that life consisted of a few simple signals and decisions; that death took root at the moment of birth and man's only recourse thereafter was to water and tend it; that propagation was a fiction; consequently, society was a fiction too: that fathers and teachers, by virtue of being fathers and teachers, were guilty of a grievous sin. Therefore, his own father's death, when he was eight, had been a happy incident, something to be proud of.

On moonlit nights his mother would turn out the lights and stand naked in front of the mirror! Then he would lie awake for hours, fretted by visions of emptiness. An ugliness unfurled in the moonlight and soft shadow and suffused the whole world. If I were an amoeba, he thought, with an infinitesimal body, I could defeat ugliness. A man isn't tiny or giant enough to defeat anything.

As he lay in his bed, ships' horns often screeched like nightmares through his open window. When his mother had been gentle, he was able to sleep without looking. On those nights, the vision appeared in his dreams instead.

He never cried, not even in his dreams, for hard-heartedness was a point of pride. A large iron anchor withstanding the corrosion of the sea and scornful of the barnacles and oysters that harass the hulls of ships, sinking polished and indifferent through heaps of broken glass, toothless combs, bottle caps, and prophylactics into the mud at harbor bottom—that was how he liked to imagine his heart. Someday he would have an anchor tattooed on his chest.

The most ungentle night of all came toward the end of summer vacation. Suddenly: there was no way of knowing it would happen.

His mother left early in the evening, explaining that she had invited Second Mate Tsukazaki to dinner. To thank him, she said, for having shown Noboru around his ship the day before. She was wearing a kimono of black lace over a crimson under-robe; her obi was white brocade: Noboru thought she looked beautiful as she left the house.

At ten o'clock she returned with Tsukazaki. Noboru let them in and sat in the living room with the tipsy sailor, listening to stories about the sea. His mother interrupted at ten-thirty, saying it was time for him to go to bed. She hurried Noboru upstairs and locked the bedroom door.

The night was humid, the space inside the chest so stuffy he could scarcely breathe: he crouched just outside, ready to steal into position when the time came, and waited. It was after midnight when he heard stealthy footsteps on the stairs. Glancing up, he saw the doorknob turning eerily in the darkness as someone tried the door; that had never happened before. When he heard his mother's door open a minute later, he squeezed his sweating body into the chest.

The moonlight, shining in from the south, was reflected back from one pane of the wide-open window. Tsukazaki was leaning against the window sill; there were gold-braid epaulets on his white short-sleeved shirt. His mother's back came into view, crossed the room to the sailor: they embraced in a long kiss. Finally, touching the buttons on his shirt, she said something in a low voice, then turned on the dim floor lamp and moved out of sight. It was in front of the clothes closet, in a corner of the room he couldn't see, that she began to undress. The sharp hiss of the sash unwinding, like a serpent's warning, was followed by a softer, swishing sound as the kimono slipped to the floor. Suddenly the air around the peephole was heavy with the scent of Arpège. She had walked perspiring and a little drunk through the humid air and her body, as she undressed, exhaled a musky fragrance which Noboru didn't recognize.

The sailor was still at the window, staring straight at Noboru. His sunburned face was featureless except for the eyes that glittered in the lamplight. By comparing him with the lamp, which he had often used as a yardstick, Noboru was able to estimate his height. He was certainly no more than five feet seven, probably a little less. Not such a big man.

Slowly, Tsukazaki unbottoned his shirt, then slipped easily out of his clothes. Though he must have been nearly the same age as Noboru's mother, his body looked younger and more solid than any landsman's: it might have been cast in the matrix of the sea. His broad shoulders were square as the beams in a temple roof, his chest strained against a thick mat of hair, knotted muscle like twists of sisal hemp bulged all over his body: his flesh looked like a suit of armor that he could cast off at will. Then Noboru gazed in wonder as, ripping up through the thick hair below the belly, the lustrous temple tower soared triumphantly erect.

The hair on his rising and falling chest scattered quivering shadows in the feeble light; his dangerous, glittering gaze never left the woman as she undressed. The reflection of the moonlight in the background traced a ridge of gold across his shoulders and conjured into gold the artery bulging in his neck. It was authentic gold of flesh, gold of moonlight and glistening sweat. His mother was taking a long time to undress. Maybe she was delaying purposely.

Suddenly the full long wail of a ship's horn surged through the open window and flooded the dim room — a cry of boundless, dark, demanding grief; pitch-black and glabrous as a whale's back and burdened with all the passions of the tides, the memory of voyages beyond counting, the joys, the humiliations: the sea was screaming. Full of the glitter and the frenzy of night, the horn thundered in, conveying from the distant offing, from the dead center of the sea, a thirst for the dark nectar in the little room.

Tsukazaki turned with a sharp twist of his shoulders and looked out toward the water.

It was like being part of a miracle: in that instant everything packed away inside Noboru's breast since the first day of his life was released and consummated. Until the horn sounded, it was only a tentative sketch. The finest materials had been prepared and all was in readiness, verging on the unearthly moment. But one element was lacking: the power needed to transfigure those motley sheds of reality into a gorgeous palace. Then, at a signal from the horn, the parts merged into a perfect whole.

Assembled there were the moon and a feverish wind, the incited, naked flesh of a man and a woman, sweat, perfume, the scars of a life at sea, the dim memory of ports around the world, a cramped breathless peephole, a young boy's iron heart — but these cards from a gypsy deck were scattered, prophesying nothing. The universal order at last achieved, thanks to the sudden, screaming horn, had revealed an ineluctable circle of life — the cards had paired: Noboru and mother — mother and man — man and sea — sea and Noboru . . . .

He was choked, wet, ecstatic. Certain he had watched a tangle of thread unravel to trace a hallowed figure. And it would have to be protected: for all he knew, he was its thirteen-year-old creator.

"If this is ever destroyed, it'll mean the end of the world," Noboru murmured, barely conscious. *I guess I'd do anything to stop that, no matter how awful!* [pp. 9-16].

After his mother, now married to the sailor, discovers Noboru's peephole, his doom is sealed. The leader of his gang sees the sailor as a betrayer, a sickening example of fatherhood: "Fathers are the flies of this world. They hover around our heads waiting for a chance, and when they see something rotten, they buzz in and root in it. Filthy, lecherous flies broadcasting to the whole world that they've screwed our mothers. And there's nothing they won't do to contaminate our freedom and our ability..." (p. 116). The murder of the sailor follows. Noboru's gang arranges to dismember the sailor, the novel ending with the latter drinking tea saturated with sleeping pills and the gang leader donning rubber gloves for the operation (Goldstein and Goldstein, 1970).

In Mishima's earlier novel, *The Temple of the Golden Pavilion*, Mizoguchi was thirteen—like Noboru—when he witnessed the primal scene between his mother and an uncle, while his father also watched. The latter, who died an early tubercular death, was a poor Zen priest in an outlying village on a lonely seacoast. Mizoguchi is the narrator and central character and begins the story by telling of his sense of alienation. Dana (1970) points out that he has stuttered since birth, and "sound," Mizoguchi relates, "is like a key to a door that separates my inner world from the world outside" (Mishima, 1959, p. 5). It is perhaps as a result of his viewing the primal scene, particularly in the destructive situation of his awareness of his father's knowledge of his mother's betrayal as well as his own oedipal betrayal, that Mizoguchi sees life in the sensual world as distorted, misshapen, a series of betrayals. It is seen in Uiko's mocking rejection of Mizoguchi; in his mother's infidelity; in Kashiwagi's cruelty; in Tsurukawa's death; in the strange fate of the woman who taught flower arrangement; in the hypocrisy of the life of the Abbott Superior of the Temple; in Mizoguchi stomping on the stomach of the pregnant Japanese prostitute on the command of an American G.I. (Dana, 1970).

There is a special reason that I have until now avoided writing about my mother. I do not particularly feel like touching on what relates to my mother.

Concerning a certain incident, I never addressed a single word of reproof to Mother. I never spoke about it. Mother probably did not even realize that I knew about it. But ever since that incident occurred, I could not bring myself to forgive her.

It happened during my summer holidays when I had gone home for the first time after entering the East Maizuru Middle School and after being entrusted to my uncle's care. At that time, a relative of Mother's called Kurai had returned to Nairu from Osaka, where he had failed in his business. His wife, who was the heiress of a well-to-do family, would not take him back into their house, and Kurai was obliged to stay in Father's temple until the affair subsided.

We did not have much mosquito netting in our temple. It was really a wonder that Mother and I did not catch Father's tuberculosis, since we all slept together under the same net; and now this man Kurai was added to our number. I remember how late one summer night a cicada flew along the trees in the garden, giving out short cries. It was probably those cries that awakened me. The sound of the waves echoed loudly, and the bottom of the light-green mosquito net flapped in the sea breeze. But there was something strange about the way in which the mosquito net was shaking.

The mosquito net would begin to swell with the wind, then it would shake reluctantly as it let the wind filter through it. The way in which the net was blown together into folds was not, therefore, a true reflection of how the wind was blowing; instead, the net seemed to abandon the wind and to deprive it of its power. There was a sound, like the rustling of bamboo, of something rubbing against the straw mats; it was the bottom of the mosquito net as it rubbed against the floor. A certain movement, which did not come from the wind, was being transmitted to the mosquito net. A movement that was more subtle than the wind's; a movement that spread like rippling waves along the whole length of the mosquito net, making the rough material contract spasmodically and causing the huge expanse of the net to look from the inside like the surface of a lake that is swollen with uneasiness. Was it the head of some wave created by a ship as it plowed its way far off through the lake; or was it the distant reflection of a wave left in the wake of a ship that had already passed this place?

Fearfully I turned my eyes to its source. Then, as I gazed through the darkness with wide-open eyes I felt as though a gimlet was drilling into the very center of my eyeballs.

I was lying next to Father; the mosquito net was far too small for four people, and in my sleep I must have turned over and pushed him over to one corner. Accordingly, there was a large white expanse of crumpled sheet separating me from the thing I now saw;

and Father, who lay curled up behind me, was breathing right down my neck.

What made me realize that Father was actually awake was the irregular, jumping rhythm of his breath against my back; for I could tell that he was trying to stop himself from coughing. All of a sudden my open eyes were covered by something large and warm, and I could see nothing. I understood at once. Father had stretched his hands out from behind to cut off my vision.

This happened many years ago when I was only thirteen, but the memory of those hands is still alive within me. Incomparably large hands. Hands that had been put round me from behind, blotting out in one second the sight of that hell which I had seen. Hands from another world. Whether it was from love or compassion or shame, I do not know; but those hands had instantaneously cut off the terrifying world with which I was confronted and had buried it in darkness.

I nodded slightly within those hands. From that nodding of my small head, Father could instantly tell that I had understood and that I was ready to acquiesce; he removed his hands. And, afterwards, just as those hands had ordered, I kept my eyes obstinately closed, and thus lay there sleeplessly until morning came and the dazzling light from outside forced its way through my eyelids.

Please remember that years later, when Father's coffin was being carried out of the house, I was so busy *looking* at the dead face, that I did not shed a single tear. Please remember that with his death I was freed from the fetters of his hands, and that by looking intently at his face, I was able to confirm my own existence. To this extent did I remember to wreak my proper revenge on those hands, that is, on what the people of this world would call love; but so far as Mother was concerned, apart from the fact that I could not forgive her for that memory, I never once thought of avenging myself on her [Mishima, 1959, pp. 54-56].

Mizoguchi felt protected and excluded from a normal relationship with life, even as his father's hands tried to protect him from the real knowledge of his mother's illicit relationship with his uncle. The denial of sexuality and its sublimation through violence and arson mark Mizoguchi's behavior. He felt his mother to be mortally dangerous to him, the hatred and aggression attached to her image being deflected onto other objects. Behind the image of the denigrated father lay an idealized father, a role frequently attributed to a religious figure, or to

God himself, or more often, the fantasy of an idealized phallus (McDougall, 1972, p. 374), and thus Mizoguchi attempts to gain, to retain, or to control this idealized paternal phallus. His sadistic hatred for his mother, together with the desperate need for her, as seen in the pathetic act of his sucking at the breast of a woman, is vented in his need to destroy his world — the Golden Temple — by arson. Repeatedly through the novel Mizoguchi expresses hatred for his mother, with frequent reference to her "small," "cunning," "hollow eyes."

As a junior at college, and as an acolyte, he is doing poorly at both and is thinking about burning down the Golden Temple. He runs away, is brought back to school by a policeman, and encounters his worried mother. He reflects, "I was hardly ever deceived by my instinctive feelings and the sight of her small, cunning, sunken eyes now brought home to me how justified I had been in my hatred for my Mother. Drawn-out hatred over the fact that she should have given birth to me in the first place, memories of that deep affront to which she had exposed me — an affront which, as I have already explained, did not leave me any room for planning my revenge, but instead, simply isolated me from Mother. Those bonds had been hard to break. Yet now, while I sensed that she was half immersed in maternal grief, I abruptly felt that I had become free. I do not know why, but I felt that Mother could never again threaten me" (p. 199). With this, Mizoguchi feels free to set fire to the Temple, with himself in it, as a lover commits double suicide with a mistress, even as the Goldsteins (1970, p. 123) suggest.

The child's sexual experiences are linked up with masturbation fantasies and obtain representation and abreaction along with them in play. "Among such re-enacted experiences the primal scene plays a very important part and generally occupies the foreground of the picture in early analysis. It is, as a rule, only after a good deal of analysis has been done and both the primal scene and the child's genital trends have been to some extent uncovered that we come to representations of its pre-genital experiences and fantasies" (Klein, 1932, p. 32). Felix Krull, the confidence man in Thomas Mann's *Confessions of Felix Krull* (1954), practiced self-deception as a lad. He loved to dress up in a variety of costumes and to pose for his artist-godfather. He had an active fantasy life, in which he played Kaiser and Prince, and which was encouraged by his philandering father and giddy mother. Breast-fed by a wet nurse, he grew up isolated from his mother and older sister, Olympia, and from peers because of the family's lack of respectability. His early life as a poseur and deceiver was further manifested in his deception in his violin playing, in forging his father's name in order to play truant, feigning illness to avoid school, swiping chocolates from a delicatessen, and beating the draft by feigning epilepsy at his physical exam. These deceptions may have been prompted, in part, by the primal scene which he did not quite see, but which his extensive fantasy was equal to: "[My mother and sister] lived in unusual intimacy. I recall seeing my mother measure Olympia's thigh with a tape measure, which gave me to think for several hours. Another time, when I was old enough to have some intuitive understanding of such matters though no words to express them in, I watched unseen and saw my mother and sister flirting with a younger painter who was doing some work about the house. He was a dark-eyed lad in a white smock and they painted upon him a green moustache with his own paint. In the end they raised him to such a pitch that they fled giggling up the attic stairs and he pursued them thither" (p. 14).

The child often overhears or eavesdrops on the adult's sexual activities. "If the child sleeps in a room adjoining that of his parents, his imagination elaborates on the sounds coming from the adjacent room (*Nebenzimmer-Erotica*). Mother's groaning, her position during the act ... then become building stones for his sadistically determined infantile sex theory, a theory soon to be enriched by at first vague and obscure, later more elaborated, rape fantasies" (Stekel, 1952, pp. 49-50). The earliest memories of Martinez, a G.I. in Mailer's *The Naked and the Dead* (1948), are of the sounds of the primal scene: "Teacher likes me, Momma likes me, big fat Momma with the smell; her arms are great and her breasts are soft; at night in the two little rooms there is the sound of Momma and Poppa" (p. 55). Cramped quarters forced sex into the open for Sammy Glick in *What Makes Sammy Run* by Budd Schulberg (1941). "Sammy remained a virgin until he was eleven. But no storks ever nested in his childhood fancy. When he was still in his cradle he could hear the creaking of bedsprings and his parents' loud breathing in the same room" (p. 194). And in Gwen Davis's (1969) *The Pretenders,* fourteen-year-old Harry visits a prostitute, Wilma, just after his mother has given him offense.

The man in his long underwear sat in a chair by the window, looking at a newspaper folded in his lap. He did not look up as Wilma led Harry to the bed at the far side of the room. She reached up and tugged at the fabric hung with rings like a shower curtain, and pulled it across the rod, separating them from the rest of the small parlor.

"Is he going to stay there?" Harry said.

"He can't see anything."

"He can hear," Harry said, remembering the stories all the boys had about listening to parental mattresses squeaking in the close-quartered darkness, recalling the times he had strained his own ears for familiar repulsive signals on the other side of the door [p. 178].

The fantasies of overhearing parental intercourse exist along with the reality and probably have their source in infantile sexual investigation (Nunberg, 1955). Supported by infantile sexual curiosity, these fantasies may perhaps appear more intensively in instances where the curiosity finds no satisfaction whatsoever in reality. Some children try to deny their knowledge of sexual activity between their parents and consequently have to obliterate much of the outer world as well. Children rarely, if ever, consciously think of their parents in the act of sex or as having a sex potential. In Robert Byrne's (1970) *Memories of a Non-Jewish Childhood,* the protagonist could not imagine his parents having intercourse.

When I was in the eighth grade my parents were in their fifties and overweight and I couldn't for the life of me imagine them engaged in sexual congress. My cousin from Wahpeton several years before had tried to convey to me the basic outline of how babies were conceived, but I fought against the idea. I couldn't picture mom and dad doing such a thing. Taking off their clothes and lying down on top of each other? Ridiculous. They didn't even dance. What he was trying to tell me, in fact, was disgusting, and if he hadn't been bigger than I was I would have beat hell out of him for putting the thought in my head. Not that he ever mentioned my mom and dad; in his examples he was always careful to use two hypothetical people from Wahpeton.

As time went by and evidence favoring my cousin's theory continued to come in, I finally had to admit that he probably had something. I myself was proof that my parents had fooled around with each other in some manner at least once, and my having a brother tended to suggest that there had been another occasion. An only child might have been able to entertain the possibility of a virgin birth, but belief in two in a row was too much to ask even of the most devout [p. 110].

In *Somewhere in England* by R. Gadney (1971), a friend of the protagonist's father had described his mother as "the sexiest English-woman east of Rome. Normally it would have been the bluff man's choice of Rome that would have worried [David] Peto. That his mother might be sexy was afterwards the observation that disturbed him" (p. 13). Another teenager, Ann Chapin in John O'Hara's (1955) *10 North Frederick,* was beginning to experience maturing sexual urges, and along with them came the realization that she was not the product of an immaculate conception.

> She was in the stage where what *she* was discovering and experiencing was unique, notwithstanding her complete knowledge of the act which, performed by her parents, had caused her existence. She thought about it little enough, but when she did she thought of her father visiting her mother in total darkness, without visual or tactile enjoyment or prolonged excitement such as she herself had enjoyed, and achieving the ultimate embrace (which she had not yet achieved) in the fashion of all married couples. So far she had not been able, or permitted herself, to imagine her father in the positions of love-making. It was easier for her to imagine her mother making love with an anonymous, featureless figure that was her father, but not Father. She was convinced otherwise, but it was not impossible for her to imagine her mother as a partner in love-making with almost any man; and except for the dirty trick it would have been on her father, she would not have been irreparably shocked if her mother had used her body for pleasure with another man. To Ann a woman's body was designed for two related purposes, pleasure and child-bearing, and her mother as a woman was no different from any other woman. As the wife of Father, however, she owed him complete fidelity, and there was nothing to indicate that she had betrayed that trust. She knew that when *she* got married she was not going to fool around [pp. 309-310].

The child character, made compulsory in fiction by the restrictions of gentility and the fear of sex, according to Fiedler (1960), is first used in Henry James's *What Maisie Knew* "to confront rather than evade experience. James' novel ... is a kind of initiation story, though it deals not with a full-scale initiation from innocence to maturity but with a quasi initiation that ends in a withdrawal. In the Jamesian version of the Fall of Man, at any rate, there are four actors, not three: the man, the woman, the serpent, and the child presumably watching from behind the tree. The Peeping Child is only a junior version of the Peeping Tom ... that has a special appeal to the American imagination. In *What Maisie Knew* James not only invents the fable, but sets the technique for presenting it; and, indeed, the vicarious ocular initiation presupposes the convention of controlled point of view. Once James has shown how to do it, novelist after novelist sets himself to portraying the corrupt world as reflected in the innocent eye. Eye to the crack in the door, ear attuned from the bed where he presumably sleeps — curious or at idle play — the innocent bystander stumbles upon the murderer bent over the corpse, the guilty lovers in each other's arms, the idolized jockey in a whorehouse, a slattern on his knee.... The end of innocence via ocular initiation is bafflement and nausea; beyond the cry of the child at the window, it is hard to imagine a real acceptance of adult life and sexuality, hard to conceive of anything but continuing flight or self-destruction.... It is around these crises that our literature compulsively circles: the stumbling on the primal scene, mother and father caught in the sexual act (or, less dramatically, the inference of that scene from creaking springs and ambiguous cries); or the discovery of heterosexual 'treachery' on the part of some crush, idolized in innocent homosexual adoration" (pp. 320-321).

Children fantasy a good deal about their bodies and those of siblings and parents, particularly those parts of the body adults are not supposed to think about. Yet, it is "hard to accept as normal and virtually universal such lurid fantasies as the belief that the mother has a phallus; the confusion of womb and anus, giving birth and defecation; the fear of castration; and particularly the child's fears and fantasies about his parents' sexual intercourse. Even harder to accept is the idea that the child in us, our unconscious self, still thinks about these things, still reacts to reality in ways shaped by these grotesque drives and fantasies" (Holland, 1966, p. 284). The first paragraph of *Virginia Fly Is Drowning,* by Angela Huth (1973), begins, "Virginia Fly was raped, in her mind, on average twice a week. These imaginings came at no particular time of day: she was never prepared for them and yet never surprised by them. They vanished as quickly as they came, and left her with no ill effects. One moment there would be this glorious vision of a man's hand running down the length of her body, causing the kind of shiver down her spine that sent her fingers automatically to do up the three buttons of her cardigan, and the next minute she would hear herself saying, with admirable calm, 'Miranda, I think it's your turn to wipe the blackboard.' "

Virginia was a thirty-one-year-old English spinster schoolteacher, living with her parents and maintaining a correspondence with an American for twelve years—a man she had never met but from whom she received hundreds of letters written illegibly in green ink on onionskin paper. When she was twenty-three, Virginia's mother thought it was time to "have a little talk about the facts of life."

"My virginity's still intact, if that's what you're asking."

"You gave me quite a little turn, for a moment. I know they all do it, these days. But, you know, when you're a mother, you don't quite like to think of your own daughter ..."

"I suppose not," said Virginia. "Same as you don't quite like to think of your own parents."

Mrs. Fly looked up at her daughter with shock in her eyes, but reacted calmly. Her original plan thwarted, with gallant spontaneity she decided to change her tactics.

"Well, there's obviously no need for us to go into technicalities— you probably know more about them than I do, what with all those books they have to-day." She gave a small laugh. "No, what I'd like to talk about is more the spiritual side. Nobody talks about that so much these days." She wove her needle expertly in and out of the threads.

"What about it?" asked Virginia, to end a pause whose length indicated her mother had lost track.

"Well, dear, how can I put it?—What I'm trying to say is this. The, er, act, shall I call it, doesn't end when it's over."

"Oh?" Virginia, for once, felt herself to be scoring.

"What I'd like you to know is, once you've experienced it, once you've been fulfilled, nothing is ever quite the same again." She looked at her daughter with unusual severity. "Quite dull girls have been known to radiate, once they have experienced love ..." Virginia felt a hot stone of nausea rise in her throat. "I mean, take your father and I. In the old days—I'll always remember experiencing quite a little after-glow."

At the thought of her parents doing anything which would give them a little after-glow, Virginia got up, went to the lavatory and was very sick. It occurred to her briefly that her mother was either mad, drunk on fantasy, or had been too influenced by the romantic novels she endlessly read. Virginia knew for a fact that they never undressed in front of each other, never went into the bathroom when the other was in the bath, and turned off the television if sex came into the programme. Indeed, her own conception must have been pretty miraculous, she thought, and poured herself a small glass of neat whiskey to try to abolish the loathsome thought of her parents' bodies flailing about in the dark.

By then Mrs. Fly realised that her plan had gone wrong some-where, and, when Virginia took her chair again, she changed the conversation to the planting out of bulbs [pp. 16-17].

Virginia's intense disgust betokened a reaction formation, such as shows up occasionally in many persons in dreams or in symptomatic acts. The disgust of hysterics in response to sexual temptation may be looked upon as an extreme denial of unconscious receptive sexual strivings: "I not only do not want to take anything into my body; I even want to spit or vomit something out of my body" (Fenichel, 1945, p. 139).

The traumatic effect of the primal scene upon the child is rendered by three situations which are generally simultaneous: the union of the parents in itself signifies for the child that he is overlooked and that they are doing things between themselves and not with him; the spectacle offered by the couple appears brutal and like a struggle; the child is passing through a phase of intensely sadistic pregenital im-pulses, with all his aggression projected upon the parents, thus intensi-fying the idea of brutality if he shoud happen to witness the primal scene, and he imagines it as intensely destructive (Perestrello, 1954). With primal-scene observation, the pregenital and the genital im-pulses of the child are merged. Powerful pregenital impulses may be experienced, resulting in bed-wetting and defecation, accompanied by sadistic fantasies directed toward the copulating parents (Klein, 1932, p. 192). A not uncommon reaction to the primal scene is an oral one, i.e., it is conceived of as a cannibalistic feast, and that it is often the event reproduced in adult depressions and elations (Lewin, 1950), moods which were prominent in Edward Lear's life, for example.

The Wolf Man and other cases of Freud's show how primal-scene traumata are bound to be at the core of psychoneurosis, which is in agreement with the findings cited by Horney (1923), Mahler (1942), Bonaparte (1945), Devereux (1951), O. E. Sperling (1956), Fliess (1956), Niederland (1958), M. Sperling (1964), Chasseguet-Smirgel (1970), and Jaffe (1971), *inter alia.* The symptoms resulting from witnessing the primal scene are well documented in the literature of both psychology and fiction. They include nightmares, night terrors, intellectual inhibition, learning difficulties, compulsive lying, and the development of pseudo stupidity or intellectual dullness because of a need to display the absence of knowledge of sexual matters which would otherwise be overwhelming. Other symptoms include hyper-activity, extreme restlessness, distractibility, and inability to concentrate. A less common consequence is the development of either homo-sexuality or transvestite tendencies. A specific instinctual temptation that may be suggested by the state of sleep is the remembrance of a primal scene, which took place at night when the child was supposed to be asleep. Fenichel (1945, pp. 321, 347) points out that since belated motor discharge of exciting impressions is a typical symptom of traumatic neuroses, it is understandable that tics frequently occur in neuroses developed under the influence of a frightening primal scene, and that voyeurs are fixated on such experiences as primal scenes or the sight of adult genitals that aroused castration anxieties. Analysis of a group of patients who, in addition to their psycho-neurotic disturbances, had been suffering for several years from head-aches of both the common and the migraine type, revealed to Pere-strello (1954, p. 219), that the headaches were related to fantasies of the primal scene and to the specific way in which the ego attempted to elaborate the situation.

Pierre, in Herman Melville's (1852) novel of the same name, defends himself against his feminine identification and homosexual threat by paranoid relations with other men. "*Pierre* is idealized to the extent that the hero spends his youthful paradise alone with his beautiful bountiful mother untroubled by rival father or siblings. [But] the paradise is lost when he discovers the presence of an earlier sibling and the lechery of the sainted father. This is, in effect, the discovery of the primal scene, against which (and his own sexuality) the hero had so stoutly defended himself" (Kligerman, 1953).

Susanna, in *Raintree County*, by Ross Lockridge, Jr. (1948), has forged a marriage with John Shawnessy out of a false pregnancy. Her mother, a severely disturbed woman, knew about her husband's infidelity with his black slave, Henrietta. Susanna discovers that her mother was responsible for setting the mansion on fire, which caused the death of Henrietta, her father, and her mother. History repeats itself when Susanna sets fire to her home, immolating her two-year-old baby and herself. In one of her lucid moments between psychotic breakdowns, Susanna tells John of a scene she witnessed in 1832 when she was six years old.

> I peeped up over the landing into the upper floor of the cabin, and there were two people on the bed together, and the light from the big fire on the riverbank burned right in through the window, and it made the woman's skin all dusky and scarlet like wine, and the man's skin pale white against it. I don't think I'd ever seen grown people without clothes on before then. I didn't quite understand it at the time, but I knew I oughtn't to be there, and I slipped down the stair and went back to the house, and no one ever knew what I saw. So then, Susanna went on, still talking softly to the dark night, I had some dim notion of what it was like between Daddy and Henrietta. And I was proud and glad because I loved them both. I didn't feel so strong then the difference between the races. That came later. Then, a few days later Henrietta came up to the house to live—Daddy was that headstrong [p. 347].

Christian Jan Romansky, a sane, civilized, apolitical university professor living in early Nazi days in Richard Bankowsky's novel, *The Barbarians at the Gates* (1972), succumbs to the charms of Dorit Wünderling, the gentile wife of a Jewish banker. Christian and his wife Claudia have a son Jan, a sensitive boy who has been pressured into joining a Hitler Youth group and who, in order to prove himself and his loyalty to the group, feels he has to outdo everyone else.

> After Christian had paid the check and they were back out in the car park, she said there was no time. Both of them should have been home an hour ago. She wouldn't even allow him into her roadster with her. And amid promises of writing to each other and of her phoning him from London to make love to him long distance, with tears rolling down her beautiful face, she climbed into his car after him just to kiss him one last time, she said, and suddenly they found themselves making love right there out in the neon glare of the car park like schoolchildren.
>
> The two little houses, abutting right on to the perimeter of the tiny car park, seemed to glare at them out of lightless eyes, as she whispered she didn't care who saw them. She hoped in fact the whole world could see how perfectly they pleased each other, even sitting up like that completely clothed and only slightly unbuttoned.
>
> Neither of them ever suspected, oh God, how could they?—that

the educational system could possibly have been so efficient, could possibly have taught such magnificent discipline and self-sacrifice that after almost three hours (for he must have pulled his car out of the darkened garage at about eight that evening) his little soldier and former devotee of innocence and beauty who had learned well the motto, "Clench your teeth, boys. Endure!" and who could march fifteen miles a day and knew all about flying and parachutes and military geography and camouflage and ambush, could be lying there absolutely silent on the floor in the back of his father's car [p. 125].

It was not, Claudia wrote to him, as though they really had to make a choice between their father in Poland or their brother in Germany. Or she between her husband or her son. Jan, though he was only twelve, was of the mental age of a superior adult, and, having endured and survived the rigors and discipline of the Jung-volk, was very much a man. Jan really had no time for family life in his religious dedication to the service of his *Gruppenleiter* and Führer, and he had asked permission of her to go and live in the Youth barrack. She had granted his request, knowing that he would have no choice but to disobey her if she refused. She knew Jan loved them and would like to continue living with them, but he had no choice. He loved his father too, she wrote. Much more than even the child could ever imagine.

"It is pathetic how he refused to listen to news from you. How he insists that his brother and sister must not even mention their father's name when he is visiting. And how he storms out of the room whenever I begin reading your letters aloud. But he never quite closes the door behind him and always finds some reason to linger a little longer than necessary in the hall. He has no choice, Christian, the poor child. You have to believe me, darling. If anything, he loves you more than any of us. And you know how we all love you. Despite everything, we love you and can't go on living without you. You're their father, darling, my husband" [p. 153].

Jan's reaction to witnessing the primal scene was a sense of betrayal, of disillusionment, and ultimately depression. In an attempt to fill the sudden void thus created in identity feeling, the sexual need became a desperate attempt to ward off rage and murderous or suicidal impulses. Jan actually made a suicide attempt, though it was unsuccessful.

A category of fiction that neatly embraces many of the factors inherent in the primal scene is the mystery story. In an analysis of its characteristics, Pederson-Krag (1949) pointed out its unique feature: the intense curiosity the detective story arouses, which is related to the human capacity for curiosity which reaches its first and most intense expression in the primal scene. "The first element of the detective story is the secret crime. Carrying the parallel further, the victim is the parent for whom the reader (the child) had negative oedipal feelings. The clues in the story, disconnected, inexplicable and trifling, represent the child's growing awareness of details it had never understood, such as the family sleeping arrangements, nocturnal sounds, stains, incomprehensible adult jokes and remarks. The criminal of the detective drama appears innocuous until the final page. In real life he was the parent toward whom the child's positive oedipal feelings were directed, the one whom the child wished least of all to imagine participating in a secret crime. . . . Whether the reaction to the primal scene has been denial or acceptance, with or without participation, the repressed memory is in every instance charged to some degree with painful affect. The mystery story attempts to present a more satisfying, less painful primal scene from the standpoint of the unconscious. This fictional primal scene satisfies the voyeurs who, like the Wolf Man, gazed with strained attention at the scene of parental coitus. The voyeur is never entirely satisfied with his peeping which he has the compulsion endlessly to repeat, like the detective story addict who rereads the same basic mystery tale without tedium. In the gradual revelation of clues that make up the bulk of the narrative, the reader is presented with one significant detail after another, a protracted visual forepleasure. Finally the crime is reconstructed, the mystery solved, that is, the primal scene is exposed. The reader has no need to take part in this by directly identifying with the characters because the gratification is obtained from being a passive onlooker. . . . In participating in the detective-story version of the primal scene, the reader's ego need fear no punishment for libidinal or aggressive urges. In an orgy of investigation, the ego, personified by the great detective, can look, remember and correlate without fear and without reproach in utter contrast to the ego of the terrified infant witnessing the primal scene" (pp. 209-213, *passim*).

The extent of the primal-scene trauma varies in terms of the psychic content of the aroused excitement and its intensity, and the child's age and previous history. Whatever the reaction, it inevitably entails anxiety, against which the ego tries to defend itself by resorting to various mechanisms (isolation, obsessive control, paranoid expulsion, manic denial) aimed at internal control in an omnipotent manner. Early sexual observations of parents in the sexual act tend to have a lasting effect, whether on the conscious or unconscious level, for the impression gathered is that sexuality is dangerous and brutal. It floods the child with inappropriate excitement beyond his capacity to understand or discharge.

TECHNICAL REFERENCES

Barker, W. J. (1966), The nonsense of Edward Lear. *Psychoanalytic Quarterly,* 35:568-586.

Bonaparte, M. (1945), Notes on the analytical discovery of the primal scene. *The Psychoanalytic Study of the Child,* 1:119-125. New York: International Universities Press.

Chasseguet-Smirgel, J. (1970), *Feminine Sexuality. New Psychoanalytic Views.* Ann Arbor, Mich.: University of Michigan Press.

Dana, R. (1970), The stutter of eternity. A study of the themes of isolation and meaninglessness in three novels by Yukio Mishima. *Critique,* 12:87-102.

Devereux, G. (1951), *Reality and Dream. Psychotherapy of a Plains Indian.* New York: International Universities Press.

Eissler, K. R. (1962), On the metaphysical of the preconscious: A tentative contribution to psychoanalytic morphology. *The Psychoanalytic Study of the Child,* 17:9-41. New York: International Universities Press.

Fairbairn, W. R. D. (1956), Considerations arising out of the Schreber case. *British Journal of Medical Psychology,* 29:113-127.

Fenichel, O. (1945), *The Psychoanalytic Theory of Neurosis.* New York: Norton.

Fiedler, L. (1960), *Love and Death in the American Novel.* London: Paladin, 1970.

Fliess, R. (1956), *Erogeneity and Libido.* New York: International Universities Press.

Frank, A. (1969), The unrememberable and the unforgettable. *The Psychoanalytic Study of the Child,* 24:48-77. New York: International Universities Press.

———— & Muslin, H. (1967), The development of Freud's concept of primal repression. *The Psychoanalytic Study of the Child,* 22:55-76. New York: International Universities Press.

Freud, S. (1896a), Heredity and the aetiology of the neuroses. *Standard Edition,* 3:141-156. London: Hogarth Press, 1962.

———— (1896b), Further remarks on the neuro-psychoses of defence. *Standard Edition,* 3:159-185. London: Hogarth Press, 1962.

———— (1896c), The aetiology of hysteria. *Standard Edition,* 3:189-221. London: Hogarth Press, 1962.

———— (1898), Sexuality in the aetiology of the neuroses. *Standard Edition,* 3:261-285. London: Hogarth Press, 1962.

———— (1900), The interpretation of dreams. *Standard Edition,* 4 & 5. London: Hogarth Press, 1953.

———— (1905), Three essays on the theory of sexuality. *Standard Edition*, 7:125-243. London: Hogarth Press, 1953.

———— (1915a), Repression. *Standard Edition*, 14:141-158. London: Hogarth Press, 1957.

———— (1915b), The unconscious. *Standard Edition*, 14:159-215. London: Hogarth Press, 1957.

———— (1916-1917), Introductory lectures on psycho-analysis. *Standard Edition*, 16. London: Hogarth Press, 1963.

———— (1918), From the history of an infantile neurosis. *Standard Edition*, 17:3-122. London: Hogarth Press, 1955.

———— (1919), A child is being beaten. *Standard Edition*, 17:177-204. London: Hogarth Press, 1955.

———— (1926), Inhibitions, symptoms and anxiety. *Standard Edition*, 20:77-174. London: Hogarth Press, 1959.

Goldstein, B. & Goldstein, S. (1970), Observations on *The Sailor Who Fell from Grace with the Sea. Critique*, 12:116-126.

Greenacre, P. (1955), *Swift and Carroll. A Psychoanalytic Study of Two Lives.* New York: International Universities Press.

Hoffman, D. (1972), *Poe Poe Poe Poe Poe Poe Poe.* Garden City, N. Y.: Doubleday.

Holland, N. (1966), *Psychoanalysis and Shakespeare.* New York: McGraw-Hill.

Horney, K. (1923), On the genesis of the castration complex in women. In: *Feminine Psychology.* New York: Norton, 1973, pp. 45-47.

Izner, S. M. (1959), On the appearance of primal scene content in dreams. *Journal of the American Psychoanalytic Association*, 7:317-328.

Jaffe, D. S. (1971), The role of ego modification and the task of structural change in the analysis of a case of hysteria. *International Journal of Psycho-Analysis*, 52:375-399.

Kanzer, M. (1955), Gogol—A study on wit and paranoia. *Journal of the American Psychoanalytic Association*, 3:110-125.

Klein, M. (1932), *The Psychoanalysis of Children.* London: Hogarth Press, 1963.

Kligerman, C. (1953), The psychology of Herman Melville. *Psychoanalytic Review*, 40:125-143.

Lewin, B. D. (1950), *The Psychoanalysis of Elation.* New York: Norton.

Mahler, M. S. (1942), Pseudo imbecility, the magic cap of invisibility. *Psychoanalytic Quarterly*, 11:149-164.

McDougall, J. (1972), Primal scene and sexual perversion. *International Journal of Psycho-Analysis*, 53:371-384.

Niederland, W. G. (1958), Early auditory experiences, beating fantasies, and primal scene. *The Psychoanalytic Study of the Child*, 13:471-504. New York: International Universities Press.

Nunberg, H. (1955), *Principles of Psychoanalysis. Their Application to the Neuroses.* New York: International Universities Press.

Pederson-Krag, G. (1949), Detecive stories and the primal scene. *Psychoanalytic Review*, 18:207-214.

Perestrello, D. (1954), Headache and primal scene. *International Journal of Psycho-Analysis*, 35:219-223.

Róheim, G. (1920), Die Urszene in Traume. *International Zeitschrift für Psychoanalyse*, 6:337-339.

Sachs, H. (1935), Edgar Allan Poe. *Psychoanalytic Quarterly*, 4:294-306.

Sarlin, C. N. (1963), Feminine identity. *Journal of the American Psychoanalytic Association*, 11:790-816.

Schachtel, E. (1947), On memory and childhood amnesia. *Psychiatry*, 10:1-26.

Schechner, R. (1968), In warm blood: *The Bacchae. Educational Theatre Journal*, 20:415-424.

Sperling, M. (1964), The analysis of a boy with transvestite tendencies: A contribution to the genesis and dynamics of transvestitism. *The Psychoanalytic Study of the Child*, 19:470-493. New York: International Universities Press.

Sperling, O. E. (1956), Psychodynamics of group perversion. *Psychoanalytic Quarterly*, 25:56-65.

Stekel, W. (1952), *Patterns of Psychosexual Infantilism*. New York: Liveright.

LITERARY REFERENCES

Bankowsky, Richard (1972), *The Barbarians at the Gates*. Boston: Little, Brown.

Braddon, Russell (1972), *The Thirteenth Trick*. New York: Norton, 1973.

Byrne, Robert (1970), *Memories of a Non-Jewish Childhood*. New York: Stuart.

Carroll, Lewis (1876), *The Hunting of the Snark and Other Poems and Verses*. New York: Harper, 1903.

——— (1881), Jabberwocky. In: *Through the Looking Glass*. New York: McGraw-Hill, 1946.

Davis, Gwen (1969), *The Pretenders*. New York: New American Library, 1970.

Gadney, R. (1971), *Somewhere in England*. New York: St. Martin's.

Gogol, Nikolai (1835), Vij. In: *The Collected Tales and Plays of Nikolai Gogol*, ed. L. J. Kent. New York: Pantheon, 1964, pp. 338-374.

Horwitz, Julius (1973), *The Married Lovers*. New York: Dial.

Huth, Angela (1973), *Virginia Fly Is Drowning*. New York: Coward, McCann & Geoghegan, 1973.

Huxley, Aldous (1932), *Brave New World*. New York: Harper & Row, 1946.

James, Henry (1908), *What Maisie Knew*. New York: Doubleday, 1954.

Lear, Edward (1866), The adventures of Mr. Lear, the Polly and the Pusseybite. In: *Teapots and Quails and Other Nonsense*, ed. A. Davidson & P. Hofer. Cambridge, Mass.: Harvard University Press, 1954.

Lockridge, Ross Jr. (1948), *Raintree County*. Boston: Houghton, Mifflin.

Mailer, Norman (1948), *The Naked and the Dead*. New York: Rinehart.

Mann, Thomas (1954), *Confessions of Felix Krull, Confidence Man*. New York: Knopf, 1955.

Melville, Herman (1852), *Pierre*. New York: Grove, 1957.

Mishima, Yukio (1959), *The Temple of the Golden Pavilion*. New York: Knopf.

——— (1963), *The Sailor Who Fell from Grace with the Sea*. New York: Knopf, 1965.

Nabokov, Vladimir (1955), *Lolita*. New York: Putnam's.

Neeley, Richard (1972), *The Sexton Women*. New York: Putnam's.

O'Brien, Edna (1965), *August Is a Wicked Month*. New York: Simon & Schuster.

O'Hara, John (1955), *10 North Frederick*. New York: Random House.

Poe, Edgar Allan (1843), The tell-tale heart. In: *The Best Tales of Edgar Allan Poe*. New York: Modern Library, 1924, pp. 357-363.

Schulberg, Budd (1941), *What Makes Sammy Run*. New York: Bantam.

Suyin, Han (1962), *Winter Love*. New York: Putnam's.

Updike, John (1968), *Couples*. New York: Knopf.

CHAPTER TWO

The Phallic Woman

In 1663, the anonymous Englishman who identified himself only by the elliptical address "A Person of Quality" gave a fairly realistic description of the effect the phallic woman has on man:

> An uxurious man is one that hath left all the world for a woman, and all women for a thing called a wife, with which idol he is so effeminate bewitched that he forgets his annual worship at Jerusalem, and is tied up with the golden calf at home. This Delilah is his devotion, this ruler his religion, this Eve the only edge to his appetite, and he will taste any fruit she tempts him to (though sour grapes). This man is never his own man but in thought, for his actions intended are either diverted and writhed by her simple will, or else wholly violated and broken by her supposed wisdom. He can be no good commonwealth man, he is so confined to her canopy; nor a good churchman, he is so tied to her canons; nor a wise man, to be vanquished with her wilfulness. He thinks himself as safe in her favours as Adam in the first form and hopes to merit Olympus by making a goddess of Diana; the which he is assured by his faith in her fair promises and his obedience to her sacred Oracles. In fine, he is good-for-nothing but to multiply mankind, and consequently, sin and (which is fittest for him) not when he purposeth, but when she pleaseth.. [p. 389].

The phallic woman has been variously defined as one who diminishes a man, who tears down man's ego and self-respect, makes him feel powerless and incapacitated, a woman who has to subjugate a man emotionally and assume his role in the relationship in order to

50

keep control over him, who is dominant, overwhelming, aggressive, and, at times, vicious. She exists beyond sex-typing or sexist assumptions. The image of the phallic woman may be that of the gum-chewing, chain-smoking, whiskey-swilling, snappy-retorting American mother-frump. Or, it may take the form of a female sure of herself, physically strong, with a gigantically voluptuous body which is hard, slim, long, and smooth—i.e., phallic. She has existed in one form or another, in various stereotypes, since the Creation. She is the fantasy of the adult male's erotic picture of the little boy's impression of the woman, or older girl, who, in her great power, damaged his masculinity (Stoller, 1968).

For the unconscious, the mother is often a giantess. Memories of the large size of the mother's pelvic region are frequently found in men. "The image of the mother emerging from behind these memories perfectly corresponds to the first sculptures of the paleolithic age: huge breasts, a huge pelvis and huge external genitals. When ... the picture that represents the maternal body is repressed, the image of the giant mother continues to live in the unconscious. The huge genital organ inhering in this memory suffers an illusionary misinterpretation due to incest prohibition and castration fear. What happens is not simply the creation of an imagined penis or that of a picture of a displaced mama; neither—in the case of boys—does a conclusion *per analogiam* take place, but the actual picture of huge external female genitals is interpreted as a penis and complemented suitably" (Hermann, 1949, p. 303).

In his paper on Gulliver, Ferenczi (1928) wrote: "One of my male patients recalls having used a small female creation of fantasy in his youthful masturbation fantasies, which he always carried in his pocket and took out from time to time in order to play with it." This, Fenichel (1936) declared, "was the phallus fantasied as a girl. Furthermore, Gulliver encounters the giant women who despite their feminine nature manifest clear evidences of the symbolism of erection—and one recalls too the frequent fairy tales of giant girls. Naturally one does not overlook the fact that giant women also represent the adult mother, by comparison with whom the little child feels so small; but it is Ferenczi himself who describes why in all these fantasies the giant, or the dwarf, represents *also* a penis. Once one has become aware of the fantasy of the phallus girl, one finds in literature the most varied representations of it" (p. 320).

Brunswick (1943) described a male patient who accused her of lying, whereas the lie was really the patient's lie, i.e., the fantasy of a woman with a penis. When the patient's little sister was born, he remarked that the whole area of the baby's genital (meaning the *mons Veneris* and the *labia majora*) was protuberant—as protuberant as a penis. "The absence of pubic hair further emphasized its phallic appearance. Much as this patient consciously enjoyed the female genital, he was aware of an aversion to pubic hair. The entire genital of the young female child thus was labeled phallic by the patient and accepted on that basis" (p. 460). Many men find the *mons pubis,* the clitoris, and the vagina mysterious and repulsive, and are inspired by feelings of horrified disgust at the "bleeding gash" of a pitiless, all-powerful woman. Men's unconscious fear of women is based on the early distortion of fact that women are castrated and on their infantile dependence on such creatures for care and love. Wherever primitive man institutes a taboo, wrote Freud (1918, pp. 198-199), "he fears some danger, and it cannot be disputed that a generalized dread of woman is expressed in all these rules of avoidance. Perhaps this dread is based on the fact that woman is different from man, and therefore apparently for ever incomprehensible and mysterious, strange and therefore apparently hostile. The man is afraid of being weakened by the woman infected with her femininity and of then showing himself incapable."

Just as Pandora let loose old age and vice, the evils of the world, so Eve was made responsible for man's mortality and fall from grace. "This interpretation of the origin of undesirable things was to prove very useful for a long time to come, and it served a double purpose. On the one hand it allowed man to assert his domination that much more forcibly; he literally had the whip hand and could go on punishing woman for what she was supposed to have done, thus justifying his domination ... on the other hand it allowed him to externalize all flaws and weaknesses in himself and make woman the embodiment of them, leaving him strong and intact and morally superior. And since sexuality is always the Achilles heel in this arrangement, not only do the strongest taboos surround sex, but it is woman's sexuality that he most loathes and fears" (Figes, 1970, p. 42). The dreams of every male analysand reveal the dread of women, which in actuality is dread of the vagina thinly disguised under abhorrence due to the absence of the penis in women. The boy "feels or instinctively judges that his penis is much too small for his mother's genital and reacts with the dread of his own inadequacy, of being rejected and derided.... a menace to his self-respect" (Horney, 1932, p. 356). It is a psychiatric commonplace for certain male patients to describe the impression of their penis encountering the glans of another penis while having intercourse. Abraham (1920) discovered that some of his male patients had the idea that women had a hollow penis which the smaller male penis could penetrate. This fantasy has an oral origin, through an unconscious equating of penis and breast, a fantasy that contributes to the formation of the image of the phallic mother (David, 1970).

As Fenichel suggested, the fantasy of the phallic woman is to be found almost everywhere in literature, as is a latent mythology predicated on the dread of women. One of the earliest illustrations in American fiction is Washington Irving's (1819) *Rip Van Winkle*. Dame Van Winkle is a terrible virago, so much the opposite of Rip that she probably represents his superego which berates and criticizes him for all his failures. Heiman (1959) pointed out that *Rip Van Vinkle* was written when Irving was thirty-six years old, at the end of a two-year depression following his mother's death and the failure of his business: "Irving had been strongly attached to his mother and painfully aware that she had not lived to see him successful in anything. *Rip Van Winkle* expresses aggression Irving had never felt free to show, for he tended to neutralize his aggressive drives and desexualize his libidinal ones. The 'sleeper' motif was his attempt to cope with anxieties about castration and rejection" (p. 16).

The literary tradition predicated on a dread of woman is a long one. "Throughout *Oedipus Rex*, great stress is laid on Clytemnestra's masculine personality traits and behavior. She knows 'how to dip hot steel.' In her 'woman's heart/ A man's will nurses hope.' She demonstrates her superior will when she makes her husband walk on the purple carpet against his wishes. She claims to use 'a woman's words,' but the Chorus says, 'Madam, your words are like a man's.' And Cassandra asks, 'What? will cow gore bull?' The issue, from Orestes' point of view, is the role confusion generated by the mother's aggressive sexual behavior, combined with the preoedipal fear of the threatening, castrating, phallic mother" (Rogers, 1970, p. 124). It is significant that with reference to her use of a hunter's net to snare her husband before the kill, Clytemnestra is repeatedly compared to a spider, a common dream symbol of the phallic mother. Orestes himself likens her to "a sting ray or an adder," and his dream depicts his mother possessing a phallus.

The fantasy of the devouring mother often symbolizes the mother as cat, tiger, lioness, or sphinx, along with spider, or snake woman or Dragon Lady. In Henry Fielding's (1742) *Adventures of Joseph Andrews,* for example, Lady Booby's mirror image is Mrs. Slipslop. In her near rape of Joseph, an epic simile elevates her to a hungry tigress, a voracious pike, and an executioner (Weinbrot, 1970). March, the ambivalent young lady in D. H. Lawrence's (1923) *The Fox,* is far more aggressive than one would think. As the story progresses, she takes on, like Henry, the major male character, the cunning, beauty, and destructiveness of the fox, which symbolizes the furtive yet powerful desires of the characters (Levin, 1967). The predatory female, the massacre of lovers, and, in particular, the slaying of the lover by the woman, is found in numerous novels. Cleopatra, in Gautier's story, *One of Cleopatra's Nights* (1915), grants the enjoyment of this particular night to the extremely beautiful lion-hunter, Meïamoun; she dances for him, and is on the point of preventing him from drinking the cup of poison when the arrival of Mark Antony seals the young man's fate. "Certain elements of the story should be noticed. The young man is beautiful, wild, and chaste, and falls in love with Cleopatra because she is unattainable ... of irresistible charm ... and the knowledge of her body is an end in itself, beyond which life has nothing to offer. Cleopatra, like the praying mantis, kills the male whom she loves. These are elements which were destined to become permanent characteristics of [this type] of Fatal Woman.... The lover is usually a youth, and maintains a passive attitude; he is obscure, and inferior either in condition or in physical exuberance to the woman, who stands in the same relation to him as do the female spider, the praying mantis, etc., to their respective mates; sexual cannibalism is her monopoly.... The perfect incarnation of this type of woman is Herodias. But she is not the only one: Helen, the Helen of Moreau, of Samain, of Pascoli, closely resemble her. The ancient myths, such as that of the Sphinx, of Venus and Adonis, of Diana and Endymion, were called in to illustrate this type of relationship, which was to be so insistently repeated..." (Praz, 1933, pp. 205-206).

All Zola's women seem to be phallic: old Geneviève in *Madeleine*

Férat, Clorinde in *Son Excellence Eugène Rougon,* Rosemonde of *Paris* eagerly awaiting the execution of Salvat, and Nana, who is described by Leonard (1963-1964, p. 150) "as a great animal of a woman, with a heavy blond mane and a covering of downy hair over her body." Nana's greatest satisfactions derive from the downfall of the men with whom she has become involved. She insists, Leonard continues, on playing the role of a woolly bear while Count Muffat acts a dog, achieving thereby, Zola wrote, vengeance on society through turning all whom she meets into animals, a pack of dogs chasing after a bitch not in heat, who turns and mocks them. In one of Zola's most striking metaphors, Nana is a giant mouth, eating up the countryside, swallowing farms, villas, fields, mills, streams, and forests; she "eats" men. Perhaps it is appropriate to recall that Fanny Hill calls vaginas "our nether mouths." Nana's primary role in the novel is that of an ineluctably insatiable vagina.

The figure of the phallic woman was successfully incarnate in all ages and all literatures, an archetype which united in itself all forms of man-eating techniques, the ferocious hunt for bed partners, the predatory stalking of the incompetent male, the greed for power, love, and control. There is not only the Cleopatra who massacred in the morning the lovers who had passed the night with her, but also La Belle Dame Sans Merci, the Mona Lisa, the Carmen of Merimée. They all took pleasure in the torment of their ascendancy, their ability to inflict pain, and their keen awareness of their destructive capabilities. In the *Trionfo della Morte,* D'Annunzio (1896) portrayed Ippolita Sanzio as doomed: " 'Cruelty lurks hidden in her love,' he thought. 'There is something destructive in her, which becomes the more evident the more violent her orgasm. . .' And he saw again in memory the terrific, almost Gorgon-like vision of her as she often appeared to him, when, convulsed by a spasm or inert in final exhaustion, he had looked at her through half-closed eyelids" (p. 353). At one moment, Ippolita becomes a gigantic, phallic woman, attaining almost mythological stature.

In "The Planter of Malata," a short story by Joseph Conrad (1916), Renouard is a passive, semi-inarticulate man paired with a cold and forbidding androgynous female, Felicia Moorsam. She is endowed with a frightening, incinerating potential and with lethal attributes which provoke Renouard to an untimely suicide by drowning. Renouard is described as "penetrated" and "vanquished" by his beloved, a woman of "tremendous power"; formerly so resourceful and brave in the face of adversity, he now behaves as if he were engaged in secret complicity with his would-be destroyer (Meyer, 1964). "Felicia Moorsom faced him suddenly, her splendid black eyes full on his face as though she had made up her mind at last to destroy his wits once and for all" (Conrad, p. 205). "What a glorious struggle with this Amazon..." (p. 185).

Fiedler (1960) finds in the whole of American literature a pantheon of portraits of women who are dreaded. Lady Brett Ashley in Hemingway's (1926) *The Sun Also Rises* is presented "not as an animal or as a nightmare but quite audaciously as a goddess, the bitch-goddess with a boyish bob ... The Lilith of the Twenties. No man embraces her without being in some sense castrated, except for Jake Barnes, who is unmanned to begin with; no man approaches her without wanting to be castrated, except for Romero, who thinks naïvely that she is—or can easily become—a woman.... Certainly, Romero's insistence that she let her hair grow out has something to do with it: 'He wanted me to grow my hair out. Me, with long hair. I'd look so like hell.... He said it would make me more womanly....' To yield up her cropped head would be to yield up her emancipation from female servitude, to become feminine rather than phallic, and this Brett cannot do. Her lovers are unmanned and degraded..." (p. 298). In the work of William Faulkner, mother, sisters, and wives all use their sexuality with cold calculation to achieve their inscrutable ends. Hightower, "the scared and stinking refugee from life in *Light in August,* cries out in despair that the husband of a mother, whether he be the father or not is already a cuckold.... What woman has ever suffered from any brute as men have suffered from good women?" (Fiedler, p. 299). The very names of Faulkner's women, Fiedler indicates, tend toward allegory. Dewy Dell in *As I Lay Dying* suggests "both a natural setting and woman's sex, her sex as a fact of nature, while Temple Drake [in *Sanctuary*] evokes both a ruined sanctuary and the sense of an unnatural usurpation: woman become a sexual aggressor—more drake than duck.... Faulkner's dewiest dells turn out to be destroyers rather than redeemers, quicksands disguised as sacred groves.... Temple is disconcertingly almost a man, almost phallic; and indeed, at the moment of her rape by Popeye, it is difficult to tell which one is the phallus bearer, to whom the bloody corncob really belongs. 'Then I thought about being a man,' Temple says later, 'and as soon as I thought it, it happened.... It made a kind of plopping sound, like blowing a little rubber tube wrong-side outward.... I could feel it, and I lay right still to keep from laughing about how surprised he was going to be...' " (pp. 299-301).

In Robert Penn Warren's (1946) *All the King's Men,* Jack Burden's mother seems to him "a woman without heart, who loved merely power over men and the momentary satisfaction to vanity or flesh which they could give her." She is, in short, according to Fiedler, the conventional bitch of contemporary American fiction. The epitome, perhaps, of the phallic mother is seen in *Man and Boy,* by Wright Morris (1951). An obsessive-compulsive tidy housewife, who pares her toenails with a knife stolen from her husband, she is universally called "Mother," although her only son died before the action begins. "She has, in effect, killed him, driven 'the Boy' before her merciless, unremitting, and unsympathetic love, first into the household refuge of the bathroom, then to the more universal sanctuary of the war, in which he has died a hero's death. Early in the game she has wrested from 'the Boy' the gun, given to him by his defeated father as a token of manhood; and having no other way of making a big bang, 'the Boy' ended by blowing himself up" (Fiedler, 1960, p. 309).

The machinations of Laura Bingham, an aging star of theater and television, a "terrible bitch," most of whose "beauty comes off with cold cream," pales in comparison. She is an incidental bed partner of Harold's in Malone's (1973) *The Corruption of Harold Hoskins,* who finds "she's been to bed with half the good-looking young men in the city. She never goes to bed with any of them twice, so there's no question of them using her. Instead, she uses them. She makes you feel like a soiled piece of kleenex when you leave" (p. 95). The inescapable inference here is that the double standard exists, acceptable if the man discards the woman as he would a used tissue, but not the reverse. Darley, the narrator in Durrell's (1957) *Justine,* admired Justine because "She talked like a man and I talked to her like a man [pp. 15-16] ... I will say only that in many things she thought as a man, while in her actions she enjoyed some of the free vertical independence of the masculine outlook [p. 17] ... It was as if men knew at once that they were in the presence of someone who could not be judged according to the standards they had hitherto employed in thinking about women [p. 71] ... [Selflessness] is what Justine loved in me—not my personality. Women are sexual robbers, and it was this treasure of detachment she hoped to steal from me..." (p. 200). But Darley, like many men, is mistaken about Justine's "masculinity." In *Mountolive* (1959), she explains: she had given him the notes for *Moeurs,* an autobiographical novel written by her first husband. "I used to copy out all Arnauti's notes for *Moeurs* in my own handwriting when he broke his wrist. I have given them to Darley as my diary ... He accepts them as mine, and says, not unnaturally, that I have a masculine mind..." (pp. 207-208). And Kit's friend in *What Makes Sammy Run,* by Budd Schulberg (1941), says to her, "You think more like a man than any woman I've ever known—and most men." To which she replies, "If you think that's a compliment, you're crazy. Every time a man discovers that a woman thinks, the only way he can explain it is that she happens to have a male mind" (p. 117).

Lady Cicely Wanfete in *Captain Brassbound's Conversion* (1913) is one of Shaw's monumental women, something more than a man, something less than female. Professor Henry Higgins in *My Fair Lady* asks, "Why can't a woman be more like a man?" Squire Western's sister, the aunt of Tom's beloved Sophia in Henry Fielding's (1749) *Tom Jones* (p. 230), is described as a "masculine person, which was near six foot high, [which] added to her manner and learning, possibly [preventing] the other sex from regarding her, notwithstanding her petticoats, in the light of a woman." Emma Bovary came to scorn her second lover, whom she intimidated and lorded over. "He was her mistress," Flaubert remarked, without indulging in speculation on the feminine submissiveness of Léon or on the virility of Emma (Peyre, 1962). Baudelaire was less discreet in his essay that analyzed her imagination, her generous and masculine way of giving herself: " 'Madame Bovary, through all that is most energetic and most ambitious in her, and also all that is most dreamy, has remained a man' " (*ibid.,* p. 344). Just so is Bella Mount in Meredith's (1859) *The Ordeal of Richard Feverel.* She has been paid by Lord Mountfalcon to keep Richard in London, by seducing him if necessary. She offers Richard a wide variety of sexual entertainment. One moment she is warmly feminine and the next "She was cold as ice, she hated talk about love" (p. 476). Richard says, "She's very like a man, only much nicer" (p. 455). Her conversation at times is "manlike" and she loves to masquerade as a man: "Wasn't it a shame to make a woman of me when I was born to be a man?" (p. 475). And the rapist in Connell's (1966) *The Diary of a Rapist* mutters to himself as he glances at his wife who is sitting at the vanity table, plucking a hair from her chin, "I don't know why she felt like pulling that hair, should think she'd let it grow, there's nothing she wants more than to be a man" (p. 7).

It is reasonable to presume that every situation of psychological castration must involve a symbiotically castratable relationship. Richard Feverel is castration-prone, and the rapist a latent homosexual. To the daughter of an overly dominant, excessively strong father, femininity may seem inevitably linked with weakness and inferiority, while masculinity is seen as strong and superior. Thus, such a daughter may well begin to take on behavioral patterns imitative of the father; and these patterns, when she encounters men her own age, may make her attempt to be extremely aggressive and controlling, traits unconsciously encouraged by both her parents. The transvestitism of Bella Mount is a symbolic form of denial of castration fear through creation of a phallic woman. Identification of oneself with an autonomous phallus, wrote Chasseguet-Smirgel (1970), results in a pathological form of secondary narcissism. "The woman who identifies with the phallus desires only to be desired. She establishes herself as a phallus; this implies impenetrability and therefore withdrawal from any relations with an external erotic object. The phallus/woman resembles, more than any other woman, what Freud (1914) described as the narcissistic woman whose fascination, similar to that of a child, is linked with her 'inaccessibility,' like the 'charm of certain animals which seem not to concern themselves about us, such as cats and the large beasts of prey.' Further on, Freud mentions the 'enigmatic nature' and the 'cold and narcissistic' attitude these women have toward men. Rather than seeing in this the essence of women's object relations, I see it as an identification with an autonomous phallus. Is it not true that men admire the phallus in these women more than the women themselves?" (pp. 123-124).

Paul Bowles' (1952) *Let It Come Down* contains a portrait of such a woman, Daisy, the Marquesa de Valverde, whose husband the Marquis is her third. She justified her behavior:

> If you had spent your childhood astride a horse, riding with your four brothers around the fifty thousand acres of estancia, it was natural that you should become the sort of woman she had become, and you could hardly expect men to feel protective toward you. As a matter of fact, it was often quite the reverse: she sometimes found her male friends looking to her for moral support. [In a reflective

mood, Daisy wondered,] What did it mean ... to be what your friends called a forceful woman? Although they intended to mean it as such, they did not manage to make it a flattering epithet; she knew that. It was adverse criticism. If you said a woman was forceful, you meant that she got what she wanted in too direct a manner, that she was not enough of a woman, that she was un-subtle, pushing. It was almost as much of an insult to say that a man had a weak character. Yet her closest friends were in the habit of using the word openly to describe her; "even to my face," she thought, with mingled resentment and satisfaction. It was as if, in accepting the contemporary fallacy that women should have the same aims and capacities as men, they assumed that any quality which was a virtue in a man was equally desirable in a woman. But when she heard the word "forceful" being used in connection with herself, even though she knew it was perfectly true and not intended as derogation, she immediately felt like some rather ungraceful predatory animal, and the sensation did not please her [pp. 206-207].

Thus there is a kind of woman who, because she will not admit the lack of what she considers the most important organ, behaves, feels, and often thinks as though she were a man, in this way developing a masculine type of character. The bewilderment and feelings of in-feriority of such women are the manifestations of a profound shock dating back to the time of the first realization of the organ deficiency. The female often compensates and attempts to drown her profound depression and dissatisfaction by violent aggression and hostility against men in general.

"I wonder," says the narrator in Stephen Vizinczey's (1965) *In Praise of Older Women,* "what kind of life would I have had if it hadn't been for my mother's tea-and-cookie parties? Perhaps it's because of them that I've never thought of women as my enemies, as territories I have to conquer—which I believe is the reason why they were friendly to me in turn. I've never met those she-devils modern fiction is so full of: they must be too busy with those men who look upon women as fortresses they have to attack and trample underfoot" (pp. 17-18). The she-devils are nowhere to be found more accurately and subtly portrayed than in Eudora Welty's (1941) short story, "Petrified Man." Jones (1957) clues the reader in by giving emphasis to the title of the story itself. Although there is a specific petrified man in the story itself, the title pointedly omits the definite article, suggesting that the story deals with debilitated and castrated men in general. The women in the story dominate the men and train them for "petrified servility ... they will conquer with whatever weapons [they command] any recalcitrant male who will not submit to their seemingly inevitable control." In their conversations, Leota, the beautician, and Mrs. Fletcher disparage the mention of any husband whose name crops up. Mrs. Fletcher's reaction to her pregnancy is one of horror and disgust, for in attempting to dominate man, she feels somehow that the womanly act of childbearing is debasing. The females in "Petrified Man" seem "to be trying to be something other than real women. Because they have gone so far toward unsexing the men, they themselves must hide their own sex as well" (Jones, 1957, pp. 1-3).

Gatiss, in talking to George Dancer, the dandy in Derek Marlowe's *A Dandy in Aspic* (1966), says:

Women, Dancer, are destructive animals. One can meet a beautiful woman one day and she will kiss your feet the next. You surrender your identity to them, allow them to share your waking moments in rapidly enlarging installments, and soon you will find they are using you. They wave their neuroses before you like a leper's bell, knowing you cannot ignore them, and you suffer them their self-pity and their pathetic bleats of negative living until one day you find yourself eaten by them, degraded, scoured out, tied to the rack of their pathetic nullity. Women use us, and the only way to treat them is to use *them*. Use them to sleep with, use them to cook for you, use them to run errands, but never, never allow yourself to enter that mental tic of their femininity. If you do, you are nothing. Your own laughingstock... [p. 167].

"The standard female in the fiction of Norman Mailer is aggressive, belittling to men, dominating and castrating ... such as Guinevere in *Barbary Shore*, Dorothea and Lulu in *The Deer Park*, the infamous Denise in "The Time of Her Time," Deborah, the great bitch of *An American Dream*, and Alice Jethroe in *Why Are We in Vietnam?*" (Gordon, 1969, p. 5). In Mailer's (1941) short story, "Maybe Next Year," the young boy narrator is trapped in a circle of misery, plagued and mistreated by a domineering, nagging mother and a uxurious, cruel father. He is "acutely conscious of his inferior status, longs for power, which involves usurping the father's role and winning the undivided affection of the mother ... [who] is viewed as fearful. His father is so henpecked that the son fears his mother will do to him what she seems to have done to his father, that is, emasculate him" (Gordon, 1969, pp. 5-6).

The phallic mother is clearly distinguishable from the oedipal mother. The former is a much more terrible image and stems from the pregenital level of experience; the latter is typically passive and ineffectual, since on this level the father is the real object of fear. The classical portrait of the seductive yet castrating mother who denies any sexual awareness on either her part of her child's is readily recognizable in Mrs. Portnoy, in Philip Roth's (1969) *Portnoy's Complaint*. "What? For your little thing?" she asks when her son wants a built-in jockstrap for his bathing trunks. As Portnoy tells his analyst, "Maybe she only said it once ... but it was enough for a lifetime!" The narrator's voice in Virginia Woolf's *To the Lighthouse* (1927) creates a view of Mrs. Ramsay that none of the characters in the novel have of her. Sometimes it seems to come from Mrs. Ramsay's fantasies of herself, sometimes it seems to "issue from above, or from the surrounding atmosphere." Wherever it has its origin, the narrator's dominant fantasy is partly that of the phallic mother: "Mrs. Ramsay is both female and male, the Lighthouse in both its masculine and feminine associations, in its phallic and in its maternal role" (Corsa, 1971).

The fantasy of the mother with a penis is constructed from the idea of the primal scene, whether it has really been observed or merely imagined. "Furthermore, in the course of development, the early fantasies are reconstructed in relation to later experiences. Masochistic, oral, anal, or phallic fantasies formed around the image of the phallic mother, or the father-mother, can be reconstructed around the oedipal image of the father in a classical, passive homosexual pattern" (David, 1970, p. 62). The origin of the fantasy of the woman with a penis began in an attempt to deny the vagina, the wound, the absence of the penis, that is, in castration anxiety. For the mother is feared and hated as well as desired and envied, with the child possibly wishing to play the passive partner to the mother with a penis, leading to castration fears. This is particularly notable from the clinical material on the transvestite play of children which appears to be the result of an identification with a phallic mother as a means of handling severe castration threats (Friend et al., 1954).

The mother in D. H. Lawrence's (1913) *Sons and Lovers* is the dominant personality, aside from Paul Morel. The first victim of her destructive love is not Paul, nor his older brother William, but the father, Walter Morel. What Gertrude does to her husband is reduce him to a child by her refusal or inability to accept the only kind of maturity, simple and animal, of which he is capable, thus symbolically emasculating him (Hardy, 1964). Lawrence never directly attributes Morel's unmanning to anyone but the man himself: "He had denied the God in him." His characterization of Paul, the son, is based on the premise that an individual often depersonalizes other people because he feels they are depersonalizing him (Laing, 1966). Paul depersonalizes Miriam and Clara primarily because he experiences such fears in his contacts with the two women, without understanding that his fears are largely fears of the phallic mother. He tells Clara that Miriam "seems to draw me and draw me, and she wouldn't leave a single hair of me free to fall out and blow away—she'd keep it" (Lawrence, 1913, p. 227). He fears that she drags all "his strength and energy into herself. . . . She wanted to draw all of him into her" (p. 194). At the end of the novel, Paul tells Miriam ". . . you love me so much, you want to put me in your pocket. And I should die there smothered" (p. 417). He thinks that in staying with her, he would be "stifling the inner, desperate man . . . denying his own life" (p. 418).

One of the most remarkably drawn phallic mothers and phallic wives is Anne Crump in Ludwig Lewisohn's (1926) autobiographical novel, *The Case of Mr. Crump*. Springing from "an atmosphere of raw sensuality and stentorian cant," the legitimacy of her birth in question, arrogant, vain and ruthless, Mrs. Crump assumes an air of contemptuous superiority over her castratable husband, Herbert. He is twenty-four, she forty-three, already married, and the mother of several children. She becomes "a vicarious refuge" in place of his own mother; with instinctive duplicity she prepares a trap and persuades him that she has become necessary to him and, when finally married, refrains from no deception, falsehood, open brutality, slander, theft, and degradation to keep him (Bragman, 1931). In her treatment of Herbert, Mrs. Crump adopts "the physical attitude behind the typical gesture of the eighteenth century, the Hogarthian wench: chin thrust forward, hair dishevelled, arms akimbo. 'What, darn your socks? I never yet darned socks for any man! Why, Jesus Christ, I don't darn my own stockings. Why don't you make money, and hire servants, God damn you!' " (Lewisohn, p. 23). An iron "instinct forbade her to admit anything that could be construed as a diminution of her condescension to any member of the male sex" (pp. 17-18). A protective, shielding attitude toward Anne was unthinkable. "You cannot protect an engine. It goes over you or you hide behind it and let it go over others.... Mrs. Crump asserted, without fear of contradiction, that all men were cowards, though they would like immensely to be bullies and that she for her part, in the words of her sacred mother, was not afraid of the face of clay..." (p. 21). When her first husband, Harrison Vilas, contracted gonorrhea, Mrs. Crump said, "I'm accustomed to being wanted, not to chasing after a mere man," (p. 25) and would dwell on the incident with triumphant vindictiveness. Anne Vilas, while courting Herbert Crump, "did her best to enmesh Herbert in soft, strong tentacles, to play upon the physical habit established between them, upon his compassion, upon his sense of honor" (p. 109). Underneath her pathos were "hardness, iron determination and an aggressive lack of shame posing as helplessness" (p. 113). Crump realizes that Anne has a real tenderness for him, "but the aliveness of that feeling is dependent on my being here—her object, her thing, slave, prisoner, merged with her family, serving her interests; it depends on the exclusion of my parents, of my art except as an impersonal means of winning bread, of friends, interests, occupations beyond these walls. She operates with the most primitive instincts of the wife and mother animal toward its mate" (p. 163). The self-pitying motif in the novel reveals Crump's oedipal needs and unconscious sadomasochistic desires.

Hannah Gonen, in *My Michael* by Amos Oz (1972), is an Israeli Madame Bovary, but rather than fleeing to romantic infidelity like Emma, she resorts to schizophrenia. She is a driven woman, seeing reality in the high-intensity flashes of a disturbed poetic vision. In the logic of her obsessions, everything she undergoes or thinks is transformed by the weird alchemy of her sexual preoccupations, her apprehension of pain and humiliation, her growing fear of losing touch with reality. Throughout the novel Hannah gradually abandons herself to fantasies of controlling like slaves two Arab boys, twins she played with as a girl. "When I was nine I still used to wish I could grow up as a female instead of a male. As a child I always played with boys and I always read boys' books. I used to wrestle, kick and climb" (p. 8). Then she recalls the twin Arabs, Halil and Aziz. "I was a princess and they were my bodyguard, and I was a conqueror and they were my officers.... I ruled over the twins. It was a cold pleasure, so remote" (p. 9). Hannah is obsessed with erotic fantasies, symbolic castration and phallicisms, and especially with conflicted ideas about strength. On her first date with Michael, whom she later marries, she thinks, "I am not particularly strong, but I am stronger than this young man" (p. 10). Her father, whose aphorisms she recalls throughout the novel, "often used to say: Strong people can do almost anything they want to do, but even the strongest cannot choose what they want to do" (p. 8). She thinks of Palmach men and of "thick-limbed tractor drivers coming all dirty from the Negev like marauders carrying off the women of some captured city" (p. 12). As a child, while ill with diptheria, she had phallic sadistic fantasies of being "a general on a train. Troops loyal to me commanded the high ground. I was an emperor in hiding. An emperor whose authority was undiminished by distance and isolation . . . I used to carry my dreams over into the works of waking. . . . I was a queen. My cool mastery was challenged by open rebellion. I was captured by the mob, imprisoned, humiliated, tortured" (p. 20). While reading a novel, Hannah thinks, "If I were Tamar I would make Ammon crawl to me on his knees for seven nights" (p. 22). On her second date with Michael, she tells him of her passion for boys' books and games and how she hates being a girl. "Even now I sometimes long to meet a man like Michael Strogoff. Big and strong, but at the same time quiet and reserved. He must be silent, loyal, subdued, but only controlling the spate of his inner energies with an effort" (p. 28).

While the pair are out strolling, Hannah's hands become cold and Michael says jokingly, "Cold hands, warm heart." "My father had warm hands *and* a warm heart. He had a radio and electrical business, but he was a bad businessman. I remember him standing doing the washing-up with my mother's apron round him. Dusting. Beating bedspreads. Expertly making omelettes. Absently blessing the Hanukah lights. Treasuring the remarks of every good-for-nothing. Always trying to please. As if everyone was judging him, and he, exhausted, was forever being forced to do well in some endless examination, to atone for some forgotten shortcoming." Michael says: "The man you marry will have to be a very strong man" (pp. 29-30). In the first week of their marriage, Hannah has conflicted, ambivalent feelings of being ravished. "If my husband had attacked me like a man dying of thirst I should have been ashamed of myself. If Michael had approached me as if I were a delicate instrument, or like a scientist handling a test tube, why was I upset?" (p. 55). The repressed wish to be a male is here found in the sublimated form of an abiding fantasy life. The phallic woman has not worked through the Oedipus complex successfully, and her capacity to love is imperfect. The oral and anal periods are marked by narcissism and ambivalence, which are, optimally, overcome in the genital phase. The genital character has a capacity for affectionate love which makes other people valuable to her, or him. "We are thus led to the conclusion," wrote Abraham (1925), "that the definite character development in each individual is dependent upon the history of his Oedipus complex, and particularly on the capacity he has developed for transferring his friendly feelings on to other people or on to his whole environment. If he has failed in this, if he has not succeeded in sufficiently developing his social feelings, a marked disturbance of his character will be the direct consequence" (p. 410).

The action in Herman Melville's (1854) short story, "I and My Chimney," reproduced below in a slightly abridged version, turns on the affection of the narrator for his beloved old chimney, which he describes in proud detail, and his lengthy dispute with his wife who wants to remove it entirely from the house.

I and my chimney, two gray-headed old smokers, reside in the country. We are, I may say, old settlers here; particularly my old chimney, which settles more and more every day.

Though I always say, *I and my chimney,* as Cardinal Wolsey used to say, *I and my King,* yet this egotistic way of speaking, wherein I take precedence of my chimney, is hardly borne out by the facts; in everything, except the above phrase, my chimney taking precedence of me.

Within thirty feet of the turf-sided road, my chimney—a huge, corpulent old Harry VIII of a chimney—rises full in front of me and all my possessions. Standing well up a hill-side, my chimney, like Lord Rosse's monster telescope, swung vertical to hit the meridian moon, is the first object to greet the approaching traveler's eye, nor is it the last which the sun salutes. My chimney, too, is before me in receiving the first-fruits of the seasons. The snow is on its head ere on my hat; and every spring, as in a hollow beech tree, the first swallows build their nests in it.

But it is within doors that the pre-eminence of my chimney is most manifest. When in the rear room, set apart for that object, I stand to receive my guests (who, by the way, call more, I suspect, to see my chimney than me), I then stand, not so much before, as, strictly speaking, behind my chimney, which is, indeed, the true host. Not that I demur. In the presence of my betters, I hope I know my place.

From this habitual precedence of my chimney over me, some even think that I have got into a sad rearward way altogether; in short, from standing behind my old-fashioned chimney so much, I have got to be quite behind the age, too, as well as running behind-hand in everything else. But to tell the truth, I never was a very forward old fellow, nor what my farming neighbors call a forehanded one. Indeed, those rumors about my behindhandedness are so far correct, that I have an odd sauntering way with me sometimes of going about with my hands behind my back. As for my belonging to the rear-guard in general, certain it is, I bring up the rear of my chimney—which, by the way, is this moment before me—and that, too, both in fancy and in fact. In brief, my chimney is my superior; my superior by I know not how many heads and shoulders; my superior, too, in that humbly bowing over with shovel and tongs, I much minister to it; yet never does it minister, or incline over to me; but, if anything, in its settlings, rather leans the other way.

My chimney is grand seignior here—the one great domineering object, not more of the landscape, than of the house; all the rest of which house, in each architectural arrangement, as may shortly appear, is, in the most marked manner, accommodated, not to my wants, but to my chimney's, which, among other things, has the centre of the house to himself leaving but the odd holes and corners to me.

But I and my chimney must explain; and, as we are both rather obese, we may have to expatiate.

*   *   *

Most houses here, are but one and a half stories high; few exceed two. That in which I and my chimney dwell, is in width nearly twice its height, from sill to eaves—which accounts for the magnitude of its main content—besides, showing that in this house, as in this country at large, there is abundance of space, and to spare, for both of us.

The frame of the old house is of wood—which but the more sets forth the solidity of the chimney, which is of brick. And as the great wrought nails, binding the clapboards, are unknown in these degenerate days, so are the huge bricks in the chimney walls. The architect of the chimney must have had the pyramid of Cheops before him; for, after that famous structure, it seems modeled, only its rate

of decrease towards the summit is considerably less, and it is trun-
cated. From the exact middle of the mansion it soars from the
cellar, right up through each successive floor, till, four feet square,
it breaks water from the ridgepole of the roof, like an anvil-headed
whale, through the crest of a billow. Most people, though, liken it,
in that part, to a razed observatory, masoned up.

*   *   *

Large as the chimney appears upon the roof, that is nothing to its
spaciousness below. At its base in the cellar, it is precisely twelve
feet square; and hence covers precisely one hundred and forty-four
superficial feet. What an appropriation of terra firma for a chimney, and what a huge load for this earth! In fact, it was only because
I and my chimney formed no part of his ancient burden, that that
stout peddler, Atlas of old, was enabled to stand up so bravely under
his pack. The dimensions given may, perhaps, seem fabulous. But,
like those stones at Gilgal, which Joshua set up for a memorial of
having passed over Jordan, does not my chimney remain, even unto
this day?

Very often I go down into my cellar, and attentively survey that
vast square of masonry. I stand long, and ponder over, and wonder
at it. It has a druidical look, away down in the umbrageous cellar
there, whose numerous vaulted passages, and far glens of gloom,
resemble the dark, damp depths of primeval woods. So strongly did
this conceit steal over me, so deeply was I penetrated with wonder at
the chimney, that one day—when I was a little out of my mind, I
now think—getting a spade from the garden, I set to work, digging
round the foundation, especially at the corners thereof, obscurely
prompted by dreams of striking upon some old, earthen-worn memorial of that by-gone day when, into all this gloom, the light of
heaven entered, as the masons laid the foundation-stones, perad-
venture sweltering under an August sun, or pelted by a March
storm. Plying my blunted spade, how vexed was I by that ungracious
interruption of a neighbor who, calling to see me upon some business, and being informed that I was below, said I need not be
troubled to come up, but he would go down to me; and so, without
ceremony, and without my having been forewarned, suddenly discovered me, digging in my cellar.

"Gold digging, sir?"

"Nay, sir," answered I, starting, "I was merely—ahem!—merely—
I say I was merely digging—round my chimney."

"Ah, loosening the soil, to make it grow. Your chimney, sir, you regard as too small, I suppose; needing further development, especially at the top?"

"Sir!" said I, throwing down the spade, "do not be personal. I and my chimney—"

"Personal?"

"Sir, I look upon this chimney less as a pile of masonry than as a personage. It is the king of the house. I am but a suffered and inferior subject."

In fact, I would permit no gibes to be cast at either myself or my chimney; and never again did my visitor refer to it in my hearing, without coupling some compliment with the mention. It well deserves a respectful consideration. There it stands, solitary and alone —not a council-of-ten flues, but, like his sacred majesty of Russia, a unit of an autocrat.

Even to me, its dimensions, at times, seem incredible. It does not look so big—no, not even in the cellar. By the mere eye, its magnitude can be but imperfectly comprehended, because only one side can be received at one time; and said side can only present twelve feet, linear measure. But then, each other side also is twelve feet long; and the whole obviously forms a square; and twelve times twelve is one hundred and forty-four. And so, an adequate conception of the magnitude of this chimney is only to be got at by a sort of process in the higher mathematics, by a method somewhat akin to those whereby the surprising distances of fixed stars are computed.

It need hardly be said, that the walls of my house are entirely free from fire-places. These all congregate in the middle—in the one grand central chimney, upon all four sides of which are hearths —two tiers of hearths—so that when, in the various chambers, my family and guests are warming themselves of a cold winter's night, just before retiring, then, though at the time they may not be thinking so, all their faces mutually look towards each other, yea, all their feet point to one centre; and, when they go to sleep in their beds, they all sleep round one warm chimney, like so many Iroquois Indians, in the woods, round their one heap of embers. And just as the Indians' fire serves, not only to keep them comfortable, but also to keep off wolves, and other savage monsters, so my chimney, by its obvious smoke at top, keeps off prowling burglars from the towns— for what burglar or murderer would dare break into an abode from whose chimney issues such a continual smoke—betokening that if the inmates are not stirring, at least fires are, and in case of an alarm, candles may be lighted, to say nothing of muskets.

But stately as is the chimney—yea, grand high alter as it is, right worthy for the celebration of high mass before the Pope of Rome, and all his cardinals—yet what is there perfect in this world? Caius Julius Caesar, had he not been so inordinately great, they say that Brutus, Cassius, Antony, and the rest, had been greater. My chimney, were it not so mighty in its magnitude, my chambers had been larger. How often has my wife ruefully told me, that my chimney, like the English aristocracy, casts a contracting shade all round it. She avers that endless domestic inconveniences arise—more particularly from the chimney's stubborn central locality. The grand objection with her is, that it stands midway in the place where a fine entrance-hall ought to be. In truth, there is no hall whatever to the house—nothing but a sort of square landing-place, as you enter from the wide front door. A roomy enough landing-place, I admit, but not attaining to the dignity of a hall. Now, as the front door is precisely in the middle of the front of the house, inwards it faces the chimney. In fact, the opposite wall of the landing-place is formed solely by the chimney; and hence—owing to the gradual tapering of the chimney—is a little less than twelve feet in width. Climbing the chimney this part, is the principal stair-case—which, by three abrupt turns, and three minor landing-places, mounts to the second floor, where, over the front door, runs a sort of narrow gallery, something less than twelve feet long, leading to chambers on either hand. This gallery, of course, is railed; and so, looking down upon the stairs, and all those landing-places together, with the main one at the bottom, resembles not a little a balcony for musicians, in some jolly old abode, in times Elizabethan. Shall I tell a weakness? I cherish the cobwebs there, and many a time arrest Biddy in the act of brushing them with her broom, and have many a quarrel with my wife and daughters about it.

*   *   *

Ah, a warm heart has my chimney.

How often my wife was at me about that projected grand entrance-hall of hers, which was to be knocked clean through the chimney, from one end of the house to the other, and astonish all guests by its generous amplitude. "But, wife," said I, "the chimney—consider the chimney: if you demolish the foundation, what is to support the superstructure?" "Oh, that will rest on the second floor." The truth is, women know next to nothing about the realities of architecture. However, my wife still talked of running her entries and partitions. She spent many long nights elaborating her plans; in imagination building her boasted hall through the chimney, as though its high mightiness were a mere spear of sorrel-top. At last, I gently reminded her that, little as she might fancy it, the chimney was a fact—a sober, substantial fact, which, in all her plannings, it would be well to take into full consideration. But this was not of much avail.

And here, respectfully craving her permission, I must say a few words about this enterprising wife of mine. Though in years nearly old as myself, in spirit she is young as my little sorrel mare, Trigger, that threw me last fall. What is extraordinary, though she comes of a rheumatic family, she is straight as a pine, never has any aches; while for me with the sciatica, I am sometimes as crippled up as any old apple tree. But she has not so much as a toothache. As for her hearing—let me enter the house in my dusty boots, and she away up in the attic. And for her sight—Biddy, the housemaid, tells other people's housemaids, that her mistress will spy a spot on the dresser straight through the pewter platter, put up on purpose to hide it. Her faculties are alert as her limbs and her senses. No danger of my spouse dying of torpor. The longest night in the year I've known her lie awake, planning her campaign for the morrow. She is a natural projector. The maxim, "Whatever is, is right," is not hers. Her maxim is, Whatever is, is wrong; and what is more, must be altered; and what is still more, must be altered right away. Dreadful maxim for the wife of a dozy old dreamer like me, who dotes on seventh days as days of rest, and, out of a sabbatical horror of industry, will, on a week-day, go out of my road a quarter of a mile, to avoid the sight of a man at work.

That matches are made in heaven, may be, but my wife would have been just the wife for Peter the Great, or Peter the Piper. How she would have set in order that huge littered empire of the one, and with indefatigable painstaking picked the peck of pickled peppers for the other.

But the most wonderful thing is, my wife never thinks of her end. Her youthful incredulity, as to the plain theory, and still plainer fact of death, hardly seems Christian. Advanced in years, as she knows she must be, my wife seems to think that she is to teem on, and be inexhaustible forever. She doesn't believe in old age. At that strange promise in the plain of Mamre, my old wife, unlike old Abraham's, would not have jeeringly laughed within herself.

Judge how to me, who, sitting in the comfortable shadow of my chimney, smoking my comfortable pipe, with ashes not unwelcome at my feet, and ashes not unwelcome all but in my mouth; and who am thus in a comfortable sort of not unwelcome, though, indeed, ashy enough way, reminded of the ultimate exhaustion even of the most fiery life; judge how to me this unwarrantable vitality in my wife must come, sometimes, it is true, with a moral and a calm, but oftener with a breeze and a ruffle.

If the doctrine be true, that in wedlock contraries attract, by how cogent a fatality must I have been drawn to my wife! While spicily impatient of present and past, like a glass of ginger-beer she overflows with her schemes; and, with like energy as she puts down her foot, puts down her preserves and her pickles, and lives with them in a continual future; or ever full of expectations both from time and space, is ever restless for newspapers, and ravenous for letters. Content with the years that are gone, taking no thought for the morrow and looking for no new thing from any person or quarter whatever, I have not a single scheme or expectation on earth, save in unequal resistance of the undue encroachment of hers.

Old myself, I take to oldness in things; for that cause mainly loving old Montaigne, and old cheese, and old wine; and eschewing young people, hot rolls, new books, and early potatoes, and very fond of my old claw-footed chair, and old club-footed Deacon White, my neighbor, and that still nigher old neighbor, my betwisted old grape-vine, that of a summer evening leans in his elbow for cosy company at my window-sill, while I, within doors, lean over mine to meet his; and above all, high above all, am fond of my high-manteled old chimney. But she, out of that infatuate juvenility of hers, takes to nothing but newness; for that cause mainly, loving new cider in autumn, and in spring, as if she were own daughter of Nebuchadnezzar, fairly raving after all sorts of salads and spinaches, and more particularly green cucumbers (though all the time nature rebukes such unsuitable young hankerings in so elderly a person, by never permitting such things to agree with her), and has an itch after recently-discovered fine prospects (so no grave-yard be in the background), and also after Swedenborgianism, and the Spirit Rapping philosophy, with other new views, alike in things natural and unnatural; and immortally hopeful, is forever making new flower-beds even on the north side of the house, where the bleak mountain wind would scarce allow the wiry weed called hardhack to gain a thorough footing; and on the road-side sets out mere pipestems of young elms; though there is no hope of any shade from them, except over the ruins of her great granddaughters' gravestones; and won't wear caps, but plaits her gray hair; and takes the Ladies' Magazine for the fashions; and always buys her new almanac a month before the new year; and rises at dawn; and to the warmest sunset turns a cold shoulder; and still goes on at odd hours with her new course of history, and her French, and her music; and likes young company; and offers to ride young colts; and sets out young suckers in the orchard; and has a spite against my elbowed old grape-vine, and my club-footed old neighbor, and my claw-footed old chair, and above all, high above all, would fain persecute, unto death, my high-manteled old chimney. By what perverse magic, I a thousand times think, does such a very autumnal old lady have such a very vernal young soul? When I would remonstrate at times, she spins round on me with, "Oh, don't you grumble, old man (she always calls me old man), it's I, young I, that keep you from stagnating." Well, I suppose it is so. Yea, after all, these things are well ordered. My wife, as one of her poor relations, good soul, intimates, is the salt of the earth, and none the less the salt of my sea, which otherwise were unwholesome. She is its monsoon, too, blowing a brisk gale over it, in the one steady direction of my chimney.

Not insensible of her superior energies, my wife has frequently made me propositions to take upon herself all the responsibilities of my affairs. She is desirous that, domestically, I should abdicate; that, renouncing further rule, like the venerable Charles V, I should retire into some sort of monastery. But indeed, the chimney excepted, I have little authority to lay down. By my wife's ingenious application of the principle that certain things belong of right to female jurisdiction, I find myself, through my easy compliances, insensibly stripped by degrees of one masculine prerogative after another. In a dream I go about my fields, a sort of lazy, happy-go-lucky, good-for-nothing, loafing, old Lear. Only by some sudden revelation am I reminded who is over me; as year before last, one day seeing in one corner of the premises fresh deposits of mysterious boards and timbers, the oddity of the incident at length begat serious meditation. "Wife," said I, "whose boards and timbers are those I see near the orchard there? Do you know anything about them, wife? Who put them there? You know I do not like the neighbors to use my land that way; they should ask permission first."

She regarded me with a pitying smile.

"Why, old man, don't you know I am building a new barn? Didn't you know that, old man?"

This is the poor old lady that was accusing me of tyrannizing over her.

To return now to the chimney. Upon being assured of the futility of her proposed hall, so long as the obstacle remained, for a time my wife was for a modified project. But I could never exactly comprehend it. As far as I could see through it, it seemed to involve the general idea of a sort of irregular archway, or elbowed tunnel, which was to penetrate the chimney at some convenient point under the stair-case, and carefully avoiding dangerous contact with the fire-places, and particularly steering clear of the great interior flue, was to conduct the enterprising traveler from the front door all the way to the dining-room in the remote rear of the mansion. Doubtless it was a bold stroke of genius, that plan of hers, and so was Nero's when he schemed his grand canal through the Isthmus of Corinth. Nor will I take oath, that, had her project been accomplished, then, by help of lights hung at judicious intervals through the tunnel, some Belzoni or other might have succeeded in future ages in penetrating through the masonry, and actually emerging into the dining-room, and once there, it would have been inhospitable treatment of such a traveler to have denied him a recruiting meal.

But my bustling wife did not restrict her objections, nor in the end confine her proposed alterations to the first floor. Her ambition was of the mounting order. She ascended with her schemes to the second floor, and so to the attic. Perhaps there was some small ground for her discontent with things as they were. The truth is, there was no regular passage-way up stairs or down, unless we again except that little orchestra-gallery before mentioned. And all this was owing to the chimney, which my gamesome spouse seemed despitefully to regard as the bully of the house.

*   *   *

Now, of all these things and many, many more, my family continually complained. At last my wife came out with her sweeping proposition—in toto to abolish the chimney.

"What!" said I, "abolish the chimney? To take out the back-bone of anything, wife, is a hazardous affair. Spines out of backs, and chimneys out of houses, are not to be taken like frosted lead-pipes from the ground. Besides," added I, "the chimney is the one grand permanence of this abode. If undisturbed by innovators, then in future ages, when all the house shall have crumbled from it, this chimney will still survive—a Bunker Hill monument. No, no, wife, I can't abolish my back-bone."

So said I then. But who is sure of himself, especially an old man, with both wife and daughters ever at his elbow and ear? In time, I was persuaded to think a little better of it; in short, to take the matter into preliminary consideration. At length it came to pass that a master-mason—a rough sort of architect—one Mr. Scribe, was summoned to a conference. I formally introduced him to my chimney. A previous introduction from my wife had introduced him to myself. He had been not a little employed by that lady, in preparing plans and estimates for some of her extensive operations in drainage. Having, with much ado, extorted from my spouse the promise that she would leave us to an unmolested survey, I began by leading Mr. Scribe down to the root of the matter, in the cellar. Lamp in hand, I descended; for though up stairs it was noon, below it was night.

We seemed in the pyramids; and I, with one hand holding my lamp overhead, and with the other pointing out, in the obscurity, the hoar mass of the chimney, seemed some Arab guide, showing the cob-webbed mausoleum of the gread god Apis.

"This is a most remarkable structure, sir," said the master-mason, after long contemplating it in silence, "a most remarkable structure, sir."

"Yes," said I, complacently, "every one says so."

"But large as it appears above the roof, I would not have inferred the magnitude of this foundation, sir," eying it critically.

Then taking out his rule, he measured it.

"Twelve feet square; one hundred and forty-four square feet! Sir, this house would appear to have been built simply for the accommodation of your chimney."

"Yes, my chimney and me. Tell me candidly, now," I added, "would you have such a famous chimney abolished?"

"I wouldn't have it in a house of mine, sir, for a gift," was the reply. "It's a losing affair altogether, sir. Do you know, sir, that in retaining this chimney, you are losing, not only one hundred and forty-four square feet of good ground, but likewise a considerable interest upon a considerable principal?"

"How?"

"Look, sir," said he, taking a bit of red chalk from his pocket, and figuring against a whitewashed wall, "twenty times eight is so and so; then forty-two times thirty-nine is so and so—ain't it, sir? Well, add those together, and subtract this here, then that makes so and so," still chalking away.

To be brief, after no small ciphering, Mr. Scribe informed me that my chimney contained, I am ashamed to say how many thousand and odd valuable bricks.

"No more," said I fidgeting. "Pray now, let us have a look above."

In that upper zone we made two more circumnavigations for the first and second floors. That done, we stood together at the foot of the stairway by the front door; my hand upon the knob, and Mr. Scribe hat in hand.

"Well, sir," said he, a sort of feeling his way, and, to help himself, fumbling with his hat, "well, sir, I think it can be done."

"What, pray, Mr. Scribe; *what* can be done?"

"Your chimney, sir; it can without rashness be removed, I think."

"*I* will think of it, too, Mr. Scribe," said I, turning the knob, and bowing him towards the open space without, "I will *think* of it, sir; it demands consideration; much obliged to ye; good morning, Mr. Scribe."

"It is all arranged, then," cried my wife with great glee, bursting from the nighest room.

"When will they begin?" demanded my daughter Julia.

"To-morrow?" asked Anna.

"Patience, patience, my dears," said I, "such a big chimney is not to be abolished in a minute."

Next morning it began again.

"You remember the chimney," said my wife.

"Wife," said I, "it is never out of my house, and never out of my mind."

"But when is Mr. Scribe to begin to pull it down?" asked Anna.

"Not to-day, Anna," said I.

"*When,* then?" demanded Julia, in alarm.

Now, if this chimney of mine was, for size, a sort of belfry, for ding-donging at me about it, my wife and daughters were a sort of bells, always chiming together, or taking up each other's melodies at every pause, my wife the keyclapper of all. A very sweet ringing, and pealing, and chiming, I confess; but then, the most silvery of bells may, sometimes, dismally toll, as well as merrily play. And as touching the subject in question, it became so now. Perceiving a strange relapse of opposition in me, wife and daughters began a soft and dirge-like, melancholy tolling over it.

At length my wife, getting much excited, declared to me, with pointed finger, that so long as that chimney stood, she should regard it as the monument of what she called my broken pledge. But finding this did not answer, the next day she gave me to understand that either she or the chimney must quit the house.

Finding matters coming to such a pass, I and my pipe philosophized over them awhile, and finally concluded between us, that little as our hearts went with the plan, yet for peace's sake, I might write out the chimney's death-warrant and, while my hand was in, scratch a note to Mr. Scribe.

Considering that I, and my chimney, and my pipe, from having been so much together, were three great cronies, the facility with which my pipe consented to a project so fatal to the goodliest of our trio; or rather, the way in which I and my pipe, in secret, conspired together, as it were, against our unsuspicious old comrade—this may seem rather strange, if not suggestive of sad reflections upon us two. But, indeed, we sons of clay, that is my pipe and I, are no whit better than the rest. Far from us, indeed, to have volunteered the betrayal of our crony. We are of a peaceable nature, too. But that love of peace it was which made us false to a mutual friend, as soon as his cause demanded a vigorous vindication. But I rejoice to add, that better and braver thoughts soon returned, as will now briefly be set forth.

To my note, Mr. Scribe replied in person.

Once more we made a survey, mainly now with a view to a pecuniary estimate.

"I will do it for five hundred dollars," said Mr. Scribe at last, again hat in hand.

"Very well, Mr. Scribe, I will think of it," replied I, again bowing him to the door.

Not unvexed by this, for the second time, unexpected response, again he withdrew, and from my wife and daughters again burst the old exclamations.

The truth is, resolve how I would, at the last pinch I and my chimney could not be parted.

"So Holofernes will have his way, never mind whose heart breaks for it," said my wife next morning, at breakfast, in that half-didactic, half-reproachful way of hers, which is harder to bear than her most energetic assault. Holofernes, too, is with her a pet name for any fell domestic despot. So, whenever, against her most ambitious innovations, those which saw me quite across the grain, I, as in the present instance, stand with however little steadfastness on the defence, she is sure to call me Holofernes, and ten to one takes the first opportunity to read aloud, with a suppressed emphasis, of an evening, the first newspaper paragraph about some tyrannic day-laborer who, after being for many years the Caligula of his family, ends by beating his long-suffering spouse to death, with a garret door wrenched off its hinges, and then, pitching his little innocents out of the window, suicidally turns inward towards the broken wall scored with the butcher's and baker's bills, and so rushes headlong to his dreadful account.

Nevertheless, for a few days, not a little to my surprise, I heard no further reproaches. An intense calm pervaded my wife, but beneath which, as in the sea, there was no knowing what portentous movements might be going on. She frequently went abroad, and in a direction which I thought not unsuspicious; namely, in the direction of New Petra, a griffin-like house of wood and stucco, in the highest style of ornamental art, graced with four chimneys in the form of erect dragons spouting smoke from their nostrils the elegant modern residence of Mr. Scribe, which he had built for the purpose of a standing advertisement, not more of his taste as an architect, than his solidity as a master-mason.

At last, smoking my pipe one morning, I heard a rap at the door, and my wife, with an air unusually quiet for her, brought me a note. [It is a letter from Mr. Scribe in which it is conjectured that somewhere concealed in the chimney is a secret chamber.]

*   *   *

But all this time I was quietly thinking to myself: Could it be hidden from me that my credulity in this instance would operate very favorably to a certain plan of theirs? How to get to the secret closet, or how to have any certainty about it at all, without making such fell work with the chimney as to render its set destruction superfluous? That my wife wished to get rid of the chimney, it needed no reflection to show; and that Mr. Scribe, for all his pretended disinterestedness, was not opposed to pocketing five hundred dollars by the operation, seemed equally evident. That my wife had, in secret, laid heads together with Mr. Scribe, I at present refrain from affirming. But when I consider her enmity against my chimney, and the steadiness with which at the last she is wont to carry out her schemes, if by hook or by crook she can, especially after having been once baffled, why, I scarcely knew at what step of hers to be surprised.

Of one thing only was I resolved, that I and my chimney should not budge.

In vain all protests. Next morning I went out into the road, where I had noticed a diabolical-looking old gander that, for its doughty exploits in the way of scratching into forbidden inclosures, had been rewarded by his master with a portentous, four-pronged, wooden decoration, in the shape of a collar of the Order of the Garotte. This gander I cornered, and rummaging out its stiffest quill, plucked it, took it home, and making a stiff pen, inscribed the following stiff note:

Chimney Side, April 2.

Mr. *Scribe.*

Sir:—For your conjecture, we return you our joint thanks and compliments, and beg leave to assure you, that

We shall remain,

Very faithfully,

The same,

I AND MY CHIMNEY.

Of course, for this epistle we had to endure some pretty sharp raps. But having at last explicitly understood from me that Mr. Scribe's note had not altered my mind one jot, my wife, to move me, among other things said, that if she remembered aright, there was a statute placing the keeping in private houses of secret closets on the same unlawful footing with the keeping of gunpowder. But it had no effect.

A few days later, my spouse changed her key.

It was nearly midnight, and all were in bed but ourselves, who sat up, one in each chimney-corner; she, needles in hand, indefatigably knitting a sock; I, pipe in mouth, indolently weaving my vapors.

It was one of the first of the chill nights in autumn. There was a fire on the hearth, burning low. The air without was torpid and heavy; the wood, by an oversight, of the sort called soggy.

"Do look at the chimney," she began; "can't you see that something must be in it?"

"Yes, wife. Truly there is smoke in the chimney, as in Mr. Scribe's note."

"Smoke? Yes, indeed, and in my eyes, too. How you two wicked old sinners do smoke!—this wicked old chimney and you."

"Wife," said I, "I and my chimney like to have a quiet smoke together, it is true, but we don't like to be called names."

"Now, dear old man," said she, softening down, and a little shifting the subject, "when you think of that old kinsman of yours, you *know* there must be a secret closet in this chimney."

"Secret ash-hole, wife, why don't you have it? Yes, I dare say there is a secret ash-hole in the chimney; for where do all the ashes go to that we drop down the queer hole yonder?"

"I know where they go to; I've been there almost as many times as the cat."

"What devil, wife, prompted you to crawl into the ash-hole! Don't you know that St. Dunstan's devil emerged from the ash-hole? You will get your death one of these days, exploring all about as you do. But supposing there be a secret closet, what then?"

"What, then? why what should be in a secret closet but—"

"Dry bones, wife," broke in I with a puff, while the sociable old chimney broke in with another.

"There again! Oh, how this wretched old chimney smokes," wiping her eyes with her handkerchief. "I've no doubt the reason it smokes so is, because that secret closet interferes with the flue. Do see, too, how the jambs here keep settling; and it's down hill all the way from the door to this hearth. This horrid old chimney will fall on our heads yet; depend upon it, old man."

"Yes, wife, I do depend on it; yes, indeed, I place every dependence on my chimney. As for its settling, I like it. I, too, am settling, you know, in my gait. I and my chimney are settling together, and shall keep settling, too, till, as in a great feather-bed, we shall both have settled away clean out of sight. But this secret oven; I mean, secret closet of yours, wife; where exactly do you suppose that secret closet is?"

"That is for Mr. Scribe to say."

"But suppose he cannot say exactly; what, then?"

"Why, then he can prove, I am sure, that it must be somewhere or other in this horrid old chimney."

"And if he can't prove that; what, then?"

"Why, then, old man," with a stately air, "I shall say little more about it."

"Agreed, wife," returned I, knocking my pipe-bowl against the jamb, "and now, to-morrow, I will a third time send for Mr. Scribe. Wife, the sciatica takes me; be so good as to put this pipe on the mantel."

"If you get the step-ladder for me, I will. This shocking old chimney, this abominable old-fashioned old chimney's mantels are so high, I can't reach them."

No opportunity, however trivial, was overlooked for a subordinate fling at the pile.

[There follows a technical discussion between the narrator and Mr. Scribe concerning the measurements of the chimney and the rooms off it on each floor.]

*   *   *

"Sir," said I, "really I am much obliged to you for this survey. It has quite set my mind at rest. And no doubt you, too, Mr. Scribe, must feel much relieved. Sir," I added, "you have made three visits to the chimney. With a business man, time is money. Here are fifty dollars, Mr. Scribe. Nay, take it. You have earned it. Your opinion is worth it. And by the way," as he modestly received the money— "have you any objections to give me a—a—little certificate—something, say, like a steam-boat certificate, certifying that you, a competent surveyor, have surveyed my chimney, and found no reason to believe any unsoundness; in short, any—any secret closet in it. Would you be so kind, Mr. Scribe?"

"But, but, sir," stammered he with honest hesitation.

"Here, here are pen and paper," said I, with entire assurance. Enough.

That evening I had the certificate framed and hung over the dining-room fire-place, trusting that the continual sight of it would forever put at rest at once the dreams and strategems of my household.

But, no. Inveterately bent upon the extirpation of that noble old chimney, still to this day my wife goes about it, with my daughter Anna's geological hammer, tapping the wall all over, and then holding her ear against it, as I have seen the physicians of life insurance companies tap a man's chest, and then incline over for the echo. Sometimes of nights she almost frightens one, going about on this phantom errand, and still following the sepulchral response of the chimney, round and round, as if it were leading her to the threshold of the secret closet.

"How hollow it sounds," she will hollowly cry. "Yes, I declare," with an emphatic tap, "there is a secret closet here. Here, in this very spot. Hark! How hollow!"

"Pshaw! wife, of course it is hollow. Who ever heard of a solid chimney?"

But nothing avails. And my daughters take after, not me, but their mother.

Sometimes all three abandon the theory of the secret closet, and return to the genuine ground of attack—the unsightliness of so cumbrous a pile, with comments upon the great addition of room to be gained by its demolition, and the fine effect of the projected grand hall, and the convenience resulting from the collateral running in one direction and another of their various partitions. Not more ruthlessly did the Three Powers partition away poor Poland, than my wife and daughters would fain partition away my chimney.

But seeing that, despite all, I and my chimney still smoke our pipes, my wife reoccupies the ground of the secret closet, enlarging upon what wonders are there, and what a shame it is, not to seek it out and explore it.

"Wife, said I, upon one of these occasions, "why speak more of that secret closet, when there before you hangs contrary testimony of a master-mason, elected by yourself to decide. Besides, even if there were a secret closet, secret it should remain, and secret it shall. Yes, wife, here for once I must say my say. Infinite sad mischief has resulted from the profane bursting open of secret recesses. Though standing in the heart of this house, though hitherto we have all nestled about it, unsuspicious of aught hidden within, this chimney may or may not have a secret closet. But if it have, it is my kinsman's. To break into that wall would be to break into his breast. And that wall-breaking wish of Momus I account the wish of a church-robbing gossip and knave. Yes, wife, a vile eaves-dropping varlet was Momus."

"Moses? — Mumps? Stuff with your mumps and your Moses!"

The truth is, my wife, like all the rest of the world, cares not a fig for my philosophical jabber. In dearth of other philosophical companionship, I and my chimney have to smoke and philosophize together. And sitting up so late as we do at it, a mighty smoke it is that we two smoky old philosophers make.

But my spouse, who likes the smoke of my tobacco as little as she does that of the soot, carries on her war against both. I live in continual dread lest, like the golden bowl, the pipes of me and my chimney shall yet be broken. To stay that mad project of my wife's, naught answers. Or, rather, she herself is incessantly answering, incessantly besetting me with her terrible alacrity for improvement, which is a softer name for destruction. Scarce a day I do not find her with her tape-measure, measuring for her grand hall, while Anna holds a yard-stick on one side, and Julia looks approvingly on from the other. Mysterious intimations appear in the nearest village paper, signed "Claude," to the effect that a certain structure, standing on a certain hill, is a sad blemish to an otherwise lovely landscape. Anonymous letters arrive, threatening me with I know not what, unless I remove my chimney. Is it my wife, too, or who, that sets up the neighbors to badgering me on the same subject, and hinting to me that my chimney, like a huge elm, absorbs all moisture from my garden? At night, also, my wife will start as from sleep, professing to hear ghostly noises from the secret closet. Assailed on all sides, and in all ways, small peace have I and my chimney.

Were it not for the baggage, we would together pack up, and remove from the country.

What narrow escapes have been ours! Once I found in a drawer a whole portfolio of plans and estimates. Another time, upon returning after a day's absence, I discovered my wife standing before the chimney in earnest conversation with a person whom I at once recognized as a meddlesome architectural reformer, who, because he had no gift for putting up anything, was ever intent upon pulling down; in various parts of the country having prevailed upon half-witted old folks to destroy their old-fashioned houses, particularly the chimneys.

But worst of all was, that time I unexpectedly returned at early morning from a visit to the city, and upon approaching the house, narrowly escaped three brickbats which fell, from high aloft, at my feet. Glancing up, what was my horror to see three savages, in blue jean overalls, in the very act of commencing the long-threatened attack. Aye, indeed, thinking of those three brickbats, I and my chimney have had narrow escapes.

It is now some seven years since I have stirred from home. My city friends all wonder why I don't come to see them, as in former times. They think I am getting sour and unsocial. Some say that I have become a sort of mossy old misanthrope, while all the time the fact is, I am simply standing guard over my mossy old chimney; for it is resolved between me and my chimney, that I and my chimney will never surrender [pp. 373-408].

The narrator's tone of whimsical obeisance-deference before his chimney cuts deeper than a casual reading would indicate, Woodruff (1960) believes. The theme of the story revolves around the wife's attempt to destroy the chimney, and it is this interpretation by Woodruff that is primarily relied on here. At first she plans to knock a hole through to make an entrance hall. " 'But wife,' said I, 'the chimney—consider the chimney: if you wish to demolish the foundation, what is to support the superstructure?' " (Melville, p. 384). It is the almost gutted cry of the harassed male protecting his tenderest parts. Her wish to strip the narrator of his prerogatives is frankly stated: "She is desirous that, domestically, I should abdicate; that, renouncing further rule, like the venerable Charles V, I should retire into some sort of monastery. But indeed, the chimney excepted, I have little authority to lay down. By my wife's ingenious application of the principle that certain things belong of right to the female jurisdiction, I find myself, through my easy compliances, insensibly stripped by degrees of one masculine prerogative after another" (pp. 387-388). In his fear of castration, the narrator reports, "I live in continual dread lest, like the golden bowl, the pipes of me and my chimney shall yet be broken" (p. 406). The wife's "terrible alacrity for improvement" is but "a softer name for destruction." One of the symbols of the wife's rejection of what the chimney stands for is her passion for cleanliness. She can "spy a spot on the dresser straight through the pewter platter" (p. 384), and is always sending the maid to destroy the cobwebs her husband cherishes (p. 383), another reference to spider symbolism, wherein the spider represents the wicked mother who possesses the male genital (Abraham, 1922).

Their incompatibility is marked, Woodruff continues, for she is a scheming, narcissistic, castrating woman, while he is easy-going and pliant, wondering whether "the doctrine be true, that in wedlock contraries attract" (Melville, p. 385). Feeling that "Whatever is, is wrong," and "must be altered right away" (p. 385), she is a kind of quester. She has affinities with the arch-quester, Ahab, destroyer of what is; she is, in fact, a domesticated Ahab bent on her own "mad project" of hunting down and killing the chimney which, rising through each successive floor, "breaks water from the ridge-pole of the roof, like an anvil-headed whale, through the crest of a billow" (p. 378). While at first her plan involves mutilation—"the general idea of a sort of irregular archway, or elbowed tunnel, which was to penetrate the chimney" (p. 388)—(the vagina penetrating the penis), her ambition came finally to embrace the "sweeping proposition—in toto to abolish the chimney" (p. 391).

Another conflict between the couple which Woodruff makes apparent is to be found in the husband who reveres "oldness" and the wife who "takes to nothing but newness." Although she is "historically" old as the narrator—"a very autumnal old lady"—the wife cultivates the newness of a "vernal young soul," "young company," and "offers to ride young colts." She plaits her gray hair in the youthful manner and always "buys her new almanac a month before the new year" (Melville, p. 387). Ruthlessly opposed to anything with a past, Woodruff declares, whether it be a "club-footed old neighbor," a "claw-footed old chair," or even the "high-manteled old chimney" itself, she tells her husband that " 'it's I, young I, that keep you from stagnating' " (Melville, p. 387).

The emphasis on the differences in approach to age and the defensiveness of the narrator probably indicate a sexual impotence which he cannot bring himself to admit. He must resort to boasting: "The preeminence of my chimney is most manifest." It is the *"King,"* the "true host" of the house in which the narrator stands "not so much before, as, strictly speaking, behind my chimney" (pp. 373-374). "As the story moves to the main thematic conflict between the wife's determination to mutilate and destroy the chimney and the narrator's equally strong determination to save his 'grand seignior' (p. 374), the ruler-ruled analogy is explored with increasing intensity" (Woodruff, 1960, p. 284). The narrator permits himself to be awed by the "incredible" size of his chimney. The only way to get a proper idea of its dimensions is "by a method somewhat akin to those whereby the surprising distances of fixed stars are computed" (Melville, p. 382). The chimney's "immensity" gives him a sense of his place. The top of the chimney, which resembles a "razed observatory, masoned up" (p. 378) (the eye of the penis?), is much less a source of contemplation than its 144 square feet at the base: "Large as the chimney appears upon the roof, that is nothing to its spaciousness below" (p. 380). So impressed is the narrator with "that vast square of masonry" (erection?) that he makes periodic trips to the cellar where, he says, "I stand long, and ponder over, and wonder at it" (p. 380) (like the boy masturbating?). In almost every imagistic pattern he employs, the narrator forces the reader back to the chimney's centrality and size. There is a "huge, corpulent old Harry VIII of a chimney" (p. 373), and if this is not sufficiently explicit, the "I" and his chimney "are both rather obese" (p. 374). The wife continues to plot against her husband's virility, but the story has no resolution. In the end, the narrator is still on the defensive against the predatory female, Woodruff concludes.

The woman-like-a-man of childhood male, transvestite and homosexual fantasies, the unconscious acting out of the mother with a penis by many females, and the legend of the vagina dentata are universals, to be found in all cultures. The primitive fear of total emasculation, implying an absolute loss of will, is the reversal of the male-dominant hierarchy. The primordial archetype of the Great Mother took form in the imagination of man as monstrous and inhuman — a composite of chimerical creatures such as griffins, sphinxes, harpies, and phallic

and bearded mothers (Neumann, 1955). The myth of the vagina dentata appears in literally hundreds of tales which have been rooted out
by anthropologists and folklorists (Devereux, 1969; Lederer, 1968;
Frazer, 1900). Elwin (1941) found that it is reported both as legend
and as dream in every tribe examined in central India. This parallel
psychological development is established in some respects among
peoples as diverse as the Baiga of India, the Chilcotin of northwest
America, and the Ainu of Japan. The legends appear to be related to a
fear of the dangers of sexual intercourse that arise not only from the
toxic character of menstrual blood and the possibility of venereal con-
tagion, but from the fear of exposure to hostile magic and witchcraft
during intercourse, the dread of castration, and the fear of impotence.
A typical Hindu legend reads:

> There was a Rakshasa's (demon's) daughter who had teeth in her
> vagina. When she saw a man, she would turn into a pretty girl,
> seduce him, bite off his penis, eat it herself and give the rest of his
> body to her tigers. One day she met seven brothers in the jungle
> and married the eldest so that she could sleep with them all. After
> some time she took the eldest boy to where the tigers lived, made
> him lie with her, cut off his penis, ate it and gave his body to the
> tigers. In the same way she killed six of the brothers till only the
> youngest one was left. When his turn came, the god who helped him
> sent him a dream. "If you go with the girl," said the god, "make an
> iron tube, put it into her vagina and break her teeth." This the boy
> did... [Elwin, 1941, p. 443].

That which destroys man is the vulva, a Maori saying goes (Róheim,
1945). Cannibalistic impulses are projected onto the vagina, which is
the object of intense fear, all kinds of infernal attributes being ascribed
to it; or it is regarded as a big trap into which men can fall and be
swallowed (Reich, 1939; Christoffel, 1956). In Jean-Paul Sartre's
(1948) "Erostratus," the paranoid homosexual protagonist of the story
indulges in sadistic sexual fantasies, some of which are acted out with
prostitutes. "One night I got the idea of shooting people. It was a
Saturday evening, I had gone out to pick up Lea, a blonde who works
out in front of a hotel on the rue Montparnasse. I never had intercourse with a woman: I would have felt robbed. You got on top of
them, of course, but they eat you up with their big hairy mouth and,
from what I hear, they're the ones—by a long shot—who gain on the

deal" (p. 43). David, the bisexual narrator in James Baldwin's (1956) *Giovanni's Room,* has left his homosexual lover to return to his fiancée. He is, however, having second thoughts. "A body which had been covered with such crazy, catty-cornered bits of [underwear] began to seem grotesque. I sometimes watched her naked body move and wished that it were harder and firmer. I was fantastically intimidated by her breasts, and when I entered her I began to feel that I would never get out alive" (p. 209).

David's wish for Helen's body to be harder and firmer may indicate his unconscious equating of her body with a penis, and the anxiety about not "getting out alive" may represent fear of the devouring vagina. The fantasy of "returning to the mother" is a genitally colored repressive variant of the Chronos myth: in place of active penetration of the woman, the man is swallowed in toto (Lewin, 1933). The knowledge that the whole body may serve as a symbol for the phallus dates back to Freud's discovery that in the manifest content of a dream, the penis may be represented by the dreamer's own body or by the body of another. When the body represents a phallus, it means that a person has in fantasy eaten a phallus and identified himself with it. In a case reported by Karpman (1950), the patient, a twenty-seven-year-old pedophilic offender, had difficulties centering around a phobia with respect to female pubic hair. It was traced to a traumatic episode at the age of seven when a neighbor enticed him into her house where she stripped him and herself, placed him on top of her, and went through the motions of coitus. His outstanding impression and his greatest fear in connection with this experience were occasioned by the woman's thick growth of pubic hair, in which it seemed to him that he was going to be swallowed up. This painful memory was repressed, but resulted in the development of a subsequent distaste for and fear of pubic hair, in reaction to which he endeavored to have intercourse with women only in the dark or after he had persuaded them to allow him to shave off their pubic hair.

Sexual obsessions run throughout J.-K. Huysman's (1884) novel, *Against Nature.* During a temporary loss of potency, the eccentric Duc Jean des Esseintes reveals his sexual weakness as a cause for feelings of inferiority toward women. In describing a painting of Salome, he says, "In this she was altogether female, obedient to her passionate cruel woman's temperament; active and alone, the more refined the more savage and the more hateful the more exquisite: she was shown awakening man's sleeping passions, powerfully bewitching and subjugating his will with the unholy charm of a great venereal flower sprouting in sacrilegious beds and raised in impious fields" (p. 68). The passage reveals more than the mere outpouring of the misogynist. The emotional and physical revulsion of the female is obvious. But then, in a dream, a repulsive woman attempts to embrace the Duc. He is helpless. "He made a superhuman effort to disengage himself from her embrace, but with an irresistible movement she seized him and clung to him, and haggardly he saw the savage Nidularium blossom yawning under her open thighs and bleeding from its saber-like blades" (p. 106). Thus, the vagina appears a menacing, bladed instrument, possessing a lethal sexuality, capable of castration.

For some men, oral intercourse allows them to deny the genital of their partner and, simultaneously, the unacceptable aspect of their motivation. Thus they can fantasize the female as a dangerous trap; by avoiding vaginal contact, they can avoid the danger of castration. One of the women in John LeCarré's (1961) *Call for the Dead* is referred to as "a sort of Moby Dick . . . a bit [like a] white man-eating whale" (p. 97), conjuring up visions of huge, gobbling teeth. Durrell (1959), in *Mountolive,* also alludes to a sea beast with sharp, emasculating teeth. Pursewarden, the English consular official in the novel, has promised Melissa 1,000 piasters if she will go to bed with him. She is a tubercular dancehall taxi-girl, the mistress of Darley who has been sleeping with Justine, who in turn has been sleeping with Pursewarden. Pursewarden had had incestuous relations with his blind sister and is, as a seeming consequence, impotent with Melissa. They are in bed together. " 'Now,' she said angrily, determined not to lose the piasters which in her imagination she had already spent, already owed, 'now I will make you La Veuve,' and he drew his breath in an exultant literary thrill to hear once more this wonderful slang expression stolen from the old nickname of the French guillotine, with its fearful suggestion of teeth reflected in the concealed metaphor for the castration complex. La Veuve! The shark-infested seas of love which closed over the doomed sailor's head in a voiceless paralysis of the dream, the deep-sea dream which dragged one slowly downwards, dismembered and dismembering . . . until with a vulgar snick the steed fell, the clumsy thinking head ('use your loaf') smacked dully into the basket to spurt and wriggle like a fish..." (p. 172).

In an earlier novel by Durrell (1937), *The Black Book,* Lobo is obsessed by the devouring female. The narrator, too, has similar problems. In a surrealist fantasy about a woman he believes he is in love with, he talks about his "aquarium of feelings.... When she comes it's all pearls and icicles emptied from her womb into the snow. The penis looks like a dolphin with many muscles and black humor.... The figure suddenly broken into a sticky tip that is all female.... Under my thews, trapped in bracts and sphincters, a unique destruction. She is weeping. Her spine has been liquefied, drawn out of her. She is filleted, the jaw telescoped with language, eyes glassy. Under my mouth a rouged vagina speaking a barbaric laughter and nibbling my tongue" (pp. 43-44). Sylvia Tietjens, in Ford Madox Ford's (1925) *No More Parades,* is one of the most powerful characters the author has drawn. She is the end of the virile tradition in literature, the bitch heroine prototype to come. If the male is impotent, her husband reflects with a shudder, "Perhaps the future of the world then was to women?" According to Wagner (1967, pp. 83-84), "This woman, who is successively described as a snake, a crocodile, an immense cat, and repeatedly as a bird of prey, hates men, yet is 'man-mad.' ... She discomfits lovers like a man out shooting. She boasts that she has killed Tietjens' father and mother and corrupted the boy he believes to be his son. Sylvia is necessary to Tietjens since she is really a man." In *The Last Post* (1928), one of the novels in Ford's tetrology of the Tietjens family, Sylvia is arguing with an old retainer of her husband's, Gunning. The latter told her that Christopher, her husband from whom she is separated, "would tan her hide if she so much as disturbed her brother by a look; he would hide her within an inch of her life. As he had already done. Sylvia said that by God he never had; if he said he had, he lied. Her immediate reaction was to resent the implication that she was not as good a man as Christopher" (p. 230). But Ford did not single out Sylvia as the solitary object of his feelings toward the female sex, for in the same work he generalized, "The dominion of women over those of the opposite sex was a terrible thing" (p. 73).

Alison's parents, in *The Freedom Trap* by Desmond Bagley (1972), separated before her birth. She lived with her mother until the latter died when Alison was ten years old; thereafter, she lived with her father. He had always wanted a boy, and so taught Alison to shoot, scuba-dive, and fly a jet. "'I was a bit of a tomboy,'" she understates to her boy friend, and then asks him, "'Do you know what I am, Owen?' 'You're a lovely woman, Alison.' 'No, I'm a Venus fly-trap.

Vegetables—like women—are supposed to be placid. They're not supposed to be equipped with snapping jaws and sharp teeth. Have you ever watched a fly alight on a Venus fly-trap?' " (p. 194).

The *horror feminae* Alison characterized herself as is sharply delineated in Edgar Allan Poe's (1835) short story, "Berenice," in which Egaeus is obsessed by her teeth. In his unconscious, the vagina is equipped with teeth, and thus a source of danger in being able to bite and castrate. "Mouth and vagina are equated . . . and when Egaeus yields to the morbid impulse to draw Berenice's teeth, he yields both to the yearning for the mother's organ and to be revenged upon it, since the dangers that hedge it about make him sexually avoid all women as too menacing. His act is therefore a sort of retributive castration inflicted on the mother whom he loves, and yet hates, because obdurate to his sex-love for her in infancy" (Bonaparte, 1949, pp. 24-25).

During the brightest days of her unparalleled beauty, most surely I had never loved her. In the strange anomaly of my existence, feelings with me, *had never been* of the heart, and my passions *always were* of the mind. Through the grey of the early morning— among the trellised shadows of the forest at noonday—and in the silence of my library at night, she had flitted by my eyes, and I had seen her—not as the living and breathing Berenice, but as the Berenice of a dream—not as a being of the earth, earthy, but as the abstraction of such a being—not as a thing to admire, but to analyze—not as an object of love, but as the theme of the most abstruse although desultory speculation. And *now*—now I shuddered in her presence, and grew pale at her approach; yet bitterly lamenting her fallen and desolate condition. I called to mind that she had loved me long, and, in an evil moment, I spoke to her of marriage.

And at length the period of our nuptials was approaching, when, upon an afternoon in the winter of the year,—one of those unseasonably warm, calm, and misty days which are the nurse of the beautiful Halcyon,—I sat (and sat, as I thought, alone) in the inner apartment of the library. But uplifting my eyes I saw that Berenice stood before me.

Was it my own excited imagination—or the misty influence of the atmosphere—or the uncertain twilight of the chamber—or the grey draperies which fell around her figure—that caused in it so vacillating and indistinct an outline? I could not tell. She spoke no word, and I—not for worlds could I have uttered a syllable. An icy chill ran through my frame; a sense of insufferable anxiety oppressed me; a consuming curiosity pervaded my soul; and sinking back upon the chair, I remained for some time breathless and motionless, with my eyes riveted upon her person. Alas! its emaciation was excessive, and not one vestige of the former being lurked in any single line of the contour. My burning glances at length fell upon the face.

The forehead was high, and very pale, and singularly placid; and the once jetty hair fell partially over it, and overshadowed the hollow temples with innumerable ringlets now of a vivid yellow, and jarring discordantly, in their fantastic character, with the reigning melancholy of the countenance. The eyes were lifeless, and lustreless, and seemingly pupil-less, and I shrank involuntarily from their glassy stare to the contemplation of the thin and shrunken lips. They parted; and in a smile of peculiar meaning, *the teeth* of the changed Berenice disclosed themselves slowly to my view. Would to God that I had never beheld them, or that, having done so, I had died!

. . . .

The shutting of a door disturbed me, and, looking up, I found that my cousin had departed from the chamber. But from the disordered chamber of my brain, had not, alas! departed, and would not be driven away, the white and ghastly *spectrum* of the teeth. Not a speck on their surface — not a shade on their enamel — not an indenture in their edges — but what that period of her smile had sufficed to brand in upon my memory. I saw them *now* even more unequivocally than I beheld them *then*. The teeth! — the teeth! — they were here, and there, and everywhere, and visibly and palpably before me; long, narrow, and excessively white, with the pale lips writhing about them, as in the very moment of their first terrible development. Then came the full fury of my *monomania,* and I struggled in vain against its strange and irresistible influence. In the multiplied objects of the external world I had no thoughts but for the teeth. For these I longed with a phrenzied desire. All other matters and all different interests became absorbed in their single contemplation. They — they alone were present to the mental eye, and they, in their sole individuality, became the essence of my mental life. I held them in every light. I turned them in every attitude. I surveyed their characteristics. I dwelt upon their peculiarities. I pondered upon their conformation. I mused upon the alteration in their nature. I shuddered as I assigned to them in imagination a sensitive and sentient power, and even when unassisted by the lips, a capability of moral expression. Of Mad'selle Sallé it has been well said, *"que tous ses pas étaient des sentiments,"* and of Berenice I more seriously believed *que toutes ses dents étaient des idées. Des idées!*—ah here was the idiotic thought that destroyed me! *Des idées!*—ah *therefore* it was that I coveted them so madly! I felt that their possession could alone ever restore me to peace, in giving me back to reason.

And the evening closed in upon me thus—and then the darkness came, and tarried, and went—and the day again dawned—and the mists of a second night were now gathering around—and still I sat motionless in that solitary room; and still I sat buried in meditation, and still the *phantasma* of the teeth maintained its terrible ascendancy as, with the most vivid and hideous distinctness, it floated about amid the changing lights and shadows of the chamber. At length there broke in upon my dreams a cry as of horror and dismay; and thereunto, after a pause, succeeded the sound of troubled voices, intermingled with many low moanings of sorrow, or of pain. I arose from my seat and, throwing open one of the doors of the library, saw standing out in the ante-chamber a servant maiden, all in tears, who told me that Berenice was—no more. She had been seized with epilepsy in the early morning, and now, at the closing in of the night, the grave was ready for its tenant, and all the preparations for the burial were completed.

.   .   .   .

I found myself sitting in the library, and again sitting there alone. It seemed that I had newly awakened from a confused and exciting dream. I knew that it was now midnight, and I was well aware that since the setting of the sun Berenice had been interred. But of that dreary period which intervened I had no positive—at least no definite comprehension. Yet its memory was replete with horror—horror more horrible from being vague, and terror more terrible from ambiguity. It was a fearful page in the record of my existence, written all over with dim, and hideous, and unintelligible recollections. I strived to decipher them, but in vain; while ever and anon, like the spirit of a departed sound, the shrill and piercing shriek of a female voice seemed to be ringing in my ears. I had done a deed—what was it? I asked myself the question aloud, and the whispering echoes of the chamber answered me, *"what was it?"*

On the table beside me burned a lamp, and near it lay a little box. It was of no remarkable character, and I had seen it frequently before, for it was the property of the family physician; but how came it *there,* upon my table, and why did I shudder in regarding it?

These things were in no manner to be accounted for, and my eyes at length dropped to the open pages of a book, and to a sentence underscored therein. The words were the singular but simple ones of the poet Ebn Zaiat, *"Dicebant mihi sodales si sepulchrum amicae visitarem, curas meas aliquantulum fore levatas."* Why then, as I perused them, did the hairs of my head erect themselves on end, and the blood of my body become congealed within my veins?

There came a light tap at the library door, and pale as the tenant of a tomb, a menial entered upon tiptoe. His looks were wild with terror, and he spoke to me in a voice tremulous, husky, and very low. What said he? — some broken sentences I heard. He told of a wild cry disturbing the silence of the night — of the gathering together of the household — of a search in the direction of the sound; — and then his tones grew thrillingly distinct as he whispered me of a violated grave — of a disfigured body enshrouded, yet still breathing, still palpitating, still *alive!*

He pointed to my garments; — they were muddy and clotted with gore. I spoke not, and he took me gently by the hand; — it was indented with the impress of human nails. He directed my attention to some object against the wall; — I looked at it for some minutes; — it was a spade. With a shriek I bounded to the table, and grasped the box that lay upon it. But I could not force it open; and in my tremor it slipped from my hands, and fell heavily, and burst into pieces; and from it, with a rattling sound, there rolled out some instruments of dental surgery, intermingled with thirty-two small, white and ivory-looking substances that were scattered to and fro about the floor [Poe, 1835, pp. 352-356].

The loss of teeth is here linked with a repressed recollection of early incestuous wishes. The dread Egaeus feels for Berenice is explicit in the apprehension he shows her. "During the brightest days of her unparalleled beauty, most surely I had never loved her.... And *now* — I shuddered in her presence, and grew pale at her approach" (p. 352). Nevertheless, he plans to marry her, only to shrink from her glassy stare and to fix on her thin and shrunken lips. "They parted; and in a smile of peculiar meaning, *the teeth* of the changed Berenice disclosed themselves slowly to my view" (p. 353). He describes the teeth in great detail "in the full fury of my *monomania,"* for he is unable to erase the dread of castration except pitiably in the upward displacement of the chimera of the *vagina dentata.*

The salvation of the human race, states the apostle of androgyny (Heilbrun, 1973), lies in a movement away from sexual polarization and "the prison of gender toward a world in which individual roles of personal behavior can be freely chosen. The ideal toward which we should move is best described by the term 'androgyny.' This ancient Greek word from andro (male) and gyn (female) — defines a condition under which the characteristics of the sexes, and the human impulses expressed by men and women, are not rigidly assigned. Androgyny seeks to liberate the individual from the confines of the appropriate ... Androgyny suggests a spirit of reconciliation between the sexes; it suggests, further, a full range of experience open to individuals who may as women, be aggressive, as men, tender; it suggests a spectrum upon which human beings choose their places without regard to propriety or custom" (pp. x-xi). Survival, continues Heilbrun, depends upon moving away from the dominant, "ideal" characteristics associated with masculinity. While placing less stress on sexual polarization and the prison of sex seems an unarguable good, no allowance has been made for Freud's doctrine of bisexuality, implicit in which is "the warning against too schematic an apposition to femininity in woman and masculinity in man. It is well recognized that no man exists whose masculine traits are not accompanied by more or less obviously feminine characteristics, and that likewise there are no women who fail to show masculine tendencies" (Lampl-de Groot, 1933, p. 19).

The lecherous academic dean in Alan Lelchuk's (1973) novel, *American Mischief,* is disturbed by "the way that our own culture had distorted and abused the word 'civilized' in relation to men and women. Just look around; how weak and unmanly the men had become, how aggressive and unfeminine the women. Why not? Did anyone of experience and honesty really believe, for example, that a real, live woman — Our Gal Sundays to the contrary — could find happiness and satisfaction with, say, a Princeton Ph.D. in English? How could that graduate cope with her? Would his school tie be as useful upon her thigh as another fellow's tongue? Would her hips and ass arouse him as much as a solid heroic couplet would? And how in the world would he be able to *take charge* of a woman, tame her? When she growled at him like a lioness in heat, and reached for her flesh with a nail-polished paw, what was he to do, recite *The Rape of the Lock?*" (p. 122).

D. H. Lawrence's (1928) *Lady Chatterley's Lover* demonstrates, if nothing else, the resexualization of women, a resurgence still in progress. Females have moved from the Victorian era, the period in which nice ladies felt nothing sexual, to an era in which the woman is actually aggressive, so aggressive in demanding her sexual due that she is beginning to strike terror in the heart of the male (Calderone, 1971). The Victorian attitude which insisted that the woman has no sexual appetite at all and must make no demands is a defense against the fear of the opposite extreme—that woman is all appetite, all demands. The fear of the uncontrolled woman, wrote Figes (1970), keeps recurring in one form or another. Today's woman, "armed with The Pill, is often regarded as rapacious because she is no longer deterred from un-bridled sexuality by the fear of unwanted children . . . The opposite of domination is to be dominated, and bands of Amazons, women who use men only for the act after having conquered them in war, and who slay all boys at birth, haunt the minds of men in mythology" (p. 50).

The distorted conception of woman and her sexuality, of what she is and what she is supposed to be, the thesis of the natural superiority of women or the dominant role played by masculine sexuality, need to be examined without bias to determine the common and distinguishing psychosocial characteristics of both sexes. It is not only the vicissitudes of a poorly resolved oedipal conflict that are responsible for the distorted concept of woman and her sexuality and for man's miscon-ceptions of the giant phallic woman, but also the persistence of an archaic oral relationship, strongly marked by an ambivalence wherein libidinal and aggressive features are intimately entwined. The per-sistence of misconceptions looks like revenge for the radical narcissistic wounds inflicted by the mother, states David (1970, p. 50), and follows, for both sexes, from the situation of the baby at the breast. Is this revenge, he asks rhetorically, not the source of the "racial" dis-crimination shown toward women, as well as the root of the maso-chistic attitude many women have toward men?

TECHNICAL REFERENCES

Abraham, K. (1920), Manifestations of the female castration complex. In: *Selected Papers.* New York: Basic Books, 1953, pp. 338-369.
———— (1922), The spider as a dream symbol. In: *Selected Papers.* New York: Basic Books, 1953, pp. 326-332.
———— (1925), Character formation of the genital level of libido development. In: *Selected Papers.* New York: Basic Books, 1953, pp. 407-417.
Bonaparte, M. (1949), *The Life and Works of Edgar Allan Poe. A Psychoanalytic Interpretation.* London: Imago.

Bragman, L. J. (1931), The case of Ludwig Lewisohn. *American Journal of Psychiatry*, 11:319-331.

Brunswick, R. M. (1943), The accepted lie. *Psychoanalytic Quarterly*, 12:458-464.

Calderone, M. (1971), Sex education. In: *Sex American Style*, eds. F. Robinson & N. Lehrman. Chicago: Playboy Press, pp. 278-333.

Chasseguet-Smirgel, J. (ed.) (1970), *Feminine Sexuality. New Psychoanalytic Views.* Ann Arbor, Mich.: University of Michigan Press.

Christoffel, H. (1956), Male genital exhibitionism. In: *Perversions: Psychodynamics and Therapy*, eds. S. Lorand & M. Balint. New York: Random House, pp. 243-264.

Corsa, H. S. (1971), *To the Lighthouse:* Death, mourning, and transfiguration. *Literature & Psychology*, 21:115-131.

David, C. (1970), A masculine mythology of femininity. In: *Feminine Sexuality*, ed. J. Chasseguet-Smirgel. Ann Arbor, Mich.: University of Michigan Press, pp. 47-67.

Devereux, G. (1969), *Reality and Dream. Psychotherapy of a Plains Indian.* New York: New York University Press.

Elwin, V. (1941), The vagina dentata legend. *British Journal of Medical Psychology*, 19:439-453.

Fenichel, O. (1936), The symbolic equation: Girl = phallus. In: *Collected Papers*, Second Series. New York: Norton, pp. 15-16.

Ferenczi, S. (1928), Gulliver fantasies. In: *Final Contributions to Psycho-Analysis*. New York: Basic Books, 1955, pp. 41-60.

Fiedler, L. (1960), *Love and Death in the American Novel.* London: Paladin, 1970.

Figes, E. (1970), *Patriarchal Attitudes.* New York: Stein & Day.

Frazer, J. G. (1900), *The Golden Bough. A Study in Magic and Religion.* London: Mason.

Freud, S. (1914), On narcissism: An introduction. *Standard Edition*, 14:69-102. London: Hogarth Press, 1957.

———— (1918), The taboo of virginity. *Standard Edition*, 11:191-208. London: Hogarth Press, 1957.

Friend, M. R., Schiddel, L., Klein, B., & Dunaeff, D. (1954), Observations on the development of transvestitism in boys. *American Journal of Orthopsychiatry*, 24:563-575.

Gordon, A. (1969), *The Naked and the Dead.* The triumph of impotence. *Literature & Psychology*, 19(3/4):3-13.

Hardy, J. E. (1964), *Man in the Modern Novel.* Seattle: University of Washington Press.

Hays, H. R. (1964), *The Dangerous Sex. The Myth of Feminine Evil.* New York: Pocket Books, 1965.

Heilbrun, C. G. (1973), *Toward A Recognition of Androgyny.* New York: Knopf.

Heiman, M. (1959), Rip Van Winkle: A psychoanalytic note on the story and its author. *American Imago*, 16:3-47.

Hermann, I. (1949), The giant mother, the phallic mother, obscenity. *Psychoanalytic Review*, 36:302-306.

Horney, K. (1932), The dread of women. *International Journal of Psycho-Analysis*, 13:348-360.

Jones, W. M. (1957), Welty's "Petrified Man." *Explicator*, 15(4):21.

Karpman, B. (1950), A case of paedophilia (legally rape) cured by psychoanalysis. *Psychoanalytic Review*, 37:235-276.

Laing, R. D. (1966), *The Divided Self.* Baltimore: Penguin.

Lampl-de Groot, J. (1933), Problems of femininity. In: *The Development of the Mind.* New York: International Universities Press, 1965, pp. 19-46.

Lederer, W. (1968), *The Fear of Women.* New York: Grune & Stratton.

Leonard, F. M. (1963-1964), *Nana:* Symbol and action. *Modern Fiction Studies,* 9:149-158.

Levin, G. (1967), The symbolism of Lawrence's *The Fox. College Language Association Journal,* 11:135-141.

Lewin, B. D. (1933), The body as phallus. In: *Selected Writings.* New York: Psychoanalytic Quarterly, Inc., 1973, pp. 28-47.

Meyer, B. C. (1964), Death and Conrad's heroes. *Columbia University Forum,* 7: 14-19.

Neumann, E. (1955), *The Great Mother. An Analysis of the Archetype.* New York: Pantheon, 1963.

Peyre, H. (1962), *Madame Bovary.* In: *Varieties of Literary Experience,* ed. S. Burnshaw. New York: New York University Press, pp. 331-352.

Praz, M. (1933), *The Romantic Agony.* New York: Medidian, 1956.

Reich, W. (1939), Quoted by L. C. Hirning in: Clothing and nudism. In: *Sex and Society Today,* ed. A. Ellis & A. Abarbanel. New York: Ace Books, 1967, p. 109.

Rogers, R. (1970), *A Psychoanalytic Study of the Double in Literature.* Detroit: Wayne State University Press.

Róheim, G. (1945), Aphrodite, or the woman with a penis. *Psychoanalytic Quarterly,* 14:350-390.

Stoller, R. (1968), *Sex and Gender.* New York: Science House.

Wagner, G. (1967), Ford Madox Ford: The honest Edwardian. *Essays in Criticism,* 17:75-88.

Weinbrot, H. W. (1970), Chastity and interpolation: Two aspects of *Joseph Andrews. Journal of English & German Philology,* 69:14-31.

Woodruff, S. C. (1960), Melville and his chimney. *Publication of the Modern Language Association,* 65:283-292.

LITERARY REFERENCES

Bagley, Desmond (1972), *The Freedom Trap.* Garden City, N.Y.: Doubleday.

Baldwin, James (1956), *Giovanni's Room.* New York: Dell, 1964.

Bowles, Paul (1952), *Let It Come Down.* New York: Random House.

Connell, Evan S. (1966), *The Diary of a Rapist.* New York: Simon & Schuster.

Conrad, Joseph (1916), The planter of Malata. In: *Tales of the East and West,* ed. M. D. Zabel. Garden City, N.Y.: Hanover House, 1958, pp. 161-213.

D'Annunzio, Gabriel (1896), *Trionfo della Morte.* In: *Gazzetta Litteraria,* p. 353.

Durrell, Lawrence (1937), *The Black Book.* New York: Dutton.

———— (1957), *Justine.* New York: Dutton, 1961.

———— (1959), *Mountolive.* New York: Dutton.

Faulkner, William (1930), *As I Lay Dying.* New York: Smith.

———— (1931), *Sanctuary.* New York: Smith.

———— (1932), *Light in August.* New York: Smith.

Fielding, Henry (1742), *Adventures of Joseph Andrews.* New York: Oxford, 1929.

———— (1749), *Tom Jones.* New York: Modern Library, 1931.

Flaubert, Gustave (1857), *Madame Bovary.* New York: Scribner's, 1930.

Ford, Ford Madox (1925), *No More Parades.* New York: New American Library, 1964.

——— (1928), *The Last Post.* New York: Boni.

Gautier, Théophile (1915), *One of Cleopatra's Nights.* New York: Brentano.

Hemingway, Ernest (1926), *The Sun Also Rises.* New York: Scribner's.

Huysmans, Joris-Karl (1884), *Against Nature.* Baltimore: Penguin, 1959.

Irving, Washington (1819), *Rip Van Winkle.* New York: Winston, 1928.

Lawrence, D. H. (1913), *Sons and Lovers.* New York: Viking, 1932.

——— (1923), *The Fox.* In: *Captain's Doll; Three Novelettes.* New York: Seltzer.

——— (1928), *Lady Chatterley's Lover.* New York: Knopf, 1932.

LeCarré, John (1961), *Call for the Dead.* London: Penguin, 1964.

Lelchuk, Alan (1973), *American Mischief.* New York: Farrar, Straus & Giroux.

Lewisohn, Ludwig (1926), *The Case of Mr. Crump.* New York: Farrar, Straus, 1947.

Mailer, Norman (1941), Maybe next year. In: *Short Fiction.* New York: Dell, 1967.

——— (1951), *Barbary Shore.* New York: New American Library.

——— (1955), *The Deer Park.* New York: Putnam.

——— (1965), *An American Dream.* New York: Dial.

——— (1967), *Why Are We in Vietnam?* London: Panther, 1970.

——— (1968), The time of her time. In: *American Short Stories Since 1945,* ed. J. Hollander. New York: Harper & Row.

Malone, John (1973), *The Corruption of Harold Hoskins.* New York: Charterhouse.

Marlowe, Derek (1966), *A Dandy in Aspic.* New York: Putnam.

Melville, Herman (1854), I and my chimney. In: *Selected Writings of Herman Melville.* New York: Modern Library, 1952, pp. 373-408.

Meredith, George (1859), *The Ordeal of Richard Feverel.* New York: Modern Library, 1927.

Morris, Wright (1951), *Man and Boy.* New York: Knopf.

Oz, Amos (1972), *My Michael.* New York: Knopf.

A Person of Quality (1663), Characters; or wit and the world in their proper colours. In: *A Book of 'Characters,'* ed. R. Aldington. New York: Dutton.

Poe, Edgar Allan (1835), Berenice. In: *The Best Tales of Edgar Allan Poe.* New York: Modern Library, 1924, pp. 347-356.

Roth, Philip (1969), *Portnoy's Complaint.* New York: Random House.

Sartre, Jean-Paul (1948), Erostratus. In: *Intimacy and Other Stories.* Norwalk, Conn.: New Directions.

Schulberg, Budd (1941), *What Makes Sammy Run.* New York: Random House.

Shaw, George Bernard (1931), *Captain Brassbound's Conversion.* New York: Dodd.

Sophocles (c. 429), *Oedipus Rex.* New York: Modern Library, 1929.

Swift, Jonathan (1726), *Gulliver's Travels.* New York: Black, 1932.

Vizinczey, Stephen (1965), *In Praise of Older Women.* New York: Ballantine, 1967.

Warren, Robert Penn (1946), *All the King's Men.* New York: Harcourt Brace.

Welty, Eudora (1941), Petrified man. In: *The Rinehart Book of Short Stories,* ed. C. L. Cline. New York: Holt, Rinehart & Winston, 1961, pp. 292-307.

Woolf, Virginia (1927), *To the Lighthouse.* New York: Harcourt Brace, 1931.

Zola, Emile (1868), *Madeleine Ferat.* In: *Works of Emile Zola.* New York: Black, 1928.

——— (1876), *Son Excellence Eugène Rougon.* In: *Works of Emile Zola.* New York: Black, 1928.

——— (1880), *Nana.* New York: Bantam, 1954.

——— (1894-1895), *Paris.* London: Chatto, 1932.

CHAPTER THREE

Anal Eroticism

The number of novels that unintentionally demonstrate the validity of Freud's theory of the anal character and anal eroticism seems limitless. Fictional corroboration can be found in the works of Cervantes, Rabelais, Swift, Rousseau, Balzac, Strindberg, Frank Norris, Zola, Djuna Barnes, Mailer, Philip Roth, James Purdy, Stanley Elkin, John Barth, John Updike, John Fowles, Jean Genet, and Günter Grass, to cite but a few.

Certain neurotics, wrote Freud (1908) in his description of the anal character, present three particularly pronounced character traits: a love of orderliness, a parsimony which easily turns to miserliness, and an obstinacy which may become angry defiance. He established the fact that the primary pleasure in emptying the bowels and in its products is especially emphasized in these people; that after successful repression, their coprophilia either becomes sublimated into pleasure in painting, modeling, or similar activities, or proceeds to a special love of cleanliness as a reaction formation; and finally that for them money can become the unconscious equivalent of feces.

If Freud had had available to him Frank Norris' novel, *McTeague, a Story of San Francisco*, written in 1899, some nine years before he presented his theory of anality, he would have had a classic reference. Point by point, *McTeague* seems to develop Freud's thesis. While Norris knew the psychology of his day, it was not Freud's. Instead, he turned to the then accepted theory of Lombroso that criminality resulted from heredity and degeneracy rather than from other factors. His hero, McTeague, closely resembled the atavistic type Lombroso had termed "L'Uomo Delinquente," a man with marvelous physical agility, lacking in moral sensibility, with relative dullness in sense impression, but animal-like in the enjoyment of the sensuous and the sensual. Accordingly, the overwhelming force of McTeague's life was hereditary; from his alcoholic father he inherited bestial tendencies, for McTeague himself turned to sadistic practices, drink, and eventually murder. As for Trina, his wife, she was no less a victim of heredity than McTeague. Of Swiss Alpine stock, her strong racial instinct for hoarding became a way of life. "She had all the instinct of a hardy and penurious mountain race—the instinct which saves without any thought, without any idea of consequences—saving for the sake of saving, hoarding without knowing why" (p. 134). Thus, although Norris wrote from an erroneous psychological premise, he nonetheless presented a consistent picture of the anal-erotic character, as will be seen.

McTeague is the story of a great dumb brute of a man who has learned dentistry in a brief apprenticeship with a journeyman practitioner. Since he has no diploma, he loses his license; without an occupation, he begins a steady slide downhill, becomes an alcoholic, maltreats his wife, steals the money she has hoarded, and, after it is gone, returns to beg her for a handout. When Trina refuses to help, his last remaining self-control slips and he murders her.

Just before their marriage, Trina had won $5,000 in a lottery, an event that determines the further course of the narrative. Trina becomes a miser, a spirit concentrated on greed, her sole purpose in life devoted to amassing and keeping her money intact. "Her five thousand dollars invested in Uncle Oelbermann's business was a glittering splendid dream which came to her almost every hour of the day as a solace and a compensation for all her unhappiness [pp. 307-308] . . . Her avarice had grown to be her one dominant passion, her love of money for the money's sake brooded in her heart, driving out by degrees every other natural affection" (p. 354).

As Trina's avarice developed, McTeague's hatred of her began. His main ambition was to possess a huge gilded tooth to hang outside his dental parlor. In point of fact, the aura of gold permeates the novel. (Norris once told William Dean Howells [1902] that he originally thought of calling his novel *The Golden Tooth*.) McTeague confined his canary in a gilt cage. He grew up at the site of a gold mine and later discovered gold near places called Gold Gulch and Gold Mountain. Early in the novel, McTeague is described as having "a heart of gold."

Maria Macapa continually babbled about an imaginary hundred-piece gold dinner service, and she filched gold foil from McTeague's office. Zerkow was paranoid about gold. Trina had gold fillings in her teeth and counted gold pieces until they were worn smooth, sometimes sleeping with them and wallowing in them like an infant in a soiled diaper. Even the sun streaming into Trina's room looked like gold coins. The obsession with money is the dominant theme of the novel and, as it progresses, the relation between feces and money becomes clear.

In the building up of sexual life and mental activity in general, the many instinctual trends which comprise anal erotism play an extraordinarily important role: "one of the most important manifestations of the transformed erotism derived from this source is to be found in the treatment of money, for in the course of life this precious material attracts on to itself the psychical interest which was originally proper to faeces, the product of the anal zone. We are accustomed to trace back interest in money, in so far as it is of a libidinal and not a rational character, to excretory pleasure, and we expect normal people to keep their relations to money entirely free from libidinal influences and regulate them according to the demands of reality" (Freud, 1918, p. 72).

For Trina, the demands of reality were fixated at an infantile stage of development. Although she recognized the danger of her hoarding, she could not stop. " 'I didn't use to be so stingy,' she told herself. 'Since I won in the lottery I've become a regular little miser. It's growing on me, but never mind, it's a good fault, and, anyhow, I can't help it' " (Norris, p. 210). Nor did her rationalization help.

. . . Trina suffered a reaction after the quarrel. She began to be sorry she had refused to help her husband, sorry she had brought matters to such an issue. One afternoon as she was at work on the Noah's ark animals, she surprised herself crying over the affair. She loved her "old bear" too much to do him an injustice, and perhaps, after all, she had been in the wrong. Then it occurred to her how pretty it would be to come up behind him unexpectedly, and slip the money, thirty-five dollars, into his hand, and pull his huge head down to her and kiss his bald spot as she used to do in the days before they were married.

Then she hesitated, pausing in her work, her knife dropping into her lap, a half-whittled figure between her fingers. If not thirty-five dollars, then at least fifteen or sixteen, her share of it. But a feeling of reluctance, a sudden revolt against this intended generosity, arose in her.

"No, no," she said to herself. "I'll give him ten dollars. I'll tell him it's all I can afford. It *is* all I can afford."

She hastened to finish the figure of the animal she was then at work upon, putting in the ears and tail with a drop of glue, and tossing it into the basket at her side. Then she rose and went into the bedroom and opened her trunk, taking the key from under a corner of the carpet where she kept it hid.

At the very bottom of her trunk, under her bridal dress, she kept her savings. It was all in change — half dollars and dollars for the most part, with here and there a gold piece. Long since the little brass match-box had overflowed. Trina kept the surplus in a chamois-skin sack she had made from an old chest protector. Just now, yielding to an impulse which often seized her, she drew out the match-box and the chamois sack, and emptying the contents on the bed, counted them carefully. It came to one hundred and sixty-five dollars, all told. She counted it and recounted it and made little piles of it, and rubbed the gold pieces between the folds of her apron until they shone.

"Ah, yes, ten dollars is all I can afford to give Mac," said Trina, "and even then, think of it, ten dollars — it will be four or five months before I can save that again. But, dear old Mac, I know it would make him feel glad, and perhaps," she added, suddenly taken with an idea, "perhaps Mac will refuse to take it."

She took a ten-dollar piece from the heap and put the rest away. Then she paused:

"No, not the gold piece," she said to herself. "It's too pretty. He can have the silver." She made the change and counted out ten silver dollars into her palm. But what a difference it made in the appearance and weight of the little chamois bag! The bag was shrunken and withered, long wrinkles appeared running downward from the draw-string. It was a lamentable sight. Trina looked longingly at the ten broad pieces in her hand. Then suddenly all her intuitive desire of saving, her instinct of hoarding, her love of money for the money's sake, rose strong within her.

"No, no, no," she said. "I can't do it. It may be mean, but I can't help it. It's stronger than I." She returned the money to the bag and locked it and the brass match-box in her trunk, turning the key with a long breath of satisfaction.

She was a little troubled, however, as she went back into the sitting-room and took up her work [pp. 208-210].

At times, when she knew that McTeague was far from home. she would lock her door, open her trunk, and pile all her little hoard on her table. By now it was four hundred and seven dollars and fifty cents. Trina would play with this money by the hour, piling it, and repiling it, or gathering it all into one heap, and drawing back to the farthest corner of the room to note the effect, her head on one side. She polished the gold pieces with a mixture of soap and ashes until they shone, wiping them carefully on her apron. Or, again, she would draw the heap lovingly toward her and bury her face in it, delighted at the smell of it and the feel of the smooth, cool metal on her cheeks. She even put the smaller gold pieces in her mouth, and jingled them there. She loved her money with an intensity that she could hardly express. She would plunge her small fingers into the pile with little murmurs of affection, her long, narrow eyes half closed and shining, her breath coming in long sighs.

"Ah, the dear money, the dear money," she would whisper. "I love you so! All mine, every penny of it. No one shall ever, ever get you. How I've worked for you! How I've slaved and saved for you! And I'm going to get more; I'm going to get more, more, more; a little every day" [p. 308].

The arguments between McTeague and Trina increased in frequency and intensity, with Trina becoming more obdurate and defiant. Her defiance sprang from anal eroticism and served a narcissistic purpose as she felt herself becoming unloved, and it formed an important ego reaction against the money demands made by McTeague. Freud (1916-1917) predicted that intense gratification or frustration at a particular stage of psychosexual infantile development would lead to certain enduring character patterns and that, given anxiety or stress, an individual would tend to regress to the stage at which gratification or frustration was greatest. Trina is typical of the anal-erotic personality: messy,[1] hostile, infantile, obstinate, procrastinating, selfish, unfeeling toward others, all expressions of unbridled primitive instinctual impulses.

The three salient traits that Freud (1908) stipulated—orderliness, parsimoniousness, and obstinacy—were spelled out by Beloff (1957) to include collecting, punctuality, procrastination, quasi sadism in personal relations, conscientiousness, pedantry, feelings of superiority, omnipotence and irritability, contempt for others, a desire to domi-

---

[1] The anal character, with his cleanliness, love for order, defiance, and miserliness, sharply deviates from the pronounced anal-erotic, who is tolerant on the matter of dirt (Ferenczi, 1914).

neer, and a desire for personal autonomy. In the following passage, once again from Norris' *McTeague*, the anal characteristic of procrastination is shown in Trina's behavior. She has just received a letter from her mother, asking for money.

"And, say, Mac," continued Trina, pouring the chocolate, "what do you think? Mamma wants me — wants us to send her fifty dollars. She says they're hard up."

"Well," said the dentist, after a moment, "well, I guess we can send it, can't we?"

"Oh, that's easy to say," complained Trina, her little chin in the air, her small pale lips pursed. "I wonder if mamma thinks we're millionaires?"

"Trina, you're getting to be regular stingy," muttered McTeague. "You're getting worse and worse every day."

"But fifty dollars is fifty dollars, Mac. Just think how long it takes you to earn fifty dollars. Fifty dollars! That's two months of our interest."

"Well," said McTeague, easily, his mouth full of mashed potato, "you got a lot saved up."

Upon every reference to that little hoard in the brass match-safe and chamois-skin bag at the bottom of her trunk, Trina bridled on the instant.

"Don't *talk* that way, Mac. 'A lot of money.' What do you call a lot of money? I don't believe I've got fifty dollars saved."

"Hoh!" exclaimed McTeague. "Hoh! I guess you got nearer a hundred *an'* fifty. That's what I guess *you* got."

"I've *not,* I've *not,*" declared Trina, "and you know I've not. I wish mamma hadn't asked me for any money. Why can't she be a little more economical? *I* manage all right. No, no, I can't possibly afford to send her fifty."

"Oh, pshaw! What *will* you do, then?" grumbled her husband.

"I'll send her twenty-five this month, and tell her I'll send the rest as soon as I can afford it."

"Trina, you're a regular little miser," said McTeague.

"I don't care," answered Trina, beginning to laugh. "I guess I am, but I can't help it, and it's a good fault."

Trina put off sending this money for a couple of weeks, and her mother made no mention of it in her next letter. "Oh, I guess if she wants it so bad," said Trina, "she'll speak about it again." So she again postponed the sending of it. Day by day she put it off. When her mother asked her for it a second time, it seemed harder than ever for Trina to part with even half the sum requested. She an-

swered her mother, telling her that they were very hard up themselves for that month, but that she would send down the amount in a
few weeks.

"I'll tell you what we'll do, Mac," she said to her husband, "you
send half and I'll send half; we'll send twenty-five dollars altogether.
Twelve and a half apiece. That's an idea. How will that do?"

"Sure, sure," McTeague had answered, giving her the money.
Trina sent McTeague's twelve dollars, but never sent the twelve that
was to be her share. One day the dentist happened to ask her about
it.

"You sent that twenty-five to your mother, didn't you?" said he.

"Oh, long ago," answered Trina, without thinking [pp. 250-252].

In the first year of their marriage, Trina was a tidy housekeeper,
"sponging off the oilcloth table-spread, making the bed, puttering
about with a broom or duster or cleaning rag" (p. 192). As her avarice
developed, her housekeeping deteriorated, so that by their fourth
anniversary, "Trina was not quite so scrupulously tidy now as in the
old days" (p. 287). When McTeague was barred from practicing
dentistry, they moved to a one-room apartment, but Trina continued
to look for cheaper quarters until she found a back room over the
kitchen in someone else's home. " 'We can have it dirt cheap,' she told
McTeague. 'I'm going to take it. It'll be money in my pocket' " (p.
334). So they did, and Trina's regression to the anal stage was almost
complete. "She who had once been of a cat-like neatness, now slovened
all day about the room . . . her slippers clap-clapping after her as she
walked . . . She even neglected her hair . . . What odds was it that she
was slatternly, dirty, coarse? . . . The one room grew abominably
dirty, reeking with the odors of cooking and of 'non-poisonous' paint.
The bed was not made until late in the afternoon, sometimes not at
all. Dirty, unwashed crockery, greasy knives, sodden fragments of
yesterday's meals cluttered the table, while in one corner was the heap
of evil-smelling, dirty linen. Cockroaches appeared in the crevices of
the woodwork, the wallpaper bulged from the damp walls and began
to peel. Trina had long ago ceased to dust or to wipe the furniture with
a bit of rag. The grime grew thick upon the window panes and in
corners of the room. All the filth of the alley invaded their quarters
like a rising muddy tide" (pp. 334-337).

In the unconscious, Abraham (1921) stated, a disordered room
represents the bowel filled with feces.

The anal-erotic quality of Trina's obsession becomes explicit in the

following psychologically exacting passage. Trina had added to her
hoard of gold by working meanly at whittling wooden toys for her
Uncle Oelbermann and smearing them with a supposedly nontoxic
paint. As part of his vengeful, sadistic behavior toward Trina, Mc-
Teague had bitten her fingers until they bled. When she touched the
paint, her fingers became infected, necessitating amputation and
reducing her to work as a scrubwoman in order to replenish the four
hundred dollars she had hoarded and which McTeague had stolen.
Her obsessive-compulsive needs forced her to redeem the lottery money
from the uncle, change the check into gold, fondle the pieces, and
ultimately to sleep with them in the nude, "taking a strange and
ecstatic pleasure in the touch of the smooth flat pieces the length of her
entire body" (p. 361).

. . . She would wake at night from a dream of McTeague revelling
down her money, and ask of the darkness, "How much did he spend
to-day? How many of the gold pieces are left? Has he broken either
of the two twenty-dollar pieces yet? What did he spend it for?"
  The instant she was out of the hospital Trina had begun to save
again, but now it was with an eagerness that amounted at times to a
veritable frenzy. She even denied herself lights and fuel in order to
put by a quarter or so, grudging every penny she was obliged to
spend. She did her own washing and cooking. Finally she sold her
wedding dress, that had hitherto lain in the bottom of her trunk.
  The day she moved from Zerkow's old house, she came suddenly
upon the dentist's concertina under a heap of old clothes in the
closet. Within twenty minutes she had sold it to the dealer in
second-hand furniture, returning to her room with seven dollars in
her pocket, happy for the first time since McTeague had left her.
  But for all that the match-box and the bag refused to fill up;
after three weeks of the most rigid economy they contained but
eighteen dollars and some small change. What was that compared
with four hundred? Trina told herself that she must have her money
in hand. She longed to see again the heap of it upon her work-table,
where she could plunge her hands into it, her face into it, feeling the
cool, smooth metal upon her cheeks. At such moments she would see
in her imagination her wonderful five thousand dollars piled in
columns, shining and gleaming somewhere at the bottom of Uncle
Oelbermann's vault. She would look at the paper that Uncle Oelbermann had given her, and tell herself that it represented five thousand dollars. But in the end this ceased to satisfy her, she must have

the money itself. She must have her four hundred dollars back again, there in her trunk, in her bag and her match-box, where she could touch it and see it whenever she desired.

At length she could stand it no longer, and only day presented herself before Uncle Oelbermann as he sat in his office in the wholesale toy store, and told him she wanted to have four hundred dollars of her money.

"But this is very irregular, you know, Mrs. McTeague," said the great man. "Not business-like at all."

But his niece's misfortunes and the sight of her poor maimed hand appealed to him. He opened his check-book. "You understand, of course," he said, "that this will reduce the amount of your interest by just so much."

"I know, I know. I've thought of that," said Trina.

"Four hundred, did you say?" remarked Uncle Oelbermann, taking the cap from his fountain pen.

"Yes, four hundred," exclaimed Trina, quickly, her eyes glistening.

Trina cashed the check and returned home with the money — all in twenty-dollar pieces as she had desired — in an ecstasy of delight. For half of that night she sat up playing with her money, counting it and recounting it, polishing the duller pieces until they shone. Altogether there were twenty twenty-dollar gold pieces.

"Oh-h, you beauties!" murmured Trina, running her palms over them, fairly quivering with pleasure. "You beauties! *Is* there anything prettier than a twenty-dollar gold piece? You dear, dear money! Oh, don't I *love* you! Mine, mine, mine — all of you mine."

She laid them out in a row on the ledge of the table, or arranged them in patterns — triangles, circles, and squares — or built them all up into a pyramid which she afterward overthrew for the sake of hearing the delicious clink of the pieces tumbling against each other. Then at last she put them away in the brass match-box and chamois bag, delighted beyond words that they were once more full and heavy.

Then, a few days after, the thought of the money still remaining in Uncle Oelbermann's keeping returned to her. It was hers, all hers — all that four thousand six hundred. She could have as much of it or as little of it as she chose. She only had to ask. For a week Trina resisted, knowing very well that taking from her capital was proportionately reducing her monthly income. Then at last she yielded.

"Just to make it an even five hundred, anyhow," she told herself. That day she drew a hundred dollars more, in twenty-dollar gold pieces as before. From that time Trina began to draw steadily upon her capital, a little at a time. It was a passion with her, a mania, a veritable mental disease; a temptation such as drunkards only know.

It would come upon her all of a sudden. While she was about her work, scrubbing the floor of some vacant house; or in her room, in the morning, as she made her coffee on the oil stove, or when she woke in the night, a brusque access of cupidity would seize upon her. Her cheeks flushed, her eyes glistened, her breath came short. At times she would leave her work just as it was, put on her old bonnet of black straw, throw her shawl about her, and go straight to Uncle Oelbermann's store and draw against her money. Now it would be a hundred dollars, now sixty; now she would content herself with only twenty; and once, after a fortnight's abstinence, she permitted herself a positive debauch of five hundred. Little by little she drew her capital from Uncle Oelbermann, and little by little her original interest of twenty-five dollars a month dwindled.

One day she presented herself again in the office of the wholesale toy store.

"Will you let me have a check for two hundred dollars, Uncle Oelbermann?" she said.

The great man laid down his fountain pen and leaned back in his swivel chair with great deliberation.

"I don't understand, Mrs. McTeague," he said. "Every week you come here and draw out a little of your money. I've told you that it is not at all regular or business-like for me to let you have it this way. And more than this, it's a great inconvenience to me to give you these checks at unstated times. If you wish to draw out the whole amount let's have some understanding. Draw it in monthly install-ments of, say, five hundred dollars, or else," he added, abruptly, "draw it all at once, now, today. I would even prefer it that way. Otherwise it's—it's annoying. Come, shall I draw you a check for thirty-seven hundred, and have it over and done with?"

"No, no," cried Trina, with instinctive apprehension, refusing, she did not know why. "No, I'll leave it with you. I won't draw out any more."

She took her departure, but paused on the pavement outside the store, and stood for a moment lost in thought, her eyes begin-ning to glisten and her breath coming short. Slowly she turned about and reentered the store; she came back into the office, and stood trembling at the corner of Uncle Oelbermann's desk. He looked up sharply. Twice Trina tried to get her voice, and when it did come to her, she could hardly recognize it. Between breaths she said:

"Yes, all right—I'll—you can give me—will you give me a check for thirty-seven hundred? Give me *all* of my money."

A few hours later she entered her little room over the kindergarten, bolted the door with shaking fingers, and emptied a heavy canvas sack upon the middle of her bed. Then she opened her trunk, and taking thence the brass match-box and the chamois-skin bag added their contents to the pile. Next she laid herself upon the bed and gathered the gleaming heaps of gold pieces to her with both arms, burying her face in them with long sighs of unspeakable delight.

It was a little past noon, and the day was fine and warm. The leaves of the huge cherry trees threw off a certain pungent aroma that entered through the open window, together with long thin shafts of golden sunlight. Below, in the kindergarten, the children were singing gayly and marching to the jangling of the piano. Trina heard nothing, saw nothing. She lay on her bed, her eyes closed, her face buried in a pile of gold that she encircled with both her arms.

Trina even told herself at last that she was happy once more. McTeague became a memory—a memory that faded a little every day—dim and indistinct in the golden splendor of five thousand dollars.

"And yet," Trina would say, "I did love Mac, loved him dearly, only a little while ago. Even when he hurt me, it only made me love him more. How is it I've changed so sudden? How *could* I forget him so soon? It must be because he stole my money. That is it. I couldn't forgive anyone that—no, not even my *mother*. And I never—never will forgive him."

What had become of her husband Trina did not know. She never saw any of the old Polk Street people. There was no way she could have news of him, even if she had cared to have it. She had her money, that was the main thing. Her passion for it excluded every other sentiment. There it was in the bottom of her trunk, in the canvas sack, the chamois-skin bag, and the little brass match-safe. Not a day passed that Trina did not have it out where she could see and touch it. One evening she had even spread all the gold pieces between the sheets, and had then gone to bed, stripping herself, and had slept all night upon the money, taking a strange and ecstatic pleasure in the touch of the smooth flat pieces the length of her entire body [pp. 355-361].

By a process of condensation, Lawrence Durrell (1957), in the "Consequential Data" finale of his *Justine*, wrote about Georges Pombal, a minor official in the French consulate, "Pombal asleep in full evening dress. Beside him on the bed a chamber-pot full of banknotes he had won at the casino" (p. 251). And Dean Bernard Kovell of Cardozo College, the juggler of six mistresses in Alan Lelchuk's (1973) *American Mischief*, fantasies about the New York Stock Exchange, "Oh, it was funny stuff to see such unconscious mixtures of fantasy and reality concerning women, emperors, cash, machines, American business. At one point, when I went to the bathroom to defecate, I had an urge to pretend that I was shitting stocks instead of feces" (p. 50).

Based on the dream material of patients, Abraham (1920) deduced that along with the primitive idea of the omnipotence of thoughts, there is a parallel of the idea of the functions of bladder and bowel. Both ideas express the same narcissistic overestimation of the self. "The idea of the omnipotence of defecation . . . recalls the myths of the Creation, in which a human being is produced from earth and clay, *i.e.,* from a substance similar to excrement. The Biblical myth of the Creation has two different accounts concerning this. In the 'Elohistic' version God created the universe and also human beings by means of his command, 'Let there be', *i.e.* by the omnipotence of his thought, will, or deed. In the 'Jahvistic' version a human being is created out of a clod of earth into which God breathes; so that here [is] expressed the more primitive idea of the omnipotence of the products of the bowel" (Abraham, 1920, pp. 320-321). Thus the functions, not just the products, of excretion are overestimated, in the sense of possessing great and unlimited power to create or destroy. The Grimm brothers' (1851) so-called household story, "The Table, the Ass and the Stick," is illustrative of this. The ass spits forth gold coins when the magic words are spoken; the table is covered with food (bread = money = feces) upon pronouncing, "Table, be spread" and the stick punishes the thieving innkeeper. In the story, as will be seen, the angry tailor drives his three sons from his house for a reason beyond their control, which may be considered aggression by the father against his sons' genitality. According to Huss (1975, p. 167), "the deceived and angry tailor and the suave and deceiving innkeeper are obverse sides of the same repressive father imago, while the master joiner, miller, and turner are at the other end of the spectrum as the nurturing father to be identified with. The three sons, as they are forced into regression, come to represent the different stages of sexual development in a single individual: the eldest son exhibits orality in his command of the magic table that is a cornucopia of nourishment; and the second son continues the maturation into the next phase—anality—by his control of the ass that spits gold coins, a common displacement type of dream symbol for feces (the appropriate orifice becoming replaced by its opposite for the sake of decorum). Finally, mature genitality is illustrated by the third son's successful use of the stick and sack."

There was once a tailor who had three sons and one goat. And the goat, as she nourished them all with her milk, was obliged to have good food, and so she was led every day down to the willows by the water-side; and this business the sons did in turn. One day the eldest took the goat to the churchyard, where the best sprouts are, that she might eat her fill, and gambol about.

In the evening, when it was time to go home, he said, "Well, goat, have you had enough?"

The goat answered,

> "I am so full,
> I cannot pull
> Another blade of grass—ba! baa!"

"Then come home," said the youth, and fastened a string to her, led her to her stall, and fastened her up.

"Now," said the old tailor, "has the goat had her proper food?"

"Oh," answered the son, "she is so full, she no more can pull."

But the father, wishing to see for himself, went out to the stall, stroked his dear goat, and said,

"My dear goat, are you full?" And the goat answered,

> "How can I be full?
> There was nothing to pull,
> Though I looked all about me—ba! baa!"

"What is this that I hear?" cried the tailor, and he ran and called out to the youth,

"O you liar, to say that the goat was full, and she has been hungry all the time!" And in his wrath he took up his yard-measure and drove his son out the house with many blows.

The next day came the turn of the second son, and he found a fine place in the garden hedge, where there were good green sprouts, and the goat ate them all up. In the evening, when he came to lead her home, he said,

"Well, goat, have you had enough?" And the goat answered,

> "I am so full,
> I could not pull
> Another blade of grass—ba! baa!"

"Then come home," said the youth, and led her home, and tied her up.

"Now," said the old tailor, "has the goat had her proper food?"

"Oh," answered the son, "she is so full, she no more can pull."

The tailor, not feeling satisfied, went out to the stall, and said, "My dear goat, are you really full?" And the goat answered,

> "How can I be full?
> There was nothing to pull,
> Though I looked all about me—ba! baa!"

"The good-for-nothing rascal," cried the tailor, "to let the dear creature go fasting!" and, running back, he chased the youth with his yard-wand out of the house.

Then came the turn of the third son, who, meaning to make all sure, found some shrubs with the finest sprouts possible, and left the goat to devour them. In the evening, when he came to lead her he said,

"Well, goat, are you full?" And the goat answered,

> "I am so full,
> I could not pull
> Another blade of grass—ba! baa!"

"Then come home," said the youth; and he took her to her stall, and fastened her up.

"Now," said the old tailor, "has the goat had her proper food?"

"Oh," answered the son, "she is so full, she no more can pull."

But the tailor, not trusting his word, went to the goat and said, "My dear goat, are you really full?" The malicious animal answered,

> "How can I be full?
> There was nothing to pull,
> Though I looked all about me—ba! baa!"

"Oh, the wretches!" cried the tailor. "The one as good-for-nothing and careless as the other. I will no longer have such fools about me;" and rushing back, in his wrath he laid about him with his yard-wand, and belaboured his son's back so unmercifully that he ran away out of the house.

So the old tailor was left alone with the goat. The next day he went out to the stall, and let out the goat, saying,

"Come, my dear creature, I will take you myself to the willows."

So he led her by the string, and brought her to the green hedges and pastures where there was plenty of food to her taste, and saying to her,

"Now, for once, you can eat to your heart's content," he left her there till the evening. Then he returned, and said,

"Well, goat, are you full?"

She answered,

"I am so full,
I could not pull
Another blade of grass — ba! baa!"

"Then come home," said the tailor, and leading her to her stall, he fastened her up.

Before he left her he turned once more, saying,

"Now, then, for once you are full." But the goat actually cried,

"How can I be full?
There was nothing to pull,
Though I looked all about me — ba! baa!"

When the tailor heard that he marvelled, and saw at once that his three sons had been sent away without reason.

"Wait a minute," cried he, "you ungrateful creature! It is not enough merely to drive you away — I will teach you to show your face again among honourable tailors."

So in haste he went and fetched his razor, and seizing the goat he shaved her head as smooth as the palm of his hand. And as the yard-measure was too honourable a weapon, he took the whip and fetched her such a crack that with many a jump and spring she ran away.

The tailor felt very sad as he sat alone in his house, and would willingly have had his sons back again, but no one knew where they had gone.

The eldest son, when he was driven from home, apprenticed himself to a joiner, and he applied himself diligently to his trade, and when the time came for him to travel his master gave him a little table, nothing much to look at, and made of common wood;

but it had one great quality. When any one set it down and said, "Table, be covered!" all at once the good little table had a clean cloth on it, and a plate, and knife, and fork, and dishes with roast and boiled, and a large glass of red wine sparkling so as to cheer the heart. The young apprentice thought he was set up for life, and he went merrily out into the world, and never cared whether an inn were good or bad, or whether he could get anything to eat there or not. When he was hungry, it did not matter where he was, whether in the fields, in the woods, or in a meadow, he set down his table and said, "Be covered!" and there he was provided with everything that heart could wish. At last it occurred to him that he would go back to his father, whose wrath might by this time have subsided, and perhaps because of the wonderful table he might receive him again gladly. It happened that one evening during his journey home he came to an inn that was quite full of guests, who bade him welcome, and asked him to sit down with them and eat, as otherwise he would have found some difficulty in getting anything.

"No," answered the young joiner, "I could not think of depriving you; you had much better be my guests."

Then they laughed, and thought he must be joking. But he brought his little wooden table, and put it in the middle of the room, and said, "Table, be covered!" Immediately it was set out with food much better than the landlord had been able to provide, and the good smell of it greeted the noses of the guests very agreeably. "Fall to, good friends," said the joiner; and the guests, when they saw how it was, needed no second asking, but taking up knife and fork fell to valiantly. And what seemed most wonderful was that when a dish was empty immediately a full one stood in its place. All the while the landlord stood in a corner, and watched all that went on. He could not tell what to say about it; but he thought "such cooking as that would make my inn prosper." The joiner and his fellowship kept it up very merrily until late at night. At last they went to sleep, and the young joiner, going to bed, left his wishing-table standing against the wall. The landlord, however, could not sleep for thinking of the table, and he remembered that there was in his lumber room an old table very like it, so he fetched it, and taking away the joiner's table, he left the other in its place. The next morning the joiner paid his reckoning, took up the table, not dreaming that he was carrying off the wrong one, and went on his way. About noon he reached home, and his father received him with great joy.

"Now, my dear son, what have you learned?" said he to him.

"I have learned to be a joiner, father," he answered.

"That is a good trade," returned the father; "but what have you brought back with you from your travels?"

"The best thing I've got, father, is this little table," said he.

The tailor looked at it on all sides, and said,

"You have certainly produced no masterpiece. It is a rubbishing old table."

"But it is a very wonderful one," answered the son. "When I set it down, and tell it to be covered, at once the finest meats are standing on it, and wine so good that it cheers the heart. Let us invite all the friends and neighbours, that they may feast and enjoy themselves, for the table will provide enough for all."

When the company was all assembled, he put his table in the middle of the room, and said, "Table, be covered!"

But the table never stirred, and remained just as empty as any other table that does not understand talking. When the poor joiner saw that the table remained unfurnished, he felt ashamed to stand there like a fool. The company laughed at him freely, and were obliged to return unfilled and uncheered to their houses. The father gathered his pieces together and returned to his tailoring, and the son went to work under another master.

The second son had bound himself apprentice to a miller. And when his time was up, his master said to him,

"As you have behaved yourself so well, I will give you an ass of a remarkable kind: he will draw no cart, and carry no sack."

"What is the good of him then?" asked the young apprentice.

"He spits out gold," answered the miller. "If you put a cloth before him and say, 'Bricklebrit,' out come gold pieces."

"That is a capital thing," said the apprentice, and, thanking his master, he went out into the world. Whenever he wanted gold he had only to say "Bricklebrit" to his ass, and there was a shower of gold pieces, and so he had no cares as he travelled about. Wherever he came he lived on the best, and the dearer the better, as his purse was always full. And when he had been looking about him about the world a long time, he thought he would go and find out his father, who would perhaps forget his anger and receive him kindly because of his gold ass. And it happened that he came to lodge in the same inn where his brother's table had been exchanged. He was leading his ass in his hand, and the landlord was for taking the ass from him to tie it up, but the young apprentice said,

"Don't trouble yourself, old fellow, I will take him into the stable myself and tie him up, and then I shall know where to find him."

The landlord thought this was very strange, and he never supposed that a man who was accustomed to look after his ass himself could have much to spend; but when the stranger, feeling in his pocket, took out two gold pieces and told him to get him something good for supper; the landlord stared, and ran and fetched the best that could be got. After supper the guest called the reckoning, and the landlord, wanting to get all the profit he could, said that it would amount to two gold pieces more. The apprentice felt in his pocket, but his gold had come to an end.

"Wait a moment, landlord," said he, "I will go and fetch some money," and he went out of the room, carrying the tablecloth with him. The landlord could not tell what to make of it, and, curious to know his proceedings, slipped after him, and as the guest shut the stable-door, he peeped in through a knothole. Then he saw how the stranger spread the cloth before the ass, saying, "Bricklebrit," and directly the ass spat out gold, which rained upon the ground.

"Dear me," said the landlord, "That is an easy way of getting ducats; a purse of money like that is no bad thing."

After that the guest paid his reckoning and went to bed; but the landlord slipped down to the stable in the middle of the night, led the gold-ass away, and tied up another ass in his place. The next morning early the apprentice set forth with his ass, never doubting that it was the right one. By noon he came to his father's house, who was rejoiced to see him again, and received him gladly.

"What trade have you taken up, my son?" asked the father.

"I am a miller, dear father," answered he.

"What have you brought home from your travels?" continued the father.

"Nothing but an ass," answered the son.

"We have plenty of asses here," said the father. "You had much better have brought me a nice goat!"

"Yes," answered the son, "But this is no common ass. When I say, 'Bricklebrit,' the good creature spits out a whole clothful of gold pieces. Let me call all the neighbours together. I will make rich people of them all."

"That will be fine!" said the tailor. "Then I need labour no more at my needle;" and he rushed out himself and called the neighbours together. As soon as they were all assembled, the miller called out to them to make room, and brought in the ass, and spread his cloth before him.

"Now, pay attention," said he, and cried, "Bricklebrit!" but no gold pieces came, and that showed that the animal was not more scientific than any other ass.

So the poor miller made a long face when he saw that he had been taken in, and begged pardon of the neighbours, who all went home as poor as they had come. And there was nothing for it but that the old man must take to his needle again, and that the young one should take service with a miller.

The third brother had bound himself apprentice to a turner; and as turning is a very ingenious handicraft, it took him a long time to learn it. His brother told him in a letter how badly things had gone with them, and how on the last night of their travels the landlord deprived them of their treasures. When the young turner had learnt his trade, and was ready to travel, his master, to reward him for his good conduct, gave him a sack, and told him that there was a stick inside it.

"I can hang up the sack, and it may be very useful to me," said the young man. "But what is the good of the stick?"

"I will tell you," answered the master. "If any one does you any harm, and you say, 'Stick, out of the sack!' the stick will jump out upon them, and will belabour them so soundly that they shall not be able to move or to leave the place for a week, and it will not stop until you say, 'Stick, into the sack!'"

The apprentice thanked him, and took up the sack and started on his travels, and when any one attacked him he would say, "Stick, out of the sack!" and directly out jumped the stick, and dealt a shower of blows on the coat or jerkin, and the back beneath, which quickly ended the affair. One evening the young turner reached the inn where his two brothers had been taken in. He laid his knapsack on the table, and began to describe all the wonderful things he had seen in the world.

"Yes," said he, "you may talk of your self-spreading table, gold-supplying ass, and so forth; very good things, I do not deny, but they are nothing in comparison with the treasure that I have acquired and carry with me in that sack!"

Then the landlord opened his ears.

"What in the world can it be?" thought he. "Very likely the sack is full of precious stones; and I have a perfect right to it, for all good things come in threes."

When bedtime came the guest stretched himself on a bench, and put his sack under his head for a pillow, and the landlord, when he thought the young man was sound asleep, came, and, stooping down, pulled gently at the sack, so as to remove it cautiously, and put another in its place. The turner had only been waiting for this to happen, and just as the landlord was giving a last courageous pull, he cried, "Stick, out of the sack!" Out flew the stick directly, and laid to heartily on the landlord's back; and in vain he begged for mercy; the louder he cried the harder the stick beat time on his back, until he fell exhausted to the ground. Then the turner said,

"If you do not give me the table and the ass directly, this game shall begin all over again."

"Oh dear, no!" cried the landlord, quite collapsed; "I will gladly give it all back again if you will only make this terrible goblin go back into the sack."

Then said the young man, "I will be generous instead of just, but beware!" Then he cried, "Stick, into the sack!" and left him in peace.

The next morning the turner set out with the table and the ass on his way home to his father. The tailor was very glad indeed, to see him again, and asked him what he had learned abroad.

"My dear father," answered he, "I am become a turner."

"A very ingenious handicraft," said the father. "And what have you brought with you from your travels?"

"A very valuable thing, dear father," answered the son. "A stick in a sack!"

"What!" cried the father. "A stick! The thing is not worth so much trouble when you can cut one from any tree."

"But it is not a common stick, dear father," said the young man. "When I say, 'Stick, out of the bag!' out jumps the stick upon any one who means harm to me, and makes him dance again, and does not leave off till he is beaten to the earth, and asks pardon. Just look here, with this stick I have recovered the table and the ass which the thieving landlord had taken from my two brothers. Now, let them both be sent for, and bid all the neighbours too, and they shall eat and drink to their hearts' content, and I will fill their pockets with gold."

The old tailor could not quite believe in such a thing, but he called his sons and all the neighbours together. Then the turner brought in the ass, opened a cloth before him, and said to his brother,

"Now, my dear brother, speak to him." And the miller said, "Bricklebrit!" and immediately the cloth was covered with gold pieces, until they had all got more than they could carry away. (I tell you this because it is a pity you were not there.) Then the turner set down the table, and said,

"Now, my dear brother, speak to it." And the joiner said, "Table, be covered!" and directly it was covered, and set forth plentifully with the richest dishes. Then they held a feast such as had never taken place in the tailor's house before, and the whole company remained through the night, merry and content.

The tailor after that locked up in a cupboard his needle and thread, his yard-measure and goose, and lived ever after with his three sons in great joy and splendour [Grimm and Grimm, 1851, pp. 149-158].

In his paper on dreams in fairy stories, Freud (1913b) stated, "It is not surprising to find that psycho-analysis confirms our recognition of the important place which folk fairy tales have acquired in the mental life of our children. In a few people a recollection of their favorite fairy tales takes the place of memories of their own childhood; they have made the fairy tales into screen memories" (p. 281). Thus, "The Table, the Ass and the Stick" has been tidied up for today's readers so that with the change of one letter in the English language, the ass now spits instead of shits (a similar change occurs in the original German). But even so, it is forever wedded to the cloacal, no matter from which end the gold erupts. In the preface to the German edition of Bourke's *Scatologic Rites of All Nations,* Freud (1913a) wrote, "Folklore had adopted a quite different method of research, and yet it has reached the same results as psycho-analysis. It shows us how incompletely the repression of coprophilic inclinations has been carried out among various peoples at various times and how closely at other cultural levels the treatment of excretory substances approximates to that practised by children. It also demonstrates the persistent and indeed ineradicable nature of coprophilic interests, by displaying to our astonished gaze the multiplicity of applications — in magical ritual, in tribal customs, in observances of religious cults and in the art of healing — by which the old esteem for human excretions has found new expression" (p. 337).

Although Ferenczi (1928), Grant Duff (1937), Karpman (1942, 1949), and Greenacre (1955) have dealt extensively with Jonathan Swift's excursions into his unconscious use of the scatological equivalents of money in *Gulliver's Travels* (1726) and *Tale of a Tub* (1704), none has written on Swift's most direct acknowledgments of the equation. According to Lee (1971, pp. 70-71):

In several poems and one satire on a proposal to establish a National Bank in Dublin, Swift used the direct connection, "money-excrements," and "Bank-posteriors," with related matters such as flatulency and privy employed as figures of speech for money and the Bank. *The Wonderful World of Wonders* (1720) is an extended riddle on the posterior, describing but not identifying it. The piece concludes, "There is so general an Opinion of his Justice, that sometimes very *hard cases* are left to his Decision: And while he *sits* upon them, he carries himself exactly *even between both Sides,* except where some *knotty Point* arises; and then he is observed to *lean* a little to the *Right,* or *Left,* as the *Matter* inclines him; his Reasons for it are so manifest and convincing, that every man approves them."

Implicit in the satire is the metaphor for money and gold. In the verse-riddle of posteriors, *Because I Am by Nature Blind,* there is the financial metaphor of purse for buttocks:

> "I'm too *profuse* some Cens'rers cry
> And all I get, I let it *fly:*
> While others give me many a Curse
> Because too *close* I hold my *Purse.*"

In *The Wonderful World of Wonders,* Swift wrote, "He has the Reputation to be a *close, griping, squeezing* Fellow; and that when bags are *full,* he is often needy; yet, when the Fit takes him, as fast as gets, he lets it fly ... He hath been constituted by the *higher* Powers in the Station of *Receiver-General;* in which Employment, some have censured him for playing fast and loose. He is likewise *Overseer* of the *Golden Mines,* which he daily inspects, when his health will permit him ... In *Politicks,* he always submits to what is *uppermost* ... In him we may observe the true Effects and Consequences of Tyranny in a State: For, as he is a great *Oppressor* of all below him, so there is no body more *oppressed* by those *above* him: Yet in his Time, he hath been so highly in Favour, that many *illustrious Persons* have been entirely indebted to *him* for their Preferments ... He hath from his own Experience the true *Point,* wherein all human Actions, Projects, and Designs do chiefly *terminate;* and how *mean* and *sordid* they are *at the Bottom*" (pp. 281-284, *passim*).

Lee asserts that the entire essay rests on the metaphor of excrement equaling money, for "we can easily see the reference to 'Golden Mines' as the excremental pile and the Bank as the posteriors that discharge these golden mines at a privy" (p. 71).

Swift made use of scatology more than any other major author in English literature, but he was following literary precedents, all of them known to him. Lee (1971) traces the use of scatology from Aristophanes' *The Clouds* (423 B.C.) to the satires of Lucilius, the poetry of Catullus, the epigrams of Martial, the invective of Juvenal, the imagery of Dante, and the "histories" of Rabelais. The fascination that the elementary processes of the toilet held for Swift is evident to every reader. The appalling collection of data from *Gulliver's Travels* alone, that which appears in Karpman's (1942) article, gives clinical validation of this and cannot fail to be interpreted as an indication of the author's fixation at the anal-sadistic stage of libidinal development. "No person," Karpman educes, "could write with such obvious gusto of urine and feces, dirt and body odors, stable smells, the stench of decomposition and excrement, moles, hairs, anal orifices, flatus and cow manure unless he were impelled to do so by unconscious neurotic drives.... His picture of the hogs plowing the earth with their snouts and manuring it at the same time with their dung is highly suggestive of the psychic process engaged in by the author himself. His nose and his anus were apparently the two bodily organs which afforded him the greatest sensory delight" (p. 29).

Swift's coprophilic interests were inextricably bound up with sadism, invariably depicted by acts of gross humiliation inflicted by means of dirt. In the Fourth Voyage, the Yahoos void their excretion upon Gulliver; he wades through cow dung; he crawls upon his belly and licks the dust in the throne room Luggnagg.

> At last I beheld several animals in a field, and one or two of the same kind sitting in trees. Their shape was very singular, and deformed, which a little discomposed me, so that I lay down behind a thicket to observe them better. Some of them coming forward near the place where I lay, gave me an opportunity of distinctly marking their form. Their heads and breasts were covered with a thick hair, some frizzled and others lank; they had beards like goats, and a long ridge of hair down their backs, and the foreparts of their legs and feet, but the rest of their bodies were bare, so that I might see their skins, which were of a brown buff colour. They had no tails, nor any hair at all on their buttocks, except about the anus; which, I presume, nature had placed there to defend them as they sat on the ground; for this posture they used, as well as lying down, and often stood on their hind feet. They climbed high trees, as nimbly as a squirrel, for they had strong extended claws before and behind, terminating in sharp points, and hooked. They would often spring, and bound, and leap with prodigious agility. The females were not so large as the males; they had long lank hair on their heads, and only a sort of down on the rest of their bodies, except about the

anus, and pudenda. Their dugs hung between their fore-feet, and often reached almost to the ground as they walked. The hair of both sexes was of several colours, brown, red, black, and yellow. Upon the whole, I never beheld in all my travels so disagreeable an animal, or one against which I naturally conceived so strong antipathy. So that thinking I had seen enough, full of contempt and aversion, I got up and pursued the beaten road, hoping it might direct me to the cabin of some Indian. I had not gone far when I met one of these creatures full in my way, and coming up directly to me. The ugly monster, when he saw me, distorted several ways every feature of his visage, and stared as at an object he had never seen before; then approaching nearer, lifted up his forepaw, whether out of curiosity or mischief, I could not tell. But I drew my hanger, and gave him a good blow with the flat side of it, for I durst not strike him with the edge, fearing the inhabitants might be provoked against me, if they should come to know that I had killed or maimed any of their cattle. When the beast felt the smart, he drew back, and roared so loud, that a herd of at least forty came flocking about me from the next field, howling and making odious faces; but I ran to the body of a tree, and leaning my back against it, kept them off, by waving my hanger. Several of this cursed brood getting hold of the branches behind leaped up into the tree, from whence they began to discharge their excrements on my head: however, I escaped pretty well, by sticking close to the stem of the tree, but was almost stifled with the filth, which fell about me on every side [1726, pp. 181-182].

Defecating on somebody has deep atavistic meaning. It is an evil charm, inexorable and deadly. Hartogs (1967) reported on the belief in anal magic by a primitive tribe of bush Negroes in the jungles of Surinam, one remarkably akin to Gulliver's experience. "The bush Negroes proved themselves brave, gentle, and adept in all phases of animal capture except one. They showed a seemingly unaccountable fear of animals that had climbed into trees. The reason for their reluctance to go after treed beasts was that these animals, either in terror or as a natural defense, often defecated on the men coming after them. Invariably, this produced panic and despair on the part of the befouled rescuer. The men appeared genuinely stricken with horror, and neither reassurance . . . nor the quick removal of the offending offal could console them. Not only did the beshitted men remain despondent for many hours, but fellow tribesmen often taunted them for their misfortune.... Their horror [was based on the belief] that the animal's excrement carried an evil spell, that it was a tangible malediction, an anal curse. No recourse availed the man on whom it fell" (p. 127).

Swift's sadistic anality is apparent in several other passages in *Gulliver's Travels*, in one of which an academician asks Gulliver to assist him in an experiment for which he had a weekly allowance of "a vessel filled with human ordure, about the bigness of a Bristol barrel." In another, Swift described the disease known as "Yahoo's evil," for which he said, "the cure prescribed is a mixture of their own dung and urine, forcibly put down the Yahoo's throat."

> I went into another chamber, but was ready to hasten back, being almost overcome with a horrible stink. My conductor pressed me forward, conjuring me in a whisper to give no offence, which would be highly resented, and therefore I durst not so much as stop my nose. The projector of this cell was the most ancient student of the Academy. His face and beard were of a pale yellow; his hands and clothes daubed over with filth. When I was presented to him, he gave me a very close embrace (a compliment I could well have excused). His employment from his first coming into the Academy was an operation to reduce human excrement to its original food, by separating the several parts, removing the tincture which it receives from the gall, making the odour exhale, and scumming off the saliva. He had a weekly allowance from the society of a vessel filled with human ordure, about the bigness of a Bristol barrel [pp. 145-146].

*   *   *

> I was complaining of a small fit of the colic, upon which my conductor led me into a room, where a great physician resided, who was famous for curing that disease by contrary operations from the same instrument. He had a large pair of bellows with a long slender muzzle of ivory. This he conveyed eight inches up the anus, and drawing in the wind, he affirmed he could make the guts as lank as a dried bladder. But when the disease was more stubborn and violent, he let in the muzzle while the bellows were full of wind, which he discharged into the body of the patient, then withdrew the instrument to replenish it, clapping his thumb strongly against the orifice of the fundament; and this being repeated three or four times, the adventitious wind would rush out, bringing the noxious along with it (like water into a pump) and the patient recovers. I saw him try both

experiments upon a dog, but could not discern any effect from the former. After the latter, the animal was ready to burst, and made so violent a discharge, as was very offensive to me and my companions. The dog died on the spot, and we left the doctor endeavouring to recover him by the same operation [p. 147].

"If the Yahoos were all his personal enemies," wrote Huxley (1929), "that was chiefly because they smelt of sweat and excrement, because they had genital organs and dugs, groins and hairy armpits; their moral shortcomings were secondary" (p. 103). Huxley concluded that Swift's greatness lies in the intensity, almost insane violence, of that "hatred of the bowels which is the essence of his misanthropy and which underlies the whole of his work" (p. 110). This ascribes a simplistic motivation to Swift's anal eroticism. He had learned, through early abandonment by his mother and from his rearing by a severe yet seductive nurse who subjected him to early and rigid bowel control, who stressed cleanliness, and who taught him to read at an astonishingly early age, the lessons of hatred of all animal processes and functions. This was the foundation of his misanthropy and misogyny, of his rejection of and his alienation from the whole animal heritage of mankind (Roberts, 1956). Swift, according to Greenacre's (1955) construction, retained a confusion of identity of his own body and a fascinating interest in the female body which later on led to a loathing disdain for its uncleanliness. He gave the most striking example of this paradoxical, almost oxymoronic, coexistence of repulsion and attraction. He hated bowels and, at the same time, bowels constituted the central comic aspect of his life work.

Swift may very well have been influenced in his writings by the example of François Rabelais who lived some 200 years before him. Like Swift's sadistically anal thrusts at the scientists and philosophers of his day, Rabelais' characters also engaged in such incredible activities as "extracting farts from a dead donkey, and selling them at fivepence a yard." Another philosopher fermented "a great tub of urine in horse-dung" to produce a distillation with which he lengthened the lives of kings and princes "by a good six or nine feet." Rabelais' satire of the conventional world view included his ridicule of the medieval scholastic learning as represented by the Library of St. Victor. Pantagruel, in *Gargantua and Pantagruel* (1522), visited the famous library and cited a long catalog of some 139 books, including *The Art of Farting Decently in Public, Tartaret, on Methods of*

Shitting, and *The Greek Prepositions Discussed by the Turdicants.*
"Rabelais used scatology to ridicule, as an anal-aggressive expression
directed at most of the institutions and attitudes of the day. Through
scatology he put to flight the medieval; he heaped dung on useless
philosophy; he beleaguered the oppressive walls of monasteries and the
church" (Lee, 1971, p. 83).

Rabelais was ordained a priest in the Franciscan order, but later
turned to the practice of medicine; the influence of these two professions is clear in his work. He set out quite consciously "to make light of
the very virtues upon which society places such deadly serious emphasis—cleanliness, orderliness, and logic. . . . He ridiculed society's fear
of the bodily functions, of dirt, and all that is not clean . . . dealing
ironically with the taboo on excrement and the bodily functions"
(Kronhausen and Kronhausen, 1969, p. 54). One of Rabelais' more
scathing uses of scatological satire is revealed in the sketch of the infant
Gargantua at fecal play, which shows him wallowing in filth, displaying the typical omnipotent feelings of the anal personality.

> He was always rolling in the mud, dirtying his nose, scratching his
> face, and treading down his shoes; and often he gaped after flies, or
> ran joyfully after the butterflies of whom his father was the ruler. He
> pissed in his shoes, shat in his shirt, wiped his nose on his sleeve,
> snivelled into his soup, paddled about everywhere, drank out of his
> slipper, and usually rubbed his belly on a basket. He sharpened his
> teeth on a shoe, washed his hands in soup, combed his hair with a
> wine-bowl, sat between two stools with his arse on the ground, ate his
> biscuit without bread, but as he laughed and laughed as he bit, often
> spat in the dish, blew a fat fart, pissed against the sun, ducked under
> water to avoid the rain, struck the iron while it was cold, had empty
> thoughts, put on airs, threw up his food or, as they say, flayed the fox,
> mumbled his prayers like a monkey, returned to his muttons, and
> turned the sows out to hap. He would beat the dog in front of the lion,
> put the cart before the oxen, scratched where he did not itch . . .
> [I, xi, 62].

A massive reaction formation to this kind of behavior is depicted in
the famous Chapter 13 of *Gargantua and Pantagruel,* in a conversation between Gargantua and his father. The erotic quality of Gargantua's anality is marked, as in the phrase, "the softness of the silk
was very voluptuous and pleasant to my fundament."

How Gargantua's wonderful understanding became known to his Father Grangousier, by the invention of a torchecul or wipe-breech.

About the end of the fifth year, Grangousier, returning from the conquest of the Canarians, went by the way to see his son Gargantua. There was he filled with joy, as such a father might be at the sight of such a child of his: and whilst he kissed and embraced him, he asked many childish questions of him about divers matters, and drank very freely with him and with his governesses, of whom in great earnest he asked, amongst other things, whether they had been careful to keep him clean and sweet? To this Gargantua answered, that he had taken such a course for that himself, that in all the country there was not to be found a cleanlier boy than he. How is that, said Grangousier? I have, answered Gargantua, by a long and curious experience, found out a means to wipe my bum, the most lordly, the most excellent, and the most convenient that ever was seen. What is that, said Grangousier, how is it? I will tell you by and by, said Gargantua. Once I did wipe me with a gentlewoman's velvet mask, and found it to be good; for the softness of the silk was very voluptuous and pleasant to my fundament. Another time with one of their hoods, and in like manner that was comfortable. At another time with a lady's neckerchief, and after that I wiped me with some ear-pieces of hers made of crimson satin, but there was such a number of golden spangles in them (turdy round things, a pox take them) that they fetched away all the skin off my tail with a vengence. Now I wish St. Anthony's fire burn the bum-gut of the goldsmith that made them, and of her that wore them! This hurt I cured by wiping myself with a page's cap, garnished with a feather after the Switzers' fashion.

Afterwards, in dunging behind a bush, I found a March-cat, and with it I wiped my breech, but her claws were so sharp that they scratched and exulcerated all my perinee. Of this I recovered the next morning thereafter, by wiping myself with my mother's gloves, of a most excellent perfume and scent of the Arabian Benin. After that I wiped me with sage, with fennel, with anet, with marjorum, with roses, with gourd-leaves, with beets, with colewort, with leaves of the vine-tree, with mallows, wool-blade, which is a tail-scarlet, with lettuce and with spinage leaves. All this did very great good to my leg. Then with mercury, with pursly, with nettles, with comfrey, but that gave me the bloody flux of Lombardy, which I healed by wiping me with my braguette. Then I wiped my tail in the sheets, in the coverlet, in the curtains, with a cushion, with arras hangings, with a green carpet, with a table cloth, with a napkin, with a handkerchief, with a combing cloth; in all which I found more pleasure than do the mangy dogs when you rub them. Yea, but, said Grangousier, which torchecul did you find to be the best? I was coming to it, said Gargantua, and by and by shall you hear the *tu autem,* and know the whole mystery and knot of the matter. I wiped myself with hay, with straw, with thatch-rushes, with flax, with wool, with paper, but,

> Who his foul tail with paper wipes,
> Shall at his ballocks leave some chips.

What, said Grangousier, my little rogue, has thou been at the pot, that thou dost rhyme already? Yes, yes, my lord the king, answered Gargantua. I can rhyme gallantly, and rhyme till I become hoarse with rheum. Hark, what the privy says to the skiters:

> Shittard
> Squittard
> Crakard
>   Turdous,
> Thy bung
> Hath flung
> Some dung
>   On us:
> Filthard
> Crackard
> Stinkard,
> St. Anthony's fire seize on thy toane,
>   If thy
>   Dirty
>   Dounby
>   Thou do not wipe, ere
>   thou be gone.

Will you have any more of it? Yes, yes, answered Grangousier. Then said Gargantua,

A ROUNDELAY

In shitting yesterday I did know
The sess I to my arse did owe:
The smell was such came from that slunk,
That I was with it all bestunk:

O had but then some brave Signor
Brought her to me I waited for,
          In shitting!
I would have cleft her water-gap,
And join'd it close to my flip-flap,
Whilst she had with her fingers guarded
My foul nockandrow, all bemerded
          In shitting.

Now say that I can do nothing! By the Merdi, they are not of my making, but I heard them of this good old grandam, that you see here, and ever since have retained them in the budget of my memory.

Let us return to our purpose, said Grangousier. What, said Gargantua, to skite? No, said Grangousier, but to wipe our tails. But, said Gargantua, will not you be content to pay a puncheon of Breton wine, if I do not blank and gravel you in this matter, and put you to a non-plus? Yes truly, said Grangousier.

There is no need of wiping one's tail, said Gargantua, but when it is foul; foul it cannot be, unless one have been a skiting; skite then we must, before we wipe our tails. O my pretty little waggish boy, said Grangousier, what an excellent wit thou hast? I will make thee very shortly proceed doctor in the jovial quirks of gay learning and that, by G—, for thou hast more wit than age. Now, I prythee, go on in this torcheculatife, or wipe-bummatory discourse, and by my beard, I swear, for one puncheon, thou shalt have threescore pipes, I mean of the good Breton wine, not that which grows in Britain, but in the good country of Verron. Afterwards I wiped my bum, said Gargantua, with a kerchief, with a pillow, with a pantoufle, with a pouch, with a pannier, but that was a wicked and unpleasant torchecul; then with a hat. Of hats, note, that some are shorn, and others shaggy, some velveted, others covered with taffities, and others with satin. The best of all these is the shaggy hat, for it makes a very neat abstersion of the fecal matter.

Afterwards I wiped my tail with a hen, with a cock, with a pullet, with a calf's skin, with a hare, with a pigeon, with a cormorant, with an attorney's bag, with a montero, with a coif, with a falconer's lure. But, to conclude, I say and maintain, that of all torcheculs, arse-wisps, bumfodders, tail napkins, bung-hole cleansers, and wipe-breeches, there is none in the world comparable to the neck of a goose, that is well downed, if you hold her neck betwixt your legs. And believe me therein upon mine honour, for you will thereby feel in your knuckle a most wonderful pleasure, both in regard of the softness of the said down, and of the temperate heat of the goose, which is easily communicated to the bum-gut, and the rest of the inwards, in so far as to come even to the regions of the heart and brains. And think not, that the felicity of the heroes and demigods in the Elysian fields consisteth either in their Asphodele, Ambrosia, or Nectar, as our old women here used to say; but in this, according to my judgment, that they wipe their tails with the neck of a goose, holding her head betwixt their legs, and such is the opinion of Master John of Scotland, alias Scotus [pp. 16-18].

In John Barth's mock-heroic, parodistic, costumed historical romance, *The Sot-Weed Factor* (1961), Ebenezer, a poet manqué, unwittingly interfered in a private argument between two piratical-looking sailors at an inn. They threatened to shoot him, and in his desperation he fouled his breeches and fainted. On his recovery in a stable to which he had been removed, he was faced with the problem of cleaning himself up, since he was "all beshit and must be scrubbed." He ran through the possibilities, rejecting each in turn: the plentiful straw, his coat, shirt, and stockings. " 'What doth this teach us,' he reflected with pursed lips, 'if not that one man's wit is poor indeed? Fools and wild beasts live by mother wit and learn from experience; the wise man learns from the wits and lives of others. Marry, is't for naught I spent two years at Cambridge . . . if native wit can't save me, then education shall!' " (p. 188). Accordingly, he searched his education for succor, beginning with his memory of history, including Herodotus, Thucydides, Polybius, Suetonius, and Sallust among others, but finding no answer. Next, he summoned to mind the philosophers, Aristotle, Epicurus, Zeno, Augustine, and the rest and found none advanced specific counsel for his homely, practical predicament.

He did not even consider physics, astronomy, and the other areas of natural philosphy, for the same reason; nor did he crack his memory on the plastic arts, for he knew full well no Phidias or Michelangelo would deign to immortalize a state like his, whatever their attraction for human misery. No, he resolved at last, it was to literature he must turn for help, and should have sooner, for literature alone of all the arts and sciences took as her province the entire range of man's experience and behavior—from cradle to grave and beyond, from emperor to hedge-whore, from the burning of cities to the breaking of wind—and human problems of every magnitude: in literature alone might one find catalogued with equal care the ancestors of Noah, the ships of the Achaians——

"And the bum-swipes of Gargantua!" he exclaimed aloud. "How is't I did not think of them till now?" He reviewed with joy that chapter out of Rabelais wherein the young Gargantua tries his hand, as it were, at sundry swabs and wipers—not in desperation, to be sure, but in a spirit of pure empiricism, to discover the noblest for good and all—and awards the prize at last to the neck of a live white goose; but hens and guineas though there were a-plenty in the yard around the stable, not a goose could Ebenezer spy. "Nor were't fit," he decided a moment later, somewhat crestfallen, "save in a comic or satiric book, to use a filly fowl so hardly, that anon must perish to please our bellies. Good Rabelais surely meant it as a jest." In like manner, though with steadily mounting consternation, he considered what other parallels to his circumstances he could remember from what literature he had read, and rejected each in turn as inapplicable or irrelevant. Literature too, he concluded with heavy heart, availed him not, for though it afforded one a certain sophistication about life and release from one's single mortal destiny, it did not, except accidentally, afford solutions to practical problems. And after literature, what else remained? [pp. 189-190].

The solution to Ebenezer's dilemma came when he casually picked up his poetry notebook and saw in it what none of his previous efforts had led him to. Although he was unable to identify with Gargantua, Ebenezer did with Don Quixote and, like him, encountered shock after cruel shock. While the comedy of the two spurious manuscript journals in *The Sot-Weed Factor*, Captain John Smith's *Secret Historie* and *The Private Journall of Sir Henry Burlingame*, is not sexual, it relies heavily on Smith's being covered with urine or excrement. But unlike Don Quixote, the scales of delusional innocence dropped gradually from Ebenezer's eyes until the falseness of his stance became evident even to him and he was then able to grow out of the anal stage. The absurd worlds of Ebenezer and Don Quixote include the Man of La Mancha's Sancho Panza and Henry Burlingame, who functioned as Ebenezer's foil. Like Ebenezer, Sancho loses his stool over his horse in a moment of terror. Like Ebenezer, Don Quixote is a romance-deluded man in a real, unidealized world. He puts words and ideas into disastrous practice, a travesty of the romantic hero: old, poor, with creaky horse and shabby equipment, knighted in an innyard, cowardly in the face of the commonplace sounds of night.

The purgings and pummelings meted out to this ordinary Spanish hidalgo are tastes of reality opposed to his romantic illusions. What is sometimes seen in Don Quixote is the wondrous prototype of a hero striving for fulfillment of an ideal, attributing to him a yearning for truth which is lacking in the crude world of reality. Those who are more reality-oriented, who accept rather than deny their instincts, see Don Quixote as an anachronistic caricature of the castrated father of the child's nonsexual period (Deutsch, 1934). At the "father's" side is the mother—Sancho Panza, the fat, greedy, nurturing figure, who in touchingly maternal manner takes care of Don Quixote's excretory functions. If Don Quixote is about reality and illusion, then the only realities the addled Knight of the Sorrowful Figure possessed were the senses of smell and hearing.

Much about this time, whether it was the coolness of the night, or that Sancho had eaten some loosening food at supper, or, which seems more probable, that nature, by a regular impulse, gave him notice of her desire to perform a certain function that follows the third concoction, it seems, honest Sancho found himself urged to do that which nobody could do for him; but such were his fears that he durst not for his life stir the breadth of a straw from his master; yet, to think of bearing the intolerable load that pressed him so, was to him as great an impossibility. In this perplexing exigency (with leave be it spoken) he could find no other expedient but to take his right hand from the crupper of the saddle, and softly untying his breeches, let them drop down to his heels; having done this, he as silently took up his shirt, and exposed his posteriors, which were none of the least, to the open air: but the main point was how to ease himself of this terrible burden without making a noise; to which purpose he clutched his teeth close, screwed up his face, shrunk up his shoulders, and held in his breath as much as possible: yet see what misfortunes attend the best projected undertakings! When he had almost compassed his design, he could not hinder an obstreperous sound, very different from those that caused his fear, from unluckily bursting out. "Hark!" cried Don Quixote, who heard it, "what noise is that, Sancho?" "Some new adventures, I will warrant you," quoth Sancho, "for ill-luck, you know, seldom comes alone." Having passed off the thing thus, he even ventured the other strain, and did it so cleverly, that without the least rumor or noise, his business was done effectually, to the unspeakable ease of his body and mind.

But Don Quixote having the sense of smelling as perfect as that of hearing, and Sancho standing so very near, or rather tacked to him, certain fumes, that ascended perpendicularly, began to regale his nostrils with a smell not so grateful as amber. No sooner the unwelcome steams disturbed him, but, having recourse to the common remedy, he stopped his nose, and then, with a snuffling voice, "Sancho," said he, "thou art certainly in great bodily fear." "So I am," quoth Sancho; "but what makes your worship perceive it now more than you did before?" "Because," replied Don Quixote, "thou smellest now more unsavorily than thou didst before." "Ho! that may be," quoth Sancho; "but whose fault is that? you may even thank yourself for it. Why do you lead me a wild-goose chase, and bring me at such unseasonable hours to such dangerous places? you know I am not used to it." "Pray thee," said Don Quixote, still holding his nose, "get thee three or four steps from me; and for the future take more care, and know your distance; for I find, my familiarity with thee has bred contempt." "I warrant," quoth Sancho, "you think I have been doing something I should not have done." "Come, say no more," cried Don Quixote, "the more you stir, the worse it will be."

This discourse, such as it was, served them to pass away the night; and now Sancho, feeling the morning arise, thought it time to untie Rozinante's feet, and do up his breeches; and he did both with so much caution that his master suspected nothing [Cervantes, 1605, pp. 189-191].

Sancho Panza's fears and feelings of helplessness in the face of the bullying Don Quixote are typical of the neurotically constipated individual. His "libido has been displaced from the genital to the anal zone, and [he deplores] the inhibition of the bowel function just as though it were a genital impotence ... One is tempted to speak of an *intestinal* impotence" (Abraham, 1921, pp. 375-376). Philip Roth's *Portnoy's Complaint* (1969) depicts a weak, screaming, physically constipated father and a phallic, screaming, mentally constipated mother. Alexander Portnoy's earliest recollection of his father, he related on the analytic couch, was of mineral oil, milk of magnesia, Ex-Lax, All-Bran, and dried fruits, used to relieve his constipation. "He used to brew dried senna leaves in a saucepan, and that, along with the suppository melting invisibly in his rectum, comprised *his* witchcraft ... And then hunched silently above the empty glass, as though listening for distant thunder, he awaits the miracle ..." (p. 3). But no miracle came. When the announcement of the explosion of the first atom bomb was made, his father remarked, " 'Maybe that would do the job.' But all catharses were in vain . . . his *kishkas* were gripped by the iron hand of outrage and frustration. Among his other misfortunes, I was his wife's favorite" (pp. 3-4).

Henderson, in Saul Bellow's *Henderson the Rain King* (1959), also had psychosomatic manifestations resembling conversion hysteria of an anal order: aggressiveness, hemorrhoids, and accident-proneness. Disorders within Henderson's personality included extreme dependency needs and an id-dominated ego, the inability to control his aggressive impulses or to accept mortality. His extreme acquisitiveness is an anal-retentive substitute for the loss of nourishment from a loving mother (Moss, 1970). With the Wariri, Henderson learned about the aggressive quality of his anal-sadistic impulses and the need to control them. Moss (p. 58) points out these illustrations:

> The Wariri often presented buttocks to Henderson's view: trying to reach the Wariri King Dahfu, he complains, "But the wives were between us with their naked thighs, and their behinds toward me . . ." (p. 176). Speaking of some Wariri tribesmen, Henderson notes, "Their behinds were pitted like colanders" (p. 152). There are references to Henderson sitting . . . as if on a toilet: "My position on the three-legged stool suggested that I was crouching there to avoid questioning . . . And I kept wiping or rubbing my nose with my Woolworth bandana" (p. 159). He often mentioned his dirty undershorts and need for a bath: ". . . my crouching position with my belly against my bare knees (incidentally, I badly needed a bath, as sitting in this posture made me aware)" (pp. 160-161). "This left me in my jockey underpants, which were notably travel-stained" (p. 197). Disparaging himself, he remarks, "I don't even deserve to be chronicled on toilet paper" (p. 211).

Ronnie, the protagonist in Kingsley Amis's *I Want It Now* (1968), also depreciated himself in an anal-sadistic fashion. He had tried to manipulate Simon into marriage because of her money only to find he really loved her. He won her after an arduous chase, including defying a phallic mother, a homosexual rival, and his own anality. He confesses to Simon, "Very odd, this whole thing. I was a shit when I met you. I still am in a lot of ways. But because of you I've had to give up trying to be a dedicated, full-time shit. I couldn't make it, hadn't the strength of character. Which is a pity in a way, because when you fall back into the ranks of the failed shits or amateur shits or incidental shits you start taking on responsibility for other people" (p. 254). The infantile pleasure Ronnie associated with his sadistic anality and the regret expressed in his reluctance to leave irresponsibility behind him is typical of the anal personality's need to hold on to whatever he can. As Dr. Matthew Mighty O'Connor, the transvestite, bogus physician in Djuna Barnes' *Nightwood* (1937) noted about Jenny, she "is so greedy that she wouldn't give her shit to the crows" (p. 106) and thus vitiate her defenses.

The relationship of anal traits to castration anxiety found in the Wolf Man (Freud, 1918) is also found in the work of Norman Mailer. Anal-phallic symbolism pervades his fiction, from his earliest short story, "Maybe Next Year" (1941), to his novel, *Why Are We in Vietnam?* (1967). In an analysis of the latter, Aldridge (1968) states, "There are two kinds of obscenity in the novel: scatological and fornicatory. Sometimes, in the mixed metaphors of evacuation and buggrey, the two cohabit. But the scatological predominates. D. J.'s talk is primarily lingual bowel movement, and this has its quirky appropriateness. For over the years Mailer has evolved a sort of eschatology of scatology, a highly idiosyncratic metaphysics of feces. Excrement represents to him the organic form of defeat and dread. It is linked in his mind to the work of the Devil, who is engaged in unremitting warfare with God to determine the ascendancy of death or life in the universe, a contest which on the human level becomes the individual's unremitting struggle against dread. Closely related to this is the concept of apocalyptic orgasm which Mailer first explored in his famous essay, 'The White Negro.' The apocalyptic orgasm so passionately sought after by the hipster is not merely the ultimate sexual spasm. It may be a physical consummation devoutly to be wished for, but it is above all else a psychomystical experience whereby new circuits of energy are generated in the self which in turn come into connection with circuits operating throughout the universe. Finally, therefore, it is a means of attaining oneness with God. But for this to become possible, the Devil in us must first be vanquished. Hence, behind every apocalyptic orgasm is an apocalyptic defecation. From one exit we ejaculate toward divinity. From the other we evacuate the Devil's work. The route to salvation is thus from anus to phallus, from organic excretion to organic ecstasy. If there is in fact a Great Chain of Being, Mailer's advice would obviously be to pull it. The evolution toward the eschatology of scatology has been a completely natural development for Mailer, for what has always most deeply concerned him is what he himself [in *Why Are We in Vietnam?*, 1967, p. 214] calls 'the worst lust, the excretory lust' " (p. 96).

The opening paragraph of *Why Are We in Vietnam?* is indicative of Mailer's preoccupation with anality and genital sexuality, two forces united in his unconscious as destructive, befouling, and potentially uncontrollable, and against which he must defend himself:

> Hip hole and hupmobile, Braunschweiger, you didn't invite Geiger and his counter for nothing, here is D. J. the friendLee voice at your service — hold tight young America — introductions come. Let go my dong, Shakespeare, I have gone too long, it is too late to tell my tale, may Batman tell it, let him declare there's blood on my dick and D. J. Dicktor Doc Dick and Jek has got the bloods, and has done animal murder, out out damn fart, and murder of the soldierest sort, cold was my hand and hot [p. 6].

When D. J. announces "there's blood on my dick" and "out out damn fart," he is saying "that the evil of the phallus and the anus is inescapable" (Gordon, 1969, p. 6).

In his analysis of Mailer's first novel, *The Naked and the Dead* (1948), Gordon (1969, pp. 6-12), said that virtually all of Mailer's heroes are impotent murderers who feel they deserve to be castrated. "Ultimately, this is a shaky manner of dealing with a castrating, anally constricted image of the mother, and a father who is perceived as impotent yet cruel. Every one of Mailer's stories represents an unconscious working out of this dilemma, a shifting of the variables in an endless search for a viable solution. As Rojack in *The American Dream* [p. 15] puts it, 'I had my fill of walking about with a chest full of hatred and a brain jammed to burst, but there is something manly about containing your rage. It is so difficult.... The exhilaration comes I suppose from possessing such strength. Besides, murder offers the promise of vast relief. It is never unsexual'. The phallic imagery here is right on the surface, though the inevitably linked anal imagery is slightly hidden: 'containing your rage' sounds like restricting a bowel movement. When the dammed-up force of the organ of the orifice is released it destroys..." (p. 6).

The Naked and the Dead is a mercilessly realistic view of men at war, Gordon continues, "littered with corpses and filled with the fecal stench of human putrefaction. Mailer's fragmented narrative ... develops a group consciousness by shifting between the inner thoughts of more than a dozen soldiers. The spectre of death is omnipresent, and the violent struggle to preserve their lives and their manhood consumes them ... 'Power' and 'control' are the two most frequently employed words in the novel, but the terms next highest in frequency are 'impotent rage' and 'failure.' The truth of the novel is revealed in its title: those who are stipped *naked* and are yet sexually *dead*. The essential characteristics of the protagonists are ... fear of impotence and castration coupled with anal regression and latent homosexuality. Like the long-suffering child, they put a clamp on their emotions, for the expulsion of emotion itself is anal. 'There was something nasty, unclean about the emotion Roth was showing. Red always curdled before emotion' [p. 500]. Feelings must therefore be smothered until they can no longer be controlled.... There is no cessation of struggle.... The cycle is suggested in the first incident in the book, when a soldier retreats to the latrine, looking for relief, and finds none. In a primitive physical sense, relieving one's bowels is connected with destruction, for the men who die first lose control of their sphincter. Hennessy, Wilson, and Roth all break the cardinal rule of the soldiers, which is 'Keep a tight asshole.' Diarrhea presages disaster, impotence and death. When the wounded Wilson finds himself about to defecate on his stretcher, he feels it as intense pain, and fights it 'with a childish fear of punishment, and then relapses into the heat and pleasure of voiding....' Sexual images fill his head and impart 'a lazy sensuality to his loins,' but an attempt to urinate is prevented by his painful syphilis, so that 'it shattered the images, left him aware and troubled and perplexed, conscious for the first time of the way he had soiled himself. He had a picture of his loins putrefacted and a deep misery ran through him' [p. 545].

"The protagonists attempt to cope with their unresolved castration anxiety through a drive toward omnipotence. General Cummings indulges in a battle plan which is pure homosexual fantasy: 'His mind kept picturing the pincers of a frontal assault and an invasion from the rear' [p. 332], that is, overpowering the enemy through simultaneous emasculation and buggery. As Cummings admits, 'Man's deepest urge is omnipotence. When we discover that the universe is not us, it's the deepest trauma of our existence' [p. 282]. The oedipal implications of such a statement are self-evident. In a similar fashion, Croft says, 'I hate everything which is not myself' [p. 142]. Lt. Hearn is horrified with himself when he discovers his own attraction toward the ruthless power of the effeminate Cummings. 'Divorced of all the environmental trappings ... he was basically like Cummings' [p. 342]. As he comes later to realize, leadership is:

> as filthy as everything else. And he enjoyed it now. After the unique excitement, call it the unique ecstasy, of leading the man.... Beyond Cummings, deeper now, was his own desire to lead the platoon. It had grown, ignited suddenly, become one of the most satisfying things he had ever done ... when he searched himself he was just another Croft.
>
> That was it. All his life he had flirted with situations, jobs, where he could move men, and always ... he had dropped things when they were about to develop, cast off women because deep within him he needed control and not mating [pp. 503-504].

"Even in this confrontation, we can see the constant shift between anal and phallic metaphors: from 'filthy,' with its hint of fecal, to the overtly sexual 'unique excitement,' 'unique ecstasy,' 'desire,' 'grown,' 'ignited suddenly,' 'satisfying,' and 'flirted,' back to the anal in 'dropped things,' concluding with the highly charged word 'control' and a sudden switch into the sexual realm with 'mating.' The two layers of castration anxiety and anal anxiety seem to coexist, even in the structure of the prose, and are subsumed under a desire for control, for omnipotence.

"Cummings himself gropes with distaste through the 'slimy walls of a muddy tent' [p. 96], and Hearn repeats his action later on in the novel with a similar response. Hearn opens the hatch door of a ship, and shock; he had forgotten how unbearable a ship's hold could become. And of course it stank. He felt like an insect crawling through the entrails of a horse. "Damn," he muttered in disgust' [p. 268] ... The equation between the anus and the lethal vagina becomes evident in a later episode. The platoon is on patrol, significantly headed for the 'Japanese rear' [p. 396]. Suddenly, they encounter a fecal jungle, 'a tunnel whose walls were composed of foliage and whose roadbed was covered with slime.' They are 'absorbed' in the stench, which released a 'stifled horror, close to nausea' [p. 396] ... They progress upriver 'with the motions of salmon laboring upstream for the spawning season' [pp. 406-407]. It is a struggle upstream all the way for Mailer in *The Naked and the Dead,* and the journey into the anus is a particularly chancy trip, filled with 'stimulations and terrors' [p. 398], because one might not return with an intact member. Sodomy promises immense power, but it also entails the risk of retaliatory castration.

"Every character in *The Naked and the Dead*," Gordon concludes, "is a projection of and an advertisement for that grand egomaniac, Mailer himself. No wonder that he later writes of his first novel as though it were some vast public excretion: 'There was nothing left in the first twenty-four years of my life to write about; one way or another, my life seemed to have been mined and melted into the long reaches of the book. And so I was prominent and empty, and I had to begin life again.'" Twelve years later, in a public conversation with R. D. Laing, Mailer (1972) described himself as 'a stingy person.'

In the discussion of *The Naked and the Dead*, the passage quoted about the platoon on patrol duty exploring a fecal jungle in which there was a tunnel whose roadbed was covered with slime reveals striking anal imagery. Exploring, while it shows genital influences, is associated with anal curiosity and is paralleled especially by the fascination for caves and the lure of buried treasure, symbolizing the curiosity for both the concealed passage and the valuable feces (Menninger, 1943). In *Dog Years* by Günter Grass (1953), two high-school chums, Eddi Amsel, a good-natured student who may or may not be half-Jewish, and his old buddy, Walter Matern, explore the passageways of the city's sewer system, an entrance to which Eddi has found by lifting a small rectangle out of the floorboards in the locker room of their school's gymnasium. The narrative begins with the recollections of Brauxel, the foreman of a mysterious mine some 2,500 feet below the earth's surface: "Who, having relieved himself after breakfast, is standing here contemplating his excrement? A thoughtful, anxious man in search of the past. Why keep ogling a smooth and weightless death's head?" (p. 73). From this direct association with feces, Brauxel's thoughts wander to the adventures of Eddi and Walter as they crawled, during the Nazi regime, through a shaft not far from the locker-room urinal into the municipal sewage system. It is a passage replete with anal imagery. The boys are "cramped" as they proceed through the "dry, foul-smelling" tunnels; they come upon a "bifurcation" in the wall which is "stopped up" with bricks, and which, when the boys open it up, slopes downward, leading them along a crumbling and dripping path under the medieval church. One of the boys has to squat in order to see better; they come across dead stinking animals and putrefaction. And, as the episode ends, an equivalence is questioned between identity and excrement.

So the Grinder—Amsel invented the name, fellow students have taken it up—so the Grinder goes first. In his left hand he holds an army flashlight, while in his right he holds a stick intended to frighten away or, as the case may be, destroy rats. There aren't many rats. The masonry is rough crumbly dry to the touch. The air cool but not glacial, more on the drafty side, though it is not clear where the draft is blowing from. Their steps do not echo as in the municipal sewers. Like the passageway leading to it, this man-high corridor slopes steeply downward. Walter Matern is wearing his own shoes, for Amsel's patent-leather shoes had suffered enough as they were crawling through the low passageways. So that's where the draft and ventilation were coming from: from that hole! They might almost have missed it if Amsel hadn't. It was on the left. Through the gap, seven bricks high, five bricks wide, Amsel pushes the Grinder. Amsel himself has a harder time of it. Holding his flashlight between his teeth, the Grinder tugs Amsel through the hole, helping to transform Amsel's almost new school clothes into the customary school rags. Both stand there for a moment panting. They are on the spacious floor of a round shaft. Their eyes are drawn upward, for a watery light is trickling down from above: the pierced, artfully forged grating on top of the shaft is inserted in the stone floor of the Church of the Trinity: they will investigate that another time. Four eyes follow the diminishing light back down the shaft, and at the bottom —the flashlight points it out to them—what lies in front of the tips of four shoes but a skeleton!

It lies doubled up, incomplete, with interchanged or telescoped details. The right shoulder blade has stove in four ribs. The sternum is driven into the right ribs. The left collarbone is missing. The spinal column is bent above the first lumbar vertebra. The arrangement of the arms and legs is exceedingly informal: a fallen man.

The Grinder stands rigid and allows himself to be relieved of the flashlight. Amsel begins to throw light on the skeleton. Without any intention on Amsel's part, effects of light and shadow are produced. With the tip of one patent-leather shoe—soon Brauxel will have no need to speak of patent leather—he draws a circle through the dry, only superficially crusted dust, circumscribing all the fallen members, moves back, lets the cone of electric light follow the line, screws up his eyes as he always does when he sees something likely to serve as a model, tilts his head, waggles his tongue, covers one eye, turns around, looks behind him over his shoulder, conjures up a pocket mirror from somewhere, juggles with light, skeleton, and mirror image, directs the flashlight behind him under a sharply bent arm, tips the mirror slightly, stands briefly on tiptoes in order to lengthen the radius, then squats by way of comparison, stands again facing his model without mirror, corrects the line here and there, exaggerates the fallen man's pose with sketching shoe, still with his shoe erases and draws new lines to undo the exaggeration, harmonizes, sharpens, softens, strives for dynamic balance ecstasy, concentrates all his powers on sketching the skeleton, preserving the sketch in his memory, and perpetuating it at home in his diary. Small wonder that after all his preliminary studies are concluded, Amsel is taken with the desire to pick up the skull from between the skeleton's incomplete collarbones, and quietly put it into his school satchel with his books and notebooks and Hedwig Lau's crumbling shoe. He wants to carry the skull to the Vistula and put it on one of his scarecrows that are still in the framework stage, or if possible on the scarecrow that he has just sketched in the dust. His hand with its five pudgy, ludicrously spread fingers is already hovering over the vestiges of collarbone; it is about to reach into the eye sockets, the safest way to lift a skull, when the Grinder, who has long stood rigid, giving little sign of his presence, begins to grind several of his teeth. In his usual way: from left to right. But the acoustics of the shaft magnify and multiply the sound so forbodingly that Amsel stops in the middle of his skulduggery, looks behind him over his rounded back, and turns the flashlight on his friend.

The Grinder says nothing. His grinding is plain enough. It means: Amsel should not spread his little fingers. Amsel shouldn't take anything away. The skull is not to be removed. Don't disturb it. Don't touch it. Place of skulls. Golgotha. Barrow. Gnashing of teeth.

But Amsel, who is always at a loss for meaningful props and accessories, who is always short on what he needs most, is again preparing to dispatch his hand skullward and again — for it isn't every day that you find a skull — outspread fingers can be discerned amid the shimmering dust of the flashlight beam. At this point the stick which thus far had struck nothing but rats descends on him, once maybe twice. And the acoustics of the shaft amplify a word uttered between blow and blow: "Sheeny!" Walter Matern calls his friend "Sheeny!" and strikes. Amsel falls sideways beside the skeleton. Dust rises and takes its time about settling. Amsel picks himself up. Who can cry such fat, convulsively rolling tears? But even as the tears roll from both his eyes and turn to beads of dust on the floor of the shaft, Amsel manages to say with a grin somewhere between good-natured and mocking: *"Walter is a very silly boy."* Imitating the teacher's voice, he several times repeats this sentence from his first-year English book; for always, even when tears are flowing, he has to imitate somebody, himself if need be: *"Walter is a very silly boy."* And then in the idiom of the Island: "This here is my head. Didn't I find it? I just wanna try it out. Then I'll bring it back."

But the Grinder is in no mood to be spoken to. The sight of the haphazardly disposed bones makes his face shrink toward the inside corners of his eyebrows. He folds his arms, leans on his stick, freezes in contemplation. Whenever he sees anything dead: a drowned cat, rats he has slain with his own hand, gulls slit open with a throw of his knife, when he sees a bloated fish rolled in the sand by the lapping of the waves, or when he sees a skeleton which Amsel wants to deprive of its skull, his teeth start in from left to right. His bullish young face twists into a grimace. His gaze, ordinarily dull to stupid, becomes piercing, darkens, gives an intimation of directionless hatred: theatrical ambiance in the passages, dungeons, and shafts beneath the Gothic Church of the Trinity. Twice the Grinder pounds his own forehead with his fist, bends down, reaches out, raises the skull to himself and his thoughts, and contemplates it while Eduard Amsel squats down to one side.

Who is squatting there, obliged to relieve himself? Who is standing there, holding a stranger's skull far out in front of him? Who looks behind him with curiosity, examining his excrement? Who stares at a smooth skull, trying to recognize himself? Who has no worms, but did once from salad? Who holds the light skull and sees worms that will one day be his? Who, who? Two human beings, pensive and troubled. Each has his reasons. They are friends. Walter Matern puts the skull back down where he found it. Amsel is scratching again in the dirt with his shoe, looking and looking. Walter Matern declaims high-sounding words into the void: "Let's be going now. This is the kingdom of the dead. Maybe that's Jan Bobrowski or Materna that our family comes from." Amsel has no ear for words of conjecture. He is unable to believe that Bobrowski the great robber, or Materna, robber, incendiary, and ancestor, ever gave flesh to this skeleton. He picks up something metallic, scratches at it, spits on it, rubs it off, and exhibits a metal button, which he confidently identifies as the button of one of Napoleon's dragoons. He dates the button from the second siege and puts it in his pocket. The Grinder does not protest, he has scarcely been listening, he is still with the robber Bobrowski or his ancestor

Materna. The cooling feces drive the friends through the hole in the wall. Walter Matern goes first. Amsel squeezes through the hole backwards, his flashlight turned upon the death's-head [pp. 75-78].

Anal curiosity becomes intimately linked with influences from the genital phase in its expressions as sublimations in the adult. But the careful attention Eddi and Walter paid in planning their explorations, the meticulous research into what their needs would be, and the organizational efficiency and enjoyment of it, are primary representations of anal sublimations. Perhaps the link between anal eroticism and genital sexuality is revealed in Grass's phrase, "strives for dynamic balance ecstasy." Freud (1908, p. 174) has written about the superstition which associates the finding of treasure with defecation, "and everyone is familiar with the figure of the 'shitter of ducats,' " usually a small chocolate man who expelled a gold piece from his anus and which used to hang on many Christmas trees in Austria. Steve Fraser, the protagonist in *State of Siege* by Eric Ambler (1956), is passing by a small fair in a mythical Malayan country. "A carousel had been set up, and a small stage on which two Indian conjurors were performing . . . One of the conjurors was holding a tin chamber pot, while the other pretended to defecate coins into it. As the coins clattered into the pot, the crowd applauded happily" (p. 38). Grass's preocupation with feces and treasure, while not as blunt as the *Dukatenscheisser* or the Indian conjurors, renders anal currency in more sublimated form.

The Specialist, by Chic Sale (1929), is a humorous sketch of "the champion privy builder of Sangamon County" and describes the building of a "four-holer" and the "eight-holer." A similar publication by Greer, entitled *Gems of American Architecture,* carries illustrations of various types of outdoor toilets with descriptions of each. The word "gems" in the title equates wealth and power with the privy (Menninger, 1943). A satirical social commentary about the building of a privy is found in *The Scandals of Clochemerle* by Gabriel Chevallier (1937), which is, at its core, a sustained renal eructation. Within the first seven pages of the novel, the plot is exposed: the Mayor of Clochemerle wants to build a urinal at public expense directly opposite the town church. With this determined, the anal-urethral-erotic aspects of the novel come at once to the fore. Early on, there is reference to the "pestiferous exhalations" of the village schoolmaster, who is also the Mayor's secretary and town clerk. His bad breath was so virulent that the city council would quickly give its consent in order "to close the schoolmaster's mouth" and shut off his "odorous eloquence." Cloche-merle depends on wine growing for its survival and "the heat of that October gave more body to the odor of new wine that bloated over the whole countryside." When Sidonie Sauvy's stomach swelled "because of a stoppage of the bowels" (p. 39), the salad oil prescribed did its job so well that it provided "a smell in the street like on the days when the casks are emptied." A local saying about the family of the notary, Girodot, was they "are a breed that do their lovemaking in the slits of money boxes" (p. 45). The Girodots were yellow-complexioned, shri-veled, and constipated. The notary himself was "a skinflint and moneygrubber, a talebearing sneak with some extremely nasty habits" (p. 45). His mind was invariably concerned with money.

In 1921 Girodot, who was a methodical man and kept entries of all transactions, had the curiosity to make a reckoning of all his expenditures occasioned by the war. By this is meant gifts to individ-uals and subscriptions to charitable objects. He made a minute examination of his old notebooks, and thereby reached a total, between the month of August 1914 and the end of 1918, of nine hundred and twenty-three francs fifteen centimes which he would not have disbursed except for the war (though he had made no reductions in his customary almsgiving or his contributions to church expenses). It should at the same time be mentioned that this gener-osity found compensation in the increased value of all his property. In conjunction with these calculations, he made a computation of his total assets. By an estimate, at their current value, of his Cloche-merle vineyards, his house, his notary's practice, his property at Dombes, his Charollais estates, his woods, and his investments, he calculated that his fortune amounted to four million six hundred and fifty thousand francs (as against an estimate of about two million two hundred thousand francs in 1914), in spite of a loss of sixty thousand francs in Russian securities [p. 46].

Girodot's preoccupation with statistics and money is typical of the other burghers of the town, and it is for this reason that they can center their attention on the device of the urinal. "In the brain of Clochemerle's inhabitants, the idea of profit hammered away with the rhythmical insistence of the blood in their arteries" and "not a single person would you find there who was free from care where money was concerned" (pp. 48-49). Meanwhile, the urinal had been built in secret, covered with tarpaulin to hide the work in progress. At the dedication, with the populace still unaware of what the new edifice was, there appeared a full panoply of a children's choir, the fire brigade, a parade, politicos, and a bottle of urine with which to baptize the convenience. The honor of making first use of the urinal was courteously and ever so innocently given to a local political notable, an ex-Minister of State who had had serious trouble with his kidneys.

Chevallier's satire is based on the indisputable fact that the human mind must live in, and be conditioned by, the human body. The focus on a fundamental function of man gives rise for an opportunity to present a malevolent, savage, scatological picture of French small-town life and manners. What Chevallier did for the French, James Joyce has done for Molly Bloom in his *Ulysses* (1918). The long soliloquy at the end of the novel presents Molly trying to fall asleep, but she is preoccupied with anal-erotic thoughts. The absence of punctuation marks points to a release from the slight hold which the social amenities ordinarily have upon her. Molly's mind flows through present and past without pause. The device of one continuous, loose sentence, which runs for forty-five pages, is reminiscent of a diarrhetic outpouring. Sixteen anal-erotic instances mark the book's coda, as Molly's thoughts race through her love affairs—both innocent and adulterous—concern about her daughter Milly, the price of kidneys, her husband's sexual pecadillos, and a host of related matters.

> . . . M Bloom youre looking blooming Josie used to say after I married him well its better than Breen or Briggs does brig those awful names with bottom in them like Mrs. Ramsbottom or some other kind of bottom . . . my hole is itching me always when I think of him I feel I want to feel some wind in me go easy not to wake him . . . I wish hed sleep in some bed by himself with his cold feet on me give us room even to let a fart . . . wheres the chamber gone easy Ive a holy horror of its breaking under me after that old commode. . . . Thats a very nice invention too by the way only I like letting myself down after in the hole as far as I can squeeze and pull the chain then to flush it nice cool pins and needles still theres something in it I suppose I always used to know by Millys when she was a child whether she had worms or not . . . Im young still can I its a wonder Im not an old shrivelled hag before my time living with him so cold never embracing me except sometimes when hes asleep the wrong end of me not knowing I suppose who he has any man thad kiss a womans bottom Id throw my hat at him after that hed kiss anything unnatural where we havent 1 atom of any kind of

expression in us all of us the same 2 lumps of lard before ever I do that to a man pfooh the dirty brutes the mere thought is enough . . . it wasnt my fault we came together when I was watching the two dogs up in her behind in the middle of the naked street . . . if he wants to kiss my bottom Ill drag open my drawers and bulge it right out in his face as large as life he can stick his tongue 7 miles up my hole as hes there my brown part . . . Ill tighten my bottom well and let out a few smutty words smellrump or lick my shit or the first mad thing comes into my head . . . then Ill wipe him off me just like a business . . . [pp. 746-776, *passim*].

Molly Bloom has been seen by various critics as an adulterous nymphomaniac with possibly twenty-four lovers in an eighteen-year period, as a fertility goddess, a Circe, a Penelope, a bored, frustrated housewife in provincial Dublin, and a mediated projection of Joyce's own sexual anxieties about phallic women. No matter which, Molly is a gusty, plain-spoken person of abundant sexual vigor, with a husband afflicted with grave sexual inhibitions and problems. In Joyce's own description, Molly is "sane full amoral fertilisable untrustworthy engaging shrewd limited prudent indifferent" (Gilbert, 1957). At heart a blunt and honest person, Molly opens all three orifices in the course of her monologue, spending a good deal of the time squatting on the chamber pot. While she is frank about her own animal functions, she is disgusted by a soldier's exhibitionism and by her one experience of the filth in a men's lavatory. Penis envy, disgust with women's functions, and narcissistic delight are mixed as she sits on the pot: "I bet he never saw a better pair of thighs than that look how white they are the smoothest place is right there between this bit here how soft like a peach easy God I wouldnt mind being a man and get up on a lovely woman O Lord what row youre making like the jersey lily easy O how the waters come down at Lahore" (p. 755). In the liquid medium of her thoughts, she recalls she is heavy enough to break a commode during an amorous experiment; she remembers her husband's excitement caused by "my muddy boots hed like me to walk in all the horse dung I could find" (p. 730); kissing her bottom she describes as "the usual" for him; she knows she can sexually stimulate him by spitting out cruel obscenities — "smellrump or lick my shit," just the thing for the masochistic Poldy. In this climactic episode, Molly becomes the motion of life itself, self-befouling, self-purifying, an enormous imago in which to give and retain, to void and restrain, and in which she achieves some kind of stasis.

In Joyce's last novel, *Finnegans Wake* (1939), his desire to reveal and, at the same time, his compulsion to conceal the sexual symbolism result in the scatological subtlety of a nonmalicious practical joke. "As usual, when Joyce comes to the sexual climax of whatever tale he is telling, he increases the linguistic anthropomorphizing of parts of the body, muddles the narrative by heightened metaphor and, through obscure combinations, provides for multiple interpretations of action. The Jarl is made to act, but what does he do? It is clear that his orduring with thunder is defecation, and, in *Finnegans Wake,* defecation always stands for creation" (Solomon, 1969, p. 11). All this partially concealed erotic imagery contributes to the scatological humor of the book. It is psychologically consistent as well, however, with Freudian dream theory and the primal significance to the sexual drive.

In one of the dramas in *Finnegans Wake,* the twins Shem and Shaun play the roles of Butt and Taff—both names scatologically meaning-ful—who are soldier buddies. The tale of how Buckley shot the Rus-sian general dramatizes the oedipal wish of the son(s) to replace the father. Solomon (1969) presents the background and interprets the action. The original anecdote was "another of John Joyce's stories about an Irish soldier, Buckley, who tried twice to shoot a Russian general in the Crimean War before he actually fired. The first time, he was bedazzled by the general's uniformed splendor; the second time, the general was squatting to defecate, and Buckley's pity for such human helplessness made him lower his gun. But when the general started to wipe himself with a piece of turf, Buckley's respect and pity vanished and he fired. Joyce went on to make the turf Irish and the general insulting Ireland. The account in *Finnegans Wake* is turned into a vaudeville skit on a TV screen, Taff operating as a foil or straightman for the comedian Butt, who pretends to be recalling a war-time incident of many years ago. But the story is also the narrative of a Freudian drama ... with its Oedipal atmosphere" (p. 43). As small boys, appalled to witness the "bigness" of the father, Butt and Taff, in reminiscence, describe the disgusting grandeur of the general. Solomon concludes that "this funny and charmingly naive description of HCE's natural recovery after defecation, and re-tumefaction after devitalization, is one of the prime sex-defecation symbols of the the-matic essence of *Finnegans Wake,* applied at this point to give final meaning to the replacement story of Buckley's shooting the Russian general. HCE, behind the outhouse door, can watch his own bodily parts in action and understand the larger mysteries of life. Joyce's philosophic optimism is continually illuminated on the sexual level by his humorous treatment of such actions of the bodily parts of both man and woman, each part assuming a human name and interacting with the other members of the genital family" (p. 49). Perhaps the most direct paean of praise for manure and its transmutation is expressed by Ernest Godwit, an English farmer and minor poet, who is talking with some friends in a pub in Gloucestershire in *Bored to Death* by Michael Delving (1975). "The muck on my boots, although it stinks, grows roses. Why, my dear, there's nothing more romantic than manure! You know what we say in Gloucestershire—'where there's muck, there's money.' Think of that miraculous transformation of foul excrement into an enrichment of the earth, into food and flowers, and then into thick wads of banknotes which a poor sod like me can spend in the delights of bread and beer and cheese" (p. 13).

It is language, of course, which is the chief instrument of psychoanalysis, and sex a major field of its scientific and therapeutic interest. It was this that made Stone (1954) say, in his paper on the principal obscene word of the English language, that the investigation of an obscene word would seem "a natural psycho-analytic undertaking, especially when it is considered that obscene language, as a special variant of slang, lives and thrives in relation to conventional language, without official notice, in much the same sense that infantile sexuality lived and throve—in child and adult—before Freud brought it to scientific attention" (p. 30). In order for Joyce to express the universal nature of his characters, he needed a language that could present several different meanings simultaneously. In *Through the Looking Glass,* Lewis Carroll (1872) has Humpty Dumpty explain the language of dreams, taking as his text the opening lines of the "Jabberwocky" poem: "Twas brillig, and slithy toves/ Did gyre and gimble in the wabe...". "Slithy," says Humpty Dumpty, "means 'lithe and slimy.' 'Lithe' is the same as 'active.' You see it's like a portmanteau—there are two meanings packed up into one word." In *Finnegans Wake,* Joyce 'constantly uses portmanteau words, but he is seldom content with only two meanings. He alters the English language in an effort to make it do the work of music, where a number of related themes can be sounded at once" (Litz, 1966, p. 103).

The enormous use of scatological language to reflect the

unconscious can be seen in jocular references to the excretory process. Abraham (1921) gives several examples: the toilet seat is often referred to as "the throne"; some people like to read during defecation, and for many of them the toilet is not only the "library" but a true place of "production"; in Spanish, "the common expression for [defecation], 'regir el vientre' ('to rule the belly'), which is used quite seriously, clearly indicates the pride taken in the functioning of [the] bowels" (p. 375). More modern samples of oral expressions colored by anal experiences are suggested by Menninger (1943). He's a "stinker," or, "that's a dirty, stinking trick"; the braggart or the bore is sometimes referred to as a "bag of wind" or a "blow-hard," often consciously equated with flatus (Bergler, 1936), or the more direct "verbal diarrhea" and "running off at the mouth," and, the most explicit of all, "scared shitless," physiological actions in the forms of constipation and diarrhea in response to fear or anger. Such coprophilic profanity is regularly equated with feces in many jokes, which represents oral soiling. In a like category are such familiar expressions as "mud-slinging," referring to verbal feces, belching, picking one's teeth in public, and nose-picking. Less camouflaged is the Bronx cheer, "that marvelously direct, bottom-glorifying and thought-shunting all-purpose negative comment" (Hartogs, 1967, p. 114). People often talk about being "cleaned out" when they have no more money, and a common expression for payday in the armed forces is "the day the eagle shits." In German-speaking countries the merchant makes use of the representation of money by excrement when he employs the same word for his day's "takings" as the hunter for the deposit of animals, namely, Lösung or "droppings" (Sterba, 1968). Whenever he saw his father come into the room, one of Freud's patients thought of the obsessive word, "father-arse," along with an accompanying picture of the father sans head or chest, but simply the lower part of the trunk. "Father-arse" was explained as "a jocular Teutonizing of the honorific title of 'patriarch'. [The German for father is Vater; for arse, arsch; hence, Vaterarsch, Patriarch.] The obsessive image is an obvious caricature. It recalls other representations which, with a derogatory end in view, replace a whole person . . . his genitals" (Freud, 1916, p. 337), or other organs, viz., I am all ears.

In Tom Jones, Henry Fielding's novel of 1749, Tom, thought to be a bastard, has unsuitably professed his love to the gentlewoman, Sophia, when her father, Squire Western, comes upon them. He is incensed and has to be restrained. Fielding has some universal comments to make about "that language which passes between country gentlemen who embrace opposite sides of the question."

The moment Sophia was departed Jones advanced in a very suppliant manner to Mr. Western, whom the parson held in his arms, and begged him to be pacified; for that while he continued in such a passion it would be impossible to give him any satisfaction.

"I wull have satisfaction o' thee," answered the squire. "So doff thy clothes. *At unt* half a man, and I'll lick thee as well as wast ever licked in thy life." He then bespattered the youth with abundance of that language which passes between country gentlemen who embrace opposite sides of the question, with frequent applications to him to salute that part which is generally introduced into all controversies that arise among the low orders of the English gentry, at horseraces, cock-matches, and other public places. Allusions to this part are likewise often made for the sake of the jest. And here, I believe, the wit is generally misunderstood. In reality, it lies in desiring another to kiss your a— for having just before threatened to kick his; for I have observed very accurately that no one ever desires you to kick that which belongs to himself, nor offers to kiss this part in another.

It may likewise seem surprising that in the many thousand kind invitations of this sort, which every one who hath conversed with country gentlemen must have heard, no one, I believe, hath ever seen a single instance where the desire hath been complied with. A great instance of their want of politeness; for in town nothing can be more common than for the finest gentlemen to perform this ceremony every day to their superiors without having that favour once requested of them [pp. 255-256].

At the literary level, Aldridge (1968) suggests, scatological obscenity is a means of clearing the psychic bowels of defeat and dread. "It is a way of ridding ourselves of the blocked aggressions, the spiritual constipations, which goad us to violence even as they inhibit our powers of creative rejuvenation.... The literary use of obscenity may also be a means of renewing vital contact between those portions of the population who habitually repress their aggressive impulses, and those to whom obscenity is part of the accepted vernacular language and thus constitutes a natural and healthy mode of release for those impulses. Ideally, the function of obscenity would be to mediate between the superego and the id..." (p. 97). Within the past decade or so, the great gap between accepted sexual behavior and freedom to express it in words has been bridged to some extent. Henry Miller has complained that for the last three hundred years, English language and literature have been stifled; they are pallid, lacking integration and totality. Anglo-Saxons have been deprived, literally speaking, of the natural and normal expressions of sex that can counteract unnatural feelings of guilt. What is being portrayed now is the sensational exposure of sex, an overreaction and overemphasis following three centuries of starvation. As a result, the treatment of sex in modern literature has became dull and routine, no longer even shocking the reader's sensibilities. Sex as cliché, sex so ritualized and stereotyped, ceases to titillate; rather, it becomes a device to produce for dramatic effect when the author cannot create literature. Sexual accomplishment becomes a cover for imaginative impoverishment. War novels, for example, abound in four-letter words. They serve sometimes as a necessary defense against anxieties concerning impotence induced by enforced sexual abstinence. In reverting to obscenity, the soldier surmounts his castration fears and flaunts his virility in front of his peers whose approval he needs. Obscenity helps deny the fear of failure and is a way of self-assurance as well as a consolation. It may also be a way of dealing not only with the basic and related fears of castration and impotence but of "incest as well. It is a form of response to the psychic wound shared by virtually all men: the fear of becoming a 'motherfucker' and being castrated as punishment for breaking the primal taboo against incest" (Hartogs, 1967, p. 113).

The earliest reference to the word "crap" in the *Oxford English Dictionary* is "crappe siftings," used in 1440 to mean the grain trodden underfoot in the barn and mingled with the straw and dust — the chaff, the husk of grain, a meaning now obsolete. By 1700, "crap" was used as a slang word for money. Kelley (1950) reports that a thieves' dictionary, published in 1719, defined "crap" as money. In 1775 "crap" was a slang term for "crop" — something that is "given off" by "Mother Earth"; "crap," therefore, represents feces, money, originally described by Freud as a true copro-symbol.

But language need not always be overtly scatological; such meaning is frequently expressed in covert, unconscious ways. Anal-erotic speech is the most distinctly observable type of "regressive partial-erotic language" (Fliess, 1956). "It is the language collateral to compulsive speech . . . The language shows . . . a peculiar monotony, and is extremely halting. In order to characterize it more accurately than by merely calling it 'verbal constipation,' one may state that the small vertical punctuation marks — comma, semicolon, colon and period — have, in this language, become 'malignant.' They not only pervade it excessively, but they have left their normal positions — framing clauses, ending a part of the whole of a sentence, introducing specification of content, etc. — and now separate any word or series of words from the next.... A further characteristic, rarely missing in regressive anal-erotic language, is the frequent interpolation of a quasi interjection as 'er,' 'uh,' or 'ah,' and imitative, so it appears, of flatus.... [The verbalization is halting because the individual's speech] has to emulate the peristaltic characteristics of a regressively sexualized anal-erotic zone. The pauses thus obtained are ... manifestations of anal-erotic silence, imitating a closure of the powerful sphincter ani" (pp. 290-292).

Fenichel (1945) maintains that a genetic relation exists between time and feces as well as between money and feces. The child acquires the ideas of order and disorder regarding time from the intervals at which defecation takes place and from how long the process takes. Thus, disturbances in anal personality may lead to stinginess or prodigality with either time or money, and sometimes both attitudes alternate. Tarachow (1966) states that words and thoughts are flatus and stool and that time limits are the command to defecate. "The feeling of time slowing or stopping is the postponement of the bowel movement. Obsessive procrastination is the struggle against giving up the stool. Obsessive rumination is playing with the stool within the body. Free time is after the bowel movement, i.e., after the narcissistic defeat. Obsessively monotonous speech is a bowel movement without the assistance of the subject and without the sphincter action which segments the stool. Obsessive undoing is the return of the stool to the body. Coprophagia and smearing have the same meaning. Giving a train of thought in separate installments is a bowel movement in installments..." (pp. 693-694).

A most curious result of anal eroticism, Jones (1918, p. 691) wrote, "is the tendency to be occupied with the reverse side of various things and situations. This may manifest itself in many different ways; in marked curiosity about the opposite or back side of objects and places — e.g. in the desire to live on the other side of a hill because it has its back turned to a given place; in the proneness to make numerous mistakes as to right and left, east and west; to reverse words and letters in writing. . . ." The displacement of libido from the genital to the anal zone is the prototype of all these "reversals" (Abraham, 1921, p. 390). James Joyce was primarily a wordsmith, a maker of metaphors with multiple meanings, using the primitive strength of onomatopoeia to evoke powerful visual and scatological images. In *A Portrait of the Artist as a Young Man* (1916), there is a typical example: "suck was a queer word . . . But the sound was ugly . . . And [when the water] had all gone down slowly the hole in the basin had made a sound like that: suck. Only louder. To remember that and the white look of the lavatory made him feel cold and then hot. There were two cocks that you turned and water came out: cold and hot. He felt cold and then a little hot; and he could see the names printed on the cocks. That was a very queer thing" (p. 11). The young schoolboy, Stephen Daedalus, retreated from the cold abstraction of mathematical thought as he grew up to the mystery of the multiplicity of language, and of the rhythmical order of words, of the nature of verse. The sentences in the spelling book were "like poetry but they were only sentences to learn the spelling from" (p. 10); his chum Fleming had written a verse about him in a geography book and "he read the verses backward but then they were not poetry" (p. 16); he held esthetic discussions to know whether words were being used according to literary tradition or according to the tradition of the marketplace, asking such rhetorical questions as, "What is that beauty which the artist struggles to express from lumps of earth" (p. 189). Stephen's constant concern with language, to know and control the word, was an anal preoccupation with which he had the power to give or not, to control and to achieve omnipotence, and to maintain a secret or private vocabulary that had meaning primarily only for him. Its unconscious application is seen in his reading the poetry backward.

The two protagonists in Günter Grass's *Dog Years,* Eddi Amsel and Walter Matern, had transferred to a new school where they were subjected to the traditional hazing of newcomers. In their anxieties about isolation and acceptance, Eddi developed a secret language.

> . . . At most little Probst and Heini Kadlubek, the son of a coal dealer, were privileged to listen while Walter Matern maintained a long dark staring silence and Eduard Amsel developed his secret language, giving new names to the new surroundings.
> "I tnod ekil eht sdrib ereh."
> I don't like the birds here.

"Sworraps ni eht ytic tnera sworraps ni eht yrtnuoc."

Sparrows in the city aren't sparrows in the country. "Draude Lesma sklat sdrawkcab."

With fluent ease he stood long and short sentences word for word on their heads and was even able to speak the new backward language with the broad accent of the Island: Dootendeetz (death's-head) became Zteednetood. With the help of a tongue molded to the Low German language, he smoothed out an awkward *c,* an unpronounceable *ps,* the difficult *sch,* and a tongue-twisting *nr,* and rendered "Liebarchen" (my friend) by the simplified "Nahkrabeil." Walter Matern caught his meaning and gave brief, equally reversed and usually correct answers: "Good idea — doog aedi." And impatient of shillyshallying: "Sey ro on?" Little Probst was flabbergasted. But Heini Kadlubek, known as "Kebuldak," proved to be not at all backward at learning to talk backward [p. 89].

Some time later, Amsel filled his garden with storm-trooper scarecrows, mechanical robots that marched and *heiled* in unison. He was visited by a dozen hooded hoodlums who proceeded to knock out his teeth. Amsel thought he recognized one of the fists. "From Amsel's red-foaming mouth, a question blows bubbles: 'Is it you? Si ti uoy?' "

Certain psychophysical reactions, mouth-related activities, and bowel-related behavior are often considered to be expressions in the adult of the early influences of oral and anal eroticism on character formation. In early infancy, the feelings connected with the bowel functions are primarily erotic, and expressions from this early period in later life are also preponderantly erotic. Abraham (1917) and Menninger (1943) made differentiations between the action of evacuation, which in general symbolizes achievement, and the product of evacuation. While no fixed formula holds, the character formations equated with the act are most commonly expressed in attitudes, and those concerned with the product are manifest in interests and in symbolic equivalents. While part of the anal-erotic character is repressed or sublimated or an admixture, some remains in its original form, thus presenting extremely diverse personality structures. Out of it develop the anal character traits portrayed by Freud as well as the picaresque contributions to esthetic and literary interests of the creative writer who presents, through scatological writing, a sense of human continuity. As Balthazar, the homosexual physician, says after a long and tiresome argument with Justine in Lawrence Durrell's

(1957) *Justine:* "Ah! my dear, after all the work of the philosophers on his soul and the doctors on his body, what can we say we really know about a man? That he is, when all is said and done, just a passage for liquids and solids, a pipe of the flesh" (p. 89).

TECHNICAL REFERENCES

Abraham, K. (1917), The spending of money in anxiety states. In: *Selected Papers.* New York: Basic Books, 1953, pp. 299-302.

———— (1920), The narcissistic evaluation of excretory processes in dreams and neurosis. In: *Selected Papers.* New York: Basic Books, pp. 318-322.

———— (1921), Contributions to the theory of the anal character. In: *Selected Papers.* New York: Basic Books, 1953, pp. 370-392.

Aldridge, J. W. (1968), From Vietnam to obscenity. *Harpers,* 236:91-97.

Beloff, H. (1957), The structure and origin of the anal character. *Genetic Psychology Monographs,* 55:141-172.

Bergler, E. (1936), On obscene words. *Psychoanalytic Quarterly,* 5:226-248.

Deutsch, H. (1934), Don Quixote and Quixotism. *Psychoanalytic Quarterly,* 6:215-222, 1937.

Fenichel, O. (1945), *The Psychoanalytic Theory of Neurosis.* New York: Norton.

Ferenczi, S. (1914), The ontogenesis of the interest in money. In: *Sex in Psychoanalysis.* New York: Basic Books, 1950, pp. 319-332.

———— (1928), Gulliver phantasies. In: *Final Contributions to Psychoanalysis.* New York: Basic Books, 1955, pp. 41-60.

Fliess, R. (1956), *Erogeneity and Libido, Psychoanalytic Series,* Vol. 1. New York: International Universities Press.

Freud, S. (1908), Character and anal erotism. *Standard Edition,* 9:168-175. London: Hogarth Press, 1959.

———— (1913a), The excretory functions in psycho-analysis and folklore. *Standard Edition,* 12:333-337. London: Hogarth Press, 1958.

———— (1913b), The occurrence in dreams of material from fairy tales. *Standard Edition,* 12:279-287. London: Hogarth Press, 1958.

———— (1916), A mythological parallel to a visual obsession. *Standard Edition,* 14:337-338. London: Hogarth Press, 1958.

———— (1916-1917), Introductory lectures on psycho-analysis. *Standard Edition,* 15, 16. London: Hogarth Press, 1963.

———— (1918), From the history of an infantile neurosis. *Standard Edition,* 17:3-122. London: Hogarth Press, 1955.

Gilbert, S. (ed.) (1957), *Letters of James Joyce.* New York: Viking.

Gordon, A. (1969), *The Naked and the Dead:* The triumph of impotence. *Literature and Psychology,* 19(3/4):3-13.

Grant Duff, I. F. (1937), A one-sided sketch of Jonathan Swift. *Psychoanalytic Quarterly,* 6:238-259.

Greenacre, P. (1955), *Swift and Carroll: A Psychoanalytic Study of Two Lives.* New York: International Universities Press.

Hartogs, R. (1967), *Four-Letter Word Games. The Psychology of Obscenity.* New York: Evans.

Howells, W. D. (1902) Frank Norris. *North American Review,* p. 733.

Huss, R. (1975), Grimm's *The Table, the Ass and the Stick:* A drama of the phallic stage. *Psychoanalytic Review,* 62:167-171.

Huxley, A. (1929), *Do What You Will; Essays.* New York: Doubleday, Doran.

Jones, E. (1918), Anal-erotic character traits. In: *Papers on Psycho-Analysis.* Boston: Beacon Press, 1961, pp. 680-704.

Karpman, B. (1942), Neurotic traits of Jonathan Swift, as revealed by *Gulliver's Travels. Psychoanalytic Review,* 29:26-45, 165-184.

———— (1949), A modern Gulliver: A study in coprophilia. *Psychoanalytic Review,* 36:162-185, 260-282.

Kelley, D. M. (1950), Note on the symbol interpretation of the word crap in coprophilia. *Psychoanalytic Review,* 37:71-72.

Kronhausen, P. & Kronhausen, E. (1969), *Erotic Fantasies. A Study of the Sexual Imagination.* New York: Grove.

Lee, J. N. (1971), *Swift and Scatological Satire.* Albuquerque: University of New Mexico Press.

Litz, A. W. (1966), *James Joyce.* New York: Twayne.

Mailer, N. (1960), *Advertisements for Myself.* New York: Signet.

———— (1967), The crazy one: Interview. *Playboy,* Oct., p. 214.

———— (1972), Conversation with R. D. Laing. Channel 13, Nov. 8.

Menninger, W. G. (1943), Characterologic and symptomatic expressions related to the anal phase of psychosexual development. *Psychoanalytic Quarterly,* 12:161-195.

Moss, J. (1970), The body as symbol in Saul Bellow's *Henderson the Rain King. Literature and Psychology,* 20:51-61.

Roberts, D. R. (1956), A Freudian view of Jonathan Swift. *Literature and Psychology,* 6(1):8-17.

Solomon, M. C. (1969), *External Geomater. The Sexual Universe of Finnegans Wake.* Carbondale, Ill.: Southern Illinois University Press.

Sterba, R. (1968), *Introduction to the Psychoanalytic Theory of the Libido.* New York: Brunner.

Stone, L. (1954), On the principal obscene word of the English language. *International Journal of Psycho-Analysis,* 35:30-56.

Tarachow, S. (1966), Coprophagia and allied phenomena. *Journal of the American Psychoanalytic Association,* 14:685-699.

LITERARY REFERENCES

Ambler, Eric (1956), *State of Seige.* New York: Knopf.

Amis, Kingsley (1968), *I Want It Now.* New York: Harcourt, Brace & World.

Barnes, Djuna (1937), *Nightwood.* Norfolk, Conn.: New Directions, 1946.

Barth, John (1961), *The Sot-Weed Factor.* Garden City, N.Y.: Doubleday.

Bellow, Saul (1959), *Henderson the Rain King.* New York: Viking.

Carroll, Lewis (1872), *Through the Looking Glass.* New York: McGraw-Hill, 1946.

Cervantes, Miguel de (1605), *Don Quixote de la Mancha.* New York: Random House.

Chevallier, Gabriel (1937), *The Scandals of Clochemerle.* New York: Bantam.

Delving, Michael (1975), *Bored to Death.* New York: Scribner's.

Durrell, Lawrence (1957), *Justine.* New York: Dutton.

Fielding, Henry (1749), *The History of Tom Jones, a Foundling.* New York: New American Library, 1963.

Grass, Günter (1963), *Dog Years.* New York: Harcourt, Brace & World.

Grimm, J., & Grimm, W. K. (1851), The table, the ass and the stick. In: *Household Stories.* New York: Macmillan, 1886, pp. 149-158.

Joyce, James (1916), *A Portrait of the Artist as a Young Man.* New York: Viking, 1964.

_____ (1918), *Ulysses.* New York: Random House, 1934.

_____ (1939), *Finnegans Wake.* London: Faber & Faber.

Lelchuk, Alan (1973), *American Mischief.* New York: Farrar, Straus & Giroux.

Mailer, Norman (1941), Maybe next year. In: *Short Fiction.* New York: Dell, 1967.

—— (1948), *The Naked and the Dead.* New York: Rinehart.

—— (1959), The white Negro. In: *Advertisements for Myself.* New York: Putnam's.

—— (1965), *The American Dream.* New York: Dial.

—— (1967), *Why Are We in Vietnam?* New York: Putnam's.

Norris, Frank (1899), *McTeague, a Story of San Francisco.* New York: International, 1900.

Rabelais, François (1552), *Gargantua and Pantagruel.* Chicago: Encyclopedia Britannica, 1952, pp. 16-18.

Roth, Philip (1969), *Portnoy's Complaint.* New York: Random House.

Sale, Chic (1929), *The Specialist.* New York: Putnam's, 1931.

Swift, Jonathan (1704), *Tale of a Tub.* New York: Dutton, 1909.

—— (1720), *The Wonderful World of Wonders.* In: *Prose Works,* ed. H. Davis. Oxford: Blackwell, 1939.

—— (1721), *Because I Am by Nature Blind.* In: *Collected Poems,* ed. J. Horrell. Cambridge: Harvard University Press, 1958.

—— (1726), *Gulliver's Travels.* New York: Long & Smith, 1933.

CHAPTER FOUR

Olfactory Eroticism

There is, naturally, a close relation between anal and olfactory eroticism in many of their manifestations: libidinal, emotional, psychosomatic, and esthetic. But odors have, in addition, a peculiarly suggestive power, sometimes evoking childhood memories long dormant. The recognition of odors reawakens a large charge of psychic energy which is attached to smelling or being smelled. The particularly nostalgic quality of memories aroused by odors is due to their connection with the earliest oral satisfaction and its accompanying love relationship (Fitzherbert, 1959). Breast imagery appears in the dream screen (Lewin, 1953; Spitz, 1955) which is visual; but other screen memories may consist of a smell (Grinstein, 1961; Friedman, 1959). Since the infantile image of the breast must include not only the appearance (Smythies, 1956) but also the odor of this organ, then the adult breast image and its derivatives should also contain an odor (Gorman, 1964).

Gorman states that olfaction is an autonomous ego function, and is also a component instinct, comparable to oral, anal, and genital factors, originating at one time in a physical stimulus but promptly converted into a sensory impression, which in turn becomes incorporated in a psychological reaction (pp. 24, 85). In 1897, Freud (1887-1902) wrote to Fliess (apologizing for his crude way of putting it) that "current memory stinks just as an actual object may stink; and just as we turn away our sense organ (the head and the nose) in disgust, so do the preconscious and our conscious apprehension turn away from the memory. This is *repression*" (p. 232). He later said, "The conjecture which goes deepest, however ... is to the effect that, with the assumption of an erect posture by man and with the depreciation of his sense of smell, it was not only his anal eroticism which threatened to fall a victim to organic repression, but the whole of his sexuality" (Freud, 1930, p. 106n). In the case of the obsessional-neurotic Rat Man, Freud (1909) commented, "when he was a child he had recognized every one by their smell, like a dog; ... in his childhood he had been subject to strong coprophilic propensities.... I have come to recognize that a tendency to taking pleasure in smell, which has become extinct since childhood, may play a part in the genesis of neurosis" (pp. 247, 247n). In relating fetishism to olfaction, Freud (1905) observed, "Psycho-analysis has shown the importance, as regards the choice of a fetish, of a coprophilic pleasure in smelling which has disappeared owing to repression" (p. 155n). And in his last publication, Freud (1930) declared that civilization had progressed toward cleanliness as a result of the repression of anality: anal eroticism is from the first subjected to the very "organic repression" that initiated cultural development, and that it undergoes further modifications under the influence of the social factor that comes into play with the fact that, "in spite of all man's developmental advances, he scarcely finds the smell of his *own* excretions repulsive, but only that of other people's" (p. 100n). Freud's observations on olfactory activity thus led him to penetrate the phenomenon of repression and the laws of the unconscious, after having focused on anality and fetishism.

Odor plays an unconscious role in all love manifestations of civilized humanity, as it does consciously among animals, primitives, and many non-European races. The range of variations of the sexual influences of smell is considerable. In a few people, olfactory sympathy or antipathy is so pronounced, wrote Ellis (1906), that is exerts a decisive role in their relations while in others smell has no part, coming into love play only as an additional stimulus; and with still others, smell leaves the individual neutral or indifferent unless the odor happens to be marked. In order to determine affective reaction to odors, Moncrieff (1966) investigated the psychogalvanic reflex. He found that an unpleasant odor caused a more pronounced reflex than a pleasant one; that the reflexes vary from one individual to another; and parallel with the same individual, different kinds of responses can be caused by different odors. Stein, Ottenberg, and Roulet (1958) presented a series of odorous substances consisting of synthetic feces, synthetic sweat, and amyl acetate to a group of 300 children between the ages of three and twelve. Almost all of the three- and four-year-olds rated the odors as pleasant. There was a significant decrease at the age of five in the percentage of pleasant reactions to the odors. The data suggest that although adult olfactory preferences may have their roots in pregenitality, the significant changes in olfactory preferences first appear during the oedipal phase, and then become consolidated and persist during latency. Thus the threshold for perception to a given odor varies from time to time and from individual to individual, ranging from complete anosmia to hyperosmia. As with other attributes, people vary, some being predominantly olfactory types, others less so, but liable nevertheless to respond to odors in their sexual life from time to time depending on past experiences.

Although the neopallium in man has superseded and overgrown the primitive olfactory "brain," the olfactory input has intimate connections with emotions and behavior as well as visceral control via neural and humoral pathways (Schneider, 1971). Despite the fact that the sense of smell has been subject to greater repression and atrophy than all the other sense organs, olfaction is endowed with greater affectivity than any of them (Brill, 1932). "When man assumed an erect posture and turned his nose away from the earth," Brill writes (pp. 37-38), "smell fell more or less into disuse, which increased... when the first sexual taboos were established. But, as the first taboos were primarily of an incestuous nature and smell was still an active sex function, primitive man was under special stress to curb this sense. This was especially the case during rutting, which made itself felt first through the sense of smell. The hypnotic sex-attractive odour given off by the female in 'heat' must have been one of man's greatest temptations to violate the incest taboo." But smell is still considered as a sense of primitive search, drive and odorous identification of objects playing a significant role in many human reactions to perfume, food, and foul odors (Papez, 1959), involving activity in erogeneity and its sublimations.

Whereas there are no scent organs in man comparable to those in other mammals, all men and women are odorous. The sources of odor include general skin odor, hair and scalp, breath, armpit, feet, perineum, in men the odor of preputial smegma, in women the mons veneris, the vulvar smegma, the vaginal mucus, and the menstrual odor. A special sublimation path of anal eroticism branches off from certain smells, such as gas, asphalt, and turpentine, and fondness for substances with agreeable odors such as perfume, occurs by means of a reaction formation (Ferenczi, 1914). Ferenczi concludes, "there can be no question that esthetics in general has its principal root in repressed anal eroticism" (p. 274).

An example of this kind of estheticism is seen in *The Picture of Dorian Gray,* Oscar Wilde's novel of 1891. Its opening paragraph reads: "The studio was filled with the rich odour of roses, and when the light summer wind stirred amidst the trees of the garden there came through the open door the heavy scent of the lilac, or the more delicate perfume of the pink-flowering thorn" (p. 107). Dorian came under the wayward tutelage of the effete, bisexual Lord Henry Wotton, against whom he had been warned. At one point, "Lord Henry went out to the garden, and found Dorian Gray burying his face in the great cool lilac-blossoms, feverishly drinking in their perfume as if it had been wine. He came close to him, and put his hand upon his shoulder. 'You are quite right to do that,' he murmured. 'Nothing can cure the soul but the senses, just as nothing can cure the senses but the soul' " (p. 120). Dorian became fascinated with esthetics. Lord Henry advised him to live by the senses, for hedonism was the only way to recreate life and save it from the rigidities of puritanism. So Dorian ventured out, seeking revelation through the five senses, including an effort to determine what influence smell had on the emotions.

> He sought to elaborate some new scheme of life that would have its reasoned philosophy and its ordered principles, to find in the spiritualising of the senses its highest realisation.
>
> The worship of the senses has often, and with much justice, been decried, men feeling a natural instinct of terror about passions and sensations that seem stronger than themselves, and that they are conscious of sharing with the less highly organised forms of existence. But it appeared to Dorian Gray that the true nature of the senses had never been understood, and that they had remained savage and animal merely because the world had sought to starve them into submission or to kill them by pain, instead of aiming at making them elements of a new spirituality, of which a fine instinct for beauty was to be the dominant characteristic. As he looked back upon man moving through History, he was haunted by a feeling of loss. So much had been surrendered! and to such little purpose!

There had been mad, wilful rejections, monstrous forms of self-torture and self-denial, whose origin was fear, and whose result was a degradation infinitely more terrible than that fancied degradation from which, in their ignorance, they had sought to escape, Nature, in her wonderful irony, driving out the anchorite to feed upon the wild animals of the desert and giving to the hermit the beasts of the field as his companions.

Yes: there was to be, as Lord Henry had prophesied, a new Hedonism that was to recreate life, and to save it from that harsh, uncomely puritanism that is having, in our own day, its curious revival. It was to have its service of the intellect, certainly; yet, it was never to accept any theory or system that would involve the sacrifice of any mode of passionate experience. Its aim, indeed, was to be experience itself, and not the fruits of experience, sweet or bitter as they might be. Of the asceticism that deadens the senses, as of the vulgar profligacy that dulls them, it was to know nothing. But it was to teach man to concentrate himself upon the moments of a life that is itself but a moment.

*   *   *

It was the creation of such worlds as these that seemed to Dorian Gray to be the true object, or amongst the true objects, of life; and in his search for sensations that would be at once new and delightful, and possess that element of strangeness that is so essential to romance, he would often adopt certain modes of thought he knew to be really alien to his nature, abandon himself to their subtle influences, and then, having, as it were, caught their colour and satisfied his intellectual curiosity, leave them with that curious indifference that is not incompatible with a real ardour of temperament, and that indeed, according to certain modern psychologists, is often a condition of it.

*   *   *

But he never fell into the error of arresting his intellectual development by any formal acceptance of creed or system, or of mistaking, for a house in which to live, an inn that is but suitable for the sojourn of a night, or for a few hours of a night in which there are no stars and the moon is in travail. Mysticism, with its marvellous power of making common things strange to us, and the subtle antinomianism that always seems to accompany it, moved him for a season; and for a season he inclined to the materialistic doctrines of the *Darwinismus* movement in Germany, and found a curious pleasure in tracing the thoughts and passions of men to some pearly cell in the brain, or some white nerve in the body, delighting in the conception of the absolute dependence of the spirit on certain physical conditions, morbid or healthy, normal or diseased. Yet, as has been said of him before, no theory of life seemed to him to be of any importance compared with life itself. He felt keenly conscious of how barren all intellectual speculation is when separated from action and experiment. He knew that the senses, no less than the soul, have their spiritual mysteries to reveal.

And so he would now study perfumes, and the secrets of their manufacture, distilling heavily-scented oils, and burning odorous gums from the East. He saw that there was no mood of the mind that had not its counterpart in the sensuous life, and set himself to discover their true relations, wondering what there was in frank-incense that made one mystical, and in ambergris that stirred one's passions, and in violets that woke the memory of dead romances, and in musk that troubled the brain, and in champak that stained the imagination; and seeking often to elaborate a real psychology of perfumes, and to estimate the several influences of sweet-smelling roots, and scented pollen-laden flowers, of aromatic balms, and of dark and fragrant woods, of spikenard that sickens, of hovenia that makes men mad, and of aloes that are said to be able to expel melancholy from the soul [pp. 165-169, *passim*].

But for Dorian Gray, the olfactory function was crowded out by more intellectual sense modalities. Still, olfaction is linked to ancient memories having vast emotional reverberations, none so clearly revealed perhaps as in the *Remembrance of Things Past* of Marcel Proust (1913). What a magnet for Mnemosyne the madeleine was for Proust! In the first volume, *Swann's Way*, it was through the taste and smell of the madeleine that Proust recaptured the past most realistically. The smell of this pastry triggered off associations amounting to total recall, revivifying the supple tissues in Proust's memory so that he lived once again the cobwebbed pains and joys of earlier days. His curiosity, turned back in time, ran a gamut from the most primitive aspects of his sense of smell to scientific curiosity, esthetic analysis, and philosophical inquiry. "The sense of smell and taste of things remain poised a long time," Proust wrote, "like souls, ready to remind us, waiting and hoping for their moment, amid the ruins of all the rest; and bear unfalteringly, in the tiny and almost impalpable drop of their essence, the vast structure of recollection" (Miller, 1956, p. 36).

In the introduction to *Remembrance of Things Past,* Krutch (1934) wrote that the novel "is cast into the form of an autobiography in which, nevertheless, the narrator himself plays a role not very much larger than that of certain other characters. It begins with his account of how he was accustomed to spend his sleepless nights in an effort to recapture the elusive memory of certain events in his childhood and it describes what some of these fragmentary memories were. Presently it tells how one of them was suddenly recaptured in its entirety when the taste of a little cake brought back a certain instance in childhood connected with the same taste and then, abandoning this incident until the last volume of the whole work, the narrator launches into the recollections of his youth. Gradually the tragic story of a certain M. Swann detaches itself and the history of his jealousy-wrecked life is told in full. Meanwhile the narrator has been growing up. He moves in aristocratic circles and becomes absorbed in the study of manners and their meaning. He falls in love . . . meets many other persons . . . and in particular the powerful M. Charlus whose greatness and final downfall constitute perhaps the most impressive of all the single stories. Presently the social organization whose traditions he has been studying with such care disintegrates; he himself falls deeper and deeper into his illness and suddenly we realize that we are back again where we started. The author is ready to begin the writing of his book and we learn at last the real significance of the little cake. Through an extraordinary series of psychological adventures the past has been recaptured—not merely remembered but totally recalled. . ." (pp. viii-ix).

> I feel that there is much to be said for the Celtic belief that the souls of those whom we have lost are held captive in some inferior being, in an animal, in a plant, in some inanimate object, and so effectively lost to us until the day (which to many never comes) when we happen to pass by the tree or to obtain possession of the object which forms their prison. Then they start and tremble, they call us by our name, and as soon as we have recognised their voice the spell is broken. We have delivered them: they have overcome death and return to share our life.
>
> And so it is with our own past. It is a labour in vain to attempt to recapture it: all the efforts of our intellect must prove futile. The past is hidden somewhere outside the realm, beyond the reach

of intellect, in some material object (in the sensation which that material object will give us) which we do not suspect. And as for that object, it depends on chance whether we come upon it or not before we ourselves must die.

Many years had elapsed during which nothing of Combray, save what was comprised in the theatre and the drama of my going to bed there, had any existence for me, when one day in winter, as I came home, my mother, seeing that I was cold, offered me some tea, a thing I did not ordinarily take. I declined at first, and then, for no particular reason, changed my mind. She sent me out for one of those short, plump little cakes called 'petites madeleines,' which look as though they had been moulded in the fluted scallop of a pilgrim's shell. And soon, mechanically, weary after a dull day with the prospect of a depressing morrow, I raised to my lips a spoonful of the tea in which I had soaked a morsel of the cake. No sooner had the warm liquid, and the crumbs with it, touched my palate than a shudder ran through my whole body, and I stopped, intent upon the extraordinary changes that were taking place. An exquisite pleasure had invaded my senses, but individual, detached, with no suggestion of its origin. And at once the vicissitudes of life had become indifferent to me, its disasters innocuous, its brevity illusory—this new sensation having had on me the effect which love has of filling me with a precious essence; or rather this essence was not in me, it was myself. I had ceased now to feel mediocre, accidental, mortal. Whence could it have come to me, this all-powerful joy? I was conscious that it was connected with the taste of tea and cake, but that it infinitely transcended those savours, could not, indeed, be of the same nature as theirs. Whence did it come? What did it signify? How could I seize upon and define it?

I drink a second mouthful, in which I find nothing more than in the first, a third, which gives me rather less than the second. It is time to stop; the potion is losing its magic. It is plain that the object of my quest, the truth, lies not in the cup but in myself. The tea has called up in me, but does not itself understand, and can only repeat indefinitely with a gradual loss of strength, the same testimony; which I, too, cannot interpret, though I hope at least to be able to call upon the tea for it again and to find it there presently, intact and at my disposal, for my final enlightenment. I put down my cup and examine my own mind. It is for it to discover the truth. But how? What an abyss of uncertainty whenever the mind feels that some part of it has strayed beyond its own borders; when it, the seeker, is at once the dark region through which it must go seeking, where all its equipment will avail it nothing. Seek? More than that: create. It is face to face with something which does not so far exist, to which it alone can give reality and substance, which it alone can bring into the light of day.

And I begin again to ask myself what it could have been, this un-remembered state which brought with it no logical proof of its existence, but only the sense that it was a happy, that it was a real state in whose presence other states of consciousness melted and vanished. I decide to attempt to make it reappear. I retrace my thoughts to the moment at which I drank the first spoonful of tea. I find again the same state, illumined by no fresh light. I compel my mind to make one further effort, to follow and recapture once again the fleeting sensation. And that nothing may interrupt it in its course I shut out every obstacle, every extraneous idea, I stop my ears and in-hibit all attention to the sounds which come from the next room. And then, feeling that my mind is growing fatigued without having any success to report, I compel it for a change to enjoy that distrac-tion which I have just denied it, to think of other things, to rest and refresh itself before the supreme attempt. And then for the second time I clear an empty space in front of it. I place in position be-fore my mind's eye the still recent taste of that first mouthful, and I feel something start within me, something that leaves its resting-place and attempts to rise, something that has been embedded like an anchor at a great depth; I do not know yet what it is, but I can feel it mounting slowly; I can measure the resistance, I can hear the echo of great spaces traversed.

Undoubtedly what is thus palpitating in the depths of my being must be the image, the visual memory which, being linked to that taste, has tried to follow it into my conscious mind. But its strug-gles are too far off, too much confused; scarcely can I perceive the colourless reflection in which are blended the uncapturable whirling medley of radiant hues, and I cannot distinguish its form, cannot invite it, as the one possible interpreter, to translate to me the evi-dence of its contemporary, its inseparable paramour, the taste of cake soaked in tea; cannot ask it to inform me what special circum-stance is in question, of what period in my past life.

Will it ultimately reach the clear surface of my consciousness, this memory, this old, dead moment which the magnetism of an identical moment has travelled so far to importune, to disturb, to raise up out of the very depths of my being? I cannot tell. Now that I feel nothing, it has stopped, has perhaps gone down again into its darkness, from which who can say whether it will ever rise?

Ten times over I must essay the task, must lean down over the abyss. And each time the natural laziness which deters us from every difficult enterprise, every work of importance, has urged me to leave the thing alone, to drink my tea and to think merely of the worries of to-day and of my hopes for to-morrow, which let themselves be pondered over without effort or distress of mind.

And suddenly the memory returns. The taste was that of the little crumb of madeleine which on Sunday mornings at Combray (because on those mornings I did not go out before church-time), when I went to say good day to her in her bedroom, my aunt Léonie used to give me, dipping it first in her own cup of real or of lime-flower tea. The sight of the little madeleine had recalled nothing to my mind before I tasted it; perhaps because I had so often seen such things in the interval, without tasting them, on the trays in pastry-cooks' windows, that their image had dissociated itself from those Combray days to take its place among others more recent; perhaps because of those memories, so long abandoned and put out of mind, nothing now survived, everything was scattered; the forms of things, including that of the little scallop-shell of pastry, so richly sensual under its severe, religious folds, were either obliterated or had been so long dormant as to have lost the power of expansion which would have allowed them to resume their place in my consciousness. But when from a long-distant past nothing subsists, after the people are dead, after the things are broken and scattered, still, alone, more fragile, but with more vitality, more unsubstantial, more persistent, more faithful, the smell and taste of things remain poised a long time, like souls, ready to remind us, waiting and hoping for their moment, amid the ruins of all the rest; and bear unfaltering, in the tiny and almost impalpable drop of their essence, the vast structure of recollection.

And once I had recognized the taste of the crumb of madeleine soaked in her decoction of lime-flowers which my aunt used to give me (although I did not yet know and must long postpone the discovery of why this memory made me so happy) immediately the old grey house upon the street, where her room was, rose up like the scenery of a theatre to attach itself to the little pavilion, opening on to the garden, which had been built out behind it for my parents (the isolated panel which until that moment had been all that I could see); and with the house the town, from morning to night and in all weathers, the Square where I was sent before luncheon, the streets along which I used to run errands, the country roads we took when it was fine. And just as the Japanese amuse themselves by filling a porcelain bowl with water and steeping in it little crumbs of paper which until then are without character or form, but, the moment they become wet, stretch themselves and bend, take on colour and distinctive shape, become flowers or houses or people, permanent and recognisable, so in that moment all the flowers in our garden and in M. Swann's park, and the water-lilies on the Vivonne and the good folk of the village and their little dwellings and the parish church and the whole of Combray and of its surroundings, taking their proper shapes and growing solid, sprang into being, town and gardens alike, from my cup of tea [Proust, 1913, pp. 34-36].

Proust's style arises out of an obsession to preserve with the utmost precision a perception or feeling he has experienced. His fervored, detailed account very nearly describes a sexual as well as an esthetic curve. Thus, in virtually a free-association method, Proust relived, in the emotional labyrinths of memory, his own lost past — not the pallid English transformation but the much more meaningful original French title, *A la Recherche du Temps Perdu.* It was a search, fervid and at times frantic, for something irrevocably *perdu*, a reunion with the beloved mother imago. It was as early as 1899 that Hughlings Jackson wrote, "Smell has been called the most suggestive of all senses; and smells have remarkable power in calling up remembrance of past scenes" (p. 156), a sentence evocative of the English title.

In an equally evocative prose essay on olfactory memories, Glenway Westcott (1971) gives his personal recollections of odors from childhood through adulthood. "Hyperaesthesia I must admit to, affecting many of my sentiments and ideals and my style of writing as well as my potential of bodily pleasure and displeasure [He had lost much of his sense of smell because of excessive cigarette smoking.] Nevertheless, even now, the things that I enjoy the smell of are a great resource and a daydream to me ... The more extraordinarily we enjoy pleasant olfactory experiences, the less we are apt to hold our breath about what sickens us and what we hate and fear.... I believe that in my case simple hedonism, desire and gratitude having to do with sensuousness and sexuality, has somewhat saved me from what Auden has called the 'glare of Nothing, our pernicious foe.' Worst of all, the nothing in the flesh due to bad habit; the nothing in the brain, when one's work-morality and talent have disappointed one; the nothing in the whining heart, envious and jealous. When it has come to that, one goes on living in order to smell and to taste and to hear and to see and to touch" (pp. 186-191, *passim*).

Odors of course evoke not only sentiment and lust and various remembrances but fear as well, especially childish, or atavistic, irrational fear.

Some years ago my friend Will Chandlee came from Philadelphia to spend a spring afternoon with me, misty and warm, almost hot, and we walked up toward Jug Mountain on an abandoned road and came to a small stone ruin with an old seedling apple tree thrust up through it, and poison ivy cloaking it; and there three or four young rat snakes had come out of hibernation and lay on the largest stone, like a loose knot or an indecipherable monogram, gradually coming to their senses. Will picked up one of them and played with it, and afterward, on our way down out of the mountain, with a mischievous smile, narrowing his thick eyelashes, held out his rosy fingers for me to sniff.

Until that moment I don't think it had occurred to me that snakes had an odor; and the surprise of the smell of my friend's fingers verged on fright, although I hadn't been consciously afraid of snakes since my childhood in Wisconsin. And the form that the fright took was a wild over-stimulation of memory: all the reptiles that had ever impressed me in rapid succession with almost simultaneous effects, overlapping somewhat, like flash photos, like a triple or quadruple or quintuple dream: a garter snake that I stoned to death at age six or seven, for which my mother reproved me and sent me to bed hungry; a cobra that I watched through plate glass in the Snake House in the Bronx, upright on its pedestal of tail, until it began to watch me and finally struck at me, that is, at the plate glass, bruising its round nose; and a heavy old cottonmouth encountered by Somerset Maugham and me when walking along a rice marsh in South Carolina, which tried to bar the way to us—with a good-sized stick that I had noticed on the levee and went back for, I was able to push it down the embankment—all these creatures in and out of my mind so swiftly that when the daydream ceased, there Will was still holding out his soiled, strong fingers.

One year at Stone-blossom we had a five-foot black racer, a beauty, glossy-skinned and white of chin, as though bearded, with a most beautiful swaying, dancing motion. Once or twice it came up on the front steps and twined itself into the iron railing. My house-keeper, Anna, was afraid of it, and I was afraid that she would incite her brother to destroy it. I gave her a talking-to on the subject. "Black racers are the natural enemies of copperheads," I said.

There were (perhaps still are) copperheads in our part of New Jersey. A friendly acquaintance of mine, a retired career woman, bought a stone house and barn in our hills and found a family of the venomous, thick-set, bright-brown, four-nostrilled creatures entrenched in a fallen stone wall, and it took years of vigilance with her shotgun to rid herself of them.

"We don't want copperheads," I firmly told my small, co-resident, superstitious, foreign female. "The friendly and strong black racer will protect us," I insisted.

"Well, I guess, if it's so, what you say, we'd better not do anything to it." Upon which she took her vacuum cleaner and dustmop and started upstairs, but turned, half way up, and spoke again. This time she called my reptilean protégé *he* instead of it, with emphasis. "You know, *he* caused all the trouble between the men and the women. You know that, don't you?"

Yes, I knew it, but I didn't (I don't) believe it. The widespread if not universal snake-horror is not, in my opinion, sexual or antisexual. A snake does not even resemble a penis; it resembles a stray bit of intestine [pp. 183-185].

Despite Westcott's disclaimer of the sexual symbolism of the snake, the evidence of the relation between it and anal regression is too well established to accept the denial at face value (Garma, 1955). For the narrator and for Ernest Pontifex in Samuel Butler's *The Way of All Flesh* (1885), oedipal anxieties were recreated by the smell of furniture polish. "Of all the rooms in the house [Ernest] hated the dining-room the worst. It was here that he had to do his Latin and Greek lessons with his father. It had a smell of some particular kind of polish or varnish which was used in polishing the furniture, and neither I nor Ernest can even now come within range of the smell of this kind of varnish without our hearts failing us" (p. 154).

Olfaction plays a strong role in human sexual development and is a crucial factor in the evolution of the Oedipus complex (Freeman, 1969). The sense of smell is available for use immediately at birth and the infant utilizes it more instinctually than the adult. The responses to smell — along with the tactile reponse — are among the infant's first experiences. His earliest gratifications have, among their components, "the smell of the mother's breasts and of milk. It is probable that the rooting reflex in the infant — that is, the food-finding reflex — which is stimulated by tactile sensations is also facilitated by smell sensations" (Wayne and Clinco, 1959, p. 68). In earliest childhood, at a time when mobility and motility are still very limited, and the child can perceive only the immediate environment, the sense of smell and the sense of touch, which act only upon the most immediate surroundings, retain the greatest sphere on, and have the most decisive importance to, his orientation in a still extremely limited world (Wulff, 1946).

The infant's excretion brings the entire surface of its buttocks and lower limbs in contact with urine and feces, a contact which seems unpleasant and repugnant to adults, "whose repressions have removed them from the infantile reaction to these processes. They cannot appreciate the sources of pleasure on which the libido of the infant can draw, in whom the stream of warm urine on the skin and contact with the warm mass of faeces produce pleasurable feelings. The child only begins to give signs of discomfort when the excreted products grow cold against its body. It is the same pleasure which the child seeks when it handles its faeces at a somewhat later period" (Abraham, 1921, p. 372). The further development of this infantile tendency is seen in the mud pies the child makes, which are now the deodorized dejecta; the interest in sand, a distorted and dehydrated symbol of feces; putty and clay molding, a more realistic sublimation of the now repressed fecal odor and interest; and eventuates in collecting pebbles, marbles (Ferenczi, 1914) and comic books. Concurrent with the repression and the sublimation of anal and olfactory sensations are the unconscious incestuous wishes. Between the ages of two and five, children react to odors with libidinal excitement (Bieber, 1959) and this, of course, is during the initial statement of the oedipal conflict. The incest taboo which begins to manifest itself during this time produces repression of olfaction. The olfactory imagery the schoolboy Stephen Daedalus evoked in *A Portrait of the Artist as a Young Man* by James Joyce (1916) was, "When you wet the bed first it is warm then it gets cold. His mother put on the oilsheet. That had the queer smell. His mother had a nicer smell than his father" (p. 7). It was the oilcloth, not the urine, that smelled peculiarly to the boy, and it was the mother, not the father, who smelled better. Proust had a similar recollection. In *Jean Santeuil* (1952), the forerunner to his *Remembrance of Things Past,* he wrote, "The odor of the waiter's napkin reminds him of his mother putting him to bed in a clean white nightshirt and clean white sheets." Proust's mother, even when he was forty years old, tucked him in bed at night in sheets especially warmed in the oven and prepared warm drinks to help him sleep (Burchell, 1928).

In his paper on introjection and transference, Ferenczi (1909) developed the theme of the oedipal conflict that runs through Dmitri Merezchkovski's novel, *Peter and Alexis* (1905). The relationship is characteristically depicted between a terrible and mighty despot and a hopelessly submissive son caught up in a love-hate relation that made him incapable of rebellion. In the daydreams of the Crown Prince, Alexis saw himself as a child, with his father before his bed.

> He stretches out his arms to his father with a fond, sleepy smile, and cries out, "Papa, Papa, my darling." Then he jumps up and flings himself round his father's neck. Peter embraces him so tightly as to hurt the child, presses him to himself, kisses his face, his neck, his bare legs, and his whole warm sleepy body. Despite the Czar's brutal educational methods with the boy and the repression of every impulse to sentiment, the Czarevitch's face glowed with bashful joy when he gazed at the familiar, horrible and dear face, with the full, almost bloated cheeks, with the curled, pointed moustache . . . with the charming smile on the dainty, almost feminine tender lips; he looked into the large, dark, clear eyes, which so fascinated him that he used to dream about them, as a love-sick youth would dream about the eyes of a beautiful woman. He recognized the odor familiar from his childhood, a mixture of strong tobacco, spirits, sweat, and something else, not disagreeable, a smell of soldiers' barracks, one that pervaded his father's working rooms and office. He felt the touch, also known to him from childhood, of the not very smoothly shaven chin with a little cleft in the middle that formed such a curious exception, almost comical, in the gloomy countenance [pp. 26-27].

Acting out of the incestuous wish, which stimulates a powerful olfactory reaction, is seen in *G,* the nameless hero of John Berger's (1972) novel, when he is seduced at the age of fifteen by his Aunt Beatrice. She flees to India to try to escape an incestuous relationship with her brother, but returns to his farm upon the death of her impotent husband. "She is a mythical figure whom he [G] has always been assembling part by part, quality by quality. Her softness—but not the extent of its area—is more familiar than he can remember. Her heated sweating skin is the source of warmth he felt in Miss Helen's clothes. . . . The whiteness of her body is what has signalled his nakedness to him

whenever he has glimpsed a white segment through the chance dis-
array of petticoat or skirt. Her smell is the smell of fields which, in the
early morning, smell of fish although many miles from the sea. . . . He
has seen drawings on walls asserting how she lacks a penis and testicles.
The dark beard-like triangle of hair makes their absence simpler and
more natural than he foresaw. . ." (p. 106). The narrator in Kingsley
Amis's *Girl, 20* (1971) thought he had detected an incestuous relationship between Penny and her symphony conductor father, Roy. Penny
reminded him of Roy's mistress, seventeen-year-old Sylvia who "ex-
uded a curious smell, not unlike that of damp hay" (p. 62). Some time
later, the narrator told how ". . . I caught a strong physical reminder
of Sylvia [when he tried to seduce Penny]. It was gone before I could
do more than decide tentatively where it had originated: face, hair,
figure, clothes, smell. In the last-named department Penny was offering a good deal of, though nothing more than, the consequences of
warm female flesh; perhaps she was a secret washer as well as a secret
listener to music." Penny did secretly love music, but would not give
her father the satisfaction of admitting it. "Excellent, but if I had
glimpsed a resemblance elsewhere between the two girls, it was unlikely, or possible, or conceivable, that Roy had too. Perhaps an incestuous fixation had been transformed into a. . ." (p. 83). And there, the
narrator leaves off, fearful perhaps to express the inexpressible.

It is sometimes overlooked that opportunities for intimate contacts
with the excretory functions of others are limited almost to the family
circle and to the earliest years of a child's life (Kubie, 1937). "Fathers
and Sons," by Ernest Hemingway (1933) is the last in the series of the
Nick Adams short stories. Nick represents Hemingway's persona; he
recalls obsessively whatever has scraped his sensibilities. Thinking back
upon his boyhood, Nick, now thirty-eight and a writer, cannot stop his
flow of "remembering the earliest times before things had gone badly
and [he] was not good at remembering." As he drives through the countryside, his thoughts are flooded with his initiation into sex with an
Indian girl, and his physician father's suicide. Dr. Adams served as
Nick's only teacher until the boy was fifteen. After that, Nick recalls,
his father "shared nothing with him." Indeed, Nick symbolically discards his father when he suffers a whipping rather than don Dr.
Adams' underwear. He could not stand his father's odor, and one
night walked alone in the dark to the Indian camp in order to get rid
of the smell. "Nick loved his father but hated the smell of him and

once he had to wear a suit of his father's underwear that had gotten too small for his father it made him feel sick and he took it off and put it under two stones in the creek and said that he had lost it. He had told his father how it was when his father had made him put it on but his father had said it was freshly washed. It had been, too. When Nick had asked him to smell of it his father sniffed it indignantly and said that it was clean and fresh. When Nick came home from fishing without it and said he lost it he was whipped for lying" (p. 265).

The sublimation of the oedipal conflict is also apparent in the behavior of motherless Jonas, a college dropout, in Seymour Epstein's *Caught in That Music* (1967). He had returned from playing handball in the neighborhood schoolyard on a Sunday morning to find the apartment he lived in with his father and sister empty. Debbie was an unconscious, incestuous mother substitute, and Solomon, their father, a wise, permissive man. Many of the phrases in the passage cited below are symbolic of the incest taboo, such as in "the cloistered seclusion of the closed drawers and locked breakfronts." The juxtaposition of the description of Debbie's bedroom, followed by Jonas's description of where he sleeps is also relevant. And it was the olfactory sense that stirred the unconscious incestuous wish.

> He left the kitchen and made a tour of the silent apartment, not merely pausing to glance into each room, but entering and sampling the special odor each distilled. The kitchen had a blending of melons, milk and soap powder; the dining room: lemon oil and the cloistered seclusion of closed drawers and locked breakfronts; Solomon's room: Baum Bengué; Debbie's room: the commingling of perfumes and powders which she kept on her dresser. Jonas slept in the living room, on the sofa that opened into a bed.... Finally, the bathroom, which gave out an acrid pungency from the oilclothy shower and window curtains put up by Debbie [p. 12].

The experimental work of Harlow (1958) and Harlow and Zimmerman (1959) on rearing infant monkeys seems to indicate that the body warmth of a monkey, even an artificial one constructed with a wire body covered with terrycloth and heated by electric light bulbs, is the most important contributing element in the developmental welfare of the babies. They show, further, that young monkeys need to have a mother to whom they can literally cling at the same time as they experience body warmth. These findings are important contributions to the understanding of human infants, but it may be risky to apply them literally. "It is obvious that the arboreal life of monkeys demands the development and persistence of clinging far beyond the requirements of humans. It is my impression, however, that in early psychoanalytic theory, anchored too strongly to libido theory, there was too exclusive an emphasis on orality, in the first phase of life, and that the importance of clinging, touch, smell, vision, and kinesthetic stimulation was insufficiently appreciated" (Greenacre, 1966, p. 749).

By 1970, Harlow and Suomi were hinting at agreement with Greenacre, suggesting that olfaction is a cue: "Infant monkeys soiled the bodies of the original cloth surrogates with such efficiency and enthusiasm as to present a health problem. . . . [Yet] infant monkeys seldom soil their real mothers' bodies" (p. 161). Since odorous substances adhere to surfaces, and because terrycloth would differentially absorb cage and other odors relative to wire mothers, olfactory cues may be contributing to the contact-comfort effect. It appears that odor may have been a confounding variable in this classic study.

Although the mother's odor becomes associated with the mother herself, the infant learns he cannot possess her attention or person as he would like, or in terms of oral needs, consume her. Repression occurs in an attempt to cope with his unfulfilled wish (Freud, 1915). Simultaneously, the infant is forced to repress perception of odors and foods and natural and artificial odors associated with mother (Gorman, 1964, p. 76). In the next development, bowel and bladder training generates an atmosphere of unpleasantness related to excretions and odors. Parental training puts taboos on the infantile curiosity and this, for some children, fixates sexual development at the anal level, eroticizing the olfactory sense. Olfaction then becomes displaced on or substituted for sexuality. In his search for the lost mother, the homosexual narrator in *Confessions of a Mask* by the Japanese novelist, Yukio Mishima (1958), recalled his youthful pursuit of a masculine identity that perforce recalled latent fecal memories. At first he identified with a collector of night soil and wanted to become one too. His memory of the night-soil collector is linked with his later responses to armored heroes and male bodies. "The odor of sweat is simultaneously like the breeze of Mishima's repeated seascapes and like the air 'burned into gold' and often associated with fire. . . . Images of 'senuous craving' in *Confessions* are later transformed into the sweaty scene of a firemen's festival. . . . There is also a clear association . . . in this novel [that] links not only the sea and sweat but also butchered bodies and a romantic ideal—St. Sebastian, martyred heroes, and knights-in-armor. Here too are the tattooed chests, the obsessive tufts of under-arm hair, the first attempts to savor the sensations of the flesh.... *Confessions* thus offers a useful gloss to the remarkable frequency with which characters in Mishima's world are beaded, pearled, or just plain dripping with sweat—indiscriminately the result of passion, fear, or exercise. In Japan's proletarian literature of the 1920's, sweat was at least functional—an essential aspect of the sufferings of the workers. In the tales of 'Sensationalist' Akutagawa, sweat, smells, and blood have a metaphysical implication, and are rendered with the stylized gestures of a *kabuki* performance, in the glittering tones of the Aesthetes. But in Mishima the fascination seems to be with the sweat itself, and meaning is to be found in the night-soil-and-soldiers-and-beloved-Omi associations of *Confessions of a Mask*" (Boardman, 1970, p. 108).

His occupation ... At that instant, in the same way that other children, as soon as they attain the faculty of memory, want to become generals, I became possessed with the ambition to become a night-soil man. The origin of this ambition might have been partly in the dark-blue jeans, but certainly not exclusively so. In time this ambition became still stronger and, expanding within me, saw a strange development.

What I mean is that toward his occupation I felt something like a yearning for a piercing sorrow, a body-wrenching sorrow. His occupation gave me the feeling of "tragedy" in the most sensuous meaning of the word. A certain feeling as it were of "self-renunciation," a certain feeling of indifference, a certain feeling of intimacy with danger, a feeling like a remarkable mixture of nothingness and vital power—all these feelings swarmed forth from his calling, bore down upon me, and took me captive, at the age of four. Probably I had a misconception of the work of a night-soil man. Probably I had been told of some different occupation and, misled by his costume, was forcibly fitting his job into the pattern of what I had heard. I cannot otherwise explain it.

Such must have been the case because presently my ambition was transferred with those same emotions to the operators of hana-densha—those streetcars decorated so gaily with flowers for festival days—or again to subway ticket-punchers. Both occupations gave me a strong impression of "tragic lives" of which I was ignorant and from which it seemed I was forever excluded. This was particularly true in the case of the ticket-punchers: the rows of gold buttons on the tunics of their blue uniforms became fused in my mind with the odor which floated through the subways in those days—it was like the smell of rubber, or of peppermint—and readily called up mental associations of "tragic things." I somehow felt it was "tragic" for a person to make his living in the midst of such an odor. Existences and events occurring without any relationship to myself, occurring at places that not only appealed to my senses but were moreover denied me—these, together with the people involved in them, constituted my definition of "tragic things." It seemed that my grief at being eternally excluded was always transformed in my dreaming into grief for those persons and their ways of life, and that solely through my own grief I was trying to share in their existences [Mishima, pp. 13-14].

His choice of occupations, night-soil collector and ticket puncher in a subway, is a measure of his desire to return to the mother's womb and to the fecal odors of infancy so that the anxieties aroused by homosexual desires would be eradicated in the pleasant and irresponsible anal period.

Just as Proust was troubled by all kinds of odors and went to great lengths to avoid them out of the unconscious fear of oedipal revival and acting out, George Orwell, the author of *1984* (1949), *Animal Farm* (1946), and *Down and Out in Paris and London* (1933), was acutely sensitive to dirt and smells: "he was disgusted by dogs' messes on pavements and horse dung in the streets; his nostrils caught the whiff of sweat, bad breath, stale beer and unwashed armpits..." (Stansky and Abrahams, 1972, p. 123). And Mersault, the passionless Raskolnikov of *The Stranger* (1965), who reappears in Albert Camus' (1972) *A Happy Death*, was terrified and haunted by the smell of the phallic cucumbers he found "on every corner" in Prague. The erotically stimulating potential of fecal odors is revealed repeatedly in Swift's *Gulliver's Travels* (1726). At almost no time are the anal-erotic, infantile ideas to which Swift returned again and again justified by the narrative. "This misanthropic Anglican clergyman did not dwell in his imagination upon rape and seduction, but upon subjects of urination, defecation and body odors" (Karpman, 1942, p. 31). His psychosexual infantilism surfaced in reveling in dirt for its own sake when the needs of the situation did not demand it—an indication of how his coprophilic interests broke through the barriers of censorship. This involved perverse olfactory gratifications, for Swift took a sensuous delight in foul odors and was obssessively preoccupied with them, as the passages in the chapter on anal eroticism reveal.

A case of olfactory-sexual fixation and compulsive paraphiliac behavior was reported by Ujhely (1953), with the suggestion that renifleurism is a substitute for homosexuality. The patient, a middle-aged man, attempted to establish contact between his nose and a female's buttocks for sexual satisfaction. He had been AWOL during World War II, spending five weeks at a French farmhouse. In the stockade, the soldier sought relief in fantasies about a French girl, especially her buttocks. While in prison, he was unable to have an erection unless he recalled the olfactory impression of perfume and body odor of the French girl. Leopold Bloom, Molly's husband in James Joyce's *Ulysses* (1918), had not had relations with his wife in ten years but liked to lie at the far end of their bed and kiss her buttocks and the "smellow-yellow furrow" (p. 68) between them, reminiscent of Ujhely's soldier patient. While the latter was seemingly impotent unless the anal olfactory stimulation inspired him, Leopold was not necessarily so. That he was anal-retentive as well as olfactory-stimulated is seen in this passage where, after breakfast one morning, Mr. Bloom ventures to the toilet.

He kicked open the crazy door of the jakes. Better be careful not to get these trousers dirty for the funeral. He went in, bowing his head under the low lintel. Leaving the door ajar, amid the stench of mouldy limewash and stale cobwebs he undid his braces. Before sitting down he peered through a chink up at the nextdoor window. The king was in his countinghouse. Nobody.

Asquat on the cuckstool he folded out his paper turning its pages over on his bared knees. Something new and easy. No great hurry. Keep it a bit. . . .

Quietly he read on, restraining himself, the first column and, yielding but resisting, began the second. Midway, his last resistance yielding, he allowed his bowels to ease themselves quietly as he read, reading still patiently that slight constipation of yesterday quite gone. Hope it's not too big bring on piles again. No, just right. So. Ah! Costive one tabloid of cascara sagrada. Life might be so. It did not move or touch him but it was something quick and neat. Print anything now. Silly season. He read on, seated calm above his own rising smell. . . [p. 68].

Even as Leopold sat on the throne, the knowledge of his cuckoldom hit him; the satisfaction he derived from his phallic stool, bearing witness to the low self-esteem in which he held himself, made his impotency to do anything about his wife's infidelity more bearable. In their discussion of colostomy patients, Orbach, Bard, and Sutherland (1957) state that inability to control evacuation or the expulsion of flatus with their attendant odors has important connections to other sources of low self-esteem and fears of unacceptability in the life experiences of such people. When the person's opinion of himself is primarily a derogatory one, being dirty constitutes another basis for maintaining this opinion and reinforces his anticipation of unfriendly, nongiving reactions by others.

Odors which are themselves obnoxious are more acceptable in disguised forms, especially in foods and particularly when the associations to the original unacceptable products are sufficiently remote (Bergler, 1955). Thus the individual may detest every smell even remotely resembling that of feces, but in food terms, such as chocolate, he may love it. Predilictions for scent derive directly from anal eroticism. "The love of pleasant smells derives from that of bad, which were originally the good smells to the child before education repressed its pleasure in them into its opposite, disgust . . . This pleasure in these first odoriforous substances survives . . . in many people . . . in the prediliction for strong cheeses, 'high' meat and game. In civilized man . . . the infantile pleasure in smells produced by the bowels is largely transformed into pleasure in scents. . . . The anal origin of this prediliction for scents we find further attested to in the popular belief that by-products of fecal matter enter into their composition" (Bonaparte, 1949, p. 221).

Body odors change drastically with variations in diet and at times of emotional stress. A chronically disordered digestion, unsound eating habits, carious teeth, and excessive smoking or drinking are often indicated by harsh and offensive body odors (Otto and Otto, 1972). Further, certain foods create body odors. The ingestion of any animal fat produces butyric acid, which, in turn, gives the carnivore a distinctive odor. Americans, who are heavy meat eaters, are accustomed to it, but they smell bad to Japanese because they eat ten times more meat. In turn American men complain about the fishy odor of Japanese girls (*Playboy*, 1972). In Kevin Klose and Philip A. McCombs' (1974) mystery novel, *The Typhoon Shipments*, Siddler, a U.S. customs agent, enters Cholon, the Chinese sector of Saigon. "His senses focused on fish, because fish is what you smell when you drive out to

Cholon. You smell fish in a thousand varieties and stages of decay. You smell the essence of Vietnam, its people, and its economy. Siddler's mind, which had been a blank until then, fluttered into a kind of rough focus and he told himself he was glad he didn't smell like a fish. He had the Western smell; his sweat and his stool had the red-meat smell, which is different from the fish smell" (p. 102).

Odors come from decomposition and decay and food and body odors reflect this process. Personal emanations can be a source of pleasure to a lover or of repugnance, a decidedly idiosyncratic matter. Van de Velde (1926) reported that Islam recognizes the intense sexual repulsion which can be caused by offensive body odor and has made it one of four grounds for divorce—"When her husband is an Akbar, that is, when he suffers from bad breath, or purulent rhinitis, or ozoena (stink-nose)" (p. 27). Praz (1933), quoting one of the Goncourt brothers, stated that " 'A passion for something does not derive from its goodness or its pure beauty, but above all from its corruption. One may love a woman madly for her whoring, for the meanness of her spirit, for the unscrupulousness of her head, heart and sensuality; one may have the exorbitant appetite of a glutton for her ripe and stinking odor. At bottom, the quality which arouses passion is the *gaminess* of beings and things' " (p. 45).

According to Ellis (1906, p. 88) the very marked sexual fascination which odor, associated with the men they love, exerts on women easily passes unperceived, but body odor of men is, in many instances, highly agreeable and sexually attractive. Moon Lady, First Wife in Chin P'ing Mei's (1609) novel, said to one of the secondary wives after their husband died, "You ought to have a little more regard for good form and discretion! You should take me as an example of how one should conduct oneself as a widow. The time for foolish dalliance is past. It was different when the house was still filled with the odor of man. Aren't you ashamed in front of the servants? You are getting yourself talked about..." (p. 675). Molly Bloom, in *Ulysses,* resented her husband's ten-year masochistic sexual abstinence with her after the death of their son, Rudi. No wonder she mused, "I wish hed even smoke a pipe like father to get the smell of a man" (Joyce, 1918, p. 737).

The gaminess Goncourt was talking about is seen explicitly in Puddu, the Sicilian archaeological digger who worked for Millie in Alan Friedman's *Hermaphrodeity* (1972). "Puddu's memorable powerful body odor that was animal and vegetable both. I frowned. I had perspired freely for days myself. This was something else. . . . My first impression had been accurate. I breathed him. We breathed together . . . I confess the smell of the man still weighs on me. I came in time to associate it not only with the odor of terrorism, kidnappings, bomb-throwings, and knife-stickings, but with the man's saintliness as well, his unwashed odor of sanctity in the service of the oppressed people. Then, however, it only distracted me, and I frankly despised myself for being American, hygienic, stout-hearted, and at bottom insensitive" (pp. 315-316). Marcia Smith, in the middle of an adulterous love affair with Frank, penned him a note in John Updike's *Couples* (1968): "Dear Frank, whom I want to call dearest and can't. Back from the beach, a quick note, for you to have while I'm in Maine. I drove home from our view of Nahant and took the children to the beach and as I lay there the sun baked a smell of you out of my skin and I thought, that's him. I smelled my palms and there you were again. . . . In love and haste, M." (p. 134). And Zorba, the Greek in Nikos Kazantzakis' (1952) novel, declared: "Well, I think every man has his own smell. We don't notice it much because smells mingle all together and we can't tell which is yours and which is mine, really . . . All we know is that there's a foul smell and that's what we call 'humanity' . . . I mean the 'human stench.' There are people who sniff at it as if it was lavender. It makes me want to spew. Anyway, let's get on, that's another story. . ." (p. 167). "Every man," wrote Cyrus L. Sulzberger (1973) in *The Tooth Merchant,* "is aware of the special smell of his woman, sometimes like musk, sometimes like amber, sometimes like mist, sometimes like dawn, sometimes like evening. Araxie smelled like the fouli flowers in a Mediterranean fig orchard" (p. 165).

As a rule, civilized man dislikes any odor emanating from human beings. A short story by Somerset Maugham (1922), called "Democracy," prompted Brill (1932, p. 41) to show how in the tale body odors divide man from man because each unwittingly thinks of the other's undue proximity, and an obtrusive smell lowers one's estimate of its human source. The story is about a pompous Chinese aristocrat who is carried to an inn by coolies. Because things are not exactly to his liking, he berates the innkeeper and the servants—yet shortly thereafter, changes completely, becoming friendly, chatting amicably with them, and quietly smoking his waterpipe with the coolies on an equal footing. "In the East," the story continues, "man is man's equal in a sense you find neither in Europe nor in America. Position and wealth put a man in a relation of superiority to another that is purely adventitious, and they are no bar to sociability" (Maugham, pp. 141-142). Maugham speculates why this should be true in the despotic caste-conscious East and not true in the democratic West. It is this sense, he claims, that divides men. In the West, "we are divided from our fellows by our sense of smell. The working man is our master, inclined to rule us with an iron hand, but it cannot be denied that he stinks" (p. 142).

Kubie (1937) feels that it is the immediate unconscious assumption that the body smell arises internally that gives it its great emotional significance. Maugham asserts that the democracy of the Chinese is based on the uniformity of the toilet habits of rich and poor in that country, and on the ubiquity of bad smell. "The cess pool . . . rang the bell of democracy." Discussing the proximity senses, Marcuse (1962) observes that smell and taste succumb to the rigidly enforced taboos on too intense bodily pleasure. The pleasure of smell and taste is much more of a bodily, physical nature, hence also more akin to sexual pleasure, than is the more sublime pleasure aroused by sound and the least bodily pleasure, the sight of something beautiful (Schachtel, 1947). Smell and taste give, as it were, unsublimated pleasure *per se* as well as unrepressed disgust. They relate (and separate) people immediately, without generalized and conventionalized forms of consciousness, to the effectiveness of organized domination, with a society that tends to isolate people, to put distance between them, and to prevent spontaneous relations and natural animal-like expression of such relations (Marcuse, 1962).

The odor of the armpit is the most powerful in the human body. Ovid (41 B.C.-17 A.D.), in his *Ars Amandi,* Book III, wrote that it was scarcely necessary to remind a lady that she must not keep a goat in her armpits: *Ne trux caper iret in alas.* Ellis (1906, p. 81) cited the sketch, "Le Gousset," by Joris-Karl Huysmans (1880) which bespeaks a fetishistic interest in the varying odors of women's armpits. "I have followed this fragrance in the country behind a group of women gleaners under the bright sun. It was excessive and terrible; it stung your nostrils like an unstoppered bottle of alkali; it seized you, irritating your mucous membrane with a rough odor which had in it something of the relish of wild duck cooked with olives and the sharp odor of the shallot. On the whole, it was not a vile or repugnant emanation; it united, as an anticipated thing, with the formidable odors of the landscape; it was the pure note, completing with the human animals' cry of heat the odorous melody of beasts and woods." Huysmans then spoke of the odor of feminine armpits in the ballroom. "There the aroma is of ammoniated valerian, of chlorinated urine, brutally accentuated sometimes, even with a slight scent of prussic acid about it, a faint whiff of overripe peaches." The women were more seductive when their perfume filtered through their garments. "The appeal of the balsam of their arms is then less insolent, less cynical, than at the ball where they are more naked, but it more easily uncages the animal in man. Various as the color of the hair, the odor of the armpit is infinitely divisible; its gamut covers the whole keyboard of odors, reaching the obstinate scents of syringa and elder, and sometimes recalling the sweet perfume of the rubbed fingers that have held a cigarette. Audacious and sometimes fatiguing in the brunette and the black woman, sharp and fierce in the red woman, the armpit is heady as some sugared wines in the blondes." Stephen Daedalus in Joyce's *A Portrait of the Artist as a Young Man* (1916) though less so than Huysmans, was also affected by the wild smell of a girl about whom he was thinking: "It was not thought nor vision though he knew vaguely that her figure was passing homeward through the city. Vaguely first and then more sharply he smelt her body. A conscious unrest seethed in his blood. Yes, it was her body he smelt: a wild and languid smell: the tepid limbs over which his music had flowed desirously and the secret soft linen upon which her flesh distilled odour and a dew" (p. 233).

The rhetorical questions raised by Brill (1932, p. 9) about the use of perfumes by women have their answers in the questions themselves: are they used as a direct outlet, as a gratification for their own olfactory sense, as a disguise for their own natural odors, or perhaps as a direct stimulus for sexual attraction? Or are they used because of the widespread and generalized anxiety to counteract body odors? In many cases, perfumes have the same sexual effects as the primitive body odors. The use of perfume has an ancient history, and played an important role in the lives of both sexes. The Bible abounds with references to ointments and potions, both sacred and sensual. "Thou anointest my head with oils; my cup runneth over," wrote the best songwriter of ancient Israel. And his son, who followed the path of his father, set in his penchant for secular dalliance, picked up his Shulamite in a litter that came up from the desert "like pillars of smoke, perfumed with myrrh and frankincense, with all the powders of the merchant." In the royal harem at Shushan, the *Book of Esther* relates, it was the custom to subject the women to a prolonged course of perfuming before they were admitted to the presence of the king: "Six months with oil of myrrh and six months with sweet odors." Ellis (1906, p. 94) cited two Middle East books, *The Perfumed Garden of Sheik Nefzaoui* and *The Arabian Nights.* According to the first, perfumes were used by men as well as women to heighten the act of intercourse; according to the second, they were used as an aphrodisiac. In the story of Kamaralzaman from *The Arabian Nights,* one passage reads, "With fine incense I will perfume my breasts, my belly, my whole body so that my skin may smell more sweetly in thy mouth, O apple of my eye!"

The seduction of Gold Lotus is the point of departure in Chin P'ing Mei's (1609) *The Adventurous History of Hsi Men and His Six Wives.* "Since Gold Lotus, when listening recently beneath the Malachite Veranda, had heard Hsi Men expressing his admiration for the smooth hips and buttocks of the Sixth [Wife], she had secretly obtained an oil subtly perfumed with jasmine, and with this, during the last few days, she had liberally anointed her body. Now, as she lay before him in her rosy nudity, it seemed to him that her skin was softer and smoother than usual, and that it exhaled a peculiarly delicious perfume" (pp. 340-341). The sensuous delight with which Cherie, in the novel of the same name by Edmond de Goncourt (1884), finds in perfume is expressed in "The intimately happy emotion which the young girl experienced in reading *Paul et Virginie* and other honestly amorous books she sought to make more complete and intense and penetrating by soaking the book with scent, and the love-story reached her senses and imagination through pages moist with liquid perfume." In a later chapter, de Goncourt remarked, "Perfume and love impart delights which are closely allied." Throughout the fantasy world of the *Brave New World* of Aldous Huxley (1932), the scent organ, like the synthetic music machine, plays a large role in stimulating sexual feeling. "The scent organ was playing a delightfully refreshing Herbal Capriccio— rippling arpeggios of thyme and lavender, of rosemary, basil, myrtle, tarragon; a series of daring modulations through the spice keys into ambergris; and a slow return through sandalwood, camphor, cedar and newmown hay (with occasional subtle touches of discord—a whiff of kidney pudding, the faintest suspicion of pig's dung) back to the simple aromatics with which the piece began.... Sunk in their pneumatic stalls, Lenina and the Savage sniffed and listened" (pp. 198-199).

Contemporary novels are quick to use perfumes to heighten sexual foreplay and sexual acts. In Arthur Arent's *The Laying On of Hands* (1969), the narrator relates, "She was leaning over me now, rubbing the back of my neck with the wet towel. I got a whiff of Bellodgia. She was the kind it stayed with. Other women were always dabbing themselves. Not Joan. Body chemistry. You find the right perfume that likes your body chemistry and you are set for life. She was leaning over me and I was looking for cleavage only there never was any with Joan. No matter how far over she leaned. You got it all or nothing with Joan. Interesting about body chemistry, though" (p. 57). And in *Nightwood*, Djuna Barnes (1937) wrote that "The perfume that her body exhaled was of the quality of that earth-flesh, fungi, which smells of captured dampness and yet is so dry, overcast with the odor of oil of amber, which is an inner malady of the sea, making her seem as if she had invaded a sleep incautious and entire" (p. 34). The amber Barnes mentions is the subject of a chapter in Herman Melville's (1851) *Moby Dick.*

Now this ambergris is a very curious substance, and so important as an article of commerce, that in 1791 a certain Nantucket-born Captain Coffin was examined at the bar of the English House of Commons on that subject. For at that time, and indeed until a comparatively late day, the precise origin of ambergris remained, like amber itself, a problem to the learned. Though the word ambergris is but the French compound for grey amber, yet the two substances are quite distinct. For amber, though at times found on the sea-coast, is also dug up in some far inland soils, whereas ambergris is never found except upon the sea. Besides, amber is a hard, transparent, brittle, odourless substance, used for mouthpieces to pipes, for beads and ornaments; but ambergris is soft, waxy, and so highly fragrant and spicy that it is largely used in perfumery, in pastilles, precious candles, hair-powders, and pomatum. The Turks use it in cooking, and also carry it to Mecca, for the same purpose that frankincense is carried to St. Peter's, in Rome. Some wine merchants drop a few grains into claret, to flavour it.

Who would think, then, that such fine ladies and gentlemen should regale themselves with an essence found in the inglorious bowels of a sick whale! Yet so it is. By some, ambergris is supposed to be the cause, and by others the effect, of the dyspepsia in the whale. How to cure such a dyspepsia it were hard to say, unless by administering three or four boat-loads of Brandreth's pills, and then running out of harm's way, as labourers do in blasting rocks.

I have forgotten to say that there were found in this ambergris, certain hard, round, bony plates which at first Stubb thought might be sailors' trouser buttons; but it afterwards turned out that they were nothing more than pieces of small squid bones embalmed in that manner.

Now that the incorruption of this most fragrant ambergris should be found in the heart of such decay; is this nothing? Bethink thee of that saying of St. Paul in Corinthians, about corruption and incorruption; how that we are sown in dishonour, but raised in glory. And likewise call to mind that saying of Paracelsus about what it is that maketh the best musk. Also forget not the strange fact that of all things of ill-savour, Cologne water, in its rudimental manufacturing stages, is the worst.

I should like to conclude the chapter with the above appeal, but cannot owing to my anxiety to repel a charge often made against whalemen, and which, in the estimation of some already biassed minds, might be considered as indirectly substantiated by what has been said of the Frenchman's two whales. Elsewhere in this volume the slanderous aspersion has been disproved, that the vocation of whaling is throughout a slatternly, untidy business. But there is another thing to rebut. They hint that all whales always smell bad. Now how did this odious stigma originate?

I opine, that it is plainly traceable to the first arrival of the Greenland whaling ships in London, more than two centuries ago. Because those whalemen did not then, and do not now, try out their oil at sea as the Southern ships have always done; but cutting up the fresh blubber in small bits, thrust it through the bungholes of large casks, and carry it home in that manner; the shortness of the season in those icy seas, and the sudden and violent storms to which they are exposed, forbidding any other course. The consequence is, that upon breaking into the hold, and unloading one of these whale cemeteries, in the Greenland dock, a savour is given forth somewhat similar to that arising from excavating an old city graveyard, for the foundations of a Lying-in Hospital.

I partly surmise also, that this wicked charge against whalers may be likewise imputed to the existence on the coast of Greenland, in former times, of a Dutch village called Schmerenburgh or Smeerenberg, which latter name is the one used by the learned Fogo Von Slack, in his great work on *Smells*, a text-book on that subject.

As its name imports (*Smeer,* fat: *berg,* to put up), this village was founded in order to afford a place for the blubber of the Dutch whale fleet to be tried out, without being taken home to Holland for that purpose. It was a collection of furnaces, fat-kettles, and oil sheds; and when the works were in full operation certainly gave forth no very pleasant savour. But all this is quite different with a South Sea Sperm Whaler; which in a voyage of four years perhaps, after completely filling her hold with oil, does not, perhaps, consume fifty days in the business of boiling out; and in the state that it is casked, the oil is nearly scentless. The truth is, that living or dead, if but decently treated, whales as a species are by no means creatures of ill odour; nor can whalemen be recognised, as the people of the middle ages affected to detect a Jew in the company, by the nose. Nor indeed can the whale possibly be otherwise than fragrant, when, as a general thing, he enjoys such high health; taking abundance of exercise; always out of doors; though, it is true, seldom in the open air. I say, that the motion of a Sperm Whale's flukes about water dispenses a perfume, as when a musk-scented lady rustles her dress in a warm parlour. What then shall I liken the Sperm Whale to for fragrance, considering his magnitude? Must it not be to that famous elephant, with jewelled tusks, and redolent with myrrh, which was led out of an Indian town to do honour to Alexander the Great? [pp. 302-304].

Most of the good perfumes used today have as their base ambergris, civet, or musk. The last is extracted from the glands of a tiny male musk deer of the high Himalayas. "It has always been associated by the Chinese with sexual attraction and was regarded as an aphrodisiac. Now there are many different kinds, classified as macrocyclic, steroid, nitro, indane, naphthalense and benzene musks. The fact that the odor of musk is somehow of sexual significance to humans, and probably always has been, is shown by the remarkable sex differentiation in ability to smell musklike chemicals such as pentadecanolide. Over fifty per cent of men cannot smell this substance at all and the rest cannot smell it in dilutions of more than one part per million of air. Yet all normal women are sensitive to it in dilutions of one part per billion. During the course of the menstrual cycle the women's sensitivity increases so that during ovulation some women can detect one part per quadrillon, an almost unbelievably small concentration, comparable to the dilution at which the male gypsy moth is able to smell his lady's lure. Although the reason for this unique female ability to perceive musk is not clear, it is obviously related to hormones. Women whose ovaries have been removed are about one thousand times less sensitive, but when given estrogen treatments they regain their normal sensitivity. It is possible that if we were not drowned in an olfactory flood-wave of artificial smells, such as those of air pollution, cosmetics and cigarette smoke, the sexual facets of natural musklike odors might be of clearer importance to us" (Carr, 1972, pp. 154-155).

Musk, as well as the other odorous substances of animal origin, such as ambergris, fixates all personal odors, whether genital or other, and enhances them; when used in concentrated form, it dominates and obliterates all other odors and displays its specific male and sexual characteristics (Van de Velde, 1926, p. 39). The work *musk* is Persian taken from the Sanskrit meaning testicle (Schneider, 1971) and lavender, from the Latin *lavare* meaning to wash: "This ambivalence is further evident in the ancient notion that perfumes represent the odor of sanctity as opposed to the suggestion of evil by foul odors" (p. 160). The exaggerated form current perfume advertising takes is as farfetched as the ancient belief about it.

Carr's demonstration that women have great olfactory acuity in smelling musk underscores the fact that women have greater smell acuity in general than men, and it varies with the menstrual cycle. Experiments with macaque monkeys indicate that secreted odors may be the agent responsible in controlling reciprocal mating behavior related to the menstrual cycle (Money, 1965). The odor or odors of menstruation have certain common characteristics in all women, but vary so widely in intensity and personal peculiarities that they have an individuality of their own as well as a threefold effect on the sexual impulse: "It may be wholly repellent; distinctly pleasant; or conditionally pleasant, i.e., slightly repellent at first, but attractive, even delightful, when a certain pronounced stage of tension and desire has been reached" (Van de Velde, 1926, p. 30). However, men have generally reacted with hostile apprehension to these organic odors. "For men, there has often seemed to be something excessively physical about women — too many secretions and smelly fluids: witness the *'inter urinam et faeces nascimur'* of St. Augustine, and the principal horror of menstruation and birth-fluids; witness the Indian maiden Satyavati, whose name means 'Truth,' but who was yet known ... as 'Fishy Smell.' ... Homosexual slang refers to woman as 'fish' " (Lederer, 1968, p. 248). Ferenczi (1933) refers "to the peculiar fact that the genital secretion of the female among the higher mammals and in man, the erotically stimulating effect which ... may be traceable to infantile reminiscences, possesses a distinctly fishy odor (odor of herring brine), according to the description of all physiologists; this odor of the vagina comes from the same substance (trimethylamine) as the decomposition of fish gives rise to" (p. 57). At a reception at the English embassy in Madrid in Lawrence Robbin's (1975) *A Certain Protocol,* some hors d'oeuvres are passed around. " 'If you think *that* was good,' Baskin said, 'try this,' and held a fish-paste cracker under Towner's nose. The old whore-muff odor of fish-paste caught him on an inward gasp. His eyes crossed. His scotum tightened..." (p. 112). The female beast only permits the male animal to approach during the periods of heat; man, on the other hand, usually abstains during menstrual periods. Not only are these periods devoid of attraction but they entail a prohibition. "Whether this is physical or moral, whether .one must see it as a temporary disgust of the flesh, a survival of ancient religious precepts, or a disapproval of the spirit—the fact remains that ... the sexual appetite, while still remaining all-powerful, is no longer attached so closely to the olfactory nerves which hitherto held it in leash" (Gide, 1911, p. 96). The Lemnian husbands, mythology relates, preferred Tracian slave women to their lawful wives whom they had come to detest because Aphrodite had inflicted them with a foul smell when they neglected to pay honor to the goddess (Engle, 1942).

The findings of brain stimulus studies on cerebral representation of sexual functions reveal that excitation in a region involved in oral mechanisms readily spills over into others concerned with genital functions. This close neural relationship, states McLean (1965, p. 209), "helps in understanding the intimate interplay of behavior in oral and sexual spheres, examples of which we are accustomed to see in the activities of our domestic animals. Such an interplay is readily taken for granted in animals, but one has only to consider the last fifty years of Freudian psychiatry to realize the trouble that it may lead to in human affairs. If there is any neural offender that can be blamed for this situation, then the olfactory sense, more than any other, must be considered the culprit." Such findings attest to the close organization of olfactory and sexual functioning of the brain. Anxieties arising out of menstrual and vaginal odors can represent a projective mechanism in which sexual impulses rejected as unacceptable are also interpreted as alienating others. The odor is feared, according to Orbach, Bard, and Sutherland (1957), because it can signify to others that sexual feelings and desires have not been suppressed as unworthy. "In other instances the fear can represent the outcome of indoctrination about the significance of the genitals and menstruation ... Sexual expression can be conceived as dirty and animal-like (subhuman) and menstruation as capable of contaminating others. . . . Finally, the fear of communicating sexual odors to others in addition to signifying disowned sexual life may represent an extension of the condemnation of anal odors to include odors which emanate from any bodily orifice" (p. 169).

When the whole organism is stimulated and ready for coitus, the vaginal odor is increased by the lubricating secretions of the accessory glands of the vulva, which may excite the male lover or repel him. "We felt each other's bodies," George reported about himself and Catherine in *Slaves* by Roderick Thorp (1972). "Her breasts were soft, empty-feeling, so I moved my hands down. She was soft all over, the softest woman I have ever touched; her pubic hair made me think of the hair on a baby's head. She was wet. I wanted to lick her, but the wetness turned me off. I wasn't ready to struggle with an odor. I wanted to kiss her thighs and her ass, and the realizations excited me terribly" (p. 84). Subsequently, George met a man in Italy who told him, "Never had any luck with Italian quiff. Their snatches smell bad to me" (p. 121). In fellatio and cunnilingus the heightened odors from the partner are not always the attraction; rather the enjoyment stems from the method of sexual activity (Sagarin, 1961). Gorman (1964, p. 73) considers olfactory genital stimuli as part of the continuously bombarding volleys of odors that symbolize both feeding, which is necessary for survival of the individual, and sexuality, which is fundamental for the survival of the species. Genital olfactory stimuli recall both the search for food and the striving for sex-linked gratifications.

The defensiveness of some women about vaginal odors is reflected in *Ulysses,* when Molly Bloom recalls a professional visit to Dr. Collins for a gynecological examination: ". . . always smelling around those filthy bitches all sides asking me if what I did had an offensive odour what did he want me to do but the one thing gold maybe what a question if I smathered it all over his wrinkly old face for him with all my compriment I suppose hed know then and could you pass it easily pass. . ." (Joyce, 1918, p. 755). And Millie, in Friedman's *Hermaphrodeity* (1972) ruminates, "I felt (*very* frankly) that the strong smell of deteriorating biological waste carried out to sea by the flow of her [Venice's] canals matched the familiar, terribly pleasant sniff in the dark of my radical medical comical tragical cloacal honey-haired cunt" (p. 286). De Beauvoir (1953) expresses for many the ambivalent feelings about the fetid quality of the vagina: "The sex organ of a man is simple and neat as a finger; it is readily visible and often exhibited to comrades with proud rivalry; but the female sex organ is mysterious even to the woman herself, concealed, mucous, and humid, as it is; it bleeds each month, it is often sullied with body fluids, it has a secret and perilous life of its own. Woman does not recognize herself in it, and this explains in large part why she does not recognize its desires as hers. These manifest themselves in an embarrassing manner. Man 'gets stiff,' but woman 'gets wet'; in the very word there are chilled memories of bedwetting, of guilty and involuntary yielding to the need to urinate. Man feels the same disgust at involuntary nocturnal emissions; to eject a fluid, urine or semen, does not humiliate; it is an active operation; but it is humiliating if the liquid flows out passively, for then the body is no longer an organism with muscles, nerves, sphincters under control of the brain and expressive of a conscious subject, but is rather a vessel, a container, composed of inert matter and but the plaything of capricious mechanical forces. If the body leaks—as an ancient wall or a dead body may leak—it seems to liquefy rather than to eject a fluid: a horrible decomposition" (p. 164).

The idea of semen as a dirty excretion, the conscious feeling that some women have of being soiled by the man during intercourse, is used to obscure the deep personal pain it causes the woman to regard her own genitalia as even dirtier (Kubie, 1937, p. 396). The odor of semen is distasteful to many people because it is unconsciously equated with the bodily excretions of urine and feces, and thus becomes disgusting on that ground. Van de Velde (1926) generalizes that, "the odor of semen is exciting and stimulating to women, and unpleasant, even nauseating, to men. But the mental associations are here so powerful that they may completely displace or negate the primary sensory impression, so that most men feel no repulsion at the odor of their own semen, but pronounced nausea at that of other men's. For a woman in coitus the odor of the beloved man's semen is delightful and excites her anew; but that of an unloved mate fills her with loathing" (p. 32).

In Chapter 94 of Melville's *Moby Dick,* which is called "A Squeeze of the Hand," Ishmael is granted a vision of the nature of love while he and his shipmates are busy squeezing the sperm of Stubb's whale. The analysis by Fiedler (1960, p. 345) suggests that "Though Melville is deliberately playing from the start with the double meaning of the word 'sperm' (he comments on how 'in old times sperm was such a favorite cosmetic,' knowing well enough that it was semen not blubber which the medieval cosmeticians prized), the passage seems for a while an idyllic prose poem: 'As I bathed my hands among the soft, gentle globules of infiltrated tissue ... as they richly broke to my fingers ... as I snuffed up that uncontaminated aroma ... I forgot all about our horrible oath; in that inexpressible sperm, I washed my hands and heart of it ... I felt divinely free from ill will or petulance or malice of any sort whatever. ...' In sperm, that is to say, Ishmael has washed himself clean of the pledge to destroy and pursue, his implication in the blasphemous quest of Ahab; it is a counterbaptism to that of fire. But the passage moves on to even more explicit and embarrassing erotic images, until at last (surely, not without a certain sly humour) Ishmael calls upon the whole world to perform a similar service of love: 'nay, let us squeeze ourselves into each other; let us squeeze ourselves universally into the very milk and sperm of kindness.' Beyond this there is only the comic version of the 'angels of paradise, each with his hands in a jar of spermaceti'. ..."

That whale of Stubb's so dearly purchased, was duly brought to the *Pequod's* side, where all those cutting and hoisting operations previously detailed, were regularly gone through, even to the baling of the Heidelburgh Tun, or Case.

While some were occupied with this latter duty, others were employed in dragging away the larger tubs, so soon as filled with the sperm; and when the proper time arrived, this same sperm was carefully manipulated ere going to the try-works, of which anon.

It had cooled and crystallised to such a degree, that when, with several others, I sat down before a large Constantine's bath of it, I found it strangely concreted into lumps, here and there rolling about in the liquid part. It was our business to squeeze these lumps back into fluid. A sweet and unctuous duty! No wonder that in old times this sperm was such a favourite cosmetic. Such a clearer! such a sweetener! such a softener! such a delicious mollifier! After having my hands in it for only a few minutes, my fingers felt like eels, and began, as it were, to serpentine and spiralise.

Squeeze! squeeze! squeeze! all the morning long; I squeezed that sperm till I myself almost melted into it; I squeezed that sperm till a strange sort of insanity came over me; and I found myself unwittingly squeezing my co-labourers' hands in it, mistaking their hands for the gentle globules. Such an abounding, affectionate, friendly, loving feeling did this avocation beget; that at last I was continually squeezing their hands, and looking up into their eyes sentimentally; as much as to say, — "Oh! my dear fellow-beings, why should we longer cherish any social acerbities, or know the slightest ill-humour or envy! Come; let us squeeze hands all round; nay, let us all squeeze ourselves into each other; let us squeeze ourselves universally into the very milk and sperm of kindness."

Would that I could keep squeezing that sperm for ever! For now, since by many prolonged, repeated experiences, I have perceived that in all cases man must eventually lower, or at least shift, his conceit of attainable felicity; not placing it anywhere in the intellect or the fancy; but in the wife, the heart, the bed, the table, the saddle, the fireside, the country; now that I have perceived all this, I am ready to squeeze case eternally. In thoughts of the visions of the night, I saw long rows of angels in paradise, each with his hands in a jar of spermaceti [Melville, 1851, pp. 307-308].

Olfaction as a primary source of sexual arousal in the child up to the age of five is also true for many adults, however repressed the erotogenic response to odors may be. Most people believe themselves to be unresponsive to olfactory arousal cues. But clinical evidence reveals that while an awareness of sexual responses to odors is usually repressed, it surfaces when the fears creating the repression are resolved (Bieber, 1970). While the sense of smell has become weak in the course of human evolution, smell can act as a powerful symbol for sexual readiness. In a letter to Fliess, Freud (1887-1902) wrote, "So long as the sense of smell (and of taste) is dominant, hair, faeces and the whole surface of the body—and blood as well, have a sexually exciting effect (pp. 186-187). But those odors which are most heavily charged with libidinal meaning are the most powerfully repressed at each level of the psychosexual development. Gorman (1964, pp. 64-70) showed that the anal, oral, and genital components of the biologic striving for pleasure all participate in the process of stimulating and being stimulated by smell.

Although there is a paucity of studies that deal with the relationship of olfaction and sex, there is evidence that during sexual arousal sensory perception, including that for odor, is heightened but appears to be ignored, at least on a conscious level, even though these sensations may add to total gratification (Schneider, 1971, p. 168). Stekel (1922) has said that certain body odors cause erotic stimulation and may be conducive to normal intercourse. Smell is a trenchant theme in Updike's (1968) *Couples*. Piet, a building contractor, was remodeling Foxy and Ken Whitman's house, all the while carrying on an adulterous affair with Foxy. In a letter to Piet, she writes: "My lover!—My whole house breathes of you, and the salt and wind is you, and the rumpled sheets whose scent is sweetest and subtlest—of us—is you. I have been all open windows and blowing curtains and blue view these last hours—so much yours I must write and tell you, though Ken is downstairs waiting to go to the little-Smiths. In a few minutes I will see you. But surrounded by others. Accept this kiss" (p. 261). Colette at thirteen was a guest at a peasant wedding, and was filled with confusion when a friend took her to see the nuptial chamber. Acute, threatening, olfactory perceptions broke through the dammed-up libidinal surgings of the adolescent girl. "The young couple's room! The curtained bed, olfactory perceptions broke through the dammed-up libidinal surgings of the adolescent girl. "The young couple's room! The curtained bed, high and narrow, the bed stuffed with feathers, piled with goosedown pillows, the bed that will be the termination of a day steaming with sweat, incense, the breath of cattle, the smell of cooking. . . . Soon the young couple will be here. I had not thought of this. They will sink into this deep featherbed. . . . They will engage in that obscure struggle about which my mother's frank words and the life of the barnyard had taught me too much and too little. And then what? I was frightened by this chamber and this bed which I had never thought of " (Colette, quoted in de Beauvoir, 1953, p. 164).

It is proof of the close connection between the sense of smell and the sexual organs that the expression of pleasure produced by olfaction resembles the expression of sexual pleasures. "Make the chastest woman smell the flowers she likes best . . . and she will close her eyes, breathe deeply, and, if very sensitive, tremble all over, presenting an intimate picture which otherwise she never shows, except perhaps to her lover" (Friedman, 1959, p. 309). In the famous flower passage in *Sons and Lovers* by D. H. Lawrence (1913), Mrs. Morel's reaction to the touch and scent of the flowers is almost literally orgasmic. In every sense, it is more really sexual—the terror of her situation all her life—than anything which she ever experienced with her husband (Hardy, 1964). Dizzy with the scent, she "herself melted out like scent into the shiny, pale air . . . in a kind of swoon." When she came to herself, she looked "languidly" about her; and going inside, she is described in the final scene exactly in the attitude of a woman returned from a tryst with her lover, in the secretiveness of remembered passion, noting the guilty stains still upon her. The scene upon which this is based is preceded by a row between Mr. and Mrs. Morel. He comes home drunk, to be called by her a "despicable liar," and to be outraged by the indictment that the "house is filthy with you." Morel screams at her to get out and it is at this point that she wanders into the garden, "seared with passion . . . trembling in every limb."

She became aware of something about her. With an effort she aroused herself to see what it was that penetrated her consciousness. The tall white lilies were reeling in the moonlight, and the air was charged with their perfume, as with a presence. Mrs. Morel gasped slightly in fear. She touched the big, pallid flowers on their petals, then shivered. They seemed to be stretching in the moonlight. She put her hand into one white bin: the gold scarcely showed on her fingers by moonlight. She bent down to look at the binful of yellow pollen; but it only appeared dusky. Then she drank a deep draught of the scent. It almost made her dizzy.

Mrs. Morel leaned on the garden gate, looking out, and she lost herself awhile. She did not know what she thought. Except for a slight feeling of sickness, and her consciousness in the child, herself melted out like scent into the shiny, pale air. After a time the child, too, melted with her in the mixing-pot of moonlight, and she rested with the hills and lilies and houses, all swum together in a kind of swoon.

When she came to herself she was tired for sleep. Languidly she looked about her; the clumps of white phlox seemed like bushes spread with linen; a moth ricochetted over them, and right across the garden. Following it with her eye roused her. A few whiffs of the raw, strong scent of phlox invigorated her. She passed along the path, hesitating at the white rose-bush. It smelled sweet and simple. She touched the white ruffles of the roses. Their fresh scent and cool soft leaves reminded her of the morning-time and sunshine. She was very fond of them. But she was tired, and wanted to sleep [Lawrence, p. 24].

On the genital level flowers seem to be a fairly consistent symbol for heterosexuality, probably arising from the fact that they are pollinated by insects who enter the blossom in symbolic coitus. Furthermore, flowers have the advantage of being objects of great beauty which thus makes possible a sublimation of what seems to the neurotic the grosser aspects of sexual intercourse (Wormhoudt, 1950). In many cases, Ellis (1906, p. 104) reported, the odor of flowers produces not only a highly pleasurable but a distinctly voluptuous effect, reflected in the phrase from John Steinbeck's *Cannery Row* (1945), "... at night the flowers smelled of love and excitement, an incredibly sweet and moving odor" (p. 29).

The association of sexual excitement with the sense of smell is portrayed more directly in this atavistic bedroom scene from *The Second Stone* by Leslie Fiedler (1963).

He closed his eyes, then, as he had not when feeling her; for he sensed that not in her but in the fastness of his own head there must lurk images for her savor: mango, grape leaf, fennel, artichoke or pomegranate. It seemed to him at last that she tasted of no taste but of a color, tasted white, the unflavor of the inside of an orange peel, or the pip.

She heaved herself over for him when he had finished with her front, turned to his mouth her back; and sighed. Surely, she was awake though not yet ready to confess it. He worked this time from sole to crown, lapping upward always, against the grain. Lost in her hair at last, he shifted to his nose, his tongue weary, his chin slobbered, his whole mouth strained and sore. He laughed a little to himself at the notion of a tired tongue, and thought that Hilda roused to ask, "What? What?" But he could not be sure. Her odors also baffled him, what odors of her own persisted beneath the scents of her tobacco and perfume, so modest and austere he felt rebuffed.

He thought of how generous Selma was in this regard, how animal: giving her rankest self as freely to the nose as to the eye, the ear, the fingertips. She smacked of jungle odors, the effluvia of great cats, or, sometimes, of the tidal flats, the shallow edges of the sea where life began in squalor and in stink. But Hilda, even where her body's insides met the air, insisted on discretion. It was not, Clem knew, a matter of deodorants only, of things bought in drugstores, but of an attitude, a stance.

Her mouth, a little open now, smelled faintly of excitement, of the special saliva that flows in women's mouths, not to moisten food or speech, but only for the sake of love. And her sex released a dry aroma like that of last year's hay, of the mustiness of haylofts before the new year's crop is carried in.

"I love you, dearest love," he almost said aloud. "Dear heart, dear beauty, beauty's bounty, summer's honey, honey's breath." He might have made a poem, but sniffed her flesh instead; and thought how afterwards, catching the scent of some passing girl, even before he'd told himself it smacked of her, he'd feel his breathing stop and lean against a wall to brace his buckling knees. "I'll marry her," he thought, "why not? I'll follow her to the States, and when she needs me, I'll be there."

But even as he spoke it in his head, he heard the answer, "No, Clem, write a book instead. A book!" He laughed, yet saw the title in the air: *My Second Best Bed;* and lying with his nose upon her spine, composed the opening sentence, "At first, Hilda, one hand pressed against the wall, had only retched."

He could not call her Hilda, of course, though no other name would really do, no other name but — Selma. "At first Selma, etc. etc." That would be a gas! He did not cease to smell her as he changed her name, baptized her out of life and into myth. Somehow she must survive the fading of the senses: sight and taste and touch and smell. He felt that he must memorize her inch by inch, savor and flavor, texture and line, so that, exiled to home, on lonely afternoons or just before falling asleep, he would be able to reconstruct her from whatever scrap the hazard of remembering gave him for a start.

Sight, touch, taste, smell; he knew there was another sense he had not yet used, but he could not recall it. He counted on his fingers: smell, taste, touch, sight. But there *had* to be five, and the fifth was — The dinging of a distant churchbell, the sound of matins, cued him in. Hearing. Hearing. He bent his ear to listen to her innards as she slept now, curled up on one side. In the early stillness, he could hear distinctly the catch and the release of breath, the pulse and thumping of the heart, the noise of peristalsis, even, he imagined, the creaking of a joint [pp. 214-215].

On a similarly atavistic order, and as erotic in its way is a subtheme found in Frank Norris' *McTeague* (1899), the smell of Trina's hair and "the sweet, fleshly aroma" that was "redolent of youth and freshness." Returning from a Sunday picnic which he had spent with Trina and her family, McTeague was invited to stay overnight. To make space for him, Trina gave up her own room and McTeague wandered through it, poking about everywhere. Some years later, their love dissipated, McTeague remembered when "even the smell of her wonderful odorous hair had sent a sensation of faintness through him" (p. 189). McTeague was unable to articulate his love for Trina when they first met; he was uncouth and crass. Later, his expression of love took the form of primitive sniffing, and this is what he did as he explored Trina's bedroom. His behavior resembled man's remote ancestors for whom smell was a more erotic stimulus than sight.

He saw into her daily life, her little ways and manners, her habits, her very thoughts. And was there not in the air of that room a certain faint perfume that he knew, that recalled her to his mind with marvellous vividness?

As he put the candle down upon the bureau he saw her hairbrush lying there. Instantly he picked it up, and, without knowing why, held it to his face. With what a delicious odor was it redolent! That heavy, enervating odor of her hair—her wonderful, royal hair! The smell of that little hairbrush was talismanic. He had but to close his eyes to see her as distinctly as in a mirror. He saw her tiny, round figure, dressed all in black—for, curiously enough, it was his very first impression of Trina that came back to him now—not the Trina of the later occasions, not the Trina of the blue cloth skirt and white sailor. He saw her as he had seen her the day that Marcus had introduced them: saw her pale, round face; her narrow, half-open eyes, blue like the eyes of a baby; her tiny, pale ears, suggestive of anaemia; the freckles across the bridge of her nose; her pale lips; the tiara of royal black hair; and, above all, the delicious poise of the head, tipped back as though by the weight of all that hair—the poise that thrust out her chin a little, with the movement that was so confiding, so innocent, so nearly infantile.

McTeague went softly about the room from one object to another, beholding Trina in everything he touched and looked at. He came at last to the closet door. It was ajar. He opened it wide, and paused upon the threshold.

Trina's clothes were hanging there—skirts and waists, jackets, and stiff white petticoats. What a vision! For an instant McTeague caught his breath, spellbound. If he had suddenly discovered Trina herself there, smiling at him, holding out her hands, he could hardly have been more overcome. Instantly he recognized the black dress she had worn on that famous first day. There it was, the little jacket she had carried over her arm the day he had terrified her with his blundering declaration, and still others, and others—a whole group of Trinas faced him there. He went farther into the closet, touching the clothes gingerly, stroking them softly with his huge leathern palms. As he stirred them a delicate perfume disengaged itself from the folds. Ah, that exquisite feminine odor! It was not only her hair now, it was

Trina herself—her mouth, her hands, her neck; the indescribably sweet, fleshly aroma that was a part of her, pure and clean, and redolent of youth and freshness. All at once, seized with an unreasoned impulse, McTeague opened his huge arms and gathered the little garments close to him, plunging his face deep amongst them, savoring their delicious odor with long breaths of luxury and supreme content [pp. 78-79].

Olfactory signals play a significant role between man and woman. Of especial meaning is the use of smell as social communication between mother and child (Wickler, 1969). The importance of odor, stated Greenacre (1969), "depends probably largely on the fact that it adds a potent intangible link between the infant and the breast, in that it is usually compounded by body smells from both sources. But further, it is biologically grounded in the general importance of smell in the first months of life. For until the baby can maintain an upright position in walking, he functions locomotorwise pretty much like a quadruped, with the nose closer to the ground and to his own genitoexcretory area than he will later on. . . . Observations of nurslings indicate that the young baby may find the breast by nosing it out as much or more than from a sense of touch. This capacity for communion through odors, first aroused in relation to the mother—her breast and general environment—later becomes externalized and extended to the outer world to include emphasis on airborne sensations. . . . With the gaining of bowel control, through spontaneous maturational processes, fortified perhaps by the demands of bodily comfort associated with walking, and by the dividends of familial social approval, a more sophisticated awareness of odor develops with air in general. This contributes to the already developing sense of the relation between intangible mental imagery and concrete objects. By then the child is aware of his thoughts, has some idea of time and of his own memory, and can differentiate dreams from events. This is a period which is significantly vulnerable to disturbance in the early life of the future fetishist" (pp. 318-319).

Thus smell helps to furnish the sensory life of the infant and lays down the foundation of subsequent fetishism. Fetishist symbolism, as the foot, shoe, slipper, or furs, often seems to depend on sexual experiences in childhood, according to Freud (1905). "Psycho-analysis has cleared up one of the remaining gaps in our understanding of fetishism. It has shown that . . . the choice of a fetish [depends on] a coprophilic pleasure in smelling which has disappeared owing to repression. Both the feet and hair are objects with a strong smell which have been exalted into fetishes after the olfactory sensation has become unpleasurable and been abandoned. Accordingly, in the perversion that corresponds to foot-fetishism it is only dirty and evil-smelling feet that become sexual objects" (p. 155n). The fetish "becomes literally a restitutive stopgap with which the mother is endowed, and through incorporation mainly by touch, vision, and smell the fetishist attains enough semblance of body integrity to permit some kind of genital functioning" (Greenacre, 1969, pp. 169-170). In her discussion of the forms and functions of the transitional object and the fetish, Greenacre posits that both are inanimate objects adopted and utilized by the person to aid in maintaining a psychophysical balance under conditions of strain: "The transitional object appears in and belongs to infancy, and is generally relinquished when infancy merges into childhood" (p. 315). In infancy, the transitional object "must be part of the baby's intimate environment and be ready at hand. This appeal of the familiar depends not only on visibility but even more on texture and odor. The preferred transitional object is commonly something soft which has been used in the infant's care, e.g., an old blanket, warmly impregnated with body odors, or a bit of wool or fluff, which may be a reduced version of the blanket, or actually a piece of it.... Durability is a built-in requirement commensurate with the degree of familiarity demanded. Individuality of odor (or blend of odors) seems especially important. Many infants will reject a beloved object if it has been washed and only become reconciled when it has again attained its familiar smelliness." In the transitional object, "blend of odors seems to be a fusion of me-odors and mother-odors..." (pp. 316-317).

Wulff (1946), in his paper on fetishism and object choice in early childhood, cites an example of a mother who gave her four-year-old boy a colored checkered handkerchief to take to bed with him for a cold he then had. "After this he demanded this handkerchief again and again, smelled of it, and refused to be parted from it.... This handkerchief he often stuffed into his pyjama leg and pressed against his genitals, saying that in this way it could not get lost. After being freshly laundered, the handkerchief gave him no pleasure; its use was pleasurable only when it had a mixture of odors which had to do with his mother—from her eau de cologne, her pocketbook, her linen cupboard, etc. It often happened that he would awaken at night and cry, 'Handkerchief!', and then finding it, would lay it over his nose, and immediately fall quietly to sleep" (p. 457). Thus, the fetish was connected with the mother's body, with her odor, and was a mother substitute. When the boy stuffed the handkerchief (the mother) into his pyjamas, he iden-tified the fetish with his genital, transferred therewith a portion of his narcissistic libido to the fetish, and converted it into object libido, but at the same time the dread of losing the penis—castration anxiety—was apparently also carried over to the fetish.

In the *Dog Years* by Günter Grass (1963), Eddi Amsel found intoler-able the fresh-smelling underwear which his loving mother insisted he wear. He swapped regularly with his best friend, Walter Matern, an example of how early infantile anal-erotic tendencies manifest them-selves in later life by using garments which have already been worn, retaining the warmth and odor of the body.

Brauxel has an unblunting distaste for unused razor blades. A handy-man who formerly, in the days of the Burbach Potash Co. Inc., worked in the mine and opened up rich salt deposits, breaks in Brauksel's razor blades and delivers them to him after using them once. Thus Brauksel has no need to overcome a revulsion which, though not directed against razor blades, was equally innate and equally strong in Eduard Amsel. He had a thing about new, new-smelling clothes. The smell of fresh underwear compelled him to fight down incipient nausea. As long as he attended the village school, natural limits were imposed on his allergy, for the apparel in which the small fry of Schiewenhorst as well as Nickelswalde weighed down the school benches was baggy, worn, and much mended. Sankt Johann High School had higher vestimentary stand-ards. His mother obliged him to put on new and new-smelling clothes: the green velvet cap has already been mentioned, in addi-tion there were polo shirts, sand-gray knee breeches of expensive material, a blue blazer with mother-of-pearl buttons, and—possibly at Amsel's request—patent-leather shoes with buckles; for Amsel had no objection to buckles or patent leather, he had no objection to mother-of-pearl buttons or blazer, it was only the prospect of all these new things actually touching his skin, the skin, it should not be forgotten, of a scarecrow builder, that gave him the creeps, espe-cially as Amsel reacted to fresh underwear and unworn clothes with an itching rash; just as Brauxel, if he shaves with a fresh blade, must fear the onset of the dread barber's itch.

Fortunately Walter Matern was in a position to help his friend. His school clothes were made of turned cloth, his high shoes had already been twice to the shoemaker's, Walter Matern's thrifty mother had bought his high school cap secondhand. And so for a good two weeks the trip in the narrow-gauge railway began with the same ceremony: in one of the freight cars, amid unsuspecting cattle on their way to the slaughterhouse, the friends changed clothes. The shoes and cap presented no problem, but though Walter Matern was hardly emaciated, his jacket, knee breeches, and shirt were too tight for his friend. Yet uncomfortable as they were, they were a blessed relief, because they had been worn and turned, because they smelled old and not new. Needless to say, Amsel's new clothes hung down limp and loose on his friend's frame, and patent leather and buckles, mother-of-pearl buttons, and the ridiculous blazer looked odd on him. Amsel, with his scarecrow builder's feet in rough, deeply furrowed clodhoppers, was nevertheless delighted at the sight of his patent-leather shoes on Walter Matern's feet. Walter Matern had to break them in until Amsel pronounced them worn and found them just as cracked as the cracked patent-leather shoe that lay in his school satchel and meant something.

To anticipate, this exchange of clothing was for years a component, though not the cement, of the friendship between Walter Matern and Eduard Ansel. Even handkerchiefs, which his mother had slipped lovingly into his pocket, fresh and folded hem to hem, had to be initiated by his friend, and the same went for socks and stockings. And the exchange didn't stop at clothing; Amsel betrayed similar feelings about new pencils and pens: Walter Matern had to sharpen his pencils, take the shape off his new erasers, break in his Sütterlin pens — he would assuredly, like Brauksel's handyman, have had to initiate Amsel's new razor blades if reddish down had already ripened on Amsel's freckleface [pp. 71-72].

Joyce, in *A Portrait of the Artist as a Young Man* (1916), depicts two different kinds of fetishistic behavior patterns in Stephen Daedalus. When he was ten, "Mother was sitting at the fire with Dante waiting for Brigid to bring in the tea. She had her feet on the fender and her jewelly slippers were so hot and they had such a lovely warm smell!" (p. 10). When odors normally felt to be repulsive become pleasurable, the olfactory sense becomes a source of erotic pleasure and takes precedence over genitally focused desires. Respiratory incorporation plays an important role in fixation on anal erotism and smelling (Bak, 1953). The second manifestation of Stephen Daedalus' fetishism occurred at two different times when he was at school, away from home and mother.

"He crouched down between the sheets, glad of their tepid glow" (Joyce, p. 21). And later, when he was in an agony of self-pity for his initial failure as a poet, he retreated from the world temporarily into the womb: "Shrinking from that life he turned towards the wall, making a cowl of his blanket" (p. 221). The transitional object itself, Greenacre (1960, p. 208) states, "is a monument to the need for . . . contact with the mother's body, which is so touchingly expressed in the infant's insistent preference for an object which is lasting, soft, pliable, warm to the touch, but especially in the demand that it remain saturated with body odors."

In Joyce's *Ulysses* (1918), Molly recalls her first meaningful romance with Jack Joe Harry Mulvey: ". . . weeks and weeks I kept the handkerchief under my pillow for the smell of him there was no decent perfume to be got in that Gibraltar only that cheap peau despagne that faded and left a stink on you more than anything else" (p. 747). Peau d'Espagne, which Molly noted with such scorn in her subtle pun, is a highly complex and luxurious perfume, "often the scent of sensuous persons . . . which most nearly approaches the odor of a woman's skin" (Ellis, 1906, p. 99). Hirschfeld (1935) cites the case of a fetishist who, after he cut the lock of a woman's hair, went home and kissed it repeatedly, pressing it to his nose and cheeks and breathing in its precious fragrance. In fetishism, the object is often selected because its odors are anal or genital in nature. Millie, the hermaphrodite in Friedman's (1972) *Hermaphrodeity,* reminisces in her old age: "And the smell of my feet, which has gotten stronger with age like cheese — well, would it really shock you if I said I liked it?" (p. 4). In Genet's (1953) *Funeral Rites,* Riton is in love with Erik and hopes his love will be returned:

> With infinite delicacy Riton took his handkerchief from his pocket, wet it silently with saliva, and slipped it through his fly and between his legs, which were slightly drawn up so that he could clean his "bronze eye" properly.
> "You think he'll stick it up me? Oh well, you never know." He wanted less to be ready for the act than to be ready for love. He rubbed a little, then took out the handkerchief so as to wet it again, happy to smell beneath his nostrils and on his lips the odor of sweat and shit. This discreet and careful grooming enchanted him [pp. 152-153].

Some men crave the smell of a definite zone of the body. The smell of linen, underwear, worn apparel, and the like may also become sexual stimulants (Stekel, 1922). Most people, however, are unaware of their fetishisms. "This is what endows the sudden falling in love with a sense of mystery in the minds of lovers. They do not know that what attracted and bound them to their love objective as a particular odor or bodily part, some characteristic gesture or motion, and they rationalize this attraction by referring to psychic qualities such as similar tastes, mutual understanding, harmonious convictions, etc." (Stekel, 1926, p. 30).

The smell of leather has a curiously stimulating sexual influence on many people. It is an odor, says Ellis (1906, pp. 100-102), "which seems to occupy an intermediate place between the natural body odors and . . . artificial perfumes. . . . Possibly it is to this fact that its occasional sexual influence is owing, for . . . there is a tendency for sexual allurement to attach to odors which are not specifically personal body odors but yet related to them. . . . Shoe fetishism, perhaps the most frequent of sexual fetishistic perversions, is greatly favored, if indeed, it does not owe its origin to the association of the foot and of the shoes. . . . The secret of the influence [of leather] . . . is that leather is animal skin and . . . may thus vaguely stir the olfactory sensibilities which had been ancestrally affected by the sexual stimulation of the skin odor. . . ."

The relation of the nose to fetishism is as well documented as the physiological relation of the nose to the genitalia, which in turn reflects its psychological grounding. Since Freud (1918) pointed it out, the bi-sexual nature of symbols and of psychogenic organic symptoms is well known (Abraham, 1920; Jones, 1938). Evidence includes nosebleeds with menstruation, acute nasal congestion and increased nasal secretions during sexual intercourse, sneezing associated with coitus, and sexual excitation in general. "Acute or chronic nasal congestion also markedly lowers the threshold of olfactory sensitivity and serves as an efficient deodorant, particularly in people who retain a strong olfactory sensitivity" (Wilson, 1948, p. 339). In describing Gogol's fictional work, Nabokov (1944) declares a nasal leitmotif runs throughout it. "It is hard to find any other author who has described with such gusto smells, sneezes and snores. . ." (p. 9). Characters fondle their own and each other's noses, one drunkard tries to saw off the nose of another, and a madman discovers that the inhabitants of the moon are noses. In the short story, "The Nose" (1835), there is a phallic displacement upward. All the evidence indicates Gogol's nasal obsession as a displacement of sexual conflicts. Studies assessing the motivation behind rhinoplasty suggest unconscious themes of heterosexual conflicts (Book, 1971). The attempt to disguise or conceal the offending organ may be prompted because of the smelling of unacceptable sexual odors. Sexual conflicts as well can be displaced onto the nose, and rhinoplasty may then become an unconscious symbolic solution.

In their study of the psychophysiological role of odors as they affect asthmatics, Stein and Ottenberg (1958) used nineteen odorants which were classified as having oral, anal, and genital qualities, fourteen of which belonged to the anal group. The asthmatics blocked associations to all classes of odors significantly more than did the controls. Other asthmatics reported attacks that were related to odors or events having anal symbolism. The hypothesis presented was that the asthmatic attack was a defense against odors that reactivated childhood anal conflicts. Kepecs, Robin, and Monro (1958) found that patients with asthma reacted more strongly to odor than to other stimuli, with anal responses predominating. Dunbar (1938) also reported overaccentuation of anal-sadistic qualities of asthmatics. Jarvis (1969) described a patient whose anal-phallic defenses led to an overinvestment in flatus, "shooting" diarrhea, and toilet noises. The overevaluation of flatus was symbolically connected with words, breath, and fertilization, which has been explored by Jones (1951). The patient's erotization and aggressive use of intestinal functioning, its smells and noises, were of primary importance in the early onset of asthma. Wilson's (1948) asthmatic and hay fever patients demonstrated an extremely acute sense of smell when they were free of symptoms, but their acuity became very much lessened with the advent of either symptom. He concluded that a psychological component was involved, based on displacement of sexual curiosity from the visual to the olfactory sphere.

At the age of two, with the birth of a younger brother, Theodore Roosevelt experienced his first asthmatic attack. A synergistic relationship between mother and child developed. The neurotic infantilism of the mother led to an adient response by the boy, and the asthma further facilitated the infantilizing process. The strong attachment for the mother and the sublimated libidinal gratifications were secondary gains. These were offset by marked conflict over anality; in Roosevelt there was relinquishment of anal pleasures through both the intestinal tract and the respiratory outlet. His aggression and anger were revealed in his obsessional hobby of wild-game hunting and stuffing birds and animals. Until his fourteenth year, and continuing in a diminishing vein for several additional years, Roosevelt identified himself as a sickly, incapacitated child, preoccupied with morbid and solitary activities, and retreating from heterosexual and peer object relations. The maternal symbiosis persisted even with marriage; his first wife replicated his mother. His sister Corinne served as an unconscious, sublimated displacement for his unresolved and frustrated oedipal wishes. He survived the rivalry with his father through the processes of reaction formation, identification, and sublimation (Kiell, 1963).

No less distressed by his asthmatic condition was Marcel Proust who suffered a severe form of it from childhood on. Miller (1956) states, in his analytic study of Proust:

> To a large extent we may piece together an account of Proust's own insights in regard to his homosexuality, including his realization of his abnormal interest in his mother, his renunciation of interest in girls, his strong identification with the women in the family, probably also his secret wish for, and fear of, a truly virile male partner. But we find available very much less self-analysis regarding Proust's asthma, except that it seemed the penalty for artistic achievement. The conflicts that were symbolically represented by his asthmatic symptoms seem to have been most obscure to him, least verbalized, most deeply related to the earliest, inarticulate levels of body expression, including the vague "Proustian" symbols connected with the sea, rooms, or air. Proust recognized that some emotional components of his asthma did exist, and he tied them up inconclusively with his homosexuality. He knew, only too early, the nostalgic importance of breathing and of odors. Fragrances of Combray recall most vividly for Marcel the reality of childhood days. . . . Evil odors are frequently his villains: for instance the poisonous smell of the staircase that separated Marcel from his mother, in Swann's Way—or the odor of asparagus by which Françoise tortured Eulalie. Flowers...were prime messengers of love and beauty for the real Marcel Proust, but flowers and the perfume of princesses were especially intolerable to him in later life . . . In general, he seems to have connected flowers with forbidden, alluring odors, and unconsciously with female sexuality [pp. 189-190].

Proust, as is known, buried himself in a cork-lined, sound-proof room, which may have been a defense to protect himself, during asthma attacks, against explosive materials from the instinctual drives. Krichhauff (1956) in his study of the inner world of the asthmatic found that the attacks expressed antagonistic, aggressive strivings against the environment, a view of the world providing nothing and endangering existence. Powerful feelings of guilt were released, and orality and aggression were linked. Numerous expressions made by the neurotic asthmatics illustrated their particular sensitivity to smell and their feelings of emptiness. Anality played a large role. Strong dependency feelings and mother fixations, as with Proust, were expressed through complaining about money. In large measure, Proust radically suppressed his oral and anal impulses, and thereby his sense of smell, consequently narrowing his affective range. Sublimation occurred by concentrating on the controlled manners of social intercourse in high society.

Anxieties about smell, and particularly anxieties about smell related to sexuality, are reflected not only in the homosexual, where pleasure is deeply repressed, often to the extent of estheticism (Ferenczi, 1914) as with Proust, but in a variety of ways. For example, Pombal in Lawrence Durrell's (1957) *Justine,* a minor consular official in the French diplomatic service, entertained colleagues with cocktail parties in order to insure his job and to curry favor with a superior. However, he found the boredom and expense of the parties excruciating and explained to his roomate, Darley, in tones of misery, the origin of this function: "The cocktail party—as the name implies—was originally invented by dogs. They are simply bottom-sniffings raised to the rank of formal ceremonials" (p. 172). On another level, of anxiety, Stephen Daedalus, in Joyce's (1916) *A Portrait of the Artist as a Young Man,* listened—along with the other schoolboys—in chapel to the Father's sermon on the foulness of hell.

> The horror of this strait and dark prison is increased by its awful stench. All the filth of the world, all the offal and scum of the world, we are told, shall run there as to a vast reeking sewer when the terrible conflagration of the last day has purged the world. The brimstone too which burns there in such prodigious quantity fills all hell with its intolerable stench; and the bodies of the damned themselves exhale such a pestilential odour that as saint Bonaventura says, one of them alone would suffice to infect the whole world. The very air of this world, that pure element, becomes foul and unbreathable when it has been long enclosed. Consider then what must be the foulness of the air of hell. Imagine some foul and putrid corpse that has lain rotting and decomposing in the grave, a jellylike mass of liquid corruption. Imagine such a corpse a prey to flames, devoured by the fire of burning brimstone and giving off dense choking fumes of nauseous loathesome decomposition. And then imagine this sickening stench,

multiplied a millionfold and a millionfold again from the millions upon millions of fetid carcasses massed together in the reeking darkness, a huge and rotting human fungus. Imagine all this and you will have some idea of the horror of the stench of hell [p. 120].

This stench, the priest concluded, was one of the greatest horrible physical torments to which the damned are subjected. Differently perceived, the greatest horror might very well have been the anxieties the priest aroused in the malleable minds of the youngsters, brought about by his emphasis on smell. It was a different story when Flaubert found "the greatest poetic synthesis" in a Jaffe cemetery where the fragrance of lemon blossoms mingled with the stench of the rotting cadavers (Praz, 1933, p. 29), or in William Faulkner's subtle and gruesome treatment of the odors of decay and death in "A Rose for Emily." "The noun *rose* does not appear in the short story itself; but when the bridal suite is broken open after Miss Emily's death, there was a 'thin, acrid pall . . . upon the valance curtains of faded rose color, upon the rose-shaded lights. . . .' The adjectival use of *rose* at the end of the story harks back to the title and links the idea of local curiosity [and] admiration for Emily with the perverted love-death of the bridal chamber" (Going, 1957-1958).

Hemingway's description of the smell of death, with its heavily scored accent on sexuality, in *For Whom the Bell Tolls* (1940), is another anxiety-producing account, as Pilar tried to make Robert Jordan and the other guerrillas understand. There are several ingredients in recognizing the smell of death, Pilar instructs the men. The first is to put the "nose up against the brass handle of a screwed-tight porthole on a rolling ship that is swaying under you so that you are faint and hollow in the stomach and you have part of that smell" (p. 244). The men joke about this until Pilar goes on to elaborate the second criterion for smelling death. It is to go to the *matadero* before dawn, stand on the wet pavement in the mist, and "wait for the old women who . . . drink the blood of the beasts who are slaughtered. When such an old woman comes out of the matadero, holding her shawl around her, with her face grey and her eyes hollow, set in the warm waxen white of her face as the sprouts grow from the seed of a bean, not bristles, but pale sprouts in the death of her face; put your arms around her, *Inglés,* and hold her to you and kiss her on the mouth and you will know the second part that odour is made of" (p. 244). The men joke, in their fear: "That one has taken my appetite . . . that of the sprouts was too much." Pilar is relentless.

"Kiss one [she insists]. Kiss one, *Inglés,* for thy knowledge's sake and then, with this in thy nostrils, walk back up into the city and when thou seest a refuse pail with dead flowers in it plunge thy nose deep into it and inhale so that the scent mixes with those thou hast already in thy nasal passages" (p. 245). Here Robert Jordan facetiously asks Pilar what kind of flowers. Undeterred, she responds, "Chrysanthemums," and proceeds remorselessly to the fourth level of recognition, which is to go along the streets of the prostitutes, "smelling what thou wilt smell where they are sweeping out the *casas de putas* and emptying the slop jars into the drains and, with this odour of labour lost mixed sweetly with soapy water and cigarette butts only faintly reaching the nostrils, thou shouldst go on to the Jardín Botánico where at night those girls who can no longer work in the houses do their work against the iron gates of the park and the iron picket fences and upon the sidewalks. It is there in the shadow of the trees against the iron railings that they will perform all that a man wishes; from the simplest request at a remuneration of ten centimos up to a peseta for that great act that we are born to and there, on a dead flower bed that has not yet been plucked out and replanted, and so serves to soften the earth that is so much softer than the sidewalk, thou will find an abandoned gunny sack with the odour of the wet earth, the dead flowers, and the doings of that night. In this sack will be contained the essence of it all, both the dead earth and the dead stalks of the flowers and their rotted blooms and the smell that is both the death and the birth of man. Thou will wrap this sack around thy head and try to breathe through it . . . and then, if thou hast not lost any of the previous odours, when thou inhalest deeply, thou wilt smell the odour of death-to-come as we know it" (pp. 245-246.)

Durrell, too, in his *Clea* (1960) links the smell of death to sexuality. Clea "feared . . . that the vulgar blood-soaked reality of this war world which spread around her might one day poison and infect our own kisses. Is it fastidious to want to keep your head, to avoid this curious sexual rush of blood to the head which comes with war, exciting the women beyond endurance? I would not have thought the smell of death could be so exciting to them!" (p. 104).

Obsessive anxieties about odors are in constant play in the fiction of Norman Mailer. As Hyman (1966, p. 277) details in *An American Dream* (1965): the "characters emanate a curious melange of odors. Before he cleanses himself by strangling Deborah, Rojack smells 'like the rotten, carious shudder of a decayed tooth.' Deborah's smell is compounded of 'sweet rot,' 'burning rubber,' and 'a bank.' The Nazi maid has 'a thin high constipated smell.' A pair of detectives give off, respectively, 'a kind of clammy odor of rut,' and 'the funk a bully emits when he heads for a face-to-face meeting.' Ganucci exudes 'an essence of disease, some moldering from the tree of death.' Cherry smells 'of something sweet and strong,' among its elements 'the back seats of cars.' The principal detective smells 'sour with use, and also too sweet.' Shago's odor is 'a poisonous snake of mood which entered my lungs like marijuana,' and later 'a smell of full nearness as if we'd been in bed for an hour.' Kelly emits 'some whiff of the icy rot and iodine in a piece of marine nerve left to bleach on the sand,' varied by 'stench [that] comes from the devotion to the goat.' " Mailer dwells obsessively on the reek of putrefaction, body stench, vomit and other excreta, and the foul offensiveness of every human presence, which relates aptly to his theme that God and Satan are at war and Satan is winning. This excerpt from his *The Deer Park* (1955) is indicative of Mailer's obsession:

> Once we were dressed, Lulu told me she could smell herself. "I have the most awful body odor, Sugar."
> "All I can smell is your perfume."
> "No, you have no sense of smell. I tell you, I know it's there. That happens to people, they suddenly develop terrible smells and they have them for the rest of their lives."
> "Where do you pick up these witches?"
> "I know someone it happened to. Sugar, I have to take a bath."
> She bathed, she bathed again. She got me to powder her; she had now decided the smell was somewhere in the room. "Oh, it's awful," she cried aloud.
> For several days she was taking baths all the time. Then she decided she had breast cancer, she ordered me to search for a lump. I told her to see a doctor... [pp. 143-144].

Lawrence Durrell's work is also marked by a pervasive preoccupation with odors. In *Justine* (1957) alone, the first of the Alexandria Quartet, a book of some 250 pages, there are forty-seven references to odors, about one for every five pages. For example, Justine "could not help but remind me of that race of terrific queens which left behind them the ammoniac smell of their incestuous loves to hover like a cloud over the Alexandrian subsconscious" (p. 11). Justine recalled in her diary an olfactory memory of her childhood in the dense Attarine Quarter of polyglot Alexandria: "The old money-lender drunk and snoring, drawing in with every breath the compost-odours, soil, excrement, the droppings of bats; gutters choked with leaves and breadcrumbs softened by piss; yellow wreaths of jasmine, heady, meretricious" (p. 55). Darley, the narrator and one of Justine's lovers, remembered "The smell of the sweat-lathered Berberinis, like that of some decomposing staircarpet" (p. 15). Walking through the Egyptian quarter of the town, "the smell of flesh changes — ammoniac, sandal-wood, saltpetre, spice, fish" (p. 59). Another time, riding in a taxi with Justine, "In that palpitant moist heat, dense from the rising damps of the river and aching with the stink of rotten fruit, jasmine and sweating black bodies, I caught sight of the very ordinary man in the taxi next to us" (p. 74), a man who he later discovered had traumatized Justine by raping her when she was too young to understand what was happening. An illustration from Durrell's *Balthazar* (1958), the second volume in the Alexandria Quartet, depicts how Scobie, an expatriate, transvestite Englishman, "paused to inhale the draught of cooking Arab bread from the doorway of a shop and the old man exclaimed 'It smells like mother's lap!" (p. 50). Scobie was nearing seventy, yet the odor of baking bread instantaneously betrayed a sexual memory of his mother.

The tyranny of the unconscious denies many people the pregenital satisfactions of olfaction; yet despite the apparent denial, olfactory sensitivity is far greater than is commonly supposed, and olfactory phenomena figure more importantly in human functioning than is commonly recognized (Wayne and Clinco, 1959, p. 65). It is not rare for transitory olfactory illusions to appear in the analytic hour (Ferenczi, 1912). Patients, in the course of a vivid recollection, may "smell" the odor that was present at the event (Bieber, 1959, p. 851). "Through smell, taste, touch we apprehend each other, ignite each other's minds," Clea told Darley after her first experience of sexual intercourse with a man in Syria, as Durrell relates in his novel, *Clea* (1960).

Information conveyed by the body's odors after orgasm, breath, tongue-taste — through these one "knows" in quite primeval fashion. Here was a perfectly ordinary man with no exceptional gifts but in his elements, so to speak, how good for me; he gave off the odours of good national objects: like newly baked bread, roasting coffee, cordite, sandalwood.... Paracelsus says that thoughts are acts. Of them all, I suppose, the sex act is the most important, the one in which our spirits most divulge themselves. Yet one feels it is a sort of clumsy paraphrase of the poetic, the noetic, thought which shapes itself into a kiss or an embrace. Sexual love *is* knowledge, both in etymology and in cold fact; "he knew her" as the Bible says! Sex is the joint or coupling which unites the male and female ends of knowledge mere-ly—a cloud of unknowing! We women know that ... [pp. 112-113].

While olfactory cues as a means of sexual attraction can be observed in many animals, Western man utilizes smell cues to a minimum. Considering olfaction along phylogenetic lines, researchers have related odors to mating of ants (Cavill and Robertson, 1965); pheromonal communication for signaling mates in extremely sensitive and female moths have been known to attract males over long distances (Bute-nandt, 1963); chemical signals are of primary importance in sexual attraction with beetles (Henzell and Lowe, 1970); in male hamsters, there is total elimination of sexual activity via olfactory bulb excision (Murphy and Schneider, 1970). The work on releaser and primer pheromones, demonstrated to be widespread in all social insects, suggests that such chemical communication is also to be found in both higher and lower organisms. Indeed, Regnier and Law (1968) think it possible that pheromonal systems might be present in man, "and it is even possible that man has generally lost awareness of them because he has developed other effective communicative systems" (p. 550). Com-fort (1971) also writes about the likelihood of human pheromones. In point of fact, Michael, Bonsall, and Warner (1974) report the actual presence of pheromones in humans, a possibility heretofore subject only to speculation. Their team isolated aromatic chemicals from the vagi-nal secretions of young women, identifying several volatile aliphatic acids such as acetic acid, propanic acid, and butanic acid in the secre-tions they collected. These same substances in rhesus monkeys act as sex attractants. Whether or not they attract human males is not yet known and Michael asserts that determining the effects of the chemical signals in humans will be difficult. Although the sense of smell has too long been ignored in studies of human and infrahuman species, and has been relegated to a role of little importance, recent experimental studies using olfaction as a dependent variable have begun to take their proper place in the literature. As these studies progress, we might predict that anthropocentric bias will yield to surer scientific certainty.

TECHNICAL REFERENCES

Abraham, K. (1920), Manifestations of the female castration complex. In: *Selected Papers.* New York: Basic Books, 1953, pp. 338-369.

_____ (1921), Contributions to the theory of the anal character. In: *Selected Papers.* New York: Basic Books, 1953, pp. 370-392.

Bak, R. C. (1953), Fetishism. *Journal of the American Psychoanalytic Association,* 1:285-298.

Beauvoir, S. de (1953), *The Second Sex.* New York: Knopf.

Bergler, E. (1955), G. Bose's psychology of smell and a case of "stink neurosis." *Samiksa,* 9:2-8.

Bieber, I. (1959), Olfaction in sexual development and adult sexual organization. *American Journal of Psychotherapy,* 13:851-859.

_____ (1970), Sexual response to odors. *Medical Aspects of Human Sexuality,* 4(10): 170.

Boardman, G. R. (1970), Greek hero and Japanese Samurai: Mishima's new aesthetic. *Critique,* 12:103-115.

Bonaparte, M. (1949), *Psychoanalytic Interpretations of Stories by Edgar Allen Poe.* London: Imago.

Book, H. W. (1971), Sexual implications of the nose. *Comprehensive Psychiatry,* 12:450-455.

Brill, A. A. (1932), The sense of smell in the neuroses and psychoses. *Psychoanalytic Quarterly,* 1:7-42.

Burchell, S. C. (1928), Marcel Proust, an interpretation of his life. *Psychoanalytic Review,* 15:300-303.

Butenandt, A. (1963), Proceedings of the society for endocrinology. *Endocrinology,* 27(9): ix-xvi.

Carr, D. W. (1972), *The Forgotten Senses.* Garden City, N.Y.: Doubleday.

Cavill, G. W. K. & Robertson, P. L. (1965), Ant venoms, attractants, and repellents. *Science,* 149:1337-1345.

Comfort, A. (1971), The likelihood of human pheromones. *Nature,* 230:432-433, 479.

Dunbar, H. F. (1938), Psychoanalytic notes relating to syndromes of asthma and hay fever. *Psychoanalytic Quarterly,* 7:25-68.

Ellis, H. (1906), *Studies in the Psychology of Sex,* Vol. 2, New York: Random House, 1936.

Engle, B. S. (1942), The Amazons in ancient Greece. *Psychoanalytic Quarterly,* 11:512-554.

Ferenczi, S. (1909), Introjection and transference. In: *Sex in Psycho-Analysis.* New York: Basic Books, 1955, pp. 35-93.

_____ (1912), Transitory symptom-construction during analysis. In: *Sex in Psycho-Analysis.* New York: Basic Books, 1955, p. 193-211.

_____ (1914), The ontogenesis of the interest in money. In: *Sex in Psycho-Analysis.* New York: Basic Books, 1955, pp. 319-331.

_____ (1933), *Thalassa: A Theory of Genitality.* New York: Psychoanalytic Quarterly, 1938.

Fiedler, L. (1960), *Love and Death in the American Novel.* London: Paladin, 1970.

Fitzherbert, J. (1959), Scent and the sexual object. *British Journal of Medical Psychology,* 32:206-209.

Freeman, S. K. (1969), Discussion: Odor and communication. *Annals of the New York Academy of Science,* 163:406-412.

Freud, S. (1887-1902), *The Origins of Psychoanalysis.* New York: Basic Books, 1954.

_____ (1905), Three essays on the theory of sexuality. *Standard Edition,* 7:125-243. London: Hogarth Press, 1953.

_____ (1909), Notes upon a case of obsessional neurosis. *Standard Edition,* 10:153-249. London: Hogarth Press, 1955.

_____ (1915), On narcissism. *Standard Edition,* 14:69-102. London: Hogarth Press, 1953.

_____ (1918), From the history of an infantile neurosis. *Standard Edition,* 17:3-122. London: Hogarth Press, 1955.

_____ (1930), Civilization and its discontents. *Standard Edition,* 21:59-145. London: Hogarth Press, 1953.

Friedman, P. (1959), Some observations on the sense of smell. *Psychoanalytic Quarterly,* 28:307-329.

Garma, A. (1955), Serpentine ornamentation and anal regression. *American Imago,* 12:293-297.

Gide, A. (1911), *Corydon.* New York: Farrar, Strauss, 1950.

Going, W. T. (1957-1958), Faulkner's *A Rose for Emily. Explicator,* 16(27).

Gorman, W. F. (1964), *Flavor, Taste and the Psychology of Smell.* Springfield, Ill.: Thomas.

Greenacre, P. (1960), Considerations regarding the parent-infant relationship. In: *Emotional Growth.* New York: International Universities Press, 1971, pp. 199-224.

_____ (1966), Problems of overidealization of the analyst and of analysis: Their manifestations in the transference and countertransference relationship. In: *Emotional Growth.* New York: International Universities Press, 1971, pp. 743-761.

_____ (1969), The fetish and the transitional object. In: *Emotional Growth.* New York: International Universities Press, 1971, pp. 315-334.

Grinstein, A. (1961), Freud's dream of botanical monography. *Journal of the American Psychoanalytic Association,* 9:480-503.

Hardy, J. E. (1964), *Man in the Modern Novel.* Seattle: University of Washington Press.

Harlow, H. (1958), The nature of love. *American Psychologist,* 13:673-685.

_____ & Suomi, S. J. (1970), Nature of love. *American Psychologist,* 25:161-168.

_____ & Zimmerman, R. R. (1959), Development of affectual responses in infant monkeys. *Science,* 146:421-432.

Henzell, R. F. & Lowe, M. D. (1970), Sex attractant of the grass grub beetle. *Science,* 168:1005-1006.

Hirschfeld, M. (1935), *Sex in Human Relationships.* London: Lane.

Hyman, S. E. (1966), *Standards.* New York: Horizon Press.

Jackson, J. H. (1899), Warnings of a crude sense of smell. In: *Selected Writings of J. Hughlings Jackson,* Vol. 2, ed. J. Taylor. New York: Basic Books, 1958, p. 156.

Jarvis, V. (1969), On a note on "the pill" and emotional conflict. *Psychoanalytic Quarterly,* 38:639-642.

Jones, E. (1938), The theory of symbolism. In: *Papers on Psycho-Analysis.* Boston: Beacon Press, 1961, pp. 87-144.

_____ (1951), The madonna's conception through the ear. In: *Essays in Applied Psycho-Analysis,* Vol. 2. New York: International Universities Press, 1964, pp. 266-357.

Karpman, B. (1942), Neurotic traits in Jonathan Swift as revealed in *Gulliver's Travels. Psychoanalytic Review,* 29:26-45, 165-184.

Kepecs, J. G., Robin, M. & Munro, C. (1958), Responses to sensory stimulation in certain psychosomatic disorders. *Psychosomatic Medicine,* 20:351-365.

Kiell, N. (1963), Effects of asthma on the character of Theodore Roosevelt. In: *The Asthmatic Child. Psychosomatic Approach to Problems and Treatment,* ed. H. I. Schneer. New York: Hoeber Medical Division, Harper & Row, pp. 84-102.

Krichhauff, G. (1956), The asthmatic and his inner world. *Zeitschrift fur Psychosom-atische Medicin,* 2:118-126.

Krütch, J. W. (1934), Introduction. *Remembrance of Things Past,* by M. Proust. New York: Random House.

Kubie, L. (1937), The fantasy of dirt. *Psychoanalytic Quarterly,* 6:388-425.

Lederer, W. (1968), *The Fear of Women.* New York: Grune & Stratton.

Lewin, B. D. (1953), Reconsideration of the dream screen. *Psychoanalytic Quarterly,* 22:174-199.

Marcuse, H. (1962), *Eros and Civilization.* New York: Vintage.

McLean, P. D. (1965), New findings relevant to the evolution of psychosexual functions of the brain. In: *Sex Research, New Developments,* ed. J. Money. New York: Holt, Rhinehart & Winston, pp. 197-218.

Michael, R. P., Bonsall, R. W. & Warner, P. (1974), Human vaginal secretions: Volatile fatty acid content. *Science,* 186:1217-1219.

Miller, M. L. (1956), *Nostalgia: A Psychoanalytic Study of Marcel Proust.* Boston: Houghton Mifflin.

Moncrieff, R. W. (1966), *Odour Preference.* New York: Wiley.

Money, J. (1965), Psychosexual differentiation. In: *Sex Research. New Developments,* ed. J. Money. New York: Holt, Rhinehart & Winston, pp. 3-23.

Murphy, M. R. & Schneider, G. E. (1970), Olfactory bulb removal eliminates mating behavior in the male golden hamster. *Science,* 16:302-303.

Nabokov, V. (1944), *Nikolai Gogol.* London: Nicholson & Watson, 1947.

Orbach, C. E., Bard, M. & Sutherland, A. M. (1957), Fears and defensive adaptations to the loss of anal sphincter control. *Psychoanalytic Review,* 44:121-175.

Otto, H. A. & Otto, R. (1972), *Total Sex.* New York: Wyden.

Papez, J. (1959), Neuroanatomy. In: *American Handbook of Psychiatry,* Vol. 2, ed. S. Arieti. New York: Basic Books, pp. 1585-1619.

Playboy (1972), Playboy advisor. *Playboy,* 19(3):41.

Praz, M. (1933), *The Romantic Agony.* New York: Meridian, 1956.

Regnier, F. E. & Law, J. H. (1968), Insect pheromones. *Journal of Lipid Research,* 9:541-551.

Sagarin, E. (1961), The sense of smell and sex. In: *The Encyclopedia of Sexual Behavior,* Vol. 2, ed. A. Ellis & A. Abarbanel. New York: Hawthorne, pp. 976-978.

Schachtel, E. (1947), On memory and childhood amnesia. *Psychiatry,* 10:1-26.

Schneider, R. A. (1971), The sense of smell and human sexuality. *Medical Aspects of Human Sexuality,* 5(5):157-168.

Smythies, J. R. (1956), The experience and description of the human body. *Brain,* 76:132.

Spitz, R. A. (1955), The primal cavity. *The Psychoanalytic Study of the Child,* 10:215-240. New York: International Universities Press.

Stansky, P. & Abrahams, W. (1972), *The Unknown Orwell.* New York: Knopf.

Stein, M. & Ottenberg, P. (1958), Role of odors in asthma. *Psychosomatic Medicine,* 20:60-65.

——— ——— & Roulet, N. (1958), A study of the development of olfactory preferences. *Archives of Neurology & Psychiatry,* 80:264-266.

Stekel, W. (1922), *Patterns of Psychosexual Infantilism.* New York: Liveright, 1952.

——— (1926), *Frigidity in Women,* Vol. 1. New York: Boni & Liveright.

Ujhely, V. A. (1953), An unusual case of renifleurism. *American Journal of Psychotherapy,* 7:68-71.

Van de Velde, T. H. (1926), *Ideal Marriage. Its Physiology and Technique.* New York: Random House, 1941.

Wayne, G. G. & Clinco, A. C. (1959), Psychoanalytic observations on olfaction, with special reference to olfactory dreams. *Psychoanalysis & Psychoanalytic Review,* 46(4):65-79.

Wickler, W. (1969), *The Sexual Code. The Social Behavior of Animals and Men.* Garden City, N.Y.: Doubleday.

Wilson, G. W. (1948), A further contribution to the study of olfactory representation with particular reference to transvestitism. *Psychoanalytic Quarterly,* 17:322-329.

Wormhoudt, A. (1950), *The Demon Lover; A Psychoanalytic Approach to Literature.* New York: Exposition.

Wulff, M. (1946), Fetishism and object choice in early childhood. *Psychoanalytic Quarterly,* 15:450-471.

LITERARY REFERENCES

Amis, Kingsley (1971), *Girl, 20.* New York: Harcourt Brace Jovanovitch.

Arent, Arthur (1969), *The Laying on of Hands.* Boston: Little, Brown.

Barnes, Djuna (1937), *Nightwood.* Norfolk, Conn.: New Directions.

Berger, John (1972), *G.* New York: Viking.

Butler, Samuel (1885), *The Way of All Flesh.* London: Dent, 1933.

Camus, Albert (1965), *The Stranger.* New York: Knopf.

_____ (1972), *A Happy Death.* New York: Knopf.

Chin P'ing Mei (1609), *The Adventurous History of Hsi Men and His Six Wives.* New York: Putnam's, 1940.

Durrell, Lawrence (1957), *Justine.* New York: Dutton.

_____ (1958), *Balthazar.* New York: Dutton.

_____ (1960), *Clea.* New York: Dutton.

Epstein, Seymour (1967), *Caught in That Music.* New York: Viking.

Faulkner, William (n.d.), A rose for Emily. In: *Collected Stories of William Faulkner.* New York: Random House, pp. 119-130.

Fiedler, Leslie (1963), *The Second Stone.* New York: Stein & Day.

Friedman, Alan (1972), *Hermaphrodeity.* New York: Knopf.

Genet, Jean (1953), *Funeral Rites.* New York: Grove, 1969.

Gogol, Nikolai (1835), The nose. In: *The Overcoat and Other Tales of Good and Evil.* Toronto: McCloud. 1957.

Goncourt, Edmond de (1884), *Cherie.* Paris: Flamarion, 1920.

Grass, Günter (1963), *Dog Years.* New York: Harcourt, Brace & World, 1965.

Hemingway, Ernest (1933), Fathers and sons. In: *The Nick Adams Stories.* New York: Scribner's, 1972.

_____ (1940), *For Whom the Bell Tolls.* New York: Scribner's.

Huxley, Aldous (1932), *Brave New World.* New York: Harper & Row.

Huysmans, Joris-Karl (1880), Le Gousset. In: *Croquis Parisiens.* Paris: Plon-Nourrit.

Joyce, James (1916), *A Portrait of the Artist as a Young Man.* New York: Viking, 1964.

_____ (1918), *Ulysses.* New York: Random House, 1934.

Kazantzakis, Nikos (1952), *Zorba the Greek.* New York: Simon & Schuster.

Klose, Kevin & McCombs, Philip A. (1974), *The Typhoon Shipments.* New York: Norton.

Lawrence, D. H. (1913), *Sons and Lovers.* New York: Viking, 1962.

Mailer, Norman (1955), *The Deer Park.* New York: Putnam's.

_____ (1965), *An American Dream.* New York: Dial.

Maugham, W. Somerset (1922), Democracy. In: *On a Chinese Screen*. New York: Doran, pp. 140-143.

Melville, Herman (1851), *Moby Dick*. Chicago: Encyclopedia Britannica, 1952.

Merezchkovski, Dmitri S. (1905). *Peter and Alexis, the Romance of Peter the Great*. New York: Putnam's.

Mishima, Yukio (1958), *Confessions of a Mask*. Norwalk, Conn.: New Directions.

Norris, Frank (1899), *McTeague. A Story of San Francisco*. New York: International, 1900.

Orwell, George (1933), *Down and Out in Paris and London*. New York: Harcourt Brace Jovanovitch, 1972.

_____ (1946), *Animal Farm*. New York: Harcourt Brace Jovanovitch, 1954.

_____ (1949), *1984*. New York: New American Library.

Proust, Marcel (1913), *Swann's Way*. New York: Random House, 1934.

_____ (1952), *Jean Santeuil*. New York: Simon & Schuster, 1956.

Robbins, Lawrence (1975), *A Certain Protocol*. New York: Harper & Row.

Steinbeck, John (1945), *Cannery Row*. New York: Viking.

Sulzberger, Cyrus L. (1973), *The Tooth Merchant*. New York: Quadrangle.

Swift, Jonathan (1726), *Gulliver's Travels*. New York: Long & Smith, 1933.

Thorp, Roderick (1972), *Slaves*. New York: Evans.

Updike, John (1968), *Couples*. New York: Knopf.

Westcott, Glenway (1971), The odor of rosemary. *Prose*, 2:171-204.

Wilde, Oscar (1891), *The Picture of Dorian Gray*. In: *The Works of Oscar Wilde*. New York: Black, 1927, pp. 107-256.

CHAPTER FIVE

Male Homosexuality

It is difficult to escape the logic of psychoanalytic theory about homosexuality, particularly when it is confirmed by the creative, intuitive writers of fiction in their portraits of the homosexual personality. Nevertheless, the controversy surrounding the subject, in terms of etiology, dynamics, and treatment, is pervasive, with answers almost as varied as there are individuals concerned with it. From Irving Bieber et al. (1962) to Marmor (1965), Socarides (1968), Ellis (1965), Hooker (1965), and Money (1963), almost endlessly, diagnosis and causes range over an immense spectrum. Homosexuality is by far the most common sexual deviation and as such is prone to overgeneralization. Etiology is unclear, it is suggested, mainly because a number of different phenomena are grouped under the term and because neither genetics, nor endocrinology, nor heredity can account for it. Thus it is felt the deepest morass is found in the causes of homosexuality.

The homosexual himself feels it is wisest to eschew it as presently unanswerable, as a political tactic designed to perpetuate barbaric legal and social discriminations, and as a convenient intellectual outlet for heterosexual condescension (Duberman, 1972). "It is currently possible to cite expert opinion 'proving' that sexual orientation results from prenatal hormonal programming, the psychodynamics of the family structure, or an innate bisexual potential variably activated or repressed according to individual experience, such as confinement in prison, and social climate, which in the United States is sex-negative and homophobic" (p. 6).

Duberman is correct when he asserts there is almost every kind of

217

proof for the causes of homosexuality, depending upon one's orientation. Homosexuality is seen by Hornstra (1967) primarily as a defense against anxiety and not as a search for sexual satisfaction. Rather than viewing it as a result of the oedipal conflict, he holds the disturbance to be one that originates much earlier in the "primeval situation." Gillespie, Pasche, and Wiedeman (1964) feel that although psychoanalytic theory has focused primarily on the oedipal triangle, there must be genetic factors at work. According to Marmor (1967), homosexuality develops as an adaptational response to certain kinds of environmental circumstances including psychodynamic, sociocultural, biological, and specific situational factors. For homosexuality to result, three major factors are needed: impaired gender identity; fear of sexual activity with the opposite sex; and some experience with homosexuality. Horowitz (1964) asserts that homosexuality may be used as an antisocial, antiparental form of acting out, or as a defense against identity diffusion. In her report, Toby Bieber (1967) emphasizes the view that inversion is a pathologic adaptation of submission and heterosexual renunciation arising out of early fears established in family life. The perception of threat from women is a nuclear paranoid mechanism. Homosexuals displace their fear of men to the less frightening feminine object.

Irving Bieber et al. (1971) do not regard homosexuality as a mental illness but rather as a psychologically rooted sexual disorder in the same sense that a chronically frigid woman or impotent man evolves a neurotic condition. Homosexuality develops out of unconscious and unrealistic fears that sexual gratification, or a sexually fulfilling, sustained love relationship with a woman will invite punishment and injury. Homosexuality is thus maladaptive because it is based on fears that are not realistic, not because of cultural unacceptability. Theorizing that heterosexuality is an acquired trait requiring the repression of certain homosexual tendencies natural to human beings, West (1968) maintains that although physical and hereditary factors play a large part in governing the strength of sexual urges psychological factors are more decisive in determining their direction. In a symposium dealing with the causes of homosexuality (Kinsey, Reichert, Cauldwell, and Mozes, 1955), Kinsey indicates these factors as leading to homosexual behavior: "the basic physiologic capacity of every mammal to respond to any sufficient stimulus; the accident which leads an individual into his or her first sexual experience with a person of the same sex; the conditioning effects of such experience; and the indirect but powerful conditioning which the opinions of other persons and the social codes may have on an individual's decision to accept or reject this type of sexual contact" (p. 559). Reichert, in the same discussion, says that an interplay of causes — hormonal imbalance, influence of surroundings, fear of pregnancy, doing what is forbidden, and sexual curiosities of children — may establish homosexual patterns. Mozes (1951) holds that homosexuality is an arrest in sexual development, a fixation caused by excessive emotion in the parent-child relationship and by being subjected to highly adverse parental influences. Inborn traits may render some persons more susceptible to this form of maladjustment.

It is patent that there are not too many points of agreement about how a homosexual orientation develops and is maintained. Castration anxiety, identity loss, antisexuality, and puritanism all enter the picture. Some authors are inclined to view a person's genetic endowment as the chief predisposing factor giving rise to homosexuality. Others emphasize parental relations — with different assessments of those relations — as the most crucial variable (Weinberg and Bell, 1972). A difficulty in explaining homosexuality arises because some practitioners, like Willis (1967), feel its highly fluid and complex transactional aspects have been neglected or ignored. Even in the same individual, homosexual behavior may represent a wide variety of complex adaptive or defensive coping transactions which vary from one set of circumstances to another, and so a new theory and a new technique of treatment are needed for each patient and for each occasion. Homosexuality must be understood, according to Wolman (1967), as a human search for identity and affection. For many men, homosexuality is the end of a deeply personal search for authentic sexuality and not a second best for the kind of heterosexual union that substitutes conquest and surrender for real intimacy. Many homosexuals themselves feel that to talk about comradeship and friendship in a homosexual relationship is inadequate; to mention affection debases it with physical undertones. It is for such reasons that homosexuals have generally been understood, they claim, in two-dimensional patterns only.

While it is difficult to draw conclusions about homosexuality, what kinds of people become homosexual, the classification of homosexuals according to etiology and to overt behavior, and the difficulty of treating homosexuals with psychotherapy, there is no question that Freud radically changed the clinical interpretation of it. Rather than regarding homosexuality merely as a pathological phenomenon, Freud brought homosexuality within the framework of classic psychoanalytic concepts of human development. In a letter to a woman who had written him concerning her son's homosexuality, he explained that homosexuality is "a variation of the sexual function produced by a certain arrest of sexual development," and is "nothing to be ashamed of, no vice, no degradation, it cannot be classified as an illness" (Freud, 1935, p. 786). In childhood, homosexuals go through a phase of "very intense but short-lived fixation to a woman (usually their mother), and that, after leaving this behind, they identify themselves with the woman and . . . proceed from a narcissistic basis, and look for a young man who resembles themselves and whom they may love as their mothers loved *them*" (Freud, 1905, p. 145). The creative writer on the subject tends to bear Freud out.

Among the factors Money (1963) reviews in the genesis of homosexuality are chromosomes, gonads, hormones, genital morphology and body image, sex assignment, gender identity, psychosexual neutrality and differentiation, imprinting, and family and culture patterns. The final determination of an individual's gender identity, Money concludes, is a neurocognitional function; the process takes place primarily after birth and the fundamentals are completed before puberty. Pare (1965) assesses conflicting and inconclusive studies on genetic factors in homosexuality and finds that although environment and genetics both seem to play roles, the degree to which genetic and environmental factors are important, in homosexuality as a whole and in any individual, remains uncertain. Perloff (1949, 1963) flatly states that homosexuality is purely a psychological condition, with no correlation between the choice of sex object and the level of hormone excretion. Furthermore, the so-called "sex hormones" are not important in the determination of sexual mannerisms and attitudes. Gentele, Lagerholm, and Lodin (1960), among many other investigators, find no significant chromosomal sex differences between heterosexual and homosexual males. Savitsch (1958), a surgeon, portrays "genuine homosexuality" as an inherent, unalterable biological condition, with environmental factors contributing little. Ford and Beach (1951) declare homosexual tendencies have a definite biological basis and appear to exist in a large majority of both sexes, although these tendencies may never be recognized and no overt homosexual behavior may ever occur.

Sufficient criteria for the identification of an adult homosexual include preferential erotic attraction to members of his own sex whether or not he engages in overt sexual relations with them. Homosexuality, states another definition, refers exclusively to overt behavior between two individuals of the same sex; the behavior must be patently sexual, involving erotic arousal and, in most instances at least, resulting in satisfaction of the sexual urge. Van den Haag (1963) defines a homosexual as a person who finds his exclusive or main sexual gratification in sexual relations with persons of his own sex. Buki (1964) defines homosexuality as a sexual impulse that, because of developmental defects, has remained immature or has undergone deviation in the course of maturation. And Cappon (1965) points out that the root of the word homosexual is the Greek *homos,* meaning "same" and not the Latin *homo,* meaning "man."

Thus Yuichi, the beautiful young male homosexual in Yukio Mishima's *Forbidden Colors* (1968), says, ". . . I can't love a woman. Do you know what I mean? My body can love them, but my interest in them is purely intellectual. I have never wanted a woman since the day I was born. I have never seen a woman and wanted her. . ." (p. 24). For most psychiatric patients the appearance of homosexuality in their treatment stirs up a peculiar kind of dread, a threat to their gender identity (Greenson, 1964). Except for the overt homosexual and the bisexual, other homosexual types have doubts about what their assigned sexual role is, and their sexual activities are reparative, calculated to restore the gender image by fusion with a person of the same sex (Gershman, 1968). The preference for a sexual partner of the same sex is the only common denominator in homosexuality; it is not a single entity or condition. Homosexual behavior which is situational, incidental, or neurotic in nature may be entirely unrelated to a person's self-perception of gender role; effeminate "passive" homosexuality in males, masculine "aggressive" homosexuality in females, and transvestitism, however, are all directly related to gender role inversion (Hampson, 1964).

Gender role, which is determined primarily by social learning during the earliest years of a child's life, is not automatically set by "instinct" nor by the body's anatomy or physiology; instead, "an individual's gender role, including erotic orientation, becomes established during the process of growing up as a result of a myriad of life experiences subtly imposed and governed by the cult of which he or she is a member" (Hampson, 1964, p. 501). Role rehearsal in childhood play and fantasy facilitates this aspect of personality development. The core of gender identity is fixed by age three and is the result of early infant-mother interaction. Sex differentiation into male identity is disturbed or hampered in the early infantile period by conflicts involving separation from the mother or by fears and prohibitions involved in patterning oneself after the image of the father (Knight, 1965).

The homosexual theme is not new in literature. Goethe wrote that homosexuality is as old as humanity itself, and can therefore be considered natural, a more enlightened viewpoint than most people even today are willing to accept. But our ignorance of the subject is still abysmal. Gide, in 1911, wrote exultantly about homosexuality: "Rage to your heart's content! Repress! Oppress! You will never suppress it!" (p. 145). D. H. Lawrence, on the other hand, railed against both male and female homosexuality: " 'Flat-chested, crop-headed, chemicalized women, of indeterminate sex. And wimbly-wambly young men, of sex still more indeterminate' " (Praz, 1933, p. 287). Since Fiedler (1948), every college student studying the American novel knows that the relation between Huck Finn and Nigger Jim, between Ishmael and Queequeg, Robinson Crusoe and Friday, and Chingachgook and Natty Bumpo forms "one long daisy chain of failed queers while the principal occupation of our national literature has been disguised but obsessive homosexuality" (p. 40).

American fiction of more recent vintage is characterized by Martin Hoffman (1968, p. 165) as "bipolar" imagery evoked of the "gay world" and of personal homosexual relations. He defines the gay world as that part of homosexual life that is a world in itself, an organized society with its own language and mores. It is that part of homosexuality which most conforms to and provides the stereotypes of homosexual life, the "queen," the "queer bar," and the "world of swish." The over-all picture that emerges from psychiatric writing on homosexuality, from the lips of homosexuals themselves, and from the novelist, is that the homosexual's life is a barren one. His sex life is likely to be loveless one-night stands, often with little or no communication; his life, even when filled with friends, is basically lonely; rarely is there any long-term, mutual commitment between two persons. The human beings who emerge from Gore Vidal's *The City and the Pillar Revisited,* John Rechy's *City of the Night,* and James Baldwin's *Giovanni's Room* exist in a lonely, lover-starved culture, and seek to define themselves in the destructive context of that culture. "This context manifests itself in their consciousness through a sense of lost innocence, a fear of experience, of love, and the dangers of love, and through a sense and fear of emasculation. Their behavior is presented in terms of unbreakable patterns. And as characters they are ultimately unable to love" (M. Hoffman, 1968, p. 167). The illegal catch-as-catch-can nature of much homosexual life breaks down other conventional attitudes.

The gay world is a sexual marketplace. The homosexual bar is where homosexuals can negotiate sexual experiences and where sexual frustrations are focused. The gay world is bound together by one thing: sexuality. It makes all homosexuals brothers and sisters; they have nothing in common other than this (I. Bieber et al., 1971). The homosexual man who does not find his way into the gay world, or who rejects it, runs grave risks in trying to act out his sexual impulses elsewhere. But the gay world can be a trap, too. People may spend too much time there, or commit themselves to it so much that they cut themselves off from important nonsexual experiences common to the straight world. "Unlike other subcultures, the homosexual community has very limited content. It may reduce the problems of access to sexual partners and reduce guilt by providing a structure of shared values, but the shared-value structure is often far too narrow to transcend other areas of value disagreement. The college-trained professional and the bus boy, the WASP and the Negro slum dweller may meet in sexual congress, but similarity of sexual interests does not eliminate the larger social and cultural barriers. The subculture is such a small world, however, that it constrains most members to participate in it only on a limited basis, reducing their anxiety and conflicts in the sexual sphere and increasing the quality of their performance in other aspects of social life. But the fact remains that the homosexual community is in itself an impoverished cultural unit" (Simon et al., 1971, p. 78).

The signs, the argot, the evasions, the frustrations, the humor, the joys, and the grief of the gay world of the male homosexual are seen in microcosm in the gay bar descriptions in a number of novels. James Baldwin (1956) describes the Parisian gay bar in which David first met Giovanni, in *Giovanni's Room,* as more than ordinarily crowded and noisy. "All the habitués were there and many strangers, some looking, some just staring.... There were the usual paunchy, bespectacled gentlemen with avid, sometimes despairing eyes, the usual knife-blade lean, tight-trousered boys. One could never be sure, as concerns these latter, whether they were after money or blood or love. They moved about the bar incessantly, cadging cigarettes and drinks, with something behind their eyes at once terribly vulnerable and terribly hard" (pp. 37-38). The young male hustler from the Far West who comes to New York City in John Rechy's *City of Night* (1962) "discovered the bars: on the west side, the east side, in the Village; one in Queens — appropriately — where males danced with males, holding each other intimately, male leading, male following . . . and it was in that bar that I first saw flagrantly painted men congregate and where a queen boy-girl camped openly with a cop . . . But because most of those bars attracted large numbers of youngmen who went there to meet others like themselves for a mutual nightlong, unpaid, sexsharing — or for the prospect of an 'affair' — the bars made me nervous, then...." (p. 56). John Lynch, the latent homosexual detective on a stake-out for a murderer in *Cruising,* by Gerald Walker (1970), soliloquizes, ". . . you go into a gay bar . . . and it's dead quiet, except maybe for a little music. You notice all those eyes turn to size you up. They look at you for thirty seconds, then they look away. Almost nobody is talking to anybody. Oh, a table here or there will be gabbing or giggling, but most of them stand around by themselves not even looking at anyone else. Everybody's waiting for somebody else to make the first move. It's like a meeting room filled with strangers waiting for the m.c. to get things started" (pp. 154-155).

The bar is not the only place where men seek impersonal sex. Called "tearooms" in the argot of the homosexual subculture, public restrooms are accessible to and easily recognized by those who wish to engage in anonymous sexual encounters (Humphreys, 1970). In *Numbers,* by John Rechy (1967), Johnny enters a movie whose marquee lights proclaim that it is open all night "and there's a balcony. Johnny knows — just as anyone who has hung out in gay bars knows — what that means. The hunting shadows in the dark . . . the frantic moving in and out of the toilet" (pp. 39-40). Johnny enters and climbs to the balcony when "suddenly, the heavy mood lifts. Instantly it's converted to euphoria. He's like someone reacting to a powerful stimulant — like an alcoholic returning to his liquor, an addict to his drug: spuriously renewed, as if the storm that raged is over but within the calm, the devastation remains" (p. 74). As he prowls the balcony, allowing himself to be seen, "wanting those on the top rows to hope he'll make himself available," he plays a sadistic, teasing game, sprawling on his seat in a casual, sexually inviting pose until he is approached, permitting the stranger a liberty but then abruptly rejecting him. Another prowler takes the man's place, and still another until Johnny permits a "youngman" to fellate him. Others "have witnessed the scene — a scene not rare but not common even in such a balcony, where the groping is usually done as an end in itself or as an invitation for completion in the restroom. Now, as if Johnny's sexual release has made them restless, there's a silent moving among those others — as if they're playing a game of musical chairs without music" (p. 82).

Norman, the modern Candide in Gavin Lambert's *Norman's Letters* (1966), who is in wild flight from mother and reality, reports how he "walked to Picadilly Circus and prowled for an hour or two. A man with a foreign accent propositioned me outside a church in Soho. I liked the exotic look of him, then felt a sudden alarm and rushed away. He called out after me, sounding annoyed, in a language I didn't understand . . ." (p. 25). The public places where homosexual contact takes place include not only the gay bars, toilets, and movie balconies, but also shower rooms, parks, steam baths, and beaches, which is indicative of the striking degree of promiscuity found in the homosexual world. Since the sexual relations in the gay life are transitory, the sexually active homosexual constantly needs new partners in order to obtain a reasonable amount of sexual satisfaction (M. Hoffman, 1968). Promiscuity among homosexuals is more the rule than the exception; a significantly higher precentage of homosexuals than heterosexuals are promiscuous. Serious pathological mechanisms may be acted out in homosexual promiscuity; for example, the compulsive search for a gigantic male organ and the unconcern with the person to whom it is attached. "Various psychodynamics may be delineated, such as a desire to get strength or masculinity magically from a large penis. It is also a way of attempting to repair a defective sense of masculinity, or a way of symbolically castrating the father figure so as for once and for all to destroy his threatening power. . . . I have spoken to homosexuals who have had fellatio with twenty men on one day, but they experienced little gratification themselves. Their reward was fatigue and disgust. Loneliness is common among homosexuals and much cruising is motivated by the need for human contact. In such encounters, the individual is oriented to pleasing his partner in any way desired. Personal sexual pleasure is but a second consideration" (I. Bieber et al., 1971, p. 78).

The hustler in Rechy's *City of Night* hungered for affection and love he never got. When he turned to "the world of males, on the streets, it was *I* who would be desired in those furtive relationships, without desiring back.... The money I got in exchange for sex was a token indication of one-way desire: that I was wanted enough to be paid for, on my own terms. Yet with that childhood-tampered ego poised flimsily on a structure as wavering and ephemeral as that of the streets (and a further irony: that it was only here that I could be surfeited, if anywhere), it needed more and more reassurance in numbers: a search for reassurance which at times would backfire sharply—insidiously wounding that devouring narcissism..." (p. 54). The distortions and rationalizations are transmuted in Rechy's second novel, *Numbers,* in which the protagonist says, "So much intimacy and ... you ... just ... walk ... away ... without a word, Johnny thinks suddenly. All these people. What are they really like? Does anyone ever get to *know* anyone else? Does anyone ever want to? I don't know anybody's name.... Yet: here I am! And that's only part of the Fear" (p. 184).

Gershman (1964, p. 32) feels that the homosexual's lack of a sense of identity "is but part of his general feelings of deadness and meaninglessness. While the latter are existential problems that face all human beings, for the homosexual they are particularly poignant and crucial ... In the homosexual, lack of love and real meaning result in depression, withdrawal, and resignation on the one hand, and, on the other, a frantic, hysterical clamor for sex." The homosexual, middle-aged pianist in Merle Miller's *What Happened* (1972) muses, "I know less about my mother than I know about dozens of boys I've spent the night with, spent an hour with.... Dozens? Hundreds? Thousands. How many thousands? Four or five years ago I made a list of all those I could remember. I refuse to repeat the number, and I hadn't even begun.... I met a man in Rio once, a rich, dreadful man, a *deputado,* and he had kept a record, he said, since he was sixteen. The number was 6,280. And he had never seen anybody twice.... That was the reason he was so dreadful. That was the reason he was sad" (pp. 167-168). In Rechy's *Numbers,* Johnny Rio experiences an insatiable craving for love, manifested by fellation. He has a narcissistic need to "make it" again and again; no sooner does he finish with one experience than he must embark upon another. As he walks swiftly on the paths of the mountain park, he feels, "there's no doubt he's the main attraction in the park" (p. 130). All the men are looking to fellate him; if he does not believe this "the hideous feeling of rejection can descend on him like an axe cutting him down" (p. 130) and thus castrate him. Rather than run such risks, Johnny moves "along, rather than waiting for a man to choose between him and someone else" (p. 138). "He's never been able to reconcile himself to the fact that no one in the world, no matter how desirable, will *always* be preferred" (p. 149). After being fellated three times within a few minutes by three different strangers, Johnny feels "a screaming need still unfulfilled" (p. 155). After sixteen fellated him in five days, there still remained "a physical demand for the park — a craving as commanding as those triggered by hunger, thirst" (p. 161).

The basic prerequisite of homosexual acting out seems to be a weak ego structure based upon a narcissistic and prenarcissistic disposition. This accounts for the fact that narcissistic projection plays an outstanding part in the choice of homosexual partners, who owe their high though transient value to their function as substitutes for the ego and the archaic parental images that were introjected early in life (Bychowski, 1954). The value of sex to James Baldwin — and Yukio Mishima, as well — lies in its very intimacy, the opportunity it offers to express, and finally anneal, the violence and despair of outcastness; and the best of their work vibrates with the belief that the barriers will come down only when access is allowed to one another across all abysses, sexual and racial. Their "world is taut with angry loneliness and fevered curiosities of the isolated, to whom touch itself is the only comprehensive act of communication. In Baldwin's novels, indeed, touching the body of the other is treated as the only way to annul its power of intensifying the individual's loneliness, simply by being out of reach" (Holmes, 1971, p. 22). Not all who would be are Narcissus. "Many who lean over the water," wrote Sartre (1949, p. 1), "see only a vague human figure. Genet sees himself everywhere; the dullest surfaces reflect his image; even in others he perceives himself, thereby bringing to light their deepest secrets...." But the easy assertion sometimes found in gay liberation circles and throughout the counterculture that promiscuity and the ability to appreciate varieties of human eroticism are the equivalents of liberation are readily refuted (Altman, 1972).

The homosexual's dominant neurotic drive is sadomasochistic. Narcissistic displacement, guilt feelings, and defensive sadistic impulses are laid bare repeatedly in fiction. George Lionel, the prodigiously talented concert pianist in Miller's (1972) *What Happened,* diagnosed his own self-destructive bent in terms of social attitudes toward his homosexuality. "I wanted so much to conform," he rationalized. His self-image was further diminished by a hostile community, by his mother, and an inevitably disastrous marriage. His reaction was an abiding dislike for himself that was translated into compulsive promiscuity. Even in his palmiest moments, when he was most adored, Lionel was forever cruising, and forever being beaten, robbed, and discarded. "Love, love, love. It keeps being spoken of. By me. I cannot move without love, eat without it, breathe without it. It has motivated every conscious effort of my life. I have had always to make everybody love me. But the minute it happens, he has to be punished for making the mistake of loving me. And people who are dying to meet me have to be punished, too" (p. 22).

Gide, like Genet, took sadistic pleasure in priding himself on his own humiliation, and in violating and shocking the modesty of others. "The result of this complex psychological formation was that Gide took up the attitude of a 'martyr of pederasty,' thus satisfying his homosexual and his algolagnic desires at the same time. . . . Certain passages from *The Immoralist* [1902] may be quoted to illustrate this. Michel, when he discovers that the Arab boy Moktir is a thief, instead of being angry is delighted, and makes the thief his favorite; he is fascinated by the corrupt peasant, Bute, and by the poachers whom he accompanies in their nocturnal expeditions; . . . he finds pleasure in telling lies; he possesses Marceline after a violent struggle in which he subdues and binds a drunken coachman" (Praz, 1933, p. 366). Homosexuality in *The Immoralist,* according to Korges (1970, p. 135), "is a metaphoric index of Michel's ironically increasing self-interest and cruelty . . . The central pattern of the book is an alternation of sickness and health, physical and spiritual. In Part I, Michel is nursed by his wife, but he is also corrupted by the Arab boys she mothers. In Part III, the wife is nursed by Michel, and she is the victim of his attraction to a boy. The wife's maternal good works are finally the cause of her mortal pain, as she utters one of the most poignant speeches in modern fiction: 'Oh, you can wait a little longer, can't you?' But he cannot." "I know now—I have found out at last what gives me my special value. It is a kind of stubborn perseverance in evil," says Michel (Gide, pp. 194-195).

Homosexuality involves public opinion and social prejudice, and society can generate the homosexual's promiscuity by creating anxieties which inhibit stable relationships. "Heterosexual prejudices fostered by stereotypic notions of homosexuality produce great pressure on homosexuals. In response to this, a homosexual community develops where counterstereotypic images of homosexuality are produced. Among these counterimages may be found beliefs that inversion has a hereditary base, that it is natural . . . or that homosexuals have special positive qualities such as unusual creative abilities" (Greenzweig, 1954). It also fosters a mystique about what homosexuals do, creating anxieties masked by a thin layer of humor. In Seymour Epstein's *Caught in That Music* (1967), the reader is never quite sure whether Jonas, who has completed two years of college, is serious or not when he asks his mistress, Ruth, "What do homosexuals do to each other. I don't understand what they do." When Ruth tells him they kiss, he complains, "You don't take my ignorance seriously enough. I really and truly do not know what fairies do to each other." "The same thing men and women do, only to each other," Ruth says, walking into the kitchen. "But they can't do the *same* thing because one of them hasn't got the same equipment." "Well, then, use your imagination." "I'm using my imagination, Ruth. Doesn't it hurt?" "Please stop it, Jonas. Don't be such a baby" (p. 154). Lynch, the latent homsexual detective in *Cruising* by Gerald Walker (1970) tries to imagine what homosexuals do. "Two men lie together, he thought, it didn't make much sense. What did two men *do*? How did they act toward each other? If they nuzzled their faces together, wouldn't their beards rub? The thought of another man's beard against his made Lynch uncomfortable. He remembered when he was a kid Uncle Phil used to give him the old sandpaper treatment, but now was something else. Nor could Lynch see any of the other things either. He just couldn't understand taking it in the ass or blowing. What a man wanted was to get *in*. He didn't want anyone getting into *him*. There was nothing like good old-fashioned screwing, Lynch thought, and he could even do without that if he had to" (p. 40).

Pursewarden, in Lawrence Durrell's *Clea* (1960), asks the rhetorical question, "How, since the Greeks, has [love] got mixed up with the cloaca maxima?" (p. 132). Norman, who loved an Arab youth, Ahmin, in Lambert's (1966) novel, *Norman's Letters,* recalls in one of his letters to the boy, "I gasped with pleasure at our shivering nakedness when we embraced; I hooted with pain when you came through the back door. And I believe, Ahmin, you enjoyed my pain. Will you be happy to know I still feel it, like a remarkable wine that lingers on the palate, or a very high note of music echoing somewhere in the hills?" (p. 10). Some of the objections to male homosexuality, and the lack of objection to Lesbianism, is on esthetic grounds, according to Masters (1962). He writes, "The role of the anus in homosexuality accounts for some hostility and repugnance, the anus being regarded by many persons solely as an excremental orifice. There is also the fact that most persons have been forced to suppress or repress the erotic feelings associated with defecation which were once natural to them, so that it might be said that those who continue to preserve the connection between the anus and eroticism arouse in us an unconscious resentment..." (p. 146). Although many people may overcome this resentment and agree that homosexuality should be accepted as a fact of life and that a laissez-faire attitude be developed, enlightened attitudes are hard to come by.

The homosexual role has not been a constant in all cultures. It exists only in certain societies and only emerged in England toward the end of the seventeenth century (McIntosh, 1968). Although constituting only one chapter in *The Adventures of Roderick Random,* Tobias Smollett's classic novel of 1748, the meeting between Lord Strutwell and Roderick is probably the earliest portrait of a homosexual in any English fiction that has survived (Cory, 1956). Gullible Roderick Random, new to London, was almost taken in by a homosexual who was after both his body and his money. Earl Strutwell's speech to Roderick is a perfect parody of cliché homosexual apologetics and seduction pieces, including a statement that although homosexuality " 'is generally decried, and indeed condemned by our laws ... it prevails not only over all the East, but in most parts of Europe; in our own country it gains ground apace, and in all probability will become in a short time a more fashionable vice than simple fornication' " (Smollett, p. 339). In Smollett's view, the socioeconomic class structure was closely related to homosexuality (Bruce, 1965); and in *Roderick Random,* he set down a very recognizable homosexual role, wherein the reader's expectation of homosexual behavior is fulfilled and where the description of the behavior is sufficiently accurate to satisfy psychological expectations.

Baffled hitherto in my matrimonial schemes, I began to question my talents for the science of fortune-hunting and to bend my thoughts towards some employment under the government, with the view of procuring which, I cultivated the acquaintance of Lords Straddle and Swillpot, whose fathers were men of interest at court. I found these young noblemen as open to my advances as I could desire. I accompanied them in their midnight rambles and often dined with them at taverns, where I had the honour of paying the reckoning.

I one day took the opportunity, while I was loaded with protestations of friendship, to disclose my desire of being settled in some sinecure, and to solicit their influence in my behalf. Swillpot, squeezing my hand, said I might depend upon his service, by G-d. The other swore that no man would be more proud than he to run my errands. Encouraged by these declarations, I ventured to express an inclination to be introduced to their fathers, who were able to do my business at once. Swillpot frankly owned he had not spoke to his father these three years, and Straddle assured me his father, having lately disobliged the minister by subscribing his name to a protest in the House of Peers, was thereby rendered incapable of serving his friends at present, but he undertook to make me acquainted with Earl Strutwell, who was hand and glove with a certain person who ruled the roost. This offer I embraced with many acknowledgements, and plied him so closely, in spite of a thousand evasions, that he found himself under a necessity of keeping his word and actually carried me to the levee of this great man, where he left me in a crowd of fellow-dependents, and was ushered to a particular closet audience, from whence in a few minutes he returned with his lordship, who took me by the hand, assured me he would do me all the service he could, and desired to see me often. I was charmed with my reception, and, although I had heard that a courtier's promise is not to be depended upon, I thought I discovered so much sweetness of temper and candour in this earl's countenance that I did not doubt of finding my account in his protection. I resolved, therefore, to profit by this permission, and waited on him next audience day, when I was favoured with a particular smile, squeeze of the hand, and a whisper, signifying that he wanted half an hour's conversation with me tete-à-tete, when he should be disengaged, and for that purpose desired me to come and drink a dish of chocolate with him tomorrow morning. This invitation, which did not a little flatter my vanity and expectation, I took care to observe, and went to his lordship's house at the time appointed. Having rapped at the gate, the porter unbolted and kept it half open, placing himself in the gap, like soldiers in a breach, to dispute my passage. I demanded to know if his lord was stirring? He answered with a surly aspect, "No." "At what hour does he commonly rise?" said I. "Sometimes sooner, sometimes later," said he, closing the door upon me by degrees. I then told him, I was come by his lordship's own appointment; to which this Cerberus replied, "I have received no orders about this matter," and was upon the point of shutting me out when I recollected myself all of a sudden, and, slipping a crown into his hand, begged as a favour that he would inquire and let me know whether or not the earl was up. The grim janitor relented at the touch of my money, which he took with all the indifference of a tax-gatherer, and showed me into a parlour, where, he said, I might amuse myself till such time as his lord should be awake. I had not sat ten minutes in this place when a footman entered, and without speaking stared at me; I interpreted this piece of his behaviour into, "Pray, sir, what is your business?" and asked the same question I had put to the porter when I accosted him first. The lackey made the same reply, and disappeared before I could get any further intelligence. In a little time he returned, on pretence of poking the fire, and looked at me again with great earnestness, upon which I began to perceive his meaning, and, tipping him with half a crown, desired he would be so good as to fall upon some method of letting the earl know that I was in the house. He made a low bow, said "Yes, sir," and vanished. This bounty was not thrown away, for in an instant he came back and conducted me to a chamber where I was received with great kindness and familiarity by his lordship, whom I found just risen, in his morning gown and slippers. After breakfast, he entered into a particular conversation with me about my travels, the remarks I had made abroad, and examined me to the full extent of my understanding. My answers seemed to please him very much; he frequently squeezed my hand, and, looking at me with a singular complacency in his countenance, bade me depend upon his good offices with the ministry in my behalf. "Young men of your qualifications," said he, "ought to be cherished by every administration. For my own part, I see so little merit in the world that I have laid it down as a maxim to encourage the least appearance of genius and virtue to the utmost of my power— you have a great deal of both and will not fail in making a figure one day, if I am not mistaken, but you must lay your account with mounting by gradual steps to the summit of your fortune. Rome was not built in a day. As you understand the languages perfectly

well, how would you like to cross the sea as secretary to an embassy?"
I assured his lordship with great eagerness that nothing could be more
agreeable to my inclination. Upon which he bade me make myself
easy, my business was done, for he had a place of that kind in his view.
This piece of generosity affected me so much that I was unable for
some time to express my gratitude, which at length broke out in my
own unworthiness and encomiums on his benevolence. I could not
even help shedding tears at the goodness of this noble lord, who no
sooner perceived them than he caught me in his arms, and hugged
and kissed me with a seemingly paternal affection. Confounded at
this uncommon instance of fondness for a stranger, I remained a few
moments silent and ashamed, then got up and took my leave, after he
had assured me that he would speak to the minister in my favour that
very day, and desired that I would not for the future give myself the
trouble of attending at his levee, but come at the same hour every day
when he was at leisure, that is, three times a week.

Though my hopes were now very sanguine, I determined to conceal my prospect from everybody, even Strap, until I should be more
certain of success, and, in the meantime, give my patron no respite
from my solicitations. When I renewed my visit, I found the street
door open to me as if by enchantment, but in my passage towards the
presence room I was met by the valet de chambre, who cast some
furious looks at me, the meaning of which I could not comprehend.
The earl saluted me at entrance with a tender embrace, and wished
me joy of his success with the premier, who, he said, had preferred his
recommendation to that of two other noblemen very urgent in behalf
of their respective friends, and absolutely promised that I should go to
a certain foreign court, in quality of secretary to an ambassador and
plenipotentiary, who was to set out in a few weeks on an affair of vast
importance to the nation. I was thunderstruck with my good fortune,
and could make no other reply than kneel, and attempt to kiss my
benefactor's hand, which submission he would not permit, but,
raising me up, pressed me to his breast with surprising emotion, and
told me he had now taken upon himself the care of making my
fortune. What enhanced the value of the benefit still more was his
making light of the favour, and shifting the conversation to another
subject. Among other topics of discourse, that of the *Belles-Lettres*
was introduced, upon which his lordship held forth with great taste
and erudition and discovered an intimate knowledge of the authors
of antiquity. "Here's a book," said he, taking one from his bosom,
"written with great elegance and spirit, and though the subject may
give offence to some narrow-minded people, the author will always be

held in esteem by every person of wit and learning." So saying, he put into my hand Petronius Arbiter and asked my opinion of his wit and manner. I told him that, in my opinion, he wrote with great ease and vivacity, but was withal so lewd and indecent that he ought to find no quarter or protection among peoples of morals and taste. "I own," replied the earl, "that his taste in love is generally decried, and indeed condemned by our laws, but perhaps that may be more owing to prejudice and misapprehension than to true reason and deliberation. The best man among the ancients is said to have entertained that passion; one of the wisest of their legislators has permitted the indulgence of it in his commonwealth; the most celebrated poets have not scrupled to avow it. At this day it prevails not only over all the East, but in most parts of Europe; in our own country it gains ground apace and in all probability will become in a short time a more fashionable vice than simple fornication. Indeed, there is something to be said in vindication of it, for, notwithstanding the severity of the law against offenders in this way, it must be confessed that the practice of this passion is unattended with that curse and burden upon society which proceeds from a race of miserable and deserted bastards, who are either murdered by their parents, deserted to the utmost want and wretchedness, or bred up to prey upon the commonwealth. And it likewise prevents the debauchery of many a young maiden, and the prostitution of honest men's wives, not to mention the consideration of health, which is much less liable to be impaired in the gratification of this appetite than in the exercise of common venery, which, by ruining the constitutions of our young men, has produced a puny progeny that degenerates from generation to generation. Nay, I have been told that there is another motive, perhaps more powerful than all these, that induces people to cultivate this inclination, namely, the exquisite pleasure attending its success."

From that discourse, I began to be apprehensive that his lordship, finding I had travelled, was afraid I might have been infected with this spurious and sordid desire abroad, and took this method of sounding my sentiments on the subject. Fired at this supposed suspicion, I argued against it with great warmth, as an appetite unnatural, absurd, and of pernicious consequence, and declared my utter detestation and abhorrence of it in these lines of the satirist:

Eternal infamy the wretch confound
Who planted first that vice on British ground!
A vice! that, 'spite of sense and nature, reigns,
And poisons genial love, and manhood stains.

The earl smiled at my indignation, told me he was glad to find my opinion of the matter so conformable to his own, and that what he had advanced was only to provoke me to an answer, with which he professed himself perfectly well pleased.

After I had enjoyed a long audience, I happened to look at my watch, in order to regulate my motions by it, and his lordship, observing the chased case, desired to see the device and examine the execution, which he approved with some expressions of admiration. Considering the obligations I lay under to his lordship, I thought there could not be a fitter opportunity than the present to manifest in some shape my gratitude; I therefore begged he would do me the honour to accept of the watch as a small testimony of the sense I had of his lordship's generosity, but he refused it in a peremptory manner and said he was sorry I should entertain such a mercenary opinion of him, observing at the same time, that it was the most beautiful piece of workmanship he had ever seen, and desiring to know where he could have such another. I begged a thousand pardons for the freedom I had taken, which I hoped he would impute to nothing else than the highest veneration for his person, let him know that, as it came to my hand by accident in France, I could give him no information about the maker, for there was no name on the inside, and once more humbly entreated that he would indulge me so far as to use it for my sake. He was still positive in refusing it, but was pleased to thank me for my generous offer, saying it was a present that no nobleman need be ashamed of receiving, though he was resolved to show his disinterestedness with regard to me, for whom he had conceived a particular friendship, and insisted, if I was willing to part with the watch, upon knowing what it had cost, that he might at least indemnify me by refunding the money. On the other hand, I assured his lordship that I should look upon it as an uncommon mark of distinction if he would take it without further question, and rather than disoblige me he was at last persuaded to put it in his pocket, to my no small satisfaction, who took my leave immediately, after having received a kind squeeze and an injunction to depend upon his promise.

Buoyed up with my reception, my heart opened; I gave away a guinea among the lackeys who escorted me to the door, flew to the lodgings of Lord Straddle, upon whom I forced my diamond ring as an acknowledgement for the great service he had done me, and from thence hied me home, with an intent of sharing my happiness with honest Strap. I determined, however, to heighten his pleasure by depressing his spirits at first and then bringing in the good news with double relish. For this purpose, I affected the appearance of disappointment and chagrin and told him in an abrupt manner that I had lost the watch and diamond. Poor Hugh, who had been already harassed into a consumption by intelligence of this sort, no sooner heard these words than, unable to contain himself, he cried, with distraction in his looks, "God in heaven forbid!" I could carry on the farce no longer, but, laughing in his face, told him everything that had passed, as above recited. His features were immediately unbended, and the transition so affecting that he wept with joy and called my Lord Strutwell by the appellations of Jewel, Phoenix, *Rara avis*, praising God that there was still some virtue left among our nobility. Our mutual congratulations being over, we gave away to our imaginations, and anticipated our happiness by prosecuting our success through the different steps of promotion till I arrived at the rank of a prime minister, and he to that of my first secretary.

Intoxicated with these ideas, I went to the ordinary, where, meeting with Banter, I communicated the whole affair in confidence to him, concluding with my assurance that I would do him all the service in my power. He heard me to an end with great patience, then regarding me a good while with a look of disdain, pronounced, "So your business is done, you think?" "As good as done, I believe," said I. "I'll tell you," replied he, "what will do it still more effectually, a halter!—'Sdeath! if I had been such a gull to two such scoundrels as Strutwell and Straddle I would without any more ado tuck myself up." Shocked at this exclamation, I desired him, with some confusion to explain himself, upon which he gave me to understand, that Straddle was a poor contemptible wretch who lived by borrowing and pimping to his fellow peers; that, in consequence of this last capacity, he had doubtless introduced me to Strutwell, who was so notorious for a passion for his own sex that he was amazed his character had never reached my ears; and that, far from being able to obtain for me the post he had promised, his interest at court was so low that he could scarce provide for a superannuated footman once a year in the customs or excise. That it was a common thing for him to amuse strangers whom his jackals ran down with such assurances and caresses as he had bestowed on me until he had stripped them of their cash and everything valuable about them—very often of their chastity—and then leave them a prey to want and infamy. That he allowed his servants no other wages than that part of the spoil which they could glean by their industry, and the whole of his conduct towards me was so glaring that nobody who knew anything of mankind could have been imposed upon by his insinuations.

I leave the reader to judge how I relished this piece of information, which precipitated me from the most exalted pinnacle of hope to the lowest abyss of despondence, and well-nigh determined me to take Banter's advice and finish my chagrin with a halter. I had no room to suspect the veracity of my friend, because, upon recollection, I found every circumstance of Strutwell's behaviour exactly tallying with the character he had described. His hugs, embraces, squeezes, and eager looks, were now no longer a mystery, no more than his defence of Petronius, and the jealous frown of his valet de chambre, who, it seems, had been the favourite pathic of his lord [pp. 335-342].

This is the first account of homosexuality in European fiction since Petronius laid the groundwork for further explorations. The attitudes of homosexuals themselves toward their homosexuality is revealed in a number of novels. Emancipation, lust, guilt, shame, fear of exposure, self-hatred are some of the feelings expressed. David, the protagonist and Giovanni's lover in Baldwin's *Giovanni's Room* (1956), is talking in a bar to an older homosexual acquaintance, Jacques.

"Tell me," I said at last, "is there really no other way for you but this? To kneel down forever before an army of boys for just five dirty minutes in the dark?"

"Think," said Jacques, "of the men who have kneeled down before you while you thought of something else and pretended that nothing was happening down there in the dark between your legs."

I stared at the amber cognac and at the wet rings on the metal. Deep below, trapped in the metal, the outline of my own face looked upward hopelessly at me.

"You think," he persisted, "that my life is shameful because my encounters are. And they are. But you should ask yourself *why* they are."

"Why are they—shameful?" I asked him.

"Because there is no affection in them, and no joy. It's like putting an electric plug in a dead socket. Touch, but no contact. All touch, but no contact and no light."

I asked him: "Why?"

"That you must ask yourself," he told me... [pp. 75-76].

Later in the story, when David confirms his homosexual relation with Giovanni, he passes a sailor in the street who "seemed—somehow—younger than I had ever been, and blonder and more beautiful, and he wore his masculinity as unequivocally as he wore his skin ... He gave me a look contemptuously lewd and knowing ... I felt my face flame, I felt my heart harden and shake as I hurried past him ... I wondered what he had seen in me to elicit such instantaneous contempt ... I knew that what the sailor had seen in my unguarded eyes was envy and desire: I had seen it often in Jacques' eyes and my reaction and the sailor's had been the same. But if I were still able to feel affection and if he had seen it in my eyes, it would not have helped, for affection, for the boys I was doomed to look at, was vastly more frightening than lust" (pp. 121-123). It was Crowley (1968) who said, "Show me a happy homosexual and I'll show you a gay corpse" (p. 84). Both the novelist and the psychiatrist have remarked about rarely observing evidence of a sense of contentment and satisfaction in the homosexual, although these are qualities frequently to be seen in the heterosexual population. Prewitt, in James Jones' *From Here to Eternity,* comments, "I've heard a lot of talk about 'great love' between homos, but I aint never seen it. I think it's more like hate, probably" (1951, p. 386). Balthazar, the homosexual physician in Durrell's (1957) *Justine,* justifies his homosexuality by thanking "God I have been spared an undue interest in love. At least the invert escapes this fearful struggle to give oneself to another. Lying with one's own kind, enjoying an experience, one can still keep free the part of one's mind which dwells in Plato, or gardening, or the differential calculus. Sex has left the body and entered the imagination now" (p. 93).

Most homosexuals live very much like heterosexuals, according to Allen and Martin (1971, p. 171). "They fall in love, live together, call home if they are going to be late, give each other gifts, quarrel, make up, and make love." For those with a more stable relationship, happiness may be achieved. But the devastating effect of fear of public discovery and censure remains, despite the changes in the social and moral climate in the Western world in recent years with respect to consensual homosexual acts. The perception of homosexuality as a threat to the stability of the social order and to the male's image of manhood and his relentless efforts to preserve this image (Mazur, 1968) is often reflected in the homosexual panic which on occasion seizes many men. "She wasn't terribly interested in sex," says the protagonist in Jim Harrison's *Wolf. A False Memoir* (1971), "but I was insistent in my own neurotic confusion—a number of homosexuals had made passes and I was worried that there was something in my conduct that made them see the potential homosexual in me. So I was bent on proving I wasn't queer to myself by getting into every girl in the Village I could get my hands on" (p. 195). He had a tremendous need to demonstrate his masculinity to himself in order to avoid being stigmatized as a homosexual. Jim, in Gore Vidal's (1948) *The City and the Pillar Revisited*, "went through several stages after his discovery that there were indeed many men who liked other men. His first reaction was disgust and alarm. He scrutinized every one carefully. Was he one? After a while, he could identify the obvious ones by their tight, self-conscious manner, particularly when they moved, neck and shoulders rigid. After a time, as the young men grew used to Jim, they would talk frankly about themselves. Finally, one tried to seduce him. Jim was quite unnerved, and violent in his refusal. Yet afterward he continued to go to their parties, if only to be able to experience again the pleasure of saying no" (pp. 72-73).

Irving Bieber et al. (1962) declare that the central causative factors in homosexuality are located in the family, with the parents acting as the chief designers of the homosexual pattern. Constitutional factors are not involved in the etiology of homosexuality; rather, it is a condition patterned within the family. Most male homosexuals are characterized by one particular type of parent-child relationship: a mother who has an inappropriate intimate relationship with her son (I. Bieber, 1968). These mothers are controlling and seductive, yet sexually repressive; their husbands are either absent or hostile, detached and sexually competitive (T. Bieber, 1967), thus making the father a central, decisive figure in the development of homosexuality in the son (I. Bieber, 1965). It is the father who emerges as the one who is hated, held in contempt and often feared. Most homosexuals love their mothers; they were often the only human beings such men ever loved. But the relationship is more likely than not an inappropriately intimate and overclose one, in which the mother prefers the son to her husband. She acts in a paradoxical, double-bind fashion: often, on the surface, she is puritanical; yet she will be intimate and seductive with her son. "She may share his bed far beyond the time a boy snuggles in bed with his mother; she may appear in various stages of undress. . . . In contrast, the father communicates hostility openly or in hidden ways. Of all his children, he is least fond of this boy, although he may have a pretty good relationship with his other sons. He plays a crucial role in the development of homosexuality. Most male homosexuals love their mother but will tell you: 'I hated my father' . . . 'He wasn't there' . . . 'I don't want any part of him' " (I. Bieber et al., 1971, p. 72). There is sufficient evidence to warrant the conclusion that the adult male homosexual often had a childhood in which there was an excessively close and abnormal, strong mother-son relationship, with a father who was usually either passive, weak, and ineffective or abusive, hostile, rejecting, and indifferent to the son (Brown, 1963). Works by Freud (1905), Hamilton (1936), Brill (1940), Bychowski (1956), West (1959), and Socarides (1968) support Irving Bieber's view of the close-binding, overintimate mother, and hostile, rejecting father.

The pathological character of the relationship of the mother and the homosexual male is substantiated in Baldwin's novel, *Giovanni's Room* (1956), Speicher's *Lower and Lower* (1973), Selby's *Last Exit to Brooklyn* (1957), Lambert's *Norman's Letters* (1966), Lawrence's *Sons and Lovers* (1913), Miller's *What Happened* (1972), Rechy's *City of Night* (1962), McHale's *Farragon's Retreat* (1971), and Joseph Hansen's *Death Claims* (1973), among others. In the last-named novel, the relationship between Mrs. Cochran, the seventy-five-year-old mother and her successful television-star son, Wade, typifies the close mother-son unit. Mrs. Cochran has lived with her boy all his life; he is unmarried, a closet homosexual unbeknownst to his Bible-quoting mother, who is so blinded by her enveloping love that she naïvely brags that Wade " 'wouldn't hurt me by trifling with women.' " Dave, an insurance investigator and himself a homosexual, has tracked Wade down as the possible murderer in a case he has been working on, and it is he, ironically, who has to break the news to the mother.

Dave took a grim breath and let it out. "Mrs. Cochran—Peter Oats is a homosexual. Do you know what that means?"

She sniffed, her mouth twitched. "I've lived a long time mister. I've seen and heard just about everything a woman of seventy-five could be expected to, and a mite more than most. I know what you're talking about." She turned her face away. "What's it got to do with my son?"

"Maybe nothing," Dave said. "I could be wrong. But I don't think I am. He's in his thirties. He's never married. There's a lot of publicity about him in the magazines. None of it ever mentions a woman. No woman except you."

"He's attached to me," she flared. "He wouldn't hurt me by trifling with women. What other woman could have made him what I did?

He's got everything a man could ask for in this world. And he's doing good with it. He's serving Jesus Christ with it. Not like the rest of them, with their drink and their night clubs and their divorces."

"Right," Dave said. "But when John Oats called, he went. Arena Blanca's fifty miles from here and it was a rainy night. But he got in that yellow Lotus of his and he went there. There's got to be a reason."

"He wasn't afraid. He's afraid of no man. He's got no cause to be afraid." Her warped fingers gripped hard on the book in her lap. "He'd seen this boy Peter in this play, you say. They'd taken supper together. It must have been to talk business. The boy's an actor."

"It wasn't the boy who called. Anyway, your son told me he wasn't interested in Peter as an actor. He pretended he hardly remembered him. He said they'd had a meal together—once. That wasn't true. Shall I tell you what I think was true?"

She didn't say yes, but she waited.

"I think your son fell in love with Peter Oats. He's beautiful and gentle. I think Peter fell in love with him. I think they slept together at that motel. And I think they wanted to go on sleeping together. It couldn't be here. But it could be up at that lodge of his, where no one goes but himself."

Her dry lips moved, but no speech came.

"The boy went home and packed his belongings. That much is fact. He talked to his father. On that I haven't the facts. His father refused to discuss it with the girl whose house he and Peter were sharing. But it upset him badly. And I think I know what it was. Peter had a weakness for honesty. He and his father had been good friends. I think he told him he was a homosexual, that he'd found a man to love and was going to live with him. He gave his father the phone number here. Obviously he also gave him the name of the man—your son's name."

"Did he know his father was a dope fiend?" She was trembling. Her voice scratched like an old phonograph record. "If he did, it was a wicked thing to do. A terrible thing. He's destroyed my son."

"I think he was like you," Dave said. "If he'd paid attention, he would have noticed changes in his father, something wrong. But he loved the man and it blinded him—I'm sorry. He didn't see because he didn't want to see. No, I don't think he knew his father was an addict."

But she wasn't listening. She was grinding the words out under her breath. "Destroyed my son. My wonderful son. Destroyed him." She jerked her head up and was fierce again. "That boy can't be handsome, he can't be gentle. You're lying. He'd plotted with his father to get money out of Wade." Her jaw thrust forward, the pinched nostrils flared [pp. 142-143].

Even when Mrs. Cochran is compelled to accept the distasteful fact of her son's homosexuality, she protects herself by denial: " 'It was like you claimed it was between them. Love, you called it. I can't accept that. Bible doesn't and I can't. Lived my whole life by the Word of God. Raised him by it. He knew better, knew he was in the wrong — otherwise he'd have spoke to me about it' " (p. 156). Her puritanical views are further advanced when she says, " 'Love don't let you doubt. *Believeth all things*. First Corinthians, thirteen, seven. . . . They lay down together in abomination' " (p. 157). Her son's homosexuality was fixated on the wish for the mother-child unity, signaling an attempt to regress to the undifferentiated phase and a total destruction of the self in a union with the mother, a situation to be avoided at any cost. In Selby's *Last Exit to Brooklyn* (1957), George's (Georgette's) mother fixation precluded any erotic relation with other women. George is brought home by Vinnie, a petty criminal whom he loves and who has playfully cut George's leg with a knife. There is considerable bleeding and pain, which George would like to ease by taking a benzedrine tablet. He is prevented from doing so because of the watchful eyes of his adoring, protective mother and the contemptuous presence of his brother Arthur, who is jealous of his mother's love for George.

It throbs and pains. I can feel it squeezing up my leg and it hurts. It hurts dreadfully. It does. It really does. I need something for the pain. O Jesus I cant stay down. I cant get out. Not even Soakie. She might have *something*. Let her in. I cant get out. Out. Up — (the door banged and her Mother looked up and noticed first the strange look on her sons face, the staring eyes; then the blood on his slacks and as he ran to him she collapsed on Mothers shoulder, crying, wanting to cry on Mothers shoulder and have her listen and stroke her hair (I love him Mother. I love him and want him.); and knowing that she must scare her Mother so she would be protected by her sympathy, and perhaps Mother would get her to bed (she wanted to run to the bed, but she knew she had to hobble to impress her), get her to bed before her brother came in the room. She might be able to hide the bennie. She had to try! Her Mother staggered and they hobbled toward the bed (mustnt run), wanting her Mother near, wanting the comfort; and feeling calmer, safer, as her Mothers face paled and her hands shook; yet calculating just how far she could go with the scene so Mother would be properly concerned yet still capable of protecting her from Arthur . . . and she may yet be able to hide the bennie) . . .

Why couldn't he be out. Why did he have to be home. If only he were dead. You sonofabitch die. DIE (Whats the matter with mommys little girl. Did ooo stub oo little toesywoesy Georgieworgit? Dont touch me you fairy. Dont touch me. Look whos calling someone a fairy. Aint that a laugh. Ha! You freak. Freak FREAK FREAK FREAK! Why you rotten punk—Georgette leaned more heavily upon Mother and swung the injured leg from side to side, groaning. Please Arthur. Please. Leave your brother alone. Hes hurt. Hes passing out from loss of blood. Brother? Thats a goodone. Please—Georgette groaned louder and started sliding from Mothers neck (if only she could get to the bed and hide the bennie. Hide the bennie. Hide the bennie); please, not again. Not now. Just call the doctor. For me. Please.) If he had stayed out. Or had just gone to the kitchen . . . Georgie porgie puddin n pie . . . Why do they do this to me? Why wont they leave me alone??? (Arthur looked at his brother and grunted with disgust then went to the phone and Georgette tried frantically to get the bennie out of her pocket but her slacks were so tight she couldnt get her hand in and she was afraid to move away from her Mother so she could get her hand in her pocket. She fell on the bed and rolled on her side and tried to get them out and under the mattress or even the pillow (yes, the pillow) but her Mother thought she was rolling with pain and held her hands trying to comfort and soothe her son, telling him to try to relax, the doctor will be here soon and you will be alright. Dont worry darling. Youll see. Everything will be alright . . . and then her brother came back, looked at his Mother then the ripped slacks and blood and said they had better take the pants off and put a little mercurochrome on the leg and Georgette tried to yank her hands free, but her Mother gripped tighter, trying to absorb her sons pain, and Georgette fought furiously, trying to hold her slacks and keep her brother from pulling them off. She screamed and kicked, but when she did the pain really throbbed through her leg, and she tried biting her Mothers hands but her brother pushed her head down (the G string! The bennie!!!). Stop. Stop! Go away. Dont let him. Please dont let him. It will be alright son. The doctor will be here soon. Nobody wants to hurt you. You rotten fairy, stop. Stop! You queer sonofabitch. STOP, but brother loosened the belt and grabbed her pants by the cuffs and Georgette screeched and her Mothers tears fell on her face, begging Arthur to be careful; and Arthur pulled them slowly yet still tore loose the clot from the wound and blood started oozing, then flowing down the leg and Georgette fell back crying and screaming, and Arthur let the pants fall to the floor and stared at his brother . . . watching the blood roll to the sheet, the leg jerk . . . listening to his brother crying and wanting to laugh with satisfaction, and even happy to see the misery on his Mothers face as she looked at Georgette and lifted his head in her arms and stroked his head, humming, shaking tears from her face . . . Arthur wanting to lean over and punch his face, that goddamn face covered with makeup, wanting to tear at the leg and listen to his fairy brother wail . . . He straightened up and stood silently at the foot of the bed for a moment halfhearing the sobs and his thoughts, then stepped around to the side and started yanking the Red Spangled G String. You disgusting degenerate. In front of my Mother you have the nerve to lay here with this thing on. He yanked, and slapped Georgette across the face, Mother pleading, crying, soothing, and Georgette rolled and clawed as the tight G String scraped along her leg, and Mother begged Arthur to leave his brother alone — BROTHER? — but he tugged and yanked, yelling above them until it was off and he flung it from him into another room. How can you hold him like that. Hes nothing but a filthy homosexual. You should throw him out in the street. Hes your brother son. You should help him. Hes my son (hes my baby. My baby) and I love him and you should love him. She rocked with Georgettes head cradled in her arms and Arthur stormed out of the house and Georgette rolled over on her back trying to reach the slacks and the bennie, but her Mother held her, continuing to tell her son that it would be alright. Everything will be alright.) [pp. 36-38].

In D. H. Lawrence's *Sons and Lovers*, the love that would have been a beautiful gift for her husband the mother gave to the son, and it soured. The father of the protagonist in Rechy's *City of Night* was fifty years old when the latter was born; he was a caretaker in a public park, an unpredictably violent man, threatening to set the mother and son on fire (p. 16) and then again, being erratically tender with his son. At one point, the son says to his father, "I hate you — you're a failure — as a man, as a father!" (p. 17). But he has a great love for his mother, and the memory of her dots the pages of the book. He describes her as "a beautiful Mexican woman who loves me fiercely and never once understood about the terror between me and my father" (p. 14). He mentions his "Mother's blind carnivorous love" (p. 15), and when he returns home from military service he still finds "my Mother and her hungry love" (p. 19). In flight from the unconscious incestuous wish, he lands in New York City. As he stands in front of the public library in Bryant Park, he says, "I felt a change within me: a frantic lonesomeness that sometimes took me, paradoxically, to the height of elation, then flung me into depression. The figure of my Mother standing by the kitchen door crying, watching me leave, hovered ghostlike over me, but in the absence of that overwhelming tearing love—away from it if only physically—I felt a violent craving for something indefinable" (p. 31).

Perhaps no novelist has drawn a truer Bieberian portrait of a close-binding, castrating mother or of a weak, ineffectual father than has Merle Miller in his *What Happened*. Looking backward from his most recent emotional collapse and institutionalization, George Lionel assembles the fragments of a tormented life. "I despise people who claim they had happy childhoods. They're all liars. I was disenchanted the instant I leapt out of the womb, in full control of my faculties, like Minerva, which, not at all incidentally, was the name my mother had picked out for me. That and a crib lined in pink satin. She wouldn't let me out of that crib until I was sixteen or so. And I thought she would never let me graduate from breast feeding. I used to leave teeth marks all over things. I was sure that the milk was laced with arsenic. You can see what I mean about tits, though. Do you wonder that since Mums at last put them away, I haven't been near a pair..." (p. 9). George recognizes the exaggeration but asks, "Who needs to?" In describing his father, George says that for him to "volunteer to do anything, to leave the house even, except to go to work, was unprecedented. He was the least aggressive, most inward man I have ever known; he was a man destined to lose, and he was the shyest man I have ever known.... I could never love anybody who wasn't shy" (p. 13). And later, "My father was impractical. I grant you that, too. And he was weak" (p. 149). And his epitaph, "said to himself more than to my mother or me, 'I keep asking myself what I did wrong, but the real question is what I ever did right'" (p. 151).

The fear of women, and the feeling of repugnance for them, is apparent in Baldwin's homosexual novels, where physical intimacy is the means to emotional fulfillment. But with it there is always risk and mundanity, a "stink" of reality which results from a loss of purity, loss of the idealized image (Alexander, 1968, p. 11). "His characters reveal an unconscious conviction that women are either mothers or whores, and the imagery strongly depicts a kind of sexual attraction" which reveals an inordinate fear and distaste for females. To David's statment (in *Giovanni's Room*), "You don't seem to have a very high opinion of women," Giovanni responds, "Oh, women! There is no need, thank heaven, to have an opinion about women. Women are like water. They are tempting like that, and they can be that treacherous, and they can seem to be that bottomless, you know?—and they can be that shallow. And that dirty. . ." (Baldwin, p. 105). In males, it is often the reaction to castration anxiety that causes homosexuality; the anxiety is provoked by the sight of female genitals, and the reaction is fear and avoidance (Fenichel, 1945).

The resurrection of the amniotic past is frequently, if unconsciously, brought to life in a number of novels dealing with male homosexual physical relations. In *Giovanni's Room,* the symbolic return to the watery womb is seen in the description of Giovanni's room. It is literally dark; its windows have been painted over; it is messy and cluttered, full of Giovanni's "regurgitated life." The sea imagery Baldwin renders makes it seem that David exists as if in a comfortable, floating prenatal state. ". . . life in that room seemed to be occurring beneath the sea, time flowed past indifferently above us . . . It became, in a way, every room I had ever been in and every room I find myself in hereafter will remind me of Giovanni's room . . . Life in that room seemed to be occurring underwater, as I say, and it is certain that I underwent a sea-change there" (p. 112).

Hart Crane's *Voyages* (1966) concludes with these lines:

oh brilliant kids, frisk with your dog, Fondle you
shells and sticks, bleached By time and the elements;
but there is a line You must not cross nor ever trust
beyond its Spry cordage of your bodies to caresses
Too lichen-faithful from too wide a breast. The
bottom of the sea is cruel [p. 35].

These images, Alexander (1968) explains, "suggest . . . seduction from a maternal force, unperceived by the innocent children but seen and spoken of from a vantage point of a somewhat fatalistic adulthood: They must not trust their bodies to the sea's caresses, 'Too lichen-faithful from too wide a breast'; yet their exuberant and spontaneous play with a dog and with toys of 'shells and sticks' may put them in danger. But the speaker's perception and advice seem absolute: 'there is a line You must not cross' because, ultimately, 'the bottom of the sea is cruel' . . . The shells and sticks the children 'fondle' in play may be the male genitalia, innocent playthings in childhood but empowered emblems of adulthood as one matures. The sea, certainly maternal 'breast,' and comforting 'caresses,' suggests the first prenatal water in which one floated and that first powerful source of nourishment and care, the mother. Yet there is danger in trusting the 'cordage' of one's body (in remaining attached, in a figurative umbilical sense) to this comfort which comes from a breast 'too wide' and 'too lichen-faithful' (faithful, perhaps, to an earlier and more fundamental love—the father). Thus the urge to 'go far' in playing near the sea, while open to literal interpretation (or to being read as a death-wish), seems also to mean the strong attraction of unconscious incestuous impulses of a male towards his mother—this is the line one must not cross. And the finality of the last line—'the bottom of the sea is cruel'—implies that annihilation would result from following through such an urge" (pp. 12-13). And the death wish is, of course, a variation on the oedipal desire to return to the womb.

Chaste male love as the ultimate emotional experience is seen in Mark Twain's (1884) *Adventures of Huckleberry Finn* (Fiedler, 1948). In the novel, the homosexual need to be embraced in the purifying waters of the womb is presented. The fugitive slave and the teenager lie side by side on a raft borne by a swift-flowing river, a passage that takes place in and out of darkness and moist mist. The water-womb imagery is spelled out, almost, in William Burroughs' *The Wild Boys* (1971). Burroughs, whom Phillips (1965) called, along with Genet, the "new immoralists," has achieved the degradation of the senses, with scarcely any concessions to existing taste or sensibility in the choice of images or metaphors, amounting to a biological nightmare, an orgy of annihilation. Burroughs is obsessed with anal intercourse—nearly every page of the novel mentions the buttocks, rectum, anus, and anal penetration—and well might have the subtitle, *The Compleat Book of the Anus.* In one scene, two boys have been swimming naked in a pond. "He dries his prong with a handkerchief and rubs Vaseline on it. 'Stick your ass up Johnny.' I raise myself out of the water and he dries me with the handkerchief and rubs the Vaseline inside. Then he hitches his hands under my hips and pulls me up and my belly goes loose under the water and it is inside me I am spurting off into the cold water feeling his hot gobs inside" (p. 109). Rechy's protagonist in *City of Night* revels in the danger of detection in the last moments of exiled excitement: "In Central Park — as a rainstorm approached — once, one night in that park, aware of an unbearable exploding excitement within me mixed with unexplainable sudden panic, I stood against a tree and in frantic succession — and without even coming — I let seven night figures go down on me. And when, finally, the rain came pouring, I walked in it, soaked, as if the water would wash away whatever had caused the desperate night-experience" (p. 57).

The sexual fantasies of Kochan, the adolescent narrator in Yukio Mishima's *Confessions of a Mask* (1958), do not always succeed, as when he imagines enacting "the double role of both Omi and myself . . . There is no doubt that Omi himself was involved in my sexual desire, but neither could it be denied that this desire was directed mainly toward my own armpits" (p. 88). At this point, Kochan masturbates, copulating symbolically not with Omi but with himself. "I knelt down in the water and surrendered myself to a wave . . . When the wave receded, my corruption had been washed away . . . together with the countless living organisms . . . microbes, seeds of marine plants, fish eggs — my myriad spermatazoa had been engulfed in the foaming sea and carried away" (p. 89). Dana (1970, p. 90) interprets the sea "as the amniotic waters, the waters of birth, bearing 'seeds of marine plants,' 'fish eggs,' even human sperm, [it] represents that vast and mysterious life-force to which Kochan would give himself over, if he could. But the sea and water are employed not only as symbols of sexuality and birth, but as images of violent death, solitude, and self-love." Thus, water as a cleansing force for the homosexual's guilt, and his need to be reunited with the mother in intimate, womblike embrace, is an unconscious device frequently used by the novelist to help understand affect, and to transmute the incestuous wish into a purifying, innocent, and beneficent symbolism.

Ferenczi (1933), in his theory of genitality, assumes an identification between sperm and the ego, eventuating in a threefold identification in coitus: identification of the whole organism with the genital, identification with the partner, and identification with the sexual secretion. The purpose of the sex act can be only "to return to the mother's womb [p. 18] . . . The human being is dominated from the moment of birth onwards by the continuous regressive trend toward the reestablishment of the intrauterine situation, and holds fast to this unswervingly . . ." (p. 20).

Many primitive cosmogonic myths which represent the earth as rising out of the sea include in them elements which permit such a cosmogony to be interpreted as a symbolic representation of birth; this is illustrated, with many examples, in Rank's *Inzestmotiv,* and Róheim was able to provide me with many instances from the wealth of his ethnological material. And certainly the psychoanalytic day's work supplies gross examples of regression to the mother symbolism of earth or of water. In many nursery tales we have the direct transference to the earth of the love for the mother which has been renounced in the passing of the oedipus complex, acts of coitus carried out through the digging of holes in the earth, or an attempt at, as it were, total regression by creeping bodily into a hollow in the earth. Nor shall I ever forget the instance of the young homosexual with an indissoluble fixation upon his mother, who in adolescence lay on the bottom of a bathtub filled with warm water in order to be able to maintain this archaic aquatic status or foetal situation breathed through a long tube protruding from the water which he held in his mouth.

The interpretation of being rescued from water or of swimming in water as a representation of birth and as a representation of coitus, an interpretation given in an earlier chapter and one moreover which is current in psychoanalysis, demands therefore a phylogenetic interpretation in addition; falling into the water would again be the more archaic symbol, that of the return to the uterus, while in rescue from water the birth *motif* or that of exile to a land existence seems to be emphasized. One is also tempted to explain the various deluge myths as a reversal, of a sort familiar to psychoanalysis, of the true state of affairs. The first and foremost danger encountered by organisms which were all originally water-inhabiting was not that of inundation but of desiccation. The raising of Mount Ararat out of the waters of the flood would thus be not only a deliverance, as told in the Bible, but at the same time the original catastrophe which may have only later on been recast from the standpoint of land-dwellers. For the psychoanalyst, at all events, it is of course not difficult to recognize Ararat, the Earth, on a deeper level of its symbolism, as simply the doublet of the Ark of Noah, and both as symbolic representations of the uterus from which all the higher animals have their origin; it should only be added that this mythological material also requires a supplemental interpretation from the phylogenetic standpoint.

Now we should like to ask for just such a supplemental interpretation in behalf of the explanations which have been given in preceding chapters, explanations wherein the several phenomena connected with coitus were conceived as symbolic actions in which the individual reexperiences the pleasure of intrauterine existence, the anxiety of birth, and the subsequent pleasure in surmounting this latter danger successfully. Since the individual identifies himself with the phallus inserted in the vagina and with the spermatazoa swarming into the body of the female, he also repeats symbolically the danger of death which his animal ancestors victoriously overcame in the geological cataclysm of the drying up of the sea [pp. 48-49].

*   *   *

The possession of an organ of copulation, the development within the maternal womb, and the circumvention of the great danger of desiccation — these three thus form an indestructible biological unity which must constitute the ultimate basis of the symbolic identity of the womb with the sea and the earth on the one hand, and of the male member with the child and the fish on the other [p. 50].

*   *   *

In much closer accord with the psychoanalytic conception regarding the determination and motivation of all biological and mental phenomena is the supposition that the amniotic fluid represents a sea "introjected," as it were, into the womb of the mother — a sea in which as the embryologist R. Hertwig says, "the delicate and easily injured embryo swims and executes movements like a fish in water" [p. 56].

It is no coincidence that womb-amniotic fluid symbolism is related by the novelist to the homosexual, just as the homosexual emerging from the shadows is referred to as coming out of the closet. Millions of homosexuals have kept themselves hidden in the closet-womb, ashamed of what they are or fearful of society's punishment and relatives' and friends' rejection, or unwilling to associate with other, more obvious homosexuals. But the testimony of many of those who acknowledge their sexual preference reveals a sense of relief in terms of achieving an identity heretofore denied. It sometimes develops into a militant or messianic fervor to educate people that homosexuals are human or that there are alternatives to the present nuclear family and that attitudes of straight people, due to ignorance, must be changed. Lawrence Durrell's

The Black Book (1940) has a closet homosexual, Tarquin, who, much like Scobie in the Alexandria Quartet, is a likeable if grotesque comic figure, a "nymph bursting from the wrappings."

> "This is a new beginning," says Tarquin. "Up to now I have been floundering, I did not know my direction. Now it is all quite different"
> He has discovered that he is a homosexual. After examining his diary, having his horoscope cast, his palm read, his prostate fingered, and the bumps on his great bald cranium interpreted.
> "From now on it is going to be different. I am going to sleep with whom I want and not let my conditioned self interfere with me. I have finished with morals, don't you think? I am that I am, and all that kind of stuff. One must be bold enough to face up to oneself, eh? I am grateful for Science having made it possible. I shall let my female half come out in full view. Untrammeled, what do you say?" [pp. 146-147].

His words run parallel to those in Shakespeare's *Much Ado About Nothing*, "I can not hide what I am!" and to Simmel's, in *Cain '67* (1971), "No one can be what one is not" (p. 376), but such platitudes take on a different hue when raised by the homosexual. Miller (1971), in acknowledging his homosexuality in the autobiographical *On Being Different,* writes: "When I was a child in Marshalltown, Iowa, I hated Christmas almost as much as I do now, but I loved Halloween. I never wanted to take off the mask, I wanted to wear it everywhere, night and day, always. And I suppose I still do. I have often used liquor, which is another kind of mask, and more recently, pot" (p. 6). In his autobiographical novel, *What Happened* (1972), Miller declares that the "thing about being a member of the underground: you never know how much the nonmember knows. Or suspects. You have to play it by ear. I suppose people in the Mafia have the same problems. And the early Christians" (p. 197). James Baldwin (1972), at the age of forty-eight, lamented, "What in the world was I now but an aging, lonely, sexually dubious, politically outrageous, unspeakable erratic freak" (p. 184). E. M. Forster's posthumous, autobiographical homosexual novel, *Maurice* (1913), is an account of two closest homosexuals who never emerge from the closet. Clive, the more intellectual member of the duo, adapts easily to the compromise of marriage and being a proper citizen, precisely because his cleverness helps him rationalize matters. Maurice, a plodder in every way, cannot knuckle down, falls in love with an illiterate gamekeeper, throws up everything, and goes off to live in the greenwood. The following conversation takes place in *The Money Murders,* by Eugene Franklin (1972):

> I held out my hand. "I'm Larry Howe..."
> We shook hands. "I'm Marcel Proust. That's my legal name. I changed it to avoid problems."
> "Problems?"
> "Mainly the problem of embarrassing my parents. I've come out."
> "Liberating the gay?"
> "I see you're not with it."
> "No. But I'm not a homophobe."
> He smiled. "But you wouldn't want your brother to marry one?"
> That stumped me. "I'd take a strong stand with regard to my sister," I said.
> He grinned. "So would I" [pp. 67-68].

For most homosexuals who have struggled against their gayness, coming out is a long and painful process (Altman, 1972). Perhaps homosexuals have for too long been accomplices in the silence surrounding them. The influence of the gay liberation movement, the loosening of society's views of what is considered deviant behavior, and the trend of psychiatrists and society to accept homosexuality as an alternate life style rather than a sickness, may coalesce to help the closet homosexual open the door.

While the closet homosexual is fully aware of his third sex status and keeps it hidden from most people, the latent homosexual may never be conscious of his sexual urges. Sometimes latent homosexuality is masked by exaggerated virility in men, as cited earlier in Harrison's *Wolf. A False Memoir.* Sometimes it is the strong repressive forces that prevent men from knowing what their real sexual feelings are. Such a man is Harry Black in Hubert Selby's *Last Exit to Brooklyn.* Harry is touching his eight-month-old son's penis, pulling his hand away when his wife enters the room. As she bends down to change the baby's diaper, it looks to him as if she were about to put his penis in her mouth. "His stomach knotted, a slight nausea starting" (p. 117). Later, in bed with his wife, an unreasoning anger and hatred for her overpowers him and, when he is forced to have intercourse with her, he performs the act sadistically in a parody of rape. He feels nauseated at the ordeal and is gripped by an anxiety attack. Prior to marriage, he customarily vomited and shed tears after running from a woman he had been with. His sadistic nightmares terrorize him. When the workers in his plant go out on strike and he is put in charge of a store-front strike head-quarters, Harry panics with so many men about him. He escapes to a nearby bar, and hears a "high-pitched feminine voice . . . of a fairy" (p. 148), and cannot tear himself away from staring and listening. Subsequently, he meets some of the men who were with the homo-sexual and casually asks them "who that fruit was" (p. 155), to which comes the rejoinder, "Why you wanna meeter?" (p. 156). Harry's de-fenses surface and he cannot stop bragging about his sexual prowess with women. Ginger, a homosexual in drag, excites Harry as he looks at him and caresses his beer glass, "licking his lips not knowing exactly what he was doing, his body reacting and tingling, aware of nothing but a lightness, almost a giddiness, and a fascination. And a feeling of power and strength" (p. 179). Ginger recognizes Harry's excitement and passion, provoking him, and treating him with sadistic contempt and teasing. A few days later, Harry is picked up in a bar by a male homosexual prostitute, Alberta, who brings him to "her" apartment where he allows himself to be seduced—quite willingly.

> Harry flopped onto the bed and rolled over and kissed her chin. She laughed and guided him to her mouth. He pushed at her side and at first Alberta was puzzled, trying to understand what he was trying to do, then realized that he was trying to turn her over. She giggled again. You silly you. You never have fucked a fairy before, have you? Harry grumbled, still fumbling and kissing her neck and chest. We make love just like anybody else honey, a little peeved at first then once more relishing the charm of having a cherry. Just relax, rolling over on her side and kissing him, whispering in his ear. When she finished the preparations she rolled back onto her back, Harry rolling over on her, and moved rhythmically with Harry, her legs and arms wrapped around him, rolling, squirming, groaning [p. 195].

Upon waking the next morning, Harry was no longer a latent homo-sexual, but he was still a closet homosexual, with his fears and con-fusion overshadowed by his momentary feeling of happiness. Unlike his feelings toward Mary, his wife, he was not angry or hating, he did not want to destroy.

Johnny Rio, the homosexual in Rechy's *Numbers,* had learned early about the quick anger of the latent homosexual. "... as with all truly sexually desirable men, he attracts both sexes—even among his own sex, some who will never recognize that attraction, who will feel it, disguised, only as a certain anger and resentment toward him. Johnny is used to that type of man, usually married, who will try to quarrel with him instantly" (p. 18).

What Hacker (1952) calls the Ishmael complex manifests itself in the form of masculine fellowship, but it is carefully sublimated in order not to violate cultural normative standards. Fiedler (1948) calls attention to this expression in a number of classics: *Moby Dick, Huckleberry Finn, Two Years Before the Mast,* and the *Leatherstocking Tales.* In each of these works an outcast American lad is found in some isolated primitive expanse, such as the broad Mississippi, the virgin forest, a deserted shore, the vast sea, in company of an older, not wholly civilized, male associate from whom the young man receives lavish affection that is reciprocated in large measure. The common theme of an isolated, aim-inhibited, homosexual relationship between a declassed American lad and an outcast of a different ethnic background is explicitly rendered in Herman Melville's *Moby Dick* (1851). "Not by chance phrase or camouflaged symbol," wrote Fiedler (1948), "but in a step-by-step exposition, the Pure Marriage of Ishmael and Queequeg is set before us: the initial going to bed together and the first shyness overcome, that great hot tomahawk-pipe accepted in a familiarity that dispels fear; next, the wedding ceremony itself (for in this marriage like so many others the ceremonial follows the deflowering), with the ritual touching of foreheads; then, the queasiness and guilt the morning after the *official* First Night, the suspicion that one has joined himself irrevocably to his own worst nightmare; finally, a symbolic portrayal of the continuing state of marriage through the image of the 'monkey rope' which binds the lovers fast waist to waist..." (p. 145).

Ishmael has been told by the landlord of the Spouter Inn that the only available space remaining is a double bed which he would have to share with a harpooner, otherwise not identified by the landlord, but who is, of course, the primitive Queequeg. Ishmael, the narrator, ponders his dilemma, initially deciding to chance sleeping with the stranger, then changing his mind.

> No man prefers to sleep two in a bed. In fact, you would a good deal rather not sleep with your own brother. I don't know how it is, but

people like to be private when they are sleeping. And when it comes to sleeping with an unknown stranger, in a strange inn, in a strange town, and that stranger a harpooneer, then your objections indefinitely multiply. Nor was there any earthly reason why I as a sailor should sleep two in a bed, more than anybody else; for sailors no more sleep two in a bed at sea than bachelor kings do ashore. To be sure they all sleep together in one apartment, but you have your own hammock, and cover yourself with your own blanket, and sleep in your own skin. The more I pondered over this harpooneer, the more I abominated the thought of sleeping with him [Melville, p. 13].

Ishmael overprotests, toys with the idea of sharing the bed, and, to be sure, changes his mind again.

I considered the matter a moment, and then upstairs we went, and I was ushered into a small room, cold as a clam, and furnished, sure enough, with a prodigious bed, almost big enough indeed for any four harpooneers to sleep abreast.

"There," said the landlord, placing the candle on a crazy old sea-chest that did double duty as a washstand and centre-table; "there, make yourself comfortable now, and good-night to ye." I turned round from eyeing the bed, but he had disappeared.

Folding back the counterpane, I stooped over the bed. Though none of the most elegant, it yet stood the scrutiny tolerably well. I then glanced round the room; and besides the bedstead and centre-table, could see no other furniture belonging to the place, but a rude shelf, the four walls, and a papered fireboard representing a man striking a whale. Of things not properly belonging to the room, there was a hammock lashed up, and thrown upon the floor in one corner; also a large seaman's bag, containing the harpooneer's wardrobe, no doubt in lieu of a land trunk. Likewise, there was a parcel of outlandish bone fish-hooks on the shelf over the fireplace, and a tall harpoon standing at the head of the bed.

But what is this on the chest? I took it up, and held it close to the light, and felt it, and smelt it, and tried every way possible to arrive at some satisfactory conclusion concerning it. I can compare it to nothing but a large door mat, ornamented at the edges with little tinkling tags something like the stained porcupine quills round an Indian moccasin. There was a hole or slit in the middle of this mat, the same as in South American ponchos. But could it be possible that any sober harpooneer would get into a door mat, and parade the streets of any Christian town in that sort of guise? I put it on, to try it, and it weighed me down like a hamper, being uncommonly shaggy and thick, and I thought a little damp, as though this mysterious harpooneer had been wearing it of a rainy day. I went up in it to a bit of glass stuck against the wall, and I never saw such a sight in my life. I tore myself out of it in such a hurry that I gave myself a kink in the neck.

I sat down on the side of the bed, and commenced thinking about this head-peddling harpooneer, and his door mat. After thinking some time on the bedside, I got up and took off my monkey-jacket, and then stood in the middle of the room thinking. I then took off my coat, and thought a little more in my shirt-sleeves. But beginning to feel very cold now, half undressed as I was, and remembering what the landlord said about the harpooneer's not coming home at all that night, it being so very late, I made no more ado, but jumped out of my pantaloons and boots, and then blowing out the light tumbled into bed, and commended myself to the care of heaven.

Whether that mattress was stuffed with corn-cobs or broken crockery, there is no telling, but I rolled about a good deal, and could not sleep for a long time. At last I slid off into a light doze, and had pretty nearly made a good thing offing towards the land of Nod, when I heard a heavy footfall in the passage, and saw a glimmer of light come into the room from under the door.

"Lord save me," thinks I, "that must be the harpooneer, the infernal head-pedlar." But I lay perfectly still, and resolved not to say a word till spoken to. Holding a light in one hand, and that identical New Zealand head in the other, the stranger entered the room, and without looking towards the bed, placed his candle a good way off from me on the floor in one corner, and then began working away at the knotted cords of the large bag I before spoke of as being in the room. I was all eagerness to see his face, but he kept it averted for some time while employed in unlacing the bag's mouth. This accomplished, however, he turned round—when, good heavens! what a sight! Such a face! It was of a dark, purplish, yellow colour, here and there stuck over with large, blackish looking squares. Yes, it's just as I thought, he's a terrible bedfellow; he's been in a fight, got dreadfully cut, and here he is just from the surgeon. But at that moment he chanced to turn his face so towards the light, that I plainly saw that they could not be sticking-plasters at all, those black squares on his cheeks. They were stains of some sort or other. At first I knew not what to make of this; but soon an inkling of the truth occurred to me. I remembered a story of a white man—a whaleman too—who, falling among the cannibals, had been tattooed by them.

I concluded that this harpooneer, in the course of his distant voyages, must have met with a similar adventure. And what is it, thought I, after all! It's only his outside; a man can be honest in any sort of skin. But then, what to make of his unearthly complexion, that part of it, I mean, lying round about, and completely independent of the squares of tattooing. To be sure, it might be nothing but a good coat of tropical tanning; but I never heard of a hot sun's tanning a white man into a purplish yellow one. However, I had never been in the South Seas; and perhaps the sun there produced these extraordinary effects upon the skin. Now, while all these ideas were passing through me like lightning, this harpooneer never noticed me at all. But, after some difficulty having opened his bag, he commenced fumbling in it, and presently pulled out a sort of tomahawk, and a sealskin wallet with the hair on. Placing these on the old chest in the middle of the room, he then took the New Zealand head—a ghastly thing enough—and crammed it down into the bag. He now took off his hat—a new beaver hat—when I came nigh singing out with fresh surprise. There was no hair on his head—none to speak of at least—nothing but a small scalp-knot twisted up on his forehead. His bald purplish head now looked for all the world like a mildewed skull. Had not the stranger stood between me and the door, I would have bolted out of it quicker than ever I bolted a dinner.

Even as it was, I thought something of slipping out of the window, but it was the second floor back. I am no coward, but what to make of this head-peddling purple rascal altogether passed my comprehension. Ignorance is the parent of fear, and being completely nonplussed and confounded about the stranger, I confess I was now as much afraid of him as if it was the devil himself who had thus broken into my room at the dead of night. In fact, I was so afraid of him that I was not game enough just then to address him, and demand a satisfactory answer concerning what seemed inexplicable in him.

Meanwhile, he continued the business of undressing, and at last showed his chest and arms. As I live, these covered parts of him were checkered with the same squares as his face; his back, too, was all over the same dark squares; he seemed to have been in a Thirty Years' War, and just escaped from it with a sticking-plaster shirt. Still more, his very legs were marked, as if a parcel of dark green frogs were running up the trunks of young palms. It was now quite plain that he must be some abominable savage or other shipped aboard of a whaleman in the South Seas, and so landed in this Christian country. I quaked to think of it. A pedlar of heads too—

perhaps the heads of his own brothers. He might take a fancy to mine — heavens! look at that tomahawk!

*   *   *

All these queer proceedings increased my uncomfortableness, and seeing him now exhibiting strong symptoms of concluding his business operations, and jumping into bed with me, I thought it was high time, now or never before the light was put out, to break the spell in which I had so long been bound.

But the interval I spent in deliberating what to say, was a fatal one. Taking up his tomahawk from the table, he examined the head of it for an instant, and then holding it to the light, with his mouth at the handle, he puffed out great clouds of tobacco smoke. The next moment the light was extinguished, and this wild cannibal, tomahawk between his teeth, sprang into bed with me. I sang out, I could not help it now; and giving a sudden grunt of astonishment he began feeling me.

Stammering out something, I knew not what, I rolled away from him against the wall, and then conjured him, whoever and whatever he might be, to keep quiet, and let me get up and light the lamp again. But his guttural responses satisfied me at once that he but ill comprehended my meaning.

"Who-e debel you?" — he at last said — "You no speak-e, dam-me, I kill-e." And so saying the lighted tomahawk began flourishing about me in the dark.

"Landlord, for God's sake, Peter Coffin!" shouted I. "Landlord! Watch! Coffin! Angels! Save me!"

"Speake-e! tell-ee me who-ee be, or dam-me, I kill-e!" again growled the cannibal, while his horrid flourishings of the tomahawk scattered the hot tobacco ashes about me till I thought my linen would get on fire. But thank heaven, at that moment the landlord came into the room light in hand, and leaping from the bed I ran up to him.

"Don't be afraid now," said he, grinning again. "Queequeg here wouldn't harm a hair of your head."

"Stop your grinning," shouted I, "and why didn't you tell me that infernal harpooneer was a cannibal?"

"I thought ye know'd it; — didn't I tell ye, he was a peddlin' heads around town? — But turn flukes again and go to sleep. Queequeg, look here — you sabbee me, I sabbee you — this man sleepe you — you sabbee?"

"Me sabbee plenty" — grunted Queequeg, puffing away at his pipe and sitting up in bed.

"You gettee in," he added, motioning to me with his tomahawk, and throwing the clothes to one side. He really did this in not only a civil but a really kind and charitable way. I stood looking at him a moment. For all his tattooings he was on the whole a clean, comely looking cannibal. "What's all this fuss I have been making about," thought I to myself — "the man's a human being just as I am: he has just as much reason to fear me as I have to be afraid of him. Better sleep with a sober cannibal than a drunken Christian."

"Landlord," said I, "tell him to stash his tomahawk there, or pipe, or whatever you call it; tell him to stop smoking, in short, and I will turn in with him. But I don't fancy having a man smoking in bed with me. It's dangerous. Besides, I ain't insured."

This being told to Queequeg, he at once complied, and again politely motioned me to get into bed — rolling over to one side as much as to say — "I won't touch a leg of ye."

"Good-night, landlord," said I; "you may go."

I turned in, and never slept better in my life.

*   *   *

Upon waking next morning about daylight, I found Queequeg's arm thrown over me in the most loving and affectionate manner. You had almost thought I had been his wife. The counterpane was of patchwork, full of odd little parti-coloured squares and triangles; and this arm of his tattooed all over with an interminable Cretan labyrinth of a figure, no two parts of which were of one precise shade — owing I suppose to his keeping his arm at sea unmethodically in sun and shade, his shirt-sleeves irregularly rolled up at various times — this same arm of his, I say, looked for all the world like a strip of that same patchwork quilt. Indeed, partly lying on it as the arm did when I first awoke, I could hardly tell it from the quilt, they so blended their hues together; and it was only by the sense of weight and pressure that I could tell that Queequeg was hugging me.

My sensations were strange. Let me try to explain them. When I was a child, I well remember a somewhat similar circumstance that befell me; whether it was a reality or a dream, I never could entirely settle. The circumstance was this. I had been cutting up some caper or other — I think it was trying to crawl up the chimney, as I had seen a little sweep do a few days previous; and my stepmother who, somehow or other, was all the time whipping me, or sending me to bed supperless, — my stepmother dragged me by the legs out of the chimney and packed me off to bed, though it was only two o'clock in the afternoon of the 21st June, the longest day in the year in our hemisphere. I felt dreadfully. But there was no help for it, so upstairs I went to my little room in the third floor, undressed myself as slowly as possible so as to kill time, and with a bitter sigh got between the sheets.

I lay there dismally calculating that sixteen entire hours must elapse before I could hope to get out of bed again. Sixteen hours in bed! the small of my back ached to think of it. And it was so light too; the sun shining in at the window, and a great rattling of coaches in the streets, and the sound of gay voices all over the house. I felt worse and worse — at last I got up, dressed, and softly going down in my stockinged feet, sought out my stepmother, and suddenly threw myself at her feet, beseeching her as a particular favour to give me a good slippering for my misbehaviour; anything indeed but condemning me to lie abed such an unendurable length of time. But she was the best and most conscientious of stepmothers, and back I had to go to my room. For several hours I lay there broad awake, feeling a great deal worse than I have ever done since, even from the greatest subsequent misfortunes. At last I must have fallen into a troubled nightmare of a doze; and slowly waking from it — half steeped in dreams — I opened my eyes, and the before sunlit room was now wrapped in outer darkness. Instantly I felt a shock running through all my frame; nothing was to be seen, and nothing was to be heard; but a supernatural hand seemed placed in mine. My arm hung over the counterpane, and the nameless, unimaginable, silent form or phantom, to which the hand belonged, seemed closely seated by my bedside. For what seemed ages piled on ages, I lay there, frozen with the most awful fears, not daring to drag away my hand; yet ever thinking that if I could but stir it one single inch, the horrid spell would be broken. I knew not how this consciousness at last glided away from me; but waking in the morning, I shudderingly remembered it all, and for days and weeks and months afterwards I lost myself in confounding attempts to explain the mystery. Nay, to this very hour, I often puzzle myself with it.

Now, take away the awful fear, and my sensations at feeling the supernatural hand in mine were very similar, in their strangeness, to those which I experienced on waking up and seeing Queequeg's pagan arm thrown round me. But at length all the past night's events soberly recurred, one by one, in fixed reality, and then I lay only alive to the comical predicament. For though I tried to move his arm — unlock his clasp — yet, sleeping as he was, he still hugged me tightly, as though naught but death should part us twain. I now strove to rouse him — "Queequeg!" — but his only answer was a snore. I then rolled over, my neck feeling as if it were in a horse-collar; and suddenly felt a slight scratch. Throwing aside the counterpane, there lay the tomahawk sleeping by the savage's side, as if it were a hatchet-faced baby. A pretty pickle, truly, thought I; abed here in a strange house in the broad day, with a cannibal and a tomahawk! "Queequeg! — in the name of goodness, Queequeg, wake!" At length, by dint of much wriggling, and loud and incessant expostulations upon the unbecomingness of his hugging a fellow male in that sort of style, I succeeded in extracting a grunt; and presently, he drew back his arm, shook himself all over like a Newfoundland dog just from the water, and sat up in bed, stiff as a pike-staff, looking at me... [pp. 17-24, *passim*].

The depiction of latent homosexuality in fiction is legion; it is seen in D. H. Lawrence's (1922) *Aaron's Rod,* Sherwood Anderson's (1923) short story, "The Man Who Became a Woman," and Leo Tolstoy's (1891) *The Kreutzer Sonata,* among others. The Tolstoy work shows that latent homosexuality has great potential for demoralization, despair, self-hatred, sadistic violence, and escalation of individual psychopathology. This is true not only for the latent but the overt homosexual, in terms of his promiscuity, need to be punished, regret at being homosexual, the sadistic quality of his love, the fear of social disapproval or rejection, the inability to experience a conventional family life, feelings of guilt and shame, or fear of potential trouble with the law. These factors suggest a depersonalization and a compulsive quality about the sexual activity of many homosexuals that is extremely costly to them. Latent homosexuality is closely related to paranoia, according to Freud (1911), who hypothesized that psychotic symptoms develop as a defense against emerging unconscious wishes. His theory of the etiology of paranoia rests upon his concept of narcissism, wherein libido is withdrawn from objects and turned on one's self. In paranoia, the person tries to free himself from this state, but is unable to go beyond his homosexual fixations. Others say that while many cases of paranoia have a manifest homosexual component, it is probably not justified to attribute it to all cases; the acceptance of Freud's theory tends to prevent the exploration of other possible etiological factors and obstructs progress toward a clearer understanding of paranoia as a symptom complex with a diverse etiology. A number of studies of the hypothesized link between homosexuality and paranoid disorders have been made, some of which show their relatedness (Aronson, 1952; Klaf and Davis, 1960; Norman, 1948; Kitay et al., 1963); others demonstrate their unrelatedness (Meketon et al., 1962; Friberg, 1964; Planansky and Johnson, 1962; Salzman, 1960); and still others produced inconclusive results (Moore and Selzer, 1963; Nitsche et al., 1956; Walters, 1955; Zamansky, 1958).

Novelists tend to agree with the traditional Freudian view which holds that paranoid development is based on latent or repressed homosexuality. Henry James, in *The Turn of the Screw* (1898), catches the thread of paranoid psychopathology, as the governess, aided by Mrs. Grose, weaves the fabric of her delusional system around the presumed homosexual relations of the departed servants and children (Aldrich, 1967). The frantic resistance to recognizing his latent homosexuality, the sadistic behavior he acts out with prostitutes, the virile symbolism of the fondling of the gun by the narrator in Jean-Paul Sartre's (1948) short story, "Erostratus," are illustrative of useful defenses against the unacceptable homosexual impulse, and the regressive disorganization of the ego. With the repressed homosexuality, appeared the paranoid delusions. Johnny Rio's obsessive need to be fellated, in Rechy's *Numbers,* is a search for replenishment of his vitality, a renewal of potency, for the erect penis is an especially powerful object, particularly if the mother treats the son as the penis she lacks. Johnny has a compulsive need to act out the dominant male over the submissive female, to defeat the other competitive "youngmen" who are also cruising in Griffith Park, to prevent, however temporarily, an acute outbreak of homosexual anxiety. The most likely expression of this anxiety is in the form of a paranoid projection. The aggressive, obsessive quality of subjecting his competitors to defeat is symbolic of his need to castrate the competitor and make a woman—a homosexual—of him, before the table can be turned.

The title of Rechy's novel, *Numbers,* has a double meaning. In homosexual argot, a "number" refers to a potential, actual, or merely desired person in vagrant sex. The theme of Rechy's book is Johnny's obsession with numbers and with counting as a device to shut off his obsessively intrusive ideation about death and self-destruction. Near the end of the novel, when he is acutely aware of the cruising young-men in the park who have now become his enemies, the repressed thoughts of death and destruction force themselves to the surface as he says to himself, "The season of sex and death is about to end. Death? Why did he think of death? The superstitious part of him is chilled by that odd slip in his thoughts. He tries to find a 'reason' for it.... The crushed bugs on the windshield, the birds smashed on the highway: the specter of death that marked his entrance to the city of lost angels..." (p. 217). On his drive from his home in Laredo to revisit Los Angeles, the scene of his spectacular earlier homosexual activities, Johnny counts the bugs crushed against the windshield of his car, the number of automobiles he passes on the road, the number of dead birds he sees on the highway. He reviews the number of women with whom he has had intercourse, the number of men who have fellated him in movie theaters and how many in how many days. He counts the physical exercises he does in multiples of seven because seven is his lucky number. When he arrives in Los Angeles, he begins the doomed count of men who fellate him and then panders to his obsession, "Just one more to make it three; like yesterday" (p. 136). After sixteen men have fellated him in five days, Johnny makes up rule number one: it "can't be the same one twice" (p. 201). Frantically determined to achieve some goal, some finality, he arbitrarily decides on thirty fellators within ten days.

He develops free-floating anxieties. Even though he "was struck by the anonymous horror, the emotional carnage of the sexual hunt in the park, and he resolved never to return" (p. 178), the next day finds him on the prowl again. "The fear that kept him away yesterday had not abated. Until he felt the Fear of the park so acutely, no reason for his actions was needed; there was no crisis. But now an action exists, without a reason—with, instead, many reasons against the action; and this signals a crisis. Of course he's aware of all this only as a festering irritation, something which blisters his consciousness and makes him feel that he's 'floating'—drifting, afraid, in what has become a hostile but deceptively welcoming sea: the Park" (p. 178). Again, there is a reference to the amniotic sea, the safety of the metaphoric womb-park. Johnny becomes oppressed and depressed: so many left to fellate him on his self-made schedule and so little time! The waves of sexual excitement, as three men fellate him within twenty minutes, drown his terror, but only momentarily.

As the time draws shorter for his goal to be accomplished, his obsession with numbers increases and he finds himself inventorying what each of the twenty-three strangers look like; when he fails to recall several, he becomes further depressed; when later he remembers, he is elated. But the paranoid ideation takes over when the top of the highest hill in the park "seems to tremble in wrath. Crazily, Johnny imagines God perched with his heavenly rifle on just such a height to 'catch' those whose numbers are up: *Pingggggggg!* God shoots! And Number Infinte-billion, Six Million, Eight Hundred and Sixty-six Thousand, Three Hundred and Seventy-two crumples over. And now Number Infinite-billion, Six Million, Eight Hundred and Sixty-six Thousand, Three Hundred and Seventy-*three* runs for cover! But God — the expert sniper who *never* misses — aims his rifle. Unswervingly. *Pingggggggg!* Another's number coming up!" (pp. 206-207). With God and "Numbers, numbers, numbers, numb — ..." (p. 249), the book draws to its logical, psychological conclusion from its opening, when "that day, as Johnny stood looking at himself in the mirror, he felt curiously that he had ceased to exist, that he existed only in the mirror" (p. 23).

"The principle of causality, whatever shape it may have taken in the development of modern science, requires that for every observable fact a corresponding law be established. This principle also applies to psychology.... The extension of data subjected to scientific investigation [by Freud] led to intensive scrutiny of minutest details that earlier no one would have thought either worthy of attention or decisive in hypotheses or theories about the mind.... In approaching a literary work psychoanalytically, the psychological meaning usually can be deciphered easily. To cite one conspicuous example, anyone who has studied the oedipal conflict in the clinical setting is bound to acknowledge it in Hamlet..." (Eissler, 1959, pp. 1-3). The reader of Leo Tolstoy's *The Kreutzer Sonata* (1891), will find further evidence for Freud's theory that paranoid symptomatology reflects a homosexual conflict. In the novel, Pozdnyshev has a compulsion to tell the story of his murder of his wife to a stranger on a train in which both are traveling through the night. He explains how he lived "dissolutely" as a youth, "like everybody in our class," but "I was not a seducer, had no unnatural tastes ... but I practised debauchery in a steady, decent way for health's sake.... The women I was intimate with were not mine, and I had nothing to do with them except the pleasure they afforded me. And I saw nothing disgraceful in this" (p. 125).

Thus Pozdnyshev has to make the point that he has no unnatural tastes, i.e., homosexual perversion; he has to insist the stranger understand he was pure, if unchaste, but for health reasons only; and he reveals his treatment of women merely as sex objects. He relates to his traveling companion some of his adolescent sexual, and apparently youthful, homosexual experiences, though their extent is not spelled out. "I had been depraved (when I was thirteen) by other boys" (p. 126). And at fifteen, he had made his first visit to a brothel with his older brother—probably a masking of his homosexuality even then. His young adulthood became a Don Juan period, for he was in a constant quest for sexual relations with women, another masked form of homosexuality. Nothing satisfies him since he cannot find the object of his quest. The sadistic act of showing his fiancée his diary, in which he has compulsively recorded his debauched past, reveals further evidence of Pozdnyshev's homosexuality. No only was his unceasing flight from one woman to another sadistic, but an even stronger sadism develops when a latent homosexual, such as Pozdnyshev, is bound in marriage to one woman. "I remember her horror, despair and confusion, when she learnt of it and understood it," he says when recalling to the train companion how he gave his fiancée his incriminating diary. "Unconscious but aggressive homosexual tendencies and sadism are inseparable phenomena. When one of the partners in a marriage is a homosexual, the marriage becomes a form of torture, especially when the homosexuality assumes an aggressive shape" (Velikovsky, 1937, p. 19). Pozdnyshev is a sadist. He does not know that his unceasing hatred for every woman who has yielded to him, and for that matter, all women, especially his wife, is caused by his unconscious desire for a male partner. At the end of the novel, he says, "Yes, if I had known what I know now, then everything would have been entirely different. I would not have married for . . . I would not have married at all" (p. 190). But he develops this insight for the wrong reasons. In his pathological hatred against women, his reaction to his wife is even more vehement because it is concentrated on her as the one possible release of libidinal tension. His hatred of and anxieties about women act as an effective barrier against his making a proper sexual adjustment. "I used formerly to feel uncomfortable and uneasy when I saw a lady dressed up for a ball, but now I am simply frightened and plainly see her as something dangerous and illicit. I want to call a policeman and ask for protection from the peril, and demand that the dangerous object be removed and put away . . . I am sure a time will come, and perhaps very soon, when people will understand this and will wonder how a society could exist in which actions were permitted which so disturb social tranquility as those adornments of the body directly evoking sensuality, which we tolerate for women in our society. Why, it's like setting all sorts of traps along the paths and promenades—it is even worse!" (p. 136).

Pozdnyshev sees sexual intercourse as unnatural and weddings as nothing but licensed debauchery. Intercourse is "horrid, shameful and painful. No, it is unnatural! And an unspoilt girl, as I have convinced myself, always hates it" (p. 138). And so he advocates not merely ascetic abstinence but complete coital abstinence on the part of mankind, which would lead to the extinction of the human race. In other words, Pozdnyshev is advocating passive psychic castration, a reaction observable in many neurotic trends and in certain psychoses as actual behavior. Pozdnyshev's latent homosexuality is protected by his advancing the view that the ultimate purpose of mankind is to annihilate itself gradually through universal psychic castration (Karpman, 1938, p. 21), much like Yukio Mishima's (1963) *The Sailor Who Fell from Grace with the Sea*. In the latter novel, Noboru, at thirteen, was convinced of his own genius and certain "that propagation was a fiction; consequently, society was a fiction too; that fathers and teachers, by virtue of being fathers and teachers, were guilty of a grievous sin" (p. 13). Pozdnyshev has the cruel insight of many paranoiacs when he says, "You know I am sort of a lunatic" (Tolstoy, p. 151) and a few pages later:

> Those new theories of hypnotism, psychic diseases, and hysterics are not a simple folly, but a dangerous and repulsive one. Charcot would certainly have said that my wife was hysterical, and that I was abnormal, and he would no doubt have tried to cure me. But there was nothing to cure. All this mental illness of ours occurred simply because we lived immorally. We suffered from our immoral life, and to smother our suffering we committed various abnormal acts— just what those doctors call "indications of mental disease"—hysterics. The cure for these illnesses does not lie with Charcot, nor with them. It cannot be cured by any suggestions or bromides, but it is necessary to recognize what the pain comes from. It is like sitting down on a nail: if you notice the nail, or see what is wrong in your life and cease to do it, the pain will cease and there will be nothing to smother. The wrongness of our life caused the pain, caused my torments of jealousy and my need of going out shooting, of cards,

and above all of wine and tobacco to keep myself in a constant state of intoxication... [pp. 156-157].

The paranoid mechanism functioning throughout the passage does not need elaboration, for Tolstoy intuitively painted a dynamic portrait of a latent homosexual who defended himself from the threat of his sexual drive and from castration anxiety through a paranoid reaction.

It was only in 1973 that a committee of the American Psychiatric Association began deliberating whether homosexuality should be considered a form of mental illness or whether it ought to be stricken from the Association's official *Diagnostic and Statistical Manual of Mental Disorders*. This manual, since its inception, has classified homosexuality as a sexual deviation along with fetishism, voyeurism, pedophilia, exhibitionism, and others. By the end of 1973, the Association altered the position it held for almost a century, deciding that homosexuality is not a mental disease but rather a "sexual orientation disturbance." The latter is defined as a category for those "whose sexual interests are directed primarily towards people of the same sex and who are either disturbed by, in conflict with, or wish to change their sexual orientation. This diagnostic category is distinguished from homosexuality, which by itself does not necessarily constitute a psychiatric disorder." The semantics of the statement and how it differs from the Association's previous position are not too clear. Its most likely effect is to put psychiatrists on notice that some homosexuals have adjusted to their sexual status and do not wish to change, and many homosexuals who need psychiatric help for reasons other than homosexuality may now seek professional help because they can assume that the psychiatrists will not necessarily try to "cure" them by converting them to heterosexuality.

For many years, Marmor (1965) among others, stated that homosexuality in itself merely represents a variant sexual preference of which society disapproves but for which an illness model is unwarranted. If homosexuality is an illness, as some maintain, others claim it is anchored in the social nexus. Simon et al. (1971) feel that the future treatment of homosexuals "clearly depends on what the future holds for all of us, and there seem to be two main possibilities. Some feel that the present trend toward greater permissiveness will not continue. I (and possibly others) believe that society will continue to evolve in ways that will provide greater freedom for everyone. If we're right, there's a chance that we will live to see a fundamental alteration in our whole approach to gender identification and sexual stereotypes. The meaning of masculine and feminine may well be redefined so substantially that the whole image of homosexuality will have to be rethought from scratch. A more immediate prospect is that changing attitudes will permit heterosexuals and homosexuals alike to unashamedly devote themselves . . . to the pursuit of their own personal happiness. So the futures of homosexual and heterosexual are inextricably linked. . ." (p. 191).

TECHNICAL REFERENCES

Aldrich, C. K. (1967), Another twist to *The Turn of the Screw*. *Modern Fiction Studies*, 13:167-178.

Alexander, C. (1968), The "stink" of reality: Mothers and whores in James Baldwin's fiction. *Literature and Psychology*, 18:9-26.

Allen, G. & Martin, C. G. (1971), *Intimacy. Sensitivity, Sex and the Art of Love*. Chicago: Cowles.

Altman, D. (1972), *Homosexual: Oppression and Liberation*. New York: Outerbridge & Dienstfrey.

American Psychiatric Association (1962), *Diagnostic and Statistical Manual of Mental Disorders*. Washington, D. C.: American Psychiatric Association.

Aronson, M. L. (1952), A study of the Freudian theory of paranoia by means of the Rorschach test. *Microfilm Abstracts*, 11:443-444.

Baldwin, J. (1972), *No Name in the Street*. New York: Dial.

Bieber, I. (1965), Changing concepts of the genesis and therapy of male homosexuality. Reported in: *American Journal of Orthopsychiatry*, 35:203.

———— (1968), Advising the homosexual. *Medical Aspects of Human Sexuality*, 2(3): 34-39.

———— et al. (1962), *Homosexuality: A Psychoanalytic Study*. New York: Basic Books.

———— et al. (1971), Playboy Panel. Homosexuality, a symposium on the causes and consequences—social and psychological—of sexual inversion. *Playboy*, 18:61, *passim*.

Bieber, T. (1967), The psychotherapy of homosexuality. *Psychiatric Opinion*, 4:12-15.

Brill, A. A. (1940), Sexual manifestation in neurotic and psychotic symptoms. *Psychiatric Quarterly*, 14:9-16.

Brown, D. G. (1963), Homosexuality and family dynamics. *Bulletin of the Menninger Clinic*, 27:227-232.

Bruce, D. (1965), *Radical Doctor Smollett*. Boston: Houghton Mifflin.

Buki, R. A. (1964), A treatment program for homosexuals. *Diseases of the Menninger System*, 25:304-307.

Bychowski, G. (1954), The structure of homosexual acting out. *Psychoanalytic Quarterly*, 23:48-61.

———— (1956), The ego and the introjects. *Psychoanalytic Quarterly*, 25:11-36.

Cappon, D. (1965), *Toward an Understanding of Homosexuality.* Englewood Cliffs, N.J.: Prentice-Hall.

Cory, D. W. (ed.) (1956), *Homosexuality: A Cross-Cultural Approach.* New York: Julian.

Crowley, M. (1968), *The Boys in the Band.* New York: Dell.

Dana, R. (1970), The study of eternity. A study of the themes of isolation and meaninglessness in three novels by Yukio Mishima. *Critique,* 12:87-102.

Duberman, M. (1972), Homosexual literature. *New York Times Book Review,* December 10, pp. 6-7, 28-29.

Eissler, K. R. (1959), The function of details in the interpretation of works of literature. *Psychoanalytic Quarterly,* 28:1-20.

Ellis, A. (1965), *Homosexuality. Its Causes and Cure.* New York: Stuart.

Fenichel, O. (1945), *The Psychoanalytic Theory of Neurosis.* New York: Norton.

Ferenczi, S. (1933), *Thalassa. A Theory of Genitality.* New York: Psychoanalytic Quarterly, 1938.

Fiedler, L. A. (1948), Come back to the raft ag'in, Huck honey! In: *An End to Innocence.* Boston: Beacon, 1952, pp. 142-151.

Ford, C. S. & Beach, F. A. (1951), *Patterns of Sexual Behavior.* New York: Harper.

Freud, S. (1905), Three essays on the theory of sexuality. *Standard Edition,* 7:125-243. London: Hogarth Press, 1957.

———— (1911), Psycho-analytic notes upon an autobiographical account of a case of paranoia. *Standard Edition,* 12:3-82. London: Hogarth Press, 1958.

———— (1935), A letter to "a grateful mother." *American Journal of Psychiatry,* 107: 786-787; 1951.

Friberg, R. R. (1964), *A Study of Homosexuality and Related Characteristics in Paranoid Schizophrenia.* Doctoral dissertation, University of Minnesota.

Gentele, H., Lagerholm, B. & Lodin, A. (1960), The chromosomal sex of male homosexuals. *Acta Dermato-Venereologica,* 40:470-473.

Gershman, H. (1964), Homosexuality and some aspects of creativity. *American Journal of Psychoanalysis,* 24:29-38.

———— (1968), The evolution of gender identity. *American Journal of Psychoanalysis,* 28:80-90.

Gide, A. (1911), *Corydon.* New York: Farrar, Straus & Cudahy, 1950.

Gillespie, W. H., Pasche, F. & Wiedeman, G. H. (1964), Symposium on homosexuality. *International Journal of Psycho-Analysis,* 45:203-216.

Greenson, R. R. (1964), On homosexuality and gender identity. *International Journal of Psycho-Analysis,* 45:217-219.

Greenzweig, C. J. (1954), *Society Within Society: A Descriptive and Analytical Presentation of Homosexuality as a Social Problem.* Unpublished master's thesis. New York: Brooklyn College.

Hacker, H. M. (1952), The Ishmael complex. *American Journal of Psychotherapy,* 6: 494-512.

Hamilton, G. v. T. (1936), Defensive homosexuality: Homosexuality as a defense against incest. In: *Homosexuality: A Cross-Cultural Approach,* ed. D. W. Cory. New York: Julian, 1956, pp. 354-369.

Hampson, J. L. (1964), Deviant sexual behavior: Homosexuality, transvestism. In: *Human Reproduction and Sexual Behavior,* ed. C. W. Lloyd. Philadelphia: Lea & Febiger, pp. 498-510.

Hoffman, M. (1968), *The Gay World: Male Homosexuality and the Social Creation of Evil.* New York: Basic Books.

Hoffman, S. (1964), The cities of the night: John Rechy's *City of Night* and the American literature of homosexuality. *Chicago Review,* 17:195-206.

Holmes, J. C. (1971), Revolution below the belt. In: *Sex American Style,* ed. F. Robinson & N. Lehrman. Chicago: Playboy Press, pp. 2-29.

Hooker, E. (1965), An empirical study of some relations between sexual patterns and gender identity in male homosexuals. In: *Sex Research: New Developments,* ed. J. Money. New York: Holt, Rinehart & Winston, pp. 24-52.

Hornstra, L. (1967), Homosexuality. *International Journal of Psycho-Analysis,* 48: 394-402.

Horowitz, M. J. (1964), The homosexual's image of himself. *Mental Hygeine,* 48:197-201.

Humphreys, L. (1970), *Tearoom Trade. Impersonal Sex in Public Places.* Chicago: Aldine-Atherton.

Karpman, B. (1938), *The Kreutzer Sonata:* A problem in latent homosexuality and castration. *Psychoanalytic Review,* 25:20-48.

Kinsey, A. C., Reichert, P., Cauldwell, D. O. & Mozes, E. B. (1955), The causes of homosexuality: A symposium. *Sexology,* 21:558-562.

Kitay, P. M., Carr, A. C., Niederland, W. G., Nydes, J. & White, R. B. (1963), Symposium on "Reinterpretation of the Schreber case: Freud's theory of paranoia." *International Journal of Psycho-Analysis,* 44:191-223.

Klaf, F. S. & Davis, C. A. (1960), Homosexuality and paranoid schizophrenia: A survey of 150 cases and controls. *American Journal of Psychiatry,* 116:1070-1075.

Knight, E. H. (1965), Overt male homosexuality. In: *Sexual Behavior and the Law,* ed. R. Slovenko. Springfield, Ill.: Charles C Thomas, pp. 434-461.

Korges, J. (1970), Gide and Mishima: Homosexuality as metaphor. *Critique,* 12(1): 127-137.

Marmor, J. (ed.) (1965), *Sexual Inversion: The Multiple Roots of Homosexuality.* New York: Basic Books.

——— (1967), Homosexuality. *Student Personnel Newsletter, State University College, Buffalo,* 1(3):15-34.

Masters, R. E. L. (1962), *Forbidden Sexual Behavior and Morality.* New York: Lancer.

Mazur, R. M. (1968), *Commonsense Sex.* Boston: Beacon.

McIntosh, M. (1968), The homosexual role. *Social Problems,* 16:182-192.

Meketon, B. W., Griffith, R. M., Taylor, V. H. & Wiedeman, J. S. (1962), Rorschach homosexual signs in paranoid schizophrenics. *Journal of Abnormal and Social Psychology,* 65:280-284.

Miller, M. (1971), *On Being Different: What It Means to Be a Homosexual.* New York: Random House.

Money, J. (1963), Factors in the genesis of homosexuality. In: *Determinants of Human Sexual Behavior,* ed. G. Winokur. Springfield, Ill.: Charles C Thomas, pp. 19-43.

Moore, R. A. & Selzer, M. L. (1963), Male homosexuality, paranoia, and the schizophrenias. *American Journal of Psychiatry,* 119:743-747.

Mozes, E. B. (1951), The lesbian. *Sexology,* 18:294-299.

Nitsche, C. J., Robinson, J. R., & Parsons, E. T. (1956), Homosexuality and the Rorschach. *Journal of Consulting Psychology,* 20:196.

Norman, J. P. (1948), Evidence and clinical significance of homosexuality in 100 unanalyzed cases of dementia praecox. *Journal of Nervous and Mental Disease,* 107:484-489.

Pare, C. M. B. (1965), Etiology in homosexuality: Genetic and chromosomal aspects.

In: *Sexual Inversion: The Multiple Roots of Homosexuality*, ed. J. Marmor. New York: Basic Books, pp. 70-80.

Perloff, W. H. (1949), Role of the hormones in homosexuality. *Psychosomatic Medicine*, 11:133-139.

———— (1963), The role of hormones in homosexuality. *Journal of the Albert Einstein Medical Center*, 11:165-178.

Phillips, W. (1965), The new immoralists. In: *The Perverse Imagination*, ed. I. Buchen. New York: New York University Press, 1970, pp. 139-146.

Planansky, K. & Johnson, R. (1962), The incidence and relationship of homosexual and paranoid features in schizophrenia. *Journal of Mental Science*, 108(456):604-615.

Praz, M. (1933), *The Romantic Agony*. New York: Meridian, 1956.

Salzman, L. (1960), Paranoid state-theory and therapy. *Archives of General Psychiatry*, 2:679-693.

Sartre, J-P. (1949), Foreword to J. Genet, *The Thief's Journal*. New York: Bantam, 1965.

Savitsch, E. de (1958), *Homosexuality, Transvestism and Change of Sex*. Springfield, Ill.: Charles C Thomas.

Simon, W., et al. (1971), Playboy Panel. Homosexuality, a symposium on the causes and consequences—social and psychological—of sexual inversion. *Playboy*, 18:61, *passim*.

Socarides, C. W. (1968), *The Overt Homosexual*. New York: Grune & Stratton.

Van den Haag, E. (1963), Notes on homosexuality and its cultural setting. In: *The Problem of Homosexuality in Modern Society*, ed. H. M. Ruitenbeek. New York: Dutton, pp. 291-302.

Velikovsky, I. (1937), Tolstoy's *Kreutzer Sonata* and unconscious homosexuality. *Psychoanalytic Review*, 24:18-25.

Walters, O. S. (1955), A methodological critique of Freud's Schreber analysis. *Psychoanalytic Review*, 42:321-342.

Weinberg, M. S. & Bell, A. P. (eds.) (1972), *Homosexuality; An Annotated Bibliography*. New York: Harper & Row.

West, D. J. (1959), Parental figures in the genesis of male homosexuality. *International Journal of Social Psychiatry*, 5:85-97.

———— (1968), *Homosexuality*. Chicago: Aldine.

Willis, S. E. (1967), *Understanding and Counseling the Male Homosexual*. Boston: Little, Brown.

Wolman, B. B. (1967), International treatment of homosexuality. *Psychotherapy and Psychosomatics*, 15:70.

Zamansky, H. S. (1958), An investigation of the psychoanalytic theory of paranoid delusions. *Journal of Personality*, 26:410-425.

LITERARY REFERENCES

Anderson, Sherwood (1923), The Man Who Became a Woman. In: *Short Stories*. New York: Hill & Wang, 1962.

Baldwin, James (1956), *Giovanni's Room*. New York: Dell, 1964.

Burroughs, William S. (1971), *The Wild Boys. A Book of the Dead*. New York: Grove Press.

Crane, Hart (1966), Voyages. In: *Complete Poems and Selected Letters and Prose*, ed. B. Weber. Garden City, N.Y.: Doubleday, pp. 35-41.

Durrell, Lawrence (1940), *The Black Book.* New York: Dutton, 1960.

——— (1957), *Justine.* New York: Dutton.

——— (1960), *Clea.* New York: Dutton.

Epstein, Seymour (1967), *Caught in That Music.* New York: Viking.

Forster, E. M. (1913), *Maurice.* New York: Norton, 1972.

Franklin, Eugene (1972), *The Money Murders.* New York: Stein & Day.

Gide, André (1902), *The Immoralist.* New York: Knopf, 1930.

Hansen, Joseph (1973), *Death Claims.* New York: Harper & Row.

Harrison, Jim (1971), *Wolf. A False Memoir.* New York: Simon & Schuster.

James, Henry (1898), *The Turn of the Screw.* New York: Dell, 1956.

Jones, James (1951), *From Here to Eternity.* New York: Scribner's.

Lambert, Gavin (1966), *Norman's Letters.* New York: Lancer, 1967.

Lawrence, D. H. (1913), *Sons and Lovers.* New York: Viking, 1962.

——— (1922), *Aaron's Rod.* New York: Viking, 1961.

McHale, Tom (1971), *Farragon's Retreat.* New York: Viking.

Melville, Herman (1851), *Moby Dick.* New York: Dodd, Mead, n.d.

Miller, Merle (1972), *What Happened.* New York: Harper & Row.

Mishima, Yukio (1958), *Confessions of a Mask.* Norwalk, Conn.: New Directions.

——— (1963), *The Sailor Who Fell from Grace with the Sea.* New York: Knopf.

——— (1968), *Forbidden Colors.* New York: Knopf.

Rechy, John (1962), *City of Night.* New York: Grove Press.

——— (1967), *Numbers.* New York: Grove Press.

Sartre, Jean-Paul (1948), Erostratus. In: *Intimacy and Other Stories.* New York: Berkley Medallion, 1960, pp. 41-58.

Selby, Hubert, J. (1957), *Last Exit to Brooklyn.* New York: Grove Press.

Simmel, Johannes Mario (1971), *Cain '67.* New York: McGraw-Hill.

Smollett, Tobias G. (1748), *The Adventures of Roderick Random.* New York: New American Library, 1964.

Speicher, John (1973), *Lower and Lower.* New York: Harper & Row.

Tolstoy, Leo (1891), The Kreutzer Sonata. In: *Leo Tolstoy, Short Novels,* Vol. 2, ed. E. J. Simmons. New York: Modern Library, 1966, pp. 114-194.

Twain, Mark (1884), *Adventures of Huckleberry Finn,* ed. H. N. Smith. Boston: Houghton Mifflin, 1958.

Vidal, Gore (1948), *The City and the Pillar Revisited.* New York: Dutton, 1965.

Walker, Gerald (1970), *Cruising.* Greenwich, Conn.: Fawcett Crest, 1971.

CHAPTER SIX

Female Homosexuality

It is with astonishing regularity that the published literature on female homosexuality bewails the dearth of data on it. In 1962, Socarides stated that, for a variety of reasons, overt female homosexuality was a relatively neglected clinical entity in contrast to male homosexuality. In 1965, Romm pointed out that practically every article written about female homosexuality notes this same fact. Wilbur (1965) and Kaye et al. (1967) made the same point; and Abbott and Love (1972) declared: "The Lesbian is one of the least known members of our culture. Less is known about her — and less accurately — than the Newfoundland dog" (p. 13). Martin and Lyon (1972) state that "Nonfiction books and articles are almost exclusively devoted to the male homosexual, with perhaps a chapter on or incidental mention of the Lesbian. The implication is ... that what is said applies equally to female homosexuals ... It is true that the male homosexual and the Lesbian have many common concerns.... It must be noted, however, that the Lesbian differs greatly from the male homosexual in attitudes, problems and life styles" (p. 7). That there are differences as well as similarities between the male and female homosexual is borne out not only by clinical research, but also by the creative writer.

There are historical, factual, and psychological reasons that account for the toleration of female homosexuality. Until recently — and even today — women have been and are considered less sexual creatures than men; consequently, what they do to each other is not as disturbing. Lesbian activity does not threaten the masculine establishment (Whiteley and Whiteley, 1965), nor does it excite the popular revul-

sion that accompanies male homosexuality, since the latter has traditionally been identified with anal intercourse. Chesser (1971) advances
a probable reason why lesbianism has not generated universal distaste:
the ignorance of the nature of the sexual act. It was believed that
semen contributed the whole of the embryo and the womb was merely
a receptacle in which the embryo was nourished. Further, the public is
unclear as to what constitutes female homosexuality (Pomeroy, 1965),
and because it is less well known it may be that the indulgent social
reaction to such relationships means that fewer Lesbians have guilt
reactions and thus fewer of them seek psychiatric help (Rancourt and
Limoges, 1967).

Pierre Louys (1896), in his novel, *Aphrodite,* wrote about the great
love between two Ephesian girls, Rhodis and Myrtocleia, a love which
was as acceptable in their society as was the love between the central
character and her male suitor. Alexandria, at the time the story
unfolds, had 1,400 sacred prostitutes, for the Greeks did not attach
ideas of lewdness and immodesty to sex, which are Judeo-Christian
values. In the introduction to his novel, Louys writes: ". . . sensuality is
a condition of intellectual growth, mysterious but necessary and creative. Those who have not felt profoundly the demands of the flesh,
whether to welcome or curse them, are left incapable of encompassing
the demands of the spirit." In Louys's Alexandria, sex gave people joy,
release from their worries, a psychological lift. In the passage below,
Chrysis has spent the night with the two girl lovers, when she is roused
from her sleep by Naucrates, a friend whose acceptance of the female
homosexual reveals cultural approval.

> During that night Chrysis had been awakened by a knocking at
> the door. She had slept all day between the two Ephesians — without
> the mad disorder of the bedclothes they might have been taken for
> sisters. Rhodis lay huddled against the Galilean whose perspired
> thigh rested on her. Myrtocleia was sleeping on her stomach, her
> eyes closed over one arm, her back naked.
>
> Chrysis gently disengaged herself, took a few steps on the bed, got
> off and opened her door slightly. A sound of voices came from the
> outside door.
>
> "Who is it, Djala?" she asked.
>
> "It is Naucrates who wishes to talk to you. I've told him you are
> not free."
>
> "How silly! Of course I am. Come in, Naucrates. I am in my
> room."

And she returned to her bed.

Naucrates stayed for a moment on the threshold as if afraid of being indiscreet. The two musicians opened their eyes still heavy with sleep but couldn't tear themselves from their dreams.

"Sit down," Chrysis said. "I shall put on no coquettish airs with you. I know you did not come for me. What is it?"

Naucrates was a well-known philosopher who for more than twenty years had been Bacchis's lover and had remained faithful to her, more out of indolence than sentiment. His gray hair was trimmed short, his beard tapered to a point in the Demosthenes manner and his moustache was level with the upper lip. He wore a long white garment made of a single strip of wool girted together.

"I've come to invite you," he said. "Bacchis is giving a dinner tomorrow with a feast afterwards. We shall be seven counting you. Don't fail to come."

"A feast? What is the occasion?"

"She is freeing her most beautiful slave, Aphrodisia. There will be girls dancing and playing the flute. I believe, indeed, that your two companions are among those engaged and that they shouldn't even be here now. There is a rehearsal this very moment at Bacchis's."

"Oh! That's true," Rhodis exclaimed. "It completely slipped our minds. Get up, Myrto. We are very late."

"No, not yet!" pleaded Chrysis. "How mean of you to take away my girls. If I had suspected that, I wouldn't have let you in. Oh! Look at them, they are all ready."

"Our clothing is quite simple," said the girl. "We're not beautiful enough to fuss over our toilette."

"Shall I at least see you at the temple?"

"Yes, tomorrow morning. We shall be carrying doves. I'm taking a drachma out of your purse, Chrysis. Otherwise we couldn't afford to buy them. See you tomorrow."

They ran off. Naucrates stared after them. Then he folded his arms and turning to Chrysis said in a low voice:

"So—you are behaving very nicely."

"What do you mean?"

"One girl is no longer enough for you; you need two now. And you are taking them right off the street. A fine example you set. Come now, will you tell me? What is left for us, us men to do? You all have your girl sweethearts. And when you leave their exhausting embraces, you then give us whatever little passion they are kind enough to leave you with. How long do you think this can go on? If it does, we men shall be forced to resort to Bathyllus."

"Oh, no!" Chrysis exclaimed. "I won't let you say that. I know the comparison is being made, but it has no sense. And I am amazed that you, who make a profession of thinking, don't understand its absurdity."

"And what distinction do you find between Lesbos and Bathyllus?"

"It is not a matter of difference. Quite clearly, there is no connection between the two."

"I don't say you are wrong. But I should like to know your reasons."

"I'll put it simply. When it comes to love, woman is the perfect instrument. From head to toes she is made solely, miraculously for love. *She alone* knows how to love; *she alone* knows how to be loved. Therefore, if a loving couple is made up of two women it is perfect. If it has only one it is half as good. If it has none it is simply idiotic. I have finished."

"You are hard on Plato, my girl."

"Great men and even the gods themselves are not great in all things. Athene has no understanding of commerce. Sophocles could not paint. Plato did not know how to love. And those philosophers, poets and rhetoricians who follow Plato are no better. They can be admirable in their special arts, yet in love they are all ignoramuses. Believe me, Naucrates, I feel I am right."

The philosopher shrugged. "You are a bit irreverent but I don't for a moment think you are wrong. My indignation was not genuine. There is for me something charming in the union of two young women: provided only they are both of them willing to stay feminine, to keep their hair long, expose their breasts, and not rig themselves out with artifices — as if, quite inconsistently, they envied the grosser sex whom they scorn so prettily.

"Yes, their love making is remarkable because their caresses are superficial, and their pleasure is all the more subtle. There is no violence in their embrace. They merely graze each other to taste ecstasy. Their wedding night is not bloodied; they remain virgins. By evading all brutality they are superior to Bathyllus which claims to offer an equivalent, forgetting that even at this shabby game you could compete with it. Human love is only distinguished from the brutish rutting of animals by two divine functions, the caress and the kiss. And here we must credit women, for it is they who have perfected them."

"You grant me everything," Chrysis said, still indignant. "Then why do you reproach me?"

"I reproach you for being a hundred thousand strong. Already a great number of women have perfect pleasure only with their own sex. Soon you will no longer want to receive us, even as a last resort. It is out of jealousy I scold you."

Here Naucrates decided that the exchange had lasted long enough and, abruptly, he stood up.

"I can tell Bacchis that she may count on you?"

"I shall come," Chrysis answered.

The philosopher kissed her knees and slowly departed [pp. 68-71].

De Beauvoir (1952) too points out the casual acceptance of female homosexuality as contrasted with the male variety, quoting Count de Tilly, " 'I avow that it is a rivalry which in no way disturbed one; on the contrary, it amuses me and I am immoral enough to laugh at it'" (p. 407). In his *Memoirs,* Casanova often confessed to a similar amuse-ment at female homosexuality, calling it a "trifling matter." In the Claudine novels of Colette, female homosexuality is treated largely as a sophisticated joke. Renaud, Claudine's husband, discovers his wife's Lesbian affair with Rezi and blithely refuses to be jealous. He cannot take women seriously enough to consider his wife unfaithful unless another man is involved. Peter, in Arthur Koestler's (1943) *Arrival and Departure,* is a political refugee from Nazi Germany, escaped to Lisbon and sheltered by a countrywoman, Sonia Bolgar, a psycho-analyst. Peter falls in love with Odette, who is described as childishly slender, with a boyish, unpainted mouth. She has been having a Lesbian relationship with Dr. Bolgar, who in turn is described as tall, masterful, and having a "copious bust with breasts massive but erect" (p. 21). Shortly after Peter rapes Odette, she leaves for the United States. Peter has gone to clean up her apartment and there "his eyes fell on a tiny fragment of Odette's blue notepaper near the top of the heap. He could not resist picking it out. The fragment contained only a few lines; there was a reference to him: 'Peter is . . .' with the rest of the sentence torn away; then some allusion which he could not understand, and then: '. . . It was nice for a change; I think I needed it [her rape by Peter]. But the real thing is you, and all my tenderness of. . .' . . . He felt no curiosity to collect the other pieces of the letter . . . What he had read caused him no particular shock—he had known of Odette's relations with Sonia before—only a faint physical revul-sion" (p. 164). Earlier, Peter had felt a "sadness . . . and pity for Odette, with her vacant look, her slimness and vulnerability—Odette the victim, drowned in the carniverous flower's embrace" (p. 156).

Is it justifiable to assume that male and female homosexuality are the same? In treating three female homosexuals, Zucker (1966) found different factors operating in female homosexuality as well as differences in etiology. There is a deeper and more complex feeling of rejection in the female homosexual. The sexual development of women is blocked in traditions and customs not present for men. For women, homosexuality is a means of escape. Among women one rarely finds the type of homosexual with weak inner conflicts, centering chiefly around social considerations and outward appearances, that one finds among men. The conflict itself is not the same in both sexes. According to Fenichel (1945), however, one of the causal factors of female homosexuality is a castration complex comparable to that found in the male, resulting in anxiety at the sight of the genital of the opposite sex, but with one important difference. Since the infant's earliest attachment is to the mother, the little girl's first love object is a homosexual one. Thus, in women, a homosexual attachment represents a regression to this early stage. Hence female homosexuality carries more archaic traces than does male homosexuality, and brings back not only the behavior patterns, aims, and pleasures, but also the fears and conflicts of the earliest years of life. This partially explains the fact that oral eroticism predominates in female homosexuality.

Several studies have produced useful data regarding female homosexuality. A psychoanalytically oriented clinical study by Armon (1960) of thirty female homosexuals from the Mattachine Society of Los Angeles, and thirty controls—students attending local schools—were tested to confirm six hypotheses. The first three hypotheses were not confirmed: (1) homosexual women show a stronger dependency orientation than heterosexual women; (2) they stress the aggressive features of the masculine role; (3) they reject feminine identification and show more conflict over sexual roles. The second group of hypotheses was confirmed: (1) homosexual women perceive women and female relationships with a hostile-aggressive cathexis which is not as pronounced in heterosexual women; (2) they show a more rejecting attitude toward men than heterosexual women; (3) they are more limited in personal social adjustment.

In response to a questionnaire by 123 homosexual women and a matched group of heterosexual women, Kenyon (1968) found significant differences in physical characteristics, medical histories, parental relationships, and emotional development. The homosexual women were significantly heavier than the paired group, with larger breasts, waists, and hips. Fewer homosexual women experienced premenstrual tension while significantly more of them resented menses than did the control group and preferred having a female physician. In contrast with the heterosexual women, the other group had poor relationships with their mothers, who were more likely to have had a psychiatric history; the relationship with the father was poor as well; yet they rated their parents' marriages as happy. More homosexual women reported an unhappy childhood than did heterosexual women; believed their parents would have preferred a boy; had a psychiatric history; a higher incidence of separation and divorce; and said the general family attitude to sex was rejecting, and that they had not received sexual instructions from their mothers.

Hopkins' (1969) investigation of twenty-four female homosexuals and a matched group of heterosexual women for age, intelligence, and professional or educational background, was an attempt to measure the female homosexual personality using the Cattell Sixteen Personality Factor Test. She found that the Lesbian personality, in comparison with her heterosexual female counterpart, was more independent, resilient, reserved, dominant, bohemian, self-sufficient, and composed. Poole's (1972) study of fifty adult Lesbians and fifty adult heterosexual women, matched only for age, resulted in these findings: ninety-two per cent of the heterosexual women played "grown-up lady" while seventy-six per cent of the female homosexuals rarely or never did; eighty-four per cent of the heterosexuals played mother with dolls, while twenty-two percent of the others sometimes or often did; seventy-six per cent of the heterosexuals played "having a baby" and only sixteen per cent of the matched group did; and twenty-eight per cent of the heterosexuals played "house with yourself as mother" rarely or not at all, and seventy-eight per cent of the Lesbians responded similarly. In their attitudes toward physical and sexual functions, fifty-four per cent of the heterosexuals were pleased with their original reaction to menstruation, while only eighteen per cent of the Lesbians were; forty-four per cent of the heterosexuals understood the sex act as being "dirty-strange" as opposed to "interesting-pleasant," while sixty-eight per cent of the Lesbians felt it to be "dirty-strange"; seventy per cent of the heterosexual women had "stimulating and interesting thoughts" about the genital area of the opposite sex, while only forty per cent of the homosexual females did. In terms of their mother's influence, affection, and understanding, ninety per cent of the heterosexual women reported favorably, while approximately fifty per cent of the matched group did so. And in their feelings toward their fathers, seventy-six per cent of the heterosexuals felt they were affectionate and loving, while only twenty-eight per cent of the Lesbians concurred. Thirty-two per cent of the heterosexuals stated their fathers disapproved of the subject of sex, while sixty per cent of the homosexual women expressed negative views.

Modalities emerge from this litany of statistics. Coupled with clinical data and the product of the novelist, stereotypic images of the female homosexual arise, comparable in many ways to the male homosexual, where the personality is formed in a family where the son feared and hated a detached, hostile, sexually competitive father. He was also over-attached to a controlling, seductive, yet sexually repressive mother who interfered with peer group participation and who had a poor relationship with her husband. Though inversion does not cancel out individual differences, nonetheless, a more or less typical background of family pathology is noted in case after case (T. Bieber, 1967). Similarly, the female homosexual reveals a great degree of congruency in parental relationships, family constellation, developmental growth, and affective behavior. When parents of homosexuals, male or female, are compared with parents of heterosexuals, there is almost always a clear indication of differences in attitudes and behavior (I. Bieber et al., 1971). For girls, a lack of ability to develop an identity apart from the mother leads to relationships with other women which repeat the same features (Denford, 1967). Parents of Kaye's (1967) Lesbian subjects had discouraged the development of feminine attributes, thus interfering with feminine identification. These girls developed a constellation of traits and activities they used to avoid the female role.

Female homosexuality, agrees Wilbur (1965, p. 280), is "associated with specific types of family constellation, the commonest of which probably includes a domineering, hostile, antiheterosexual mother, and a weak, unassertive, detached father." The latter is typically a submerged, pallid figure, concerned and overanxious about his daughter with his behavior frequently designated as maternal. Actually he is often quiet, withdrawn, puritanical, exploitative, feared by his daughter and physically interested in her, overtly possessive, yet tending to discourage her development as an adult. He may remain apart from emotional involvement in the family, thus not presenting a strong masculine ideal to which the daughter can relate positively. Intense oedipal problems with the father often compel the daughter to adopt homosexuality as a defense against her incestuous wishes. In such instances, the father is not perceived as hostile. The daughter may turn to him for affection and her incestuous wishes may thus become augmented. "What affection is displayed and accepted tends to come from the father, and this affection intensifies the Oedipus complex. The daughter may then adopt homosexuality as a defense against the powerful Oedipal problem and against maternal hostility, or she may succumb to the mother's antiheterosexual attitudes and give up her own heterosexual wishes. At the same time she removes herself from competitiveness with the mother" (Wilbur, 1965, p. 280).

Clea's father, in Lawrence Durrell's *Balthazar* (1958), is the proto-type of the ineffectual, pallid parent of a homosexual daughter. In the novel, Justine is forced by poverty to do a little modeling for art students at an atelier. Clea, an artist, is struck by Justine's Alexandrian beauty and engages her for a portrait, which leads to a homosexual relationship. Clea "would be in a fever all day until the appointed moment when her model met her. At four she stood before the closed door of the studio, seeing clearly through it to the corner where Justine already sat, turning over the pages of *Vogue* and smoking as she waited, legs crossed. The idea crossed her mind, 'I pray to God she has not come, is ill, has gone away. How eagerly I would welcome indif-ference!' Surprised, too, for these disgusts came from precisely the same quarters as the desire to hear once more that hoarse noble voice — they too arose only from the expectation of seeing her beloved once more. These polarities of feeling bewildered and frightened her by their suddenness . . . She tried to fall back on other pleasures, to find that none existed. She knew that the heart wearies of monotony, that habit and despair are the bedfellows of love, and she waited patiently, as a very old woman might, for the flesh to outgrow its promptings, to deliver itself from an attachment which she now recognized was not of her seeking. Waited in vain. Each day she plunged deeper. Yet all this, at any rate, performed one valuable service for her, proving that relationships like these did not answer the needs of her nature" (pp. 54-55).

While the basic and fundamental drive in Clea was toward hetero-sexuality, it was blocked by anxieties and inhibitions. Her father was of no help, doing little more than suffering visibly and asking a mutual friend to do what he could to abort the "illicit relationship" she had formed with Justine. Clea, he told their friend, was "an innocent, a goose." In helpless anguish, he confided, "I cannot bear to watch it, and I do not know what to do. It is like watching a small child skipping near a powerful piece of unprotected machinery" (p. 49).

Another such father is Leo Ackerman in Seymour Epstein's (1967) *Caught in That Music.* When he learns his Roslyn is a Lesbian, he turns to a favored young employee in his printing business, Jonas Gould, in an effort to understand how it happened, looking for some reason, denying the actuality, and seeking some comfort.

> Mr. Ackerman nodded slowly. He settled back in his chair. His face took on its flaccid, doughy look. Then he leaned forward again, his arms resting on the desk.
>
> "Jonas, listen to me," he said. "I don't know what she's told you. I won't ask you any more. I realize you're trying to spare my feelings. But let me tell you something — it's all a dream, this thing she's got in her head. She got an idea in her head. Where? Why? Ask the wind. Ask God. I don't know. But it's nonsense, and it's not only me that's saying so. She doesn't know this, but I've talked to a doctor. A very big man, here in the city. A psychiatrist. Sure there are such things in the world. Don't I know! But I asked this doctor point-blank, I told him not to pull his punches, and do you know what he said? He said that in fifty per cent of the cases it's all in the mind. Something happens in childhood. You don't like your mother. You don't like your father. Who knows? I suppose these things happen. But, I'm telling you, Jonas — I'm not kidding you, and I'm not kidding myself — that girl had a *happy* childhood! There wasn't a place I didn't take her. Every week end. Movies, museums, zoos, concerts, everything they had for children in this city, she saw. All right, maybe in spite of everything, something can still happen — " Leo slapped the palm of his hand on his desk with each word — "*but this doctor told me that in more than fifty per cent of the cases if the person goes ahead and gets married and lives a normal life, it will all disappear! All the nonsense!* . . . I don't know if you know this, Jonas — it was news to me, too — but none of us is completely male or completely female. Every man has got a little of the female in him. Every woman has got a little of the male. But I brought up this girl. I know her — " The phone on Leo's right rang. Without taking his eyes off Jonas, he picked it up, told the switchboard girl he was busy, no calls, he didn't want to be disturbed, and hung up. "Do you think I wouldn't know if there was something the matter with her? A temporary thing. An idea. Nothing more. Like

she says she wants to be a biologist. Do you think I'd stand in her way? This is nineteen forty-one. You don't do that sort of thing with grown girls anymore. But I guarantee you, that's only an idea, too. . . . Jonas, I want to ask you a question. You met Roslyn. You took her out a few times. I'm sure you behaved yourself. But you know me and I know you, so we can speak frankly to each other. Jonas, could you have sexual intercourse with Roslyn?"

Jonas stared at his employer. He wondered if fat Leo Ackerman had anticipated this scene, prepared these words. Did he know how they sounded? Did he know what he was saying? But compassion has no more genius than grief. He said, "I just didn't think of her that way."

Mr. Ackerman closed his eyes momentarily, nodded. He would go along with anything. His patience was limitless.

"Jonas, I know you. Have you ever gone out with a girl that you didn't think of her that way, even for a second? I'm asking you please not to be bashful, not to say what you think I want to hear. As a favor, please, be truthful."

Truthful! Jesus!

"I suppose it crossed my mind," Jonas said.

"What crossed your mind?"

"Sex."

"How did it cross your mind?"

Jonas wrenched himself around in his chair. "Mr. Ackerman, I'm not going to sit here and be given the third degree on that!"

"Take it easy," Mr. Ackerman said, holding up his hands in ponderous placation. "I've kidded you in the past. I know. I don't have to tell you this is different, do I? I know when a young man looks at a girl and she doesn't appeal to him, his mind turns off, like a valve. But if she does appeal to him, it does go further, in his mind. All I'm asking Jonas, is how far did it go, in your mind?"

"I don't know. I don't remember."

"I'm asking you to be truthful."

"I *am* being truthful."

"Could you have sexual intercourse with her?"

"I told you yes."

"Because you would want to? Because it would be enjoyable?"

"Why else?"

Now Mr. Ackerman leaned back again in his new, high-backed swivel chair, which, for all its newness, groaned under that weight. He pointed his finger at Jonas.

"Do you think you would have felt that way if she were a freak?

Do you? There's the whole point! That's what I'm getting at! There's your proof! A boy like you would know in a second whether he was dealing with a woman or a freak. If you felt you could have sexual intercourse with her, you could! And you would enjoy it! And she would enjoy it!"

"Mr. Ackerman—"

"Jonas, do me this one favor. Please go down to Philly. We have business there. You have a reason for going. Drop in and say hello."

Jonas suddenly felt light, unencumbered. It was truly not his affair. It had moved of its own accord far beyond any possibility of his involvement. He said, "I know what you're hoping, Mr. Ackerman, but I can tell you that nothing is going to come of it, between Roslyn and me. You can't force these things. She really doesn't want to see me."

"Did she say so?"

"Yes."

"I thought you said you were corresponding."

"We weren't."

"Then why did you say you were?"

"Because you seemed to want it so badly."

"Did you do anything to make her mad?"

"No, Mr. Ackerman."

"You didn't get along?"

"We got along."

"You don't like each other?"

"There's a difference between 'like' and what you're talking about. You know that."

"You're not giving it a chance, Jonas."

Now Jonas leaned toward Mr. Ackerman, his elbows resting on the arms of the chair. He gripped his left wrist with the fingers of his right hand. His words were not loud or specially inflected; the even emphasis of each word announced the finality.

"There is nothing there, Mr. Ackerman. I'm sorry."

"I've given you breaks, Jonas," said Mr. Ackerman.

"I've worked for them," Jonas said.

"I could throw you out on your ass."

"I'll save you the trouble."

"Where would you get a job like this?"

Jonas realized that Leo Ackerman wasn't seeing him. His eyes gazed through him at some timeless, spaceless point where fears converge.

"There's going to be a war," Jonas said. "I can get another job un-

til it comes. And when the war does come, Mr. Ackerman? Would
you want Roslyn to be a widow?"

Those same eyes returned from their private distance, and Jonas
realized with a little shock that that possibility had also entered Leo
Ackerman's calculations; that widowhood would at least be an outer
badge to wear, an emblem denying the other; and that Jonas
Gould's life, though a regrettable sacrifice, was a supportable one.
And yet this man liked him, would have known great happiness in
having him as son-in-law.

"All right," Mr. Ackerman said.

Jonas got up. "I'm sorry," he said.

Mr. Ackerman nodded.

"Do you want me here?" Jonas asked. "Or — ?"

"Jonas, I'm very upset," Mr. Ackerman said. He looked up, sup-
plicatingly. "You don't believe that about Roslyn, do you?"

There was no other answer: "Of course not" [pp. 257-260].

There are indications in the findings of the Bene-Anthony Family Relations Test applied by Bene (1965) to thirty-seven unmarried Lesbians
and eighty heterosexual married women that Lesbians tend to have
more domineering and less affectionate mothers, to be more hostile
toward them, and to see their parents as having desired a son, data
which coincide with the studies cited earlier. The mothers of Kaye's
(1967) subjects had pathological relationships: they were dominant,
somewhat puritanical, and contemptuous of their daughters, whose
developing femininity they tended not to encourage. The "typical"
mother, in Wilbur's (1965) view, is overbearing, dominant in the family, and excessively controlling: "The relationship between the mother
and the female homosexual is usually a very active one; there is a chronic struggle between them, in which the child is the loser. There are innumerable attempts by the mother to dominate, conquer, and control.
The commonest techniques are rejection or threats of rejection, depreciation, and guilt induction. The female child destined to be a
homosexual looks upon her mother with hostility and rebellion. She is
in conflict, however, because of the concomitant presence of great
longing for affection and approval from her mother. Identification
with the mother is impaired by her own hostility" (p. 275).

The Well of Loneliness by Radclyffe Hall (1928) has been described
by Havelock Ellis (1928) as possessing notable psychological and sociological significance. "So far as I know it is the first English novel

which presents, in a completely faithful and uncompromising form, one particular aspect of sexual life as it exists among us today. The relation of certain people—who while different from their fellow human beings, are sometimes of the highest character and the highest aptitudes—to the often hostile society in which they move, presents difficulties and still unresolved problems. The poignant situations which thus arise are here set forth so vividly, and yet with such complete absence of offence, that we must place Radclyffe Hall's book on a high level of distinction." The domineering, controlling parent in the novel is epitomized in the portrayal of the mother of Stephen, the homosexual daughter. When the mother discovers the daughter's sexual propensity, she tells her to leave the house. "In that letter you say things that may only be said between a man and a woman, and coming from you they are vile and filthy words of corruption—against nature, against God who created nature . . . You have presumed to use the word love in connection with this . . . I have loved your father, and your father loved me. That was *love* . . . The same roof mustn't shelter both of us..." (Hall, pp. 201-202).

In summary, Wilbur (1965, p. 276) found "in the triangular constellation of the father-mother-homosexual daughter, there is generally . . . a father who tends to be passive, inept, gentle, and detached; a mother who is dominant, domineering, guilt-inducing, and hostile; and a daughter who is hostile to her mother, cannot turn to her father because of what she perceives as his weakness, and who suffers from severe feelings of rejection and longing." Many researchers on female homosexuality, like those on male homosexuality, believe that the mechanisms and nature of sex-object choice are unknown. Marmor (I. Bieber et al., 1971) has called for caution in making statements concerning the etiology of homosexuality, heterosexuality, or any other sexual orientation. "No single, specific family background has been elicited for female homosexuality at this point in our investigation; our studies indicate that multiple causes are involved there also. No one family background can be a total explanation. Clinical experience suggests that the development of homosexuality depends on a complicated conglomeration of factors that vary in terms of quality, quantity and timing in their impact on the developing child" (pp. 72-73). Thus, in all probability, multiple causes converge in the female homosexual, and this symptom is overdetermined. In most cases, pyschological determinants are the most potent. Freud (1920) explained homosexuality in his female patient as withdrawal from men in order to remove one cause of her mother's hostility. Such withdrawal may be an element in the etiology of female homosexuality, especially if the mother is envious of her daughter, hostile to her own mate, and verbally pessimistic about the girl's future in a sexual relationship with a man. Another determining factor may be the search for an ego ideal by people whose self-images are devalued or impaired (Kaplan, 1967). The search for this ego ideal through homosexual relations may often be a substitute for the more usual ascription of this role to the father.

Romm (1965) cites an umbrella of reasons under which the female might opt for homosexuality: "When the female is rejected in her formative years by her parents; when she feels unloved, depreciated, and demeaned; when a male sibling is preferred to her; when she feels that her sex is a disappointment to her parents; or when she becomes convinced, justifiably or not, that males in our society are the favored sex, she may react with feelings of inferiority and hostility toward men. She may then take refuge in psychosexual identification with the male and may assume a masculine role in a homosexual relationship; or, in a reaction formation, she may become the helpless passive ultrafeminine partner in a homosexual relationship in which a 'masculine' and strong mother-father representative loves only her and does for her and to her what she sought from one or both parents earlier in life. Many other factors may also enter into the choice of female homosexuality: fear of growing up and assuming adult responsibilities; fear of dominance and destruction through bodily penetration; fear of mutilation and destruction by pregnancy and childbirth; defiance of parents and society; and desire to conquer and possess the mother by identifying her with the female lover..." (pp. 296-297).

The middle childhood years of the tomboy seem to play a crucial role in subsequent female homosexuality. Of 225 Lesbians studied by Riess and Gundlach (1968), seventy-eight per cent reported being tomboys as against forty-two per cent of the control group of heterosexual women. "The tomboy claims qualities usually believed to belong to men. She does not see why they cannot be hers also. She wants freedom and wants to be like those who appear to her to be free—men who seem to have the opportunity for achievement and glory within their grasp" (Abbott and Love, 1972, p. 21). Arthur and Maud Lane, married twenty-seven years in Mary Renault's (1945) novel, *The Middle Mist*, provide a constantly oscillating emotional barometer in their household, bickering and arguing more from habit than conviction.

Their two daughters are the innocent victims of their petty tyrannies and hostilities. Leo, christened Leonora, can at twenty-five be mistaken for a teen-age boy. As an adolescent, "she spent her pocket money, not on powder and rouge, but on telescopes, pocket compasses, knives fitted with screwdrivers ... [She would come home] at night dirty, and bearing trophies of rare eggs and crystal spar ... grazed knees ... a black eye" (p. 9). She was forever in the company of boys. Her father, feeling put upon by the ever-present three women, one day shouted at her, "If I had a son, I shouldn't be subjected day by day to this petty conspiracy of women...." To which Leo replied, "If I were a man I wouldn't be here. And I bloody well wish I were" (p. 4). This dialogue was the precipitating factor in prompting Leo to leave home. From then on, she lived on a houseboat near London, writing successful Westerns and maintaining a domestic ménage with a nurse who had saved her life some seven years previously. The passage below describes the feelings of comfort she derives when she is with Joe, a houseboat neighbor, and the only man with whom a sense of acceptance exists without sexual complication.

> With him, and through him only, she had the company of her kind; freely and simply, without the destructive bias of sexual attraction or rejection, he let her be what her mind had made her and her body refused. For the rest, her way of life had always seemed to her natural and un-complex, an obvious one, since there were too many women for the more fortunate of the surplus to arrange themselves; to invest it with drama or pathos would have been in her mind a sentimentality and a kind of cowardice. Because of this confidence she had got what she needed from women easily, and without sacrifice of pride. But no one, except Joe, had given her what she had wanted from men since she had swum and climbed with the boys of her Cornish home; a need as deep and as fundamental, to be a man with his friend, emotion-free, objective, concerned not with relationships but with work and things, sharing ideas without personal implication to spoil them, easily like bread or a pint of beer in a bar. She had accepted this gift from the first almost without thought, not analyzing its goodness, only feeling it to be good; it had been so elementary and wholesome a part of life that she had never questioned it till now, when it was threatened [pp. 165-166].

The female homosexual has many of the same feelings and characteristics as the male homosexual: guilt, shame, jealousy, promiscuity, hatred of the opposite sex, and masochism, among others. Zola's (1880) Nana despised and manipulated men, using them with ruthless glee, especially when she could ruin them. After Fontan, who has been living off Nana's earnings as a prostitute, throws her out, she turns to her friend Satin who expresses her utter contempt for men.

"I could have gone to Madame Robert's," said Satin. "She always has room for me.... But with you it's out of the question. She's so jealous she's silly. The other night she beat me."

When they were in their room, Nana, who had not yet given vent to her feelings, burst into tears and told about Fontan's dirty trick again and again. Satin listened sympathetically and tried to console her. She finally became even more indignant than Nana, and began denouncing men.

"Oh, the pigs! The pigs! ... You shouldn't have anything more to do with those pigs!"

She then helped Nana to undress, hovering around her like a considerate, submissive little woman. "Let's go to bed right now, darling," she said. "We'll be more comfortable.... Oh, you're so silly to be upset! They're all pigs! Don't think about them any more.... You know I like you. Stop crying, do that for your little darling."

As soon as they were in bed, she took Nana in her arms to calm her. She refused to hear Fontan's name; each time it came to Nana's lips she stopped it there with a kiss and a pretty little angry pout. Her hair hung loosely around her shoulders and she had a childish, tender beauty. Little by little, in that soft embrace, Nana dried her tears. She was touched; she began returning Satin's caresses. At two o'clock, the candle was still burning. They were both laughing softly and uttering words of love [p. 236].

It is too gross a generalization to say that all Lesbians hate men; but many do, and practically all have an antimasculine bias (Chesser, 1971). Olive Chancellor, the protagonist in Henry James' (1886) *The Bostonians,* had a "moral resource that she could always fall back upon; it had already been a comfort to her, on occasions of acute feelings, that she hated men, as a class...." Basil, for instance, "belonged to a sex to which she wished to be under no obligations" (p. 17-18, *passim*). Henry James was one of the few nineteenth-century English or American novelists to deal with sexual themes. In *The Bostonians,* the theme of female homosexuality, a recurrent one in his fiction, is portrayed, although a number of scholars of English literature have questioned whether or not Olive Chancellor is of homosexual persuasion and whether James consciously recognized the sexual significance of what he wrote (Hartsock, 1968). To a clinician, the evidence renders unabashed positive answers to both points. In his introduction to the novel, Rahv (1945) stated, "With ... prescience [James] analysed in the character of Olive Chancellor the emotional economy of the Lesbian woman. One cannot be certain that James understood her precisely as such, but in view of the fact that he worked without benefit of the many-sided psychiatric knowledge now at the novelists' disposal, his intuitive grasp of the psychic process of repression and displacement is astonishing indeed. Nor did James make the mistake so common in novels treating similar themes, the mistake of isolating the abnormal person and presenting ... her as a clinical case. Olive Chancellor is presented in the closest relation to her milieu, and her unconscious goal is made to express itself through the hysteria of Feminism..." (p. ix).

Evidence relevant to the question of James' understanding of the Lesbian factor in his novel is found in the comment in his *Notebooks* (Matthiessen and Murdock, 1961, p. 47), "The relation of the two girls should be a study of one of those friendships between women which are so common in New England." Hartsock (1968, p. 302) reports, "More pertinent evidence emerges from the novel itself with the first descriptions of Olive Chancellor." She traces these. On his first visit with Olive, Basil Ransom, a kinsman, "actually perceived ... that Miss Chancellor was a signal old maid. That was her quality, her destiny; nothing could be more distinctly written. There are women who are unmarried by accident, and others who are unmarried by option; but Olive Chancellor was unmarried by implication of her being. She was a spinster as Shelley was a lyric poet, or as the month of August is sultry. She was so essentially a celibate that Ransom found himself thinking of her as old, though when he came to look at her... it was apparent that her years were fewer than his own" (James, p. 14). Thus, James says that Olive is by nature unsuited to marriage: "Her nature was like a skiff in a strong sea" (p. 7). Concealed from Olive Chancellor herself, says Hartsock, was the desperate reaching out for an intimate relationship. "She had an immense desire to know intimately some *very* poor girl. This might seem one of the most accessible of pleasures; but in point of fact, she had not found it so. There were two or three pale shop-maidens whose acquaintance she had sought; but they seemed afraid of her, and the attempt had come to nothing. She took them more tragically than they took themselves; they couldn't make out what she wanted them to do, and they always ended by being odiously mixed up with Charlie. Charlie was a young man in a white overcoat and a paper collar; it was for him, in the last analysis, that they cared about the most" (James, p. 28).

So Olive fantasized—not of the Short-Skirts League or the feminist movement with which she was so ardently involved, but of "a friend of her own sex with whom she might have a union of soul" (p. 67); of "still winter evenings under the lamp, with falling snow outside, and tea on a little table" and "a chosen companion" (p. 73) reading there with her. While these descriptions are compatible with any normal desire for friendship, when Olive does meet a very poor girl, Verena Tarrant, the aura of the scene is one of breathless sexuality rather than feminine sociability. Olive, tremulous with excitement, looks Verena over "in a manner that caused the girl to rejoice at having put on the jacket with the gilt buttons" (p. 67). Olive asks Verena to stay with her: "'Will you be my friend, my friend of friends, beyond every one, everything, forever and forever?'" (p. 68). Comments Hartsock (1968, p. 303), "Verena, naive and a bit stupid, cannot understand Olive's insistence that each must give up everything else. From this point on, the novel traces the temporary fulfillment of Olive's hopes and their ultimate destruction when Verena returns to the normal relationship of love for Basil Ransom."

'I was certain you would come—I have felt it all day—something told me!' It was with these words that Olive Chancellor greeted her young visitor, coming to her quickly from the window, where she might have been waiting for her arrival. Some weeks later she explained to Verena how definite this prevision had been, how it had filled her all day with a nervous agitation so violent as to be painful. She told her that such forebodings were a peculiarity of her organisation, that she didn't know what to make of them, that she had to accept them; and she mentioned, as another example, the sudden dread that had come to her the evening before in the carriage, after proposing to Mr. Ransom to go with her to Miss Birdseye's. This had been as strange as it had been instinctive, and the strangeness, of course, was what must have struck Mr. Ransom; for the idea that he might come had been hers, and yet she suddenly veered round. She couldn't help it; her heart had begun to throb with the conviction that if he crossed that threshold some harm would come of it for her. She hadn't prevented him, and now she didn't care, for now, as she intimated, she had the interest of Verena, and that made her indifferent to every danger, to every ordinary pleasure. By this time Verena had learned how peculiarly her friend was constituted, how nervous and serious she was, how personal, how exclusive, what a force of will she had, what a concentration of purpose. Olive had taken her up, in the literal sense of the phrase, like a bird of the air, had spread an extraordinary pair of wings, and carried her through the dizzying void of space. Verena liked it, for the most part; liked to shoot upward without an effort of her own and look down upon all creation, upon all history, from such a height. From this first interview she felt that she was seized, and she gave herself up, only shutting her eyes a little, as we do whenever a person in whom we have perfect confidence proposes, with our assent, to subject us to some sensation.

'I want to know you,' Olive said, on this occasion; 'I felt that I must last night, as soon as I heard you speak. You seem to me very wonderful. I don't know what to make of you. I think we ought to be friends; so I just asked you to come to me straight off, without preliminaries, and I believed you would come. It is *so right* that you have come, and it proves how right I was.' These remarks fell from Miss Chancellor's lips one by one, as she caught her breath, with the tremor that was always in her voice, even when she was the least excited, while she made Verena sit down near her on the sofa, and looked at her all over in a manner that caused the girl to rejoice at having put on the jacket with the gilt buttons. It was this glance that was the beginning; it was with this quick survey, omitting nothing, that Olive took possession of her. 'You are very remarkable; I wonder if you know how remarkable!' she went on, murmuring the words as if she were losing herself, becoming inadvertent in admiration.

Verena sat there smiling, without a blush, but with a pure, bright look which, for her, would always make protests unnecessary. 'Oh, it isn't me, you know; it's something outside!' She tossed this off lightly, as if she were in the habit of saying it, and Olive wondered whether it were a sincere disclaimer or only a phrase of the lips. The question was not a criticism, for she might have been satisfied that the girl was a mass of fluent catch-words and yet scarcely have liked her the less. It was just as she was that she liked her; she was so strange, so different from the girls one usually met, seemed to belong to some queer gipsy-land or transcendental Bohemia. With her bright, vulgar clothes, her salient appearance, she might have been a rope-dancer or a fortune-teller; and this had the immense merit, for Olive, that it appeared to make her belong to the 'people,' threw her into the social dusk of that mysterious democracy which Miss Chancellor held that the fortunate classes know so little about, and with which (in a future possibly very near) they will have to count. Moreover, the girl had moved her as she had never been moved, and the power to do that, from whatever source it came, was a force that one must admire. Her emotion was still acute, however much she might speak to her visitor as if everything that had happened seemed to her natural; and what kept it, above all, from subsiding was her sense that she found here what she had been look-ing for so long—a friend of her own sex with whom she might have a union of the soul. It took a double consent to make a friendship, but it was not possible that this intensely sympathetic girl would re-fuse. Olive had the penetration to discover in a moment that she was a creature of unlimited generosity. I know not what may have been the reality of Miss Chancellor's other premonitions, but there is no doubt that in this respect she took Verena's measure on the spot. This was what she wanted; after that the rest didn't matter; Miss Tarrant might wear gilt buttons from head to foot, her soul could not be vulgar.

'Mother told me I had better come right in,' said Verena, looking now about the room, very glad to find herself in so pleasant a place, and noticing a great many things that she should like to see in detail.

'Your mother saw that I meant what I said; it isn't everybody that does me the honour to perceive that. She saw that I was shaken from head to foot. I could only say three words—I couldn't have spoken more! What a power—what a power, Miss Tarrant!"

'Yes, I suppose it is a power. If it wasn't a power, it couldn't do much with me!'

'You are so simple—so much like a child,' Olive Chancellor said. That was the truth, and she wanted to say it because, quickly, without forms or circumlocutions, it made them familiar. She wished to arrive at this; her impatience was such that before the girl had been five mintues in the room she jumped to her point—inquired of her, interrupting herself, interrupting every-thing: 'Will you be my friend, my friend of friends, beyond every one, everything, forever and forever?' Her face was full of eagerness and tenderness.

Verena gave a laugh of clear amusement, without a shade of em-barrassment or confusion. 'Perhaps you like me too much.'

'Of course I like you too much! When I like, I like too much. But of course it's another thing, your liking me,' Olive Chancellor added. 'We must wait — we must wait. When I care for anything, I can be patient.' She put out her hand to Verena, and the movement was at once so appealing and so confident that the girl instinctively placed her own in it. So, hand in hand, for some moments, these two young women sat looking at each other. 'There is so much I want to ask you,' said Olive.

'Well, I can't say much except when father has worked on me,' Verena answered, with an ingenuousness beside which humility would have seemed pretentious.

'I don't care anything about your father,' Olive Chancellor rejoined very gravely, with a great air of security.

'He is very good,' Verena said simply. 'And he's wonderfully magnetic.'

'It isn't your father, and it isn't your mother; I don't think of them, and it's not them I want. It's only you — just as you are.'

Verena dropped her eyes over the front of her dress. 'Just as she was' seemed to her indeed very well.

'Do you want me to give up — ?' she demanded, smiling.

Olive Chancellor drew in her breath for an instant, like a creature in pain; then, with her quavering voice, touched with a vibration of anguish, she said: 'Oh, how can I ask you to give up? *I* will give up — I will give up everything!'

Filled with the impression of her hostess's agreeable interior, and of what her mother had told her about Miss Chancellor's wealth, her position in Boston society, Verena, in her fresh, diverted scrutiny of the surrounding objects, wondered what could be the need of this scheme of renunciation. Oh no, indeed, she hoped she wouldn't give up — at least not before she, Verena, had had a chance to see. She felt, however, that for the present there would be no answer for her save in the mere pressure of Miss Chancellor's eager nature, that intensity of emotion which made her suddenly exclaim, as if in a nervous ecstasy of anticipation, 'But we must wait! Why do we talk of this? We must wait! All will be right,' she added more calmly, with great sweetness.

Verena wondered afterward why she had not been more afraid of her — why, indeed, she had not turned and saved herself by darting out of the room. But it was not in this young woman's nature to be either timid or cautious; she had as yet to make acquaintance with the sentiment of fear. She knew too little of the world to have learned to mistrust sudden enthusiasms, and if she had had a suspicion it would have been (in accordance with common worldly knowledge) the wrong one—the suspicion that such a whimsical liking would burn itself out. She could not have that one, for there was a light in Miss Chancellor's magnified face which seemed to say that a sentiment, with her, might consume its object, might consume Miss Chancellor, but would never consume itself. Verena, as yet, had no sense of being scorched; she was only agreeably warmed. She also had dreamed of a friendship, though it was not what she had dreamed of most, and it came over her that this was the one which fortune might have been keeping. She never held back.

'Do you live here all alone?' she asked of Olive.

'I shouldn't if you would come and live with me!' [James, pp. 66-69].

Olive's masculinity, her hatred of men, and her passion for Verena bespeak a latent homosexuality (Edel, 1962). The scene in which Olive draws Verena to her in the dark after the young girl has yielded to Ransom is one in which "horror and pity are astonishingly mixed and there is not its equal for psychological penetration in nineteenth-century fiction" (Cargill, 1961, p. 136). Olive's tragedy, according to Putt (1966), is that of self-delusion, wherein love and jealousy prompt all her behavior toward Verena. "What is specific about the homosexual symptom, aside from a prolonged uncertainty as to gender identity in childhood, is fear of the opposite sex, or fear of inadequacy in one's proper sex role, or both" (Adler, 1967, p. 72). When Peter, a new heterosexual friend of homosexual Leo in Renault's *The Middle Mist,* kisses her, she gazes "up at him with level, half-open eyes. 'Don't look at me,' he said, 'as if you had a knife in your garter.' This amused her, and she laughed. 'I don't wear garters.' 'Nor you do. What lovely stockings.' 'Do you know, Peter, I think I really like you.' Peter scented more defence-mechanisms in this, to him, needlessly guarded statement..." (p. 181).

Olive's jealousy of Verena in *The Bostonians* is an illustration of a common characteristic found in many female homosexual relationships. In Lesbian society, "where there is no marriage, no social or legal sanctions to help sustain relationships beyond the initial period of romantic love, insecurity and jealousy" are rife (Abbott and Love, 1972, pp. 80-81). The tension developing out of a Lesbian's need for love causes her feelings to become clouded with self-hate, often eventuating in hate for her partner. In *Claudine at School,* by Colette (1900), the irrational jealousy of the headmistress of a girls' school in the illustration cited here shows a double Lesbian relationship: one a rather sophisticated schoolgirl crush, the other mature homosexual feelings—Claudine for Mlle. Aimée, and Mlle. Sergent for Mlle. Aimée. Mlle. Sergent's jealousy of Claudine leads to some hysterical scenes.

'. . . tell me the truth. She doesn't want you to come any more?'

I was trembling with anguish; I gripped my hands between my knees to make them keep still. Aimée fidgeted with the cover of the Grammar and began to tear off a strip where it was gummed. As she did so, she raised her eyes towards me. They had grown scared again.

'Yes, that's it. But she didn't say it the way you said it, Claudine. Listen to me a moment. . . .'

I did not listen to a word; I felt as if I were dissolving with misery. I was sitting on a little stool on the floor, and, clasping my arms around her slim waist, I beseeched her:

'Darling, don't go away. . . . If you only knew, I'd be too utterly wretched! Oh, find some excuse, make up something, come back, don't leave me! It's sheer bliss for me, just being with you! Doesn't it give *you* any pleasure at all? Am I just like Anaïs or Marie Belhomme to you? Darling, do, *do* come back and go on giving me English lessons! I love you so much. . . . I didn't tell you . . . but now you can't help seeing I do! . . . Come back, I implore you. She can't beat you for it, that red-haired beast!'

I was burning with fever and my nerves were becoming more and more frayed at feeling that Aimée's were not vibrating in sympathy. She stroked my head as it lay on her lap and only interrupted now and then with a quavering 'my little Claudine!' At last her eyes brimmed over and she began to cry as she said:

'I'm going to tell you everything. It's too wretched—you make me too unhappy! Well, last Saturday, I couldn't help noticing *She* was being much nicer to me than usual. I thought she was getting used to me and would leave the two of us in peace so I was awfully happy and pleased. And then, towards the end of the evening, when we were correcting exercise-books at the same table, I suddenly looked up and saw she was crying. And she was looking at me in such a peculiar way that I was absolutely dumbfounded. Then, all at once, she got up from her chair and went off to bed. The next day after being awfully nice to me all day, when I was alone with her in the evening and was just going to say good night, she suddenly asked me: "You're very fond of Claudine, aren't you? And no doubt, she returns your fondness?" And, before I had time to answer, she fell into a chair beside me and sobbed. And then she took my hands and said all sorts of things that simply took my breath away....'

'What things?'

'Well ... she said to me: "My dear little thing, don't you realize you're breaking my heart with your indifference? Oh, my darling girl, how could you possibly not have noticed my great affection for you? My little Aimée, I'm jealous of the tenderness you show to that brainless Claudine who's quite definitely a little unhinged. ... If you'd only just not hate me, oh! if you'd only love me a little, I'd be a more tender friend than you could ever imagine. ...." And she looked into the very depths of my soul with eyes like red-hot pokers.'

'Didn't you answer her at all?'

'Of course not! I hadn't time to! Another thing she said was: "Do you think they're very useful to her or very kind to me, those English lessons you give her? It tears my heart every time I see the two of you go off together! Don't go there—don't ever go there again! Claudine won't give it another thought in a week's time and I can give you more affection than she's capable of feeling!" Claudine, I assure you, I no longer had any idea what I was doing. She was mesmerizing me with those crazy eyes of hers and, suddenly, the room began to go round, and my head swam; and for two or three seconds, not more, I couldn't see anything at all. I could only hear her saying over and over again, and sounding terrified "My God! ... My poor little girl! I've frightened her ... she's so pale, my little Aimée, my darling!" And, immediately after that, she helped me to undress, in the most kind, affectionate way, and I slept as if I'd spent the entire day walking.... Claudine, my poor pet, you realize there was simply nothing I could do about it!'

I was stunned. So she had passionate friendships, that volcanic Redhead! At heart, I was not tremendously surprised; it was bound to end that way. Meanwhile, I sat there, utterly overwhelmed; faced with Aimée, this frail little creature bewitched by that Fury, I did not know what to say. She dried her eyes. It seemed to me that her distress was over with her tears.

'But you ... don't love her at all?'

She answered, without looking at me:

'No, of course not. But, really, she does seem to be awfully fond of me and I never suspected it.'

Her answer froze me completely. After all, I'm not completely out of my mind yet and I understand what people are trying to say to me. I let go her hands which I was holding and I stood up. Something had been broken. Since she was unwilling to frankly admit that she was no longer with me against the other, since she was hiding her deepest thoughts, I thought all was over. My hands were ice-cold and my cheeks were burning. After a painful silence, I was the first to speak:

'Dear Aimée of the lovely eyes, I implore you to come just once more to finish up the month. Do you think she will agree?'

'Oh, yes! I'll ask her.'

She said it promptly and spontaneously, already sure of getting anything she wanted out of Mademoiselle Sergent now. How fast she was receding from me and how fast the other had triumphed! Cowardly little Lanthenay! She loved comfort like a warmth-starved cat and knew very well that her chief's friendship would be more profitable to her than mine! But I did not mean to tell her so or she would not come back for the last lesson and I still cherished a vague hope. . . . The hour was over and I escorted Aimée to the door. In the passage, I embraced her fiercely, with a touch of despair. Once I was alone, I was surprised not to find myself feeling quite as sad as I believed myself to be. I had expected a tremendous, absurd explosion but, no, what I felt was more like a chill that froze me. . . .

At supper, I broke in upon Papa's musings.

'Papa, you know those English lessons of mine?'

'Yes, I know. You're quite right to take them. . . .'

'Please listen. I'm not going to take any more.'

'Ah, they tire you, do they?'

'Yes, they get on my nerves.'

'Then you're quite right.'

And his thoughts flew back to his slugs — if they had ever left them [pp. 48-51].

Violet, in *Norman's Letter* by Gavin Lambert (1966), was betrayed by her lover, Kitty. As she recounted the unhappy details to her brother Norman, "Her voice ached. 'Oh, Kitty, Kitty. You wicked, heartless girl.' She tried to pull herself together, gave me a sheepish grin. 'Women . . .' she said. 'They twist us around their little fingers.' She sank into a chair. 'I saw them together. Locked in a passionate embrace.' And a tear glistened in the corner of one eye. 'Kitty and who?' 'Her understudy. I surprised them in the dressing room. Oh Kitty, oh my faithless darling' " (p. 69). Jenny Petherbridge, a middle-aged widow who has been married four times, as related in Djuna Barnes' (1937) *Nightwood,* steals Robin Vote from Nora in order to establish her own Lesbian relationship with Robin. Dr.

Matthew Mighty O'Connor, bogus gynecologist and garrulous trans-vestite friend, tries to explain Jenny's motivation in the "theft": Jenny "has a longing for other people's property but the moment she possesses it the property loses some of its value, for the owner's estimate is its worth. Therefore it was she took your Robin . . . She is a looter . . . She sets about collecting a destiny—and for her, the sole destiny is love, anyone's love and so her own. So only someone's love is her love" (p. 98). When Robin turned the table on Jenny and rebelled in her jealous rage, Jenny "struck Robin, scratching and tearing in hysteria, striking, clutching and crying. Slowly the blood began to run down Robin's cheeks, and as Jenny struck repeatedly Robin began to go forward as if brought to the movement by the very blows them-selves, as if she had no will, sinking down in the small [horse-drawn] carriage, her knees on the floor, her head forward as her arm moved upward in a gesture of defence; and as she sank, Jenny also, as if compelled to conclude the movement of her first blow, almost as something seen in retarded action, leaned forward and over, so that when the whole gesture was completed, Robin's hands were covered by Jenny's slight and bending breast, caught in between the bosom and the knees" (p. 76).

In 1916, Ernest Jones wrote an introduction to Ronald Firbank's novel, *Inclinations,* saying in part, "With the exception of Proust, Firbank is the one serious novelist of the twentieth century, overtly concerned with homosexuality, who avoids pathos which mars even *Les Faux-Monnayeurs* . . . In life, he feared and disliked women, his mother excepted; in his fiction his entire feminine sensibility concerned itself far more with women than men. He is perfectly at home with their talk, their affairs, their clothes. . ." (p. xi). In *Incli-nations,* Mabel Collins, a fifteen-year-old English schoolgirl of tomboy habits is carried off to Greece by Geraldine — usually called "Gerald" — O'Brookomore, a noted and formidable biographer. The famous twentieth chapter of the novel, cited in its entirety below, in which Miss O'Brookomore laments the defection of the beloved, is wickedly funny, as well as revealing of the jealous despair of the bereft woman.

"Mabel! Mabel! Mabel! Mabel!
"Mabel! Mabel! Mabel! Mabel!"

In the Paris 1913 section of Thomas Pynchon's *V* (1963), there is a passage that states a major theme in the novelist's work. "Lesbianism, we are prone to think in this Freudian period of history," he writes, "stems from self-love projected on to some other human object. If a girl gets to feeling narcissist, she will also sooner or later come upon the idea that women, the class she belongs to, are not so bad either..." (p. 407). The heroine, V., is meditating on her Lesbian passion for a young ballerina: "It was a variation on ... the Tristan-and-Iseult theme, indeed, according to some, the single melody, banal and exasperating, of all Romanticism since the Middle Ages: 'the act of love and the act of death are one.' Dead at last, they would be one with the inanimate universe and with each other. Love-play until then becomes an impersonation of the inanimate, a transvestism not between sexes but between quick and dead, human and fetish" (p. 410).

Although constituting but one scene, the behavior and conversation between Cytherea and Miss Aldclyffe in Thomas Hardy's (1871) first published novel is one of the most outspoken descriptions of Lesbianism in English literature up to the twentieth century. *Desperate Remedies* has a convoluted, elaborate, and incredible plot. Edward Springrove, a young architect, and a loose-principled adventurer named Aeneas Manston are both in love with Cytherea Graze. But Springrove is also engaged to another girl, and Manston is secretly married, as well as being the illegitimate son of Miss Aldclyffe, the lady of the manor who employs Cytherea as a companion. To add another coincidence, Miss Aldclyffe was once in love with Cytherea's father. A series of melodramatic entanglements and improbabilities follow. But the most realistic subplot Hardy devised was the Lesbian scene initiated by the tormented Miss Aldclyffe with Cytherea. In writing this explicit homosexual scene, Hardy was much advanced for the times, Miss Aldclyffe slips into Cytherea's bed and asks, with increasing passion, to be hugged and kissed. She expresses jealousy when she discovers Cytherea has been kissed by a man. "'Find a girl,'" she says sardonically, "'whose mouth and ears have not been made a regular highway of by some man or other!'" (p. 93). After telling Cytherea she loves her more than any man could, she asks the girl to put her "'hair round your mama's neck, and give me one good long kiss, and I won't talk any more in that way about your lover'" (p. 97).

Cytherea entered her bedroom, and flung herself on the bed, bewildered by a whirl of thought. Only one subject was clear in her mind, and it was that, in spite of family discoveries, that day was to be the first and last of her experience as a lady's-maid. Starvation itself could not compel her to hold such a humiliating post for another instant. 'Ah,' she thought, with a sigh, at the martyrdom of her last little fragment of self-conceit, 'Owen knows everything better than I.'

She jumped up and began making ready for her departure in the morning, the tears streaming down when she grieved and wondered what practical matter on earth she could turn her hand to next. All these preparations completed, she began to undress, her mind unconsciously drifting away to the contemplation of her late surprises. To look in the glass for an instant at the reflection of her own magnificent resources in face and bosom, and to mark their attractiveness unadorned, was perhaps the natural action of a young woman who had so lately been chidden whilst passing through the harassing experience of decorating an older beauty of Miss Aldclyffe's temper.

But she directly checked her weakness by sympathizing reflections on the hidden troubles which must have thronged the past years of the solitary lady, to keep her, though so rich and courted, in a mood so repellent and gloomy as that in which Cytherea found her; and then the young girl marvelled again and again, as she had marvelled before, at the strange confluence of circumstances which had brought herself into contact with the one woman in the world whose history was so romantically intertwined with her own. She almost began to wish she were not obliged to go away and leave the lonely being to loneliness still.

In bed and in the dark, Miss Aldclyffe haunted her mind more persistently than ever. Instead of sleeping, she called up staring visions of the possible past of this queenly lady, her mother's rival. Up the long vista of bygone years she saw, behind all, the young girl's flirtation, little or much, with the cousin, that seemed to have been nipped in the bud, or to have terminated hastily in some way. Then the secret meetings between Miss Aldclyffe and the other woman at the little inn at Hammersmith and other places: the commonplace name she adopted: her swoon at some painful news, and the very slight knowledge the elder female had of her partner in mystery. Then, more than a year afterwards, the acquaintanceship of her own father with this his first love; the awakening of the passion, his acts of devotion, the unreasoning heat of his rapture, her tacit acceptance of it, and yet her uneasiness under the delight.

Then his declaration amid the evergreens: the utter change produced in her manner thereby, seemingly the result of a rigid determination: and the total concealment of her reason by herself and her parents, whatever it was. Then the lady's course dropped into darkness, and nothing more was visible till she was discovered here at Knapwater, nearly fifty years old, still unmarried and still beautiful, but lonely, embittered, and haughty. Cytherea imagined that her father's image was still warmly cherished in Miss Aldclyffe's heart, and was thankful that she herself had not been betrayed into announcing that she knew many particulars of this page of her father's history, and the chief one, the lady's unaccountable renunciation of him. It would have made her bearing towards the mistress of the mansion more awkward, and would have been no benefit to either.

Thus conjuring up the past, and theorizing on the present, she lay restless, changing her posture from one side to the other and back again. Finally, when courting sleep with all her art, she heard a clock strike two. A minute later, and she fancied she could distinguish a soft rustle in the passage outside her room.

To bury her head in the sheets was her first impulse; then to uncover it, raise herself on her elbow, and stretch her eyes wide open in the darkness; her lips being parted in the intentness of her listening. Whatever the noise was, it had ceased for the time.

It began again and came close to her door, lightly touching the panels. Then there was another stillness; Cytherea made a movement which caused a faint rustling of the bed-clothes.

Before she had time to think another thought a light tap was given. Cytherea breathed: the person outside was evidently bent upon finding her awake, and the rustle she had made had encouraged the hope. The maiden's physical condition shifted from one pole to its opposite. The cold sweat of terror forsook her; and modesty took the alarm. She became hot and red; her door was not locked.

A distinct woman's whisper came to her through the keyhole: 'Cytherea!'

Only one being in the house knew her Christian name, and that was Miss Aldclyffe. Cytherea stepped out of bed, went to the door, and whispered back 'Yes?'

'Let me come in, darling.'

The young woman paused in conflict between judgment and emotion. It was now mistress and maid no longer; woman and woman only. Yes; she must let her come in, poor thing.

She got a light in an instant, opened the door, and raising her eyes and the candle, saw Miss Aldclyffe standing outside in her dressing-gown.

'Now you see that it is really myself; put out the light,' said the visitor. 'I want to stay here with you, Cythie. I came to ask you to come down into my bed, but it is snugger here. But remember that you are mistress in this room, and that I have no business here, and that you may send me away if you choose. Shall I go?'

'O no; you shan't indeed if you don't want to,' said Cythie generously.

The instant they were in bed Miss Aldclyffe freed herself from the last remnant of restraint. She flung her arms round the young girl, and pressed her gently to her heart.

'Now kiss me,' she said. 'You seem as if you were my own, own child!'

Cytherea, upon the whole, was rather discomposed at this change of treatment; and, discomposed or no, her passions were not so impetuous as Miss Aldclyffe's. She could not bring her soul to her lips for a moment, try how she would.

'Come, kiss me,' repeated Miss Aldclyffe.

Cytherea gave her a very small one, as soft in touch and in sound as the bursting of a bubble.

'More earnestly than that—come.'

She gave another, a little but not much more expressively.

'I don't deserve a more feeling one, I suppose,' said Miss Aldclyffe, with an emphasis of sad bitterness in her tone. 'I am an ill-tempered woman, you think; half out of my mind. Well, perhaps I am; but I have had grief more than you can think or dream of. But I am a lonely woman, and I want the sympathy of a pure girl like you, and so I can't help loving you—your name is the same as mine—isn't it strange?'

Cytherea was inclined to say no, but remained silent.

'Now, don't you think I must love you?' continued the other.

'Yes,' said Cytherea absently. She was still thinking whether duty to Owen and her father, which asked for silence on her knowledge of her father's unfortunate love, or duty to the woman embracing her, which seemed to ask for confidence, ought to predominate. Here was a solution. She would wait till Miss Aldclyffe referred to her acquaintanceship and attachment to Cytherea's father in past times: then she would tell her all she knew: that would be honour.

'Why can't you kiss me as I can kiss you? Why can't you!' She impressed upon Cytherea's lips a warm motherly salute, given as if in the outburst of strong feeling, long checked, and yearning for something to care for and be cared for by in return.

'Do you think badly of me for my behavior this evening, child? I don't know why I am so foolish as to speak to you in this way. I am a very fool, I believe. Yes. How old are you?'

'Eighteen.'

'Eighteen! . . . Well, why don't you ask me how old I am?'

'Because I don't want to know.'

'Never mind if you don't. I am forty-six; and it gives me greater pleasure to tell you this than it does to you to listen. I have not told my age truly for the last twenty years till now.'

'Why haven't you?'

'I have met deceit by deceit, till I am weary of it—weary, weary—and I long to be what I shall never be again—artless and innocent, like you. But I suppose that you, too, will prove to be not worth a thought, as every new friend does on more intimate knowledge. Come, why don't you talk to me, child? Have you said your prayers?'

'Yes—no! I forgot them to-night.'

'I suppose you say them every night as a rule?'

'Yes.'

'Why do you do that?'

'Because I have always done so, and it would seem strange if I were not to. Do you?'

'I? A wicked old sinner like me! No, I never do. I have thought all such matters humbug for years—thought so so long that I should be glad to think otherwise from very weariness; and yet, such is the code of the polite world, that I subscribe regularly to Missionary Societies and others of the sort. . . . Well, say your prayers, dear—you won't omit them now you recollect it. I should like to hear you very much. Will you?'

'It seems hardly—'

'It would seem so like old times to me—when I was young, and nearer—far nearer Heaven than I am now. Do, sweet one.'

Cytherea was embarrassed, and her embarrassment arose from the following conjuncture of affairs. Since she had loved Edward Springrove, she had linked his name with her brother Owen's in her nightly supplications to the Almighty. She wished to keep her love for him a secret, and, above all, a secret from a woman like Miss Aldclyffe; yet her conscience and the honesty of her love would not for an instant allow her to think of omitting his dear name, and so endanger the efficacy of all her previous prayers for his success by an unworthy shame now: it would be wicked of her, she thought, and a grievous wrong to him. Under any worldly circumstances she might have thought the position justified a little finesse, and have skipped him for once; but prayer was too solemn a thing for such trifling.

'I would rather not say them,' she murmured first. It struck her then that this declining altogether was the same cowardice in another dress, and was delivering her poor Edward over to Satan just as unceremoniously as before. 'Yes; I will say my prayers, and you shall hear me,' she added firmly.

She turned her face to the pillow and repeated in low soft tones the simple words she had used from childhood on such occasions. Owen's name was mentioned without faltering, but in the other case, maidenly shyness was too strong even for religion, and that when supported by excellent intentions. At the name of Edward she stammered, and her voice sank to the faintest whisper in spite of her.

'Thank you, dearest,' said Miss Aldclyffe. 'I have prayed too, I verily believe. You are a good girl, I think.' Then the expected question came.

' "Bless Owen," and whom, did you say?'

There was no help for it now, and out it came. 'Owen and Edward,' said Cytherea.

'Who are Owen and Edward?'

'Owen is my brother, madam,' faltered the maid.

'Ah, I remember. Who is Edward?'

A silence.

'Your brother, too?' continued Miss Aldclyffe.

'No.'

Miss Aldclyffe reflected a moment. 'Don't you want to tell me who Edward is?' she said at last in a tone of meaning.

'I don't mind telling; only . . .'

'You would rather not, I suppose?'

'Yes.'

Miss Aldclyffe shifted her ground. 'Were you ever in love?' she inquired suddenly.

Cytherea was surprised to hear how quickly the voice had altered from tenderness to harshness, vexation, and disappointment.

'Yes—I think I was—once,' she murmured.

'Aha! And were you ever kissed by a man?'

A pause.

'Well, were you?' said Miss Aldclyffe, rather sharply.

'Don't press me to tell—I can't—indeed, I won't, madam!'

Miss Aldclyffe removed her arms from Cytherea's neck. ' 'Tis now with you as it is always with all girls,' she said, in jealous and gloomy accents. 'You are not, after all, the innocent I took you for. No, no.' She then changed her tone with fitful rapidity. 'Cytherea, try to love me more than you love him—do. I love you more sincerely than any man can. Do, Cythie: don't let any man stand between us. O, I can't bear that!' She clasped Cytherea's neck again.

'I must love him now I have begun,' replied the other.

'Must—yes—must,' said the elder lady reproachfully. 'Yes, women are all alike. I thought I had at last found an artless woman who had not been sullied by a man's lips, and who had not practised or been practised upon by the arts which ruin all the truth and sweetness and goodness in us. Find a girl, if you can, whose mouth and ears have not been made a regular highway of by some man or another! Leave the admittedly notorious spots—the drawing-rooms of society—and look in the villages—leave the villages and search in the schools—and you can hardly find a girl whose heart has not been *had*—is not an old thing half worn out by some He or another! If men only knew the staleness of the freshest of us! that nine times out of ten the "first love" they think they are winning from a woman is but the hulk of an old wrecked affection, fitted with new sails and re-used. O Cytherea, can it be that you, too, are like the rest?'

'No, no, no,' urged Cytherea, awed by the storm she had raised in the impetuous woman's mind. 'He only kissed me once—twice I mean.'

'He might have done it a thousand times if he had cared to, there's no doubt about that, whoever his lordship is. You are as bad as I—we are all alike; and I—an old fool—have been sipping at your mouth as if it were honey, because I fancied no wasting lover knew the spot. But a minute ago, and you seemed to me like a fresh spring meadow—now you seem a dusty highway.'

'O no, no!' Cytherea was not weak enough to shed tears except on extraordinary occasions, but she was fain to begin sobbing now. She wished Miss Aldclyffe would go to her own room, and leave her and her treasured dreams alone. This vehement imperious affection was in one sense soothing, but yet it was not of the kind that Cytherea's instincts desired. Though it was generous, it seemed somewhat too rank and capricious for endurance.

'Well,' said the lady in continuation, 'who is he?'

Her companion was desperately determined not to tell his name: she too much feared a taunt when Miss Aldclyffe's fiery mood again ruled her tongue.

'Won't you tell me? not tell me after all the affection I have shown?'

'I will, perhaps, another day.'

'Did you wear a hat and white feather in Budmouth for the week or two previous to your coming here?'

'Yes.'

'Then I have seen you and your lover at a distance! He rowed you round the bay with your brother.'

'Yes.'

'And without your brother—fie! There, there, don't let that little heart beat itself to death: throb, throb: it shakes the bed, you silly thing. I didn't mean that there was any harm in going alone with him. I only saw you from the Esplanade, in common with the rest of the people. I often run down to Budmouth. He was a very good figure: now who was he?'

'I—I won't tell, madam—I cannot indeed!'

'Won't tell—very well, don't. You are very foolish to treasure up his name and image as you do. Why, he has had loves before you, trust him for that, whoever he is, and you are but a temporary link in a long chain of others like you: who only have their little day as they have had theirs.'

''Tisn't true! 'tisn't true! 'tisn't true!' cried Cytherea in an agony of torture. 'He has never loved anybody else, I know—I am sure he hasn't.'

Miss Aldclyffe was as jealous as any man could have been. She continued—

'He sees a beautiful face and thinks he will never forget it, but in a few weeks the feeling passes off, and he wonders how he could have cared for anybody so absurdly much.'

'No, no, he doesn't—What does he do when he has thought that—Come, tell me—tell me!'

'You are as hot as fire, and the throbbing of your heart makes me nervous. I can't tell you if you get in that flustered state.'

'Do, do tell—O, it makes me so miserable! but tell—come tell me!'

'Ah—the tables are turned now, dear!' she continued, in a tone which mingled pity with derision—

> 'Love's passions shall rock thee
> As the storm rocks the ravens on high,
> Bright reason will mock thee
> Like the sun from a wintry sky.

'What does he do next?—Why, this is what he does next: ruminate on what he has heard of women's romantic impulses, and how easily men torture them when they have given way to those feel-ings, and have resigned everything for their hero. It may be that though he loves you heartily now—that is, as heartily as a man can—and you love him in return, your loves may be impracticable and hopeless, and you may be separated for ever. You, as the weary, weary years pass by will fade and fade—bright eyes *will* fade—and you will perhaps then die early—true to him to your latest breath, and believing him to be true to the latest breath also; whilst he, in some gay and busy spot far away from your last quiet nook, will have married some dashing lady, and not purely oblivious of you, will long have ceased to regret you—will chat about you, as you were in long past years—will say, "Ah, little Cytherea used to tie her hair like that—poor innocent trusting thing; it was a pleasant useless idle dream—that dream of mine for the maid with the bright eyes and simple, silly heart; but I was a foolish lad at that time." Then he will tell the tale of all your little Wills and Won'ts, and particular ways, and as he speaks, turn to his wife with a placid smile.'

'It's not true! He can't he c-can't be s-so cruel—and you are cruel to me—you are, you are!' She was at last driven to desperation: her natural common sense and shrewdness had seen all through the piece how imaginary her emotions were—she felt herself to be weak and foolish in permitting them to rise; but even then she could not control them: be agonized she must. She was only eighteen, and the long day's labour, her weariness, her excitement, had completely unnerved her, and worn her out: she was bent hither and thither by this tyrannical working upon her imagination, as a young rush in the wind. She wept bitterly.

'And now think how much *I* like you,' resumed Miss Aldclyffe, when Cytherea grew calmer. 'I shall never forget you for anybody else, as men do—never. I will be exactly as a mother to you. Now will you promise to live with me always, and always be taken care of, and never deserted?'

'I cannot. I will not be anybody's maid for another day on any consideration.'

'No, no, no. You shan't be a lady's-maid, of course. You shall be my companion. I will get another maid.'

Companion—that was a new idea. Cytherea could not resist the evidently heartfelt desire of the strange-tempered woman for her presence. But she could not trust to the moment's impulse.

'I will stay, I think. But do not ask for a final answer to-night.'

'Never mind now, then. Put your hair round your mama's neck, and give me one good long kiss, and I won't talk any more in that way about your lover. After all, some young men are not so fickle as others; but even if he's the ficklest, there is consolation. The love of an inconstant man is ten times more ardent than that of a faithful man — that is, while it lasts.'

Cytherea did as she was told, to escape the punishment of further talk; flung the twining tresses of her long, rich hair over Miss Aldclyffe's shoulders as directed, and the two ceased conversing, making themselves up for sleep. Miss Aldclyffe seemed to give herself over to a luxurious sense of content and quiet, as if the maiden at her side afforded her a protection against dangers which had menaced her for years; she was soon sleeping calmly [pp. 86-97].

Hardy, like Henry James, had a conscious, intuitive understanding of women, as this scene reveals. Guerard (1964, pp. 103-105, *passim*) states that intuitive understanding may be "subconscious as well as conscious, and the 'unpleasantness' which Hardy dramatizes is unmistakably that of Lesbian attachment . . . Hardy was indignant over a relationship whose psychic discomforts he had imagined fully; in which he participated symbolically. The indignation got into the prose. But he did not know, perhaps, what the imagined relationship really signified . . . Human neuroses existed and could be dramatized long before they were explained and 'known.' Or did Hardy know what he was writing about? . . . One passage in the novel itself bears directly on the problem of deliberateness":

It was perceived by the servants of the house that some secret bond of connection existed between Miss Aldclyffe and her companion. But they were woman and woman, not woman and man, the facts were ethereal and refined, and so they could not be worked up into a taking story. Whether, as old critics disputed, a supernatural machinery be necessary to an epic or no, an ungodly machinery is decidedly necessary to a scandal.

The jealous possessiveness of the dominant partner can become fierce if threatened by heterosexual rivalry, as seen in this excerpt as well as in *The Bostonians, Nana,* and Rolland's *Annette and Sylvie,* (1922). Just as male homosexuals are compulsively preoccupied with sexuality, female homosexuals in therapy display a similar pattern. In addition to providing sexual release and gratification, the homosexual relationship appears to serve a range of defenses and reparative needs. "Although some homosexual relationships may appear stable, con-

tinuity is unusual. In some apparently stable female homosexual relationships, either or both partners secretly indulge in homosexual
relationships on the side. Discovery of such infidelity often results in a
break between the partners. Within the relationship itself, there are
a great many tensions and a tendency toward hostile eruptions that
may lead to a break in the relationship. Extreme ambivalence in both
partners leads to impermanence in homosexual partnerships. The
frequency of verbal or physical fighting between homosexual partners
and among homosexual groups suggests that there is much in
homosexual relationships that is destructive. There is certainly a
longing to develop and maintain meaningful relationships. Frequent
attempts to relate are frustrated by chronic ambivalence, hostility and
anxiety" (Wilbur, 1965, p. 279). The typical homosexual female is
described by Sprague (1962) as young, urban, comparatively well-
educated, feminine, unhappy, lonely, insecure, and tending toward
promiscuity; and a study by Sawyer (1965) of an interacting set of
black female overt homosexuals indicated that while mate stability is
highly valued, instability is the general rule.

On the other hand, Irving Bieber et al. (1971) reported that Lesbian
relationships tend to be long-lived, an opinion concurred in by Hyde
(1970), who thinks women are by and large much less promiscuous and
far more discreet than men. One of the reasons Allen and Martin
(1971) propose for society's being less condemnatory of Lesbians is that
women are reared as nestbuilders and when they mate, they remain
with one another, at least in comparable ratio to the heterosexual
married population. Autobiographical and fictional literature does
not tend to bear this out. Aaron (1972), in his autobiography, looked
back on the gay life as one in which "fidelity is almost impossible . . .
danger is essential . . . sexual contacts are impersonal and even anonymous" (p. 98).

Djuna Barnes' *Nightwood* depicts the futility of the compulsive
promiscuity of Robin Vote. *Nobody Answered the Bell,* by Rhys
Davies (1971), tells about Kenny, forty-two years old at the narrative's
opening. "After cutting herself off from her Liverpool family and
heading south at the age of eighteen, she had settled for many years in
London, sharing bedsitting rooms with a series of girls. They invariably left her, sometimes for a man" (p. 37). It was not until many years
later, when she developed a permanent liaison with Rose, that Kenny
told her, "You redeemed me. I always dreaded I would end up living

with a whore—without being one of them, if you know what I mean" (p. 38).

The promiscuity of the female homosexual, like her male counterpart, is often observed in the gay bar. "The Lesbian who goes to the bar to find community, freedom, love and ego support, finds instead competition, exploitation, degradation, and frequently loveless sex" (Abbott and Love, 1972, p. 74). There is no denial that the common reason for going to a bar is to find a love partner, but Allen and Martin (1971) ascribe a much more circumspect view to their behavior: once the Lesbian "meets someone who appeals to her, she and her prospective partner date several times . . . before they become intimate. . ." (p. 35). In Emile Zola's *Nana,* female homosexuality is explicit in the relationship between Satin and Nana. The "traditional tolerance of lesbianism [which] has a much older literary history than homosexuality made it possible for [Zola] to introduce the Sapphic episodes in *Nana*; male inversion was out of the question . . . [for] there is no doubt that [Zola] was afraid to undertake a novel on homosexuality, or even to introduce into various works the homosexual overtones he had planned in [his] notes" (Lapp, 1959, p. 280). In one scene in the novel, which is set in the 1870's, Satin brings Nana to the gay bar of Laura Piedefer and exposes her to the beady-eyed, fat women who patronize it primarily to ogle and meet young women.[1]

The next day, since Fontan had told her he would not be home for dinner, she went to see Satin early to take her out for a good meal in a restaurant. Choosing the restaurant involved a great deal of discussion. Satin suggested several that Nana thought were abominable. They finally decided to go to Laure's, a fixed-price restaurant on the Rue des Martyrs, where dinner cost three francs.

Tired of waiting until it was time for dinner, and not knowing what to do on the sidewalk, they went into Laure's twenty-minutes early. The three rooms were still empty. They sat down at a table in the room where Laure Piedefer was enthroned on a high seat behind the counter. This Laure was a lady of fifty whose swelling contours were tightly held in check by belts and corsets. Women began arriving one after another, each one leaning over the saucers to kiss Laure on the mouth with tender familiarity, while the moist-eyed monster tried to divide her attentions in such a way as to make no

---

[1] *Giovanni's Room* by James Baldwin (1956), written nearly a century later, neatly replicates the barroom scene, only this time the characters are beady-eyed, ogling, fat men.

one jealous. The waitress, however, was a tall, thin, pockmarked woman whose eyes, beneath their dark lids, flashed somber fire as she served the ladies.

The three rooms rapidly became full. There were nearly a hundred women seated wherever they could find a place for themselves. Most of them were somewhere around forty, with fat bodies, slack hips, and faces puffy with vice. And amid these bulging breasts and bellies, there were a few pretty, slender girls whose faces still looked guileless, despite the effrontery of their gestures. They were beginners who had been picked up in dance halls by some of Laure's customers, and brought to her establishment, where a multitude of fat women, excited by the smell of their youth, crowded around them and anxiously paid court to them like old bachelors, buying them delicacies. As for the men, they were few in number: ten or fifteen at most. Except for four of them who had come to see the sight and were joking in a thoroughly relaxed manner, they all maintained a humble attitude in the overwhelming flood of skirts.

"The food is good here, isn't it?" said Satin.

Nana nodded, satisfied. It was the old-fashioned, solid dinner of a provincial hotel: meat pie, chicken with rice, beans with gravy, and vanilla cream with caramel sauce. The ladies were particularly fond of the chicken with rice; they ate until they almost burst their corsets, and slowly wiped their lips. At first Nana was afraid of meeting former friends who might ask her stupid questions, but she finally stopped worrying when she saw no one she knew among that motley crowd in which faded dresses and tattered hats were to be seen side by side with elegant costumes, in the fraternity of the same perversions. For a moment she was interested by a young man with blond, curly hair and an insolent face who was sitting at a table with a group of fat women, all breathlessly eager to satisfy his slightest whim. But when the young man laughed, his chest bulged. Nana could not hold back a little cry. "Why, it's a woman!" she exclaimed.

Satin, who was stuffing herself with chicken, looked up and said, "Ah yes, I know her. . . . She's very popular. They're all after her."

Nana grimaced in disgust. She couldn't understand that yet. However, she said in a reasonable tone that there was no use arguing about tastes, because you never knew what you might like some day. And she ate her vanilla cream with a philosophical air. She saw clearly that Satin with her big, blue, virginal eyes, was causing a great stir among the women at the neighboring tables. There was, in particular, a buxom blond who was doing her best to be charming. She was aglow with excitement, and her behavior was so forward that Nana was on the point of intervening [Zola, pp. 216-218].

Many authors, including Freud (1905), Deutsch (1930), and Rado (1933), stress that masochism is basic in feminine emotionality. Freud claimed that the repression of aggression imposed on women by their constitutions and by society favored the development of strong masochistic impulses in them. A clinically accurate picture of female homosexuality has been drawn by D. H. Lawrence in his relatively obscure novelette, *The Fox* (1923), in which Lawrence shows the masochistic structure of the relationship between the two protagonists, Banford and March. The former is a small, thin, nervous, and delicate chicken-farm operator during World War I. Her partner is March, a robust thirty-year-old woman, who "had learned carpentry and joinery at the evening classes in Islington. She would be the man about the place" (p. 3). It was March who did most of the outdoor work. "When she was out and about, in her puttees and breeches, her belted coat and her loose cap, she looked almost like some graceful, loose-balanced young man" (p. 4). Banford worked about the house primarily, cooking and cleaning and acting the role of the fusspot wife: "Goodnight . . . You'll see the fire is safe, if you come up last, won't you?" (p. 28). It is not until the twenty-sixth page that her first name — Jill — is mentioned. March's first name is Ellen, but she is nicknamed Nellie, and she is called this occasionally by Banford. The constant, masculine use of last names is the first clue of the women's homosexuality, a fact only gradually brought home to the reader until it is questioned directly by Henry Grenfel, the twenty-year-old soldier who comes to the farm looking for his grandfather, the previous owner, who had died without Henry's knowledge. March is described: "arms, strong and firm-muscled" (p. 46), and "manfully climbing over the bars [of the fence] with all her packages in her arms" (p. 43). After Henry shoots the fox which had been destroying the chickens, he says to March: "He's a beauty . . . He will make you a lovely fur." "You won't catch me wearing a fox fur," she replies (p. 37). And ". . . March always outspoken and rather scolding in her tenderness, Banford murmuring rather vaguely. They were evidently good friends" (p. 43). Until, at last, Henry, who has been trying to persuade March to marry him, leave Banford, and go to Canada with him, asks March forthrightly, "Do you wish you were with Miss Banford? Do you wish you'd gone to bed with her?" (p. 52).

The typical husband-wife relation Banford and March act out is played against the stresses of the psychic-masochistic substructure of the camouflage. At one point, Henry begs March to sit down with him for a minute to discuss his marriage proposal. "No," she says, "Jill will be waiting" (p. 29). He tries to convince her to discuss the situation. Bewildered as he is by her negative attitude, but all the more determined, he presses on, even after he eavesdrops on Banford saying to March, "No, I simply couldn't stand it. I should be dead within a month. Which is just what he would be aiming at, of course. That would be just his game, to see me in the churchyard. No, Nellie, if you were to do such a thing as to marry him, you could never stop here. I couldn't, I couldn't live in the same house with him. Oh-h! I feel quite sick with the smell of his clothes. And his red face simply turns me over. I can't eat my food when he's at the table. What a fool I was ever to let him stop. One ought *never* to try to do a kind action. It always flies back in your face like a boomerang" (p. 69).

The Fox contains a series of observations which Bergler (1958) describes. The defensive pseudoaggressive dialogues and feelings between Banford and March are typical of their behavior to one another. March seems to enjoy the conflict between Banford and her competitor, Henry, and even marries him although he has been indirectly responsible for Banford's accidental death. Banford is a ready partner to the give-and-take of verbal combat as well. March places her masochism in fantasies, remains helpless against the "mocking" fox although she has a shotgun in her hands, and is equally masochistic in her relationship with Henry after he has shot the fox. Lawrence describes March's constant "injustice collecting" as representative of her hidden masochism. Even Banford refers to it when she exclaims to March, "You always feel injured. Now you're feeling injured because I won't have that boy to come and live on the farm" (p. 43). March's unvarying inner defense is the search for love, which neither she nor Banford can find in the connubial bed since "injustice collecting" is the real aim of the masochistic, homosexual personality.

Female homosexuals who function on pain inflicted and pain received are a common phenomenon. "The cell-like structure of Lesbian society leaves intact the self-hatred which a woman usually brings with her into a gay subculture. As she has been contemptuous of the Lesbian in herself, she learns from the Lesbians to be contemptuous of the Lesbian in others" (Abbott and Love, 1972, p. 80). Kenny and Rose, in Davies' *Nobody Answered the Bell* (1971), show the petty irritations of two Lesbians living together, their obstinacy, little hurtful tyrannies, hostile teasings, skittishness, their bouts of malice — as well as the calm that could infect a loved person coming within the beneficence of one's presence. Kenny is a loving serviteur with occasional flareups of jealousy and sexual demands. When Rose makes innocent contact with a delivery boy in their isolated retreat, Kenny becomes punishing and demanding.

> Rose had made no movement, though again there was a trace of cowering. Her empty eyes did not look at Kenny as, the imperviousness lingering, she whispered, 'He gave it me.'
> 'Look!' Kenny, all threat gone, stood before her again. She pulled up her fisherman's jersey, tore open her slacks, and the garment fell down her thighs, exposing the bronze-red rose tattooed below her navel. 'That's you, my sweetheart, and that's mine for always! Kiss it!' Rose made no move. Kenny took a step forward, thrust her hard, work-tautened belly towards the beloved face. 'Kiss it, my love,' she entreated in a wail. 'Why do you torture me? I would die for you.' She pressed the flower against Rose's lips. There was a yielding in the long moment of union. A power was acknowledged. When Kenny drew away she sank to her knees, crying with a choked descent into sobs, an arm before her eyes, as though in shame of her display [p. 30].

Red, the college student narrator in Han Suyin's (1962) *Winter Love*, is seducing the willing, married Mara. They are in Red's boarding-house bedroom, with Red fingering a tweed blanket her father had given her. "I became a child, lapsing into near baby-talk. Mara was my mother, and I was drowsy, and telling her things I wanted to tell her. 'I loved my daddy. He was nice to me. Even when my stepmother told him the most horrid things about me — that I should be psycho-analyzed, that I was queer, that I collected bits of string and that showed I wasn't normal — even then he was nice to me. "Never mind," he would say, "you'll be all right. Daddy knows it. That's my girl," he used to say.' " (p. 184). Red and Mara subsequently become lovers; at one point, Mara has to go off with her husband, and Red is jealous and hurt. "At Mara's return I tried to hurt her as much as her absence hurt me. When people suffer they take it out on the object of their love, because the object of their love is in their possession. They cannot stop themselves . . . Mara had hurt me; she had been with Karl for three days. There was no security with her, only the constant fear of losing her, and the bright satin heart of love gets frayed perhaps sooner, shows wear more quickly, than the hempen robes of marriage" (p. 226).

'Well, stranger?" I said when she came in breathless on the fourth day, watching the joy wipe itself out, uncertainty creep into the smile on her face; but then she decided that it was affection, I was always a bit abrupt, and she took it as it truly was, a mark of having missed her. Of course it was, but she had no idea how much I would make her pay for having missed her.

She was hugging me when I gave her the second shot: "Had a good time with Karl?"

"Oh, Red." She buried her face in my sweater, moving her head against it like a cat rubbing itself, plaintive, placatory. "Don't let's talk about it, Red. You know it's horrible. I'm back now, that's all that matters."

But I wouldn't let her push the horror away, I wouldn't give her the tenderness and peace she wanted, though I could see how thin she was after three days with him, with black shadows under her eyes. Now I can scarcely bring myself to face my own cruelty, it is my punishment, to be borne: how I held her back from me, holding her shoulders, forcing her to look at me, saying: "What did he do to you *this* time? Tell me." Adding: "He's a man, isn't he, that precious husband of yours?"

And of course it was horrible because she accepted the cruelty, she wept. She thought she deserved it because I was hurt, she thought I was so hurt in my love for her that I had to hit her with the memories she ran away from. And thus, as Rhoda had done, Mara gave me an excuse for being cruel to her, and it eased my pain to hurt her, it was nearly joy; and after that it became impossible for me to change, to stop hurting her, on and off. [pp. 226-227].

Romain Rolland (1922), in his *Annette and Sylvie,* presents two half-sisters in a homosexual attachment. Annette is the daughter of a puritanic and intellectual woman; her illegitimate half-sister Sylvie is the child of her father and his charming mistress. The girls are orphaned in their early twenties, when Annette accidentally discovers the relationship and searches Sylvie out. Annette, far more protected than the sophisticated Sylvie, "confessed the jealous suffering she had felt at discovery of the second family that her father had hidden from her, and the turmoil into which she had been thrown by the existence of a rival, a sister. With her burning frankness, she dissimulated nothing that had made her blush; her passion reawakened as she evoked it. She said, 'I hated you! ...' in so fierce a tone that she stopped, checked by the sound of her own voice" (p. 76). It is possible, wrote Socarides (1963, p. 406), "that antagonism between sisters becomes overcompensated and a mild homosexual love interwoven with a great deal of identification may develop. Beneath the latter lies the original hatred. In addition, the turning away from heterosexuality is a regression, reviving memory traces of the earlier relationship to one's mother." The sisters become very quickly aware of their "imperious and imploring" love, learning much from each other. "For this time they had given themselves completely, eager to take all and give all" (Rolland, p. 154). "Their intimacy became so necessary to them that they wondered how they had ever done without it" (pp. 164-165).

The task force on homosexuality sponsored by the National Institute of Mental Health (Livingood, 1972) recommended *inter alia* that the effects of the portrayal of homosexual behavior, attitudes, and values in literature and drama, and the public's response to such portrayal are in need of study: "The taboo on homosexuality has a variety of functions linking it not only with values concerning heterosexual behavior, but also with other aspects of the social system" (p. 3). Despite the research, the scientific study, the attempts to determine specific causal factors, and even legislation by the state or federal governments, homosexual behavior will probably never be accepted as "normal" (Knox, 1965). Abbott and Love (1972) write that "once a woman is known as a Lesbian, both she and society often feel that no other fact about her can rival the sexual identification ... No matter what a Lesbian achieves, her sexuality will remain her primary identity. The role others expect her to play distorts or negates the value of all her behavior. They may see her through a kind of filter: the same words, the same actions as before now appear to have special meanings. There is something strange about her that they did not see before her sexual preference was revealed" (p. 27).

Four major theoretical questions concerning the etiology and determinants of homosexuality are indicated by Hooker (1968): "(1) Is the human organism psychosexually neutral at birth, or are there inherent sexual predispositions? (2) What is the nature and content of the learning process by which homosexual object choice develops? (3) Are the particular periods in the developmental process, such as early childhood or adolescence, critical for homosexual object choice? (4) Are parent-child relations in the nuclear family crucial in determining whether an individual becomes homosexual, or are peer relations in childhood and adolescence, and deviant subcultures in adolescence and early adult life, of equal or possibly greater importance?" Money (1970) states that whatever the degree of a person's homosexual commitment, the behavior concerned may be partially hereditary, constitutional, and biological in its determination, and partially environmental, learned, and sociological: "In the etiology of homosexuality, one may look for prenatal preordained factors either in the genetic code or in the metabolism of the intrauterine environment . . . Postnatally, one must look for critical period experiences or exposures that may leave a permanent imprint. One needs an open mind regarding the nature of such experiences. For all that is known at present, these factors may range from a specific nutritional insufficiency to deprivation of sensory stimulation, as in congenital hearing loss, to pathology of behavioral interaction within the family, or to incapacity to relate fully with children of similar age" (p. 425).

The tyranny of genital identity, the coercive corrosion of parental power, and the psychic straightjacket of role playing can create crippling inhibitions in girls and young women. Hooker (1968, p. 13) states that "Psychoanalytic theories assume that homosexuality is a symbolic expression of unconscious psychodynamic mechanisms and that in any given case these mechanisms and symbolizations are complex and numerous. The narcissistic search for a love object symbolizing the self, the avoidance and derogation of males, the unconscious incestuous desire, the longing for love, all involve complex patterns of variables that are difficult to state as clear hypotheses." These controversial issues cannot be resolved by the research or literary evidence currently available.

TECHNICAL REFERENCES

Aaron, W. (1972), *Straight*. Garden City, N.Y.: Doubleday.

Abbott, S. & Love, B. (1972), *Sappho Was a Right-on Woman: A Liberated View of Lesbianism*. New York: Stein & Day.

Adler, K. A. (1967), Life style, gender role, and the symptom of homosexuality. *Journal of Individual Psychology*, 23:67-68.

Allen, G. & Martin, C. G. (1971), *Intimacy, Sensitivity, Sex and the Art of Love.* Chicago: Cowles.

Armon, V. (1960), Some personality variables in overt female homosexuality. *Journal of Projective Techniques,* 24:292-309.

Beauvoir, S. de (1952), *The Second Sex.* New York: Knopf.

Bene, E. (1965), On the genesis of female homosexuality. *British Journal of Psychiatry,* 111:815-821.

Bergler, E. (1958), D. H. Lawrence's *The Fox* and the psychoanalytic theory of lesbianism. *Journal of Nervous and Mental Disease,* 126:488-491.

Bieber, I. et al. (1971), Homosexuality. A symposium on the causes and consequences — social and psychological — of sexual inversion. *Playboy,* 18:61, *passim.*

Bieber, T. (1967), A female therapist's view. *Psychiatric Opinion,* 4(2): 12-15.

Cargill, O. (1961), *The Novels of Henry James.* New York: Macmillan.

Chesser, E. (1971), *Strange Loves: The Human Aspects of Sexual Deviation.* New York: Morrow.

Denford, J. D. (1967), The psychodynamics of homosexuality. *New Zealand Medical Journal,* 66:743-744.

Deutsch, H. (1930), Homosexuality. In: *The Psychology of Women: A Psychoanalytic Interpretation,* Vol. 1. New York: Grune & Stratton, 1944, pp. 325-353.

Edel, L. (1962), *Henry James: The Middle Years, 1882-1895.* Philadelphia: Lippincott.

Ellis, H. (1928), Commentary. In: *The Well of Loneliness,* by Radcliffe Hall. New York: Permabook.

Fenichel, O. (1945), *The Psychoanalytic Theory of Neurosis.* New York: Norton.

Freud, S. (1905), Three essays on the theory of sexuality. *Standard Edition,* 7:125-243. London: Hogarth Press, 1953.

———— (1920), The psychogenesis of a case of homosexuality in a woman. *Standard Edition,* 18:146-172. London: Hogarth Press, 1955.

Guerard, A. J. (1964), *Thomas Hardy.* Norfolk, Conn.: New Directions.

Hartsock, M. E. (1968), Henry James and the cities of the plain. *Modern Language Quarterly,* 29:297-311.

Hooker, E. (1968), Homosexuality. In: *National Institute of Mental Health Task Force on Homosexuality: Final Report and Background Papers,* ed. J. M. Livingood. Rockville, Md.: National Institute of Mental Health, 1972, pp. 11-21.

Hopkins, J. (1969), The Lesbian personality. *British Journal of Psychiatry,* 115:1433-1436.

Hyde, H. M. (1970), *The Love That Dared Not Speak Its Name.* Boston: Little, Brown.

Jones, E. (1916), Introduction. R. Firbank's *Inclinations.* Norfolk, Conn.: New Directions, 1951.

Kaplan, E. A. (1967), Homosexuality: A search for the ego-ideal. *Archives of General Psychiatry,* 16:355-358.

Kaye, H. E. et al. (1967), Homosexuality in women. *Archives of General Psychiatry,* 17:626-639.

Kenyon, F. E. (1968), Physique and physical health of female homosexuals. *Journal of Neurology, Neurosurgery and Psychiatry,* 31:487-489.

Knox, S. C. (1965), Another look at homosexuality. *Journal of the American Medical Association,* 193:831.

Lapp, J. C. (1959), Watcher betrayed and the fatal woman: Some recurring patterns in Zola. *Publication of the Modern Language Association,* 74:276-284.

Livingood, J. M. (ed.) (1972). *National Institute of Mental Health Task Force on Homosexuality: Final Report and Background Papers*. Rockville, Md.: National Institute of Mental Health.

Martin, D. & Lyon, P. (1972), *Lesbian/Woman*. San Francisco: Glide.

Matthiessen, F. O. & Murdock, K. B. (eds.) (1961), *Notebooks of Henry James*. New York: Oxford University Press.

Money, J. (1970), Sexual dimorphism and homosexual gender identity. *Psychological Bulletin*, 74:425-440.

Pomeroy, W. B. (1965), Why we tolerate Lesbians. *Sexology*, 31:652-655.

Poole, K. (1972), The etiology of gender identity and the Lesbian. *Journal of Social Psychology*, 87:51-57.

Putt, S. G. (1966), *Henry James: A Reader's Guide*. Ithaca, N.Y.: Cornell University Press.

Rado, S. (1933), Fear of castration in women. *Psychoanalytic Quarterly*, 2:425-475.

Rahv, P. (1945), Introduction to Henry James' *The Bostonians*. New York: Dial.

Rancourt, R. & Limoges, T. (1967), Homosexuality among women. *Canadian Nurse*, 63:42-44.

Riess, B. F. & Gundlach, R. H. (1968), Self and sexual identity in the female: A study of female homosexuals. In: *New Directions in Mental Health*, ed. B. F. Riess. New York: Grune & Stratton, pp. 205-229.

Romm, M. E. (1965), Sexuality and homosexuality in women. In: *Sexual Inversion: The Multiple Roots of Homosexuality*, ed. J. Marmor. New York: Basic Books, pp. 282-301.

Sawyer, E. (1965), *A Study of a Public Lesbian Community*. Unpublished Master's thesis. St. Louis, Mo.: Washington University.

Socarides, C. W. (1962), Theoretical and clinical aspects of overt female homosexuality. *Journal of the American Psychoanalytic Association*, 10:579-592.

————— (1963), The historical development of theoretical and clinical concepts of overt female homosexuality. *Journal of the American Psychoanalytic Association*, 11:386-414.

Sprague, W. D. (1962), *The Lesbian in Our Society*. New York: Tower.

Whiteley, C. H. & Whiteley, W. M. (1965), *Sex and Morals*. New York: Basic Books.

Wilbur, C. B. (1965), Clinical aspects of female homosexuality. In: *Sexual Inversion: The Multiple Roots of Homosexuality*, ed. J. Marmor. New York: Basic Books, pp. 282-301.

Zucker, L. J. (1966), Mental health and homosexuality. *Journal of Sex Research*, 2:111-125.

LITERARY REFERENCES

Baldwin, James (1956), *Giovanni's Room*. New York: Dell, 1964.

Barnes, Djuna (1937), *Nightwood*. Norfolk, Conn.: New Directions, 1946.

Colette (1900), *Claudine at School*. London: Penguin.

Davies, Rhys (1971), *Nobody Answered the Bell*. New York: Dodd Mead.

Durrell, Lawrence (1958), *Balthazar*. New York: Dutton.

Epstein, Seymour (1967), *Caught in That Music*. New York: Viking.

Firbank, Ronald (1916), Inclinations. In: *Three Novels*. Norfolk, Conn.: New Directions, 1951.

Hall, Radclyffe (1928), *The Well of Loneliness*. New York: Permabook, 1959.

Hardy, Thomas (1871), *Desperate Remedies.* New York: St. Martin's, 1966.

James, Henry (1886), *The Bostonians.* New York: Dial, 1945.

Koestler, Arthur (1943), *Arrival and Departure.* New York: Macmillan

Lambert, Gavin (1966), *Norman's Letter.* New York: Coward-McCann.

Lawrence, D. H. (1923), The Fox. In: *Short Novels of the Masters,* ed. C. Neider. New York: Holt, Rinehart & Winston, 1948.

Louys, Pierre (1896), *Aphrodite.* New York: Lancer, 1962.

Pynchon, Thomas (1963), *V.* New York: Modern Library.

Renault, Mary (1945), *The Middle Mist.* New York: Morrow.

Rolland, Romain (1922), *Annette and Sylvie.* New York: Holt, 1925.

Suyin, Han (1962), *Winter Love.* New York: Putnam's.

Zola, Emile (1880), *Nana.* New York: Bantam, 1964.

CHAPTER SEVEN

Transvestism and Transsexuality

The concepts of transvestism and transsexuality and their specific forms of expression have been known since antiquity and have appeared in myths and classical literature from Heroditus to Shakespeare and on to the present (Pauley, 1965). "A woman shall not wear that which pertaineth unto a man," reads Deuteronomy 22:5, "neither shall a man put on a woman's garment; for whosoever doeth these things is an abomination unto the Lord thy God." Evidence for the phenomenon of transsexualism is available in records throughout the centuries, spanning widely different cultures (Green, 1966). Classical mythology, classical history, Renaissance and nineteenth-century history along with cultural anthropology point to the pervasiveness of transsexualism.

In Greek mythology, the transsexual influence is dramatized in the designation of the goddess, Venus Castina, as responding with sympathy and understanding to the yearnings of feminine souls locked in male bodies (Bulliet, 1928). Teiresias, the great blind seer from Thebes who revealed to Oedipus that he was Laius' son and that he had married Jocasta, his own mother, was granted the singular privilege of living both as a man and a woman, for his sex was changed by order of the gods. There are several stories about Teiresias' blindness: on Mount Cyllene in Arcadia, he watched two serpents mating. With his stick, he killed the female, immediately becoming a woman and

322

subsequently a notorious harlot. Seven years later he again saw two snakes coupling, killed the male this time, and regained his own sex. When Zeus and Hera were researching whether the pleasures of sex were felt more by man or by woman, Zeus maintaining that women derived more pleasure than men, with Hera arguing the opposite, they referred the question to Teiresias who could speak from experience, since he had been both a man and a woman and had married during his seven years as a woman. Teiresias said that if the pleasures of physical love are reckoned on a scale of one to ten, men enjoy one and women the whole ten. Hera, infuriated, blinded him, but Zeus granted him the gift of prophecy. Many ancients tell the story of Teiresias: Homer in *The Odyssey*, Sophocles in *Oedipus the King* and *Antigone*, Euripides in *The Bacchants* and *The Phoenician Women*, Ovid in *Metamorphoses*, as well as Aeschylus, Apollodorous, Didorus, Hyginus, Pausanias, Pindar, and Statius. In English literature there are Tennyson's and Swinburne's "Teiresias," and T. S. Eliot's *The Wasteland*. In other Greek myths, Zeus appeared to Europa as a bull, to Leda as a swan, and to Persephone as a serpent. And as a serpent, Apollo made love to Atys.

In ancient Syria, according to Lucian (Randell, 1969), the novice priests of the Gallae traditionally castrated themselves during the rites of the Goddess Astarte when they dedicated themselves to her in states of extreme excitement. "Following the autocastration, they ran in the streets of the town carrying the severed genitals, which they threw into the doorway of any house that took their fancy. In return for this doubtful gift, the novices obtained from the householder female clothing which they wore as full-fledged priests. Lucian inferred that they lived contentedly thereafter in socially accepted female roles although their basic male sexuality was known to all" (p. 355).

Devereux (1957) in his article, "The Awarding of a Penis As Compensation for Rape," tells of a legendary horse-taming tribe in Greek mythology, the Lapiths, one of whose chiefs was "Kaineus, who—like Teiresisas—had once also been a woman, at which time he bore the name of Kainis, which is the feminine form of Kaineus. Kainis was raped by Poseidon, who then offered to make restitution by granting any request which she cared to make. Kainis chose to ask that she be changed into a man and made invulnerable, so that no one might be able to rape her. Her wish was granted and she became the man

Kaineus" (p. 398). The uncouscious fantasies of bisexuality, androgyny, and transsexualism are revealed in these myths and yield thera-
peutically relevant insights.

The concept of the nadle or transvestite in Navaho society is well
formulated and his cultural role well substantiated in the mythology.
"In the tales dealing with the creation and emergence of the Navaho
the pursuits and activities of the nadle are outlined. They are
described as wealthy and as having control of all wealth. In that part
of the Emergence Myth which tells of the quarrel between men and
women, they play a very prominent part. Because of the ability of the
nadle to perform the functions and duties of women as well as men,
they make it possible for the men to overcome the women. The outlook
of Navaho society toward the nadle is very favorable . . . The family
which counted a transvestite among its members . . . was considered
. . . as very fortunate. The success and wealth of such a family was
believed to be assured. Special care was taken in the raising of such
children and they were afforded favoritism not shown to other children
of the family. As they grew older and assumed the character of nadle,
this solicitude and respect increased, not only on the part of their
families but from the communtiy as a whole" (Hill, 1935, pp. 234-235).
But by 1935, the acculturated Navaho was ridiculing the transvestite.

Another mythical account concerns the Scythians (Green, 1966),
"whose rear guard pillaged the temple of Venus at Ascelon while
leaving Syria and Palestine, which they had invaded. The goddess was
supposed to have been so enraged that she made women of the
plunderers, and further decreed that their posterity should be similarly
affected. Hippocrates, describing the Scythian 'No-men' who resembled eunuchs, wrote: 'They not only follow women's occupations, but
show feminine inclinations and behave as women. The natives ascribe
the cause to a deity . . .' Still another account deals with the ancient
kingdom, Phrygia, where the priest of the God, Attis, is said to have
emasculated himself under a pine tree. The priests were said, following
castration, to become transvestites and perform women's tasks . . . The
Teiresias myth parallels a related folk tale in East Indian lore. According to legend in the Mahabharata, a king was transformed into a woman by bathing in a magic river. As a woman he bore a hundred sons
whom he sent to share his kingdom with the hundred sons he had had
as a man. Later, he refused to be changed back into a man because the
former king felt that 'a woman takes more pleasure in the act of love

than does a man.' Contrary to the fate of Teiresias, the transformed King was granted his wish . . . Not only were the gods empowered with the ability to change one's sex but change of sex was performed on both human and beast by witchcraft and by the intervention of demons. Witches were claimed to be the possessors of drugs that had the capacity to reverse the sex of the taker. Some said that males could be transformed into females and females into males, but it was also argued that the sex change worked in only one direction. Thus it was declared that the Devil could make males of females, but could not transform men into women because it is the method of nature to add on rather than to take away . . ." (pp. 174-175).

Contemporary transvestite and transsexual myths include David Garnett's (1922) *Lady into Fox* and Lawrence Durrell's (1968) *Tunc*. In the former, the sudden changing of Mrs. Tebrick "into a vixen is an established fact . . . The metamorphosis occurred when Mrs. Tebrick was a full-grown woman . . . The sprouting of a tail, the gradual extension of hair all over the body, the slow change of the whole anatomy by a process of growth, though it would have been monstrous, would not have been so difficult to reconcile to our ordinary conceptions, particularly had it happened in a young child. But here we have something different. A grown lady is changed straightaway into a fox . . ." (pp. 1-2). The transformation from delicate female to hirsute, phallic male is symbolically posed by Garnett, as it is in Durrell's *Tunc*. *Tunc* "has a dream-like quality, the passage of time is not quite real in it, things seem to happen magically by fearing or wishing or breaking a taboo or not breaking a spell, but the dream is, in a Freudian sense, doing dream-work. In dreams we try to escape from reality but are brought back to it. Durrell draws the reader's attention to the magical, wish-fulfilling and fear-fulfilling, element in the story . . . But as in a disturbing dream which draws attention to memories or hopes and fears one thought one had buried . . . at the end of this story" (Fraser, 1968, p. 169) it all adds up. Caradoc, an architect, is a strange, bardic, Teiresias figure who has become fat and feminine, a baggy, breasted figure. At the novel's end, he is living with a native wife on a Robinson Crusoe island, suckling two children from his ancient breasts:

Either it was Caradoc or it wasn't Caradoc, and it was only a glimpse . . . [p. 315]. As I got nearer to the big hut I saw that there was an old man sitting on the steps, an old man with a mane of white hair. He started when he saw me and gave an inarticulate cry, as if of rage . . . He was simply covered in hair, beard to his waist, high-forehead-ed sweep of mane backward, loincloth, and rough-thonged slippers made of some bark or other. His eyes were small and bloodshot, and at this moment regarded me as a cornered and wounded wild boar might. Everything seemed to come together in a confused sort of focus — you know how it is in moments of excitement? And some of the things I saw in that few seconds I didn't take in until afterward, when I was on the run. For example, that he had two small children at his breasts, *he was giving them suck*, old man. I could even see some of the milk trickling down among the hairs on his breast, white as cocoanut milk . . . [Durrell, p. 317].

One constant rule of mythology, wrote Robert Graves, is that whatever happens among the gods above reflects events on earth. The psychiatric literature deals with transvestism on four levels: female identification, fetishism, secondary narcissism, and exhibitionism. Hora (1953) saw male transvestism as a complex, overdetermined symptom, consisting of a combination of fetishism and female identification. Where masturbation is blocked, the transvestite's sexual fantasies express themselves in characterological deviations or acting out which correspond with the individual's concept of femininity, derived from his incestuous identification with his mother and consequent self-punitive, masochistic trends. The phenomenon of transvestism occurs with people who have a conscious interest in cross-dressing in public or private, involving either outer garments or only undergarments or both. The transvestite habitually prefers to wear the clothes of the opposite sex. "A male dressed as a woman cohabits not with the woman but with her clothes, and the transvestite himself represents a phallic woman under whose clothes a penis is hidden. A female transvestite unconsciously makes believe she has a penis and possesses the masculinity of her father. These perversions allow sexual energy to be discharged in private acts of psychological significance" (Goldfarb, 1970, p. 208). The transvestite may vary from the one who behaves as if he were a male and a female who live together to the one who purportedly just enjoys dressing as a fetishistic expression. "It is clinically impressive that transvestites are very concerned with their appearance as women and in many cases may masturbate as they see themselves in a mirror" (Guze, 1969, p. 174). Although transvestism may serve as a means of mechanizing, impersonalizing, and distancing sexual relations, it does not preclude the desire for heterosexual relations. Transvestism does not necessarily indicate the presence of either latent or dormant homosexuality (Rubins, 1967).

According to Benjamin (1966, p. 13), the majority of transvestites are overtly heterosexual but many may be latent bisexuals. "They 'feel' as men and know that they are men, marry, and often raise families. A few of them, however, especially when they are 'dressed,' can as part of their female role react homosexually to the attentions of an unsuspecting normal male. The transvestite's marriage is frequently endangered as only relatively few wives can tolerate seeing their husbands in female attire." Diane, the wife of Count "Tzigie" in Gwen Davis's (1969) *The Pretenders,* is one of the few.

> When she got home, the lights were out in the foyer. The servants had all gone to bed, thinking she was in the bedroom with Tzigie. That probably meant that Tzigie was sleeping. She slipped out of her Valentino shoes, made her way quietly across the apartment floors, and gently opened the door to the master suite.
>
> He was standing in front of the full-length mirror by the marble-topped console. He had on one of her black chiffon scarves and a necklace of imitation rose quartz from Kenneth Lane, with matching earrings. His dress was the black and white vinyl she had discarded before the party.
>
> "Oh," he said, and brought up his hands, as if to shield himself from his own reflection.
>
> She closed the door and locked it, behind her back, watching him the entire time. He did not move.
>
> "I'm sorry," he said. "I'm really sorry."
>
> "It's all right," she swallowed. "If it makes you happy."
>
> "I didn't think you'd be home so early."
>
> "It isn't as if you're hurting anyone, is it."
>
> "I didn't want you to know."
>
> "Why not?" Diane said. "People do all kinds of things. As long as you don't hurt anybody. You make a very good-looking woman."
>
> "You're laughing at me?"
>
> "Not at all."
>
> She looked at him in the reflection, and then she looked at him directly. "As a matter of fact, I never realized until this very moment how much like me you really looked."
>
> "I take that as a great compliment," he said.

"So you should," she said, and went to him.

That evening they made love with a ferocity they had never had before, she wanting him more than she had ever done, and he hungering to please her. Shortly after that he shaved off his moustache. From then on, she never went shopping, even for a brassiere, without his coming along. And whenever she wanted him, she had only to set out something of hers on the bed, or the chaise, so he would know, and make himself ready for her [pp. 308-309].

Transvestism is adroitly assimilated in Zola's *Nana* (1880), when the actress admits young Georges Hugon to her bedroom soaking wet with rain, dresses him up in one of her nightgowns, and finds him irresistible because he is feminine (Lapp, 1959). Georges himself is delighted with the garment and "would always wear one if he could" (Zola, p. 200).

The room was lighted by a lamp and the fire began blazing brightly.

"He'll never get dry—he's going to catch a cold," said Nana, seeing Georges shiver.

And not one dry pair of trousers in the house! She was about to call the gardener back when she had an idea. Zoé, who had been unpacking the trunks in the dressing room, brought Madame some clean clothes: a chemise, some petticoats, and a negligee.

"Why, that's perfect!" cried Nana. "Zizi can wear those! You don't mind wearing my clothes, do you? As soon as yours are dry, you'll put them on and go home right away, so your mother won't scold you. . . . Hurry; I'm going to change my clothes in the dressing room."

When she reappeared in a negligee ten minutes later, she clasped her hands in delight.

"Oh, the darling! He looks so nice dressed as a woman!"

He had put on a long nightgown, a pair of embroidered drawers and a batiste negligee trimmed with lace. In these clothes he looked like a girl, with his bare young arms and his tawny hair, still wet, hanging down his neck.

"He's as thin as I am!" said Nana, putting her arm around his waist. "Zoé, come and see how well my clothes fit him. . . . They look as though they were made for him, except that they're too loose in the chest. . . . Poor Zizi, he doesn't have as much there as I do."

"Yes, I'm a little lacking in that department," said Georges, smiling.

All three of them were gay. Nana began buttoning the negligee from top to bottom, to make him decent. She turned him around like a doll, patted him, made his skirt billow in back. And she questioned him, asking him if he was comfortable, if he was warm. Oh yes, he was quite comfortable! Nothing was warmer than a woman's nightgown; he would always wear one if he could. He moved around in it, delighted by the fine linen, by that sweet-smelling garment in which he seemed to find a little of Nana's warm life [pp. 199-200].

Rachilde (1884) picked a similar theme in the novel, *Monsieur Vénus*, as plotted by Foster (1956). Raoule, a wealthy orphaned girl of twenty-five, encounters an effeminate man of the working class a year her junior to whom she is hopelessly attracted. Her pride is stung by her weakness, and to avoid accepting Jacques as an equal she virtually buys him and subsequently maintains him in luxury. By degrees she forces him to wear feminine clothes and play a woman's part, to which he proves readily adaptable. She herself adopts the masculine costume and role. But so completely does Jacques assume the female role, that he makes advances to a handsome military officer. Jacques is described as a dazzling Titian blond, well-fleshed in breast and hips, with only his hands, voice, and coarse hair betraying his sex. Raoule herself is taller than he, with a boyish figure. She is never suspected of being female when she ventures out in men's clothes.

Two Japanese novelists, Yukio Mishima and Junichiro Tanizaki, also write about transvestism. Kochan, the narrator in Mishima's *Confessions of a Mask* (1958), is "snatched away" by his overly possessive grandmother and raised in strange isolation from his immediate family, although living in the same house, in an atmosphere "perpetually closed and stifling with the odors of sickness and old age" (p. 10). Kochan has a brief period of dressing up as a woman, first as Tenkatsu, the female magician, and then as Cleopatra. He grows up in isolation, an autistic child, with love only for the boy, Omi. To understand his attraction to transvestism, it is necessary to examine his view of "tragic things." As a child, he is attracted to the occupations of nightsoil man, streetcar operator, and subway ticketpuncher (see Chapter Three). "Aside from their possible Freudian significance, the narrator clearly senses in these roles the isolation of the people who perform them and his own isolation from them: 'Existences and events occurring without any relationship to myself, occurring at places . . . denied to me — these together with the people involved in them, consti-

tuted my definition of 'tragic things.' It seemed that my grief at being
eternally excluded was always transformed in my dreaming into grief
for those persons and their ways of life, and that solely through my own
grief I was trying to share in their existences.' What is tragic, then,
would appear to be those lives which exclude the narrator. But the
definition is not wholly narcissistic. The yearning toward these solitary
figures is an attempt 'to share their existences,' thus negating or
mitigating their exclusion from his own. When the narrator, as a boy,
dresses in his mother's clothes, he is apparently experimenting with
himself as an object of love. The failure of his adult audience to
understand the meaning of his mimicry, and moreover, their overt
disapproval of it further instructs him of his own conviction about
isolation, and in his 'own incapacity for accepting love' " (Dana, 1970,
p. 94). In an introduction to *Young Samurai* (1967, p. 9), Mishima
writes, "In our hearts, so long nurtured on the Way of Samurai, there
has arisen a strange paradox: without etiquette we have no morality."
That is a compelling thought, Korges (1970, p. 130) notes: "It reminds
one that the Samurai class was largely homosexual, that the Samurai
used make-up (as did American Indians, though we call the Indian
make-up by a tough masculine phrase — 'war paint' — apparently to
make it sound less like cosmetics the Braves applied), and the Samurai
were quite conscious of their appearance, as were the Greek warriors
who puzzled the Persian invaders by combing their hair just before
battle, preparing their bodies for the test before them."

In Tanizaki's *Diary of a Mad Old Man* (1965), the dominant theme is
the relation of sexual desire to the will to live. Tanizaki tells the story of
a seventy-seven-year-old man of exquisite tastes who suffers a stroke,
the while discovering that even though his body is breaking down, his
sexual urges are far from diminished. The first entry in his diary
reveals his attraction to transvestites during youthful times reappear-
ing in old age.

> This evening I went to the Kabuki. All I wanted to see was *Suker-
> oku*, I had no intention of staying for the rest of the program. Kanya
> as the hero didn't interest me, but Tossho was playing Agemaki and
> I knew he would make a beautiful courtesan. I went with my wife
> and Satsuko; Jokichi came from his office to join us. Only my wife and
> I knew the play, Satsuko never saw it before. My wife thinks she may
> even have seen it with Danjuro in the lead, she isn't sure. But I have a
> vivid memory of seeing him in it. I believe that was around 1897,

when I was thirteen or fourteen. It was Danjuro's last Sukeroku; he died in 1903. We were living in the Honjo district of Tokyo in those days: I still remember passing a famous print shop—what was the name of it?—with a triptych of Sukeroku in the window.

I suppose this was Kanya's first attempt at the role, and sure enough his performance didn't appeal to me. Lately all the actors cover their legs with tights. Sometimes the tights are wrinkled, which spoils the effect completely. They ought to powder their legs and leave them bare.

Tossho's Agemaki pleased me very much. I decided it was worth coming for that alone. Others may have acted the part better, but it is a long time since I have seen such a beautiful Agemaki. Although I have no homosexual inclinations, recently I've come to feel a strange attraction toward the young Kabuki actors who play women's roles. But not off stage. They don't interest me unless they're made up and in feminine costume. Still, if I stop to think of it, perhaps I must admit to a certain inclination.

When I was young I had an experience of that kind, though only once. There used to be a handsome young actor of female roles called Wakayama Chidori. He made his debut at the Masago Theater in Nakasu, and after he got a little older he played opposite Arashi Yoshizaburo. I say "older," but he was around thirty and still very beautiful: you felt as if you were looking at a woman in the prime of life, you wouldn't have believed it was a man. As the daughter in Koyo's *A Summer Gown,* I found her—or rather him—utterly captivating. Once I remarked jokingly to a teahouse mistress that I'd like to ask him out some evening, dressed just as he was for the stage, and maybe even see what he was like in bed. "I can arrange it for you," she told me—and she did! Everything went perfectly. Sleeping with him was exactly like sleeping with a geisha in the usual way. In short, he was a woman to the very last, he never let his partner think of him as a man. He came to bed in a gaudy silk undergarment, and still wearing his elaborate wig lay there in the darkened room with his head on a high wooden pillow. It was a really strange experience, he had an extraordinarily skillful technique. Yet the fact is that he was no hermaphrodite, but a splendidly equipped male. Only, his technique made you forget it.

But as skillful as he was, I have never had a taste for that sort of thing, and so my curiosity was satisfied after a single experience. I have never repeated it. Yet why, now that I am seventy-seven and no longer even capable of such relations, have I begun to feel attracted, not to pretty girls in trousers, but to handsome young men in feminine attire? Has my old memory of Wakayama Chidori simply been revived? I hardly think so. No, it seems to have some connection with the sex life of an impotent old man—even if you're impotent you have a kind of sex life . . . [pp. 3-5].

While a transvestite prefers to wear the clothes of the opposite sex, he is not transsexual except for occasional fantasies of sexual transformation. All transsexuals, however, are overt transvestites (Stoller, 1965). The transsexual syndrome is characterized by the seemingly complete identification of a person with the thoughts, feelings, and especially the sense of gender identity of a member of the opposite sex; these people do not deny the reality of their anatomic sex but feel their psychosexual identity differs from their anatomic gender through an unexplainable, unfortunate "trick of nature" (Wolf et al., 1968). Transsexuals not only want to dress like the opposite sex, they abhor the signs of their anatomic sex, especially their genitals, and they want to have their bodies altered to resemble that of the other sex; they are convinced that nature has made a mistake in their case, that they really belong to the other sex, that their bodies have developed along the wrong lines (Walinder, 1967). Thus, transsexualism is, Socarides (1970) summarized, a psychiatric syndrome characterized by an intense wish to be of the opposite sex through surgery or endocrine therapy, a belief one is basically of the opposite sex, and an imitation of behavior associated with the opposite sex. The preference for the feminine role is predicated on the conviction of belonging to the opposite sex. "This conviction is held and persists despite the painfully obvious fact of normal male anatomy and genitalia, before and after puberty, and in the absence of delusional ideation or psychosis in the majority of transsexuals studied. He is disgusted with the development of his primary and secondary sexual characteristics, to the point where the male transsexual frequently contemplates and occasionally performs self-mutilation of his genitalia. He prefers normal, heterosexual men as sexual partners, and rejects homosexual men or the idea that his sexual activity is homosexual. Feeling he belongs to the female gender, he considers it appropriate to have a love relationship with a man, and feels 'unnatural' in a relationship with a woman, considering this 'homosexual.' There is some evidence that sex or overt sexual activity, whether it be considered homosexual or heterosexual, plays a minor or secondary role. The transsexual may decide to pass and become accepted as a female, either before or after sex reassignment surgery, depending upon individual circumstances" (Pauly, 1968, p. 460).

The transsexual's obsessive feeling that he belongs to the opposite sex and his attitude toward his sex organs, which is one of disgust and revulsion, are among the chief diagnostic differentials between transsexualism and transvestism. According to Benjamin (1966), the transvestite "usually wants to be left alone. He requests nothing from the medical profession, unless he wants a psychiatrist to try to cure him. The transsexual, however, puts all his faith and future into the hands of the doctor, particularly the surgeon . . . Both can be considered symptoms . . . of the same underlying psychopathological condition, that of a sex or gender role disorientation and indecision. Transvestism is the minor though the more frequent, transsexualism the much more serious although rarer disorder" (p. 14).

Thus, transsexuals, persons who feel themselves psychologically of a different sex from their morphological gender, are differentiated from transvestites and homosexuals. The male transsexual, according to Money and Brennan (1970), wants a boy friend and a husband who is genuinely masculine in his erotic preference and behavior. "The transsexual male, despite karytotypic, hormonal and anatomical masculinity is not erotically responsive to the image of the normal female. He is, instead, responsive either to the image of the normal male or the image of himself as a female, or both. He lives in the hope of being able to evoke from a normal male the same response as a normal female would evoke. He wants a man to fall in love with him as a female. He wants to be accepted as a normal female" (p. 204). The differentiation among transvestite, transsexual, and homosexual may be described in these terms: "The transvestite feels himself to be a male and intermittently likes to have the feeling of being a woman coursing through him; the true transsexual feels himself to be both a female and a woman; and the homosexual, regardless of the degree of his effeminacy, considers himself to be a male and a man, though he clearly identifies himself as being a man of a particular class—homosexual" (Stoller, 1968, p. 159). The psychiatrist's diagnosis of transsexualism as homosexuality and the conclusion that the patient should accept himself as such are frequently iatrogenic.

In Geoff Brown's (1966) *I Want What I Want*, Roy has been living as a woman for several months, when in desperation he seeks help from a "sexologist," Mr. Waites.

The room was furnished like the austere living-room of a gentle-man of traditional taste. On the parquet floor was a large carpet with a Persian design. There were two leather arm chairs as well as high-backed Jacobean chairs. There was no desk. In the centre of the room was a long mahogany table. But against one wall there was a medical couch and there was a sink and, in a corner, a hospital screen with wheels. The fireplace was empty but the room was warm.

The young woman went past me and placed the case she was carrying on the table. She took a notebook from the pocket of her leather coat. She took her coat off and put it over the back of a chair. Then she hurried to set a chair for me.

I sat near the table. The young woman was somewhere behind me out of sight. Boyishly, Mr. Waites sat on the table with his legs swinging. He was an extremely vain man.

'I recieved a letter from Dr. Murdoch in Beverley about you, Miss Ross. He said you wouldn't discuss your problem with him. Do you think you can discuss it with me?'

'It's very difficult,' I said.

'Then take your time, and try to remember that, whether you tell me the truth or not, you'll still be getting a bill.'

'It's very simple,' I said. 'I'm a boy.'

He did not give any sign that he was surprised.

'In what way are you a boy?'

I did not know what to answer. I was dumb for a moment before I said, 'I am really a boy. I dress up like this because I like wearing women's clothes.'

'Are you sure you're a boy?'

'I think I am.'

'You're not altogether sure?'

'In some ways I'm not sure. When I'm dressed up I feel like a woman.'

'Why did you come here today dressed like that?'

'I've been dressed up all the time since the autumn of last year. I've been living as a woman.'

'I see. Well, then, we'd better make sure what you are. Do you mind getting undressed?'

'No.' I stood up. I felt that I might fall down.

'Do you want Nurse Spencer to go out of the room or would you prefer her to stay?'

'I think I'd prefer her to go out.'

He spoke to the young woman. 'If you could leave us.'

I went behind the screen. There was a chair. I started taking my clothes off. I put them on the chair. I felt ill. My arms were heavy and my hands were weak. I was slow.

When I had taken my clothes off I found that I did not want to take the bandages off. My body looked wretched enough without my poor, unwanted thing being visible.

I came out from behind the screen with my arms across my chest. I was a skinny boy. I thought that I must look ridiculous with my long hair and my painted face. I felt grotesque. It was a woman's head on the top of a boy's body. I was humiliated. I was so foolish and miserable.

Mr. Waites had got down off the table. He looked at me without surprise or contempt. I thought that he must have seen people like me before.

He asked me to take the bandages off. I did as I was told. I was a helpless monstrosity. He was methodical and careful. I wished that I could faint. The worst was when he was finding out whether I had two testicles. He examined my chest. He made me put my head back while he examined my neck. He examined my arms and hands. I wished that I was not wearing nail varnish. He stood away from me and looked me up and down. He made me turn about. He made me stand with my legs together. He asked me to walk. I walked backwards and forwards on the carpet while he watched me.

'Do you shave?'

'Yes. Just at the sides of my chin.'

'Right,' he said, 'you can get dressed.'

I went behind the screen and put the bandages back and dressed myself as quickly as I could. When I came out the young woman was back in the room. She looked at me as a patient of no extraordinary interest.

Mr. Waites was back on the table. He said to me, 'I have no doubt that you are a male. Do you understand that?'

'Yes.'

'You have an unusual number of anatomical feminine characteristics. However, I'm a sexologist, not an anatomist. I can tell you that I have no doubt at all that you are a male. Even in the best developed men there are often some feminine characteristics. I can tell you that you are not in a position to choose your sex. Do you understand?'

'Yes.'

'What do you do for a living?'

'I used to work for my father. I haven't had any work since I've been living as a woman. I've been living on some money my mother left me.'

'How much was that?'

'Five hundred pounds.'

'Then you're not very well placed?'

'No.'

'You'll have to stop pretending to be a woman or you could find yourself in serious trouble of one kind or another. Have you ever thought of going on the stage?'

'No.'

'I'd advise something like that. If you want to dress up as a woman, you might as well cash in on it. I can't pretend you haven't a very striking appearance. You might do very well on the stage. I believe there are entertainments called drag shows. It's probably not the most wholesome art form — but someone has remarked that it takes all sorts to make a world. Are you homosexual?'

'I think so.'

'Then I think your best bet is to try to get yourself into the entertainment business. I imagine you came to see me because you have ideas about wanting to change sex. Is that right?'

'Yes.'

'Forget it. There is no such thing as a change of sex. You are a male and you will always be a male. There is nothing that anybody can do about it. Do you understand that?'

'Yes.'

'If you were a female who had some abnormality, it might be possible for you to be given medical help. But you're a male. You'll just have to make the best of a bad job — which is what we all have to do' [pp. 208-210].

A questionnaire concerning the attitudes of physicians toward somatic treatment of transsexuals was administered by Green (1967) to 600 psychiatrists, 250 general practitioners, and 500 urologists and gynecologists, with a one-third over-all response. The respondents' attitudes were negative: among 168 psychiatrists, somatic treatment would be refused because eighty-six per cent would not wish to explain their actions to the local medical society, sixty-four per cent were concerned with legal implications, eighty-three per cent with morbidity rates, and ninety-four per cent objected on moral and religious grounds. Requests for treatment by transsexuals apparently threaten physicians in the security of their own sexual identifications.

Nor is the gay life a solution for the transsexual. "He does not like it. He actually dislikes homosexuals and feels he has nothing in common with them" (Benjamin, 1966, p. 42). After his visit to the sexologist, Roy said to himself bitterly, "I had told Mr. Waites that I was a homosexual. But if I were not in a male body, I would not be a homosexual. It was not my fault. Yes, it was my fault. I was what I was, and fault was in me. I was rotten. I had a cancer of masculinity" (Brown, p. 211). Earlier in the novel, Roy said, "I hated men's lavatories. They always seemed dank and, however clean they might be, one always imagined the strong amber tang of the male. I hated homosexuals most when I thought of them doing things in such places" (p. 51). When Shirley, Roy's sister, visited him after he had written to tell her about his transsexual feelings, "she put it to me delicately that I ought not to make myself look too nice or I might attract men. I said that I liked to look nice for its own sake and that I was not at all interested in men" (p. 174).

Many transsexuals have no overt sex life at all, with low libidinal energy. "The sex drive in some of them is turned inward toward their own ego. Masturbation is then occasionally practiced, but the urge for it is low and under estrogen treatment gets even lower, to the point of zero" (Benjamin, 1966, p. 49). A curious note is brought out by Guze (1969, p. 173): the transsexual patient in some ways seems to put masculinity on a pedestal and responds as if he were truly unworthy of that role; since he does not fit the cultural concept of the male, a concept he fears but loves and admires, he must be female. Thus, the homosexual step is denied. Roy, who has been masquerading as Wendy in *I Want What I Want,* has developed a relationship with Frank, a normal male about whom he fantasies.

> Frank was a good soldier. There were stories of girls who dressed up as boys to go to war with their sweethearts. I would dress up as a boy to go with Frank. I would march along by his side all day and at night I would sleep on the ground with him . . . I might save his life in battle, and he might say, "Because you have saved my life, I must forgive you everything." But he would not be able to forgive my being a boy. I would have to put my gun in my mouth and kill myself. I would be better dead — like my mother. Why can't I have my mother's body instead of its being dead and rotten in the ground? Mother, I am a woman, like you. Your suffering is over, but mine goes on and on. Frank was a good soldier. He was strong

and healthy. He had nothing to do with drag. He had nothing to do with peanuts. I was a peanut. Or was a peanut a transvestite who was not a homosexual? [p. 211].

None of the ninety-one transsexuals in Walinder's (1967) population regarded having sexual relations with members of their own sex as homosexual. "In fact, they were shocked at the idea that others thought they were homosexual. To them, sexual relations with a member of their own anatomic sex were heterosexual, not homosexual. In keeping with this, the male transsexuals sought the company of virile heterosexual men, and refused to have anything to do with homosexual men" (p. 76).

As might be expected, there are divergent opinions expressed in the literature on the etiology of transsexualism, with multifactorial theories predominating. These include a combination of constitutional, psychological, and hormonal causes (Aubert, 1947; Benjamin, 1954, 1964, 1966; Burchard, 1961; Delay et al., 1954; Roth and Ball, 1964), which are controversial, puzzling, and obscure. No genetic cause has yet been proved for any transsexual manifestation (Benjamin, 1966). Nor has any endocrine dysfunction been demonstrated associated with transsexualism (Kupperman, 1967). Since androgens enhance libido in both normal males and females, sex orientation is not dependent on endocrine or chromatin patterns, but on the psychological direction of the patient himself. Christodorescu (1971) proposed that the transsexual exhibits a psychosexual inversion characterized by the assumption of roles, attitudes, feelings, and the wearing of apparel of the opposite sex while simultaneously having an accurate perception of body image. "He considers himself a victim of nature that has made a mistake, endowing him with somatic, sexual attributes in contradiction to his feelings and affinities. The inversion is purely psychological, since there is no sign of intersexuality, either genetic, morphologic, gonadal, or hormonal" (p. 42). Green and Money (1961) indicated the possibility of an inherited predisposition for imprinting and, naturally, for its consequences. They found among their patients an "infrequency of forceful parental domination in the household" and also "relatively fragile body build."

Case histories of adult transsexuals reveal that their cross-gender identification and behavior date back to childhood. "There is considerable evidence from several sources, in particular research on anatomically intersexed children, that gender identification is established early in life. As some cross-gender behavior may be seen in many children, the recognition of a significant disorder of gender identity is a complex diagnostic task" (Green, 1968, p. 502). Green presents case-history data for nine boys, each eight years of age or younger when first diagnosed as manifesting anomalous gender-role development. In six cases, parents were able to identify clearly cross-gender behavior at age three or younger. When initially evaluated, these boys were behaving in the way adult male transsexuals retrospectively describe their behavior at a comparable age. One of the outstanding characteristics of the twenty-five transsexuals examined by Pomeroy (1967) was their isolation from other children when they were young, frequently leading to feelings of rejection, isolation, and unhappiness. While there is no common pattern that permits generalizations to be made about the intrafamily dynamics, in at least nineteen cases explored by Pauly (1965) the father was feared, often alcoholic, inconsistent, even brutal, and consequently distant, rejecting, providing a negative model for masculine identification. The mother of the male transsexual is perceived by her son as the ideal person, and an excessively close relationship develops (Pauly, 1968). Stoller (1967) gives dramatic examples from his clinical work with transsexuals of how much the mother's mood, unconscious fantasies, and expectancies can interfere with the gender identity of the child. A common factor in three cases of little boy transsexuals who, from the second year of life, showed unmistakable gross and persistent signs of feminine identification, was a mother who maintained physical contact with the child so intense as to inhibit development of concepts of separate body boundaries between mother and child. All the mothers showed a boyish femininity, were tomboys until puberty, and remained very unenthusiastic in the female sexual role. In maintaining prolonged contact with their sons quite outside the normal range in western culture, the mothers had wanted to compensate for feelings of distance they had felt from their own mothers.

"I never knew my father and I think my mother never knew him either," says Samuel Mountjoy, the narrator in William Golding's (1959) *Free Fall*, who spent considerable youthful effort asking his mother, "What was my dad, Ma?" (pp. 12-14), and never getting a satisfactory answer. His mother "was as near a whore as makes no matter" (p. 33). She was variously a charwoman, hop picker, drunk, and moviegoer.

> She did not have sexual connection for that implies an aseptic intercourse, a loveless, joyless refinement of pleasure with the prospect of conception inhibited by the rubber cup from the bathroom. She did not make love, for I take that to be a passionate attempt to confirm that the wall which parted them is down. She did none of these things . . . No. She was a creature. She shared pleasure round like a wet-nurse's teat, absorbed, gustily laughing and sighing. Her casual intercourse must have been to her what his works are to a real artist—themselves and nothing more. They had no implication. They were meetings in back streets or fields, on boxes, or gateposts and buttresses. They were like most human sex in history, a natural thing without benefit of psychology, romance or religion. Ma was enormous. She must have been a buxom girl in the bud but appetite and a baby blew her up into an elephantine woman. . . [pp. 14-15].

Samuel tumbled and crawled in the world of Rotten Row, underfed and scantily clothed, taken to school by little Evie, a liar and fantasist, whose stories took wings.

> My innocent credulity was a condition of the sights so that I learned nothing. She was, she confided to me, she was sometimes a boy. She told me that, but first she swore me to a secrecy which I violate now for the first time. The change, she said, was sudden, painful, and complete. She never knew when, but then pop! out it came and she couldn't do anything else. She had to pee the way I did. What was more, when she changed she could pee higher up the wall than any of the boys in our Row, see? I saw and was appalled. To think of Evie, putting off the majesty and beauty of her skirt and pulling on common trousers—to see her cut short the lank hair, abandon hairribbons! Passionately I implored her not to be a boy. But what could she do, she said? Hesitatingly I grasped at the only comfort. Might I perhaps change into a girl, wearing skirts and a hair-ribbon? No, she said. It only happened to her. . . [pp. 31-32].

Half of the transsexual patients studied by Pomeroy (1967) had parents who were separated by divorce or death during the subjects' childhood. Stoller (1969b) also mentions the father's absence in the transsexual cases he studied. Not only were the fathers away from home much of the time, or unavailable to their sons, but they were "unable to take part in the family as masculine men [and] their relationships with their wives [were] distant and sulking."

As Samuel reached late adolescence, the fantasy of transsexual change pursued him when he fell in love with Beatrice.

"Beatrice."

"Mm?"

"What is it like to be you?"

A sensible question; and asked out of my admiration for Evie and Ma, out of my adolescent fantasies, out of my painful obsession with discovery and identification. An impossible question.

"Just ordinary."

What is it like to hold the centre of someone's universe, to be soft and fair and sweet, to be neat and clean by nature, to be desired to distraction, to live under this hair, behind these huge unutterable eyes, to feel the lift of these guarded twins, the valley, the plunge down to the tiny waist, to be vulnerable and invulnerable? What is it like in the bath and the lavatory and walking the pavement with shorter steps and high heels; what is it like to know your body breathes this faint perfume which makes my heart burst and my senses swim?

"No. Tell me."

And you can you feel them all the way out to the rounded points? Do you know and feel how hollow your belly is? What is it like to be frightened of mice? What is it like to be wary and serene, protected and peaceful? How does a man seem to you? Is he clothed, always, jacketed and trousered, is he castrated like the plaster casts in the art room? [Golding, pp. 103-104].

James Morris, the noted British author and reporter who accompanied Sir Edmund Hilary on his historic ascent of Mount Everest, underwent surgical sex transformation and, as Jan Morris, wrote in *Conundrum* (1974):

Nobody really knows why some children, boys and girls, discover in themselves the inexpungeable belief that, despite all the physical evidence, they are really of the opposite sex. It happens at a very early age. Often there are signs of it when the child is still a baby, and it is generally profoundly ingrained, as it was with me, by the fourth or fifth year. Some theorists suppose the child to be born with it: perhaps there are undiscovered constitutional or genetic factors, or perhaps, as American scientists have lately suggested, the fetus has been affected by misdirected hormones during pregnancy. Many more believe it to be solely the result of early environment: too close an identification with one or the other parent, a dominant mother or father, an infancy too effeminate or too tomboyish. Others again think the cause to be partly constitutional, partly environmental — nobody is born entirely male or entirely female, and some children may be more susceptible than others to what the psychologists call the "imprint" of circumstance [pp. 7-8].

Psychogenic factors, according to Goldrach (1967) and Vietze (1970) play a major role in the genesis of transsexualism. The tomboy characteristics of the mothers of transsexual children studied by Stoller are generally accepted by society, whereas few parents will recognize or boast of their son's "sissy" traits. Money and Brennan's (1968) sample of six transsexual females showed that, as children, their physical energy and modes of expressing it were typically associated with the male stereotype. "Tomboyishness in the progestin-induced and the androgenital syndromes is a matter chiefly of physical energy expenditure and outdoor athletic interests of the type customarily assigned to boys. Aggressive fighting and territoriality, while not excluded from this energy expenditure, was not a notable characteristic of it. There was no accurate evidence of a predisposition to homosexual childhood sexual curiosity, play or intimacy, nor to Lesbian eroticism in prepuberty or early adolescence. Maternal doll-play in childhood and antic of a baby and child care in adulthood were both absent or weak" (p. 496). Millie, in Alan Friedman's *Hermaphrodeity* (1972), began to get a bit thinner in prepuberty, "more boyish, I felt with immense pleasure . . . and began to chase in desperate tomboy style after Sandy and his friends" (p. 11). At thirteen, she "was utterly uninterested in school, other girls . . ." (p. 16), and a little later, prior to sex reassignment surgery, said how "enormously grateful, how glad, I'd be to become male, physically, mentally, emotionally — the works — a banana split sundae with nuts, whipped cream, and cherries" (p. 25) with almost conscious use of the sexual symbolism in her choice of words. When a girl openly states her wish to be a boy, insists on dressing boyishly, has masculine mannerisms, shows no interest in doll play, strongly prefers competitive sports and male companions, as did Millie, then there are clear signposts to the possibility of serious cross-gender identification (Green, 1968).

The male counterpart of the tomboy often shows a high degree of adherence to the feminine stereotypes. Fourteen male transsexuals studied by Money and Primrose (1968) were labelled "sissies" during childhood. After puberty, they adopted a receptive role in sexual relations, often in complete disregard of their genitals; other characteristics were also consistent with a feminine gender identity. In Brown's fictional account of a male transsexual, *I Want What I Want*, Roy reminisced of his childhood play habits and reading matter.

> In the corner, under the slope of the ceiling, was the wooden fat-box that contained the dozens of pieces of the electric train set I had not particularly wanted one Christmas. I had liked playing with Shirley's doll house until my father had got rid of it. One could play a story with a doll's house. On the far side of the bed there was a wall cupboard between the flue that ran up the wall and the corner of the room. I went across and opened the cupboard. On a shelf there was an old copy of a children's book, *Chatterbox*. Some of the stories in it were intended for boys and some were intended for girls. The girls' stories were mostly about the boyish adventures of schoolgirls. I had supposed that the heroines wore the navy blue knickers that the little girls wore at the school I went to. It had been after I had gone to the grammar school that I had stopped wanting to wear the navy blue knickers and be a little girl and started wanting to grow up to wear knickers of silk and nylon and have breasts [p. 55].

Before puberty, the most frequently occurring feature among the ninety-one transsexuals Walinder (1967) studied was a feeling of belonging to the opposite sex. "The next most common feature was behaving and playing like members of the opposite sex. For boys, this meant that they played with dolls, that they chose to be the mother when playing house, that they sewed and embroidered, that they helped their mother with the house-work, and so on. It also meant that they refused to do what other boys did — that they refused, for example, to spend any time on things of a mechanical nature, play ball, play Indians and cowboys, or climb trees. . ." (pp. 39-40).

While there is much that is questionable regarding the etiology of transsexualism, there are a number of emotional and behavioral characteristics common to this population. Roth and Ball (1964) found obsessional and dysthymic features occurred significantly more often in transsexual men than in a matched control group of homosexuals. They noted also that their patients were shy and reserved, sensitive, conscientious, determined and foresightful. Ellis (1928) also pointed out the sensitive and refined nature of the subjects, and their obsessional quality has often been noted (Masson, 1939; Aubert, 1947; Alby, 1959; Randell, 1959; Israel and Geissmann, 1960). Prior to surgery, the transsexual presents a number of personality traits which place him in a severe dilemma: primarily he feels different from other males and purportedly like a female (Guze, 1969). He feels comfortable only when he can function as a woman, emotionally and physically. In *I Want What I Want*, Roy ordered a number of items of female attire from a mail-order house. He tried on a nightgown. "The nightdress produced a feeling that was a stillness. Its femininity was my femininity. I was real and desirable. It was beautiful to be gently alive and conscious of myself. The door was locked and I was safe. I had become the centre, still and alone. The nightdress was the truth about me. Whatever might be written on the birth certificate that was amongst my father's papers at home, I knew that I was female. The nightdress was correct. It was my nightdress. I had chosen it. The error of nature was not my error" (p. 101).

This "error of nature" is a common refrain among transsexuals. They become more and more convinced that nature has blundered and God has cheated them (Hofer, 1961; Benjamin, 1964; Guze, 1969). What frequently follows is a tremendous undercurrent of resentment against the Deity and authority. Roy, in *I Want What I Want*, "would be able to believe in God if [he] changed sex" (p. 173), and when he goes to church prays, "Please, God, let me be a woman" (p. 196). "In scaling the patient's behavior, one finds an intense spitefulness in almost all of the persons studied, both men and women" (Guze, 1969, p. 179). They persist more and more in outspokenly hostile demands for help from the doctor for medical measures to change their sex, whether it be hormones or plastic surgery or both (Brautigam, 1958).

In Norma Meacock's (1972) *Thinking Girl,* the female narrator, who seems to be a fetishistic transvestite, Type II, according to Benjamin's (1966, p. 22) classification as well as a true transsexual of moderate intensity, Type V, is in dire pursuit of sexual reassignment.

What did I know of dildos? I was twenty-three at the time and loved my Girly to distraction. We both had great imaginations and high hopes of a sex change by surgery in Sweden. I insisted on this to her mother. "Look," I said, "I'm really a man in disguise. They made a mistake. Nothing to worry about." She was unconvinced and turned us both out of the house. I decided to find a job that would support us. I wanted Girly to keep the home fires burning. Your true lesbian will out-male any male. She waxes pompous bolstering up tradition and lives in a no-man's land where she will cheerfully abjure woman's rights for her woman and utter all kinds of out-of-date nonsense. Fingers are fun and I was roused then as never since. At least we knew where to rub! I always lay on top through this Sapphic inability to risk being feminine, and we contorted our pelvises so cleverly that our vulvas touched. . . . I cultivated a bass voice but it never was bass enough save when I had a cold. I cut my hair in an Eton crop and she called me Leopold, after Bloom, Poldy for short, always affecting. We ceased, tacitly, to apply feminine nouns and pronouns to me and intensified their application to her. I called her my wife and sent her a valentine every year . . . I flattened my breasts with a roll-on, wore a check shirt and smoked a pipe. I relieved my brother-in-law of an old pair of trousers with flies and thought I cut quite a dash . . . Close friends sent us cuttings on sex changes and related subjects from the popular papers and told us it was a frequent phenomenon among hens. We collected stories of eighteenth-century generals whose female sex was revealed on their deathbeds. Sweden was many times reverted to and the devotion with which Girly would await the outcome of years (we guessed three) of surgical treatment.

After a year and a half we both experienced moods of depression. She wanted a baby. I wanted to give her one . . . I cried aloud in grief because my wishes were so humble: a wife, a home, a family; and forever unattainable. Neither piety nor iconoclasm availed and I began to pester doctors. They assured me I was a normal female in all corporal respects and tentatively suggested psychiatrists. I would leave in wrath swearing that in Scandinavia society was more just and rectified God's little mistakes . . . We lay in each other's arms imagining what could never be, but sweetly sometimes, without a keen edge, and I gazed at her splendid eyes and licked her pink nipples. Poldy dear Poldy, Girly dear Girly [pp. 13-16, *passim*].

Another common characteristic of the transsexual is his disgust with his body, primarily his genitals. It is a source of torment to him and he "lives only for the day when his 'female soul' is no longer being outraged by his male body" (Benjamin, 1966, p. 19). Some men try to change their appearance by plucking their eyebrows and removing facial hair, shaving their arms and legs and trimming their pubic hair to make it look feminine; others try to make their bodies look like a woman's by injecting paraffin into their breasts and by other means. Myra Breckinridge, in the novel of the same name by Gore Vidal (1968), describes her alter ego, Myron, as being intensely masculine at times, "but the feminine aspects of his nature were the controlling ones, as I knew best. He wanted men to possess him rather than the other way around. He saw himself as a woman, made to suffer at the hands of some insensitive man. Needless to say, he found partners galore. When I think of the elaborate dinners he used to cook for merchant seamen with tattoos! The continual fussing about the house, so reminiscent of the female preparing to lay her egg" (pp. 96-97). In the notebook Myra maintained as a therapeutic device, she wrote, "Myron was tortured by having been attached to those male genitals which are linked to a power outside the man who sports them, or, to be precise, they sport the man for they are peculiarly willful and separate and it is not for nothing that the simple boy so often says of his erection, partly as a joke but partly as a frightening fact, 'He's got a head of his own' [p. 246]. . . . With a swift movement of the scalpel, the surgeon freed me from the detested penis [p. 248] . . . Im Myra Myron is dead as a doornail why when I lost those ugly things it was like a ship losing its anchor and Ive been sailing ever since [p. 236] . . . . [I feel] free as a bird and perfectly happy in being the most extraordinary woman in the world" (p. 237).

Roy, in *I Want What I Want,* gives similar evidence. "It was hateful to have to shave. They were just the patches on the sides of my chin, but they would have to be gone over every morning. Hair remover would have no effect. The hairs grew because I had been born a man child. 'Let the day perish wherein I was born, and the night in which it was said, There is a man-child conceived.' I had read that even hormone treatment could fail to remove the beard. Masculinity was a hideous disorder [p. 104] . . . Men were very ugly . . . The thought of a naked man was obscene. It was difficult to imagine how anyone could be happy in a male body. It was quite impossible to imagine being positively glad to be a man . . . I realized that I was thinking of men as the opposite sex. The realisation gave me a pleasant sensation [p. 166] . . . 'There's no such thing as a good-looking man,' I told her. 'They're all ugly' " (p. 215).

This abhorrence of their own bodies can lead to self-mutilation, for the compulsion to adopt the total female role is paramount with the transsexual. "I had thought of mutilating myself with a razor blade," says Roy in *I Want What I Want*, "so that an operation to create a vagina would be the only possible repair for the damage I had done. But, of course, I did not have the stark courage for such an act. And I would almost certainly bleed to death before I could be helped. And, even if I did not bleed to death, there was the likelihood I would do damage that would make it impossible for me ever to enjoy being a woman" (p. 175). And later, Roy "wished that I had no choice but to be a girl. An operation would make it so that I had no possibility of choosing; I would always have to sit down when I used the lavatory. I always did sit down, but I had the possibility of choosing. If I were bound to one way, I would be one person. I would be a woman" (p. 216). The best Roy can do is to hide his genitals cleverly, with the help of sticking plaster and a bandage that drew the penis and scrotum between his legs. Newton (1972) describes the use of a "gaff" by female impersonators for the purpose of concealing the genitals. A gaff is "simply a strip of rubber worn between the legs and held taut by thin rubber bands over the hips, which holds the genitals tightly down and back between the legs" (p. 44).

Myron Breckinridge had "the stark courage" to do what Roy could not. "I have punished the head . . . by a literal decapitation, killing Myron so that Myra might be born" (Vidal, p. 246). "My body is, if I may say so, unusually lovely, the result of the most dedicated plastic surgeons who allowed me, at my request, to remain conscious during all stages of my transformation, even though I was warned that I might be seriously traumatized in the process. But I was not. Quite the contrary. I was enthralled, delighted, fascinated (of course the anesthetic had a somewhat intoxicating effect). And when, with one swift movement of the scalpel, the surgeon freed me from the detested penis, I amazed everyone by beginning to sing, I don't know why, "I'll be seeing you". . . hardly a fitting song since the point to the exercise is that I would *not* be seeing it or any of its equivalents . . . ever again; at least not in the way Myron saw such things. Nevertheless, I was elated, and have not for one moment regretted my decision to be unique" (p. 208). At the same time, phantom limb pain, familiar to the more traditional amputee patient, cropped up with Myron/Myra. "Look at me . . . for I am the New Woman whose astonishing history is a poignant amalgam of vulgar dreams and knife-sharp realities (shall I ever be free of the dull lingering pain that is my peculiar glory, the price so joyously paid for being Myra Breckinridge . . .)" (p. 2).

Millie/Willie, in *Hermaphrodeity* by Alan Friedman (1972), also feels various psychic pains after surgical intervention.

The destiny that followed—the happily obsessed career of bodily passion and spiritual realization I embraced with a will—in a single volume? Hardly. No . . . no matter how thick this book, if I can cram half my lifetime into its pages I'll be satisfied, believe me.

Sentimentally, I've kept a bulging manila envelope full of pictures from that far-off time. Candid-camera shots of me. Smirking on the porch. Gobbling at Thanksgiving dinner. Trying out my new boy's bike. Every time I pull the rubberband off the envelope I experience an unpleasant twinge in my groin. There I stand with a skirt on—in several photos you can see the beginnings of my girlshape under my blouse. In others taken only months later I'm wearing pants and a tie, looking skinny and afraid. There's one eloquent photograph: it's a group picture and it tells the story (Plate II). We're all standing there. Mother's fists and eyes are grimly clenched. Father's tongue is proudly flexing his mustache. And my brother Sandy's fingers are gingerly clasping my shoulder. I'm the blond sixteen-year-old up front, the one with the bright embarrassed teeth.

Anatomy is destiny, we hear from Freud by way of Napoleon. To comprehend the course of my destiny, you really ought to see the before-and-after shots of my operation. The medical close-ups of my naked saddle—these are fascinating. Caught during and after surgery, every detail of my genitals shows with clarity in this expert series of stills depicting my transition from girlhood to manhood. It's almost too graphic for words: below my mons veneris emerges first the glans of my penis, then gradually the shaft; then in the place of my girl-lips appear (photographed in four stages of emergence) my testicles. The successful procedure adopted by the surgeon was at once featured in medical journals here and abroad (Plates III-VIII).

*   *   *

For a time I was dizzy, sick from the afteraffects of anaesthesia and feverish with a sense of anticipation. It must have been the second day when Father came to visit and cried, putting his head on the foot of my bed. The third or fourth day, as soon as the ache in my groin was bearable, I stood up, without the nurse's permission, staggered gingerly into the bathroom, and locked myself in. Half a week after the operation, the bandages had been partially loosened: cautiously, I took them aside completely and — with my heart doing little scared squirrel jumps between my two tiny fluttery breasts — I examined myself.

There! God Almighty! There it hung! My swinger! Frankly, I'll admit to you I'd expected something, well, heavier, wealthier, more muscular, more dramatic. (I'd always seen Sandy's grand organ erected.) This tool of mine looked a trifle on the unambitious side. Still, even a hungry, skinny tool was a grand tool, I decided optimistically. And right there underneath . . . yes, that funny little fleshy sac of testicles. Only then did I come to appreciate the surgical skill that had made my miracle a reality: when my golden-brown hair grew in again, my curls would conceal the stitches; underneath, my familiar cleft was thoroughly blocked and hidden by the folds of the brave new sac. Only a scar was visible there. I satisfied myself that I was unenterable and undetectable unless you were a doctor who knew in advance the mystery of my locked compartment.

You know what I did next? I swung. I swung myself for the pure innocent unexampled pleasure of seeing my own tiny majesty swing. Then I commanded him to RISE! He wouldn't of course. Well, no matter. When I got back into bed I was giggling with happiness.

All in all, I made a goodlooking boy. A scrawny blue-eyed blond kid. My hands and feet were kind of small for a boy and I was medium height . . . how peculiar that felt . . . for years I'd thought of myself as a tall girl! At home, under hormone treatment, in a matter of only a few weeks my little breasts (which Mother and I called my 'boobles,' private talk somewhere between boobies and baubles) dwindled like two swollen bruises and soon receded altogether into my chest. I was deeply impressed by the mysteries of chemistry. Scissors, shears, knives — cutting my hair, clipping my nails, learning to play mumbletypeg, snipping loose threads from my underwear, which had to be perfect [pp. 24-28, *passim*].

One of the primary characteristics of transsexualism is the person's attempt to deny and change his biological sex and pass into and maintain identification with the opposite sex. The desire for a change of sex operation becomes the single theme of the transsexual's life and is pursued with obsessive determination (Pauly, 1968). Morris, the Mount Everest climber, writes of determined feelings:

> Sex has its reasons, too, but I suspect the only transsexuals who can really achieve happiness are those of the classic kind, the lifelong puzzlers, to whom it is not primarily a sexual dilemma at all—who offer no rational purpose to their compulsions, even to themselves, but are simply driven blindly or helplessly towards the operating table. Of all our fellows, we are the most resolute. Nothing will stop us, no fear of ridicule or poverty, no threat of isolation, not even the threat of death itself. . . . It is only in writing this book that I have delved so deeply into my own emotions. Yet nothing I have discovered there has shaken my conviction, and if I were trapped in that cage again nothing would keep me from my goal, however fearful its prospect, however hopeless the odds. I would search the earth for surgeons, I would bribe barbers or abortionists, I would take a knife and do it myself, without fear, without qualms, without a second thought [1974, p. 169].

Stoller (1968) holds that the word "transsexual" should not be defined in terms of a patient seeking surgical alteration of his sexual organs, but in characterological terms with a central "conviction in a biological normal person of being a member of the opposite sex" (p. 42). The request for surgical intervention is clearly secondary to this belief, which should not be confused with a psychotic delusion. But in his conviction that a mistake of nature has been made and that he is truly of the opposite sex, the transsexual demands a surgical change in his external sex characteristics. The conversion operation includes castration, penectomy, and construction of an artificial vagina and vulva for the male transsexual, and mastectomy, hysterectomy, and the creation of an artificial phallus for the female transsexual (Pauly, 1968). These procedures are, of course, irreversible as well as risky; candidates must be selected with the greatest care and, when they are, the results of the conversion operation are not only excellent but the only treatment that does any good (Stoller, 1969a). Of the cases reviewed by Pauly (1968), satisfactory outcomes of surgery were ten times more likely than unsatisfactory results. Wollman (1967) found that, without exception, every person who had undergone the painful and prolonged procedures did not regret the discomfort or the expense involved. The findings of Money and Schwartz (1969) indicate that surgical intervention in the treatment of transsexuals could serve the function of creating a more tolerable existence for them. Money (1971), remarking on the outcome of sex reassignment in twenty-four cases of transsexualism, noted that all the males and six of the females expressed complete satisfaction with the surgery. Flores and Garcia Trovato (1971) also concluded that surgical treatment produces better results than either psychotherapy or other somatotherapies. Thus, with properly selected cases, it would seem there are no regrets. Nevertheless, surgical sex reassignment is a less-than-perfect solution to the problem of transsexualism.

To approximate the female anatomical structure becomes the single theme of the male transsexual's life; surgical techniques and hormone therapy permit the partial realization of fantasies of sexual metamorphosis (Pauly, 1965). The transsexual lives a fantasy. Dr. Matthew O'Connor, the transvestite bogus gynecologist who dominates Djuna Barnes' (1937) *Nightwood* with the brilliance of his speech and the weight of his personality, is lying in his rumpled bed, wearing a woman's nightgown and a blonde wig, surrounded by empty perfume bottles. His dream is of babies and knitting in a pretty cottage. "If I had to do it again, [he tells Nora], I'd be the girl found lurking behind the army . . . Am I not the girl to know of what I speak? We go to our Houses by our nature—and our nature, no matter how it is, we all have to stand—as for me, so God has made me, my house is the pissing port. Am I to blame if I've been summoned before and this my last and oddest call? In the old days I was possibly a girl in Marseilles thumping the dock with a sailor, and perhaps it's that memory that haunts me. The wise men say that the remembrance of things past is all that we have for a future, and am I to blame if I've turned up this time as I shouldn't have been, when it was a high soprano I wanted, and deep curls to my bum, with a womb as big as the king's kettle, and a bosom as high as the bowsprit of a fishing schooner? And what do I get but a face on me like an old child's bottom—is that happiness, do you think?" (pp. 90-91). And again, "It was more than a boy like me, who am the last woman left in this world, though I am the bearded lady" (p.100). The confused protagonist in Connell's *The Diary of a Rapist* (1966) enters in his diary, "If I had one wish I'd wish to be a woman. And I'd go traveling by myself. Put on an attractive suit with a crisp white blouse, wear rings, necklaces and perfume . . ." (p. 155).

A sustained exposition of the obsessive quality of the transsexual's fantasy world is offered in Geoff Brown's *I Want What I Want* in the character of the protagonist, Roy Clark, who "becomes" Wendy Ross. He fantasied about and identified with his psychiatrist's wife: "There was day after day of being a woman. When she went into a room the gentlemen stood up. When she went to wet she had to sit down. She had no choice. She was always a woman" (p. 5). His earliest recollection of his fantasy life was: "I had often thought about the possibility when I was eight or nine. I had thought that I might be dreaming everything and the I might wake up and find I was really a little girl" (p. 8). One day, "A young girl walked on the footpath. Her hair was black The breeze folded her summer dress as she walked. She walked along pretending to be unconscious of her happiness. There was something intelligent about her movements. Perhaps she was down on the long vacation from Oxford. Perhaps she was a clever model, come home for a rest from London. The first was possible. The second seemed unlikely. She was not tall enough. I was tall enough" (p. 46). One time, Roy wished that he "would sweat like a June bride, sweating weakly and femininely from the nervousness and happiness in white satin" (p. 47). His obsession is further revealed: "I have to have women's clothes because I was a woman in the head. They could oppress me, but they could not get into my head. It was an impossibility for anyone to make me believe that it was better to be a man than a woman as it would have been for them to make me believe that the streets where I lived were better than Cottingham. In their hearts, they must know the truth themselves, but they had to keep pretending for the sake of decency — while all the time they knew that men, with their grotesque sexual organs, were always indecent. To be a man was horrible. It was ridiculous that I should have been sent to a mental hospital. It was perfectly sane for me to want to be a woman. It was my body that was wrong, not my mind" (p. 51). When Roy returned home from the hospital, he discovered that Mrs. Wilson had been living with his father during his absence and now would no longer be able to be alone with him in the house. "I would have liked to make a bargain whereby Mrs. Wilson came to live in sin with my father in exchange for my being allowed to send away for clothes and dress up when I wanted. Such a bargain was impossible. We all had to play hide-and-seek . . ." (p. 54). Roy's childhood fantasies led to sadistic imaginings of criminals who would kidnap girls, bind and gag them, and bring them to hideouts. "The criminals of my imagination were hard handsome men in dinner jackets, each with an automatic pistol slung out of sight beneath his left arm. The women were so beautiful and beautifully dressed that they were near to fainting with the mere ecstasy of being themselves. But I was the most beautiful. I would be going to the ballroom in a long Rolls Royce, softly lit. I would be poised and self-assured in a sheath dress of black satin with a stole of black chiffon about my shoulders. The chauffeur would be my body-guard as well as my driver, a silent man, as ruthless as he was loyal, ready to cut down anyone who caused me even the slightest annoyance. I would arrive at the secret ballroom and everyone would gasp. I would dance with the most successful of all the criminals, Max, cruel and handsome like a tiger" (pp. 58-59).

Herman Dudley, in the short story "The Man Who Became a Woman," by Sherwood Anderson (1923), is possessed by the fantasy that he has changed into a woman. At one point, he asks himself why he was unable to scream when some men, thinking he was a woman, attempted to rape him. "Just why I couldn't I don't know. Could it be at the time I was a woman, while at the same time I wasn't a woman? It may be that I was too ashamed of having turned into a girl and being afraid of a man to make any sound" (p. 223). It was only when his terror left him that Herman began to return to a more normal state: "It burned all that silly nonsense about being a girl right out of me ... I screamed at last and the spell ... was broken" (p. 225). While there is no question of true transsexualism being involved in the Anderson story, the obsessive quality of the sexual inversion pursued the adolescent Herman to maturity.

Perhaps of most importance to the transsexual is the self-concept of body image. Schilder (1935) suggested that recognition of one's own body developmentally involves secondary narcissism; thus the person turns from the object world to self-affection. Guze stated that the transsexual patient "seems unable to accept his own body image and invest affect in himself. His is a conflicting experience: the outer world expects him to be a man, but he feels unable to fulfill that expectation and concludes that he must be a physically malformed woman. The psychologically crippled male can escape into the rationalization of the malformed woman by denying the male. Likewise the female transsexual can deny her femaleness by claiming to be a crippled man. But why all this maneuvering? The answer lies in the fact that the transsexual has behaved like two persons. His anatomical masculine self has created a female subject that he can respond to . . . While the transvestite responds freely, masturbating as he observes his female counterpart in the mirror, the transsexual cannot do this. Why? There are several clinical hypotheses: (1) He has never reached an adequate stage of masculine development and thus he perceives his fantasy as himself. (2) He is extremely puritanical and refuses to be aroused by his image. Consequently, he must destroy himself so that his image may survive. He refuses to accept the duality, because he cannot perceive it. Rather, the transsexual perceives himself as a woman imprisoned in the male body which he experiences, or vice versa. Flugel (1950) refers to an interesting psychoanalytic suggestion made by Fenichel in 1929, that is, an unconscious refusal to accept the lack of a penis in woman and secondly, an unconscious identification of the self with the penis-possessing woman. The position seems to be a simplification, albeit a significant one, of a much more complex situation. Anatole France predicted that at some time, in a more tolerant world than his, the degree of sex distinctiveness in dress would correspond more to the degree of heterosexual or homosexual differentiation of the wearer" (Guze, 1969, pp. 174-175).

That day has not yet come. The transsexual syndrome bears, in society's judgment, the stigma of sexual deviance and is thus taboo. Inherent in this censure is the multitude of laws, social restrictions, and popular fears that tend to cloud and confuse the issue (Knorr, Wolf, and Meyer, 1968) making it inseparable from medical concerns. Psychotherapy has not proved helpful in allowing the transsexual to accept the gender identity consistent with his sexual anatomy. Sex conversion surgery is hazardous and meets with limited success. Psychotherapy has been unsuccessful, with the single exception claimed by Barlow, Reynolds, and Agras (1973) whose treatment of a diagnosed male transsexual by behavior modification eventuated in a successful change of gender identity, indicating that gender role may not be as inflexible as assumed and that radical surgery may not be the only answer. Etiological factors are still being explored. Money and Ehrhardt (1973) and Yalom, Green, and Fisk (1973), for example, are gathering evidence indicating that the predisposition to gender identity problems may actually be established in prenatal life through improper hormonal programming of the fetal brain. The frayed ends of the transsexual's life are braided into a complicated but indivisible unit. Picking out the pattern, strand by strand, is an onerous and still impossible task. The only existing certainty is that the person has no feeling of sexual ambiguity, but rather an assuredness that is absolute and irrepressible that the other sex is the desirable, natural, logical, and only one. There is the unshakable conviction that he was born with the wrong body, being feminine by gender but male by sex. Completeness can be achieved only when the one is adjusted to the other.

TECHNICAL REFERENCES

Aubert, G. (1947), *Trois cas de désir de changer de sexe.* Dissertation, University of Lausanne.

Barlow, D. H., Reynolds, E. J. & Argas, W. S. (1973), Gender identity change in a transsexual. *Archives of General Psychiatry,* 28:569-576.

Benjamin, H. (1954), Transsexualism and transvestism as psychosomatic and somatopsychic syndromes. *American Journal of Psychotherapy,* 8:219-230.

———— (1964), Clinical aspects of transsexualism in the male and female. *American Journal of Psychotherapy,* 18:458-469.

———— (1966), *The Transsexual Phenomenon.* New York: Julian Press.

Brautigam, W. (1958), Zur Phänomenologie der erotischen and sexuellen Liebe sowie ihrer Perversionen. *Nervenartzt,* 29:53-59.

Bulliet, G. (1928), *Venus Castina. Famous Female Impersonators Celestial and Human.* New York: Covici, Friede.

Burchard, J. M. (1961), *Struktur und Soziologie des Transvestismus und Transsexualismus.* Stuttgart: Enke.

Christodorescu, D. (1971), Female transsexualism. *Psychiatric Clinics,* 4:40-45.

Dana, R. (1970), The stutter of eternity. A study of the themes of isolation and meaninglessness in three novels by Yukio Mishima. *Critique,* 12:87-102.

Delay, J., Deniker, P., Lamperiere, T. & Benoit, J. C. (1954), Histoire d'un travesti: l'éonisme. *Encephale,* 43:385-398.

Devereux, G. (1957), The awarding of a penis as a compensation for rape. *International Journal of Psycho-Analysis,* 38:398-401.

Ellis, H. (1928), *Studies in the Psychology of Sex,* Vol. 7. New York: Davies.

Flores, J. R. & García Trovato, M. (1971), El síndrome transexual. *Revista de Neuro-Psiquiatria,* 34:37-57.

Flugel, J. C. (1950), *The Psychology of Clothes.* New York: International Universities Press.

Foster, J. (1956), *Sex Variant Women in Literature.* New York: Vantage.

Fraser, G. S. (1968), *Lawrence Durrell. A Critical Study.* New York: Dutton.

Goldfarb, R. (1970), *Sexual Repression and Victorian Literature.* Lewisburg, Pa.: Bucknell University Press.

Goldrach, C. (1967), Le Trans-sexualisme. *Concurs Médicale,* 88:531-535.

Green, R. (1966), Transsexualism: Mythological, historical and cross-cultural aspects. In: H. Benjamin, *The Transsexual Phenomenon.* New York: Julian Press, pp. 173-186.

_____ (1967), Physician emotionalism in the treatment of the transsexual. *Transactions of the New York Academy of Sciences,* 29:440-443.

_____ (1968), Childhood cross-gender identification. *Journal of Nervous and Mental Disease,* 147:500-509.

_____ & Money, J. (1961), Effeminacy in prepubertal boys. Summary of 11 cases. *Pediatrics,* 27:286-291.

Guze, H. (1969), Psychosocial adjustment of transsexuals: An evaluation and theoretical formulation. In: *Transsexualism and Sex Reassignment,* ed. R. Green & J. Money. Baltimore: John Hopkins Press, pp. 171-181.

Hill, W. W. (1935), Status of hermaphrodite and transvestite in Navaho culture. *American Anthropologist,* 37:273-279.

Hofer, G. (1961), Transvestitismus. *Fortschrifft für Neurologie und Psychiatrie,* 29:1-33.

Hora, T. (1953), The structural analysis of transvestitism. *Psychoanalytic Review,* 40:268-294.

Israel, L. & Geissmann, P. (1960), Le désir de changer de sexe chez les invertis psychosexuels. *Cahiers Psychiatrie,* 14:91-114.

Knorr, N. J., Wolf, S. R. & Meyer, E. (1968), The transsexual's request for surgery. *Journal of Nervous and Mental Disease,* 147:517-524.

Korges, J. (1970), Gide and Mishima: Homosexuality as metaphor. *Critique,* 12:127-137.

Kupperman, H. S. (1967), The endocrine status of the transsexual patient. *Transactions of the New York Academy of Sciences,* 29:434-439.

Lapp, J. C. (1959), Watcher betrayed and the fatal woman: Some recurring patterns in Zola. *Publication of the Modern Language Association,* 74:276-284.

Masson, J. (1939), Un cas de transvestissement. *Annales Médicale-Psychologique,* 97:132-139.

Mishima, Y. (1967), Introduction to *Young Samurai: Bodybuilders of Japan.* New York: Grove Press.

Money, J. (1971), Prefatory remarks on the outcome of sex reassignment in 24 cases of transsexualism. *Archives of Sexual Behavior,* 1:163-165.

_____ & Brennan, J. G. (1968), Sexual dimorphism in the psychology of female transsexuals. *Journal of Nervous and Mental Disease,* 147:487-499.

_____ _____ (1970), Heterosexual vs. homosexual attitudes: Male partners' perception of the feminine image of male transsexuals. *Journal of Sex Research,* 6:193-209.

_____ & Ehrhardt, A. A. (1973), *Man and Woman; Boy and Girl.* Baltimore: Johns Hopkins Press.

_____ & Gaskin, R. J. (1970), Sex reassignment. *International Journal of Psychiatry,* 9:249-269.

_____ & Primrose, C. (1968), Sexual dimorphism and dissociation in the psychology of male transsexuals. *Journal of Nervous and Mental Disease,* 147:472-486.

_____ & Schwartz, F. (1969), Public opinion and social issues in transsexualism: A case study in medical sociology. In: *Transsexualism and Sex Reassignment,* ed. R. Green & J. Money. Baltimore: John Hopkins Press, pp. 253-266.

Morris, J. (1974), *Conundrum.* New York: Harcourt Brace Jovanovich.

Newton, E. (1972), *Mother Camp: Female Impersonators in America.* Englewood Cliffs, N. J.: Prentice-Hall.

Pauly, I. B. (1965), Male psychosexual inversion: Transsexualism. A review of 100 cases. *Archives of General Psychiatry,* 13:172-181.

_____ (1968), The current status of the change of sex operation. *Journal of Nervous and Mental Disease,* 147:460-471.

Pomeroy, W. (1967), A report on the sexual histories of 25 transsexuals. *Transactions of the New York Academy of Sciences,* 29:444-447.

Randell, J. B. (1959), Transvestism and trans-sexualism—a study of 50 cases. *British Medical Journal,* 2:1448-1452.

_____ (1969), Preoperative and postoperative status of male and female transsexuals. In: *Transsexualism and Sex Reassignment,* ed. R. Green & J. Money. Baltimore: Johns Hopkins Press, pp. 355-381.

Roth, M. & Ball, J. R. B. (1964), Psychiatric aspects of intersexuality. In *Intersexuality in Vertebrates Including Man,* ed. C. N. Armstrong & A. J. Marshall. New York: Academic Press, pp. 395-443.

Rubins, J. L. (1967), The neurotic personality and certain sexual perversions. *Contemporary Psychoanalysis,* 4:53-72.

Schilder, P. (1935), *The Image and Appearance of the Human Body.* New York: International Universities Press, 1950.

Socarides, C. W. (1970), A psychoanalytic study of the desire for sexual transformation ("transsexualism"): The plaster-of-paris man. *International Journal of Psycho-Analysis.* 51:341-349.

Stoller, R. J. (1965), Passing and the continuum of gender identity. In: *Sexual Inversion,* ed. J. Marmor. New York: Basic Books, pp. 190-210.

_____ (1967), Etiological factors in male transsexualism. *Transactions of the New York Academy of Sciences,* 29:431-434.

_____ (1968), *Sex and Gender: On the Development of Masculinity and Femininity.* New York: Science House.

_____ (1969a), A biased view of "sex transformation" operations. *Journal of Nervous and Mental Disease.* 149:312-317.

_____ (1969b), Parental influences in male transsexualism. In: *Transsexualism and Sex Reassignment,* ed. R. Green & J. Money. Baltimore: Johns Hopkins Press, pp. 153-169.

Vietze, G. (1970), Zur Pathogenese des Transsexualismus: Literatur und Hallbericht. *Psychiatrie, Neurologie und medizinische Psychologie,* 22(3):81-91.

Walinder, J. (1967), *Transsexualism. A Study of Forty-Three Cases.* Goteborg, Sweden. Scandinavian University Books.

Wolf, S. R., Knorr, N. J., Hoopes, J. E. & Meyer, E. (1968), Psychiatric aspects of transsexual surgery management. *Journal of Nervous and Mental Disease,* 147:525-531.

Wollman, L. (1967), Surgery for the transsexual. *Journal of Sex Research,* 3:145-147.

Yalom, I. D., Green, R. & Fisk, N. (1973), Prenatal exposure to female hormones. Effect on psychosexual development in boys. *Archives of General Psychiatry,* 28:554-561.

LITERARY REFERENCES

Anderson, Sherwood (1923), The man who became a woman. In: *Short Stories.* New York: Hill & Wang, 1962.

Barnes, Djuna (1937), *Nightwood.* Norwalk, Conn.: New Directions, 1946.

Brown, Geoff (1966), *I Want What I Want.* New York: Putnam's, 1967.

Connell, Evan S., Jr. (1966), *The Diary of a Rapist*. New York: Simon & Schuster.

Davis, Gwen (1969), *The Pretenders*. New York: World Books.

Durrell, Lawrence (1968), *Tunc*. New York: Dutton.

Freidman, Alan (1972), *Hermaphrodeity*. New York: Knopf.

Garnett, David (1922), *Lady into Fox*. London: Chatto & Windus, 1960.

Golding, William (1959), *Free Fall*. New York: Harcourt, Brace & World, 1960.

Meacock, Norma (1972), *Thinking Girl*. New York: Dial Press.

Mishima, Yukio (1958), *Confessions of a Mask*. Norwalk, Conn.: New Directions.

Rachilde (1884), *Monsieur Vénus*. New York: Covici, Friede, 1929.

Tanizaki, Junichiro (1965), *Diary of a Mad Old Man*. New York: Knopf.

Vidal, Gore (1968), *Myra Breckinridge*. Boston: Little, Brown.

Zola, Emile (1880), *Nana*. New York: Modern Library.

CHAPTER EIGHT

Masturbation

In his *Introductory Lectures on Psycho-Analysis,* Freud (1916-1917) wrote a rather predictable scenario for an imaginary novel, dubbing it "In the Basement and on the First Floor." Two girls, so the plot goes, one the caretaker's child, the other the daughter of the wealthy owner of the house, play freely without supervision. Their games become "naughty," i.e., take on a sexual character: they play "mother and father" and stimulate each other's genitals. In subsequent years, both masturbate, but the practice affects their later lives differently. Because of their different upbringing, the caretaker's daughter is unharmed by her sexual activities, free from neurosis. The other girl acquires a sense of wrongdoing. Although she gives up her masturbatory activity after a long struggle, she retains an inner feeling of subdued depression; she is sexually repressed, and suffers a neurotic breakout (pp. 353-354).

Freud's little fiction illustrates a morality and taboo that have long existed. Strong feelings about masturbation cross economic, social, and racial lines, meeting with approval in few societies. The variety of human sexual expression, ranging from conventional intercourse to sodomy, homosexuality, bestiality, incest, and orgies, is readily found in the literature of most cultures. But the available material on masturbation in fiction or autobiographies is fitful until the mid 1960's.

An earlier version of this chapter appeared in *Masturbation: From Infancy to Senescence,* ed. I. M. Marcus & J. J. Francis. New York: © International Universities Press, 1975

By and large, it is an area of behavior which has been left alone. Certainly serious literature has avoided the topic as if no one who ever lived searched for gratification and pleasure in lonely privacy. It is rarely alluded to, even in joking terms, in literary works. The heroes of fiction and drama from Oedipus to Don Quixote to Romeo to those of Hemingway and Dreiser down to Humbert Humbert may have burned with manly passions, suffered hideous frustration in the embrace of natural or unnatural lust, but there is no record that they ever once sought surcease from this pain, or fantasized into a semblance of reality the incarnation of their desire — as most men surely do — by playing with themselves. And needless to say, that women have ever sought this secret pleasure has remained throughout the ages an idea beyond the remotest supposition [Styron, 1968, p. 99].

Styron's complaint no longer obtains. The novel without a passage on masturbation seems to be disappearing, as novelists continue to rummage more wantonly among human frailties. In Alan Friedman's (1972) *Hermaphrodeity*, Carlo masturbates Millie (p. 294); in *The Favorite Game* by Louis Cohen (1965), Shelley and Gordon "announced their betrothal in the summer, after a session of mutual masturbation on the screened porch of the Sims house at Lake George" (p. 117); "Dr Curlin smiled when I asked him why sex dominated so much of our lives. Would he smile if he found his wife masturbating with a Coca-Cola bottle?" asked Dave in *The Married Lovers* by Julius Horwitz (1973, p. 13). In a jealous huff, the boy-man dean of a Boston college in Alan Lelchuk's (1973, p. 76) *American Mischief* quit Angela's apartment when he discovered a strange pair of men's shoes in her closet. At midnight, she turned up at his quarters pleading for forgiveness, but "With a dean's icy control, I kept my hands off her and escorted her out. And with a boy's rage, I masturbated across a lascivious photo of her bikinied body. . . ." Willy in the novel *Willy Remembers* by Irvin Faust (1971) is a senile, confused, Archie Bunker-type, ninety-three-year-old man when he tells the story of his life and times. According to him, Oswald shot McKinley, Theodore Roosevelt, and Garfield. Henry and Frank Joseph are his sons. "Attorney General Mitchell, no relation to Billy, took care of all the bolshies. The first time my father caught me jerking off he beat me black and blue and I never did it again and neither did Henry. But he never had to as

he was getting plenty. Frank Joseph never jerked off in his life"
(p. 172).

A normal reaction to masturbation is found in *The Corruption of
Harold Hoskins* by John Malone (1973).

> Harold thought back to the summer of his thirteenth year, during
> which he had three times joined in a circle jerk in Mulvey's Woods
> behind his mother's farm. While he had no subsequent desire to
> repeat the experience, either on a communal or a more personal
> basis, he did not recall having found the events in any way trau-
> matic. Quite the contrary, it had all been rather fun, even funny.
> The situation had had about it an aura of a prank, like throwing
> stones at streetlights. 'A scholarly prank, the communal wank,'
> Harold thought to himself. It had been an experience divorced from
> desire, at least so far as he was concerned. Curiosity, certainly, had
> been present, but none of the desperate need to touch produced in
> him, only a year or so later, by the sight of a pair of well-developed
> breasts, nestling roundly in a low-cut bodice [pp. 55-56].

The divorced bisexual protagonist in John Speicher's (1973, p. 101)
Lower and Lower, desperate in his loneliness, says, "In my flat I
deliberated on whether I ought to masturbate, and decided not to do
so." Harrington, a middle-aged man in George V. Higgins' (1973) *The
Digger's Game*, ribs Digger who has just told him a hard-luck story.
"You're pulling your joint," he said. "God's punishing you. Pretty soon
you're gonna get hair on your hands and moles on your face and
pimples on your ass. Everbody'll be able to tell. Don't do your brains
any good, either. Keep it up, you're gonna turn simple; and you don't
have far to go, either, you was to ask me. Three Our Fathers and fifty
Hail Marys and a good Act of Contrition. Our Blessed Mother don't go
for your filthy habits, you know" (p. 21). As for novels depicting
women in the act of masturbating, there are Alix K. Shulman's
Memoirs of an Ex-Prom Queen (1972), Edna O'Brien's *August Is a
Wicked Month* (1965), Henry Sutton's *The Voyeur* (1970), John
Updike's *Couples* (1968), Marilyn Coffey's *Marcella* (1973), Hubert
Selby's *The Room* (1972), Lois Gould's *Such Good Friends* (1970),
Erica Jong's *Fear of Flying* (1973), and Kate Wilhelm's *Margaret and I*
(1971), among others, some of which will be discussed here. Novels
with masturbation scenes abound today. Masturbation threatens to
become the fashion in the novel, not as the stuff of dramatic effect or

narcissistic need but as an esthetic creed. Each work of fiction needs, it would seem, its resident masturbator. Thus the novel has come full swing, from remote symbolic reference to the act to vivid, detailed portrayals.

In James Dickey's (1970) pornographic adventure yarn, *Deliverance*, there is a cliff-hanging description. The scene takes place where Ed is scaling up from the river with his bow and arrows to kill the murderer of his buddy Drew: "I kept inching up. With each shift to a newer and higher position I felt more and more tenderness toward the wall [p. 163] . . . The urine in my bladder turned solid and painful, and then ran with a delicious sexual voiding like a wet dream, something you can't help or be blamed for [pp. 164-165] . . . Then I would begin to try to inch upwards again, moving with the most intimate motions of my body, motions I had never dared use with Martha, or any other human woman. Fear and a kind of enormous moon-blazing sexuality lifted me, millimeter by millimeter" (p. 176). A bit later, having gone some millimeters higher, Ed reveals: "It was painful, but I was going. I was crawling, but it was no longer necessary to make love to the cliff, to fuck it . . ." (p. 177).

Pope Clement VII proclaimed, "Neither touch nor be touched." The taboo against masturbation, religiously, medically, and socially purveyed, but hardly enforceable, has always been nurtured by the Judeo-Christian tradition. It is based largely on the interdiction of the old Biblical arguments for repressing sexuality. Specific for masturbation is the Old Testament story of Onan who defiled himself and his family honor by spilling his seed on the ground instead of giving it to continue his brother's line. The Biblical narrative does not make it clear whether his offense was masturbation or *coitus interruptus*. Nonetheless, Onan gave his name to a synonym for masturbation.

The Roman Catholic Church bases its ideas of concupiscence and original sin on the moral philosophy of Saint Augustine. "All men," Augustine concluded, "are born as the result of concupiscence; that is, they are conceived in sin. They also live their early years in sin, because children are not reasonable beings. Christ, being the product of virgin birth, bears no stain of original sin; ordinary mortals stand in constant danger that concupiscence will set their genitals in rebellion against God-given reason. The task of each man is to make up for his original sin by giving his will control over his impulses. . . ." Thus, Augustinian sexual restraint became Western civilization's official sexual code, the cornerstone for sexual behavior. And with the reinforcement of the religious sanction by iatrogenic medical testimony, the primitive attitude continued until fairly recently.

Such implacable morality against sexuality provided a cornucopia of guilt and a fount of repression. The thrust to repress sexuality simply drove it underground, the practice of masturbation along with it, so that with few exceptions the literature before 1900 dealt with masturbation symbolically and largely unconsciously. In modern times, the symbolism is reflected in the words of the paranoid General Jack D. Ripper in *Dr. Strangelove*, who feared the leaking away of his "precious bodily fluids," representing masturbation as loss, debility, or pollution. So, too, the slang expressions for masturbation are universally pejorative: frigging, jerking off, whacking it, beating the meat, pulling off, and jacking off. Masturbation, according to Perrin (1969), appeared to be the most indecent act known in the eighteenth century. "Dictionaries which freely define all the four-letter words — Bailey's and Perry's, for example — nevertheless shy away from listing onanism. The few that do invariably define it as 'self-pollution' or occasionally 'the crime of self-pollution'; and he who looks up 'self-pollution' to find out what this mysterious crime is does not find the term listed at all, although plenty like 'self-slaughter' are. 'Masturbation' itself is a Victorian term, although known earlier: Burton spoke of 'mastrupratious' in 1621, and Swift and Dickens each have a character known as 'Master Bates.' One of the first dictionaries to list it — Worcester's, Boston, 1861 — finally lifts a corner of the veil. Worcester defines it as 'self-pollution; onanism,' and then offers the following etymology: 'Perhaps from the Latin *manus*, the hand, and *stupro*, to ravish' " (p. 164).

Moral tales were one genre by which an author could preach about the evils of masturbation and natural emissions. Geoffrey Chaucer's (c. 1388) "The Parson's Tale" in *The Canterbury Tales* is a case in point. The parson is enumerating the sins he can think of and among them is the following.

Another form of sin appertains to lechery, and that comes often to those who are virgin and also to those who are corrupt; and this sin men call pollution, which comes in four ways. Sometimes it is due to laxness of the body; because the humours are too rank and abundant in the body of man. Sometimes it is due to infirmity;

because of the weakness of the retentive virtue, as is discussed in works on medicine. Sometimes it is due to a surfeit of food and drink. And sometimes it comes from base thoughts that were enclosed in man's mind when he fell asleep; which thing may not happen without sin. Because of this, men must govern themselves wisely, or else they may fall into grievous sin [p. 540].

Children's stories, fairy tales, folk tales, and legends were other avenues through which early literature expressed masturbatory activity. Krishna, the Pan and Narcissus of Hindu mythology, was the god of self-contemplation. Symbol of autoeroticism was Lord Krishna's practice, *hautrus* (Manual orgasm), regarded among early Greeks and Romans as devised by Hermes and Mercury, and deified as ritualistic. Women of certain Hindu sects, worshipping the female principle (yoni), stimulated the clitoris and labia in emulation of the maternal goddess Shuktee (Edwardes, 1959, p. 112)

A story can offer children direct gratification, having scoptophilic and oral aspects as well as the taking in through eyes and ears. "The excitement accompanying a thrilling story (producing red cheeks, glassy eyes, tenseness or restlessness) seems comparable to masturbation and sometimes merges into it" (Peller, 1959, p. 414). Friedländer (1942), in her work on the function of children's books in latency and pre-puberty, shows how the "child feels itself drawn to those books containing the fantasies with which the child itself is engaged. These fantasies, by their derivations from day-dreams, still testify to their original connection with masturbation . . . The adult's attitude toward the typical literature of this period leads one to suspect that the kinship of such activity with the realm of instinctual gratification, in particular masturbation, must be known to them" (p. 147).

Folk tales, of course, exist in every culture. Those that survive are the ones that best bear repetition. Some of the most loved stories remain remarkably stable in form. This suggests that what we call "plots" in fiction are ways of meeting imaginative or psychological needs that vary only slightly from culture to culture (Davis, 1953). Examples include the use of the pattern of three, spinning and rubbing stories, spiders, demons, powerful genii, witches, and mother figures.

Engle (1942) recapitulates the story of Melampus, the oldest Greek legendary physician, who cured Iphiclus, son of King Phylacus, of impotency. A vulture related that when Iphiclus was still a child, Phylacus chased him with a knife "because he was misbehaving, by unseemly play with his hands for which the father, doubtless in jest, made as if to cut the guilty member off with his knife." Failing to overtake the boy, the father struck the knife into a wild pear tree. As a consequence of his fright, Iphiclus had not the power to procreate. This legend, concludes Engle, corresponds to Freud's empirical discovery that disturbances of masculine potency result from man's unconscious fear of castration by the father. Psychoanalytic experience compels the interpretation of Iphiclus's "misbehavior" as masturbation with concomitant oedipal fantasies.

Róheim (1949) has analyzed a number of folk tales involving demons. While a mortal is sound asleep, demons, often dwarfs, appear in a room and do the work that has been left undone. The theme frequently is spinning, with the sleeper, generally a young girl, punished by her mother. The dwarfs have hanging lips, noses a yard long, snakelike feet, very thick fingers, and their faces represent a vulva displaced upward. In one tale, these symbols of masturbation appear for the last time at a wedding. In another, the king forbids his wife to spin any further, i.e., to masturbate. In the Silesian version, the dwarf is called *Knirrficker; ficken* is the German equivalent of fuck.

Three illustrations from fairy tales confirm the hidden meaning of masturbation in literature. Aladdin's discovery of the magic lamp through "accidental" rubbing is easily recognizable as the discovery of sexual pleasure through rubbing the penis. The genie who appears to do his master's bidding is like the personification of the erect penis. "We are told that Aladdin availed himself of the services of the genie to keep himself and his mother supplied with everything they needed. This detail is the familiar part of the child's fantasy. When he becomes rich and powerful he can supplant the father and give to mother all the things her heart desires. The fantasy of satisfying the mother's every wish must certainly derive from the child's envy of the father, his larger penis and his potency, and his realization that he, as child, is 'poor' in these respects; he can give nothing to his mother" (Fraiberg, 1954, p. 229).

In Hans Christian Andersen's "The Tinder Box," the soldier accidentally discovers the secret of the tinder box by striking sparks from the flint. All manner of riches are his. Like Aladdin, the soldier overrides all obstacles and obtains the beautiful princess for his own. "Through the acquisition of a magical device, the hero achieves the means of obtaining the inaccessible woman. The magical device ... is a penis which performs miracles. The rubbing of the lamp and the striking of the box ... are unmistakable allusions to the arousal of sexual sensations in the penis" (Fraiberg, p. 231). The magic lamp and the tinder box are phallic symbols that give up their secrets through accidental manipulation.

Grimm's Tale No. 31 tells of a miller who promises his daughter to the devil in return for making him rich. The devil comes to fetch the girl and orders the father to cut her hands off because otherwise he has no power to take her. The father does as bidden but the handless girl wanders away into the forest. A king finds her, marries her, and has hands of silver made to replace the real ones. The rest of the story consists of an alternating series of "love object found," and "love object lost," connected with some form of castration—hands, tongue, eyes, etc. Róheim (1945) identifies the father, husband, and devil as the same person who cuts off the girl's hands and chases her into the wide world because she refuses to comply with his wishes. The story itself is probably based on a masturbation fantasy, which is why the hands are cut off, for while the girl is masturbating, she fantasies coitus with her father.

The nursery rhyme, "Little Miss Muffet/sat on a tuffet/ Eating her curds and whey/ There came a big spider / And sat down beside her/ And frightened Miss Muffet away," masks a little girl's masturbation fantasy, an incestuous wish. It is seen in the symbolism of the muff, which is a perfect representation of the vagina, in the tuffets of hair, and in the eating of curds and whey (Sharpe, 1943). The spider chases Miss Muffet away from a pleasurable activity. The creature represents the bisexual conflict because it unconsciously resembles the fantasied bisexual genitalia, the penis embodied in the female genitals (Newman and Stoller, 1969).

More than forty years before the younger Grimm brother was born, Jonathan Swift published *Gulliver's Travels* (1726). In it, Lemuel Gulliver acts out his masturbatory fantasies which, like those of Swift, are closely interwoven with anal preoccupations rather than genital ones. Greenacre (1955) points out at least two places where Swift makes clear and extensive references, and several others where he alludes to masturbation fantasies and castration fears. In his *Memoirs of Scriblerus* (1704), Swift writes about the sagacity of Dr. Martin Scriblerus in treating a young nobleman who suffered from distempers of the mind. He was hobbled by speech affectations, spoke in verse, sought odd company. The diagnosis: young man in love. But since there was no woman involved, the doctor concluded he was in love with himself. "There are people," he said, "who discover from their youth a most amorous inclination to themselves. . . . There are some people who are far gone in this passion of self-love; they keep a secret intrigue with themselves and hide it from all the world besides. This Patient has not the least care of the Reputation of his Beloved, he is downright scandalous in his behavior with himself. . . ."

Swift's other traveling surgeon, Dr. Lemuel Gulliver, Greenacre reminds us, had his early training under a master named Bates. "My good *Master Bates,* dying in two years after and I having few friends, my business began to fail; for my conscience would not suffer me to imitate the bad practice of too many among my brethren." Greenacre raises the question whether this "apparent pun in words can possibly be significant. Swift's peculiar and varied relation to language in which punning has a conspicuous place lends support to the notion that this might even be a sly conscious trick of self-revelation. . . . In the earlier *Scriblerus* version, the confession is more explicit but is disowned through the device of attributing the disturbance to a patient; in the Gulliver account, it is admitted but concealed in the pun" (p. 99).

It is in the Third Voyage, however, that the greatest exposition of masturbation fantasies appear. Gulliver reaches an island perfectly round in shape, which floated in space, moves up and down, and is so delicately balanced that the tenderest hand can propel it. In a footnote, Greenacre (p. 100) writes, "The utilization of those current scientific fantasies of Swift's day seems . . . absolutely in keeping with elaborated masturbation fantasies, which may occur detached from masturbation or with the peculiarly prolonged and sometimes incomplete masturbation of the latency period in children who have especially little resolution of the Oedipus complex. The child, in the latency period, is especially involved with understanding the mechanics of the world around him, and when this is combined with his unresolved masturbation urges, the fantasies of the mechanics of the body are combined with unusual intensity with similar ones regarding external objects and surroundings. Such thinking may last throughout

life and is sometimes valuably productive. That Swift saw the dangers
of these ruminations limited to masturbatory states is obvious from his
descriptions of the Laputans."

Slightly more than two decades after the appearance of *Gulliver's
Travels,* John Cleland (1749) published his *Memoirs of a Woman of
Pleasure,* more familiarly known as "Fanny Hill" after its heroine.
While the theme of the *Memoirs* is unspotted female virtue, considered
as its own reward, Cleland shows how lust is sanctified by the powers of
love. Fanny is 15 years old when she is taken into Mother Brown's fancy
London brothel. In at least five separate passages, Phoebe, an experienced hand in the world's oldest profession, breaks Fanny in by having
the latter masturbate her, or indulge in mutual masturbation, or
practice on herself, until Fanny is left in an intolerably aroused semi-
satisfied condition. She is rescued from the bordello by Charles, falls in
love, and has her first experience of intercourse with him. Among the
sexual practices Charles teaches Fanny is testicular masturbation. Her
description follows:

> Presently he guided my hand lower, to that part in which nature
> and pleasure keep their stores in concert, so aptly fasten'd and hung
> on to the root of their first instrument and minister, that not improp-
> erly he might be styl'd their purse-bearer too: there he made me
> feel distinctly, through their soft cover, the cover, the contents, a
> pair of roundish balls, that seem'd to play within, and elude all
> pressure but the tenderest, from without [p. 55].

Thus Cleland indicated vividly the pleasure that exists in testicular
and scrotal stimulation. Along with the primary pleasurable aspect of
this phenomenon, Glenn (1959) stipulates a displacement from the
penis as well. Testicular pressure, producing pain, serves to evoke
masochistic gratification.

In describing the story, "The Nose," by Nikolai Gogol (1835),
Kanzer (1955) states that the Russian author's literary biographers
reveal him as a lifelong masturbator who probably never had sexual
contact with a woman. "Gogol's symbolic use of nasal imagery was by
no means entirely unconscious. The phallic connotations of the nose
were well known to his contemporaries . . . and one journal actually
rejected 'The Nose' because of the obscenity.... In his desire to
project his nose from him, he apparently tried to fight off autoerotic
temptations and to punish himself for such desires. His masturbatory

fantasies were satisfied and were even of assistance in this process by concocting ridiculous adventures for the detached nose which, freed from the rest of the body, could be permitted to follow to some extent its wayward inclinations" (p. 120).

The Victorian period, in its flight from candid sexuality, produced few if any illustrations of masturbation in fiction other than what is to be found in the pornography of the age. The latter includes Frank Harris' *My Life and Loves,* the anonymous *My Secret Life,* the serialized stories that appeared in *The Pearl, A Journal of Facetiae and Voluptuous Reading,* and the *Amatory Experiences of a Surgeon* by the pseudonymous James Campbell. These are but a few among a large number of slightly differentiated variations within a highly conventionalized form. The compelling fear of Victorian sexologists was the fear of masturbation; their pornographic productions were "written primarily for masturbators, by masturbators, and are themselves structurally and functionally very much like masturbation" (Stoehr, 1967-1968, p. 32). The nineteenth-century underworld of literature does not serve a fruitful purpose here.

Perhaps the only reference to masturbation in the "legitimate" literature of the period is concealed in decent Victorian metaphor, as interpreted by Goldfarb (1970). It is George Meredith's *The Ordeal of Richard Feverel* (1859), wherein an act of rowing, seen in the novel's context, is viewed as representing an act of masturbation. In Chapter 17, Richard sublimates his libidinal urges by writing poetry. His father, Sir Austin, considering this unmanly, burns the manuscripts and forbids him to continue, urging him to indulge in manly sports. During the night following this scene, Richard tosses fitfully in his sleep, awakens at five in the morning, and wanders outdoors. Sir Austin, discovering Richard's couch "a picture of a tempest" and the room frightfully disarranged, recognizes his son's sexual needs. By now, Richard is at the boathouse, heeding his father's advice and, symbolically, masturbating.

> Strong pulling is an excellent medical remedy for certain classes of fever. Richard took to it instinctively. The clear fresh water, burnished with sunrise, sparkled against his arrowy prow: the soft deep shadows curled smiling away from his gliding keel. Overhead solitary morning unfolded itself, from blossom to bud, from bud to flower; still delicious changes of light and colour, to whose influ-

ences he was heedless as he shot under willows and aspens, and across sheets of river-reaches, pure mirrors to his upper glory, himself the sole tenant of the stream.

After the "shot" of ejaculation, Richard feels relieved. "He had pulled through his first feverish energy." Some time later, he "lapsed into that musing quietude which follows strenuous exercise."

However obscure this passage might be, there was nothing subtle about the witty and pungent speech Mark Twain delivered to a stag dinner at the Stomach Club in Paris in 1879, entitled, "Some Thoughts on the Science of Onanism." It was so broadly humorous that even its title was suppressed by Twain's biographer (Ferguson, 1943). Another biographer (Kaplan, 1966, pp. 221-222), describes Clemens as "a Victorian gentleman who tacitly accepted a double standard even if he did not take advantage of it and who, at one and the same time, believed that prostitution was a necessary evil and occasional convenience but also denied the existence of any kind of urgent sexuality in the women of his own circle and social rank. He also made a rigid distinction between smoking-room sexuality and drawing-room purity." Thus, Clemens could be smutty and lusty, as we know from his pornographic novel, *1601*. In the talk to the Stomach Club, he contributed a salutary cynicism to the topic of masturbation, exposing with devastating irreverence the hypocritical attitudes of the day. "He paid tribute to the high antiquity of masturbation and joked that modern progress and improvement now assigned to it somewhat the same social dignity as flatulence. His talk . . . could be traced to a favorite joke of Artemus Ward's about 'playing the lone hand' " (Kaplan, 1966).[1]

Barchilon and Kovel (1966) looked at the sequence of events in Twain's *Huckleberry Finn* (1883) that were linked associatively and polarized, much as they would have been in free associations. For example, the title of Chapter 10 is "What Comes of Handlin' Snake-Skin." It deals with castration anxiety connected with masturbation through a derivative, the bad luck that befalls those who touch a snake skin. "Jim tells Huck, 'It was the worst bad luck in the world to touch a snakeskin with my hands'. Huck denies this at first but becomes convinced when his next venture with a snake leads to the near-fatal

---

[1] The speech is still unpublished, but may be read in Notebook 13 of the Mark Twain Papers in the University of California Library, at Berkeley.

biting of Jim by the snake's mate. . . . When Jim survives, 'I made up
my mind I wouldn't ever take a-holt of a snakeskin again with my
hands,' Jim underlines the theme, 'he druther see the new moon over
his left shoulder as much as a thousand times than take up a snakeskin
in his hand' " (pp. 59-60). Chapter 3, as Barchilon and Kovel point
out, contains a transparent symbol of autoeroticism. In it, Tom Sawyer
tells Huck that for the boys' gang to gain any loot, it would have to be
"done by enchantment," specifically by rubbing a lamp to invoke a
genie, in the manner of Aladdin. Huck is as skeptical as ever, and "I
thought all this over for two or three days, and then I reckoned I would
see if there was anything in it. I got an old tin lamp and an iron ring,
and went out in the woods and rubbed till I sweat like an Injun,
calculating to build a palace and sell it; but it warn't no use, none of
the genies come" (p. 18). This strikes Barchilon and Kovel "as remarkably suggestive of the pre-ejaculatory masturbation of latency"
(p. 791).

It was not until the twentieth century that novelists began to write
about masturbation, still largely in symbolic terms but more overtly
expressed. D. H. Lawrence's short story, "The Rocking Horse Winner"
(1926), is an example of exquisitely symbolic literary autoeroticism
which follows the style of the fairy tale in detail. All the ingredients are
there: the economy of language and the style, magic and primitive
thinking, animism, the wicked witch-mother and the simple son.
Indeed, the hobby horse is very common in folklore and there are
accounts of rituals in which their riders rocked themselves into a trance
in order to attain powers of prophecy—which is precisely what happens here. Certain uncanny experiences of equilibrium and space may
be remnants of infantile sexuality. Fenichel (1945) said:

> In psychoanalytic practice, we have the habit of stating, when
> sensations of this kind come up, such as unclear rotating objects,
> rhythmically approaching and receding objects, sensations of cre-
> scendo and decrescendo, that "primal scene material is approach
> ing.". . . It is well known that while falling asleep the inhibiting
> forces decrease before the drives do, and that, therefore, in this state
> the temptation to masturbate is most intense. In falling asleep, also,
> archaic types of ego feelings are regressively experienced before con-
> sciousness is lost and a high percentage of these "archaic ego feelings"
> are felt as sensations of equilibrium and space. A normal person is
> not bothered much by these sensations. He may even not be aware of

them, unless he expressly directs his attention to them. This is different in persons whose infantile masturbation is represented by these sensations, and these again are mainly persons who have had primal scene experiences. A minority of these persons may still enjoy such sensations as a kind of masturbation equivalent. The majority, after repression, are afraid of them, and in extreme cases such fears may become the cause of severe sleep disturbances [p. 215].

According to Anna Freud (1954), rocking is an autoerotic substitute for satisfactions originally provided by the mother, with the specific aim of re-establishing body contact with her. The mother in "The Rocking Horse Winner" is an infantile, spoiled creature who complains bitterly and incessantly of her husband's failure to provide for her adequately. Her little son, Paul, discovers that by riding his hobby horse furiously he can predict the winning mount in races. The gardener and Paul's uncle are privy to his secret and amass a small fortune for the boy, which Paul turns over to his mother. But it is not enough for her. Then Paul's rocking becomes frenzied, he is "wild-eyed and strange . . . his big blue eyes blazing with a sort of madness." He develops a mysterious fever; on his deathbed, he gives the name of the Derby winner. The similarities between this tale and the rubbing in "Aladdin's Lamp" and "The Tinder Box" are apparent. Paul's violent and rhythmic rocking and its climax correspond to masturbatory activity (Fraiberg, 1954), just as riding the horse ("riding" was once the word for intercourse) stands for the child's imitation of the sex act.

In his article on "Pornography and Obscenity," Lawrence (1929) made a number of observations on masturbation.

When the grey ones wail that the young man and young woman went and had sexual intercourse, they are bewailing the fact that the young man and the young woman didn't go separately and masturbate. Sex must go somewhere, especially in young people. So, in our glorious civilization, it goes in masturbation. And the mass of our popular literature, the bulk of our popular amusements just exists to provoke masturbation. . . . We prefer that the people shall masturbate. . . . Masturbation is the one thoroughly secret act of the human being, more secret even than excrementation. . . . The great danger of masturbation lies in its merely exhaustive nature. . . . In masturbation there is nothing but loss. . . . There is merely the spending away of a certain force, and no return. The body remains, in a sense, a corpse, after the act of self-abuse . . . the only positive effect of masturbation is that it seems to release a certain mental energy, in some people. But it is mental energy which manifests itself always in the same way, in a vicious circle of false and easy sympathy, sentimentalities [pp. 79-82, *passim*].

Thus, even as enlightened a creative writer as Lawrence fell prey to the still pervasive Victorian ideation on the subject. Dr. William Acton's best seller, *Functions and Disorders of the Reproductive Organs in Childhood, Youth, Adult Age and Advanced Life,* which ran through eight editions between 1857 and 1894, advised that semen plays a "most important part in the human economy" and that semen "is a highly organized fluid, requiring the expenditure of much vital force in its elaboration and its explusion" (Hale, 1971, p. 36). The model on which the notion of semen is formed is clearly that of money (Marcus, 1966). Up until the end of the nineteenth century, the chief English colloquial expression for the orgasm was "to spend," which bespeaks a complex shift to the contemporary "to come." Thus, Lawrence's very vocabulary betrayed him, retaining as it did the unconscious use of the economic motif of the nineteenth century concerning masturbation, as well as the use of Victorian moralistic labels, as in "self-abuse."

While it cannot be said that James Joyce was obsessed with masturbation, he was clearly troubled by it. West (1970) found frequent mention made of it as well in the diary and autobiography of James's brother, Stanislaus (1958). Throughout the year 1904, when James was writing his story, "The Sisters," Stanislaus often remarked about masturbation in his diary.

In Joyce's masterpiece, *Ulysses* (1918), there are at least four masturbatory passages. "Dr." Buck Mulligan, in the bacchanalian scene, jocularly diagnoses "Dr." Leopold Bloom as "prematurely bald from selfabuse, perversely idealistic in consequence, a reformed rake, and has metal teeth." In the Nausicaä scene with the fireworks on the strand, Gerty MacDowell is seated on the ground. As she leans back to watch, she reveals her "graceful beautifully shaped legs." Leopold Bloom, a voyeur with a fetish for women's underclothing, observes Gerty and her accidentally exposed undergarments. His heart pounds, his breathing becomes hoarse. A long Roman candle is fired and goes up over the trees, higher and higher. ". . . and then the Roman candle burst and it was like a sigh of O! and everyone cried O! O! in raptures and it gushed out of it a stream of rain gold hair threads and they shed and ah! they were all green dewy stars falling with golden, O so lovely!" Just as the rocket reaches its apogee and explodes, Bloom reaches a climax and ejaculates. In the free association passages that follow, he frets because the semen feels "cold and clammy. After effect not pleasant" (p. 363). And a bit later, "Lord, I am wet" (p. 365). And again, "This wet is very unpleasant. Stuck. Well the foreskin is not back. Better detach" (p. 367). And finally, "Tired I feel now. Will I get up? O wait. Drained all manhood out of me, little wretch" (p. 370). Very little has changed in the half-century since Joyce wrote this. In Gerald Green's (1971) spy spoof, *Faking It or the Wrong Hungarian,* Ben Bloodworth, a minor novelist unintentionally turned spy, has a misfire after an abortive seduction attempt. "As she left me, I went off. Out of me it came, one endless gush of spleen, liver, lights, both kidneys and thirty feet of intestine. As Joyce reminded us, through old Leopold Bloom, warm at first, cold later. I rested there, drained, deflated, gutted, a beached dead mackeral" (p. 123).

In the famous last section of *Ulysses,* in which Joyce was among the first of novelists to use the psychoanalytic technique of free association, Mollie Bloom is lying in bed and ruminating about her life. The interior monologue continues for forty-five pages, and at one point Mollie recalls when she was fifteen years old, living in Spain, and met an English naval lieutenant, one Mulveys.

> . . . that old servant Ines told me that one drop even if it got into you at all after I tried with the Banana but I was afraid it might break and get lost up in me somewhere yes because they once took something down out of a woman that was up there for years covered with limesalts theyre all mad to get in there where they come out of youd think they could never get far enough up and then theres a wonderful feeling there all the time so tender how did we finish it off yes O yes I pulled him off into my handkerchief pretending not to be excited but I opened my legs I wouldnt let him touch me inside my petticoat I had a skirt opening up the side I tortured the life out of him first tickling him I loved rousing that dog in the hotel rrrsst awokwokawok his eyes shut and a bird flying below us he was shy all the same I liked him like that morning I made him blush a little when I got over him that way when I unbuttoned him and took his out and drew back the skin it had a kind of eye in it. . . [p. 745].

Joyce's thematic concern with masturbation remained remarkably constant. In *A Portrait of the Artist as a Young Man* (1916), his description of young Stephen Daedalus's anguish with his surging libidinal urges marks another milestone in English literature, for the pattern was followed by innumerable imitators. "After Stephen's encounter with the prostitute, his barriers of 'order-elegance' give way entirely to the tides of the actual. His shame and fear mount with increasing intensity, until finally he regards even his very genitals with monumental disgust: What a horrible thing! Who made it to be like that, a bestial part of the body able to understand bestially and desire bestially? Was that then he or an inhuman thing moved by a lower soul? His soul sickened at the thought of a torpid snaky life feeding itself out of the tender marrow of his life and fattening upon the slime of lust. O why was that so? O why?" (p. 185).

Three years before *A Portrait* was published, E. M. Forster (1913) finished his autobiographical novel, *Maurice,* but publication was not permitted until 1972, after the novelist's death. In the following excerpt, Forster does not permit Maurice the sickening anguish Joyce allowed Stephen, but renders rather an intellectualized, detached sense of desolation and despair. "As soon as his body developed he became obscene. He supposed some special curse had descended on him, but he could not help it, for even when receiving Holy Communion filthy thoughts would arise in his mind. . . . He longed for smut but heard little and contributed less, and his chief indecencies were solitary. Books: the school library was immaculate. . . . Thoughts: he had a dirty little collection. Acts: he desisted from these after the novelty was over, finding that they brought him more fatigue than pleasure" (p. 23).

The presence of fecal, urinary, or masturbatory imagery is often disguised in literature not because it is wicked or evil, but rather because it is unbeautiful, unheroic, or infantile (Burke, 1963). Virginia Woolf used obvious symbolism to disguise what otherwise would have been then unpublishable. In *Mrs. Dalloway* (1925), Peter Walsh, returning from a long stay in India, goes to see an old love, Clarissa, who years before had rejected him for a rival, Richard Dalloway. According to the story Peter tells Clarissa, he has returned to England to marry a woman he met in India. However, the reader soon wonders whether Peter does not still love Clarissa, and he begins to look for clues that will help him define the relationship. Steinberg (1953) points them out:

> Putting his hand into his pocket, he [Peter] took out a large pocket-knife and half opened the blade [p. 59].
> "How heavenly to see you again!" she [Clarissa] exclaimed. He had his knife out. That's so like him, she thought [p. 60].
> ... and he took out his knife quite openly—his old horn-handled knife which Clarissa could swear he had had these thirty years—and clenched his fist upon it. What an extraordinary habit that was, Clarissa thought; always playing with his knife [p. 65].
> For Heaven's sake, leave your knife alone! She cried to herself in irrepressible irritation. . . [p. 69]. I know what I'm up against, he thought, running his finger along the blade of his knife, Clarissa and Dalloway and all the rest of them; but I'll show Clarissa—and then to his utter surprise, suddenly thrown by those uncontrollable forces thrown through the air, he burst into tears [p. 69] . . . [After leaving Clarissa, Peter sees a young woman on the street who becomes "the very woman he had always had in mind."] Straightening himself and stealthily fingering his pocket-knife he started after her. . ., this excitement, which seemed even with its back turned to shed on him a light which connected them [p. 79].

Most psychiatrists and psychologists have not been overly concerned with the varieties of methods used in masturbatory practice. For them, it is not the activity as such that engages attention, but rather "the problems which it raises for the patient's psychic economy, such as guilt, anxiety, conflict (both intrapsychic and with the surround) and a variety of symptoms" (Spitz, 1962, p. 283). However, in later footnotes to the "Three Essays," Freud (1905) pointed out not only that "masturbation represents the executive agency of the whole of infantile sexuality..." (p. 189n) but also that: "Unusual techniques in carrying out masturbation in later years seem to point to the influence of a prohibition against masturbation which has been overcome" (p. 188n). Miller (1969) declares that careful questioning about the specific technique and subsequent associations to it can lead to a surprising wealth of associations. He emphasizes the importance of the particular method of masturbation as an attempt to discharge certain unconscious fantasies while keeping them repressed. Lihn (1970) cites the case of a young man whose preferred masturbation ritual was to don his mother's panties, conceal his penis between his thighs, and with the panties apply pressure to his penis while looking at himself in the bathroom mirror, imagining himself to be a woman with a penis. This ritual was evidence of the patient's struggle between identification with his mother and establishing a separate identity from, and an object relationship with, her.

There are several fictional illustrations that describe unusual methods of masturbating. In Kingsley Amis's (1973) *The Riverside Villas Murder*, two fourteen-year-old English boys, Reg and Peter, are discussing a "newly" discovered way to masturbate. Underneath the banter, their anxiety reveals itself.

> "Hey, I had a super one in the bath last night. The old soapy-hand method. Do you do that much?"
> "A bit."
> "Do you think it does you any harm, you know, doing it?"
> "I shouldn't think so. You know Forester?"
> "Yes," said Reg, meaning he well knew who Forester was.
> "He says wasting time doesn't do you any harm as long as you don't take it too seriously."
> "Hey, that's pretty good. As far as I'm concerned, sometimes I take it seriously and sometimes I don't. I always think it's marvellous it being so easy. You know, nothing to learn or practise."
> "Same here. It's like a free strawberry sundae really" [p. 105].

A far more unusual method concerns a casual friend of the narrator in Henry Miller's (1934) *Tropic of Cancer*.

> Van Norden . . . found a new diversion. He's found that it's less annoying to masturbate. I was amazed when he broke the news to me. I didn't think it possible for a guy like that to find any pleasure in jerking himself off. I was still more amazed when he explained to me how he goes about it. He had "invented" a new stunt, so he put it. "You take an apple," he says, "and you bore out the core. Then you rub some cold cream on the inside so as it doesn't melt too fast. Try it some time. It'll drive you crazy at first. Anyway, it's cheap and you don't have to waste much time [p. 263].

Another example, from Philip Roth's (1969) seminal venture, *Portnoy's Complaint*, follows closely the masturbation technique in *Tropic of Cancer*, with the singular exception in the last sentence.

On an outing of our family association, I once cored an apple, saw to my astonishment (and with the aid of my obsession) what it looked like, and ran off into the woods to fall upon the orifice of the fruit, pretending that the cool and mealy hole was actually the legs of that mythical being who always called me Big Boy when she pleaded for what no girl in all recorded history had ever had. "Oh shove it in me, Big Boy," cried the cored apple that I banged silly on that picnic. "Big Boy, Big Boy, oh give me all you've got," begged the empty milk bottle that I kept hidden in our storage bin in the basement, to drive wild after school with my vaselined upright. "Come, Big Boy, come," screamed the maddened piece of liver that, in my own insanity, I bought one afternoon at a butcher shop and, believe it or not, violated behind a billboard on the way to a bar mitzvah lesson [pp. 18-19].

Roth gives a detailed portrait of the Portnoy family. The father is constipated, passive, hard-working but unsuccessful, the mother powerful, seductive, obsessive, castrating, and overprotective. Alexander Portnoy, the protagonist, discovers at the age of nine that he has an undescended testicle, and he describes graphically his frantic anxieties about sexual identity. While cryptorchism in itself is not pathogenic, and only becomes so within the matrix of a disturbed parent-child relationship (Blos, 1960), in the Portnoy family setting the genital defect assumed a dominant importance. As Alexander himself recognized, his obsession with masturbation and sex was the driving force of his life. As a child Portnoy masturbated, preferably on the toilet, in line with his father's constipation which emerges as a central experience leading to a negative identification. Bettelheim (1969) says, "The father cannot let go. The son cannot hold anything in, or hold on to anyone. The father, out of incessant fear for the future, chose and stuck to his job of life insurance salesman. This is internalized by his son as fear for his masculinity. And for this he finds only one defense: the excessive masturbation that seems to prove his body is working, but at the price of self-disgust. Because what he wants is not a penis that gives pleasure, but an instrument that expels its content, a seeking of self-assurance, which his kind of masturbation cannot give him" (p. 5). When Portnoy recalls masturbating into the liver which was then eaten at dinner, he has no inkling that this shows an extreme sexualization of the oral stage.

What is popularly known as the Jewish mother syndrome, given currency by *Portnoy's Complaint*, is touched on in this excerpt. Portnoy is on Dr. Spielvogel's couch, ticking off the countless ways his mother has smothered him.

> I tear off my pants, furiously I grab that battered battering ram to freedom, my adolescent cock, even as my mother begins to call from the other side of the bathroom door. . . . Doctor, do you understand what I was up against? My wang was all I really had that I could call my own. . . . Look, am I exaggerating to think it practically miraculous that I'm ambulatory? The hysteria and the superstition! The watch-its and the be-carefuls! You musn't do this, you can't do that — hold it! don't! . . . Imagine then what my conscience gave me for all that jerking off! The guilt, the fears — the terror bred into my bones! . . . Doctor Spielvogel, this is my life, my only life. . . . Why are they screaming still, "Watch out! Don't do it! Alex — no!" and why, alone on my bed in New York, why am I still hopelessly beating my meat? Doctor, what do you call this sickness I have? . . . Oh my secrets, my shame, my palpitations, my flushes, my sweats! . . . Doctor, I can't stand any more being frightened like this over nothing! Bless me with manhood! Make me brave! Make me strong! Make me whole! Enough of being a nice Jewish boy, publicly pleasing my parents while privately pulling my putz! Enough! [pp. 31-36, *passim*].

The symptom of masturbation tends to be a circular mechanism, for the lack of satisfaction in the act and the resulting damming up of libido causes further and excessive masturbation, resulting in the compulsion. Much of the whining and the exaggerated hilarity in *Portnoy's Complaint* masks a hysteria, poorly concealing the glibness and the dishonesty of self-deception and self-pity. Alexander's childhood polymorphous perversity and pure pain are relived daily in the disguises of adult behavior. The fact that he seems incapable of any sustained relationship with a woman he attributes to his overactive sexuality, though he makes perceptive and self-mocking jokes about the incestuous wishes he is unconsciously struggling with. The central experience of Alexander's consciousness is his incessant, compulsive masturbation. He might well say of himself, "I masturbate, therefore I am."

In the light of Augustine's injunctions against carnal pleasures, contemporary Catholic novelists, such as Byrne, Peters, Farrell, and McHale, among others, have dwelt on the sinfulness of masturbation and in particular the guilt feelings it arouses. In Fritz Peters' *Finistère*,

(1925), one of the earliest novels to trace with psychological accuracy the development of homosexuality from childhood on, there is a scene where young Matthew's sense of shame and guilt about masturbation is intense.

> The first time it had been terrifying, and what was worse, painful. But even with the pain there had been some compulsion that had forced him on and on. Gradually the pain had disappeared—the physical pain, at any rate. But it had been replaced by something else, something that had formed inside him, between his ribs, and hurt almost as much. It was always afterwards that he felt it, hating himself, making promises and vows for the future. But then the next time, he would be beaten again, trapped by himself, unable to resist. . . .
> He was startled by his mother's voice at the door. It was a good thing he had thought to lock it again!
> "Hurry up, darling," she said. "You're keeping us waiting!"
> "I'll be right out," he answered quickly and seized the towel from the rack behind the door. He dried himself and then tore into his clothes. His haste was not because he had delayed them, but because he had been caught—almost—and his rush to dress himself seemed to make up for his sense of shame [p. 55].

The rage and disgust a character named Marney feels for himself in Lawrence Durrell's (1937) *The Black Book* is seen in this passage. He "is fighting his dark angel," but the odds are too great.

> He is forced to his feet, forced to rock down to the lavatory and stand rigidly over the pan, furiously knocking himself off, feeling his breath patter faster and faster in his mouth, the bullets of feeling riddle him from head to foot. He holds his penis away from him, as if it were a potato being cleaned in a sink. Afterward he is forced to lean his head against the cold wall. Tiny cries of rage and disgust come from him. He is doomed. Tenderly he buttons himself up and climbs the stairs. He is afraid. The dark angel hangs over him [p. 106].

It is hardly news that neurotic symptoms and distortions arise out of the conflict about masturbation. If masturbatory acts or fantasies are considered degrading, they interfere with the person's self-concept and his ability to function with equanimity. Even though masturbation may serve to avoid an explosion, the stigma attached to it may impair

the individual's creativity (Marcus, 1962). The intense guilt feelings
and shame reactions generated by masturbation are evident in a
passage from Farrell's *Young Lonigan* (1938) which is reminiscent of
the *Finistère* excerpt. "Studs had stayed in the bathroom too long, as
he was staying most of these days. The old man bellowed that dinner
was ready. Studs came out, feeling relieved. He muttered a hasty act of
contrition, promising God and the Blessed Virgin that he would try his
hardest to break the sixth commandment by thought, word or
deed" (p. 159). Somewhat later, the father suspects Studs' behavior. In
what passes for sex education, he delivers a muted lecture, in which
nothing is called by its right name and there is the usual recipe for
salvation. The customary vulgarity of language used is all the more
vulgar because it is suggestive rather than explicit (Lipton, 1965).
" 'I'm your father and it's a father's duty to instruct his son and you see
now if you get a little itch . . . well you don't want to start . . . rubbin'
yourself . . . you know what I mean' " (p. 163). And silence, with the
boy and the father staring at each other self-consciously, and the boy
suddenly made ashamed of his own body, dashing out of the house,
needing air and sunlight in an effort to forget the whole scene.

The precocious narrator in Stephen Vizinczey's (1965) *In Praise of
Older Women* relates his fears and anxieties during early adolescence:
"Back in cadet school I had heard a lot about the dangers of sex. At
masturbation time, after the lights were turned out in the dormitory,
we used to scare each other with stories about boys who turned into
imbeciles because they played with themselves or had intercourse with
girls. I remember one tale about a kid who cracked up just from
thinking about women. By the time I got to the American Army camp
I had lost all my religious fears, but I still believed that if a boy
had a very strong sex-drive, his other faculties would be stunted. And I
worried a great deal about myself" (p. 34). Shawn, a minor character
in *What Happened* by Merle Miller (1972), is an only child after three
miscarriages; his father had been fifty when he was born, his mother
forty-four. "True, my father made a lot of money in the drug business,
and we never kept pigs in the parlor, but they are both still obsessed
with crucifixes and blotchy reproductions of the Christ Child and Our
Blessed Virgin, by the smell of incense and Hail Marys and by priests
with pimply faces and many hands, wanting to talk about the evils of
masturbation" (p. 207).

But you don't have to be Catholic or Jewish to entertain guilty and shameful feelings over masturbation. Yukio Mishima, the brilliant Japanese novelist who spectacularly committed ritual hara-kiri in 1970 after an unsuccessful attempt to incite a rightist protest movement, wrote a number of novels, most of which reveal a preoccupation with homosexuality, blood, sadism, and violent death. In one of them, significantly titled *Confessions of a Mask*, Mishima (1958) tells the tale of tubercular, anemic Kochan who liked to dress in his mother's clothes, was not allowed to play with boys, and who early on was attracted to men in tight pants. He had sadomasochistic masturbation fantasies of tying a handsome youth to a pillar, plunging a knife into his breast, and watching the blood spurt. At fourteen, Kochan's parents took him to a doctor because his hands "were the color of dead grass."

> He was an agreeable man, a friend of the family's. When they began asking him for details about my trouble, he said: "Well, let's see what the answer book has to say about anemia." The examination was over, and I was at the doctor's elbow, where I could peep into the book from which he began reading aloud. The family was seated facing him and could not see the pages of the book.
>
> "So then, next there's etiology—the causes of the disease. Hookworm—these are a frequent cause. This is probably the boy's case. We'll have a stool examination. Next there's chlorosis. But it's rare, and anyway it's a woman's disease—"
>
> At this point the book gave a further cause for anemia, but the doctor did not read it aloud. Instead, he skipped over it, mumbling the rest of the passage in his throat as he closed the book. But I had seen the phrase that he had omitted. It was 'self-pollution'.
>
> I could feel my heart pounding with shame. The doctor had discovered my secret [pp. 91-92].

Later in the novel, Kochan asked rhetorically:

> Where could I have obtained enlightenment? Novels abound in kissing scenes, but none that I had read made any reference to such a thing as erections on such occasions. This was only natural, as it is scarcely a subject to be described in a novel. . . . The period called adolescence . . . seemed to have come to pay us a sick visit. Having attained puberty, the boys seemed to do nothing but always think immoderately about women, exude pimples, and write sugary verses . . . They had read, first this study of sex, which emphasized the harmful aspects of masturbation, and then that, which spoke

reassuringly of no great harmful effects; as a result, they too appeared to finally become enthusiastic practitioners [pp. 108-109].

More than a hundred years after Cleland's vivid descriptive scenes of Fanny Hill masturbating, there is increasing depiction of female masturbation in contemporary fiction. In Erica Jong's (1973) *Fear of Flying,* the narrator recalls how she "saw Dr. Schrift for one memorable year when I was fourteen and starving myself to death in penance for having finger-fucked on my parents' livingroom couch" (p. 4). With her second husband, Bennett, a psychoanalyst lying asleep beside her, who keeps long silences and great distance from her, she touches herself to prove she is not dead.

She thinks of the first two weeks of her broken leg. She used to masturbate constantly then to convince herself that she could feel something besides pain . . . She runs her hands down her belly. Her right forefinger touches the clitoris while the left forefinger goes deep inside her, pretending to be a penis. What does a penis feel, surrounded by those soft, collapsing caves of flesh? Her finger is too small. She puts in two and spreads them . . . Lonely, lonely, lonely. She moves her fingers to that rhythm, feeling the two inside get creamy and the clitoris get hard and red . . . "Who do you think of when you masturbate?" her German analyst asked. *"Who do you sink of?" I sink therefore I am.* She thinks of no one, really, and of everyone. Of her analyst and of her father. No, not her father. She cannot think of her father. Of a man on a train. A man under the bed. A man with no face. His face is blank. His penis has one eye. It weeps. She feels the convulsions of the orgasm suck violently around her fingers. Her hand falls to her side and then she sinks into a dead sleep [p. 119].

In *Margaret and I* by Kate Wilhelm (1971), masturbation is also treated with great relevance. Margaret is a borderline schizophrenic, and in many ways like Isadora in *Fear of Flying,* sorely troubled by her sexual relationship with her husband. Often after the latter's deliberate, calculated passion, Isadora was dissatisfied enough to masturbate.

She backed into the seat of the toilet and sat down on the edge of it, spreading her legs wide apart, and tentatively at first, then harder and harder, she thrust her fingers inside her vagina as far as she could, and wished she had something she could use, she wanted to hurt herself, to be filled to choking. Her other hand left the nipple to rub savagely at the clitoris and she felt the welling, the fire raging now, and at last the final climax ripped through her, and with a sobbing cry she felt her convulsive orgasm, and the hot flow of fluid scalded her hand. She jerked it free, and fell to her knees, with her head cradled on her arms on the side of the bathtub, and she sobbed and wept, her body heaving with the violence of her reaction for many minutes [Wilhelm, pp. 184-185].

Henry Miller's Germaine, a prostitute in *Tropic of Cancer* (1934), does not experience the distress of Margaret, but rather is exuberantly narcissistic while she plays with herself.

As she stood up to dry herself, still talking to me pleasantly, suddenly she dropped the towel and, advancing towards me leisurely, she commenced rubbing her pussy affectionately, stroking it with her two hands, caressing it, patting it, patting it . . . As she flung herself on the bed, with legs spread wide apart, she cupped it with her hands and stroked it some more, murmuring all the while in that hoarse, cracked voice of hers that it was good, beautiful, a treasure, a little treasure . . . That was the only place where she experienced any life — down there where she clutched herself with both hands [pp. 39-41, *passim*].

In another novel by Mishima (1965), *The Sailor Who Fell from Grace with the Sea*, there is an opening scene in which Noboru, a thirteen-year-old voyeur, watches his widowed mother through a peephole in connecting bedrooms in their home in Yokohama. "She was only thirty-three and her slender body, shapely from playing tennis every week, was beautiful. Usually she got right into bed after touching her flesh with perfumed water, but sometimes she would sit at the dressing table and gaze into the mirror at her profile for minutes at a time, eyes hollow as though ravaged by fever, scented fingers rooted between her thighs. On these nights, mistaking the crimson of her bundled nails for blood, Noboru trembled" (p. 7). With a precocious cruelty, Noboru, who later witnesses the primal scene, murders his mother's lover.

If the anemic Kochan, in the previously cited *Confessions of a Mask,* had read Iharu Saikaku's *The Life of an Amorous Woman* (1686), he would not have had reason to complain. The heroine of the novel, a woman of great passion, is unable to satisfy her sexual needs since she lives in the house of a Samurai warrior which is bound by the strictest conventions. "One day, as I was examining a fascinating depiction by Hiskikawa of an erotic scene, I was stirred despite myself to the most intense excitement. I sought then to quench my amorous flames, now with my heel, now with the middle finger of my hand. These were cold and insensible tools indeed for stilling my wanton lust, and soon I was overcome with desire for a more solid form of love." Ivan Morris, who translated and edited this work, comments that the use of the heel is not as startling as it may seem to Western readers when one remembers the traditional Japanese sitting posture and the suppleness resulting from it. Yet, according to Kinsey, the heel is used in the United States as well.

Günter Grass has written an insightful scene in his novel *Cat and Mouse* (1961), involving a group of seven adolescent boys and one girl whose pastime it was to swim to the deck of a half-sunk barge in the harbor and dawdle the day away, occasionally diving below the water's surface in search of sunken treasure. Tulla is preoccupied with the boys' penises and seems to have an obsessive voyeuristic impulse to observe them masturbating.

Calmly, her chin in the cup of her hand, Tulla would look on when Winter or Esch, unable to contain himself, produced his modest offering. Hunching over so that the bones of her spine stuck out, she would gaze at Winter, who was always slow in getting there, and mutter: "Man, that's taking a long time!"

But when, finally, the stuff came and splashed on the rust she would begin to fidget and squirm, she would throw herself down on her belly, make little cat's eyes and look and look, trying to discover heaven-knows-what, turn over, sit up, rise to her knees, stand slightly knock-kneed over the mess, and begin to stir it with a supple big toe, until it foamed rust-red: "Boy! That's the berries! Now you do it, Atze."

Tulla never wearied of this little game—yes, game, the whole thing was all perfectly innocent. "Aw, you do it," she would plead in that whining voice of hers. "Who hasn't done it yet? It's your turn."

She always found some good-natured fool who would get to work even if he wasn't at all in the mood, just to give her something to goggle at. The only one who wouldn't give until Tulla found the right words of encouragement—and that is why I am narrating these heroic deeds—was the great swimmer and diver Joachim Mahlke. While all the rest of us were engaging in this time-honored, nay

Biblical, pursuit, either one at a time or — as the manual put it — with others, Mahlke kept his trunks on and gazed fixedly in the direction of Hela. We felt certain that at home, in his room between snowy owl and Sistine Madonna, he indulged in the same sport.

He had just come up, shivering as usual, and he had nothing to show. Schilling had just been working for Tulla. A coaster was entering the harbor under its own power. "Do it again," Tulla begged, for Schilling was the most prolific of all. Not a single ship in the roadstead. "Not after swimming. I'll do it again tomorrow," Schilling consoled her. Tulla turned on her heel and stood with outspread toes facing Mahlke, who as usual was shivering in the shadow of the pilothouse and hadn't sat down yet. A high-seas tug with a forward gun was putting out to sea.

"Won't you? Aw, do it just once. Or can't you? Don't you want to? Or aren't you allowed to?"

Mahlke stepped half out of the shadow and slapped Tulla's compressed little face left right with his palm and the back of his hand. His mouse [Adam's apple] went wild. So did the screwdriver [which always hung around his neck]. Tulla, of course, didn't shed one single tear, but gave a bleating laugh with her mouth closed; shaking with laughter she arched her india-rubber frame effortlessly into a bridge, and peered through her spindly legs at Mahlke until he said: "OK. Just so you'll shut your yap."

Tulla came out of her contortion and squatted down normally with her legs folded under her, as Mahlke stripped his trunks down to his knees. The children at the Punch-and-Judy show gaped in amazement: a few deft movements emanating from his right wrist, and his pecker loomed so large that the tip emerged from the shadow of the pilothouse and the sun fell on it. Only when we had all formed a semicircle did Mahlke's jumping Jim return to the shadow.

"Won't you let me just for a second?" Tulla's mouth hung open. Mahlke nodded and dropped his right hand, though without uncurving his fingers. Tulla's hands, scratched and bruised as they always were, approached the monster, which expanded under her questioning fingertips; the veins stood out and the glans protruded.

"Measure it!" cried Jürgen Kupka. Tulla spread the fingers of her left hand. One full span and another almost. Somebody and then somebody else whispered: "At least twelve inches!" That was an exaggeration of course. Schilling, who otherwise had the longest, had to take his out, make it stand up, and hold it beside Mahlke's. Mahlke's was first of all a size thicker, second a matchbox longer, and third looked much more grown-up, dangerous, and worthy to be worshiped.

He had shown us again, and then a second time he showed us by producing not one but two mighty streams in quick succession. With his knees not quite together, Mahlke stood by the twisted rail inside the pilothouse, staring out in the direction of the harbor buoy, a little to the rear of the low-lying smoke of the vanishing high-seas tug; a torpedo boat of the *Gull* class was just emerging from the harbor, but he didn't let it distract him. Thus he stood, showing his profile, from the toes extending just over the edge of the watershed in the middle of his hair: strangely enough, the length of his sexual part made up for the otherwise shocking protuberance of his Adam's apple, lending his body an odd, but in its way perfect, harmony.

No sooner had Mahlke finished squirting his first load over the rail than he started in all over again. Winter timed him with his waterproof wrist watch; Mahlke's performance continued for approximately as many seconds as it took the torpedo boat to pass from the tip of the breakwater to the buoy; then, while the torpedo boat was rounding the buoy, he unloaded the same amount again; the foaming bubbles lurched in the smooth, only occasionally rippling swell, and we laughed for joy as the gulls swooped down, screaming for more.

Joachim Mahlke was never obliged to repeat or better this performance, for none of us ever touched his record, certainly not when exhausted from swimming and diving; sportsmen in everything we did, we respected the rules.

For a while Tulla Pokriefke, for whom his prowess must have had the direct appeal, courted him in her way; she would always be sitting by the pilothouse, staring at Mahlke's swimming trunks. A few times she pleaded with him, but he always refused, though good-naturedly [pp. 42-49].

The plight of prisoners in dealing with their sexual frustrations is well known. Homosexuality and masturbation are the two obvious outlets available to them. As psychiatric consultant at a very large prison, Cleckly (1957) has seen little or nothing to suggest that men who enter prison with ordinary sexual orientation think of anything but the unavailable female, whether they masturbate with their hands, avail themselves of a hole in the mattress, or manipulate their genital organ against or within the body of another inmate. Monsieur Meursault, the existentialist protagonist in Albert Camus's (1965) *The*

Stranger, was jailed in Algiers after shooting an Arab thug who had waylaid him.

> I gradually became friendly with the chief jailer, who went the rounds with the kitchen hands at mealtimes. It was he who brought up the subject of women. "That's what the men here grumble about most," he told me.
>
> I said I felt like that myself. "There's something unfair about it." I added, "Like hitting a man when he's down."
>
> "But that's the whole point of it," he said; "that's why you fellows are kept in prison."
>
> "I don't follow."
>
> "Liberty," he said, "means that. You're being deprived of your liberty."
>
> It had never before struck me in that light, but I saw his point. "That's true," I said, "otherwise it wouldn't be punishment."
>
> The jailer nodded. "Yes, you're different, you can use your brains. The others can't. Still, those fellows find a way out; they do it by themselves." With which remark, the jailer left my cell. Next day I did it like the others [pp. 96-97].

The matter-of-fact approach of the jailer is carried to an extreme in Jean Genet's (1963) *Our Lady of the Flowers*, where the action occurs entirely in the fantasy world of the protagonist while he is in his prison cell. Portnoy's obsession seems almost minor by comparison, for Genet is truly obsessed with sperm, murder, betrayal, the sexual orifices, and masturbatory narcissism. His very sentences are ejaculations: "It was a good thing that I raised egoistic masturbation to the dignity of a cult! I have only to begin the gesture and a kind of unclean and supernatural transposition displaces the truth. Everything within me turns worshiper. The external vision of the props of my desire isolates me, far from the world" (p. 139). Genet finally works masturbation into a religious experience.

Masturbation fantasies often have as their core murder, perversion, or incest (Marcus, 1962). Demonstrable evidence for this is offered repeatedly in *Our Lady of the Flowers*: "All by itself the murderer's hand seeks his penis, which is erect. He strokes it through the sheet, gently at first, with the lightness of a fluttering bird, then grips it, squeezes it hard; finally he discharges into the toothless mouth of the strangled old man. He falls asleep" (p. 129).

The masturbation theme in *Our Lady* is so pervasive that Sartre

(1963) calls it an epic of masturbation. "There is only one subject: the pollution of a prisoner in the darkness of his cell; only one hero: the masturbator" (p. 11). The novel is actually a controlled waking dream, with the masturbation fantasies gradually becoming an introspective exploration, revolving around the regressive, infantile narcissism of the masturbator.

There is no question that *Our Lady* is autobiographical projection. Genet is a true maudit: convicted thief, male prostitute, pimp, black-mailer, trafficker in drugs, army deserter, stool pigeon, traitor, glori-fier of violence and torture, fascist. His novel can be viewed as mani-fest content from which inferences on the unconscious associations of masturbation can be made. Valeros (1968) makes this interpretation, concluding that Genet's masturbatory activities are temporary resolu-tions to his motivating anxieties. These anxieties stem from Genet's hunger in the first months of life, so that hunger-danger is uncon-sciously experienced as damage-murder. The self-representation involved in Genet's masturbation is basically bodily, composed mainly of tactile, olfactory, and kinesthetic sensations. Through the uncon-scious fantasies associated with masturbation, the masturbation fan-tasy proper and the autoerotic stimulation, reintegration, and refusion of the split-off parts of the self-representation are achieved. Thus, for Genet, masturbation is an attempt to deal with regressive and primi-tive conflicts, probably originating in his early infancy. The original motivating anxiety for Genet's masturbation resembles primitive, overwhelming hunger; the orgasm achieved through masturbation symbolizes primitive satisfaction at the breast.

Genet's prison cell seems to be crawling with spiders. In the discus-sion of Little Miss Muffet, the spider was interpreted as a symbol for the penis within the female genital. In *Our Lady*, the frequency with which the protagonist expresses his fear of spiders suggests unconscious castration anxiety. The multiple legs of the spider are phallic symbols. They arouse dread because they are reminders of the possibility of the loss of the penis (Newman and Stoller, 1969). Freud (1940) described this mechanism in his interpretation of the Medusa's head symbol. Sterba (1950) has a comment on the subject which might apply to Genet: "Unerring scientific intuition has made man choose two com-parisons from the animal world—the spider and the vampire—to represent the oral danger of object love and particularly the danger of being loved. Both of these are symbols to us of the oral destructive danger of being loved and represent the endangered object as a victim of oral aggression" (p. 21).

Creative writers concerned with masturbation are products of their age. Up to the nineteenth century, references to masturbation had to be veiled and camouflaged — consciously as by Swift, unconsciously as by Meredith. It was rare for a writer to escape the strictures of his society. Even D. H. Lawrence, who felt emancipated from Victorian prudery, was hoisted on its petard. Joyce was considerably more inventive, for he made wiser use of psychoanalytic theory in his fiction. More recently, *Portnoy's Complaint* was publicly discussed as much for its protrayal of a Jewish family as for its acknowledgment of the existence of masturbation in life and not for possible prurience. And with the sexual revolution of the 1970's in full swing, many authors are writing with uninhibited candidness. Kate Wilhelm's vivid description of Margaret masturbating is a measure of this freedom.

In an afterword to his novel on homosexuality, *The City and the Pillar,* Gore Vidal (1965) wrote:

> In its slow way, our society is beginning to shed many of its superstitions about the sexual act. The idea that there is no such thing as "normality" is at last penetrating the tribal consciousness, although the religiously inclined still regard nonprocreative sex as "unnatural," while the statistically inclined regard as "normal" only what the majority does. Confident that most sexual acts are heterosexual, the consensus maintains that heterosexuality, as the preferred form of erotic expression, must be "right." However, following that line of reasoning to its logical conclusion, one would have to recognize that the most frequently performed sexual act is neither hetero- nor homosexual but onanistic, and surely, even in a total democracy, masturbation would not be declared the perfect norm from which all else is deviation. In any case, sex of any sort is neither right nor wrong. It is [pp. 157-158].

TECHNICAL REFERENCES

Barchilon, J. & Kovel, J. S. (1966), Huckleberry Finn: A psychoanalytic study. *Journal of the American Psychoanalytic Association,* 14:775-814.

Bettelheim, B. (1969), Portnoy psychoanalyzed: Therapy notes found in the files of Dr. O. Spielvogel, a New York psychoanalyst. *Midstream,* 15(6):3-10.

Blos, P. (1960), Comments on the psychological consequences of cryptorchism: A clinical study. *The Psychoanalytic Study of the Child,* 15:395-429. New York: International Universities Press.

Burke, K. (1963), The thinking of the body; comments on the imagery of catharsis in literature. *Psychoanalytic Review,* 50:375-418.

Cleckly, H. (1957), *The Caricature of Love: A Discussion of Social, Psychiatric, and Literary Manifestations of Pathologic Sexuality.* New York: Ronald Press.

Davis, R. G. (ed.) (1953), *Ten Modern Masters.* New York: Harcourt, Brace & World.

Edwardes, A. (1959), *The Jewel in the Lotus.* New York: Julian Press.

Engle, B. S. (1942), Melampus and Freud. *Psychoanalytic Quarterly,* 11:83-86.

Fenichel, O. (1945), *The Psychoanalytic Theory of Neurosis.* New York: Norton.

Ferguson, D. (1943), *Mark Twain: Man and Legend.* Indianapolis: Bobbs Merrill.

Fraiberg, S. (1954), Tales of the discovery of the secret treasure. *The Psychoanalytic Study of the Child,* 9:218-241. New York: International Universities Press.

Freud, A. (1954), Problems of infantile neurosis. *The Writings of Anna Freud,* 4:327-355. New York: International Universities Press.

Freud, S. (1905), Three essays on the theory of sexuality. *Standard Edition,* 7:125-243. London: Hogarth Press, 1953.

——— (1916-1917), Introductory lectures on psycho-analysis. *Standard Edition,* 15 & 16. London: Hogarth Press, 1963.

——— (1940), Medusa's head. *Standard Edition,* 18:273-274. London: Hogarth Press, 1955.

Friedländer, K. (1942), Children's books and the function in latency and prepuberty. *American Imago,* 3:129-150.

Glenn, J. (1969), Testicular and scrotal masturbation. *International Journal of Psycho-Analysis,* 50:353-362.

Goldfarb, R. M. (1970), *Sexual Repression and Victorian Literature.* Lewisburg, Pa.: Bucknell University Press.

Greenacre, P. (1955), *Swift and Carroll: A Psychoanalytic Study of Two Lives.* New York: International Universities Press.

Hale, N. G., Jr. (1971), *Freud and the Americans: The Beginnings of Psychoanalysis in the United States, 1876-1917.* New York: Oxford University Press.

Joyce, S. (1958), *My Brother's Keeper.* New York: Viking.

Kanzer, M. (1955), Gogol—a study of wit and paranoia. *Journal of the American Psychoanalytic Association,* 3:110-125.

Kaplan, J. (1966), *Mr. Clemens and Mark Twain: A Biography.* New York: Simon & Schuster.

Lawrence, D. H. (1929), Pornography and obscenity. In: *Sex, Literature and Censorship,* ed. H. T. Moore. New York: Twayne, 1953, pp. 69-88.

Lihn, H. (1970), Fetishism: A case report. *International Journal of Psycho-Analysis,* 51:351-358.

Lipton, L. (1965), *The Erotic Revolution.* Los Angeles: Sherbourne.

Marcus, I. M. (1962), Masturbation. Panel report. *Journal of the American Psychoanalytic Association,* 10:91-101.

Marcus, S. (1966), *The Other Victorians: A Study of Sexuality and Pornography in Mid-Nineteenth-Century England.* New York: Basic Books.

Miller, I. (1969), Unconscious fantasy and masturbatory technique. *Journal of the American Psychoanalytic Association,* 17:826-872.

Newman, L. E. & Stoller, R. J. (1969), Spider symbolism and bisexuality. *Journal of the American Psychoanalytic Association,* 17:862-872.

Peller, L. (1959), Daydreams and children's favorite books: Psychoanalytic comments. *The Psychoanalytic Study of the Child,* 14:414-433. New York: International Universities Press.

Perrin, N. (1969), *Dr. Bowdler's Legacy.* New York: Atheneum.

Róheim, G. (1945), Masturbation fantasies. *Psychiatric Quarterly*, 20:656-673.
_____ (1949), Tom, Tit, Tot. *Psychoanalytic Review*, 36:365-369.
Sartre, J.-P. (1963), Introduction. *Our Lady of the Flowers*. New York: Grove.
Sharpe, E. F. (1943), Cautionary tales. *International Journal of Psycho-Analysis*, 24:41-45.
Spitz, R. A. (1962), Autoeroticism re-examined: The role of early sexual behavior patterns in personality formation. *The Psychoanalytic Study of the Child*, 17:283-315. New York: International Universities Press.
Steinberg, E. (1953), Freudian symbolism and communication. *Literature and Psychology*, 3:2-5.
Sterba, R. F. (1950), On spiders, hanging and oral sadism. *American Imago*, 7:21-28.
Stoehr, T. (1967-1968), Pornography, masturbation and the novel. *Salmagundi*, 2(2):28-56.
Styron, W. (1968), The vice that has no name. *Harper's*, 236:97-100.
Valeros, J. A. (1968), On masturbation: A study of Jean Genet's *Our Lady of the Flowers*. *Psychiatric Quarterly*, 1968, 42:252-262.
Vidal, G. (1965), An afterword. In: *The City and the Pillar*. New York: New American Library, pp. 155-158.
West, M. (1970), Old Cotter and the enigma of Joyce's "The Sisters." *Modern Philology*, 67:370-372.

LITERARY REFERENCES

Andersen, Hans Christian (n.d.), The tinder box. In: *Andersen's Fairy Tales*. New York: Grosset & Dunlap, pp. 335-343.
Amis, Kingsley (1973), *The Riverside Villas Murder*. New York: Harcourt Brace Jovanovich.
Camus, Albert (1965), *The Stranger*. New York: Knopf.
Chaucer, Geoffrey (c. 1388), The parson's tale. In: *The Canterbury Tales*. Chicago: Encyclopaedia Britannica, 1952.
Cleland, John (1749), *Memoirs of a Woman of Pleasure*. New York: Putnam's, 1963.
Coffey, Marilyn (1973), *Marcella*. New York: Charterhouse.
Cohen, Louis (1965), *The Favorite Game*. New York: Avon.
Dickey, James (1970), *Deliverance*. Boston: Houghton, Mifflin.
Durrell, Lawrence (1937), *The Black Book*. New York: Dutton.
Farrell, James T. (1938), *Young Lonigan*. New York: Modern Library.
Faust, Irvin (1971), *Willy Remembers*. New York: Avon, 1972.
Forster, E. M. (1913), *Maurice*. New York: Norton, 1972.
Friedman, Alan (1972), *Hermaphrodeity*. New York: Knopf.
Genet, Jean (1963), *Our Lady of the Flowers*. New York: Grove.
Gogol, Nikolai (1835), The nose. In: *The Overcoat and Other Tales of Good and Evil*. Toronto: McCloud, 1957.
Gould, Lois (1970), *Such Good Friends*. New York: Random House.
Grass, Günter (1961), *Cat and Mouse*. New York: Harcourt, Brace & World.
Green, Gerald (1971). *Faking It, Or The Wrong Hungarian*. New York: Pocket Book, 1972.
Higgins, George V. (1973), *The Digger's Game*. New York: Knopf.
Horwitz, Julius (1973), *The Married Lovers*. New York: Dial.

Jong, Erica (1973), *Fear of Flying*. New York: Holt, Rinehart & Winston.
Joyce, James (1916), *A Portrait of the Artist as a Young Man*. New York: Viking, 1964.
———— (1918), *Ulysses*. New York: Random House, 1934.
Lawrence, D. H. (1926), The rocking horse winner. In: *The Lovely Lady*. New York: Viking, 1933.
Lelchuk, Alan (1973), *American Mischief*. New York: Farrar, Straus & Giroux.
Malone, John (1973), *The Corruption of Harold Hoskins*. New York: Charterhouse.
Meredith, George (1859), *The Ordeal of Richard Feverel*. New York: Modern Library, 1927.
Miller, Henry (1934), *Tropic of Cancer*. New York: Grove, 1961.
Miller, Merle (1972), *What Happened*. New York: Harper & Row.
Mishima, Yukio (1958), *Confessions of a Mask*. Norwalk, Conn.: New Directions.
———— (1965), *The Sailor Who Fell from Grace with the Sea*. New York: Knopf.
O'Brien, Edna (1965), *August Is a Wicked Month*. New York: Simon & Schuster.
Peters, Fritz (1925), *Finistère*. New York: Farrar, Straus & Young.
Roth, Philip (1969), *Portnoy's Complaint*. New York: Random House.
Saikaku, Iharu (1686), *The Life of an Amorous Woman*.
Selby, Hubert (1972), *The Room*. New York: Grove Press.
Shulman, Alix K. (1972), *Memoirs of an Ex-Prom Queen*. New York: Knopf.
Speicher, John (1973), *Lower and Lower*. New York: Harper & Row.
Sutton, Henry (1970), *The Voyeur*. New York: Fawcett Crest.
Swift, Jonathan (1704), *Memoirs of Scriblerus*. New York: O'Shea, n.d.
———— (1726), *Gulliver's Travels*. New York: Long & Smith, 1933.
Twain, Mark (1883), *The Adventures of Huckleberry Finn*. New York: Farrar, Straus & Cudahy, 1962.
Updike, John (1968), *Couples*. New York: Knopf.
Vizinczey, Stephen (1965), *In Praise of Older Women*. New York: Ballantine.
Wilhelm, Kate (1971), *Margaret and I*. Boston: Little, Brown.
Woolf, Virginia (1925), *Mrs. Dalloway*. New York: Harcourt, Brace.

CHAPTER NINE

Impotence and Frigidity

In his "Contributions to the Psychology of Love. On the Universal Tendency to Debasement in the Sphere of Love" Freud (1912) wrote, "If a practising psycho-analyst asks himself on account of what disorder people most often come to him for help, he is bound to reply—disregarding the many forms of anxiety—that it is psychical impotence" (p. 179). Yet, even with today's increasing outspokenness, few people discuss impotence or frigidity outside their therapist's office. If people do speak about the subject, it is only in a risible, embarrassed, or pejorative manner. The categories of jokes on the subject are legion, perhaps because people laugh hardest at the things that frighten them most. "If she won't lay she's frigid; if she does she's a whore," quipped Sergeant William Brown in Norman Mailer's (1948) *The Naked and the Dead.* The point of William Wycherly's *The Country Wife* (1672) is that its hero, Mr. Horner, was regarded as impotent by most of the male members of the cast but quite the contrary by the ladies. Those who suffer the predicament most likely do so alone and in silence. Thus, while impotence and frigidity are common phenomena, they are kept as secret as masturbation.

There is an acute sense of vulnerability and loss of self-esteem accompanying these symptoms. Whether organic or functional, they invariably bring psychological problems in their wake. The male's concept of his masculinity is challenged; little can be as damaging as the potency factor which in turn gives rise to, as Hastings (1963) wrote, the "fear of fear. Given a few failures, the male may come to have misgivings about his potency and masculinity, and subsequent sexual trials may be approached with the dread of failure. The determination to prove his masculinity, combined with inner doubts that he can, does not provide the ideal setting for success" (p. 44). If the impotence continues for any period of time, the fear becomes magnified.

Male potency disorders are overwhelmingly psychological in origin. The most frequent factors encountered are anxiety or fear, hostility and resentment, disgust, inversion of the sex drive, inhibition, personality factors, ignorance and misinformation, and functional psychoses (Cooper, 1969a). It is a truism that sexual dysfunction is almost universal in neurotic, psychotic, and personality disorders. And as Freud indicated, impotence and premature or retarded ejaculation are among the commonest forms of sexual dysfunction in the male and are almost always the result of psychodynamic factors. Of these, premature ejaculation is the most typical potency disorder. It is known from Abraham's (1917) classic study that an urethral-anal wish to soil the woman is not consciously discernible. According to Bergler (1947), the aggression displayed in the symptom is pseudo aggression, namely refusal. The superego reproaches the ego for malicious refusal of sexual pleasure to the woman. A new defense is then set up: "I don't want to refuse, I give immediately." But this precipitate giving is really a mockery of giving, since pleasure is denied to the woman.

Ejaculatio praecox is a source of severe displeasure. The man suffers from tormenting feelings of insufficiency, experiences anxiety, is full of self-reproach, and somehow senses a lack of masculinity. In most cases there exists in the unconscious an aggressive and cruel attitude toward the woman. "In their dreams . . . these patients often produce the idea of killing a woman by copulating with her: the penis is a sadistic weapon. With *ejaculatio praecox,* the penis is robbed of its danger and can not be used in a sadistic way against the woman... There is also the fear of losing the penis through the sexual act itself. Thus while the libidinal desire and erection are present to begin with, immediately after intromission or just before bodily contact, erection disappears . . . These people are narcissistic; their true love-object is themselves" (Abraham, 1917, pp. 287-291, *passim*). There is a paradoxical sense of omnipotence in impotence.

A remarkable illustration of this is found in Ecclesiastes, which presents a picture of an urbane, cynically disillusioned man, Kohelet, whom, Zimmerman (1948, p. 301) relates, nothing ruffles and whose advice is to seek pleasure wherever it can be found: "True, there is some advantage to wisdom, and life's experience may be enriched through marriage, and pleasure should be one's main objective. Nevertheless everything, however good, however beautiful, is vain and purposeless and ultimately futile."

> Remember then thy Creator in the days of thy youth, before the evil days come, and the years draw nigh, when thou shalt say: "I have no pleasure in them"; before the sun and the light, and the moon, and the stars are darkened, and the clouds return after the rain; in the days when the keepers of the house shall tremble, and the strong men shall bow themselves, and the grinders cease because they are few, and those that look out shall be darkened in the windows, and the doors shall be shut in the street, when the sound of the grinding is low; and one shall start up at the voice of the bird, and all the daughters of music shall be brought low; also when they shall be afraid of that which is high, and terrors shall be in the way; and the almond-tree shall blossom, and the grasshopper shall drag itself along, and the caperberry shall fail; because man goeth to his long home, and the mourners go about the streets [Eccles. 12:1-5].

The passage is ripe with symbolism as Zimmerman's (pp. 302-304) exegesis details. The almond tree is an erotic symbol; the caperberry was used by the ancients as an aphrodisiac; the arms and the legs are genital equivalents; the loss of teeth represents loss of potency; the eyes are comparable to the blinding in the Oedipus legend, and are a substitute for castration; in Hebrew, the word for door is "delet," a symbol for the vagina and since the plural is used here it represents the labia of the vagina; the bird is the winged phallus of the ancients; the voice is a sign of sexual potency; height is a familiar conception and disguise for sexual intercourse; way is also a symbol for intercourse; grinder is a synonym for millstone, and in post-Biblical times the millstone bore names of obvious sexual significance, for the upper millstone was called *rekeb*, "the rider," and the nether millstone *shekeb*, "the lier-under." In short, Kohelet has let his imagination take flight, and his poetry may be interpreted as a dream, the sexual content of which is evident. Zimmerman paraphrases the passage cited so that its hidden meaning becomes clear: "Be mindful of your health while you are young, before the evil days come when you shall say you have no sexual pleasure in them; before your life is darkened by the loss of sexual powers, before your arms, legs, teeth and eyes fail, and the female doors are closed because the 'grinding' has faltered (the old man cannot penetrate the vagina because he fails in erection); the bird languishes and the voice falters (he is afraid of the sexual act because of his repeated failures), and so he pretends to despise the almond tree (sexual activity and pleasure) and even aphrodisiacs are unavailing" (p. 305). Zimmerman feels that Kohelet, seemingly so calm and composed, really is deeply disturbed. The theme of failure is dominant: "It is a loss of sexual powers, repeated under different symbols that has given Kohelet a tremendous shock . . . and crushed him. It was his sense of inadequacy, of incompetence, and finally of failure to measure up sexually, that gave rise to his pessimism and cynicism" (p. 305).

A characteristic symptom of psychogenic impotence is that it is selective in nature, that is, it occurs under one set of circumstances but not under another. This characteristic is pathognomonic; it does not occur in chemical and organic impotence (Hastings, 1963). The phenomenon of selective impotence and the apparent inhibitory effect of the vagina *per se* bring up the question of specific fantasies attached to that organ and not to other orifices of the female body. Melanie Klein (1945) indicates that in infantile fantasies the mother incorporates the father whose penis is thought to be present in the womb. Father is there—perhaps accounting for the vagina's unique danger.

Significantly, the name of the membrane guarding the vaginal orifice is derived from that of a male god, Hymen. As the myth goes, Hymen was a soft, beautiful male, who loved an Athenian maid. She and her friends were kidnapped by pirates. Because of his fairness, Hymen was mistaken for a woman and also carried off. During their abduction, Hymen stirred up his fellow captives to slay the pirates, who were drunk. Thereafter he won the maiden for his bride and became known as the protector of womanhood. Seidenberg (1951) corroborates the myth of Hymen with clinical examples of the psychopathology underlying impotence in the male. In both myth and clinical examples, weak male figures (Hymen, and the passive father) protect a woman from sexual assault and destroy (castrate) the would-be attacker. In the clinical example, the son is in danger of castration both by the strong mother and the weak father whom he fantasies as incorporated by the mother.

A psychoanalytic interpretation of Grimm's fairy tale "Sleeping Beauty" (Gustin, 1952) reveals the plight of the frigid Princess. The psychological version concerns a patriarchal King who is extremely attached to his beautiful daughter. The jealous Queen resents the King's attention to their daughter, and disguising herself as a vindictive fairy, places the curse of frigidity upon the Princess. In a desperate effort to safeguard his exclusive possession of the Princess, the frantic King castrates the competition by ordering all distaffs destroyed. Despite this effort, the curse takes effect on the Princess's fifteenth birthday. "The instant she felt the prick she fell upon the bed which was standing near and lay still in a deep sleep." This is the Princess' initiation to coitus and her first sensual awakening. She reacts by becoming frigid, going to sleep, to be awakened eventually by the virile Prince who breaks through the briar hedge (the hymen) and rescues her from the prison of lifeless sleep. "Desired by the father, resented by the mother, deemed virtuous by society, she is the victim of a triple-barreled assault. She must please her father, appease her mother, and be a well-behaved Princess" (p. 19). To seek recourse in frigidity and thus avoid the temptation of incest and the loss of her mother's affection is the only solution.

Taylor (1954, pp. 85-87) relates that "At the beginning of the twelfth century there appeared a school of poets who called themselves troubadors. Each troubador chose as the object of his affection the wife of a feudal lord and devoted to her all his poetry. In it he extolled the virtues of a relationship between a man and a woman in which the woman is placed on a pedestal. . . . The Virgin Mary was their special patron. The troubadors disclaimed any physical desire to possess their mistress; merely to see her was enough. The husbands of the ladies in question accepted the relationship and supported the troubadors in their castles. Andrew, the Chaplain at the court of Queen Alienor, set down in 1186 elaborate rules for the troubadors in the *Treatise on Love,* in which he deemed it inadvisable to love at all since 'love leads to incest'—peculiar logic indeed. Thus in the troubador we have a body of men each of whom loves and obeys a woman who is powerful and superior to himself, and with whom he may never sleep, apparently for fear of incest." Fiedler (1950, p. 50) deduced that if marriage is the enemy of love and if love leads to incest, "the beloved must be, in short, like a mother: remote, superior, unattainable, or at least attainable only with the sense of breaking the deepest taboo. No wonder the lover desires almost as much not to possess her as to possess her."

An unresolved oedipal conflict or a dominating maternal figure was early recognized by Freud (1912) as a cause for impotence. "An incestuous fixation on mother and sister, which has never been surmounted plays a prominent part in this pathogenic material and is its most universal content" (p. 180). The selective nature of the predicament enters into the situation also. The man who is fixated on his mother tends to be impotent with women he loves and idealizes, but has no difficulty with persons of a lower class. Male sexual maturity requires that the original love object be abandoned in favor of a more remote object. When this does occur, said Freud, such men have no desire to love "and where they desire they cannot love. They seek out objects which they do not need to love. . . . As soon as the condition of debasement is fulfilled, sensuality can be freely expressed" (p. 183). As a result of incestuous longings and fantasies from childhood, not actual overt acts of incest, "it can happen that a young man's sensuality becomes tied to incestuous objects in the unconscious. . . . The result is then total impotence. . ." (p. 182).

There are many ways in which selective impotence manifests itself: a man may be impotent with his wife, but no one else; impotent with a mistress, but not with his wife; impotent with women of equal social status but not with prostitutes; impotent with women, but capable of erection and ejaculation with masturbation; impotent with his wife, but potent in sexual dreams or able to achieve morning erections (Hastings, 1963). The paradox of nocturnal erections and impotence in the same man demonstrates the powerful influence psychological inhibitions, fears, and hostility have to disturb normal functions of the body. An example of potency with prostitutes and impotence with his wife is presented in John O'Hara's (1955) *10 North Frederick,* in the relationship between Lloyd Williams, lawyer, district attorney, judge, and his second wife, Lottie Franklin Williams. Isadora Zelda Wing, wife of Bennett, a psychoanalyst, is carrying on an adulterous affair with Adrian Goodlove, a British psychoanalyst in Erica Jong's (1973) *Fear of Flying.* Isadora writes, "Adrian was impotent when I wanted him in private, but he became voraciously virile in the most public places: in beach cabanas, in parking lots, in airports, in ruins, monasteries and churches. Unless he could break at least two taboos with one act, he wasn't interested at all" (p. 199).

The superstition of the Romans concerning impotence is evoked in Robert Graves' (1934) *I, Claudius.* Claudius's granduncle, the Emperor Augustus, had married his grandmother, Livia Augusta — an impious marriage that affected Augustus's conscience because he thought it displeased the gods. Here, too, selective impotence played a role, as Claudius relates.

It was always a matter of wonder that there were no children of the marriage, seeing that my grandmother had not shown herself unfruitful and that Augustus was reported to be the father of at least four natural children, besides his daughter Julia, who there is no reason for doubting was his own daughter. He was known, moreover, to be passionately devoted to my grandmother. The truth will not easily be credited. The truth is that the marriage was never consummated. Augustus, though capable enough with other women, found himself as impotent as a child when he tried to have commerce with my grandmother. The only reasonable explanation is that Augustus was, at bottom, a pious man, though cruelty and even ill-faith had been forced on him by the dangers that followed his granduncle Julius Caesar's assassination. He knew that the marriage was impious: this knowledge, it seems, affected him nervously, putting an inner restraint on his flesh.

My grandmother, who had wanted Augustus as an instrument of her ambition rather than as a lover was more glad than sorry for this impotence. She found that she could use it as a weapon for subjecting his will to hers. Her practice was to reproach him continually for having seduced her from my grandfather, whom she protested that she had loved, by assurances to her of deep passion and by secret threats to him that if she were not given up he would be arraigned as a public enemy. (This last was perfectly untrue.) Now look, she said, how she had been tricked! The passionate lover had turned out to be no man at all; any poor charcoal-burner or slave was more of a man than he! Even Julia was not his real daughter, and he knew it. All that he was good for, she said, was to fondle and fumble and kiss and make eyes like a singing eunuch. It was in vain that Augustus protested that with other women he was a Hercules. Either she would refuse to believe it or she would accuse him of wasting on other women what he denied her. But that no scandal of this should go about she pretended on one occasion to be with child by him and then to have a miscarriage. Shame and unslakable passion bound Augustus closer to her than if their mutual longings had been nightly satisfied or than if she had borne him a dozen fine children. And she took the greatest care of his health and comfort, and was faithful to him, not being naturally lustful except of power; and for this he was so grateful that he let her guide and rule him in all his public and private acts. I have heard it confidently stated by old palace officials that, after marrying my grandmother, Augustus never looked at another woman. Yet all sorts of stories were current at Rome about his affairs with the wives and daughters of notables; and after his death, in explaining how it was that she had so complete a command of his affections, Livia used to say that it was not only because she was faithful to him but also because she never interfered with his passing love-affairs. It is my belief that she put all these scandals about herself in order to have something to reproach him with.

If I am challenged as to my authority for this curious history I will give it. The first part relating to the divorce I heard from Livia's own lips in the year she died. The remainder, about Augustus's impotence, I heard from a woman called Briseis, a wardrobe-maid of my mother's, who had previously served my grandmother as a page-girl, and being then only seven years old had been allowed to over-hear conversations that she was thought too young to understand. I believe my account true and will continue to do so until it is supplanted by one that fits the facts equally well. To my way of thinking, the Sibyl's verse about "wife, no wife" confirms the matter. No, I cannot close the matter here. In writing this passage, with the idea, I suppose, of shielding Augustus's good name, I have been holding something back which I shall now after all set down. Because, as the proverb says, "truth helps the story on". It is this. My grandmother Livia ingeniously consolidated her hold on Augustus by secretly giving him, of her own accord, beautiful young women to sleep with whenever she noticed that passion made him restless. That she arranged this for him, and without a word said beforehand or after-wards, forbearing from the jealousy that, as a wife, he was con-vinced that she must feel; that everything was done very decently and quietly, the young women (whom she picked out herself in the Syrian slave-market—he preferred Syrians) being introduced into his bedroom at night with a knock and the rattle of a chain for sig-nal, and called away again early in the morning by a similar knock and rattle; and that they kept silence in his presence as if they were succubi who came in dreams—that she contrived all this so thought-fully and remained faithful to him herself in spite of his impotence with her, he must have considered a perfect proof of the sincerest love. You may object that Augustus, in his position, might have had the most beautiful women in the world, bond or free, married or un-married, to feed his appetite, without the assistance of Livia as pro-curess. That is true, but it is true nevertheless that after his marriage to Livia he tasted no meat, as he once said himself, though perhaps in another context, that she had not passed as fit for eating [pp. 20-22].

Medieval demonological literature provides a fruitful source of views relating to the causes and treatment of impotence prevalent in the Middle Ages (Cooper, 1969a). The infamous *Malleus Malleficarum* (Sprenger and Kramer, 1489), a manual of sexual psychopathology concerned primarily with impotence, sexual fantasies, and conversion hysteria, became the "scientific" basis for barrenness, impotence, and frigidity, and was used by the Church in accusing and condemning people of witchcraft. In the mass persecutions in Bamberg, Germany, between 1609 and 1633, 900 men, women, and children were burned at the stake. "Every case of impotence or sexual fantasy which came to the attention of the Inquisitors was bound to lead to death" (Taylor, 1954, p. 107). The Church wished to suppress certain sexual expressions and was always ready to accept wild stories which supported its preconceptions. "Thus," Taylor reported, "though they quite accurately distinguished loss of potency [due] to lack of semen from that due to inability to obtain an erection, they also described a third form in which the penis becomes invisible and intangible — caused by a woman casting a 'glamour' " (p. 108).

Dietary prescriptions to remedy impotence as well as for stimulating potency have persisted for centuries. In *A File on Death* by Kenneth Giles (1973), two men ring the bell of a house owned by a Señor Abajo, whom they wish to see. The door is opened by the Señor's chef who tells them the Señor is awake at the moment,

". . . but you must not tire him. I should be present, but do not take too long because I am seething his testicles in champagne." "What did you say?" [came the incredulous question]. "The Spanish can't get enough of them, sir. Of course statistically it is difficult, but I have an arrangement with a friendly slaughterhouse man in Granchester. Three lovely ones I procured yesterday and the secret is the amount of cummin in the sauce. Slice thinly, seethe in champagne, egg and breadcrumb, deep fry, prepare a white sauce. . . ." Chef Beedle's eyes glinted behind thick glasses. "I'd like to try a spoonful," said Honeybody, placated. "So you shall, in twenty minutes' time when the Señor eats." Chef Beedle recognized a kindred spirit [p. 46].

Zorba the Greek by Nikos Kazantzakis (1952) provides another illustration when an exotic dish is placed before a squeamish guest.

At this moment grandmother Anagnosti entered silently and submissively carrying the celebrated delicacy on an earthenware dish, and also a large jug full of wine. She set them on the table and remained standing with hands clasped and lowered eyes.

I felt some repugnance at having to taste this hors d'oeuvre, but, on the other hand, I did not have the courage to refuse. Zorba was watching me out of the corner of his eye and enjoying my discomfiture.

"It's the most tasty dish you could wish for, boss," he affirmed. "Don't be squeamish."

Old Anagnosti gave a little laugh.

"That's the truth, indeed it is, you try them and see. They melt in the mouth! When Prince George — may the hour be blessed for him! — visited our monastery up there in the mountains, the monks prepared a royal feast in his honor, and they served meat to every one save to the prince, who was given a plateful of soup. 'What are these? Beans?' he asked in surprise. 'White haricot beans, are they?' 'Try them, Your Highness,' said the old abbot. 'Try them and we'll talk about them afterwards.' The prince took a spoonful, two, three, he emptied his plate and licked his lips. 'What is this wonderful dish?' he said. 'What tasty beans! They're as nice as brains!' 'They're no beans, your Highness,' replied the abbot, laughing. 'They're no beans! We've had all the cocks of the neighborhood castrated!' "

Roaring with laughter, the old man stuck his fork into another morsel [p. 71].

During the eighteenth century, particularly in England and Italy, the most significant strain in the sexuality of the period seems to have been a fear of impotence (Taylor, 1954). Pombal's only preoccupation, in Durrell's (1958) novel, *Balthazar,* "is with losing his job or being *impuissant:* the national worry of every Frenchman since Jean-Jacques" (p. 27). The emergence of Don Juanism reflected the obsessive repetition of seduction, which generally derives from a need to prove one's potency. Samuel Richardson, in one of the earliest English novels, *Clarissa, or the History of a Young Lady* (1747), portrayed Lovelace as a rake and a seducer of the innocent, with no real capacity for love. While he hates matrimony, he must marry Clarissa, he must be sure that she loves him above all others, he must try her virtue to be sure that she will be a faithful wife. He tries her virtue by raping her and is thus convinced of it. In a letter to a friend, Lovelace asks rhetorically, in a hypocritical moment of abasement, "Why, why did my mother bring me up to bear no control? Why was I so educated, as that to my very tutors it was a request that I should not know what control or disappointment was? Ought she not to have known what cruelty there was in her kindness?" (p. 756).

Clarissa's entire family is aligned against her in her adamant refusal to marry dull Mr. Solmes, their choice, and they are just as set against Lovelace. Clarissa cries that if she cannot have Lovelace, she will have no one. Her parents bring pressure to bear on her refractory behavior: they banish her from her dear father's presence, they confine her to her room, they threaten her with the loss of her grandfather's inheritance, they dismiss her lifetime personal servant. But it is primarily against her brother James that Clarissa rails. She intuits something sinister in his behavior, but mistakenly puts it at the door of ambition and greed, for if she marries Solmes he may be in line for a baronetcy and certainly will add to the family property. Clarissa describes James frequently in letters to her friend, Anna Howe, in such a way as to arouse suspicion. "But my brother! What excuse can be made for his haughty and morose temper!" (p. 23). Or, "My brother heard me out with such a kind of impatience as showed he was resolved to be dissatisfied with me, say what I would" (p. 30). His opposition to her desire to become betrothed to Lovelace evinces in James an extraordinary and poorly concealed jealousy. In one of the many solemn family discussions about Clarissa's intractable feelings, she writes to Anna Howe, "My brother looked at me with scorn, having measured me, as I may say, with his eyes as I entered, from head to foot" (p. 35). She calls him "My unbrotherly accuser" (p. 29). A few weeks later, she writes a sharp note to Anna, "Meantime, give me leave to tell you, that it goes against me, in my cooler moments, unnatural as my brother is to me, to have you, my dear, who are my other self, write such very severe reflections upon him, in relation to the advantage Lovelace had over him" (p. 281). Nevertheless, her own wrath remains undiminished against James. "O my cunning brother! This is *his* contrivance. And then my anger made me recollect the triumph in his and my sister's fondness for each other, as practised before me; and the mingled indignation flashing from her eyes, as arm in arm they spoke to me, and the forced condescension playing upon their lips, when they called me Clary, and sister" (p. 366). Clarissa's own indignation boils over when she describes this scene to Anna:

> My uncle was very much displeased. But he had not the opportunity to express his displeasure, as he seemed preparing to do; for in came my brother in exceeding great wrath; and called me several vile names. His success hitherto, in his devices against me, had set him above keeping even decent measures.
>
> Was this my spiteful construction? he asked — was this the interpretation I put upon his brotherly care of me, and concern for me, in order to prevent my ruining myself?
>
> It *is*, indeed it *is*, said I: I know no other way to account for your late behaviour to me: and before your face I repeat my request to my uncle, and I will make it to my other uncle whenever I am permitted to see him, that they will confer all their favours upon you, and upon my sister; and only make me happy (it is all I wish for for!) in their kind looks and kind words.
>
> How they all gazed upon one another! — but could I be less peremptory before the man?
>
> And as to *your* care and concern for me, sir, turning to my brother; once more I desire it not. You are but my brother. My father and mother, I bless God, are both living; and, were they *not*, you have given me abundant reason to say that you are the very last person I would wish to have any concern for me.
>
> How, niece! And is a brother, an *only* brother, of so little consideration with you as this comes to? And ought he to have no concern for his sister's honour and the family's honour?
>
> *My* honour, sir! I desire none of his concern for that! It never was endangered till it had his undesired concern! Forgive me, sir — but when my brother knows how to act like a brother, or behave like a gentleman, he may deserve more consideration from me than it is possible for me now to think he does" [pp. 388-389].

Clarissa cannot reach her brother. His "marble heart was untouched" (p. 390). Even her aunt eventually comments, "Your brother, child . . . is too passionate — his zeal for *your* welfare pushes him on a little too vehemently" (p. 392). The clue to James's passion may be an early sequence in the novel, which deals with the report of a duel fought between James and Lovelace in which the former has been slightly wounded. In all likelihood, the duel is symbolic of James's need to prove his virility. Defeated by Lovelace, he is threatened; but he feels no sense of rivalry with dull Mr. Solmes. His quick temper, his hair-trigger sensitivity to Lovelace, and his extraordinary concern for Clarissa's honor, point to fears of impotence and incest.

Two years after the first volume of *Clarissa* was published, Henry Fielding's (1749) *The History of Tom Jones, A Foundling* appeared. Fielding also recognized the problem of potency disturbances. Tom Jones finds himself at an inn. The landlord has been confined to his room for half a year with gout, he drinks considerably, and his shrewish wife has taken over the management of the hostelry. He "had been married," writes Fielding delicately, "by my landlady for certain purposes which he had long since desisted from answering, for which she hated him heartily. But as he was a surly kind of fellow, so she contented herself with upbraiding him by disadvantageous comparisons with her first husband, whose praises she had eternally in her mouth... 'He was a husband to me, he was' " (pp. 360-361).

In Jonathan Swift's "Memoirs of Scriblerus" (1704a), there are invectives against "the accursed nurse" who, among other things, made the infant's ears "lie forever flat and immovable." Greenacre (1955) says this is probably a reference to impotence, both genital and auditory. Grant-Duff (1937) points out the connection between the ears and the genitals seen in a passage in Swift's *Tale of a Tub* (1704b): "If there be a protuberancy of parts in the superior region of the body, as in the ears and nose, there must be a parity also in the inferior; and therefore in that truly pious age, the males in every assembly ... appeared very forward in exposing their ears to view, and the regions about them, because Hippocrates tells us that when the vein behind the ears happens to be cut a man becomes a eunuch; and the females were nothing backwarder in beholding and edifying by them" (p. 96). That almost any part of the body might temporarily become a phallic symbol is apparent in other passages in the satire.

Many of the cases of secondary impotence reported in Masters and Johnson's (1970) *Human Sexual Inadequacy* involve men who had an early homosexual experience and tried to reverse it — unfortunately for the wives — through marriage. The lesbian experiences a similar trial. Mary Wollstonecraft, acknowledged to be the godmother of the women's liberation movement and the first English female novelist, is the author of *Mary, A Fiction* (1788). Mary has an unrequited passion for Ann. Prompted by her mother's death-bed wish and her father's importuning to marry, she does so. But the marriage is never consummated; Mary is sickened by the mere approach of her husband, a weak and egocentric youth who goes off to complete his education while Ann moves in with Mary. When her husband suggests returning, the thought of him still makes Mary ill. "There was no previous attachment to give rise to her revulsion. Her friendship with Ann had occupied her whole heart and resembled a passion" (p. 51). When Mary eventually meets her husband again, she faints at the sight of him. She runs off to the country to devote herself to good works and wait for death in which she would be reunited with Ann and "where there is neither marrying nor giving in marriage" (p. 187).

Whatever the etiology, frigidity in women, like impotence in men, is the most frequent psychosexual dysfunction (Benedek, 1959). Fenichel (1945) describes frigidity as the expression of an inhibition of a complete sexual experience, rooted in anxieties about a danger unconsciously associated with full attainment of the sexual aim — a condition completely analogous to male impotence. The male frequently assumes the cause of this to be a malicious act of will. "In contrast to impotence," Hastings (1963, p. 78) states that "the term frigidity is used to frequently describe the woman who seems to have little or no interest in becoming sexually aroused or who, in fact, rejects the idea of intercourse. Whereas the impotent male is often, if not usually, thought of as having normal sex drives but an inability to perform, the frigid female is often thought of as one who turns her back on sex. Neither men nor women tend to regard the lack or loss of erectile ability in the male as being an act of will, but rather a sorry episode over which the male has no control." Yet every single disturbance in development can become, according to Deutsch (1960), a source of frigidity. In addition, perhaps the most troublesome invasion into the sphere of sexual gratification comes from the reproductive functions and from the psychological meaning of coitus as the first act of these functions. Millett (1970), in her polemical book on sexual politics, puts the basis of frigidity on a complex of causes: the rigid conditioning of women to fear and abhor sexuality, the frequently humiliating and exploitative character in which it is presented to them, and often perhaps, the unconscious rage asserting itself at their position in a patriarchal culture.

Paulson and Lin (1970) used the Osgood Semantic Differential Rating Scale as a psychological measuring instrument, combined with factor analysis as a statistical procedure, to corroborate analytic theory that nonorganic frigidity in women is related to intense psychological conflicts. Attitudes toward the self, rejection of the psychosocial-sexual role, ambivalent and negative feelings toward a perceived inadequate body image, and resultant feelings of depression, all appear to characterize the personalities of the frigid subjects studied. Individual factors related to companionship needs, male envy, and hostility to the opposite sex were also found.

There are different types of undersexed women, different degrees of coldness. Some have fears of sex, some experience pain with sex; some women show aversion, some are passively submissive, and some pretend to enjoy intercourse (Ellis, 1966). In treating forty-one frigid women, Cooper (1969b) found a high degree of anxiety and intropunitive hostility. Clinically, the cases could be divided into immature hysterics, those angry with their husbands or men in general, and those with a generalized incapacity to sustain an affectionate relationship.

In their examination of *Villette* (1853), McCurdy (1947) and Goldfarb (1970) discovered that in Charlotte Brontë's three previous novels, *The Professor, Jane Eyre,* and *Shirley,* the heroines all find sexual fulfillment in marriage. However, Lucy Snowe, the heroine in the fourth novel, *Villette,* finds bliss not in marriage, conjugal love, and children, but in living alone, reading love letters, and waiting for a man she has never kissed. Brontë portrays a woman who represses her sexuality, as well as a male protagonist who is seemingly impotent and is attracted to Lucy for obvious psychological reasons: each would be perfectly safe with the other. M. Paul Emanuel, an austere, irritable, choleric, willful, professor of literature, nearly twice Lucy's age, calls her, "My little sister" in what seems to be one of the most passionless marriage proposals in all of literature.

> "Now, Mademoiselle Lucy, look at me, and with that truth which I believe you never knowingly violate, answer me one question. Raise your eyes; rest them on mine; have no hesitation; fear not to trust me — I am a man to be trusted."
>
> I raised my eyes.
>
> "Knowing me thoroughly now — all my antecedents, all my responsibilities — having long known my faults, can you and I still be friends?"
>
> "If monsieur wants a friend in me, I shall be glad to have a friend in him."
>
> "But a close friend I mean — intimate and real, kindred in all but blood? Will Miss Lucy be the sister of a very poor, fettered, burdened, encumbered man?"

I could not answer him in words, yet I suppose I *did* answer him; he took my hand, which found comfort in the shelter of his. *His* friendship was not a doubtful, wavering benefit—a cold, distant hope—a sentiment so brittle as not to bear the weight of a finger: I at once felt (or *thought* I felt) its support like that of some rock.

"When I talk of friendship, I mean *true* friendship," he repeated emphatically; and I could hardly believe that words so earnest had blessed my ear; I hardly could credit the reality of that kind, anxious look he gave. If he *really* wished for my confidence and regard, and *really* would give me his—why, it seemed to me that life could offer nothing more or better. In that case, I was become strong and rich: in a moment I was made substantially happy. To ascertain the fact, to fix and seal it, I asked,—

"Is monsieur quite serious? Does he really think he needs me, and can take an interest in me as a sister?"

"Surely, surely," said he; "a lonely man like me, who has no sister, must be but too glad to find in some woman's heart a sister's pure affection."

"And dare I rely on monsieur's regard. Dare I speak to him when I am so inclined?"

"My little sister must make her own experiments," said he; "I will give no promises. She must tease and try her wayward brother till she has drilled him into what she wishes. After all, he is no inductile material in some hands."

While he spoke, the tone of his voice, the light of his now affectionate eye, gave me such a pleasure as, certainly, I had never felt. I envied no girl her lover, no bride her bridegroom, no wife her husband; I was content with this my voluntary, self-offering friend. If he would but prove reliable, and he *looked* reliable, what, beyond friendship, could I ever covet? But, if all melted like a dream, as once before had happened—? [pp. 395-396].

Both characters are thus secure in their asexuality. Since M. Emanuel's proposal makes no sexual claim on her, Lucy is delighted to accept. She confides in an acquaintance, "I shall share no man's or woman's life in this world, as you understand sharing. I think I have a friend of my own, but am not sure and till I *am* sure, I live solitary." "But solitude," replies Polly, "is sadness." "Yes; it is sadness. Life, however, has worse than that. Deeper than melancholy, lies heartbreak" (p. 414). An eighteen-year-old pupil at the girl's school in Villette, where Lucy teaches, tells her, "You can't call yourself young at twenty-three; you have no attractive accomplishments—no beauty.

As to admirers, you hardly know what they are; you can't even talk on the subject; you sit dumb when the other teachers quote their conquests. I believe you never were in love, and never will be; you don't know the feeling: and so much the better, for though you might have your own heart broken, no living heart will you ever break. Isn't it all true?" In response to which Lucy rationalizes, "A good deal of it is true as gospel, and shrewd besides . . . Still, Miss Fanshawe, hapless as I am, according to your showing, sixpence I would not give to purchase you, body and soul" (p. 139). The close of the novel finds the betrothed Lucy waiting for M. Emanuel who had been away in Guadaloupe on business for three years. "Reader," says Lucy, "they were the three happiest years of my life."

Goldfarb (1970) has found a revealing letter Charlotte Brontë had written about Lucy Snowe. " 'As to the name of the heroine, I can hardly express what subtlety of thought made me decide upon giving her a cold name; but at first, I called her "Lucy Snowe" (spelt with an "e"); which Snowe I afterwards changed to "Frost." Subsequently, I rather regretted the change, and wished it "Snowe" again . . . A *cold* name she must have; partly, perhaps, on the "lucus a non lucendo" principle—partly on that of the "fitness of things," for she has about her an external coldness' " (p. 150).

"But if I feel, may I *never* express?" Lucy pleads (Brontë, p. 221). And the intellectual answer is, "Never!" An almost cursory run-through of the novel reveals the denial of affect, the cold ideation: "Loverless and inexpectant of love, I was as safe from spies in my heart-poverty as the beggar from thieves in his destitution of purse" (p. 113). "Cold, reluctant, apprehensive, I had accepted a part to please another" (p. 135). "On me school triumphs shed a cold lustre" (p. 148). "I suddenly felt colder, where before I was cold, and more powerless where before I was weak" (p. 157). "I am so cold and dull here" (p. 165). ". . . perfectly unconscious, perfectly bloodless, and nearly cold" (p. 177). "The inert force of deep, settled love she bore herself, was wonderful: it could only be surpassed by her proud impotency to care for any other living thing. Of blood, her cool veins conducted no flow; placid lymph filled and almost obstructed her arteries" (p. 203). "I felt cold and shaking" (p. 238). "Cold and fixed was [Lucy's] reply" (p. 244). "I betook myself to her cold staircase" (p. 379). "His friendship was . . . a cold, distant hope" (p. 394). "In your hand there is both chill and poison" (p. 435). "I said very little, I gave her only the crust and rind of my nature" (p. 462). "Nothing but a chilling dimness was seen or felt" (p. 478).

Villette, McCurdy (1947, p. 146) explains, was written in its entirety during the period of mourning after the death of Charlotte's brother, Bramwell, and her two remaining sisters, Emily and Anne, when, as Charlotte continually says in her letters, she underwent repeated experiences of profound depression. No doubt her own short-lived marriage, opposed by her tyrannical father, was another factor in the frigid quality of her final work.

"If you want to know more about femininity," wrote Freud (1933), "Enquire from your own experiences of life, or turn to the poets, or wait until science can give you deeper and more coherent information" (p. 135). Between Freud and Masters and Johnson, there had been comparatively little understanding of the female orgasm. Brown (1966) reviews this neglect by medicine and psychology over the first six decades of the present century, as well as the myth that the majority of females have neither the desire nor the capacity for sexual gratification, and for those who do, it is a defect that should be denied or somehow eliminated. Frigidity, according to Moreno (1969), is a failure in a relationship between a man and a woman, symptomatic of the pathology of the couple and not simply a female neurosis. The experience of pleasure for the woman is connected to the personal relationship, even if this relationship may appear superficial, occasional, and insignificant.

Such a relationship seems to exist between Julien Sorel and Mathilde de la Môle in Stendhal's *The Red and the Black* (1830). The unhappy chase Mathilde leads Julien on and her sexual inconsistencies with him prompt the belief that she is using sexual withholding as a weapon in an alternating hostile and loving relationship. It would also seem to be a sadomasochistic reaction, for Mathilde imposes as much punishment upon herself as on Julien. Mathilde, wounded in her vanity, resents him as well as herself, and therefore denies both pleasure. In her masochistic impulses, she expresses her enslavement to Julien, uttering words of adoration; in her sadism, she wants to be humiliated, for Julien is the son of a carpenter, far beneath her social class, a contemptible upstart. She alienates her ego more and more profoundly in rage at permitting the affair even to start. Mathilde was vexed at having yielded to Julien; "that is why, at times, she falls at his feet, willingly bends to his every caprice, sacrifices her hair to him; but at the same time she is revolted as much against him as against herself; we readily divine her cold as ice in his arms" (de Beauvoir, 1968, p. 400).

A contemporary example of this pendular swing is found in Lois Gould's *Such Good Friends* (1970). Julie, who finds things to criticize in her husband, ridicules him, and obviously displays her intellectual superiority, keeps her hostile attitude out of consciousness, and often marks her behavior with exaggerated tenderness (Stekel, 1927). Richard Messinger, an art director for a magazine, is dying of a hepatic coma. He had been a philanderer for most of the seven years of his marriage with Julie, compulsively keeping a secret diary, in code, of all his extramarital affairs, like an accountant figuring out his sex returns. I was *"Your* goddam bright idea I should spend my nights illustrating a fucking children's book [accuses her husband]. I'm the only art director in New York who has to break his balls free-lancing to pay the rent—pardon me, *main*tenance. You wanted a co-op? You gotta co-op. I got *Melancholy Melinda and the Magic Melon Patch*, pictures by Richard Messinger. So why don't you just mosey on to bed, okay?" (Gould, p. 8). He is too exhausted for sexual relations. While he is in the coma, Julie ruminates about her husband and her own feelings.

"It's a bitch," he'd sigh in his nicest monotone, "but I guess you've emasculated me somehow." And I'd lie there next to him, tears sliding sideways into my hair until he felt the wetness and lost his temper, because what the hell was *I* crying about. It usually happened after I'd tried touching him gently, quietly, dutifully trying to make his body respond in spite of him. He'd keep shielding his face with *The New Yorker* and say, "Please, Julie, don't. It's ... it makes me uncomfortable. I *know* you're not being aggressive, but that's the way you come on. I can't ... I don't want ... oh Christ, you act soft and tender, and I *feel* you acting. It turns me off, you know?"

Finally, I'd be able to move my hand away, hating it for being where it was, and lift my head off his chest, cringing back to my side of the bed. Then I'd wait for the inevitable aching sensation to start on the insides of my wrists. Hurt and need and helplessness. Ugly. Oh God, I must be so ugly. And then he'd slam the magazine on his night table and say, "I wish—aw, Christ, maybe I need a psychiatrist—maybe it's my fault, maybe *I'm* the one who's sick." Then he'd sigh heavily, turn off his light, turn his back to me and pretend to sleep. Or pretend not to—I never really knew.

Though I never saw it that way, it was the most beautiful solution a man could devise for keeping a fuckless marriage intact, and an unfucked wife in line. *I* was the failure. Hopelessly unfuckable. After what I'd *already* done to Richard, I couldn't even console myself by getting a lover or a divorce, now could I? So the bastard had it made.

I took up overeating, masturbation. Dexamyl, charging things at Bloomingdale's and reading textbooks on abnormal psychology. I trained myself to climb into bed with Krafft-Ebing and a whole Sara Lee fudge ripple pound cake, and I'd rip through both until I'd worked up a nice sado-masochistic fantasy, then go to work with my fingers. After a few months I'd learned to do it even with Richard lying there next to me. I was positive he never knew. Even if he did, somehow it would be less humiliating than the alternative—thrusting myself at him again, buying see-through nightgowns, stroking his body instead of mine, and trying, *trying* to understand why nothing I did produced any more reaction than that catheter they'd put on him this morning [pp. 9-10].

"This is the saddest story I have ever heard," is the opening sentence of Ford Madox Ford's ironically titled *The Good Soldier* (1915). It carries the subtitle, *A Tale of Passion,* and the book's controlling irony lies in the fact that the passionate situations are related by the narrator, John Dowell, who is himself incapable of passion, sexual or moral. Dowell is impotent in every respect so as to be almost totally self-effacing. He is a prissy, intensely conventional New Englander whose personality serves as an ironic counterpoint to a passionate tale told with deliberate horror, made all the more so because of its understatement. A man of inherited wealth, Dowell marries "a vulgar, common flirt," he comes to realize, who carried on adulterous activities for the twelve years of their married life under his nose without his ever being aware of them. His wife commits suicide, and although he could have prevented it, he is impotent to stop her. The nuptial kiss is the last sexual contact he has with Florence. He is not only gulled by her but also by his best friend, Ashburnham, the ironical "good soldier" who carries on the affair with Florence, abetted by his wife's reluctant connivance and acceptance. Dowell's impotence in all matters is pyramidal, building up until the only role he can play is nurse to a schizophrenic girl. The novel depicts serious illness, alcoholism, two suicides, and the seduction of a girl of fourteen who has an illegitimate child at fifteen. Its characters include a prostitute mother, a pimping wife, a mad girl, an American nymphomaniac, and an impotent protagonist.

The craft by which Ford erects the undercurrent of horror upon horror, narrated in the most beguiling, seductive manner, doubles the intensity of the plot. "Am I no better than a eunuch?" Dowell cries plaintively (p. 11). He explains, "You see, I suppose [Ashburnham] regarded me not so much as a man. I had to be regarded as a woman" (p. 28). As for his wife, ". . . in Florence I had at once a wife and an unattained mistress" (p. 49). While courting Florence in Connecticut he discovers, "But, if I never as much as kissed Florence, she let me discover very easily . . . her simple wants. And I could supply those wants: She wanted to marry a gentleman of leisure [with] an income of fifty thousand dollars a year . . . and — she faintly hinted — she did not want much physical passion in the affair" (p. 81). On the night he elopes with Florence, he notes, "It was the first time I had ever been embraced by a woman — and it was the last when a female embrace has had any warmth for me" (p. 85). Dowell was thirty at the time. Florence would like to tell him "that I was considerably less than a man and that what would happen was what must happen when a real male came along" (p. 120) but is only restrained by the rationalized decency of Leonora Ashburnham, whose husband is carrying on the adulterous affair with Florence. After the latter's suicide, when Florence becomes fearful of the inevitable exposure of her promiscuity, Dowell is dead-tired, feeling "practically catalepsy — was just the repose that my exhausted nature claimed after twelve years of the repression of my instincts, after twelve years of playing the trained poodle. For that was all that I had been" (p. 122). And when he finds himself hopelessly in love with and caring for Nancy, the young ward of the Ashburnhams who has fallen into a schizophrenic reaction as a result of a nearly consummated incestuous relationship with the "good soldier," Dowell comments, "She [Nancy] had frequently told me that she had no vocation; it just simply wasn't there — the desire to become a nun. Well, I guess that I was a sort of convent myself; it seemed fairly proper that she should make her vows to me. . . . [But] I didn't want to present myself to Nancy as a sort of old maid" (pp. 123-124).

Perhaps the two most famous physically impotent characters in fiction are D. H. Lawrence's Sir Clifford Chatterley, better known as Lady Chatterley's husband, and Ernest Hemingway's Jake Barnes in *The Sun Also Rises* (1926). Both were emasculated by wounds received in World War I, but whereas Hemingway used gallows humor to depict Jake's impotence, Lawrence had his characters discuss Clifford's condition seriously. They offer an interesting contrast in approach. One of Lawrence's aims in writing *Lady Chatterley's Lover* (1928) was to help release individuals from their sexual inhibitions. Hemingway, on the other hand, was primarily concerned with homosexuality and castration, masculinity, and romantic death, all dominant forces in his own life. Young (1952) suggested that Hemingway was psychologically crippled by castration anxieties and that his major works derive from this source. He suffered from a compulsive type of impotence, as Gutheil (1959, p. 722) called it, based on the unspoken death clause, "If you have successful sexual relations, you will die." Lawrence believed the reverse: "Have successful sex and you will live." Fiedler (1960) feels that from the time of Hemingway, impotence has been a central symbol in fiction, "a felt clue to the quality of American life, erotic and spiritual. Faulkner, ... Hemingway's contemporary and admirer, has exploited the same theme, conceiving as eunuchs both Flem Snopes, symbol of the new bourgeoisie, and sterile lover of money, and Popeye, the spawn of urban alleys, Prohibition, and the hysteria of the Great Depression. The self-pity, which in Hawthorne, James, and even Hemingway has softened the horror of the portrait of the American as impotent voyeur, the insistence that, for better or worse, he is an intellectual, 'one of us'..." (p. 322).

Jake Barnes, in *The Sun Also Rises,* is a worldly-wise accepter of the nature of the human condition (Cochran, 1968), reflecting an emotional insularity, cynicism, and world-weariness that mark the novel. Jake's thought after he frames his telegram to Brett who awaits his aid in the Hotel Montana in Madrid is, "That seemed to handle it. That was it. Send a girl off with one man. Introduce her to another to go off with him. Now go and bring her back. And sign the wire with love. That was it all right. I went to lunch" (Hemingway, p. 239). What could be more prosaic than such behavior; but its unreality shocks because of the ready acceptance of the intolerable. "To be sure Hemingway tells us that it is 'the War' which has afflicted Jake with the absurd wound which he examines in the mirror of his lonely room; but 'the War' is merely a convenient tag for the failure of values and faith which converted a generation of young American writers to self-hatred, bravado, and expatriation. The same forces, at any rate, which have 'emancipated' Brett have unmanned Jake; forced him into the role not only of witness to Brett's love affairs, but of pimp as well — setter-up of scenes which, beheld or imagined, can only drive him into queasy despair" (Fiedler, 1960, p. 322).

In choosing impotence as a principal plot device, Hemingway was betraying one of the most fundamental and pervasive fears he, and most men, have: the fear of losing one's manhood, which carries with it the fear of either never having had it or never fully attaining it. In Hemingway there is always "virility, strength, courage: he is the soldier searching out the eye of the battle storm; the intrepid hunter and fisherman compelled to pursue the greatest fish and stalk the most dangerous animal from the Gulf Stream to Central Africa; the athlete, swimmer, brawler, boxer; the hard drinker and hard lover who boasted that he had bedded every girl he wanted and some that he had not wanted; the lover of danger, of the bullfight, of flying, of the wartime front lines; the friend of brave men, heroes, fighters, hunters and matadors ... He sought danger because he had to, in order to escape some greater internal danger" (Yalom and Yalom, 1971, p. 487). Hemingway's unconscious castration anxieties are masked and sublimated through his novels. In *The Sun Also Rises,* Hemingway deals with impotence obliquely. His hero, Jake Barnes, is masculine in every way but the crucial one: he drinks, he dances with a whore, he goes off with the boys on a fishing trip. But he cannot escape his doom. "It was a rotten way to be wounded," he cries. And the chill horror evoked by his desexing is inescapable, following him in his thoughts, ruminations, and pursuit of the bitch-goddess Brett.

"What happened to me is supposed to be funny. I never think about it," Jake lies to her. "Oh, no. I'll lay you don't." "Well, let's shut up about it." "I laughed about it too, myself, once." She wasn't looking at me. "A friend of my brother's came home that way from Mons. It seemed like a hell of a joke. Chaps never know anything, do they?" "No," I said. "Nobody ever knows anything." I was pretty well through with the subject. At one time or another I had probably considered it from its various angles, including the one that certain injuries or imperfections are a subject of merriment while remaining quite serious for the person possessing them. "It's funny," I said. "It's very funny" [pp. 26-27].

Shortly after this scene with Brett, Jake tries to fall asleep, but his night thoughts inevitably lead him back to his inescapable fate. He recalls the liaison colonel who visited him in the Italian hospital after his plane had been shot down, and who made a speech, "You, a foreignor, an Englishman . . . have given more than your life" (p. 31). He remembers how serious the colonel was, never laughing; he brings to mind the "swell advice" of the Catholic Church: not to think about it. "Then all of a sudden I started to cry. Then after a while it was better and I lay in bed and listened to the heavy trams go by and way down the street, and then I went to sleep" (p. 32).

Hemingway achieves a symbolically pathetic ending for his protagonists.

> "Oh, Jake," Brett said, "we could have had such a damned good time together."
>
> Ahead was a mounted policeman in khaki directing traffic. He raised his baton. The car slowed suddenly pressing Brett against me.
>
> "Yes," I said. "Isn't it pretty to think so?" [pp. 258-259].

Perhaps it is Hemingway's anticlimactic attempt at a happy ending to put a band-aid on the reader's psyche when he has the policeman "raise his baton" in phallic greeting to the despairing couple.

D. H. Lawrence, too, was greatly concerned with masculinity and potency, for these assume a prominence in his work. Jim Bricknell in *Aaron's Rod* (1922) tells Lilly Rawdon that "technically" he can make love: "I'm potent all right—oh, yes." Yes, he confesses, inside he feels "the life going." The emphasis of Gudrun Brangwen's dance before the Highland cattle in *Women in Love* (1920) is on the bullocks' impotence which is related to Gerald's impotence. But their subsequent relationship is a sterile one which "leads Gudrun to the homosexual Loerke and . . . Gerald to his death in the snow, a symbol for the sterility of his cerebral, mechanical, preoccupations" (Ort, 1969, p. 38).

Clifford Chatterley, in *Lady Chatterley's Lover* (1928), is not only rendered impotent but also confined to a wheelchair because of wounds suffered in the war. Even before these events, he was never much interested in sex and perhaps this makes it easier for his father-in-law to tell him that the semi-virgin state of Lady Chatterley would inevitably prove to be intolerable. Clifford's preoccupation is with perpetuating his line. At first, he sublimates this through fecund short-story writing. Any fault-finding with the stories is looked upon with umbrage, as by a fatuous parent whose child has been criticized. "He was almost morbidly sensitive about these stories. He wanted everyone to think them good, of the best, ne plus ultra. They appeared in the most modern magazines, and were praised and blamed as usual. But to Clifford the blame was torture, like knives goading him. It was as if the whole of his being were in his stories. Connie helped him as much as she could. At first she was thrilled. He talked everything over with her monotonously, insistently, persistently, and she had to respond with all her might. It was as if her whole soul and body and sex had to rouse up and pass into these stories of his" (p. 12). When his creativity slackened, his thoughts turned to links with children and links with England. The important secret in marriage was habit, "not the occasional spasm." And for him Connie was indeed a habit, keeping up his morale, inspiring him to write, making him "sensitive and conscious of himself and his own states." In short, Lord Chatterley was a pure egoist, using his wife as a simple instrument for the maintenance of himself and his ideas in the world (McCurdy, 1940, p. 191).

"I want this wood perfect . . . untouched. I want nobody to trespass in it," said Clifford.

There was a certain pathos.. The wood still had some of the mystery of wild, old England; but Sir Geoffrey's cuttings during the war had given it a blow. How still the trees were, with their crinkly, innumerable twigs against the sky, and their grey, obstinate trunks rising from the brown bracken! How safely the birds flitted among them! And once there had been deer, and archers, and monks padding along on asses. The place remembered, still remembered.

Clifford sat in the pale sun, with the light on his smooth, rather blond hair, his reddish full face inscrutable.

"I mind more, not having a son, when I come here, than any other time," he said.

"But the wood is older than your family," said Connie gently.

"Quite!" said Clifford. "But we've preserved it. Except for us it would go . . . it would be gone already, like the rest of the forest. One must preserve some of the Old England!"

"Must one?" said Connie. "If it has to be preserved, and preserved against the new England? It's sad, I know."

"If some of the old England isn't preserved, there'll be no England at all," said Clifford. "And we who have this kind of property, and the feeling for it, *must* preserve it."

There was a sad pause.

"Yes, for a little while," said Connie.

"For a little while! It's all we can do. We can only do our bit. I feel every man of my family has done his bit here, since we've had the place. One may go against convention, but one must keep up tradition." Again there was a pause.

"What tradition?" asked Connie.

"The tradition of England! of this!"

"Yes," she said slowly.

"That's why having a son helps; one is only a link in a chain," he said.

Connie was not keen on chains, but she said nothing. She was thinking of the curious impersonality of his desire for a son.

"I'm sorry we can't have a son," she said.

He looked at her steadily, with his full, pale-blue eyes.

"It would almost be a good thing if you had a child by another man," he said. "If we brought it up at Wragby, it would belong to us and to the place. I don't believe very intensely in fatherhood. If we had the child to rear, it would be our own, and it would carry on. Don't you think it's worth considering?"

Connie looked up at him at last. The child, her child, was just an "it" to him. It ... it ... it!

"But what about the other man?" she asked.

"Does it matter very much? Do these things really affect us very deeply? ... You had that lover in Germany ... what is it now? Nothing almost. It seems to me that it isn't these little acts and little connections we make in our lives that matter so very much. They pass away, and where are they? Where ... Where are the snows of yesteryear? ... It's what endures through one's life that matters; my own life matters to me, in its long continuance and development. But what do the occasional connections matter? And the occasional sexual connections specially! If people don't exaggerate them ridiculously, they pass like the mating of birds. And so they should. What does it matter? It's the life-long companionship that matters. It's the living together from day to day, not the sleeping together once or twice. You and I are married, no matter what happens to us. We have the habit of each other. And habit, to my thinking, is more vital than any occasional excitement. The long, slow, enduring thing ... that's what we live by ... not the occasional spasm of any sort. Little by little, living together, two people fall into a sort of unison, they vibrate so intricately to one another. That's the real secret of marriage, not sex; at least not the simple function of sex. You and I are interwoven in a marriage. If we stick to that we ought to be able to arrange this sex thing, as we arrange going to the dentist; since fate has given us a checkmate physically there."

Connie sat and listened in a sort of wonder, and a sort of fear. She did not know if he was right or not. There was Michaelis, whom she loved; so she said to herself. But her love was somehow only an excursion from her marriage with Clifford; the long, slow habit of intimacy, formed through years of suffering and patience. Perhaps the human soul needs excursions, and must not be denied them. But the point of an excursion is that you come home again.

"And wouldn't you mind *what* man's child I got?" she asked.

"Why, Connie, I should trust your natural instinct of decency and selection. You just wouldn't let the wrong sort of fellow touch you."

She thought of Michaelis! He was absolutely Clifford's idea of the wrong sort of fellow.

"But men and women may have different feelings about the wrong sort of fellow," she said.

"No," he replied. "You cared for me. I don't believe you would ever care for a man who was purely antipathetic to me. Your rhythm wouldn't let you."

She was silent. Logic might be unanswerable because it was so absolutely wrong.

"And should you expect me to tell you?" she asked, glancing up at him almost furtively.

"Not at all, I'd better not know. . . . But you do agree with me, don't you, that the casual sex thing is nothing, compared to the long life lived together? Don't you think one can just subordinate the sex thing to the necessities of a long life? Just use it, since that's what we're driven to? After all, *do* these temporary excitements matter? Isn't the whole problem of life the slow building up of an integral personality, through the years? living an integrated life? There's no point in a disintegrated life. If lack of sex is going to disintegrate you, then go out and have a love affair. If lack of a child is going to disintegrate you, then have a child if you possibly can. But only do these things so that you have an integrated life, that makes a long harmonious thing. And you and I can do that together ... don't you think? ... if we adapt ourselves to the necessities, and at the same time weave the adaptation together into a piece with our steadily-lived life. Don't you agree?"

Connie was a little overwhelmed by his words. She knew he was right theoretically. But when she actually touched her steadily-lived life with him she . . . hesitated. Was it actually her destiny to go on weaving herself into his life all the rest of her life? Nothing else?

Was it just that? She was to be content to weave a steady life with him, all one fabric, but perhaps brocaded with the occasional flower of an adventure. But how could she know what she would feel next year? How could one ever know? How could one say Yes? for years and years? The little yes, gone on a breath! Why should one be pinned down by that butterfly word? Of course it had to flutter away and be gone, to be followed by other yes's and no's! Like the straying of butterflies.

"I think you're right Clifford. And as far as I can see I agree with you. Only life may turn quite a new face on it all."

"But until life turns a new face on it all, you do agree?"

"Oh, yes! I think I do, really" [Lawrence, pp. 41-43].

The narcissism of Lord Chatterley is matched, to a degree, by that of Sasha Davis Raybel, the central character in Alix K. Shulman's *Memoirs of an Ex-Prom Queen* (1972). Sasha embarks on a loveless marriage to Frank, a doctoral candidate in history at Columbia University. From the time she began to wear orthodontic appliances, Sasha has been narcissistically obsessed with the need to be beautiful and desirable. She is forever doubting her looks, although in reality she is quite beautiful. The tale of the Ugly Duckling never fails to move her to tears; she wallows in fables, searching for guidance in them. Despite the fact that she was Queen of her high school prom in suburban Cleveland at the age of fifteen, she cannot believe in her beauty although she devotes countless hours of contemplation to it. Underlying her behavior is a narcissistic defense originating in penis envy. This is a painful record of one woman's search of herself, a search that somehow can be defined only by male recognition of her physical charms. The search leads her to a psychiatrist's office, where Dr. Webber discovers Sasha is twenty-three years old, married three years, frigid with her husband, but enjoying a sideline occupation as a call girl. She finds it difficult to relate to the psychiatrist at first: "I tried to think of something both intelligent and shocking, something telling and rare, something to make this doctor know that I was not, in

Dr. John Watson's memorable words, just another ordinary 'quacking, gossiping, neighbor-spying, disaster-enjoying' neurotic frigid woman—a textbook case" (p. 189). Eventually, she does reveal herself as a classical case, to her own astonishment.

I was seeing Dr. Webber regularly, Mondays and Thursdays, after work, and though I tried to do what was expected of me, I found myself talking about everything except what really mattered. In fact, it was by observing what I was unable to say that I discovered what really mattered: whether or not he found me beautiful.

I was frantic to know but could not bring myself to ask. Even if I could someday manage the question, how would I make him answer it? And if he should miraculously answer, how could I know he was telling the truth? I couldn't even ask him if he thought me *pretty*, an easier, an almost innocent question, and one common courtesy would dictate he answer yes. But like one obsessed, I could not ask. (*Aha!* he would have said had he known my obsession, *why do you want to know?*) Instead I tried to captivate him. I concocted dreams with secret messages for him to decode. I drenched him in anecdotes and plied him with metaphors. I gave him my favorite poems to read. Leading him to the well of my beauty if he'd happened to miss it, I told him of my various conquests and seductions, exaggerating to inspire him to drink.

"It's interesting," he observed, "that the only man you say you loved is a father, as old as your own father, and forbidden to you by the mother, his wife." He ended on a question mark, hoping 1 would pick up the thread. But I wouldn't. I found his tiresome moralizing silly.

"I loved Alport before I knew he had a wife," I said. "I've been to bed with older married men with more children than he. And not for love."

Sometimes I rebuked him for the *genetic fallacy:* taking cause for value—which only proved to him that he was probably "on to something"; and sometimes, planting my profile smack in his line of vision, I penalized him with silence.

I would wait, smoking cigarette after cigarette, until he came up with a question. Usually it was, "I wonder why you are feeling hostile today?" or else it was his second-favorite conversational gambit:

"What about Frank, your husband?"

"What about him?" I would return. My husband, like my marriage, bored me, as, no doubt, I bored him. We no longer had any life in common. He was full of *no's* and *don't's* while I liked to think I lived by *yes* and *do*. Frank did nothing but study during the week and see his friends on Saturday nights. He varied neither schedule nor sentence structure. The baby talk he had always used for addressing me in public he now used in private as well. Deceiving him had led me to avoid him, and since being in therapy exempted me from his sexual advances ("I'm still frigid, Frank, so don't touch me"), our contact was minimal.

"You hardly ever mention him. Don't you think that's rather . . . uh . . . unusual?"

And then I told him once again that, not believing in romantic love and finding my husband sufficiently tolerant of my idiosyncrasies to permit me a modicum of freedom, I considered my marriage satisfactory. Apart from the sex, of course, which was my own problem.

"And Frank? Does he consider it satisfactory too?"

"He doesn't complain," I snickered. It was wrong of the doctor to call him Frank and take his side.

"Don't you think he knows about your . . . uh . . . activities?"

"Oh, no!" I was shocked. "Do you think I should tell him?"

The doctor said nothing. I knew my "activities" had no bearing on Frank. They might have, if I ever pursued them for love. But I never did. Frank, however, couldn't be expected to understand that. A conventional fellow, he would feel himself wronged and required to do something if he knew.

"What do *you* think, Sasha?" Dr. Webber asked, enigmatically stroking his beard.

"I think it would upset him terribly to know, and I'm really not out to hurt him, whatever you think. It would mess up all his plans. He'd probably feel obliged to leave me."

The doctor nodded. He seemed to like that speech better than my other one, the one in which I weighed my own ten reasons for leaving Frank. That one made Dr. Webber break all his principles and actually give me advice:

"If I were you, Sasha. I wouldn't make any drastic changes right now while you're in the middle of analysis."

He seemed to feel that the known was better than the unknown, another man would prove no better for me than this one, and a crazy nymphomaniacal penis-envying castrating masochistic narcissistic infantile fucked-up frigid bitch like me was lucky to have hooked any man at all.

Actually, Dr. Webber seemed less interested in the practical questions surrounding my marriage than in the theoretical. Over the months I had been working painstakingly at getting him to reveal his premises, but with little success. Until one day, while I was discussing a dream I'd had the night before, a chance remark I made caused him to reveal his entire theory.

That night I had dreamed a chess game in which I, a plain red pawn, had so yearned to reach the eighth rank and become queen that I had refused gambits, squandered opportunities, betrayed my team. Alone and unprotected, I went on trying for queen despite certain defeat.

"What does being queen mean to you?" asked the doctor, suppressing a yawn.

I couldn't tell him about the Bunny Hop. Knowing I had once been considered beautiful might prejudice his own answer to the question I still hoped one day to ask. "The queen is the most powerful piece on the board," I answered. "She outdoes everyone. She can move almost every way there is to move." It was rich with symbolism and also true.

"The *most* powerful? Is she more powerful than the king?" he asked with an insinuating smile.

Either he didn't play chess, or he was after something. I went along.

"In the world a king may be more powerful, but in chess the queen is more powerful. That's why as a little pawn I wanted to be a boy and as a woman I enjoy playing chess."

I was pleased with my answer, but nothing like Dr. Webber. I could tell by the way he sat up and began to scribble that he was through yawning for that session.

"Can you think of what the dream might be saying?" he prodded.

I considered. Frank had applied for a Fulbright for a year's study in Germany. I was excited at the prospect of going abroad, but apprehensive as well; perhaps the dream took on that dilemma. As I was about to suggest something along those lines, Dr. Webber, impatient to share his revelation, leaned forward, reading from his notes.

"Even as a little pawn you always wanted to be a boy. Yet you long to be a 'queen,'" he said. "You have 'betrayed your own team'— your own nature?"

Dr. Webber's crude "hints," which I had always felt free to pursue or let lie, now came thickly. He was like a prompter, trying hard not to be heard, yet unwilling to let the lines be lost and the play ruined. The more I ignored his interpretation, the more certain he became.

Didn't everything, he asked, reduce for me to queen versus king? My belligerence, my seductions, my willfulness? Did they not all point to a profound conflict within my nature? Was I not always attempting to conquer where I should yield? take where I should give? Did I not identify with my father instead of my mother? Were not my very ambitions (to be a lawyer! a philosopher!), my rejection of maternity, my fantastic need to excel, my unwillingness to achieve orgasm—were they not all denials of my own deepest, instinctive self—my feminine self?

I had never before seen Dr. Webber so animated, not even when he was advising me to do nothing rash. I felt the time had come to plunge in and pose my own question. Catching him off guard in an expansive moment seemed my best chance of getting a truthful answer. After all, self-knowledge was what I was paying for.

He was still waiting for me to agree when, as casually as I could, I said, "Do you think I'm beautiful, Doctor?" If I could learn the truth about myself now, it would be worth all this painful analysis.

Dr. Webber pounced on this question. "Why do you ask?" he asked.

"I don't know, I just wondered," I said, looking intently at the telephone and mentally dialing a number. He was impossible to pin down; already I was sorry to have asked.

He examined me closely while my cheeks went red and my hands went damp. Then he said, "We have just come to an important—a breakthrough!—discovery with this chess dream. Even if you don't acknowledge it openly, unconsciously you do acknowledge it. You ask, *Do I think you are beautiful?* You mean, *Do I think you are a woman?* Don't you see? Yes, Sasha, I think you are a woman. I *know* you are. Now *you* must begin to accept this in yourself" [pp. 190-195].

While Sasha found she could not accept the insights about her latent Lesbianism and her feelings of self-rejection as a female, they were probably crucial factors in her unsatisfactory sexual response.

Freud (1905), Stekel (1927), Fenichel (1945), Stafford-Clark (1954), Ellis (1933), and Hirschfeld (1944), among others, believed that impotence was commonly associated with homosexuality, stemming from an unresolved oedipal situation. In every case of male homosexuality, there is a childhood period of intense fixation on the mother, followed by the boy's identification with her and a search for young men resembling himself whom he wishes to love as his mother loved him. His

obsessive strivings are determined by his restless flight from the woman, resulting in sexual aversion manifesting itself, in many instances,
as heterosexual impotence. Strong incestuous fixations, particularly
those based on actual incestuous relations, are often behind this readiness to sacrifice sex (Gutheil, 1959). The young impotent man is afraid
to confront life and is dominated by the maternal figure who will show
her revenge through castration (Ranzato and Zagami, 1969).

Henry Allanbee, a twenty-three-year-old loner and the protagonist
in Desmond Cory's thriller, *Even If You Run* (1972), illustrates these
points. He is a latent homosexual, with strong masculinity strivings,
rejection of femininity, and unconscious guilt associated with aggression toward both parents. While Henry was growing up, his parents
were constantly quarreling in his presence. "The voices" in the passage
quoted below refer to his father's head-on auto collision with a truck,
in which he and his mistress, a strip-tease artist, were brought dying to
a hospital, and to his mother's histrionic complaints to Henry about
her husband's infidelities. Henry learned to control his emotions, for
therein lay safety. He occupied himself with making toy models, a
hobby he continued throughout manhood. He also collected ballistic
and war memorabilia, specializing in Nazi mementos. And his occupation: bomb expert, both assembling and detonating. He became
involved in a Spanish plot to assassinate, by bombing, a prominent
official. In the scene that follows, he meets with Ramona, a pharmacy
store owner and revolutionary. They meet at a hotel, known to be a
prostitute haven, to discuss details of the plot and avoid detection by
the Guardia Civil.

She laid down the cigarette in an ashtray. Her fingers — delicate,
competent — patted the bed.
"Come and sit down, Henry. Come and sit here."

But why, why?
And knowing why all the time. That was the worst of it.
"I can't. It won't."
His hands were hard-clenched on stiff linen; the length of his body
rigid and trembling. Ramona's shoulder was smooth and slippery
with sweat against his cheek. The muttered cry, as though unheard
by her; still she fought him, grimly, silently, as an angler steers the
salmon towards the bank, her fingers moving up and down, up and
down, always competent, always careful, clean white nurse's fingers

readying him for the operating table. Against his mouth, the anaesthetic pad of her neck, her yielding flesh. *Oh yes you can. You will.*

The voices, always the voices. From the other rooms. The corridor and the soundless wheels of the trolley. Other doors, white-painted; other rooms. Each with its narrow bed, its pink-shaded light. Creakings, moans, protestations; the white arches of lifted legs, reared in the plunging darkness. This was where it ended. The Accident Ward.

The steam, rising from the engine. The long dark tunnel. The voices, the others, the other women; the whores, the bitches he goes with. You won't understand, you can't. You're too young, Henry. But one day you'll know what all these years I've had to put up with. "Oh God. No. No. It's no good."

No, she'd said, no. We can't go on. No no no no no. The words, the protestations, becoming inaudible behind the white door, the white-painted door with the twisted handle; no no no, we can't go on, there's nothing left (the shrill accented voice changing in tone, rising in desperate denial), no no, I can't, I won't (the echoes of that denial reverberating in his lowered head, mingling with his own perplexed refusal to believe, *no, no, don't, she's the enemy, she's the others*) and the cold light of the headlamps startling him as he crouched, bewildered, in the dark-carpeted passage, the roar of the motor, the sharp reflected light streaming in through the half-open window at the head of the stairs so that he saw the leap of his own dressing-gowned shadow—gigantic, contorted—as he turned away; hearing, as he turned, blended with the rumble of the lorry that other sound, open-throated yet no longer shrill, low yet penetrating. Stop, oh stop. That noise. "Stop it. Stop it."

And the fingers at last pausing. Holding him calmly, motionlessly. "What noise?"

Henry's mouth was still wrenched open in an agonising rictus; sweat tickled his chin. He brought up his hand to wipe away the moisture, the movement freeing his jawlock; what noise? What did she mean? What noise? "I can't hear anything." He lifted his head, listening.

"You said, stop that noise."

"Did I?"

Up on one elbow. His back flexed, losing its rigidity; he was streaming with perspiration. Not just his face and neck, his whole body. Ramona, watching him; the fish diving for the deep bottom, for its covert of shimmering weeds. The fight was over. "It's no good," Henry said. "Is it?"

"It's too damned hot," Ramona said [pp. 100-101].

Henry's impotence protects his ego against the unconscious anxieties and guilt feelings he has about his parents, without the expenditure of psychic effort necessary for symptom formation (Philoppopoulos, 1967). Behind the fear of impotence lies the fear of his homosexuality, as it did with Sasha, hardly conscious or expressed by fantasies (Launay, 1969). Henry achieves potency, or power, through his occupation, bombing. Fromm (1941) states that power has a twofold meaning. "One is the possession of power over somebody, the ability to dominate him; the other meaning is the possession of power to do something, to be able, to be potent ... Thus power can mean one of two things, domination or potency.... Impotence, using the term not only with regard to the sexual sphere but to all spheres of human potentialities, results in the sadistic striving for domination..." (p. 162). Thus Henry, while disliked by his fellow conspirators as a person, was admired and trusted for his power to perform coolly under stress and to do an expert job.

Homosexual anxieties and concomitant impotency fears pursued Dave Kahn, in Seymour Epstein's *Leah* (1964), "like a man going to a guillotine—still moving, still alive, possibly still not believing in the fate facing him" on the night he approached Leah Rubel in her bed and found himself wanting. Dave's parents were ideally suited to each other, thriving on Broadway musicals, fancy restaurants and an un-ending round of entertaining. Dave was left to a long succession of maids. When Dave was twelve, his father went bankrupt and then died. The old opulence was gone, and Dave's mother turned to him. From virtually nothing, he became everything. "Life ... became a thick, cloying chocolate malted. In return, she wanted to be cut in on every thought, every action" (p. 207). The boy was the principal victim; his mother never remarried. In the scene that follows, Dave and the spinsterish Leah, who have become acquainted only recently, are discussing an unfortunate incident that occurred while they were in a bistro. Dave had felt affronted by some male homosexuals, but Leah believed their behavior had been innocuous. Dave's touchiness becomes all the more inappropriate when he attacks Leah.

"... Tonight you tried to make out like I was straight from the Middle Ages because I was repelled by a bunch of disgusting, snotty queers!"

Had he reached over and slapped her face, Leah couldn't have been more slack-jawed, bewildered, outraged with astonishment.

"I—"

"And what is more—" he cut in "—the thing the really bothers me the most is that you took *their* part after that dirty little swine deliberately, personally insulted me. I mean how damn objective can you get! You can't have a very high opinion of me, can you? And coming after what I told you—the way I feel about you—I couldn't have made that much plainer, could I? Since we met last Saturday, there haven't been many waking moments when I haven't been thinking about you—"

"Dave—" Leah rid herself of the glass she was holding. "Dave—" she was actually trembling from the wild farrago of accusation and admission, indiscriminately mixed as they were and flung at her with such dizzying suddenness. "Dave, I don't know what I've done to make you feel this way, but whatever it is I'm sorry. I had absolutely no intention . . . I hadn't the slightest idea. . . ."

"Listen," he said, his face paler than ever, and terribly drawn, so that Leah knew that however unreasonable and imagined his injury, it was deeply felt. "We're neither of us children," he went on, his whole demeanor changing again, now softly importunate and wrung with premonitions of loss. "We both know what a basic lack of respect—I mean, I've seen it between people—I'm sure you have, too. And you know it's humiliating to have made an admission—well, God damn it, you *know* what I've been admitting!—and then, to find you completely *down* on me . . . I know all this sounds terribly exaggerated, but things have happened to me, Leah, as I'm sure they have to you, and—and a man gets to be fearful. Can you understand that? Can you understand what it is, Leah, to be full of fears?"

Leah reached up and took his head between her hands. She drew him toward her lips. It was a painful, contorted kiss. *Did she know what it was to be full of fears!* This wrenched from her a storm of feeling to match his own. Yes, she could understand fears, even fears as groundless and swollen as his. And it was too much! Just—too—damn—much! To have things offered her, mangled, snatched away!

She wept, her face against his. Dave kissed her slowly, first her eyes, then her mouth, then her cheeks. She felt his open mouth against her cheek, his tongue, as if he were trying to taste the salt of her tears. "Leah," he breathed against her, drinking balm from her face. "Leah—" his hands caressing the sides of her body, moving down to her hips, buttocks. "Leah—"

They swayed together, Leah gave herself up to the sweet groping dominion of flesh, exploring his body with her own hands. "Dave, wait—" she whispered, breaking away from him.

"No!" he protested, as if it were pain to be separated for a second.

"I'll be back in a second, darling," she said, and went to the bathroom—for, as he had said, neither of them were children.

When she returned, wearing only the bathrobe that hung from a peg on the bathroom door, the room was in darkness. They found each other in the darkness, and taking Dave by the hand Leah led him to the sofa. She heard a sound escape his lips, a sound which might have meant anything—desire, love, conquest—but it was only a slight, deprecating laugh. "Now you'll have to excuse *me*," he said, and felt his way to the bathroom.

He was gone for less than a minute. The light from the bathroom exploded like a photographer's bulb when he came out, and then all was darkness again.

"Here," said Leah, to give him direction.

He was beside her, kneeling as he had done last Sunday, his hands cold as defeat, touching her, one on her pelvis, the other on her ribs, below her breast. His face, profiled against her stomach, pressed there as if in this posture of supplication he would speak to her very entrails, to some merciful part of her that would share in comradeship this wound.

"It's no use, Leah," he bled. "I can't. That's the way it is with me, I can't. That's my curse, I can't." Over and over, like a weary, penitential prayer: "I'm sorry, Leah . . . I'm sorry . . . I'm sorry . . ."

Now Leah could recognize the voice of Dave Kahn. Not the senseless, false voice of accusation, but this, his own voice made real by this grief, and the grief meeting her horrified understanding at the level where pity begins [pp. 126-128].

Jill, the eighteen-year-old runaway in *Rabbit Redux* by John Updike (1971) and Simona, the frigid depressive in *I Want It Now* by Kingsley Amis (1969), are two of a kind. Jill is a teeny-bopping drug addict whom Harry "Rabbit" Angstrom picks up in a bar and takes home because she has no place else to go. Harry's name, of course, reveals his story: he is the harried rabbit that copulates and runs, full of purgatorial *angst*. Jill's wealthy, Connecticut father died suddenly while watching a performance of the nude musical show, *Hair;* her mother had been playing around with men ever since Jill remembered. "You should be fucking my mother, she really is good with men, she thinks they're the be-all and end-all. I know she was playing around, even before Daddy died" (p. 144). Harry, separated from his wife, and twice Jill's age, is unable to rise to the occasion. Jill "glances at his groin. 'I don't turn you on exactly, do I?... I don't turn anybody on, much. No tits. My mother has nifty tits, maybe that's my trouble'" (pp. 143-144).

Competition with the mother is Simona's trouble as well in *I Want It Now*. She does not like her name, or Mona, but insists on being called Simon. Her mother, now Lady Baldock, has been married three times and is arrogantly status-conscious. Simon's father died many years previously. At twenty-six, she barely remembers him. However, she still calls mother "Mummy," and is obedient in her fashion. When the reader first meets Simon, she is unwashed and unshod, attending a posh Mayfair party and inviting Ronnie Applegard to go to bed with her. The brashness of the demand is an aggressive reaction to her mother's dominance. Ronnie, an opportunist interested in two things, self-advancement and sex, eagerly brings her to his digs where he shortly discovers she is frigid. Simon's muffled voice comes to him, "You're mad at me," to which he replies, "I might well be, yes, but I'm not ... I'm merely disappointed. I thought you were bloody attractive. Never mind. I don't know whether it's me you don't like, or men, or sex, and I'm not bothered which it is. That's your problem, love. Now in a minute I'm going round to the pub to get some cigarettes, and when I come back I'll expect to find you gone" (p. 42). Simon's difficulty is probably vaginismus, an involuntary spasm of the vaginal muscles, always psychogenic in origin. "While it protects the woman from the pain she fears, she suffers a pain which is brought about unconsciously. This is a conversion symptom. Above and beyond the sexual fantasies which the symptom may express, vaginismus achieves its unconscious goal by excluding the penis, by expelling it, or by painfully enclosing it. Sadistic and masochistic tendencies fuse in this symptom with urethral and anal eliminative and retentive tendencies. Thus, vaginismus can be compared to ejaculatio praecox or ejaculatio retardata" (Benedek, 1959, p. 735). But Ronnie's first unhappy sexual experience with Simon does not deter him from pursuing her when he discovers she comes from a wealthy family. He wangles an invitation from Lady Baldock to her Greek island villa and there finds that he and Simon have connecting rooms. "Mummy's very good about me and sex," explains Simon, "and I think she likes to know" (Amis,

p. 77). Unprincipled Ronnie is dogged in his determination to woo and win Simon:

He lay down beside her and took her in his arms. Her body stiffened slightly.

'Have you always hated it?' he asked.

'Oh yes, every time. Hated the whole bloody thing.'

'Does it make any difference whether you like the man?'

'No. Not to itself. That's always the same, right from the first time. I was only fourteen then. A girl-friend of mine had just started and she told me exactly what you did. It sounded so marvellous that I went and did it straight away. And it was horrible. I thought maybe I was too young, so I held off for a couple of years, and then tried it again. And it was just like it was the first time, horrible in exactly the same way. And it's been like that ever since. Sorry, Ronnie, but it isn't *you*, you see.'

'I do see. But what I don't see is why you keep doing it. You told me you'd had forty-four men. Is it because you hope you'll find someone it won't be horrible with?'

'Forty-five, counting you. No, after the first two I stopped hoping. Until the other day, that is. Now I've started hoping again. No, I slept around because I wanted someone. Someone to be with me. You know, a man of my own. That was part of the time. The rest of the time it wasn't as grand as that. Just someone to be with me for a while.'

'Simon, have you never come? Had an orgasm?'

Her voice grew hoarser. 'Not with men.'

'Ah.'

'No, not girls either. I tried them. By the time we got into bed I didn't want to do anything to them, and what they did to me was just as horrible as a man. Different, but easily as horrible.'

'I see.'

'Are you disgusted with me?'

'No. I was just wondering if we could use that, if I could use it.'

'Trouble is, Ronnie,' she said in a laryngitic whisper, 'you have to sort of be over here to do it, where I am. Be me, really. I only know one way to do it and it takes ages. Doesn't always work, either. Sorry. Nothing seems to be any good, does it?'

'We're making a bit of progress. It's bound to be slow.'

'Hey, wait a minute, Ronnie, can't I do it to you? I mean, you know ... Or would that be difficult?'

'Nothing could be easier, love, I can assure you of that. But wouldn't you hate it?'

'Not hate it, just not mind it. And I'll like it being nice for you. If it would be.'

'It would be.'

After that, of course, she was more relaxed than ever before, until it started being relevant again. Then, and later, and as earlier, he found his touch confined to the totally neutral areas of her, and these were not many. The arm up to the elbow, the furry forearm, he possessed undisputed; the upper arm began to be sensitive territory, and the shoulder brought a tiny but perceptible stiffening from head to foot, because shoulder was near breast, and everybody knew what came after breast. The small of the back was all right, but as a hand moved from there to the angle of the waist it came closer to everything. Face was good, neck good, throat less good, base of throat bad. Ronnie came to dread their twice-daily sessions, but only a bit, not nearly as much as Simon did. Anyway, having no visible alternative, he went on with them. Towards the end of the week she began to improve slightly, both before and during, or so he fancied. She was best, obviously, when she got interested in what they were talking about, when, in other words, she could momentarily forget the hideous fact that she was lying naked with a naked man who was all too ready, demonstrably able and therefore by definition unreservedly willing to copulate with her. Handicapped by almost total ignorance of what made women frigid, he tried some amateur psycho-analysis, asking her for instance to recall her first man and just what it was that was horrible about him.

'It wasn't him that was horrible, it was it. What he did, or maybe how he did it. When he got going. I still thought it was going to be lovely up until I suppose he really got excited, until he realized that nothing could stop him starting to do it any minute. I hadn't told him I was a virgin and that didn't come into it: he didn't hurt me. He just ... the way he used his hand on me, in such a hurry all the time, as if he was putting out a fire, or dealing with a dangerous animal. And then when he got into me, so sort of urgent, I don't mean too fast, not that at all, I think he was probably quite good and wanted to give me a nice time. It was like he and I were in some sort of terrible emergency together, trying to escape from a flood or something, almost ... like riding a horse to get out of danger, and the harder he went at me the faster we'd go. And then at the end he had to go all out for a bit or something would have got us, and then we were past, we were safe, he'd got us through. Only I'd never wanted to come along in the first place.'

Ronnie said with carefully idle curiosity, 'Did your mother ever, you know, tell you about sex, explain it to you?'

'We've never discussed it.'

'Oh,' he said, still very idly, 'I'd have thought it must keep coming up, you say she's very good about it, and things like the arrangements here, surely you and she . . .'

'No, it's all taken as read. We don't discuss it.'

'Ng. What did your father say about it? Oh, of course, he died when you were a child, didn't he? Your first stepfather, then.'

'Stavros. Well . . . he never had much to do with me. He sort of left me to Mummy, really. We never talked about anything. So . . .'

'Yes, so you've never had a man round the place much. Just boy-friends and lovers and people from outside.'

She moved slightly, apparently just for comfort, but one result was that her thighs were now farther away from his. 'I see. You mean I'd never had a chance to find out what men were like at all until I went to bed with one. And so it was all too much of a shock. There may be something in that. But can there be? Aren't you supposed to feel better right away when you know what's been making you feel bad? Isn't that what these psycho-whatnot fellows say?'

'I expect you've been to lots of them.'

'Oh no. Mummy doesn't believe in them.'

Whatever there might have been in the shock idea, Simon did not seem to feel better after being introduced to it, either right away or later. The whole thing was and continued much the same. On the afternoon of his last day, Ronnie found himself seized by the desperation that is the forerunner of despair. There seemed no thoughts in his mind when he started treating naked Simon as a naked woman, plying her with hands and mouth and body in motions no more voluntary than those of a man carried downstream by a torrent. At the last moment, as he settled himself above her, she made a movement or a sound, probably both, that activated some part of his brain. It was gone instantly without leaving the faintest recollection of itself, but he could recollect what it had reminded him of: somebody preparing to receive a physical punishment or catch a formidably heavy object. As unthinkingly as before, he stopped.

'Come on, Ronnie. What is it? I'm ready.'

'I couldn't. You'd hate it.'

'I don't mind hating it. I want you to have it.'

'I'd hate it too. Anyway, I couldn't now.'

He spoke the truth. By this time he was lying beside her and holding her in his arms. She started to cry violently.

'It makes no difference whatever we do. Nobody's ever been so nice to me and it doesn't make any difference. It'll never be right.'

He agreed with her, but said, 'One day it'll be right,' there being no other line by which to play out the next twenty hours or so.

'I'm so horrible and silly and childish and awful and selfish and babyish and scared of everyting. And you're going.'

'Only to London. Not away for good.'

'If only I could come with you.'

At this point Ronnie could not prevent himself from feeling rather sorry for Simon. Feeling sorry for people was something he was far from used to, which was perhaps why he forgot himself sufficiently to say, 'Why don't you? It would be marvellous if you did.'

'I can't.'

'Why not? You haven't got to be here.'

She shrank away from him, and when she spoke her voice had gone dead. 'Not coming.'

'Why not? Remember you agreed to tell the truth.'

'Only about sex and things.'

Ronnie started to say that in his view they had not left that topic, but this time checked himself. 'No, Simon, everything. You must see that, surely.'

'All right, then. Mummy wouldn't like it.'

'I see. What would she do if you just said you were going?'

'Well, she wouldn't prevent me, of course. But she'd be terribly upset. She wants me here with her, to help her and things.'

'I haven't seen you doing much helping. And so she's terribly upset, but you just tell her kindly that you're going and go. What can she do?'

'Ronnie, you're completely off. You don't understand a damn thing. When Mummy gets upset it's just . . . awful. She's so sensitive and she's had two husbands die and she's so brave.' There was a fresh onset of crying. 'You don't know what it's like when she really gets upset. It's not fair, she's had so much to put up with about me and everything. She gets so terribly worked up. I can't stand people getting worked up.'

'Of course not,' said Ronnie pacifically. 'Simon, quite off the track, but did your mother and what's his name, bloody shagbag, old Stavros, did they get on fairly okay?'

'Not too bad, I suppose.'

'No great dust-ups, rows, any of that?'

'Well, yes, they did, actually. Stavros wanted his own way in ab-solutely everything. Including about me. The only time he took any interest in me was when he was trying to send me away to school or something. Mummy used to stand up to him on behalf of me and he'd be furious at being crossed, and then she'd get upset, and so it went on.'

'Were you sent away to school?'

'No. Mummy stopped him doing that. What about it?'

'Just off the track.' He held her in his arms a little longer and then said, as coldly as he could, 'Don't you think your trouble is simply that you're scared stiff of your mother?'

'Ball, ballocks, shit.' No more tears now. She wriggled out of his embrace and settled in a sort of uncommitted position, by him but not with him. 'You're so completely off you'll never know it. Mr. Van Pup and Mr. Vassilikós and everybody keeps saying we're just like sisters. *You . . . wouldn't . . . know.* All my girl-friends keep say-ing they wish they got on with their mothers like I do with Mummy. We can talk about anything. You just wouldn't know.' [pp. 116-122].

Ronnie describes Simon's performance in bed with him as "you jog-ging about like an electric blender to stop me seeing how much you hate it" (p. 80). When Lady Baldock recognizes Ronnie for the fortune hunter he is, she sends him packing, quickly finding another suitor for her daughter, one Mansfield, who is, of all things, impotent. "And when you come to think of it," an acquaintance tells Ronnie, "we are dealing with a situation in which incapacity is a recommendation. What better husband for a girl who don't like it than a guy who can't do it?" Simon informs Ronnie that Mummy "wants me to marry [Mansfield] because he's the son of the man she was in love with when she was a girl before she married Daddy." To which Ronnie astutely responds, "She wanted a homosexual son who doted on his darling mother, not a heterosexual daughter . . . In a way, your mother would like you never to get married at all, so that she could keep you by her side and go on bullying you, and also because she knows you want to be married. So men appear, and sleep with you, and that's fine because she knows you don't enjoy it" (p. 171).

Another fictional mama, the more notorious Mrs. Portnoy, did not want her heir to get married either. She did a workmanlike job on Alexander, even if the figments of the latter's imagination were deliberately distorted One memory may suffice: of Mrs. Portnoy, standing over her son with a butcher's knife to make him eat, an exaggerated castrating vision of a childhood unhappily remembered. Alex, in Philip Roth's *Portnoy's Complaint* (1969), is continuously preoccupied with the need to prove his masculinity. Radomisli (1967) describes a form of object split in which the man is sexually potent with the debased woman and is sexually inhibited with the respected, esteemed woman without, however, insisting on the latter's purity and asexuality. Saul (1951) determined that for some men sexuality is an outlet for so much hostility that it means to them an attack. They are relatively impotent with women whom they respect and sexually uninhibited only with those women for whom they have no regard or sympathy. This type of man divides women into two categories; he is potent only with the degraded ones who are not identified with the incestuous object, but whom he can "attack" because he identifies with them so little. Both mechanisms, dependence and hostility, frequently occur in the same person, and are usually closely related.

Portnoy was capable of performing prodigious feats of sexuality only with the "debased" woman. One instance was the triumverate *ménage* he established in Rome with an Italian prostitute and The Monkey. "Boy, was I busy! I mean there was just so much to do. You go here and I'll go there — okay, now you go here and *I'll* go there — all right, now she goes down that way, while I head up this way, and you sort of half turn around on this . . . and so it went, Doctor, until I came my third and final time. . ." (Roth, p. 137). Portnoy was potent with women who bore no resemblance to his mother, an overpowering woman. She controlled by any tactic available: physical or emotional threat, rejection or guilt. Thus, Portnoy was afraid to love a woman in any serious way. For to love, as he loved his mother as a child, was to risk castration, rejection, or extraordinary control by another. To love was to be smothered and overwhelmed. To marry was to risk living with a woman like mother and becoming as impotent, self-effacing, and long-suffering as his father. Thus when Alex met Naomi, a native-born Israeli Sabra, who seemed as formidable as his mother, he was impotent. "It's no good," he said, "I can't get a hard-on in this place" (p. 268). "But me, I dare to steal a slightly unusual kind of a hump, and while away on my *vacation*—and now I can't get it up!" (p.

273). Portnoy could not understand what happened to him. Previously, to relieve his own sense of sexual inadequacy, he had led to bed a succession of women to prove his masculinity. The novel ends in a long, drawn-out whimper of impotent frustration, with Portnoy fantasizing a furious gun duel between himself and the police.

The usual family trinity found in Norman Mailer's fiction—the innocent, tormented son, the brutal or inept father, and the castrating mother—provide the basis for his heroes' psychic impotence. McLeod in *Barbary Shore* (1951), Eitel in *The Deer Park* (1955), and detective Roberts in *An American Dream* (1965) are the bad father figures who are impotent or compensating for their sexual inadequacy through violence. In fact, every male in the Mailerian canon, hero or villain, suffers from psychic impotence or castration anxiety, or has grave doubts about his potency (Gordon, 1969). *The Naked and the Dead* (1948), Mailer's first novel, is an explicit statement of defeat. Omnipotence, as a private motive of historical destiny, gives way to impotence (Hassan, 1961). This impotence holds, even in a physical sense, as Gordon illustrates (p. 7): "Martinez, the Mexican, is insecure, and feels incomplete as a man until he can succeed with 'white Protestant girls, firm and aloof' (p. 58). Corporal Stanley discovers he is 'inept and incapable of controlling himself. His love spasms had been quick and nervous; he had wept . . . in his wife's arms at his failure' (p. 257). Wilson, once an invincible stud, is now rotting away from venereal disease, and fears the Japanese will 'cut mah nuts off' (p. 448). As Hearn says blithely, 'If I'm afraid of having my dick cut off or something like that, I don't care to know it' (p. 304)." The fear of loss of potency and the terror of castration is pointed out in another scene by Gordon (p. 11): "When the soldiers are forced to carry a field piece through a deeply rutted jungle trail, the struggle with the gun becomes a form of forbidden sexual encounter, like sodomy: 'They felt as though they were groping their way through an endless tunnel. Their feet sank into the deep mud . . .' (p. 114). The metaphorical sodomy in turn conjures up images of castration: 'The file at last broke into separate wriggling columns like a worm cut into many parts' (ibid.) And the final impotence occurs when the men lose their grip, and the gun slides downhill."

As T. S. Eliot observed in *The Cocktail Hour,* (1950), "To men of a certain type, the suspicion that they are incapable of loving is as disturbing to their self-esteem as, in cruder men, the fear of impotence."

Multiple etiological factors usually influence the impotent male and frigid female. Those factors, according to Masters and Johnson (1970, p. 137), "that are in large measure responsible for individually intolerable levels of anxiety either prior to or during initial attempts at sexual connection are untoward maternal influences, psychological restrictions originating with religious orthodoxy, involvement of homosexual functioning, and personal devaluation from prostitution experiences." The intrapsychic conflicts projected in fiction tend to bear out the psychological analyses and give credence to the psychoaffective nature of the predicament.

TECHNICAL REFERENCES

Abraham, K. (1917), Ejaculatio praecox. In: *Selected Papers.* New York: Basic Books, 1953, pp. 280-298.

Beauvoir, S. de (1968), *The Second Sex.* New York: Knopf.

Benedek, T. F. (1959), Sexual functions in women and their disturbance. In: *American Handbook of Psychiatry,* 1, ed. S. Arieti. New York: Basic Books, pp. 727-748.

Bergler, E. (1947), Newer genetic investigations on impotence and frigidity. *Bulletin of the Menninger Clinic,* 11:50-57.

Brown, D. G. (1966), Female orgasm and sexual inadequacy. In: *An Analysis of Human Sexual Response,* ed. R. Brecher & E. Brecher. Boston: Little, Brown, pp. 125-174.

Cameron, N. (1963), *Personality Development and Psychopathology: A Dynamic Approach.* Boston: Houghton Mifflin.

Cochran, R. W. (1968), Circularity in *The Sun Also Rises. Modern Fiction Studies,* 14(3):297-306.

Cooper, A. J. (1969a), Factors in male sexual inadequacy: A review. *Journal of Nervous and Mental Disease,* 149(4):337-359.

_____ (1969b), Some personality factors in frigidity. *Journal of Psychosomatic Research,* 13(2):149-155.

Deutsch, H. (1960), Frigidity in women. In: *Neuroses and Character Types.* New York: International Universities Press, 1965, pp. 358-362.

Ellis, A. (1966), *The Search for Sexual Enjoyment.* New York: Macfadden.

Ellis, H. (1933), *Psychology of Sex.* New York: New American Library, 1954.

Fenichel, O. (1945), *The Psychoanalytic Theory of Neurosis.* New York: Norton.

Fiedler, L. A. (1960), *Love and Death in the American Novel.* London: Paladin, 1970.

Freud, S. (1905), Three essays on the theory of sexuality. *Standard Edition,* 7:125-243. London: Hogarth Press, 1953.

_____ (1912), Contributions to the psychology of love, II. On the universal tendency to debasement in the sphere of love. *Standard Edition,* 11:179-190. London: Hogarth Press, 1957.

_____ (1933), New introductory lectures on psycho-analysis. *Standard Edition*, 22: 3-182. London: Hogarth Press, 1964.

Fromm, E. (1941), *Escape from Freedom*. New York: Rinehart.

Goldfarb, R. M. (1970), *Sexual Repression and Victorian Literature*. Lewisburg, Pa.: Bucknell University Press.

Gordon, A. (1969), *The Naked and the Dead:* The triumph of impotence. *Literature and Psychology*, 19(3/4):3-13.

Grant-Duff, I. F. (1937), A one-sided sketch of Jonathan Swift. *Psychoanalytic Quarterly*, 6:238-259.

Greenacre, P. (1955), *Swift and Carroll: A Psychoanalytic Study of Two Lives*. New York: International Universities Press.

Gustin, J. C. (1952), Phantasy in frigidity. *Psychoanalysis*, 1(2):12-26.

Gutheil, E. H. (1959), Sexual dysfunctions in men. In: *American Handbook of Psychiatry*, 1, ed. S. Arieti. New York: Basic Books, pp. 708-726.

Hassan, I. (1961), *Radical Innocence*. Princeton: Princeton University Press.

Hastings, D. W. (1963), *Impotence and Frigidity*. New York: Delta.

Hirschfeld, M. (1944), *Sexual Anomalies and Perversions: Physical and Psychological Development and Treatment*. London: Aldor.

Klein, M. (1945), The Oedipus complex in the light of early anxieties. *International Journal of Psycho-Analysis*, 26:11-33.

Launay, C. (1969), Les inhibitions sexuelles chez l'adolescent. *Acta Paedopsychiatrica*, 36(1):23-26.

Masters, W. H. & Johnson, V. E. (1970), *Human Sexual Inadequacy*. Boston: Liittle, Brown.

McCurdy, H. G. (1940), Literature and personality: Analysis of the novels of D. H. Lawrence. *Character and Personality*, 8:181-203.

_____ (1947), A study of the novels of Charlotte and Emily Brontë as an expression of their personalities. *Journal of Pesonality*, 16:109-152.

Millett, K. (1970), *Sexual Politics*. Garden City, N.Y.: Doubleday.

Moreno, M. (1969), Sexual impotence in the female: Frigidity. *Rivista di Psichiatria*, 4(4):289-297.

Ort, D. (1969), Lawrence's *Women in Love*. *The Explicator*, 27(5):38.

Paulson, M. J. & Lin, T. T. (1970), Frigidity: A factor analytic study of a psychosomatic theory. *Psychosomatics*, 11:112-119.

Philippopoulos, G. S. (1969), The analysis of a case of frigidity: Psychopathology-psychodynamics. *Psychotherapy and Psychosomatics*, 15(2/4):220-230.

Radomisli, M. (1967), The phallic phase and debasement in the sphere of love. *Psychoanalytic Review*, 54(3):5-20.

Ranzato, F. P. & Zagami, E. (1969), Sexual impotence in the young and old: Psychological causes. *Rivista di Psichiatria*, 4(4):324-326.

Saul, L. J. (1951), Two observations on the split in object choice. *Psychoanalytic Quarterly*, 20:93-95.

Seidenberg, R. (1951), Psychosexual aspects of Hymen. *Psychiatric Quarterly*, 25:472-474.

Sprenger, J. & Kramer, H. (1489), *Malleus Malleficarum*. London: Rodker, 1928.

Stafford-Clark, D. (1954), The aetiology and treatment of impotence. *Practitioner,* 172:397-404.

Stekel, W. (1927), *Impotence in the Male.* New York: Liveright, 1959.

Taylor, G. R. (1954), *Sex in History.* New York: Ballantine.

Yalom, I. D. & Yalom, M. (1971), Ernest Hemingway: A psychiatric view. *Archives of General Psychiatry,* 24:485-494.

Young, P. (1952), *Ernest Hemingway: A Reconsideration.* University Park, Pa.: Penn State University Press.

Zimmerman, F. (1948), The book of *Ecclesiastes* in the light of some psychoanalytic observations. *American Imago,* 5:301-305.

LITERARY REFERENCES

Amis, Kingsley (1969), *I Want It Now.* New York: Harcourt, Brace & World.

Brontë, Charlotte (1853), *Villette.* London: Zodiac, 1957.

Cory, Desmond (1972), *Even If You Run.* Garden City, N.Y.: Doubleday.

Durrell, Lawrence (1958), *Balthazar.* New York: Dutton.

Eliot, T. S. (1950), *The Cocktail Hour.* New York: Harcourt, Brace & World.

Epstein, Seymour (1964), *Leah.* Boston: Little, Brown.

Fielding, Henry (1749), *The History of Tom Jones, A Foundling.* New York: New American Library, 1963.

Ford, Ford Madox (1915), *The Good Soldier: A Tale of Passion.* New York: Boni, 1927.

Giles, Kenneth (1973), *A File on Death.* New York: Walker.

Gould, Lois (1970), *Such Good Friends.* New York: Random House.

Graves, Robert (1934), *I, Claudius.* New York: Random House.

Hemingway, Ernest (1926), *The Sun Also Rises.* New York: Scribner's.

Jong, Erica (1973), *Fear of Flying.* New York: Holt, Rinehart & Winston.

Kazantzakis, Nikos (1952), *Zorba the Greek.* New York: Simon & Schuster.

Lawrence, D. H. (1920), *Women in Love.* New York: Viking, 1974.

―――― (1922), *Aaron's Rod.* New York: Viking, 1961.

―――― (1928), *Lady Chatterley's Lover.* New York: Knopf.

Mailer, Norman (1948), *The Naked and the Dead.* New York: Rinehart.

―――― (1951), *Barbary Shore.* New York: New American Library.

―――― (1955), *The Deer Park.* New York: Putnam.

―――― (1965), *An American Dream.* New York: Dial.

O'Hara, John (1955), *10 North Frederick.* New York: Random House.

Richardson, Samuel (1741), *Clarissa, or the History of a Young Lady,* Vol. 1. New York: Dutton, 1932.

Roth, Philip (1969), *Portnoy's Complaint.* New York: Random House.

Shulman, Alix K. (1972), *Memoirs of an Ex-Prom Queen.* New York: Knopf.

Stendahl (1830), *The Red and the Black.* New York: Modern Library, 1926.

Swift, Jonathan (1704a), Memoirs of Scriblerus. In: *The Prose Works,* ed. H. Dans. Oxford, England: Blackwell, 1939.

_____ (1704b), *Tale of a Tub*. New York: Dutton, 1909.

Updike, John (1971), *Rabbit Redux*. New York: Knopf.

Wollstonecraft, Mary (1788), *Mary, a Fiction*. London: Johnson.

Wycherley, William (1672), *The Country Wife*. Lincoln, Neb.: University of Nebraska Press, 1965.

CHAPTER TEN

Rape

Sex and violence are so close to the surface in so many people's lives that it is quite possible a large percentage of newspaper and fiction readers, as well as movie audiences, are readily titillated by the glamorous and exciting accounts portrayed in these media. The President's Commission on Law Enforcement and Administration of Justice (1967) reported the national incidence of forcible rape as increasing. A detailed interview study undertaken by the National Opinion Research Center of the University of Chicago (Ennis, 1967) found focible rape actually occurred at more than three and a half times the reported rate of 42.5 per 100,000 population. These figures suggest that, on the average, the likelihood of a serious personal attack on any American woman in a given year is about one in 500. The Washington, D.C. Crime Index for 1970-1971 showed 421 cases of rape, a thirty per cent increase over the previous twelve months, with a marked increase in daytime rapes. Over 37,000 rapes were reported in the United States in 1970. If the incidence of rape has in fact increased nationally, this might be corollary to the general increased aggression and violence.

Rape is considered by many people to be the most heinous of crimes. Depending upon the brutality of the attack and the age of the victim, the trauma and shock of only one incident, taking no more than a few minutes, can last for years (Schiff, 1972). Rape is an act of violence; there is no such thing as nonviolent rape.

Rape has been defined as unlawful sexual intercourse with a woman by force and against her will (Barnes, 1967). The legal essence of the offense is that it be committed without the woman's consent or gained by threats or false pretenses or trickery, or when the woman is stupified or unconscious from drink or drugs. Rape, as defined by Sutherland and Scherl (1970), refers to forced sexual penetration of a woman by a man, accomplished under actual or implied threat of severe bodily harm. Three elements are necessary: carnal knowledge, force, and commission without consent (Miller, 1934). The slightest penetration of the male organ is sufficient to constitute carnal knowledge; mere entrance into the vulva or labia suffices. Ejaculation may or may not take place. Thus, the word "rape," a legal term, connotes an assaultive sexual attack on an unwilling victim, with the adjective "forcible" commonly employed. Statutory rape is carnal knowledge of any girl below a legally set age, ranging from fourteen to twenty-one in the United States, with or without her consent. The essence of statutory rape is age, that is, having intercourse with a juvenile.

A survey of rape in literature would undoubtedly include references to the Bible and to Greek and Roman literature. It will be recalled that Zeus was a notorious rapist, having violated Leda while camouflaged as a swan, and Europa in the guise of a bull. Kainis, of the horse-taming tribe, was raped by Poseidon. In some instances rape was punishable, but it was not always treated under criminal law. In early cultures, rape and abduction of women tended to be ritualized, institutionalized events rather than expressions of primitive aggressiveness (Bednarik, 1968). Rape flourished in cultures where women were the property of men and where their theft under certain circumstances was tolerated, as noted by Wortis (1939). He cites an example of a socially acceptable form of rape in the romance of Thomas Malory's *Le Morte d'Arthur* (c. 1450). During the wedding feast of King Arthur and Guinevere, a lady on a white palfrey protested the theft of her brachet. "There came a knight named Hontzlake of Wentland riding all armed on a great horse, and took the lady away with him with force and ever she cried and made a great dole." When she was gone, the king was glad "for she made such a noise." According to the rules of chivalry a knight might not harm a damsel or wench if found alone, should he wish to preserve his good name. If, however, the damsel were accompanied by another knight and, if it pleased him to give combat to the knight and win the lady by arms, then he might do his will with her just as he pleased, and no shame or blame whatsoever would be held against him (Briffault, 1963).

Rape is not tolerated in today's culture, where women have ceased to be regarded as chattel and where common thievery—the rape of property—is taboo. Changing religious, moral, philosophical, and social factors define sexual patterns of behavior and individual response to these patterns. From the evidence in other societies, experiences such as rape, "carnal abuse," defloration, incest, homosexuality, or "indecent" exposure do not have the effects expected in this part of the world (Tappan, 1955). Young people who have not been exposed to parental and community hysteria about sex can better absorb the experience of a socially disapproved sexual assault without untoward consequences (Ellis, 1954; Greer, 1972). There are considerable variations even among cultures in this country in matters of open sexuality. These variations are functions of social class, ethnic group, religious background, and parental attitudes. Sexual behavior considered normal in one class is frequently thought deviant in another (Hayman et al., 1972). According to Ellis (1954): "When we label sex activity as abnormal because it seems to be injurious to mental or physical health . . . we should acknowledge that exceptionally few sex acts are dangerous or health-destroying *in themselves,* but that many become self-destructive because society insists on viewing them as such and making them so. Rape, for example, actually inflicts little or no harm on the adult victims if they are raised to view it lightly; but if they are raised to look upon it as a heinous attack, they may actually be seriously harmed by it" (p. 78). It is where severe neurotic fears have already been implanted or where they are imposed after the encounter that lasting injury may be done. This is apparent in William Faulkner's protagonist, Temple Drake, who is raped in the novel *Sanctuary* (1931). Six years after the attack, the action picks up in the sequel, *Requiem for a Nun* (1951), and Temple is still expiating for the event.

In *Letters from Iceland,* Christopher Isherwood asked his friend, W. H. Auden (1937), "What about the sex life [there]?" The response: "Uninhibited." When, in Richard Falkirk's novel, *The Chill Factor* (1971), a murder occurs in Iceland, an American visitor questions the chief of police. " 'Why is everyone in Rejkjavik saying she was raped?' 'That was the first impression. It is very difficult to destroy. We presumed too much from the torn clothing.' He ordered another drink. 'We in Iceland find this disgusting. Nothing like this has happened before.' 'And that's why people presume it must be an American?' He nodded. 'Because an Icelandic man would never have to resort to rape' " (p. 74).

Taboos are essential to the preservation of any normal pattern of sexual behavior, but both the sexual behavior pattern and its regulatory taboos are proper subjects for critical evaluation. Centuries ago, rape was part of a ritualized fertility rite in Italy. In a modern retelling of a pagan saturnalia, the infectious hilarity and the creative fantasy that permeate *Hermaphrodeity,* the novel by Alan Friedman (1972), overcome even the outrageous perpetration of a rape that befalls Millie who, with some local peasants, has just come upon an archaeological treasure trove. She relates:

> There is a footnote to this excavation. The strain of climactic discovery had evidently been too much for my men. As I was getting into bed one night they surrounded my tent to serenade me first, and then had the effrontery, with lots of jokes and lots of shouts, to come in and pull me out of my cot in my nightgown. Tugging at my hands, they insisted on leading me, over my protests, over my laughter, with lots of flashlights and song, to the nearby Cave of the Throat. I was irritated at being dragged into an unlighted cave at night by so many aroused old men. But for group morale I decided to be a good sport about the whole thing and confined my objections to nervous reprimands. When we reached the cave, they hauled me in all the way under the arch to that inflamed pink-and-purple-and-red stalagmite poking up out of the floor, engorged and glistening. They pulled my legs apart and rudely lifted my nightgown out of the way. Even Totonedu. I was paralyzed with shock: worse, I was plain speechless. With all the cackling together, intoning some unctuous local chant, and holding me up by my spread thighs over the ancient protruding deposit, rather gently they wedded me to the rock.
>
> As their boss I was outraged. As a poet, however, I was impressed to the core and upon reflection realized that I had experienced a rape that deserved reverence. How else was I to interpret it? Some obscenities are sacred, certain violations sacramental [pp. 397-398].

Impaled on the tip of the phallic stalagmite, hermaphroditic Millie became accepting and philosophical about what at first seemed an outrage. Her logical recourse was to fire all the workers, which she did, but simply to maintain discipline.

The phenomenon of rape has a long and colorful history, insights from which can be gained from the reading of plays, novels, and short stories. This is so because such fictional sources involve force, humiliation, and degradation, and can be conceived as the utmost dramatization of the conflict and fate of the personalities involved (Amir, 1971). But there is singularly little authoritative psychological material on the subject. Up until 1974, only three books (Amir, 1971; Baughman, 1966; MacDonald, 1971) were published which deal exclusively with rape; but even these are not primarily psychological in approach. However, in 1974 and 1975, at least eleven books (Astor, 1975; Brownmiller, 1975; Connell and Wilson, 1974; MacKellar, 1975; Medea and Thompson, 1974; Lynch, 1974; Russell, 1975; Schultz, 1975; Smith and Giles, 1975; Storaska, 1975; Weiss and Friar, 1975) appeared, all concerned, in *toto,* with rape.

Law books and law journals do deal extensively with the subject, mostly with problems of consent, reliability of the victims' stories, and corroborative evidence. Next to murder, rape is the most serious criminal offense on the statute books, with the states retaining, until very recently, a possible death penalty for those convicted of forcible rape. For the crimes of robbery, assault, fraud, and others, the victim's word is enough to make out a prima facie case and take to a jury. But with the crime of rape, it is not enough at all. For rape, as Lord Hale observed three centuries ago, "is an accusation easily to be made and hard to be proved, and harder to be defended by the party accused, tho never so innocent" (Anon., 1967, p. 1136). The presumption on the part of male legislators has generally been that women who complain of rape are not always to be trusted. One of the characters in *The Plot Against Roger Rider* by Julian Symons (1973) comments, ". . . you know what the police say — any woman who claims she's been raped by just one man was at least partly consenting" (p. 59). Because of the inordinate danger that innocent men will be convicted, some states have adopted the rule that the unsupported testimony of the complaining witness is not sufficient evidence to support a rape conviction. In recognition of the role psychological factors play in provoking charges of sexual misconduct, there is a marked trend on the part of many courts and legislatures to insist on corroboration in prosecution for such offenses (Katz, Goldstein, and Dershowitz, 1967).

Until 1972, the law in New York State required that the purported rape victim's testimony be corroborated in three major aspects: force and lack of consent, penetration, and the identity of the rapist, the last to be sworn to by a third-party witness. The succeeding law of 1974 in New York removed the requirement for corroborative, eyewitness testimony. But it still often will be difficult to convict a rapist in cases where the two parties are known to each other. Laws concerning rape, the major crime least reported to the police, are undergoing a fundamental revision in other states as well. The changes are being made in large measure because of vigorous lobbying by women's rights groups, which, having suffered setbacks in the fight to ratify the Federal Equal Rights Amendment and having won the battle over abortion, have made rape their number one issue. A spot check by the *New York Times* in 1975 shows that fifteen of twenty-five states have changed the rules of evidence in a rape case to exclude the introduction in the trial of material about a victim's personal sex life, either current or past, except in limited instances. The fifteen states are California, Colorado, Florida, Iowa, Ohio, Oregon, Michigan, Minnesota, Montana, Nebraska, Nevada, New Mexico, New York, Texas, and Washington. Bills providing for a similar change in trial evidence limitations have been proposed in eight other states. The changes reflect a growing national trend to view rape not as a deviant sexual offense, but as a violent crime of assault. The women's groups have fought to eliminate the kind of demeaning cross-examination that tends to put the victim, rather than the rapist, on trial, to prevent questioning by unsympathetic male interrogators whose attitudes suggest that any woman can resist rape if she really wants to. Michigan's new law dispenses with the requirement for a corroborating witness, recognizes male as well as female victims of rape, limits the admissibility of evidence of the victim's sexual conduct, and establishes four degrees of sexual assault, providing varying penalties. Although rape is less prevalent in Britain than in America, guidelines for a new law on rape are being pursued there also.

Male legislators and police officials have based their justification for placing the burden of supplying corroborative evidence on women on the need to protect innocent men. Women accuse men of rape for a number of reasons, it is believed, ranging from wishful thinking to injured pride, from the need to excuse pregnancy to guilt feelings about sexual intercourse. Thus the old law discriminated against rape victims by forcing them to produce greater evidential requirements than victims of an assault or mugging.

Slovenko (1971) states that the crime of statutory rape is one of the most obsolete concepts of the law, pointing out that a sexually experienced fifteen-year-old girl may be far more acutely aware of the implications of sexual intercourse than her sheltered cousin who is beyond the age of consent. "Nevertheless, even in circumstances where a girl's actual comprehension contradicts the law's presumption, the male is deemed criminally responsible for the act, although himself young and naive and responding to advances which may have been made him ... The law on statutory rape applies even though the girl has been divorced or is a prostitute" (pp. 160-161).

Forcible rape trials often devolve into a series of conflicting statements by the accused and the alleged victim regarding precisely what took place, whether the girl at first consented and then changed her mind, whether she misinterpreted her agreement or whether she was taken by an overpowering show of force. A racial rape aroused the latent antagonistic division of a small Alabama town in the early 1930's in *To Kill a Mockingbird,* by Harper Lee (1960). Mayella Ewell, the nineteen-year-old, friendless, illiterate daughter of Bob Ewell, a red-neck, drunken widower living hear the town dump with his eight children, accused Tom Robinson, a black married man with three children, of raping her. His court-appointed attorney was Atticus Finch, the kind of man who did something "just because he knew it was right, necessary to the harmony of things that it be done," as William Faulkner characterized two other Southern attorneys, Horace Benbow in *Sanctuary* and Gavin Stevens in *Requiem for a Nun.* All three were champions not so much of truth as of justice, or of justice as they saw it, involving themselves, often for no pay, in affairs of equity and passion. In the first passage from *To Kill a Mockingbird* quoted here, Mayella is on the witness stand, giving her version of what transpired under the cross-examination by Atticus.

> Atticus said, "Is this the man who raped you?"
> "It most certainly is."
> Atticus's next question was one word long. "How?"
> Mayella was raging. "I don't know how he done it, but he done it—I said it all happened so fast I—"
> "Now let's consider this calmly—" began Atticus, but Mr. Gilmer interrupted with an objection: he was not irrelevant or immaterial, but Atticus was browbeating the witness.
> Judge Taylor laughed outright. "Oh sit down, Horace, he's doing nothing of the sort. If anything, the witness's browbeating Atticus."
> Judge Taylor was the only person in the courtroom who laughed. Even the babies were still, and I suddenly wondered if they had been smothered at their mothers' breasts.
> "Now," said Atticus, "Miss Mayella, you've testified that the defendant choked and beat you—you didn't say that he sneaked up

behind you and knocked you cold, but you turned around and there he was—" Atticus was back behind his table, and he emphasized his words by tapping his knuckles on it. "—do you wish to reconsider any of your testimony?"

"You want me to say something that didn't happen?"

"No ma'am, I want you to say something that did happen. Tell us once more, please, what happened?"

"I told'ja what happened."

"You testified that you turned around and there he was. He choked you then?"

"Yes."

"Then he released your throat and hit you?"

"I said he did."

"He blacked your left eye with his right fist?"

"I ducked and it—it glanced, that's what it did. I ducked and it glanced off." Mayella had finally seen the light.

"You're becoming suddenly clear on this point. A while ago you couldn't remember too well, could you?"

"I said he hit me."

"All right. He choked you, he hit you, then he raped you, that right?"

"It most certainly is."

"You're a strong girl, what were you doing all the time, just standing there?"

"I told'ja I hollered'n'kicked'n'fought—"

Atticus reached up and took off his glasses, turned his good right eye to the witness, and rained questions on her. Judge Taylor said, "One question at a time, Atticus. Give the witness a chance to answer."

"All right, why didn't you run?"

"I tried to . . ."

"Tried to? What kept you from it?"

"I—he slung me down. That's what he did, he slung me down'n got on top of me."

"You were screaming all this time?"

"I certainly was."

"Then why didn't the other children hear you? Where were they? At the dump?"

No answer.

"Where were they?"

"Why didn't your screams make them come running? The dump's closer than the woods, isn't it?"

No answer.

"Or didn't you scream until you saw your father in the window? You didn't think to scream until then, did you?"

No answer.

"Did you scream first at your father instead of at Tom Robinson? Was that it?"

No answer.

"Who beat you up? Tom Robinson or your father?"

No answer.

"What did your father see in the window, the crime of rape or the best defense to it? Why don't you tell the truth, child, didn't Bob Ewell beat you up?"

When Atticus turned away from Mayella he looked like his stomach hurt, but Mayella's face was a mixture of terror and fury. Atticus sat down wearily and polished his glasses with his handkerchief.

Suddenly Mayella became articulate. "I got somethin' to say," she said.

Atticus raised his head. "Do you want to tell us what happened?"

But she did not hear the compassion of his invitation. "I got somethin' to say an' then I ain't gonna say no more. That nigger yonder took advantage of me an' if you fine fancy gentlemen don't wanta do nothin' about it then you're all yellow stinkin' cowards, stinkin' cowards, the lot of you. Your fancy airs don't come to nothin'—your ma'amin' and Miss Mayellerin' don't come to nothin', Mr. Finch—"

Then she burst into real tears. Her shoulders shook with angry sobs. She was as good as her word. She answered no more questions, even when Mr. Gilmer tried to get her back on the track. I guess if she hadn't been so poor and ignorant, Judge Taylor would have put her under the jail for the contempt she had shown everybody in the courtroom. Somehow, Atticus had hit her hard in a way that was not clear to me, but it gave him no pleasure to do so. He sat with his head down, and I never saw anybody glare at anyone with the hatred Mayella showed when she left the stand and walked by Atticus's table.

When Mr. Gilmer told Judge Taylor that the state rested, Judge Taylor said, "It's time we all did. We'll take ten minutes" [pp. 198-200].

In his summary to the all-white jury, Atticus explains that Mayella has committed no crime, merely broken a rigid and time-honored code of our society, a code so severe that whoever breaks it is hounded from our midst as unfit to live with. She is the victim of cruel poverty and ignorance, but I cannot pity her: she is white. She knew full well the enormity of her offense, but because her desires were stronger than the code she was breaking, she persisted in breaking it. She persisted, and her subsequent reaction is something that all of us have known at one time or another. She did something every child has done — she tried to put the evidence of her offense away from her. But in this case she was no child hiding stolen contraband: she struck out at her victim — of necessity she must put him away from her — he must be removed from her presence, from this world. She must destroy the evidence of her offense. . . . She must put Tom Robinson away from her. Tom Robinson was her daily reminder of what she did. What did she do? She tempted a Negro. She was white, and she tempted a Negro. She did something that in our society is unspeakable: she kissed a black man [p. 216].

Tom's testimony at the trial, given below, contradicts the statements made by Mayella. Tom's left arm is twelve inches shorter than his right, making it physically impossible for him to have punched Mayella's face as she testified, or to have throttled her; further, there is no corroborating evidence by a reliable witness as the law demanded.

As Tom Robinson gave his testimony, it came to me that Mayella Ewell must have been the loneliest person in the world. She was even lonelier than Boo Radley, who had not been out of the house in twenty-five years. When Atticus asked had she any friends, she seemed not to know what he meant, then she thought he was making fun of her. She was as sad, I thought, as what Jem called a mixed child: white people wouldn't have anything to do with her because she lived among pigs; Negroes wouldn't have anything to do with her because she was white. She couldn't live like Mr. Dolphus Raymond, who preferred the company of Negroes, because she didn't own a riverbank and she wasn't from a fine old family. Nobody said, "That's just their way," about the Ewells. Maycomb gave them Christmas baskets, welfare money, and the back of its hand. Tom Robinson was probably the only person who was ever decent to her. But she said he took advantage of her, and when she stood up she looked at him as if he were dirt beneath her feet.

"Did you ever," Atticus interrupted my meditations, "at any time, go on the Ewell property — did you ever set foot on the Ewell property without an express invitation from one of them?"

"No suh, Mr. Finch, I never did. I wouldn't do that, suh."

Atticus sometimes said that one way to tell whether a witness was lying or telling the truth was to listen rather than watch: I applied his test — Tom denied it three times in one breath, but quietly, with no hint of whining in his voice, and I found myself believing him in spite of his protesting too much. He seemed to be a respectable Negro, and a respectable Negro would never go up into somebody's yard of his own volition.

"Tom, what happened to you on the evening of November twenty-first of last year?"

Below us, the spectators drew a collective breath and leaned forward. Behind us, the Negroes did the same.

Tom was a black-velvet Negro, not shiny, but soft black velvet. The whites of his eyes shone in his face, and when he spoke we saw flashes of his teeth. If he had been whole, he would have been a fine specimen of a man.

"Mr. Finch," he said, "I was goin' home as usual that evenin', an' when I passed the Ewell place Miss Mayella were on the porch, like she said she were. It seemed real quiet like, an' I didn't quite know why. I was studyin' why, just passin' by, when she says for me to come there and help her a minute. Well, I went inside the fence an' looked around for some kindlin' to work on, but I didn't see none, and she says, 'Naw, I got somethin' for you to do in the house. Th' old door's off its hinges an' fall's comin' on pretty fast.' I said you got a screwdriver, Miss Mayella? She said she sho' had. Well, I went up the steps an' she motioned me to come inside, and I went in the front room an' looked at the door. I said Miss Mayella, this door look all right. I pulled it back'n forth and those hinges was all right. Then she shet the door in my face. Mr. Finch, I was wonderin' why it was so quiet like, an' it come to me that there weren't a chile on the place, not a one of 'em, and I said Miss Mayella, where the chillun?"

Tom's black velvet skin had begun to shine, and he ran his hand over his face.

"I say where the chillun?" he continued, "an' she says — she was laughin', sort of — she says they all gone to town to get ice creams. She says, 'Took me a slap year to save seb'm nickels, but I done it. They all gone to town.'"

Tom's discomfort was not from the humidity. "What did you say then, Tom?" asked Atticus.

"I said somethin' like, why Miss Mayella, that's right smart o'you to treat 'em. An' she said, 'You think so?' I don't think she understood what I was thinkin' — I meant it was smart of her to save like that, an' nice of her to treat 'em."

"I understand you, Tom. Go on," said Atticus.

"Well, I said I best be goin', I couldn't do nothin' for her, an' she says oh yes I could, an' I ask her what, and she says to just step on that chair yonder an' git that box down from on top of the chiffarobe."

"Not the same chiffarobe you busted up?" asked Atticus.

The witness smiled. "Naw suh, another one. Most as tall as the room. So I done what she told me, an' I was just reachin' when the next thing I knows she — she'd grabbed me round the legs, grabbed me round th' legs, Mr. Finch. She scared me so bad I hopped down an' turned the chair over — that was the only thing, only furniture, 'sturbed in that room, Mr. Finch, when I left it. I swear 'fore God."

"What happened after you turned the chair over?"

Tom Robinson had come to a dead stop. He glanced at Atticus, then at the jury, then at Mr. Underwood sitting across the room.

"Tom, you're sworn to tell the whole truth. Will you tell it?"

Tom ran his hand nervously over his mouth.

"What happened after that?"

"Answer the question," said Judge Taylor. One-third of his cigar had vanished.

"Mr. Finch, I got down offa that chair an' turned around an' she sorta jumped on me."

"Jumped on you? Violently?"

"No suh, she — she hugged me. She hugged me round the waist."

This time Judge Taylor's gavel came down with a bang, and as it did the overhead lights went on in the courtroom. Darkness had not come, but the afternoon sun had left the windows. Judge Taylor quickly restored order.

"Then what did she do?"

The witness swallowed hard. "She reached up an' kissed me 'side of th' face. She says she never kissed a grown man before an' she might as well kiss a nigger. She says what her papa do to her don't count. She says, 'Kiss me back, nigger.' I say Miss Mayella lemme outa here an' tried to run but she got her back to the door an' I'da had to push her. I didn't wanta harm her, Mr. Finch, an' I say lemme pass, but just when I say it Mr. Ewell yonder hollered through th' window."

"What did he say?"

Tom Robinson swallowed again, and his eyes widened. "Somethin' not fittin to say—not fittin' for these folks'n chillun to hear—"

"What did he say, Tom? You *must* tell the jury what he said."

Tom Robinson shut his eyes tight. "He says you goddam whore, I'll kill ya."

"Then what happened?"

"Mr. Finch, I was runnin' so fast I didn't know what happened."

"Tom, did you rape Mayella Ewell?"

"I did not, suh."

"Did you harm her in any way?"

"I did not, suh."

"Did you resist her advances?"

"Mr. Finch, I tried. I tried to 'thout bein' ugly to her. I didn't wanta be ugly, I didn't wanta push her or nothin'."

It occurred to me that in their own way, Tom Robinson's manners were as good as Atticus's. Until my father explained it to me later, I did not understand the subtlety of Tom's predicament: he would not have dared to strike a white woman under any circumstances and expect to live long, so he took the first opportunity to run—a sure sign of guilt.

"Tom, go back once more to Mr. Ewell," said Atticus. "Did he say anything to you?"

"Not anything, suh. He mighta said somethin', but I weren't there—"

"That'll do," Atticus cut in sharply. "What you did hear, who was he talking to?"

"Mr. Finch, he were talkin' and lookin' at Miss Mayella."

"Then you ran?"

"I sho' did, suh."

"Why did you run?"

"I was scared, suh."

"Why were you scared?"

"Mr. Finch, if you were a nigger like me, you'd be scared, too." [pp. 204-207].

An untrue charge of rape, which may be put forth in remarkably convincing detail as Bob Ewell did in *To Kill a Mockingbird*, is uniquely difficult to prove. If the prosecution can show that the defendant was with the victim when the alleged crime occurred, then the accused may find it impossible to establish he never attempted the attack or that the female consented to it. The adversary trial on which

American law relies so heavily to expose untruth is likely to produce, in rape cases, nothing more than two conflicting stories, both told under oath (Anon., 1967). Even when the corroborator lies, as did Mayella's father, the conflict is inevitably resolved automatically in the accuser's favor, which is what happens in the novel. It is easy for a woman to allege that she has been raped. Frequently the circumstances are fabricated by a "victim" in order to account for facts which would otherwise be awkward to explain (Barnes, 1967). About five per cent of the reported rape charges, according to the FBI, relate events that never took place. False accusations of sex crimes in general, and rape in particular, are generally believed to be much more frequent than the charges of other crimes. A woman may accuse an innocent man of rape because she is mentally ill, perhaps given to delusions; or because, having consented to intercourse, she is ashamed of herself and bitter at her partner because she is pregnant; or she prefers a false explanation to the truth simply because she hates the man whom she accuses, or for reasons of blackmail.

According to Geis (1971), there is the not uncommon female belief that women are fundamentally seducers, agreeable to rape if the proper self-excusing conditions become available. A similar belief among males is that women are apt to derive a certain satisfaction from rape, that they respond erotically to a show of force. John Updike (1971) described one of the men in his novel, *Couples* (1968), as fighting "her as a raped woman might struggle, to intensify the deed." Claudia, in William Murray's *The Americano* (1968), is an unhappily married South African girl. Beautiful and reckless, she believes she knows what she wants from life, and has the courage and moral honesty to face even the most unpleasant truths about herself. While she is holidaying at a Sicilian beach resort with her lover (the narrator), the following scene takes place.

One afternoon she caused a sensation. It was an unusually hot sunny day for that time of year and we went swimming at the public beach. Claudia appeared in a two-piece suit, a relatively modest one compared to the bikinis that now grace every beach. We had hardly settled down to sunbathe when we found ourselves surrounded by watchers, concentric, shifting rows of black-haired, beady-eyed young male faces. "I feel I'm being publicly raped," Claudia said.

"Put your towel over your shoulders," I advised her.

"Nonsense," she said, and calmly undid the straps to her bra so that her shoulders could be fully exposed to the sun. An appreciative murmur went up from the audience. Several minutes later, while we were lying on our stomachs and trying with scant success to ignore the crowd around us, a sweating policeman in black uniform loomed over us. We were thrown off the beach and fined fifteen hundred lire for creating a public disturbance.

Back in the hotel, Claudia went wild. She stripped and flung her clothes about the room, then sank into the bed and waited for me to come to her. We made furious love, like ravenous animals. "You'd like to be raped, wouldn't you?" I said to her.

"I want everything," she said. "I want almost everything to happen to me, do you understand?"

"No, but I think it's what excited me about you. This sense of grasping for everything, for every experience."

"Except pain," she said. "That I can't bear. Or inflicting it, inflicting physical pain on anything or anyone else." She paused and smiled. "It's fun pretending, though."

"If I hadn't been there this afternoon, would you—"

"Are you asking me if I would have let them attack me?"

"Yes."

"I don't know," she said. "The idea began to excite me only when we got back here."

"You frighten me, Claudia."

"Do I, darling?"

"Yes."

"Why? Because I'm honest? Most people have these feelings at one time or another, I'm sure of it. Only, I'm not ashamed to face my feelings" [pp. 127-128].

If Claudia is any example, there are apparently some women who may not feel entirely negative about a rape experience. Fantasies of being raped are exceedingly common in women and are probably universal (Menninger, 1938). Most women entertain more or less consciously at one time or another fleeting fantasies or fears that they are being or will be attacked by a man. Rape fantasies are variants of the seduction fantasies of hysterical women patients (Deutsch, 1945). What women ultimately want in intercourse is to be raped, violated, and humiliated by men (Deutsch, 1930), a viewpoint Rado (1933) agrees with. Factor (1954) reports the reaction of a twenty-eight-year-old patient to an attempted rape by an intruder in her home. She was a Catholic girl who suffered from severe periodic hemorrhagic diarrhea. She lived with her parents, docilely accepting the severe social restrictions imposed by her father. An initial hostile father transference was followed by an erotic one. At this point the attempted rape occurred. The day she appeared in court with the attacker, she had a dream from which she awakened with stomach pain and the fear that if the culprit were freed he would try to harm her or kill her. Before the dream, but following the rape attempt, her prim, sedate attitude toward the analyst changed to a seductive and exhibitionistic one. In the dream, the rapist, father, and analyst were condensed. She expressed guilt at her unconscious compliance, and the wish that the man would be punished and not she, as well as the wish for a second attempt which would be more successful. The erotic acting out increased and was related to lessening of unconscious guilt on the basis of having suffered a real attack, with the feeling, "father is guilty too." The diminution of guilt indicated by her behavior toward the analyst might alternatively be explained by Alexander's (1952) concept of the bribability of the superego. The superego winks at the behavior of the ego, and is much more complaisant toward impulses from the id.

A pride of experts—psychoanalysts, psychologists, sociologists, novelists, jurisprudents, policemen, and pornographers—has imbued Western culture and laws with the suspicion that maybe rape is not against women's will after all (Brownmiller, 1975). This mythology of rape is pervasive in the literature. Janet Angstrom, Harry's wife in John Updike's (1971) novel, *Rabbit Redux,* says, "You know what rape usually is? It's a woman who changed her mind afterward" (p. 37). Odette remarks to Peter in Arthur Koestler's *Arrival and Departure* (1943), "After all, lovemaking is only a rape by mutual consent" (p. 55). The hidden wish to be raped may be true for some women; they do not experience an inner sense of guilty involvement, nor do they contact the authorities readily, if at all. Those, however, who feel there has been no invitation, seduction, or willing compliance on their part generally make an immediate telephone call to the police or go to the nearest emergency medical facility (Sutherland and Scherl, 1970, p. 505). The extent and severity of the emotional trauma on rape victims depend on the circumstances surrounding the incident, especially threat of, or actual physical violence, previous emotional problems, and current stress (Hayman et al., 1972, p. 26). The long-range effect varies according to the type of offense and the chronological age of the victim. Those who suffer the greatest permanent damage are under seventeen and feel they have acquired temporary or permanent adverse ideas about sex (Landis, 1956). Some girls develop the fear that they have become different and unattractive to boys. These notions may persist below the level of consciousness and give rise to sexual disturbances years later (Massey, Celso-Ramon, and Emich, 1971). In Bernard Malamud's *The Tenants* (1971), Lesser and a black girl have just finished having intercourse when the following conversation takes place.

> They lay in bed, passing a cigarette back and forth.
> He asked her whether she had ever come with anybody.
> "I huff and puff with Sam to make him feel good but I don't really think I have."
> He said she would.
> "I almost did with you."
> "How long haven't you?"
> "I don't want to think about that."
> "Do you have any idea why you don't?"
> "Unless it was because I was raped when I was little, which happened to me on the cellar stairs after he dragged me down there."
> "Jesus — who?"
> "This redhead nigger neighbor boy from upstairs. His daddy was white and beat the shit out of his black mother. My mama said it got the boy so frustrated he hated everybody and wanted to hurt them. He finally got sent away" [pp. 128-129].

An in-depth study by Sutherland and Scherl (1970) of thirteen rape victims with an age range of eighteen to twenty-four, who were seen by a mental health team within forty-eight hours of the attack, revealed a striking sequence of reactions falling into three distinct phases: (1) An acute initial reaction, including shock, disbelief, dismay, agitation, and incoherence, lasting several days. (2) An apparent outward adjustment lasting weeks to months. After the immediate anxiety-arousing issues were settled temporarily, the patient returned to her usual daily pursuits. This seeming adjustment was reassuring to relatives and friends, for it looked as if the girl had dealt successfully with the experience and integrated it properly. It was the therapists' impression, however, that "this period of pseudo adjustment does not represent a final resolution of the traumatic event and the feelings it has aroused. Instead, it seemed to contain a heavy measure of denial or suppression. The personal impact of what has happened is ignored in the interest of protecting self and others. During this phase, the victim must deal with her feelings about the assailant. Anger or resentment are often subdued in the interest of a return to ordinary daily life. The victim may rationalize these feelings by attributing the act to blind chance ('It could have happened to anyone'), to 'sickness' on the part of the rapist, or to an extension of the social struggle of black against white or of poor against rich. In similar fashion and for the same reasons, the victim's doubts about her role in the assault are also set aside. (3) Phase Three begins when the victim develops an inner sense of depression and the need to talk" (pp. 507-508). The chief need of most rape victims was to abreact the dramatic event, not unlike soldiers after combat, with someone who could listen sympathetically and objectively, without excessive anxiety or a judgmental attitude (Hayman et al., 1972, p. 26). It was during this phase that the resolution of feelings aroused by rape usually occurred. Concerns which were dealt with superficially or denied successfully reappeared for more comprehensive review. The depression occurred for most of the young women who were raped.

This paradigm by Sutherland and Scherl reflects the highly volatile state of the first phase, as depicted by William Faulkner in *Sanctuary* (1931). Temple Drake, a freshman at Oxford University, was a Mississippi debutante, descendant of a long line of statesmen and soldiers proud in the annals of the state. Raped by Popeye with a corncob because he was impotent, she was subsequently abducted by him and shut up in a Memphis sporting house. A doctor had just left her after treating her for serious hemorrhaging when someone came into the room.

Temple neither saw nor heard her door when it opened. She just happened to look toward it after how long she did not know, and saw Popeye standing there, his hat slanted across his face. Still without making any sound he entered and shut the door and shot the bolt and came toward the bed. As slowly she began to shrink into the bed, drawing the covers up to her chin, watching him across the covers. He came and looked down at her. She writhed slowly in a cringing movement, cringing upon herself in as complete an isolation as though she were bound to a church steeple. She grinned at him, her mouth warped over the rigid, placative porcelain of her grimace.

When he put his hand on her she began to whimper. "No, no," she whispered, "he said I cant now he said ..." He jerked the covers back and flung them aside. She lay motionless, her palms lifted, her flesh beneath the envelope of her loins cringing rearward in furious disintegration like frightened people in a crowd. When he advanced his hand again she thought he was going to strike her. Watching his face, she saw it beginning to twitch and jerk like that of a child about to cry, and she heard him begin to make a whimpering sound. He gripped the top of the gown. She caught his wrists and began to toss from side to side, opening her mouth to scream. His hand clapped over her mouth, and gripping his wrist, the saliva drooling between his fingers, her body thrashing furiously from thigh to thigh, she saw him crouching beside the bed, his face wrung above his absent chin, his bluish lips protruding as though he were blowing upon hot soup, making a high whinnying sound like a horse [p. 90].

Nearly two hundred years earlier, Samuel Richardson wrote on a similar theme in his *Clarissa* (1748). The chief action of the book concerns Lovelace's attempts to reduce Clarissa to submission after she falls under his control. He abducts Clarissa and tricks her into living in a brothel where she becomes his prisoner — as befell Temple Drake. Lovelace cannot persuade Clarissa to do his bidding. In desperation, he drugs and rapes her. That this is no victory, Lovelace is painfully aware. Clarissa is not so sure; scrupulous beyond all reason, she suspects her deepest self of some complicity. When Richardson became irked by heretical readers who admired Lovelace and regarded Clarissa's resistance as prudish, he overstressed the external action of the novel to absolve Clarissa of any culpable feelings toward the rapist and thus limit her guilt simply to an error of judgment. Consequently, in the second and third editions of the novel, according to Dussinger (1966), Richardson whitewashed the heroine as a paragon of virtue and blackened Lovelace as an irredeemable sadist, thereby reducing the original psychological complexity of his characters. "What a situation am I in," exclaimed Lovelace, "with all my cursed inventions? I am puzzled, confounded and ashamed of myself, upon the whole. Nevertheless, she had best take care that she carries not her obstinacy much further. She knows not what revenge for slighted love will make me do" (p. 462). The novel is in the form of letters. The first is from Lovelace to his friend, John Belford, in which he relates some of the things that have happened between Clarissa and himself.

Have you, madam, any reliance upon my honour?

Still silent.

You hate me, madam! You despise me more than you do the most odious of God's creatures!

You ought to despise *me,* if I did not.

You say, madam, you are in a *bad* house. You have *no reliance* upon my honour — you believe you *cannot avoid me* ——

She arose. I beseech you, let me withdraw.

I snatched her hand, rising, and pressed it first to my lips, and then to my heart, in wild disorder. She might have felt the bounding mischief ready to burst its bars. You *shall* go — to your own apartment, if you please — but, by the great God of Heaven, I will accompany you thither!

She trembled. Pray, pray, Mr. Lovelace, don't terrify me so!

Be seated, madam! I beseech you, be seated!

I will sit down ——

Do then, madam — do then — all my soul in my eyes, and my heart's blood throbbing at my finger-ends.

I will, I will — you hurt me — pray, Mr. Lovelace, don't — don't frighten me so — and down she sat, trembling; my hand still grasping hers.

I hung over her throbbing bosom, and putting my other arm round her waist — And you say you hate me, madam — and you say you despise me — and you say you promised me nothing ——

Yes, yes, I *did* promise you — let me not be held down thus — you see I sat down when you bid me. Why (struggling) need you hold me down thus? I did promise *to endeavour to be easy till Thursday was over!* But you won't let me! How can I be easy? Pray, let me not be thus terrified.

And what, madam, *meant* you by your promise? Did you mean anything in my favour? You designed that I should, at the time, *think* you did. Did you mean anything in my favour, madam? Did you intend that I should *think* you did?

Let go my hand, sir — take away your arm from about me (struggling, yet trembling). *Why do you gaze upon me so?* [pp. 462-463].

*   *   *

But for the lady, by my soul I love her, I admire her, more than ever! I *must* have her. I *will* have her still — *with* honour, or *without,* as I have often vowed. Had she threatened ME, I should soon have been master of *one* arm, and *in both!* But for so sincere a virtue to threaten *herself,* and not offer to intimidate *any other,* and with so much presence of mind, as to distinguish, in the very passionate intention, the necessity of the act, in defence of her *honour,* and so *fairly* to disavow *lesser* occasions; showed such a deliberation, such a choice, such a principle; and then keeping me so watchfully at a distance, that I could not seize her hand so soon as she could have given the fatal blow; how impossible not to be subdued by so *true* and so *discreet* a magnanimity!

But she is not *gone.* She shall not go. I will press her with letters for the Thursday. She shall yet be mine, legally mine. For, as to cohabitation, there is now no such thing to be thought of.

The captain shall give her away, as proxy for her uncle. My lord will die. My fortune will help my *will,* and set me above everything and everybody.

But here is the curse — she despises me, Jack! What man, as I have heretofore said, can bear to be despised, especially by his wife? O Lord! O Lord! What a hand, what a cursed hand have I made of this plot!

It goes against me to say,

God bless the lady!

Near 5, Sat. Morn.

Mr. Lovelace to Miss Clarissa Harlowe
[*Superscribed to Mrs. Lovelace*]

M. Hall, Sat. Night, June 24.

My dearest Life, — If you do not impute to love, and to terror raised by love, the poor figure I made before you last night, you will not do me justice. I thought I would try to the very last moment, if, by complying with you in *everything,* I could prevail upon you to promise to be mine on Thursday next, since you refused me in earlier day. Could I have been so happy, you had not been hindered going to Hampstead, or wherever else you pleased. But when I could not prevail upon you to give me this assurance, what room had I (my demerit so great) to suppose that your going thither would not be to lose you for ever?

I will not offer to defend myself, for *wishing you to remain where you are,* till either you give me your word to meet me at the altar on Thursday; or till I have the honour of attending you, preparative to the solemnity which will make that day the happiest of my life.

The orders I have given to the people of the house are: "That you shall be obeyed in every particular that is consistent with my expectations of finding you there on my return to town on Wednesday next: that Mrs. Sinclair, and her nieces shall not, without your orders, come into your presence: that neither shall Dorcas, till she has fully cleared her conduct to your satisfaction, be permitted to attend you: but Mabel, in her place; of whom you seemed some time ago to express some liking. Will I have left behind me to attend your commands. But, as to letters which may be sent you, or any which you may have to send, I must humbly entreat that none such pass *from* or *to* you, for the few days that I shall be absent." But I do assure you, madam, that the seals of both sorts shall be sacred: and the letters, if such be sent, shall be given into your own hands the moment the ceremony is performed, or before, if you require it.

I send this by a special messenger, who will wait your pleasure in relation to the impatiently wished-for Thursday: which I humbly hope will be signified by a line [pp. 470-471].

*   *   *

MISS CLARISSA HARLOWE TO MISS HOWE

Wednesday Night, June 28.
O MY DEAREST MISS HOWE!—Once more have I escaped—but, alas! *I*, my *best self*, have *not* escaped! Oh, your poor Clarissa Harlowe! *You* also will hate me, I fear! Yet you won't when you know all!

But no more of myself! my *lost* self.

.   .   .   .   .   .

Forgive, Oh, forgive my rambling. My peace is destroyed. My intellects are touched.

O my best, my dearest, my *only* friend! What a tale have I to unfold! But still upon *self*, this vile, this hated *self*! I will shake it off, if possible: and why should I not, since I think, except one wretch, I hate nothing so much? Self, then, be banished from *self* one moment (for I doubt it *will* for no longer), to inquire after a *dearer* object, my beloved Anna Howe—whose mind, all robed in spotless white, charms and irradiates—but what would I say? [p. 481].

*   *   *

... But now, indifferent as my head was, I had little time to consider the man and his behaviour. He terrified me with his looks, and with his violent emotions, as he gazed upon me. His sentences short, and pronounced as if his breath were touched. Never saw I his abominable eyes look as then they looked — triumph in them! — fierce and wild; and more disagreeable than the women's at the vile house appeared to me when I first saw them: and at times, such a leering, mischief-boding cast! Yet his behaviour was decent — a decency, however, that I might have seen to be struggled for — for he snatched my hand two or three times, with a vehemence in his grasp that hurt me; speaking words of tenderness through his shut teeth, as it seemed; and let it go with a beggar-voiced humble accent, like the vile woman's just before; half-inward; yet his words and manner carrying the appearance of strong and almost convulsed passion!

I complained once or twice of thirst. My mouth seemed parched. At the time, I supposed that it was my terror (gasping often as I did for breath) that parched up the roof of my mouth. I called for water: some table-beer was brought to me: beer, I suppose was a better vehicle (if I were not dosed enough before) for their potions. I told the maid that she knew I seldom tasted malt-liquor: yet, suspecting nothing of this nature, being extremely thirsty, I drank it, as what came next: and instantly, as it were, found myself much worse than before; as if inebriated, I should fancy: I know not how.

His servant was gone twice as long as he needed: and just before his return, came one of the pretended Lady Betty's with a letter for Mr. Lovelace.

He sent it up to me. I read it: and then it was that I thought myself a lost creature; it being to put off her going to Hampstead that night, on account of violent fits which Miss Montague was pretended to be seized with; for then immediately came into my head his vile attempt upon me in this house; the revenge that my flight might too probably inspire him with on that occasion, and because of the difficulty I made to forgive him, and to be reconciled to him; his very looks wild and dreadful to me; and the women of the house such as I had more reason than ever, even from the pretended Lady Betty's hint, to be afraid of: all these crowding together in my apprehensive mind, I fell into a kind of frenzy.

I have not remembrance how I was for the time it lasted: but I know that, in my first agitations, I pulled off my head-dress, and tore my ruffles in twenty tatters, and ran to find him out.

When a little recovered, I insisted upon the hint he had given of their coach. But the messenger, he said, had told him that it was sent to fetch a physician, lest his chariot should be put up, or not ready.

I then insisted upon going directly to Lady Betty's lodgings.

Mrs. Leeson's was now a crowded house, he said: and as my earnestness could be owing to nothing but groundless apprehension (and O what vows, what protestations of his honour did he then make!), he hoped I would not add to their present concern. Charlotte, indeed, was used to fits, he said, upon any great surprises, whether of joy or grief; and they would hold her for a week together, if not got off in a few hours.

All impatient with grief and apprehension, I still declared myself resolved not to stay in that house till morning. All I had in the world, my rings, my watch, my little money, for a coach; or, if one were not to be got, I would go on foot to Hampstead that night, though I walked it by myself.

A coach was hereupon sent for, or pretended to be sent for. Any price, he said, he would give to oblige me, late as it was; and he would attend me with all his soul. But no coach was to be got.

Let me cut short the rest. I grew worse and worse in my head; now stupid, now raving, now senseless. The vilest of vile women was brought to frighten me.

I remember I pleaded for mercy. I remember that I said *I would be his—indeed I would be his*—to obtain his mercy. But no mercy found I! My strength, my intellects, failed me—and then such scenes followed—O my dear, such dreadful scenes!—fits upon fits (faintly indeed and imperfectly remembered) procuring me no compassion—but death was withheld from me. That would have been too great a mercy!

·   ·   ·   ·   ·   ·

Thus was I tricked and deluded back by blacker hearts of my own sex than I thought there were in the world; who appeared to me to be persons of honour: and, when in his power, thus barbarously was I treated by this villainous man!

The very hour that I found myself in a place of safety, I took pen to write to you. The apprehensions I had lain under, that I should not be able to get away; the fatigue I had in effecting my escape; the difficulty of procuring a lodging for myself;—these, together with the recollection of what I had suffered from him, and my farther apprehensions of my insecurity, and my desolate circumstances, had so disordered me, that I remember I rambled strangely in that letter.

The letter I received from your mother was a dreadful blow to me. But nevertheless it had the good effect upon me (labouring, as

I did just then, under a violent fit of vapourish despondency, and almost yielding to it) which profuse bleeding and blisterings have in paralytical or apoplectical strokes; reviving my attention, and restoring me to spirits to combat the evils I was surrounded by— sluicing off, and diverting into a new channel the overcharging woes which threatened once more to overwhelm my intellects.

* * *

And now, honoured madam, and my dearest Miss Howe, who are to sit in judgment upon my case, permit me to lay down my pen with one request, which, with the greatest earnestness, I make to you both: and that is, That you will neither of you open your lips in relation to the potions and the violences I have hinted at. Not that I am solicitous that my disgrace should be hidden from the world, or that it should not be generally known that the man has proved a villain to me: for this, it seems, everybody but myself expected from his character. But suppose as his actions by me are really of a *capital nature,* it were insisted upon that I should appear to prosecute him and his accomplices in a court of justice, how do you think I could bear that?

But since my character, *before* the capital enormity, was lost in the eye of the world; and that from the very hour I left my father's house; and since all my own hopes of worldly happiness are entirely over; let me slide quietly into my grave; and let it not be remembered, except by one friendly tear, and no more, dropped from your gentle eye, mine own dear Anna Howe, on the happy day that shall shut up all my sorrows, that there was such a creature as

Clarissa Harlowe [pp. 502-505].

Clarissa's fears about bringing charges against Lovelace are frequently justified. If a rapist is brought to trial it is likely that the victim will be called upon as a witness. When this is the case, she will be subject to cross-examination by the defending attorney. "In general it is proper to ask the prosecuting witness to testify as to whether she had previously had intercourse. Assuming that a single girl or divorcee did have previous coitus, it would not be illogical for the defending attorney to inquire as to when she last had intercourse in order to prove that any semen found in the vagina at the time of the examination after the alleged rape may be that of a previous consort. Living sperm has been demonstrated in the cervical mucus as long as ninety-six hours after intercourse. For the single girl or divorced woman, such a line of questioning could be devastating, and in a sense, would put her on trial himself" (Evrard, 1971, pp. 198-199). Shakspeare's insight into the infinite varieties of human experience brings to light the outrage, anguish, anger, blight, and despair of rape in his *Rape of Lucrece:* "The wound that nothing healeth, the scar that will despite of cure remain, leaving the spoil perplexed in greater pain. She bears the load of lust he left behind. . . ."

The hated product of outrage that women are expected to bear, as in the case of the girls in Bangladesh violated by marauding Pakistani troops in their civil war, is tantamount to a doomed life sentence. Given a uniform in the service of a war machine, a man can become capable of committing any atrocity, including rape. Fictional accounts of rape during war render some electric portrayals that reveal the emotions of the victims as Shakespeare indicated. In a subtly written horror story, "The Shadows Behind the Women," by Eddie Cohen (1960), a Bavarian traveling salesman unwittingly returns twenty years after World War II to a tiny, burnt-out peasant village in France to sell his wares, which are, ironically, toys. One of the women, upon recognizing him as a soldier-rapist and pillager, makes a rendezvous with him for midnight at a nearly destroyed mill. He keeps the tryst, only to find the appointed place crowded with the widows of men who had been mercilessly executed by the Germans and who had themselves been raped. They force the Bavarian to relive the torment they endured under his brutality when he was a Nazi soldier committing the bestial crimes. In another short story, Marcus, a survivor of a Nazi concentration camp in Brian Glanville's (1960) "The Survivor," is befriended by a London couple, Mr. and Mrs. Levinson. Marcus eventually emigrates to Israel where he joins the navy and occasionally visits the Levinsons, particularly because of his attraction to their daughter, Miriam. One drunken night, he rapes her. Mrs. Levinson throws him out of the house, screaming, "Get out! Get out of my house, you filthy refugee!" '(p. 216).

Augustin, one of Robert Jordan's fellow soldiers in the Spanish Civil War in Ernest Hemingway's *For Whom the Bell Tolls* (1940), is puzzled because Pilar keeps Maria away from all the men "as fiercely as though she were in a convent of Carmelites" (p. 276). The reader learns from Maria that previously "things were done to me . . . I fought until I could not see. I fought until — until — until one sat upon my head — and I bit him — and then they tied my mouth and held my arms behind my head — and others did things to me" (p. 70). Pilar, her true friend, tells Maria in an attempt to comfort her "that nothing is done to oneself that one does not accept and that if I loved someone it would take it all away" (p. 72). Temple Drake, in Faulkner's *Requiem for a Nun,* refers to Pilar's rationalization on three separate occasions when she attempts to expiate her guilt for her behavior after having been raped. Cunegonde, in Voltaire's *Candide* (1759), after telling of her rape, philosophizes, "A woman of honor may be ravished once, but her virtue gathers strength from such rudeness" (p. 25). She had been in her "bed and fast asleep, when it pleased heaven to send the Bulgarians to our fine castle of Thunder-ten-tronckh; they murdered my father and my brother, and cut my mother to pieces. A huge Bulgarian, six feet high, perceiving the horrible sight had deprived me of my senses, set himself to ravish me. This abuse made me come to myself; I recovered my senses, I cried, I struggled, I bit, I scratched, I wanted to tear out the huge Bulgarian's eyes, not considering that what had happened in my father's castle was a common thing in war . . ." (pp. 25-26). One of the most graphic rape scenes in war literature appears in Joseph Heller's *Catch-22* (1955), when Aarfy casually throws Michaela out of the window to her death after raping her.

Voltaire's Cunegonde had some contemporary ideas of what to do if she were raped. Storaska (1975) advises the modern woman to use her purse as a weapon against the rapist; as a penultimate resort, he suggests trying to turn the rapist's sexual desires off by picking the nose, scratching, belching, expelling flatus, vomiting, urinating, or defecating. If the victim feels endangered by serious injury or death, last-ditch defenses include the eyeball press, which may blind or kill the rapist; the testicle squeeze, which should send him into shock; and the front-thrust kick, which may cripple his knee for life. Connell and Wilson (1974), Medea and Thompson (1974), and MacKellar (1975) make similar suggestions. In Ed McBain's (1973) hilarious satire, *Hail to the Chief,* Detective Meyer Meyer of the 87th Precinct gives a lecture to a group of college coeds.

> . . . Meyer told an assorted collection of not-so-virginal college girls that a rapist was a seriously disturbed individual who was incapable of enjoying a normal sex relationship with a woman. . . . Meyer told his audience that a rapist *expects* his victim to be terrified, and that this terror-reaction adds to his own excitement.

*   *   *

"Now some of you may feel that rape is not such a terrible thing. It is a penetration by force, true, it is a violation of your body, true — but if you submit to this violation, perhaps you will not be hurt. Perhaps. But remember that part of the psychological interplay that makes rape appealing and exciting to this man is the very taking-by-force aspect of what he's doing. And where there is force involved, there is the attendant danger of being severely beaten or even killed."

*   *   *

"I don't want you to become neurotic about rape, I don't want you to start screaming if a panhandler taps you on the shoulder. He may only want a quarter for a drink, and you'll start screaming, and he'll try to shut you up, and the next thing you know he's broken your neck. That's as bad as being assaulted by a *real* rapist. I do want to frighten you a bit, however, and the first thing I want to frighten you about is hitchhiking. If you'd like to get raped, the best way to accomplish your goal is to go outside and start hitch-hiking. I can't guarantee that if you hitch a ride tonight, you'll positively be raped. But I *can* guarantee that if you hitch from the same spot at the same time each night, someone will try to rape you. It might take a week, it might take longer. But someone will try. And it will have nothing whatever to do with how you look. You can be standing on that corner wearing a potato sack, with your hair in curlers, and a fever sore on your lip, and that won't discourage the rapist. He is a sick man; you are presumably a healthy individual. Don't, for God's sake, foolishly place yourself in hazardous or vulnerable situations."

*   *   *

"Like in the song from *The Fantasticks,* there are many different kinds of rape. If you're out on a date with a man you know, and you're necking in his automobile, and he decides to take you by force, against your wishes, that's *rape* — even if you've known him since he was six years old. In a situation like that, I would advise that you stop necking for a moment, stick your finger down your throat, and vomit into his lap. The more serious rape, if rapes can be classified as to seriousness, is the one that can lead to bodily injury or death. A man jumps out at you, he threatens you at knife point. Don't begin telling him what a disgusting animal he is, don't start cutting him down to size, because he may decide to cut *you* down to size — literally. He is emotionally unstable, he does not need his ego further bruised. I've known victims who have talked themselves out of being raped by treating their attacker with human kindness, understanding, sympathy, and humility. This doesn't always work, but it may at least buy you some time until either help comes or you can effect an escape. One girl bought time by telling the rapist she *knew* he'd been following her, and thought she was the luckiest girl alive, because here she was just a plain, dumpy little thing, and he was such a big handsome man. She put her arms around his neck and got very affectionate — something totally unexpected by the rapist — and he lost his erection and was momentarily incapable of performing. By the time he got back to the business at hand, which was taking this girl by *force,* don't forget that, some people wandered up the street, and the girl was saved from attack.

"But let's suppose a man begins hitting you the moment he drags you into the bushes. Your natural reaction, even if you plan *not* to resist, even if you plan to go limp — which may cause the same thing to happen to *him* — is to turn your head away from the blows, or bring up your hands to protect your face, or in some way involuntarily show resistance or fear, which will only provoke him more. Let's say nothing you've said or done has worked, you are on the ground, he is still striking you, he is going to rape you. The question now is whether you want to be raped, and maybe killed, or whether you want to hurt this man. Only you can decide that. If you choose not to be a victim, I can tell you how to hurt him, and how to get away from him."

*   *   *

"Remember that the unexpected is the best approach. You are flat on your back, and this man is about to rape you. Instead of trying to twist away, instead of trying to shove him off you, begin to fondle him. That's right. Fondle the man. Fondle his genitals. And then drop your hand to his testicles and squeeze. Squeeze as hard as you can. You are going to hurt this man, but you are also going to end the rape that very minute. You may wonder whether he will be able to chase you afterwards, perhaps hit you harder than he did before, perhaps even kill you. I can guarantee that you can run clear to California and back, and that man will still be lying on the ground incapable of movement. This is one way of stopping a rape, if you do not choose to become a victim. There is another way, and I suspect your reaction to it will be 'I'd rather get raped.' That, of course, is up to you. I can only offer you options."

*   *   *

"Again, do the unexpected," Meyer said. "Put your hands gently on the rapist's face, palms against his temples, cradle his face, murmur words of endearment, allow him to think you're going along with his plans. Your thumbs will be close to his eyes. If you have in yourself the courage to push your thumbs into a hard-boiled egg, then you can also push them into this man's eyes. You will put out his eyes, you will blind him. But you will not be raped. There is never a moment, during a rape in progress, I can guarantee this, when you will not have the opportunity to fondle the man's genitals or to put your hands on his face. These are his vulnerable areas, and if you behave unexpectedly and do not seem to be preparing an attack, he will not suspect what is coming until it is too late. Squeezing his testicles will incapacitate him, but may not permanently injure him. Putting out his eyes is a drastic measure, and you may feel with some justification that doing this is worse than what the rapist is trying to do to you—that the means of preventing rape are worse than the crime itself. The choice is yours."

Meyer wiped his brow with his handkerchief, and then asked, "Are there any questions?" [pp. 113-117, *passim*].

Gang rape, another expression of group phallicism and fear of women projected in raw hostility, is, in its mindlessness and viciousness, akin to war rape. If a man is stronger than a woman who refuses to submit to his demands, he may use force; if he is not up to the task, he may well call on the help of other men who then share the spoils (Eidelberg, 1961). Group rape involves two or more men behaving in accord with well-established principles of collective behavior. Amir (1971, pp. 198-199), using Redl's (1942) ten-type classification of central persons, sifts out three types involved in group rape: the organizer, the seducer, and the bad influence.

Common to them all is that they develop and mobilize common group emotions, provide support for forbidden drives, and reinforce and direct them to concrete activities. The organizer is the central person characterized by the initiatory acts. The seducer not only initiates acts but is also the first to commit them. Hence, he becomes a model of behavior. In group rape this person will often be the first to rape the victim and will do more to humiliate her. The bad influence ... supports the potential of the group members for perversion by virtue of the infectiousness of the unconflicted personality's consultation upon the conflicted one. Through this method the other members are also spared guilt, anxiety, and conflict.

Anthony Burgess's nightmarish science-fiction novel, *A Clockwork Orange* (1963), is about an England of the foreseeable future, where roving bands of hoodlums practice sexual assault and acts of ultra-violence for the pure, sadistic joy of it. An amoral *malchick* (boy) named Alex, the fifteen-year-old leader of a quartet of young thugs, likes to don masks and wage surprise attacks on private homes in the country where they may rape and pummel their victims without fear of interference by the *millicents* (police).

The dynamics of group rape in *A Clockwork Orange* appear to conform to the model presented by Amir (1971, p. 110). "The existence of past aggressive behavior and actual or latent predisposition for such behavior prevails in the lower-class adolescents. This comes in a period of life when intensified sexual desires and experimentation with sex occur. On the one hand, there is a sexual identity problem and a need to repudiate bonds with the female sex, which may express itself in isolation from a constant relation to females, or in rejection of everything which may have feminine traits. Sometimes it expresses itself in actual aggression toward females and appreciation of sex only for its physical aspects, without the emotional elements which the middle class attaches to the sexual sphere. Episodically, rape and group rape will then occur."

The adolescents in the Burgess novel represent the three types in Redl's paradigm, with Alex the organizer, Dim Dim the seducer, and Georgie and Pete the bad influence. As the leader, Alex is the first to have intercourse with his victim; his gang suffers the definitional insult of dealing with already used and abused merchandise, with a homosexual motif underlying the group rape by their mutual involvement with the same object. Further, sustaining their image in front of their fellows is likely to be important in instigating and perpetuating the act of group rape. The scene below reveals the four boys invading the country home of a writer and his wife. Burgess enhances the nightmare quality of *A Clockwork Orange* through the extraordinary use of language which he explains as bits of rhyming slang and a bit of gypsy, but with most of the roots Slav. (For ease in reading, a glossary is provided in footnotes 1-13.)

> "Now for the other vesch,[1] Bog[2] help us all." So he did the strong-man on the devotchka,[3] who was still creech creech creeching[4] away in very horrowshow[5] four-in-a-bar, locking her rookers[6] from the back, while I ripped away at this and that and the other, the others going haw haw haw still, and real good horrowshow groodies[7] they were that then exhibited their pink glazzies,[8] O my brothers, while I untrussed and got ready for the plunge. Plunging, I could slooshy[9] cries of agony and this writer bleeding veck[10] that Georgie and Pete held on to nearly got loose howling bezoomny[11] with the filthiest of slovos[12] that I already knew and others he was making up. Then after me it was right old Dim should have his turn, which he did in a beasty snorty howly sort of a way with his Peebee Shelley maskie taking no notice, while I held on to her. Then there was a change-over, Dim and me grabbing the slobbering writer veck who was past struggling really, only just coming out with slack sort of slovos like he was in the land in a milkplus bar, and Pete and Georgie had theirs. Then there was like quiet and we were full of like hate, so smashed what was left to be smashed—typewriter, lamp, chairs—and Dim, it was typical of old Dim, watered the fire out and was going to dung on the carpet, there being plenty of paper, but I said no. "Out out out out," I howled. The writer veck and his zheena[13] were not really there, bloody and torn and making noises. But they'd live [p. 29].

Although the victim in group rape is invariably an outsider, she serves as a focus for the group and thus becomes an object of aggressive and sexual drives (Amir, 1971). "The existence of aggression and sexuality in the group and in each member is mobilized by the appearance of the victim, especially if she is known to the group as having a 'bad reputation,' or as being passive due to her drinking or mental condition" (p. 199). Tralala, the bitterly ironic name of the teen-age prostitute in Hubert Selby's hair-raising novel, *Last Exit to Brooklyn* (1957), is the only girl in a gang of vicious muggers and small-time thieves. Raised in an urban jungle of waterfront docks, slum houses, and shabby bars, crime and assault are accepted constants, a way of

---

[1] Thing; [2] God; [3] girl; [4] scream; [5] good; [6] arms; [7] breasts; [8] eyes; [9] hear; [10] fellow; [11] mad; [12] words; [13] wife.

life. When her gang is arrested, Tralala, feeling abandoned and lonely, subways to Times Square looking for and finding pickups among the officers, soldiers, and navy men of World War II. She gets into a drunken stupor for several weeks with numerous men. One night in a bar, still dazed by drink, she invites her doom.

... someone yelled all tits and no cunt and Tralala told him to comeon and find out and a drunken soldier banged out of a booth and said comeon and glasses fell and Jack knocked over his stool and fell on Fred and they hung over the bar nearing hysteria and Ruthy hoped she wouldnt get fired because this was a good deal and Annie closed her eyes and laughed relieved that they wouldnt have to worry about Tralala and they didnt spend too much money and Tralala still bounced her tits on the palms of her hands turning to everyone as she was dragged out the door by the arm by 2 or 3 and she yelled to Jack to comeon and she/d fuckim blind not like that fuckin douchebag he was with and someone yelled we/re coming and she was dragged down the steps tripping over someones feet and scraping her ankles on the stone steps and yelling but the mob not slowing their pace dragged her by an arm and Jack and Fred still hung on the bar roaring and Ruthy took off her apron getting ready to leave before something happened to louse up their deal and the 10 or 15 drunks dragged Tralala to a wrecked car in the lot on the corner of 57th street and yanked her clothes off and pushed her inside and a few guys fought to see who would be first and finally a sort of line was formed everyone yelling and laughing and someone yelled to the guys on the end to go get some beer and they left and came back with cans of beer which were passed around the daisychain and the guys from the Greeks cameover and some of the other kids from the neighborhood stood around watching and waiting and Tralala yelled and shoved her tits into the faces as they occurred before her and beers were passed around and the empties dropped or thrown and guys left the car and went back on line and had a few beers and waited their turn again and more guys came from Willies and a phone call to the Armybase brought more seamen and doggies and more beer was brought from Willies and Tralala drank beer while being laid and someone asked if anyone was keeping score and someone yelled who can count that far and Tralalas back was streaked with dirt and sweat and her ankles stung from the sweat and dirt in the scrapes from the steps and sweat and beer dripped from the faces onto hers but she kept yelling she had the biggest goddam pair of tits in the world and someone answered ya bet ya sweet ass yado and more came 40 maybe 50 and they screwed her and went back on line and had a beer and yelled and laughed and someone yelled that the car stunk of cunt so Tralala and the seat were taken out of the car and laid in the lot and she lay there naked on the seat and their shadows hid her pimples and scabs and she drank flipping her tits with the other hand and somebody shoved the beer can against her mouth and they all laughed and Tralala cursed and spit out a piece of tooth and someone shoved it again and they laughed and yelled and the next one mounted her and her lips were split this time and the blood trickled to her chin and someone mopped her brow with a beer soaked handkerchief and another can of beer was handed to her and she drank and yelled about her tits and another tooth was chipped and the split in her lips was widened and everyone laughed and she laughed and she drank more and more and soon she passedout and they slapped her a few times and she mumbled and turned her head but they couldnt revive her so they continued to fuck her as she lay unconscious on the seat in the lot and soon they tired of the dead piece and the daisychain brokeup and they went back to Willies the Greeks and the base and the kids who were watching and waiting to take a turn took out their disappointment on Tralala and tore her clothes to small scraps put out a few cigarettes on her nipples pissed on her jerkedoff on her jammed a broomstick up her snatch then bored they left her lying amongst the broken bottles rusty cans and rubble of the lot ... [pp. 112-114].

Amir (1971) noted two kinds of women as typical group rape victims: (1) those who become involved in group rape only because of inadvertency, that is, because they are in the wrong place at the wrong time; (2) girls or women of poor reputation like Tralala, or those who for other reasons are often not in a position to complain about the offense, like Stupid Ludmila in Jerzy Kosinski's *The Painted Bird* (1965).

When she was very young and innocent her parents ordered her to get married to the son of the village psalmist, notorious for his ugliness and cruelty. Ludmila refused, infuriating her fiancé so much that he enticed her outside the village where an entire herd of drunken peasants raped the girl until she lost consciousness. After that she was a changed woman; her mind had become addled. Since no one remembered her family and she was considered not too bright, she was nicknamed Stupid Ludmila. She lived in the forests, lured peasants into the bushes and pleased them so much with her voluptuousness that afterwards they could not even look at their fat and stinking wives [pp. 54-55].

Thus twice-raped Ludmila falls into both types Amir describes, a woman of poor reputation and in the wrong place at the wrong time. The narrator is a nine-year-old boy whose Jewish parents, caught in a Nazi round-up, have sent him to the woods to save himself. It is a gruesome scene that is related, the more horrifying, perhaps, because the deeds are narrated in the most matter-of-fact way possible, without emotionally charged adjectives that carry literary connotations and allow the reader to appreciate the horror from outside. Here the reader is forced to participate and observe directly, as the narrative calls little or no attention to itself.

> The pastures stretched directly beyond the cemetery. A few cows were foraging not far off, and several young peasants warmed themselves at a fire. To avoid being noticed we quickly crossed through the cemetery and climbed over a high wall. On the other side, where we could not be seen, Stupid Ludmila tied the dog to a tree, threatened me with a belt and commanded me to take off my pants. She herself wriggled out of her sack and, naked, pulled me toward her.
>
> After a moment of struggling and squirming, she drew my face closer to her and ordered me to lie down between her thighs. I tried to free myself but she whipped me with the belt. My screams attracted the other shepherds.
>
> Stupid Ludmila noticed the approaching group of peasants and spread her legs wider. The shepherds came up slowly, staring at her body.
>
> Without a word they surrounded her. Two of them immediately began to let down their pants. The others stood undecided. No one paid any attention to me. The dog tied to the tree was struck with a rock and lay licking its wounded back.
>
> A tall shepherd mounted the woman while she writhed below him. When he finished and rose, another man took his place. Stupid Ludmila moaned and shuddered, drawing the man to her with her arms and legs. The other men crouched nearby, looking on, snickering and jesting.
>
> From behind the cemetery appeared a mob of village women with rakes and shovels. It was led by several younger women who shouted

and waved their hands. The shepherds hitched up their pants but did not flee; instead, they held on to the desperately struggling Ludmila. The dog strained at the leash and snarled, but the thick rope did not loosen. The women came closer. I sat down at a safe distance near the cemetery wall. I then noticed Lekh running across the pastures.

He must have returned to the village and learned what was going to happen. The women were quite close now. Before Stupid Ludmila had time to get up, the last of the men fled to the cemetery wall. The women now grabbed her. Lekh was still far away. Exhausted, he had to slow down. His pace was shambling and he stumbled several times.

The women held Stupid Ludmila down flat against the grass. They sat on her hands and legs and began beating her with the rakes, ripping her skin with their fingernails, tearing out her hair, spitting into her face. Lekh tried to push through, but they barred his way. He tried to fight, but they knocked him down and hit him brutally. He ceased to struggle and several women turned him over on his back and straddled him. Then the women killed Ludmila's dog with several shovel blows. The peasants were sitting on the wall. When they moved closer to me I moved away, ready at any moment to flee into the cemetery, where I would be safe among the graves. They feared the spirits and ghouls which were said to reside there.

Stupid Ludmila lay bleeding. Blue bruises appeared on her tormented body. She groaned loudly, arched her back, trembled, trying vainly to free herself. One of the women now approached, holding a corked bottle of brownish-black manure. To the accompaniment of raucous laughter and loud encouragements from the others, she kneeled down between Ludmila's legs and rammed the entire bottle inside her abused, assaulted slit, while she began to moan and howl like a beast. The other women looked on calmly. Suddenly with all her strength one of them kicked the bottom of the bottle sticking out of Stupid Ludmila's groin. There was the muffled noise of glass shattering inside. Now all the women began to kick Ludmila. When the last woman had finished kicking, Ludmila was dead.

Their fury spent, the women went to the village chattering loudly. Lekh rose, his face bleeding. He swayed on his weak legs and spat out several teeth. Sobbing, he threw himself on the dead girl. He touched her mutilated body, crossing himself, babbling through his swollen lips.

I sat, huddled and chilled, on the cemetery wall, not daring to move. The sky grayed and darkened. The dead were whispering about the wandering soul of Stupid Ludmila, who was now asking mercy for all her sins. The moon came up. Its cold, pale, drained light illuminated only the dark shape of the kneeling man and the fair hair of dead Ludmila lying on the ground.

I slept and woke by turns. The wind raged over the graves, hanging wet leaves on the arms of the crosses. The spirits moaned, and the dogs could be heard howling in the village.

When I awoke, Lekh was still kneeling by Ludmila's body, his hunched back shaken by sobs. I spoke to him, but he paid no attention. I was too frightened to go back to the hut. I resolved to leave. Above us wheeled a flock of birds, chirping and calling from all directions [pp. 60-63].

The extent of group rape, either in the United States or elsewhere in the world, is unknown. Amir (1971) calculated that seventy-one per cent of the reported rapists in Philadelphia during 1958 and 1960 were perpetrators of group rape. Figures from Canada indicate that two thirds of the people charged with rape were allegedly involved in group offenses. In New South Wales, ninety-six per cent of the offenders convicted of rape between 1960-1967 were guilty of multiple offenses. Amir reports that younger persons were disproportionately representative in multi-offender cases.

Rape is always a dehumanizing and brutalizing phenomenon, committed by a certain kind of sadistically aggressive male. The healthy lover is one who believes enjoyable sex takes the willing cooperation of two; it is the man who refuses to believe that the act of sex is a mutual enterprise who is the latent rapist. Freud (1919) tended to view rape and all other sex deviations as neurotic symptoms, expressing the failure of the offender to resolve the Oedipus complex. The act of rape is an attack on the mother (Abrahamsen, 1960), and the victim is imbued, through the mechanism of projection, with all the feelings the boy had toward his mother: fear, aggression, incestuous wishes, and anticipation of punishment in the form of castration (Hirning, 1947). Thus, the rapist tries to extract responsiveness from the mother-victim, which he is afraid will not be given (Amir, 1971). The rapist seems motivated mainly by aggressiveness and hostility toward women, with concomitant subjugation, humiliation, and even murder (Hayman et al., 1972, p. 17) as driving forces. As a group rapists are vicious, but individually, when they aren't committing rape, they are nonaggressive, timid, and impotent (Massey, Celso-Ramon, and Emich, 1971). The deviate's inadequate sexuality transfers itself into hostility toward the female sex. He places his victim in a degraded role, belittles her and through a sense of dominance, satisfies his hostile impulses. Anne says to her husband David, in Julius Horwitz's novel, *The Married Lovers* (1973), "Rape must be the way men express their worst fear of women" (p. 23).

The peasant boy in Goethe's "The Sorrows of Werther" (1773) reflects the prescience of doom in Werther himself. The boy, a servant in the household whose mistress he loves and by whom he is rejected, rapes her; it is the only way he can achieve satisfaction of his desires. He is by no means vicious or wanton; he rues the attack and contemplates suicide.

It is even so! As Nature puts on her autumn tints, it becomes autumn with me and around me. My leaves are sear and yellow, and the neighboring trees are divested of their foliage. Do you remember my writing to you about a peasant boy shortly after my arrival here? I have just made inquiries about him in Walheim. They say he has been dismissed from his service, and is now avoided by every one. I met him yesterday on the road, going to a neighboring village. I spoke to him, and he told me his story. It interested me exceedingly, as you will easily understand when I repeat it to you. But why should I trouble you? Why should I not reserve all my sorrow for myself? Why should I continue to give you occasion to pity and blame me? But no matter: this also is part of my destiny.

At first the peasant-lad answered my inquiries with a sort of subdued melancholy, which seemed to me the mark of a timid disposition; but as we grew to understand each other, he spoke with less reserve, and openly confessed his faults, and lamented his misfortune. I wish, my dear friend, I could give proper expression to his language. He told me, with a sort of pleasurable recollection, that after my departure his passion for his mistress increased daily, until at last he neither knew what he did nor what he said, nor what was to become of him. He could neither eat nor drink nor sleep: he felt a sense of suffocation; he disobeyed all orders, and forgot all commands involuntarily; he seemed as if pursued by an evil spirit, till one day, knowing that his mistress had gone to an upper chamber, he had followed, or rather, been drawn after her. As she proved deaf to his entreaties, he has recourse to violence. He knows not what happened; but he called God to witness that his intentions to her were honorable, and that he desired nothing more sincerely than that they should marry, and pass their lives together. When he had come to this point, he began to hesitate, as if there was something which he had not courage to utter, till at length he acknowledged with some confusion certain little confidences she had encouraged, and liberties she had allowed. He broke off two or three times in his narration, and assured me most earnestly that he had no wish to make her bad, as he termed it, for he loved her still as sincerely as ever; that the tale had never before escaped his lips, and was only now told to convince me that he was not utterly lost and abandoned. And here, my dear friend, I must commence the old song which you know I utter eternally. If I could only represent the man as he stood, and stands now before me, — could I only give his true expressions, you would feel compelled to sympathize in his fate. But enough: you, who know my misfortune and my disposition, can easily comprehend the attraction which draws me towards every unfortunate being, but particularly towards him whose story I have recounted.

On perusing this letter a second time, I find I have omitted the conclusion of my tale; but it is easily supplied. She became reserved towards him, at the instigation of her brother who had long hated him, and desired his expulsion from the house, fearing that his sister's second marriage might deprive his children of the handsome fortune they expected from her; as she is childless. He was dismissed at length; and the whole affair occasioned so much scandal that the mistress dared not take him back, even if she had wished it. She has since hired another servant, with whom, they say, her brother is equally displeased, and whom she is likely to marry; but my informant assures me that he himself is determined not to survive such a catastrophe.

This story is neither exaggerated nor embellished: indeed, I have weakened and impaired it in the narration, by the necessity of using the more refined expressions of society.

This love then, this constancy, this passion, is no poetical fiction. It is actual, and dwells in its greatest purity amongst that class of mankind whom we term rude, uneducated. We are the educated, not the perverted! [pp. 72-74].

The peasant boy's assault was an explosive expression of pent-up impulse, typical of the behavior pattern of many rapists. The avenue of release was limited to him and found expression in this one regretful occurrence. It is usual in situations where the instinctual drive is very confined that it will suddenly and explosively burst out (Karpman, 1954). A study of 300 consecutive sex offenders (Brancale, Ellis, and Doorbar, 1952), accomplished by means of psychological, psychiatric, and social work interviews, together with a variety of psychometric and projective tests, clinically analyzed and correlated, revealed these findings which are extrapolated for rape: only sixteen per cent of the men convicted of statutory rape were found to be severely disturbed, but relatively high rates of disturbed behavior were found against those convicted of forcible rape. There was a clear relation between the seriousness of the sex offense and the seriousness of the offender's emotional disturbance. Hostility was evident in those convicted of sexual assault and forcible rape, and was found relatively seldom in those convicted of statutory rape. Subnormal intelligence was found in offenders convicted of statutory rape and incestuous relations and was least frequent in those convicted of forcible rape. Massey, Celso-Roman, and Emich (1971) conclude that "rapists are usually young (whereas the older man turns to molestation of children, incest, and sodomy). The backgrounds of sexual offenders involve family problems ranging from extreme repression to excessive laxity ... No predictable mental or physical type is involved. Psychoses account for a small proportion of the attacks" (p. 33).

The Brancale study classifies four main types of rapists. The first is the normal, well-adjusted male who behaves abnormally when under the influence of alcohol or drugs, or releases his pent-up impulses in an explosive manner. Sexual repression, immaturity, and feelings of inferiority may prompt an assault. The second type includes the sexual deviate but psychiatrically nondeviate offender who may be well adjusted apart from his abnormal sexual activities. He experiences sexual pleasure only when obtaining it by force; there is a strong, sadistic element attached to the pleasure. Type three is the sexual and psychiatric deviate who is impulsive, poorly controlled, or uncontrolled. The last classification encompasses the psychotic, mentally retarded, or brain-damaged. The schizophrenic, often considerably deteriorated, may assault a woman without understanding what he is doing or else is "told" to do so by hallucinations (Allen, 1962). Karpman (1954) adds a fifth category, the aggressive criminal, not a true sex offender, who is out to pillage and rob, and for whom rape is just another act of plunder.

Popeye, the Memphis gangster, procurer, and rapist in Faulkner's *Sanctuary*, was such a man. He has been proposed for various prototypes, actual, literary, and allegoric: as Freudian id, Jungian shadow, Gothic villain, amoral modernist, or simply evil personified (Slabey, 1962). Rape and impotence are not mutually exclusive in the sexually disturbed male, but rather tend to go hand in hand. Popeye's mother was seduced by a syphilitic streetcar strikebreaker who followed her home one night, made her pregnant, married and then abandoned her and the child. He was cared for by the rattled mother and a psychotic grandmother whose forte was arson. Popeye's pleasure was to butcher live love birds and kittens with a pair of scissors. At five, he was sent to a home for incorrigible boys, where he remained for five years. His behavior there was impeccable. As a man, he visited his invalid mother annually and dutifully. To assert his masculinity, he carried a revolver with him, murdered a man, corncob-raped Temple Drake, and was hanged for a murder he did not commit. He neither protested his innocence nor let himself be helped by friends, attorneys, or priests, impotent to the end, dreading the possible surfacing of his homosexuality into consciousness.

In Vidal's (1948) *The City and the Pillar Revisited*, Jim Willard and Bob Ford, two high-school boys, experience what seems to be a typical adolescent homosexual weekend, the first time for each. But it is not the last for Jim, who eventually discovers the joys and anguish of homosexual relationships with a number of men. Through the years, the memory of his first affair with Bob haunts him, until one day he meets Bob in New York and invites him to his hotel room for a drink.

As they drank beneath the harsh unshaded light of a single electric bulb, the room became stifling with summer heat. They took off their shirts. Bob's body was still muscular and strong, the skin smooth and white, not freckled, unlike most redheads.

The duet began pianissimo.

"You remember the old slave cabin?" asked Jim.

"Down by the river? Sure."

"We had a lot of fun there."

"I'll say. There was a pond, too, wasn't there? Where we swam?" Jim nodded. "Remember the last time we were there?"

"No, I don't think I do."

Could he have forgotten? Impossible. "Sure you remember. The weekend before you went North. Right after you graduated."

Bob nodded. "Yeah, I kind of remember." He frowned. "We ... we fooled around quite a bit, didn't we?"

Yes, he remembered. Now it would happen. "Yes. Kind of fun, wasn't it?"

Bob chuckled. "Kids always do that, I guess. Though it's funny, I never did, except that one time."

"Neither did I."

"So I guess we were just a couple of little queers at heart." Bob grinned.

"Did you ever . . . well, do *that* again, with anybody else?"

"Any other guy? Hell, no. Did you?"

"No."

"Let's have another drink."

Soon they were both drunk and Bob said that he was sleepy. Jim said that he was, too, and that he had better go home, but Bob insisted that he spend the night with him. They threw their clothes on the floor. Wearing only shorts, they tumbled onto the unmade bed. Bob lay sprawled on his back, arm across his face, apparently unconscious. Jim stared at him: was he really asleep? Boldly, Jim put his hand on Bob's chest. The skin was as smooth as he remembered. Lightly he touched the stray coppery hairs which grew below the deep-set naval. Then, carefully, like a surgeon performing a delicate operation, he unbuttoned Bob's shorts. Bob stirred, but did not wake, as Jim opened wide the shorts to reveal thick blond pubic hair from which sprouted the pale quarry. Slowly his hand closed around Bob's sex. He held him for what seemed a long time. Held him, until he looked up to find that the other was awake and watching him. Jim's heart stopped for a full beat.

"What the fuck are you doing?" The voice was hard. Jim could not speak. Obviously the world was ending. His hand remained frozen where it was. Bob pushed him. But he could not move.

"Let go of me, you queer."

Plainly a nightmare, Jim decided. None of this could be happening. But when Bob struck him hard in the face, the pain recalled him. Jim drew back. Bob leapt to his feet and stood, swaying drunkenly, fumbling with buttons. "Now will you get the hell out of here?"

Jim touched his face where he had been struck. His head still rang from the blow. Was he bleeding?

"Get out, you hear me?" Bob moved toward him, menacingly, fist ready. Suddenly, overwhelmed equally by rage and desire, Jim threw himself at Bob. They grappled. They fell across the bed. Bob was strong but Jim was stronger. Grunting and grasping, they twisted and turned, struck out with arms, legs, but Bob was no match for Jim and, at the end, he lay face down on the bed, arm bent behind him, sweating and groaning. Jim looked down at the helpless body, wanting to do murder. Deliberately he twisted the arm he held. Bob cried out. Jim was excited at the other's pain. What to do? Jim frowned. Drink made concentration difficult. He looked at the heaving body beneath him, the broad back, ripped shorts, long muscled legs. One final humiliation: With his free hand, Jim pulled down the shorts, revealing white, hard, hairless buttocks. "Jesus," Bob whispered. "Don't. Don't."

Finished, Jim lay on the still body, breathing hard, drained of emotion, conscious that the thing was done, the circle completed, and finished.

At last Jim sat up. Bob did not stir. He remained face-down, clutching the pillow to his face while Jim dressed. Then Jim crossed to the bed and looked down at the body he had loved with such single-mindedness for so many years. Was this all? He put his hand on Bob's sweaty shoulder. Bob shied away from him: fear? disgust? It made no difference now. Jim touched the pillow. It was wet. Tears? Good. Without a word, Jim went to the door and opened it. He looked back once more at Bob, then he turned out the light and shut the door behind him. He left the hotel, not caring where he went. For a long time he walked aimlessly, until at last he came to one of the many bars where men looked for men. He entered, prepared to drink until the dream was completely over [pp. 216-219].

Traditionally rape has been viewed as an offense one male commits on a woman. But male victims of rape at the hands of other males often feel twice imposed upon, as they have not only been subjected to forcible and painful intercourse, but further abused in being reduced to the status of a female (Millett, 1970). Much of this is evident in Genet and in the contempt homosexual society reserves for its "passive" or "female" partners. In James Dickey's *Deliverance* (1970), a quartet of Atlanta, Georgia suburbanites, out to prove their masculinity on a back-to-nature canoe trip, found their venture turned into a terrifying test of survival, with sodomy and murder at the end of the journey. The primal masculine adventure became a nightmare under the careless brutality of two hillbilly rapists, for whom conquest and degradation of the victims seemed to be at least as important as sexual release.

They both went toward Bobby, the lean man with the gun this time. The white-bearded one took him by the shoulders and turned him around toward downstream.

"Now let's you just drop them pants," he said.

Bobby lowered his hands hesitantly. "Drop . . ?" he began.

My rectum and intestines contracted. Lord God.

The toothless man put the barrels of the shotgun under Bobby's right ear and shoved a little. "Just take 'em right on off," he said.

"I mean, what's this all . . ." Bobby started again weakly.

"Don't say nothin'," the older man said. "Just do it."

The man with the gun gave Bobby's head a vicious shove, so quick that I thought the gun had gone off. Bobby unbuckled his belt and unbuttoned his pants. He took them off, looking around ridiculously for a place to put them.

"Them panties too," the man with the belly said.

Bobby took off his shorts like a boy undressing for the first time in a gym, and stood there plump and pink, his hairless thighs shaking, his legs close together.

"See that log? Walk over yonder."

Wincing from the feet, Bobby went slowly over to a big fallen tree and stood near it with his head bowed.

"Now git on down crost it."

The tall man followed Bobby's head down with the gun as Bobby knelt over the log.

"Pull your shirt-tail up, fat-ass."

Bobby reached back with one hand and pulled his shirt up to his lower back. I could not imagine what he was thinking.

"I said *up*," the tall man said. He took the shotgun and shoved the back of the shirt up to Bobby's neck, scraping a long red mark along his spine.

The white-bearded man was suddenly also naked up to the waist. There was no need to justify or rationalize anything; they were going to do what they wanted to. I struggled for life in the air, and Bobby's body was still and pink in an obscene posture that no one could help. The tall man restored the gun to Bobby's head, and the other one knelt behind him.

A scream hit me, and I would have thought it was mine except for the lack of breath. It was a sound of pain and outrage, and was followed by one of simple and wordless pain. Again it came out of him, higher and more carrying. I let all the breath out of myself and brought my head down to look at the river. Where are they, every vein stood out to ask, and as I looked the bushes broke a little in a place I would not have thought of and made a kind of complicated alleyway out onto the stream—I was not sure for a moment whether it was water or leaves—and Lewis' canoe was in it. He and Drew both had their paddles out of water, and then they turned and disappeared.

The white-haired man worked steadily on Bobby, every now and then getting a better grip on the ground with his knees. At last he raised his face as though to howl with all his strength into the leaves and the sky, and quivered silently while the man with the gun looked on with an odd mixture of approval and sympathy. The whorl-faced man drew back, drew out.

The standing man backed up a step and took the gun from behind Bobby's ear. Bobby let go of the log and fell to his side, both arms over his face.

We all sighed. I could get better breath, but only a little.

The two of them turned to me. I drew up as straight as I could and waited with the tree. It was up to them. I could sense my knife sticking in the bark next to my head and I could see the blood vessels in the eyes of the tall man. That was all; I was blank [pp. 120-122].

George Lionel, the homosexual protagonist in Merle Miller's *What Happened* (1972), goes beyond the torments of homosexuality to make it a powerful lament for all the maimed, the suffering, the insulted, and the injured. George's strong-willed mother made him go to a YMCA summer camp much against his wishes. All through public and high school, he was called "Sis" and "Sissy" by classmates and teachers. In the following excerpt, George is in a mental hospital, driven to the edge of madness after his third suicide attempt. He is ruminating about his childhood Götterdammerung when he was gang-raped at the camp. The play on words and the puns are verbal rituals in a classical attempt to control realistic events.

They started laughing, all of them, all again, and I was laughing, too; I always laughed, afraid if I didn't laugh, so laughed. And then I saw that I was laughing alone; the others where not laughing; they were looking at each other, and I saw that it was no laughing matter, scatter, and I got up, glid up, and was to start to run, stun. They always laughed when I ran, everybody laughed. See the sissy run, they said. Run, fag, run, they read ... But this time I didn't start, couldn't start, had no feet to start. Irish, McKennon he was, reached out and tripped me, hipped me. Sang, "You've got a nice little ass there, lass, crass." In the lake were bass. And he sang,

"Ass, and you don't even need a rubber." "Mass," he sang, "grass."
Only there was no grass, only needles on the brown gown. Sang,
"I'm first: I thought of it." Sang, "You hold his head and shoulders."
Sang, "You hold her feet." Sang, "And you just lay there nice and
quiet and don't make a move. Because if you do, you little sissy you,
I'll beat you so hard you are going to wish. . . ." . . . The boy never
knew how many; he went blank and back and never felt how many.
Was any, and the blood and the small snow through the fine pine
made a mud, mud and blood, and that white that wasn't snow was
some, come. No ripples in the lake, no take. No scream. Never any
scream. Never any tears [p. 287].

Brancale's fourth type of rapist, the psychotic, is personified by Earl
Summerfield, in *The Diary of a Rapist* by Evan S. Connell, Jr. (1966).
Earl kept a diary in which he recorded the unrelenting development of
his incipient schizophrenia and its culmination in the rape of a beauty
contestant he had seen in an amusement park. Earl was a civil service
employee, bored with a job that had no future, resenting his co-
workers and superiors, and feeling greatly devalued as a man. He was
married to an icy, ambitious teacher, who read the financial section of
the paper in bed, leaving little time for Earl in or out of bed. He was
filled with resentment against Bianca, although his ambivalent feelings
prompted him on occasion to surprise her, however bizarre the surprises were. The entries in the diary reveal his progressive deterioration: "Bought a camera, stripped away my clothes and took a picture
of myself in front of the mirror—stiff as a lance! I'll send her the film. I
think she'll like that" (p. 286). He spent hours looking at himself in the
bathroom mirror; he locked himself in the bedroom, symbolic perhaps
of his expressed wish to be locked up before he hurt someone. He felt
trapped and alienated, isolated, resentful, discouraged, angry, suspi-
cious, revengeful, and impotent. Simultaneously, he was fearful of his
id impulses and very much conflicted by them. "I don't know what to
think, what to believe. So confused" (p. 48). And later, "Dark forces
are at work" (p. 162). His anger began to focus on girls. He saw them as
teasing and tantalizing him as he read about them in the daily papers.
No wonder, Earl concluded, there were so many rapes and sex murders. No wonder, too, that the diary he kept was filled with references
to acts of violence, gore, blood, mutilation, death, and the rattling of
nuclear bombs. For Earl, it was a world of menace as well as a world of
pleasures denied him. He became a hater and his hate focused on a

beauty contestant, a respectable girl, living with her mother, but to Earl she was "the whore of Babylon." If she were not, how then could she make him think all those dark thoughts? There is a blank entry in the diary for July 4—the day on which Earl raped the girl in an alley near a church. The succeeding diary entries, some of which follow, show him becoming a nocturnal creature, wandering around his neighborhood in San Francisco, going into people's homes, violating their privacy as he violated his "whore of Babylon." He ruminates on his assault, recalling how powerful he felt, how "quick" when he touched the victim. He wants the authorities to come for him soon, and plaintively cries, "where are they?" He knows he is ill and he knows he cannot help himself from doing further harm unless he is caught quickly.

July 11

Who knows how our ideas come to us? From above, or below? From without, or within? Thoughts we never think. Those shears an inch from her throat, suddenly I felt a wish to marry her— I never dreamed that, God knows! I almost asked the slut. Would have, I think, but was afraid she'd start to laugh. Maybe she wouldn't laugh at me. I don't know. It's too late now, she hates me. Hates all men because of me. I didn't have any right to do what I did—it was wrong. But of course on the other hand it's what she deserved. She's a vile dirty little bitch. I should have ripped open her belly and snapped a picture of the mess—sent it to the Chronicle. Everybody ought to see exactly what she is. Exactly what she is. Everybody ought to see. That's right.

July 12

She'd point me out if she had the chance. Then who'd believe anything I tried to say? Who'd believe Earl Summerfield under those circumstances? Nobody. Not one person. If I said she joined me against the church wall, who'd listen? She joined me and that's true, but in front of others she'd act the professional Innocent—not saying anything, just pointing. That's how it would be. Oh yes! But just the same, how soon will she taunt another man?—that's what I'd like to know. I might call & ask.

Must admit to feeling garrulous this evening. It is because I haven't been found out? Eight days! La la!—well, is freedom so important? Don't know, can't seem to come to any conclusions, nothing much matters. Eight days I guess I didn't actually expect. Don't know what I expected. But who's going to say I won't have eight more? After that—who knows!

Another hour gone. Feeling much subdued & poetic. Head full of beautiful ideas.

The Devil is supposed to have a forked penis so he can commit sodomy and fornication simultaneously, yet we build gods in the image of ourselves because it's implausible to do otherwise, consequently there's no reason for me to feel upset. How can one already worn out by this corrupt world understand Incorruption? Let the human race lament & let animals rejoice, etc. Yes, that's how it is, for the world has lost its youth and the times are beginning to grow old.

That's right, I've been right all along. I wasn't wrong. And after putting up with what I have—insults thrust into my head like sticks—well, the thought escaped. Skittered off crookedly as a butterfly. But I know what I'll do next Monday, offer a theory. Predict "he" won't be caught because he's intelligent. If anybody's interested I'll elaborate, mention examples, memorize a few statistics. Also I could remind them of how easily people forget, offer to place a bet that two months from now, or less, not one of them will be able to recall her name. Or I might bet that within one year not even the police will care.

Yes, all things fade like the memory of a stranger once seen in the street. Moments of love & violence, hours of bitterest hate. True. Of millions of words addressed to me how many could I repeat? Five hundred at the most. And the faces of women—the many faces that I've seen, how many would I recognize? Thirty or forty. What have they taught me? Nothing. I've listened to them talk & watched them wherever they go, but Magnus is going to find a lump of gold in the desert before a woman will teach me anything. Small humor, less wit, no philosophy, nothing but that dull resignation to Fate. Mercy & forgiveness. No matter what we do they forgive us. How strange. Unlike the nature of a man.

Why is it they continue to love us when we treat them as we do? Nobody can be sure, there are false answers to every question.

July 13

Very late but I'm not sleepy. Might go for a walk downtown and look at posters in the windows of the travel bureaus. Or maybe just walk slowly through the streets of San Francisco breaking things till

I'm stopped. I don't care. I'm free but it doesn't interest me. Maybe I'm free against my will. I guess I can choose.

How very different I feel tonight. Remembering for instance how quick and powerful I felt as soon as I touched her. Hadn't expected anything like that, but one touch and then I was capable of—oh, I suppose of just about anything. I couldn't do it now, but that night I was able to hear the slightest sound, and it wouldn't be much trouble to run away from anybody. Fog drifting over the top of the church, cold midsummer night. Suppose what I keep thinking about the most is that she didn't seem especially surprised. Well, of course she had warnings enough, that's probably the reason. Forgot how many times I telephoned, also there were the notes. Yes. But another puzzling thing is why she wanted me to talk. Say something! Say something! On her knees in the corner trying to see my face & begging me to talk. I don't know, think I did say something. Annoyed when she asked whether I believed in God. In times like these? God doesn't mean any more to us than a tinkling cowbell.

I've never felt quite the way I do just now. I don't know what to make of it. Not a sound within this room & I feel like asking questions but am uncertain what to ask.

Holding up both hands in front of my face & somehow had the impression they were covered with black seeds. Otherwise, no sensation. Not even when I think about her. Seems like everything's slowed down. Here it is already the 13th but time's dragging. Sand sifting gradually through the atmosphere. Maybe things are going on that I don't know much about. That's possible. Yes, that's possible.

July 14

Last night went back for a look at the church but didn't get too close, simply walked by as though on my way somewhere. Didn't see anybody, no sign of police, but I won't be fooled by that. Whatever I am, I'm not a fool. Let's see—then across the street and through that vacant lot looking for her shoe. Why did I keep one, throw away the other? Didn't want her to follow, I remember that's why I took them off her feet, but going through the lot for no good reason suddenly tossed one into the weeds. Well, I suppose I was afraid they'd be found if—no, that can't be it, all I can think of now is that I didn't want to give them up completely, so kept one. Now I want them both, they'd look nice together & might help somehow. Bring her that much closer. If I need—there's Bianca coughing again! Propped up in bed, no doubt, pillows behind her back and those horn-rim glasses with a rhinestone chain looped around her neck. Smoking, squinting through the smoke while she examines stock-market reports — I don't need to look, every night's the same. I never thought it would turn out like this. We've drawn back from each other. Avoiding each other like two little organisms under a microscope. Floating in separate worlds.

Well, sing softly Earl! The night of the soul is dark, twice as dark as the ocean floor.

*   *   *

July 20

Saturday. Again today and again tonight. Angered by the way I indulge myself. God knows I didn't choose my habits, something goes through me like an electric wire & there's nothing I can do. Can't prevent myself. Now I sit here covered with perspiration and hope for a knock at the door, hope somebody discovers. Hours turn, hours turn. Why can't they find me? Do I have to go out again? After that once more? How much longer? How much longer? How much longer?

July 21

No doubt in my mind about what I should have done when I had the chance. Knowing she's alive is what I hate. Knowing that as long as she lives I won't be able to forget. I thought that I had thought of everything but forgot what I should easily have remembered — that I couldn't forget. It's like a theme out of Purgatory, or dry agonies of early Christian fathers & no help. No help from anyone.

If only she'd resisted I'm not sure what — might have killed her, might have run away in a panic — but she obeyed, did everything I ordered. Beside the wall, kneeling there quiet as a pony with soft nipples hanging down. Somehow I thought about the Queen of Sheba when I saw that shag of hair — ought to have shaved it and kept it in a box. According to the Bible this woman came to prove Solomon "with hard questions" but when she had seen him in his glory there was no spirit left in her. That probably was how she felt. Yes, otherwise she would have screamed or fought against me.

Well, here I am yawning. Tik toc tik toc tik toc! I don't know how many hours I've been absorbed in thought. Soon I suppose it'll be growing light beyond the Berkeley hills.

July 22

No reason I can't visit her again. Why not? I'm free to do as I please, nobody on earth can prevent me. For the first time I know what Freedom is. Freedom that's absolute. I used to envy people I decided were important, from Mr. Foxx on up to famous scientists, explorers, millionaire bankers, etc., but now I look down on them. Not one of them compares with me. And furthermore—this build-ing just swayed! It's quieted down now, guess it was a small earth-quake.

Remembering how she moved beneath me. She did respond, it wasn't long until she did. Not long until the senses of the body overcame her mind. They can't resist us, not one of them. I'll never know exactly what it means, they live so much inside themselves, tangled flowers fascinated by their own idleness. Plants in a green-house suffocating us. All of them, even the ugliest. Aneurine drag-ging that shriveled red leg & pausing to smile at me—it disgusts me so I can't feel pity. Why doesn't she leave me alone? If everybody would leave me alone I'd be all all right [pp. 131-139, *passim*].

Earl's torments were indeed appalling. He suffered a cornucopia of symptoms: schizophrenia, depression, hysteria, fetishism, trans-vestism, and obsessive-compulsive fantasies. No other voice but his intrudes in this diary. But for a diseased mind capable of acts absolute in their Caligulan extremity, the portrayal of the psychopath in Hubert Selby's (1971) *The Room* is unparalleled. He is an erotic bundle of sexual gelegnite, fantasizing, in these pages, the ultimate in sadistic rape of a young, beautiful woman by a pair of inhuman policemen. It is catalogued step by near-realistic, unrelenting, horrify-ing step. The fantasy then proceeds to a scene where the psychopath perversely testifies before a special committee of the United States Senate, imaginatively aware that the entire country, "perhaps the world," would know what he said about the terrors and harsh outrages that await unsuspecting women in the dark. What Selby describes is true, in varying degrees, of the sadistic rape fantasies many men oc-casionally have.

Psychiatry is peculiarly at a loss in the handling of abnormal sex offenders, although serious efforts have been made during the last half century. Wortis (1939) reported that although psychiatric and juri-dical committees were established for the psychological study of sex offenders, little agreement was reached even on the very nature of the problem. Some felt that sex offenses, being punishable crimes, should be dealt with by suitable punishment or segregation. Others felt such offenses were psychiatric diseases and should be turned over to the doctors, but "we doctors were not sure how far we could go with them in the way of treatment. Some of us felt the offenders were largely constitutionally inferior psychopaths, 'poor stuff'; others felt that at least some of the punishable perversions were intrinsically harmless constitutional variants ... Still others felt that these offenders were essentially neurotics who should be treated by a long period of analysis if they were to be helped at all" (p. 554). A generation later, Tappan (1955) indicated methods of effective treatment for sex offenders had not yet been worked out. While psychiatrists indicated that psychotherapy of some sort should be given to rapists and others, it was felt a very high percentage of deviates would not respond to treatment, with the one possible exception of individual psychotherapy. And seventeen years later at a conference of psychiatrists, social workers, psychologists, gynecologists, and police held in Washington, D.C., Hayman et al. (1972, p. 17) reported that despite the easing of sexual morality and the availability of sexual partners, the inevitability of rape will probably remain a continuing problem. There is no easy solution to the problem of rape. Under the present circumstances, even the many changes in the law enacted by the several states will not protect women from attack. Nor do current investigations into the psychology of the rapist look fruitful as preventive measures. Perhaps when the culture goes beyond the politics of rape, primal and metaphorical, will men and woman meet each other on a common ground, equals at last.

TECHNICAL REFERENCES

Abrahamsen, D. A. (1960), *The Psychology of Crime*. New York: Columbia University Press.

Alexander, F. (1952), *Dynamic Psychiatry*. Chicago: University of Chicago Press.

Allen, C. (1962), *A Textbook of Psychosexual Disorders*. London: Oxford University Press.

Amir, M. (1971), *Patterns in Forcible Rape*. Chicago: University of Chicago Press.

Anon. (1967), Corroborating charges of rape. *Columbia Law Review*, 62:1136-1148.

Astor, G. (1975), *The Charge Is Rape*. Chicago: Playboy Press.

Barnes, J. (1967), Rape and other sexual offenses. *British Medical Journal Supplement*, 2:293-295.

Baughman, L. A. (1966), *Southern Rape Complex: Hundred Year Psychosis*. Atlanta, Ga.: Pendulum.

Bednarik, K. (1968), *The Male in Crisis.* New York: Knopf, 1970.

Brancale, R., Ellis, A., & Doorbar, R. R. (1952), Psychiatric and psychological investigation of convicted sex offenders. *American Journal of Psychiatry,* 109:17-21.

Briffault, R. (1963), *The Mother.* New York: Grosset & Dunlap.

Brownmiller, S. (1975), *Against Our Will. Men, Women and Rape.* New York: Simon & Schuster.

Connell, N. & Wilson, W. (eds.) (1974), *Rape. The First Sourcebook for Women.* New York: New American Library.

Deutsch, H. (1930), The significance of masochism in the mental life of women. *International Journal of Psycho-Analysis.* 11:48-60.

———— (1945), *The Psychology of Women,* Vol. I. New York: Grune & Stratton.

Dussinger, J. A. (1966), Conscience and the pattern of Christian perfection in *Clarissa. Publication of the Modern Language Association,* 81:236-245.

Eidelberg, L. (1961), *The Dark Age.* New York: Pyramid.

Ellis, A. (1954), *The American Sexual Tragedy.* New York: Twayne.

Ennis, P. H. (1967), *Criminal Victimization in the United States: A Report of a National Survey.* Chicago: National Opinion Research Center of the University of Chicago.

Evrard, J. R. (1971), Rape: The medical, social, and legal complications. *American Journal of Obstetrics & Gynecology,* 111:197-199.

Factor, M. (1954), A woman's psychological reaction to attempted rape. *Psychoanalytic Quarterly,* 23:243-244.

Freud, S. (1919), A child is being beaten. *Standard Edition,* 17:175-204. London: Hogarth Press, 1955.

Geis, G. (1971), Group sexual assaults. *Medical Aspects of Human Sexuality,* 5(5):101, 104, 109-111, 113.

Greer, G. (1972), Interview. *Playboy,* 19(1):61-82.

Hayman, C. R. et al. (1972), Rape and its consequences. Roundtable. *Medical Aspects of Human Sexuality,* 6(2):12 *passim.*

Hirning, L. C. (1947), The sex offender in custody. In: *Handbook of Correctional Psychology,* ed. R. M. Linder & R. V. Seliger. New York: Philosophical Library, pp. 233-256.

Karpman, B. (1954), *The Sexual Offender and His Offenses.* New York: Julian.

Katz, J., Goldstein, J. & Dershowitz, A. M. (1967), *Psychoanalysis, Psychiatry and the Law.* New York: Free Press.

Landis, J. T. (1956), Experiences of 500 children with adult sexual deviations. *Psychiatric Quarterly Supplement,* 30:91-109.

Lynch, W. W. (1974), *Rape! One Victim's Story. A Documentary.* Chicago: Follett.

MacDonald, J. M. (1971), *Rape: Offenders and Their Victims.* Springfield, Ill.: Charles C Thomas.

MacKellar, J. (1975), *Rape. The Bait and the Trap.* New York: Crown.

Massey, J. B., Celso-Ramon, G. & Emich, J. P., Jr. (1971), Management of sexually assaulted females. *Obstetrics & Gynecology,* 38:29-36.

Medea, A. & Thompson, K. (1974), *Against Rape. A Survival Manual for Women: How to Avoid Entrapment and How to Cope with Rape Physically and Emotionally.* New York: Farrar, Straus & Giroux.

Menninger, K. A. (1938), *Man Against Himself.* New York: Harcourt, Brace.

Miller, J. (1934), *Miller on Criminal Law.* St. Paul, Minn.: West.

Millett, K. (1970), *Sexual Politics.* New York: Doubleday.

President's Commission on Law Enforcement and Administration of Justice (1967), *The Challenge of Crime in a Free Society.* Washington, D.C.: Government Printing Office.

Rado, S. (1933), Fear of castration in women. *Psychoanalytic Quarterly,* 2:425-475.

Redl, F. (1942), Group emotion and leadership. *Psychiatry,* 4:573-596.

Russell, D. E. H. (1975), *The Politics of Rape; the Victim's Perspective.* New York: Stein & Day.

Schiff, A. F. (1972), Rape. *Medical Aspects of Human Sexuality,* 6(5):76, 81, 82, 84.

Schultz, L. G. (ed.) (1975), *Rape Victimology.* Springfield, Ill.: Charles C Thomas.

Slabey, R. M. (1962), Faulkner's *Sanctuary. Explicator,* 21(45).

Slovenko, R. (1971), Statutory rape. *Medical Aspects of Human Sexuality,* 5:155, 158, 160-162, 166-167.

Smith, A. R. & Giles, J. V. (1975), *An American Rape: A True Account of the Giles-Johnson Case.* New York: New Republic/Dutton.

Storaska, F. (1975), *How to Say No to a Rapist—and Survive.* New York: Random House.

Sutherland, S. & Scherl, D. J. (1970), Patterns of response among victims of rape. *American Journal of Orthopsychiatry,* 40:503-511.

Tappan, P. W. (1955), Some myths about the sex offender. *Federal Probation,* 19(2):7-12.

Weiss, C. & Friar, J. (1975), *Terror in the Prisons: Homosexual Rape and Why Society Condones It.* Indianapolis: Bobbs-Merrill.

Wortis, J. (1939), Sex taboo, sex offenders and the law. *American Journal of Orthopsychiatry,* 9:554-564.

LITERARY REFERENCES

Auden, W. H. & MacNeice, L. (1937), *Letters from Iceland.* Toronto: Ryerson Press.

Burgess, Anthony (1963), *A Clockwork Orange.* New York: Norton.

Cohen, Eddie (1960), The shadows behind the women. In: *Story Jubilee,* ed. W. Burnett & H. Burnett. Garden City, N.Y.: Doubleday, 1965, pp. 147-164.

Connell, Evan S., Jr. (1966), *The Diary of a Rapist.* New York: Simon & Schuster.

Dickey, James (1970), *Deliverance.* Boston: Houghton Mifflin.

Falkirk, Richard (1971), *The Chill Factor.* Garden City, N.Y.: Doubleday.

Faulkner, William (1931), *Sanctuary.* New York: Random House.

———— (1951) *Requiem for a Nun.* New York: Random House.

Friedman, Alan (1972), *Hermaphrodeity.* New York: Knopf.

Glanville, Brian (1960), The survivor. In: *Story Jubilee,* ed. W. Burnett & H. Burnett. Garden City, N.Y.: Doubleday, 1965, pp. 210-217.

Goethe, Johann Wolfgang von (1773), The sorrows of Werther. In: *Great German Short Novels and Stories,* ed. B. A. Cerf. New York: Modern Library, 1933.

Heller, Joseph (1955), *Catch-22.* New York: Simon & Schuster.

Hemingway, Ernest (1940), *For Whom the Bell Tolls.* Baltimore: Penguin, 1955.

Horwitz, Julius (1973), *The Married Lovers.* New York: Farrar, Straus & Giroux.

Koestler, Arthur (1943), *Arrival and Departure.* New York: Macmillan, 1966.

Kosinski, Jerzy (1965), *The Painted Bird.* Boston: Houghton Mifflin.

Lee, Harper (1960), *To Kill a Mockingbird.* Philadelphia: Lippincott.

Malamud, Bernard (1971), *The Tenants.* New York: Farrar, Straus & Giroux.

Malory, Thomas (c. 1450), *Le Morte d'Arthur*. New York: Potter, 1962.

McBain, Ed (1973), *Hail to the Chief*. New York: Random House.

Miller, Merle (1972), *What Happened*. New York: Harper & Row.

Murray, William (1968), *The Americano*. New York: New American Library.

Richardson, Samuel (1748), *Clarissa, or the History of a Young Lady*. New York: Modern Library, 1950.

Selby, Hubert, Jr. (1957), *Last Exit to Brooklyn*. New York: Grove.

────── (1971), *The Room*. New York: Grove.

Symons, Julian (1973), *The Plot Against Roger Rider*. New York: Harper & Row.

Updike, John (1968), *Couples*. New York: Knopf.

────── (1971), *Rabbit Redux*. New York: Knopf.

Vidal, Gore (1948), *The City and the Pillar Revisited*. New York: Dutton.

Voltaire (1759), *Candide*. New York: Airmont, 1966.

CHAPTER ELEVEN

Pedophilia

Humbert Humbert, the extraordinary protagonist in Vladimir Nabokov's *tour de farce, Lolita* (1955), defends his behavior in the seduction of the prenubile girl in terms of living in the wrong century.

> At other times I would tell myself that it was all a question of attitude, that there was nothing wrong in being moved to distraction by girl-children. Let me remind my reader that in England, with the passage of the Children and Young Person Act in 1933, the term "girl-child" is defined as "a girl who is over eight but under fourteen years"... In Massachusetts, U.S., on the other hand, a "wayward child" is, technically, one "between seven and seventeen years of age" (who, moreover, habitually associates with vicious or immoral persons). Hugh Broughton, a writer of controversy in the reign of James the First, has proved that Rahab was a harlot at ten years of age. This is all very interesting, and I daresay you see me already frothing at the mouth in a fit; but no, I am not; I am just winking happy thoughts into a little tiddle cup. Here are some more pictures. Here is Virgil who could the nymphet sing in single tone, but probably preferred a lad's peritoneum. Here are two of King Akhnaten's and Queen Nefertiti's pre-nubile Nile daughters (that royal couple had a litter of six), wearing nothing but many necklaces of bright beads, relaxed on cushions, intact after three thousand years, with their soft brown puppybodies, cropped hair and long ebony eyes. Here are some brides of ten compelled to seat themselves on the fascinum, the virile ivory in the temples of classical scholarship. Marriage and cohabitation before the age of puberty are still not uncommon in certain East Indian provinces. Lepcha old men of

eighty copulate with girls of eight, and nobody minds. After all, Dante fell madly in love with his Beatrice when she was nine, a sparkling girleen, painted and lovely, and bejeweled, in a crimson frock, and this was in 1274, in Florence, at a private feast in the merry month of May. And when Petrarch fell madly in love with his Laureen, she was a fair-haired nymphet of twelve running in the wind, in the pollen and dust, a flower in flight, in the beautiful plain as described from the hills of Vaucluse [pp. 20-21].

These were not the only instances Humbert Humbert could have cited. Helen, whose face launched a thousand ships and the Trojan War, was but ten when carried off by Theseus; Juliet was only twelve or thirteen when she goaded Romeo. Julian, in the novel of the same name by Gore Vidal (1962), reflects, "We tend of course to think of Plato as divine, but I am afraid he was rather like our old friend Iphicles, whose passion for youths has become so outrageous that he now lives day and night in the baths, where the boys call him the queen of philosophy" (p. 21). Some four centuries later, Claudius, in Robert Graves' (1934) *I, Claudius,* put on record, "I have never at any time of my life practiced homosexuality. I do not use Augustus's argument about it, that it prevents men having children to support the State, but I have always thought it at once pitiful and disgusting to see a full-grown man, a magistrate, perhaps, with a family of his own, slobberingly uxuriously over a plump little boy with a painted face and bangles. . ." (p. 218). Some four or five decades after Octavian Augustus's death, Petronius wrote an ironic story, "I Meet Eumolpus," about the seduction of a young boy. Plutarch said the reason why freeborn Roman boys wore a gold ball around their necks when they were very young was so men could tell which boys it was all right to abuse when they found a group in the nude. Plutarch's statement is only one among many that indicate sexual abuse of boys was not limited to those over eleven or twelve years of age. Sexual abuse by pedagogues, tutors, and teachers of smaller children was common throughout antiquity (de Mause, 1974).

In the fifteenth century, Gilles de Rais, with Jeanne d'Arc, created a unified France and also admitted to having killed 3,000 children and to having had sexual relations with them. Henry the Fourth's physician, Heroard, recorded the details of the young Louis XIII's life at the beginning of the seventeenth century. It is an astonishing document, remarkable for the pedophilic behavior openly practiced, the coarseness of the jokes, the language used to and by children, the indecent gestures made in public which shocked no one and which were regarded as perfectly natural (Ariès, 1955). "This lack of reserve with regard to children surprises us: we raise our eyebrows at the outspoken talk but even more at the bold gestures, the physical contacts, about which it is easy to imagine what a modern psycho-analyst would say. The psychoanalyst would be wrong. The attitude toward sex, and doubtless sex itself, varies according to the environment, and consequently according to period and mentality. Nowadays the physical contacts described by Heroard would strike us as bordering on sexual perversion and nobody would dare to indulge in them publicly. This was not the case at the beginning of the seventeenth century" (p. 103). Ariès gives detailed evidence of open sexual molesting of children, concluding that playing with children's private parts formed part of a widespread tradition.

The later nineteenth century continued the tradition but in more subtle ways. "This was the cult of the Love of Little Girls. It originated at Oxford where professors entertained small girls at tea parties. Among its literary voices were W. E. Hentley, Francis Thompson, Robert Louis Stevenson, and Algernon Swinburne" (Kingdon, 1961). The hobby of a mathematics professor, Lewis Carroll, was to photograph little girls in the nude. Robert Browning, in *Evelyn Hope,* wrote of an adult man's love for a little girl. The contemporary novelist, Virginia Woolf, who married Freud's British publisher, was subjected to a pedophilic attack by her half-brother George Duckworth who was nineteen and she six at the time of the occurrence. Her first mental breakdown occurred seven years later with the death of her mother, her second after her father's death when she was twenty-two. When at thirty she finally married, she learned that her world was without sex. At various times before and after her marriage, she formed attachments to women that were Sapphic. She thought a husband might remove her dread of sex and make it possible for her to bear children, but one of her worst collapses occurred right after the marriage. Her family blamed her half-brother (Bell, 1972).

It seems certain that Dostoevsky was preoccupied with pedophilia: Svidrigaylov in *Crime and Punishment* is guilty of it, and in a chapter of *The Possessed* which the publisher refused to print, Stavrogin confessed to the same offense (Storr, 1964, p. 103). Sophie Kovaleskya, whose sister Dostoevsky courted, told in her reminiscences of his ac-

count of a novel he had planned in his youth (Pratt, 1971). A middle-
aged, successful, contented landowner woke early one morning, permeated by a sense of well-being. In the midst of pleasant sensations
between sleep and waking, he became aware suddenly of "a peculiar
feeling of discomfort, such as that from an internal ache or mysterious
disturbance. Very much like what a man experiences who has an old
wound, from which the bullet has not been extracted; in the same way,
he has been feeling perfectly at ease when suddenly the old wound
begins to smart. And now our landed proprietor speculates on what
this may portend. He has no ailment, he knows of no trouble, yet here
he is, utterly wretched. But there must be something to account for it,
and he urges his consciousness to the utmost... And suddenly it *does*
come to him, and he experiences it all as vividly, and as tangibly—and
with what horror in every atom of his being!—as if it had happened
yesterday instead of twenty years ago. Yet for all that twenty years it
has not once troubled him. What he remembers is how once, after a
night of debauchery, egged on by drunken companions, he had forced
a little girl of ten years old" (Mayne, 1961, p. 166). Stekel (1952) made
the assumption that Dostoevsky had visualized the perpetration of that
crime in one of his epileptic spells. "If this is the case, then Raskolnikov's murder would represent a transmutation of the victim from a
child to an old woman. Such transmutations are by no means alien to
the psychogenesis of human passions and paraphilias" (p. 298).

To bring Humbert Humbert's erudite plea up to date for understanding his behavior with Lolita, he could also have cited the widespread tradition in Moslem cultures of sexual play with children. As
Ariès pointed out, there are features in Islamic society which Heroard
would not have found surprising. Albert Memmi (1955) described one
of them in his novel, *The Pillar of Salt,* in which the young protagonist
relates an incident on a tram which is taking him to school in Tunis.

One day ... I had boarded the streetcar that passed by the high
school. As it made no better time than I did on foot, I practically
never took it, except when, as this morning, it happened to be
raining. Each new passenger who boarded the car arrived among us
wet and covered with mud, hurriedly slamming the sliding door
behind him. The car itself, all warm from its human load and
saturated with the steam of our breath, was acquiring an odd kind
of intimacy as the passengers felt drawn together by a common
feeling of well-being that contrasted with the storm beating against

the windows. A mysterious sense of communion was thus born among us. All the races of our city were represented there. Sicilian workers in patched blue overalls, with their tools at their feet, were arguing noisily; a French housewife, conscious of her own dignity, was on her way to the market; in front of me a Mohammedan sat with his son, a tiny little boy wearing a miniature fez and with his hands all stained with henna; to my left, a Djerban grocer from the South, off to restock his store, with his basket between his legs and a pencil over his ear. The rain was sweeping against the panes of the car, opaque with steam, and the drops of water fell against them like the blows of a whip. The Djerban, affected by the warmth and peace inside the tram, stirred in his seat. He smiled at the little boy, whose eyes twinkled as he turned to look at his father. The latter, flattered by this attention and grateful, reassured the child and smiled at the Djerban.

"How old are you?" the grocer asked the boy.

"Two and a half years old," the father replied.

"Did the cat gobble it up?" the grocer asked the child.

"No," the father answered. "He isn't circumcised yet, but some day soon. . . ."

"Ah, ah!"

The grocer had indeed found something to talk about to the child.

"Will you sell me your tiny little animal?"

"No!" the child responded angrily.

Quite obviously, the boy knew what the grocer meant and the same offer had already been made to him before. I, too, was familiar with this game and had played it some years ago, provoked by other aggressors and feeling the same emotions of shame and desire, revulsion, curiosity, and complicity. The child's eyes sparkled with the pleasure of the awareness of his own growing virility, and with the shock of his revulsion at this monstrous provocation. He looked toward his father, but the latter only smiled: this was a permissible game. Our neighbors in the tram watched the traditional scene with complacent approval. In this warm and human car, protected as we were against nature's aggressiveness, we were like one happy family.

"I offer you ten francs for it," the Djerban proposed.

"No!" the child protested.

A Bedouin pushed the sliding door open and hesitated as he entered. The stink of a stable and of stale cooking fats spread throughout the car, as well as of something else that I was unable to identify. Through the still open door an unpleasant draft reached us.

"Close the door!" the Sicilian masons shouted, though apparently without any hostility or clannish animosity.

The Mohammedans in the car all pricked their ears up. For a while, the little game stopped. But the Sicilians had really intended no harm and we were quite clearly, one and all, a big family of Mediterraneans. One of the Mohammedans, to show that he appreciated it, even decided to join in the fun:

"Close that door! Don't they have doors, back home on your mountainside?"

The Bedouin smiled foolishly and, without giving an answer, finally closed the door before sitting down heavily beside the French lady who, without making any display of it, grew tense and pulled herself together. She didn't actually move, but my own antennae had already detected a violent disturbance in her magnetic equilibrium. The third odor of the Bedouin now became more recognizable in the closed car: the bitter and penetrating smell of burned charcoal.

"Come on! Sell me your little tail," the Djerban began again.

The child's attention had wandered, and he now started.

"No! No!"

"I'll give you fifty francs for it."

"No!"

"One hundred francs!"

"No!"

"Ah, you're a tough number! Two hundred!"

"No!"

"Well, I'll go all the way: a thousand francs!"

"No!"

The eyes of the Djerban tried to express greed.

"And I'll throw in a bag of candy too!"

"No! No!"

"So it's no deal? Is that your last word?" shouted the Djerban, pretending now to be angry. "Repeat it once more: is it still no?"

"No!"

Then, suddenly, the Djerban threw himself on the child, pulling a terrifying face, and grabbed roughly at the boy's fly. The child defended himself with his fists, shrieking in terror that was no longer a pretense, tore the fez off his aggressor's head and began to pull at his hair. In the end, the Djerban, almost blinded and his face already bruised by the tiny hands, let go of the tiny little animal.

The boy's father was laughing out loud, the Djerban was doubled up with nervous laughter, and all our neighbors were smiling broadly. Even the lady who sat beside the Bedouin must have found it, deep inside her, quite funny. At last the child, still pale and distrustful, decided to smile at his partner in the game [pp. 166-169].

The term "pedophilia erotica" was introduced by Krafft-Ebing in 1912 to label adult behavior that manifests erotic sexual desire for children. Although pedophilia literally means love of children, it is generally used today to signify sexual deviance (Peters and Sadoff, 1970). Pedophilia is the expressed desire for immature sexual gratification with a prepubertal child. It can be heterosexual or homosexual (Mohr, Turner, and Jerry, 1964). Pedophilia includes all cases of sex play with children, whether it be pederasty, fellatio, cunnilingus, masturbation of the child or adult, and so on (Frosch and Bromberg, 1939). The pedophile engages a child sexually before the latter acquires the capacity for rebuttal. He requires the cooperation of a child partner in order to achieve sexual gratification (Lorand and Schneer, 1967).

Psychoanalytic theory sees the causes for pedophilia in the weaning process, phallic and castration anxieties, psychic impotence, and incestuous wishes, all basic to an unresolved Oedipus complex which makes the choice of an immature sexual object understandable. It is "only exceptionally that children are . . . exclusive sexual objects. . . . They usually come to play that part when someone who is cowardly or has become impotent adopts them as a substitute, or when an urgent instinct (one which will not allow of postponement) cannot at the moment get possession of any more appropriate object" (Freud, 1905, p. 148). In the House-Tree-Person test administered by Hammer (1954) to thirty-three pedophiles in Sing Sing Prison, the woman drawing was significantly older than the man. She appeared as a sexualized maternal figure. "We may, then, postulate that as a child the pedophile originally desired, psychosexually speaking, the mother-figure because she was the nearest and most significant female. Having failed to resolve his original entanglement in oedipal feelings, he now tends to view the mature female as an object arousing his forbidden oedipal attitudes [the sexualized view in the subjects' drawings of self-described fifty-year-old women by twenty-six-year-old pedophiles] . . . reflects the strikingly immature confusion of sexual and maternal figures ... The pedophile is plagued by forbidden sexual desires toward the mother-figure. His frightening desires cause [him] to renounce adult females as available sex objects and to throw himself into a regressive flight into immaturity. He falls back, or has remained fixated, upon intermediate goals in regard to both sexual object and sexual activities, the latter usually involving seeing, touching, and manipulating of a child's genitals" (pp. 352-353).

The formula Cassity (1927) arrived at, the weaning trauma, with its various hazards, apparently plays a dominant role in later pedophilic formations. Among the hazards are resulting psychic emasculation, the subsequent narcissistic effort to compensate for the imagined impotency and the eventual occurrence of the precipitating factor of the neurosis itself. All these hazards contribute extensively to the final use of the unique expedient of pedophilia, in order that the neurotic might cope more satisfactorily with the rapidly accumulating psychic entanglements. Thus the early loss of the breasts provokes strong retaliative tendencies that are alleviated by forcing the love object to gratify oral cravings and at the same time dominating and controlling it, as well as avoiding castration anxiety by choosing a love object like oneself. Selecting a little girl as an object "represents a narcissistic object choice, that is, treating these girls as they would have liked to be treated by their mothers" (Fenichel, 1945, p. 333). Thus, while the mature woman represents a maternal and therefore tabooed incestuous figure, the child represents the patient as he would prefer to be himself, that is, a small child (Hirning, 1947). This is a recurrent theme in the literature on pedophilia. Psychological tests of pedophilic patients point up the oral deprivation and need for maternal warmth, according to Kurland (1960), who adds, "Another common finding in keeping with the emphasis on oral needs was the preoccupation of each man with oral-genital perversion and its prominence in their fantasy life. This further substantiates ... the polymorphous perverse nature of these patients' pathology and their deeply rooted and fixated immaturity" (p. 402).

The analytic portrait that evolves of the pedophile is, in summary, an essentially immature, shy person who is orally deprived and in need of maternal warmth not provided by the phallic mother. The pedophile suffers from castration anxiety and an unresolved Oedipus complex, and uses pedophilia as a defensive measure against introjected and projected anxieties of early childhood in an attempt to avoid anxiety, guilt, and pain (Socarides, 1959). A hallmark of the pedophile is his immature character, with strong feelings of sexual inadequacy and impotence (Karpman, 1954), who lacks the courage to attempt sexual contact with adult women (Guttmacher, 1951). Such a man usually avoids close relationships with people his own age, does not feel grown-up, and is unable to carve out any satisfying or self-sustaining role in the adult community.

There is a second character type, according to Kopp (1962), who is quite different and for whom the offense is superficially far less fitting. "In contrast to the childlike type of pedophile, this patient presents himself as being very much a man of the world. He is self-important, self-righteous and has an air of almost arrogant independence. His life is often characterized by one or more marriages, some success in business, and an active role in the adult community" (p. 66). Nabokov's Humbert Humbert seems to fit this category. As he himself elegantly presents the unhappy picture of the pedophile, ". . . the majority of sex offenders that hanker for some throbbing, sweet-moaning, physical but not necessarily coital, relation with a girl-child, are innocuous, inadequate, passive, timid strangers who merely ask the community to allow them to pursue their practically harmless, so-called aberrant behavior, their little hot wet private acts of sexual deviation without the police and society cracking down upon them. We are not sex fiends! We do not rape as good soldiers do. We are unhappy, mild, dog-eyed gentlemen, sufficiently well integrated to control our urge in the presence of adults, but ready to give years and years of life for one chance to touch a nymphet. Emphatically, no killers are we" (pp. 89-90). Both types of pedophile basically suffer from the same core problem: they see sex as an aggressive act that might bring retaliation from a stronger, adult female. In a sense the child molester is picking on someone of his own level of sexual maturity (Kozol, 1971), and is thus regressed or fixated at an immature level of psychosexual development, whereby he obtains primary sexual gratification from a physically immature female.

After evaluating over 1,600 cases of all types of sexual offenses, Pach, Halleck, and Ehomann (1962) concluded that sexual deviation is occasionally seen in relatively intact personalities, but the majority of subjects were functioning inadequately, showing poor controls in most areas of their lives. One of the manifestations of poor control is excessive use of fantasy to defend against acting out too many suppressed urges. "How marvelous [exclaimed Humbert Humbert] were my fancied adventures as I sat on a hard park bench pretending to be immersed in a trembling book. Around the quiet scholar, nymphets played freely . . . Rope-skipping, hopscotch . . . Ah, leave me alone in my pubescent park, in my mossy garden. Let them play around me forever. Never grow up" (Nabokov, pp. 21-22). And speaking in the third person, "Again and again resourceful Humbert evoked Charlotte as seen in the raree-show on manly imagination" (p. 74). Even before the seduction of Lolita was consummated, Humbert fantasied, "Lolita, with an incestuous thrill, I had grown to regard as my child" (p. 82). He imagined all kinds of ways to get at Lolita: "It occurred to me that a prolonged confinement [for Charlotte Haze, Lolita's mother] with a nice Caesarian operation and other complications in a safe maternity ward, sometime next spring, would give me a chance to be alone with my Lolita for weeks, perhaps—and gorge the limp nymphet with sleeping pills" (p. 82), or else dose both mother and daughter thoroughly with sleeping pills in order to take advantage of Lolita (p. 96). He apostrophized, in an outburst of doggerel, "Oh Lolita, you are my girl, as Vee was Poe's and Bea Dante's, and what little girl would not like to whirl in a circular skirt and panties?" (p. 109).

In their study of the psychosexual development of Norman, a child molester, Bell and Hall (1971), working independently, made a content analysis of his 1,368 dreams recorded over a three-year period. The study includes Norman's account of himself during an extended intake, plus twenty interviews held over a seven-month period, and a battery of projective and intelligence tests. Data from institutions where the patient had been confined periodically over fifteen years were also obtained, along with letters mailed to the therapist subsequent to contact. Thus five different kinds of information were utilized: dreams, interviews, tests, institutional reports, and personal correspondence. The dream material was given the role of principal datum.

The most outstanding feature of [the patient's] personality is his extraordinary emotional immaturity. On every level of his existence, he remains a child. His infantile status is reflected in a polymorphously perverse disposition which fails to distinguish between one sexual object and another or one sexual act and another . . . Most of his sexual feelings are not acted out. In fact he is less sexually active than most males his age ... Another reflection of Norman's child-like personality is his unusual dependence upon his mother and sister for emotional security. This dependency is of long standing. During his childhood ... Norman had few friendships. Then, as now, Norman invested little of himself in others with whom he remained only superficially friendly. Another reason that Norman remains a "loner" is that his associations with other children were very painful. In fact it is reasonable to suppose that Norman's sexual activities with children represent, in part, the effort to make up for his original experience of loneliness in childhood [pp. 83-84].

The great majority of sexual acts in heterosexual pedophilia consist of the type of sex play found among children — looking, showing, fondling, and being fondled — indicating that the nature of the sexual act corresponds to the immature needs of the adult (Mohr, Turner, and Jerry, 1964), and represents "an arrested development in which the offender has never grown psychosexually beyond the immature prepubertal age..." (p. 20). In Gagnon's (1965) summary of 400 pedophilic offenses reported to the police, the sexual techniques of the pedophile varied with the degree of participation. Thirty per cent of the accidental, one-time victims were subjected to fondling of the genitalia, seventeen per cent to nongenital petting, and ten per cent to more extensive sexual contact of which nearly half involved force. "There is some evidence," Gagnon suggests, "that the younger the child is the greater the likelihood of fondling, while for the older child there is a greater likelihood of exhibition ... Among the collaborative victims a much more extensive set of [sexual] techniques occurred which involved a greater degree of cooperation. One-third of the contacts involved coitus or attempts at coitus. Forty-one per cent involved genital petting, and only 3 per cent the minimum of nongenital petting" (p. 182).

Illustrations from current fiction reveal the extent and variety of pedophilic behavior. In Joyce's (1918) *Ulysses,* Leopold Bloom sadistically teaches little girls whom he picks up on the street to say dirty words they do not understand: "Whew! Girl in Meath street that night. All the dirty things I made her say all wrong of course. My arks she called it. It's so hard to find one who. Aho! If you don't answer when they solicit must be horrible for them till they harden. And kissed my hand when I gave her the extra two shillings. Parrots. Press the button and the bird will squeak. Wish she hadn't called me sir. O, her mouth in the dark! And you a married man with a single girl!" (p. 364). If, in the short story, "A Perfect Day for Bananafish" by J. D. Salinger (1948), "the child Sybil cannot save the life of Seymour Glass, at least she illuminates for him the world of adult corruption. [Salinger] proffers Seymour Glass' erotic trifling with the golden-haired Sybil ['The young man suddenly picked up one of Sybil's wet feet, which were drooping over the end of the float, and kissed the arch'] not as one more neurotic symptom, but as an attempt to escape from sexual bondage to the freedom of love; in his work, in short, the child becomes the rival of his wife" (Fiedler, 1960, pp. 310-311).

Marceline, Michel's wife in André Gide's (1902) *The Immoralist,* innocently brings Arab boys to their villa in Biskra to amuse her husband. Their company proves not so innocent. Menalque, a friend, says to Michel, "You preferred the company of children to that of your wife" (p. 119). The flat statement is true. Michel's homosexual pedophilic taste is evident in his description of a number of little Arab boys with whom he has relations. Bachir "had charmingly turned ankles and wrists" (p. 29); "His gandourah, which had slipped down a little, showed his delicate little shoulder. I wanted to touch it. I bent down. . . " (p. 29); "He was called Lassif, was only twelve years old, was a handsome boy" (p. 50); "Lachmi [Lassif's brother, showed] a golden nudity beneath his floating garment" (p. 50). There is a pedophilic radical in the nature of all males, not just those who are homosexual but also the vast majority of men who are not (Stekel, 1952). Fleeting periodic episodes of pedophilia occur in patients with intense fears of the opposite sex concomitant with suppressed homosexual tendencies (Socarides, 1959). But the man who is sexually interested in children is rarely a homosexual with well-developed interests in adult males, and he is seldom a member of the "gay" community (SIECUS, 1970).

Gustav von Aschenbach's involvement with the beautiful Polish boy in Thomas Mann's (1913) *Death in Venice,* while genuinely homosexual, is nongenitally erotic. In the story, von Aschenbach is a symbol of order and self-discipline. His wife died early in their marriage; he has a married daughter; he is an author held in great esteem by the German nation. On his fated trip to Venice, his parched spirit is unexpectedly and disturbingly refreshed by the sight of the handsome, fourteen-year-old Tazio; he loses restraint, disintegrates, and dies. Von Aschenbach is drawn, on the psychological level, as an aging man whose rational disciplined self is overwhelmed by a late and sudden eruption of drives which had been long and ruthlessly suppressed (Gronicka, 1956). Their return causes id derivatives to emerge, and he succumbs to a dreamlike state of falling in love with Tazio and surrendering emotionally to the waves of his homoerotic impulses (Slochower, 1969). Mann gave von Aschenbach an ambiguous name, for it means both life and death. "*Bach* is a brook or stream, a life symbol; but also the root of Bacchus, or Dionysius, a death symbol here, as in *Asch,* ashes" (Traschen, 1965, p. 166), even as "the story is a delicate and dynamic interweaving of dream and analysis, of the latent and the manifest, the preconscious and the conscious" (Slochower, 1969, p. 105). The repression of homosexual impulses in most adult men is so successful that no conscious feeling of want is left. Breakdowns as serious as that of Gustav von Aschenbach are seen only in cases of severe disturbance (Vanggaard, 1969).

Humbert Humbert is another example of latent, repressed homosexuality. While institutionalized for a depressive reaction, he discovered the joys of trifling with psychiatrists. At one point he bribed a nurse and "won access to some files and discovered, with glee, cards calling me 'potentially homosexual' and 'totally impotent' " (Nabokov, p. 36). Just as Michel exults in Bachir's "charmingly turned ankles and wrists," so Humbert Humbert does with Lolita's "beautiful boy-knees" (p. 122), her "white wide little-boy shorts, the slender waist" (p. 232). Humbert brags about his "orchideous masculinity" (p. 173); before going off to murder his rival, Quilty, he compulsively "checked the arrangement of my papers, bathed and perfumed my delicate body, shaved my face and chest, selected a silk shirt and clean drawers..." (p. 270). Michel, in Gide's *The Immoralist,* is profoundly more explicit in his expressed preference for homosexual pedophilia.

> I live for next to nothing in this place. A half-caste innkeeper prepares what little food I need. The boy ... brings it to me in the evening and morning, in exchange for a few sous and a caress or two. He turns shy with strangers, but with me he is as affectionate and faithful as a dog. His sister is an Ouled-Naïl and in the winter goes back to Constantine to sell her body to passers-by. She is very beautiful, and in the first weeks I sometimes allowed her to pass the night with me. But one morning, her brother, little Ali, surprised us together. He showed great annoyance and refused to come back for five days. And yet he knows perfectly well how and on what his

sister lives; he used to speak of it before without the slightest embarrassment . . . Can he be jealous? Be that as it may, the little rascal has succeeded in his object; for, partly from distaste, partly because I was afraid of losing Ali, I have given the woman up since this incident. She has not taken offence: but every time I meet her, she laughs and declares that I prefer the boy to her. She makes out that it is he who keeps me here. Perhaps she is not altogether wrong [p. 205].

Michel's openness about his homosexual preference for little boys is validated by McCaghy's (1967) study. Only twenty-five per cent of the 181 persons who had been convicted for male child molesting used denial, compared with fifty-three per cent of those who had molested females. Homosexual offenders were more likely than heterosexual offenders to admit other undetected instances. The explanation given for this phenomenon is that since many homosexuals have already internalized images of themselves as sexual deviants, their self-concepts are not seriously threatened by accusations of child molesting. They accept their deviant role and so have less need to deny the molesting accusation or to justify their behavior as molesters. Thus the protagonist in Jean Genet's (1953) *Funeral Rites,* who senses ten-year-old Paulo's distress during the seduction process but "could think of nothing to say that would reassure him" (p. 135), except to summon up out of his narcissistic, immature personality structure the weak and meaningless compliment, "You're very good-looking." After asking the boy if he is afraid, he "laughs wildly" and forces him to sit on the bed, kisses him on the corner of his mouth, and persuades Paulo to touch his penis, a "shy token of kindness [which] magnified my gratitude" (p. 137). With Paulo's cooperation, the ultimate act, related in unrelieved detail, is completed.

The sadistic, impulse-ridden pedophile usually feels little guilt but is unsure of his masculinity. His emotional stability is precarious, with a long history of mixing sex and aggression (Finch, 1973). This type of offender has an obvious dependent or sociopathic personality structure, obtaining gratification by manipulating, demanding, or taking (Swanson, 1971). In less severe cases sociopathic features may be partially under control so that the man is functioning reasonably well until rejected by a woman. Rico, in Alberto Moravia's (1972) *Two: A Phallic Novel,* suffers nothing but humiliation, sexual and otherwise, in his attempts at sublimation, until he is in such a frenzy that he

nearly rapes and murders Virginia, the nine-year-old daughter of
Irene. Rico has spent the night with Irene, an agreed platonic eight
hours, she lying naked to his view but untouchable. His frustration is
heightened when in the morning he covertly watches Irene masturbate
ecstatically in front of a mirror. He leaves the bedroom and enters
Virginia's. "I don't know what happened to me. I don't know how I got
dressed. I crept out on tiptoe, without making any noise, behind the
back of Irene, who did not see me because she had her eyes shut. The
next door, as I knew, was that of Virginia's room. I opened it and went
in ... I was conscious that I was on the point of doing something
terrible; but at the same time I felt I should do it. . . ." (p. 345). At the
last moment, just when he puts his hand out to take hold of Virginia's
bedsheet, his superego compels him to stop, and he leaves her room
"on tiptoe."

Harry Black, the hopelessly doomed homosexual protagonist in
Hubert Selby, Jr.'s (1957) novel, *Last Exit to Brooklyn,* drunkenly
accosts ten-year-old Joey and, despite the awareness of risk, because of
the inadequacy of his impulse control leads him behind a billboard in
a vacant lot.

> He walked to the corner, slipping several times, finally having to
> crawl to the lamppost to help himself stand. He clutched the post for
> a few minutes catching his breath. A kid, about 10 years old, from
> his block walked over to him and laughed. Youre drunk Mr. Black.
> Harry touched him on the head, then stuck his hand down under
> the large collar of the kids jacket and rubbed the back of his neck.
> It was very warm. Even slightly moist. The kid laughed again. Hey,
> your hands cold. Quit it. Harry smiled his smile and pulled him
> closer. Where yagoin Joey? Up the corner to see the fellas. Harrys
> hand was warm now and Joey stopped squirming. Howya like a
> soda. You buyin? Yeah. o k. They started slowly up 57th street,
> Harrys hand still on the back of Joeys neck. When they had walked
> a few feet Harry stopped. They stood still a second then Harry
> started walking into the empty lot. Hey, where yagoin. Over there.
> Comeon. I wanna show yasomethin. What yawant ta show me?
> Comeon. They crossed the lot and went behind the large adver-
> tising sign. Whats here? Harry leaned against the billboard for a
> moment then lowered himself to his knees. Joey watched him, his
> hands in his jacket pockets. Harry reached up and opened Joeys fly
> and pulled out his cock. Hey, whatta yadoin, trying to back away.
> Harry clutched Joey by the legs and put Joeys small warm cock in

his mouth, his head being tossed from side to side by Joeys attempts to free himself, but he clung to Joeys legs, keeping his cock in his mouth and muttering please . . . please. Joey pounded him on the head and tried to kick him with his knee [pp. 225-226].

Sexual aggressors in pedophilia, according to Eaton and Vastbinder (1969, p. 440), "represent a variety of psychological disturbances: character and behavior disorders, neuroses, psychoses, mental retardation or brain damage . . . The aggressor in a consenting sexual relationship with an adolescent is probably less emotionally ill than one who sexually abuses a small child." In "Little Louise Roque," a story by de Maupassant (1903), a schizoid trait is evident in the Mayor of a French village, Renardet, a widower of six months who is tormented by unfulfilled libidinal desires. When he accidentally comes across a twelve-year-old girl bathing naked in a pond in the woods, his sexual impulses overcome his scruples and he assaults her "without understanding what he was doing." To stop her screams, he unintentionally strangles her. Tortured by the fear of discovery, his passion spent by the rape and murder, he relives the two crimes which intrude repeatedly upon his thoughts. He develops psychosomatic symptoms, insomnia, and seemingly hallucinatory experiences, but Renardet is still collected enough to play out the charade when called upon to officiate as Mayor in the investigation of the incident.

As soon as he had reached his study he sat down before his table, which his lamp, covered with a shade, lighted up brightly, and, clasping his hands over his forehead, began to cry.

He remained crying for a long time, then wiped his eyes, raised his head and looked at the clock. It was not yet six o'clock.

"I have time before dinner."

And he went to the door and locked it. He then came back and sat down before his table. He pulled out a drawer in the middle of it and, taking from it a revolver, laid it down over his papers, under the glare of the lamp. The barrel of the firearm glittered and cast reflections which resembled flames.

Renardet gazed at it for some time with the uneasy glance of a drunken man; then he rose and began to pace up and down the room.

He walked from one end of the apartment to the other, stopped from time to time and started to pace up and down again a moment afterward. Suddenly he opened the door of his dressing room, steeped a towel in the water jug and moistened his forehead, as he had done on the morning of the crime.

Then he began to walk up and down once more. Each time he passed the table the gleaming revolver attracted his glance and tempted his hand, but he kept watching the clock, thinking:

"I have still time."

It struck half-past six. Then he took up the revolver, opened his mouth wide with a frightful grimace and stuck the barrel into it, as if he wanted to swallow it. He remained in this position for some seconds without moving, his finger on the lock; then suddenly seized with a shudder of horror, he dropped the pistol on the carpet and fell back on his armchair, sobbing:

"I can't. I dare not! My God! My God! My God! How can I have the courage to kill myself?"

There was a knock at the door. He rose up in a stupefied condition. A servant said:

"Monsieur's dinner is ready."

He replied: "All right. I'm going down."

He picked up the revolver, locked it up again in the drawer, then looked at himself in the glass over the mantelpiece to see whether his face did not look too much troubled. It was as red as usual, a little redder perhaps. That was all. He went down and seated himself before the table.

He ate slowly, like a man who wants to drag on the meal, who does not want to be alone with himself.

Then he smoked several pipes in the dining room while the plates were being removed. After that he went back to his room.

As soon as he was alone he looked under his bed, opened all his cupboards, explored every corner, rummaged through all the furniture. Then he lighted the tapers over the mantelpiece and, turning round several times, ran his eye all over the apartment in an anguish of terror that made his face lose its color, for he knew well that he was going to see her as he did every night — little Louise Roque, the little girl he had violated and afterward strangled.

Every night the odious vision came back again. First it sounded in his ears like the snorting that is made by a threshing machine or the distant passage of a train over a bridge. Then he commenced to pant, to feel suffocated, and had to unbutton his shirt collar and loosen his belt. He moved about to make his blood circulate; he tried to read; he attempted to sing. It was in vain. His thoughts, in spite of himself, went back to the day of the murder, made him go through it again in all its most secret details, with all the violent emotions he had experienced from first to last.

He had felt on rising up that morning, the morning of the horrible day, a little vertigo and dizziness which he attributed to the heat, so that he remained in his room till the time came for lunch.

After the meal he had taken a siesta, then toward the close of the afternoon he had gone out to breathe the fresh, soothing breeze under the trees in the wood.

But as soon as he was outside the heavy scorching air of the plain oppressed him more. The sun, still high in the heavens, poured out on the parched, dry and thirst soil floods of ardent light. Not a breath of wind stirred the leaves. Beasts and birds, even the grasshoppers, were silent. Renardet reached the tall trees and began to walk over the moss where the Brindelle sent forth a slight, cool vapor under the immense roof of trees. But he felt ill at ease. It seemed to him that an unknown, invisible hand was squeezing his neck, and he could scarcely think rationally, having usually few ideas in his head. For the last three months, only one thought haunted him, the thought of marrying again. He suffered from living alone, suffered from it morally and physically. Accustomed for ten years past to feeling a woman near him, habituated to her presence every moment, to her embrace each successive day, he had need, an imperious and perplexing need, of incessant contact with her and the regular touch of her lips. Since Mme Renardet's death he had suffered continually without knowing why, had suffered from not feeling her dress brush against his legs every day and, above all, from no longer being able to grow calm and languid in her arms. He had been scarcely six months a widower, and he had already been looking out through the district for some young girl or some widow he might marry when his period of mourning was at an end.

He had a chaste soul, but it was lodged in a vigorous Herculean body, and carnal images began to disturb his sleep and his vigils. He drove them away; they came back again, and he murmured from time to time, smiling at himself:

"Here I am, like Saint Antony."

Having had this morning several besetting visions, the desire suddenly came into his breast to bathe in the Brindelle in order to refresh himself and reduce his feverishness.

He knew, a little farther on, of a large deep spot where the people of the neighborhood came sometimes to take a dip in the summer. He went there.

Thick willow trees hid this clear pool of water where the current rested and went to sleep for a little while before starting on its way again. Renardet, as he appeared, thought he heard a light sound, a faint splash which was not that of the stream or the banks. He softly put aside the leaves and looked. A little girl, quite naked in the transparent water, was beating the waves with both hands, dancing about in them a little and dipping herself with pretty movements. She was not a child, nor was she yet a woman. She was plump and well formed, yet had an air of youthful precocity, as of one who had grown rapidly and who was now almost ripe. He no longer moved, overcome with surprise, with a pang of desire, holding his breath with a strange, poignant emotion. He remained there, his heart beating as if one of his sensual dreams had just been realized, as if an impure fairy had conjured up before him this young creature, this little rustic Venus born of the river foam, who was making his heart beat faster.

Suddenly the little girl came out of the water and without seeing him came over to where he stood, looking for her clothes in order to dress herself. While she was gradually approaching him with little hesitating steps, through fear of the sharp pointed stones, he felt himself pushed toward her by an irresistible force, by a bestial transport of passion, which stirred up all his carnality, stupefied his soul and made him tremble from head to foot.

She remained standing some seconds behind the willow tree which concealed him from view. Then, losing his reason entirely, he opened the branches, rushed on her and seized her in his arms. She fell, too scared to offer any resistance, too much terror-stricken to cry out, and he possessed her without understanding what he was doing.

He woke up from his crime as one wakes out of a nightmare. The child burst out weeping.

He said:

"Hold your tongue! Hold your tongue! I'll give you money."

But she did not hear him; she went on sobbing.

He went on:

"Come now, hold your tongue! Do hold your tongue. Keep quiet."

She still kept shrieking, writhing in the effort to get away from him. He suddenly realized that he was ruined, and he caught her by the neck to stop her from uttering these heart-rending, dreadful screams. As she continued to struggle with the desperate strength of a being who is flying from death, he pressed his enormous hands on that little throat, swollen with cries. In a few seconds he had strangled her, so furiously did he grip her, yet not intending to kill but only to silence her.

Then he rose up, overwhelmed with horror.

She lay before him with her face bleeding and blackened. He was going to rush away when there sprang up in his agitated soul the mysterious and undefined instinct that guides all beings in the hour of danger.

It was necessary to throw the body into the water, but he did not; another impulse drove him toward the clothes, of which he made a thin parcel. Then as he had a piece of twine, he tied it up and hid it in a deep portion of the stream, under the trunk of a tree, the foot of which was immersed in the Brindelle.

Then he went off at a rapid pace, reached the meadows, took a wide turn in order to show himself to peasants who dwelt some distance away on the opposite side of the district and came back to dine at the usual hour, telling his servants all that was supposed to have happened during his walk.

He slept, however, that night—slept with a heavy, brutish sleep, such as the sleep of persons condemned to death must occasionally be. He opened his eyes at the first glimmer of dawn and waited, tortured by the fear of having his crime discovered, for his usual waking hour.

Then he would have to be present at all the stages of the inquiry as to the cause of death. He did so after the fashion of a somnambulist, in a hallucination which showed him things and human beings in a sort of dream, in a cloud of intoxication, with that dubious sense of unreality which perplexes the mind at times of the greatest catastrophes.

The only thing that pierced his heart was La Roque's cry of anguish. At that moment he felt inclined to cast himself at the old woman's feet and to exclaim:

" 'Tis I."

But he restrained himself. He went back, however, during the night to fish up the dead girl's wooden shoes, in order to carry them to her mother's threshold.

As long as the inquiry lasted, so long as it was necessary to guide and aid justice, he was calm, master of himself, sly and smiling. He discussed quietly with the magistrates all the suppositions that passed through their minds, combated their opinions and demolished their arguments. He even took a keen and mournful pleasure in disturbing their investigations, in confuting their ideas, in showing the innocence of those whom they suspected.

But from the day when the investigation came to a close he became gradually nervous, more excitable than he had been before, although he mastered his irritability. Sudden noises made him jump up with fear; he shuddered at the slightest thing, trembled sometimes from head to foot when a fly alighted on his forehead. Then he was seized with an imperious desire for motion which compelled him to keep continually on foot and made him remain up whole nights walking to and fro in his own room.

It was not that he was goaded by remorse. His brutal mind did not lend itself to any shade of sentiment or of moral terror. A man of energy and even of violence, born to make war, to ravage conquered countries and to massacre the vanquished, full of the savage instincts of the hunter and the fighter, he scarcely took count of human life. Though he respected the Church through policy, he believed neither in God nor in the devil, expecting consequently in another life neither chastisement nor recompense for his acts. As his sole creed, he retained a vague philosophy composed of all the ideas of the encyclopedists of the last century. He regarded religion as a moral sanction of the law, both one and the other having been invented by men to regulate social relations.

To kill anyone in a duel, or in a battle, or in a quarrel, or by accident, or for the sake of revenge or even through bravado would have seemed to him an amusing and clever thing and would not have left more impression on his mind than a shot fired at a hare, but he had experienced a profound emotion at the murder of this child. He had, in the first place, perpetrated it in the distraction of an irresistible gust of passion, in a sort of sensual tempest that had overpowered his reason. And he had cherished in his heart, cherished in his flesh, cherished on his lips, cherished even to the very tips of his murderous fingers, a kind of bestial love, as well as a feeling of horror and grief, toward this little girl he had surprised and basely killed. Every moment his thoughts returned to that horrible scene, and though he endeavored to drive away the picture from his mind, though he put it aside with terror, with disgust, he felt it surging through his soul, moving about in him, waiting incessantly for the moment to reappear [pp. 979-1003].

Most molestations are committed by an adult known to the child (AMA Committee, 1972), and occur at either's home. Gagnon (1965) reports:

...the social relationship between the offender and the victim varied with the type of victim. The accidental victim with only a single experience usually had it with a complete stranger ... Another quarter of these victims were acquainted with the adult, or the child had known him before the offense occurred. Eight per cent of the offenses occurred with relatives other than the father ... Among the multiple-event victims much of the same pattern holds but with a greater concentration among relatives and a slight decrease among the per cent of strangers and acquaintances. Among the collaborative victims who sustained the offense out of their own interest, only 12 per cent of the offenses were with strangers, 44 per cent with acquaintances, one-third with relatives other than the father, and 9 per cent with the father. Among the coerced victims all of the offenses were with relatives, indicating that proximity was required to make the continuation of a forced offense possible. Duress or force is commonly useful for only a single event, but if the offender is a constant physical presence to the child there seems some likelihood that the offense will be continuous [p. 184].

Mohr, Turner, and Jerry (1964) and Revitch and Weiss (1962) bear out the fact that the victim is seldom a total stranger to the offender and that there is frequent involvement of neighbors, friends of the family, and relatives as offenders.

Anna, the mistress of the narrator in *Memoirs of Hecate County* by Edmund Wilson (1942), tells him about her daughter Cecile who is being cared for by her indolent grandmother. "Anna was afraid ... that they wouldn't give Cecile milk and eggs and other things they didn't have themselves; and she was afraid that the Polish boarder would play with her when he was drunk, as Cecile had once told her he had tried to do" (p. 206). Many boys are initiated into the mysteries of sex by maids, governesses, older cousins, and the like. "Love for immature boys is a common sexual deviation among adult females. The diminution of the possibility of becoming impregnated or infected adds a great deal to the paraphilic preference given boy-lovers. Havelock Ellis was the first to point out the strange fact that on the whole more males are seduced by females than the other way around. The biographies of men willing to expose their sexual experiences confirm this fact" (Stekel, 1952, p. 61). Vilar's (1971) aphorism seems to hold; chastity in man has never been highly valued by women: "For this reason a boy can never be raped by an older woman—only seduced" (p. 79). The quixotic Armenian hero of Cyrus L. Sulzberger's (1973) novel, *The Tooth Merchant*, Kevork Sasounian, speaks seventeen languages, is described as "the world's most brilliant bum and most flamboyantly unsuccessful crook" (p. 7) and was dismissed from the faculty of Roberts College in Istambul for interfering with the boys, a practice for which the Armenian excuses himself with the observation, "Turkish civilization brews Turkish habits" (p. 7). Earlier, he had noted, "Since I was taught the value of sex at the age of ten by a one-armed German housemaid with a gimp in her left leg who also introduced me to shoplifting, my life has been richer than most" (p. 5). In Trevanian's *The Eiger Sanction* (1972), Miss Ophel, a sere, cat-loving, fluttering, fragile, and fairly well-to-do spinster, semi-officially adopts orphaned Jonathan Hemlock. "On the evening of his sixteenth birthday there was a little party, just the two of them and champagne and petits fours. Miss Ophel got a little tipsy, and a little fearful over her empty life, and very affectionate toward Jonathan. She hugged him and kissed him with her dusty lips. Then she hugged him tighter. By the next morning, she had made up a cute little nickname for it, and almost every evening thereafter she would coyly ask him to do it to her" (p. 23).

Incestuous, homosexual pedophilic delinquency is relatively rare, but it does happen, as the narrator in John Rechy's *City of Night* (1956) relates. "When I was about eight years old, my father taught me this: He would say to me: 'Give me a thousand,' and I knew this meant I should hop on his lap and then he would fondle me—intimately—and he'd give me a penny, sometimes a nickel. At times when his friends—old gray men—came to our house, they would ask for 'a thousand.' And I would jump on their laps too. And I would get nickel after nickel, going around the table. And later, a gift from my father would become a token of a truce from the soon-to-blaze hatred between us" (p. 14).

To be sure, the far more common incestuous relationship is between father and daughter, or father and stepdaughter, usually in families where the father is extremely authoritarian (Peters and Sadloff, 1970). An age-old and universal phenomenon, the Phaedra complex, refers to the sexual attraction between stepparent and stepchild, where the incest taboo is not as strong as in the natural father-daughter relationship (Massey, Garcia, and Emich, 1971). We see it in the Biblical story of Joseph and Potiphar, the Greek tragedy of Euripides, *Hippolytus,* the Roman *Phaedre* by Seneca, the French *Phèdre* of Racine, and modern versions by Sutton and Nabokov, among others. In the typical tale as told by Euripides, Phaedra is married to a much older man,

Theseus, King of Athens, who has a son, Hippolytus. Young Phaedra falls in love with him but he is appalled by the thought of a sexual relationship with his stepmother and so spurns her. She commits suicide, but not before leaving a note stating he has violated her. The King puts a curse on Hippolytus. Banished by his father, Hippolytus subsequently meets a violent death. Too late, Theseus learns his son was innocent of any wrongdoing. The King's violent death completes the tragedy.

To the usual "family romance" between parent and child, one other dimension is added when a parent remarries: the viability of the incest taboo. The degree of intimacy varies from family to family. In some groups there is much warmth and physical affection; in others, austere formality. But no doubt there is a natural tendency toward some expression of physical intimacy, for any parent can see a child in a potential sexual role, and conversely the growing child can envision the parent as a source of sexual gratification which may be apparent in smiles, hugs, and caresses as well as in the reaction formation of physical avoidance between adolescent and parent (Messer, 1969). Even though Nabokov specifically denies or derogates the oedipal nature of the Humbert-Lolita stepfather-stepdaughter relationship, it is present: the novel seems to be an elaborate oedipal smokescreen. "Humbert's obsession with nymphets in general, and Lolita in particular, is an attempt to re-experience the fresh, unspoiled love of his mother during infancy" (Hiatt, 1967, p. 365). At one point, Humbert says of his relationship with his stepdaughter, ". . . I seemed to myself as implausible a father as she seemed to be a daughter" (Nabokov, p. 176). He fantasies a dynasty: "With patience and luck I might have her produce eventually a nymphet with my blood in her exquisite veins, a Lolita the Second, who would be eight or nine around 1960, when I would still be *dans la force de l'age*" (p. 176).

Among familiars who may subject the child to sexual abuse is the schoolmaster. William Faulkner and Colette treat this aspect of pedophilia in their novels. Labove, teaching in the one-room schoolhouse in *The Hamlet* (Faulkner, 1931), is sick with desire for Eula Varner, the last of sixteen children, "already bigger than most grown women . . . Her entire appearance suggested some symbology out of the old Dionysic times—honey in sunlight and bursting grapes, the writhen bleeding of the crushed fecundated vine beneath the hard rapacious tramling goat-hoof" (p. 99). And ". . . even at nine and ten and

eleven, there was too much — too much leg, too much breast, too much
buttock; too much of mammalian female meat..." (p. 100). Eula
attended Labove's school from her eighth year until nearly her fourteenth, years he suffered silently like a "virile anchorite of old time.
The heatless lean-to room was his desert cell, the thin pallet bed on the
puncheon floor the couch of stones on which he would lie prone and
sweating in the iron winter nights, naked, rigid, his teeth clenched in
his scholar's face and legs haired-over like those of a faun" (p. 118).
The first morning Eula entered the classroom, Labove turned from the
"crude blackboard and saw a face eight years old and a body of
fourteen with a female shape of twenty ... By merely walking down
the aisle between them she would transform the very wooden desks and
benches themselves into a grove of Venus and fetch every male in the
room ... springing into embattled rivalry..." (pp. 113-114). Labove's
fantasies led him to thoughts of marriage with Eula, but he did not
want a wife and old man Varner would never agree. Yet he stayed on,
until one beserk day he chased her around the classroom and eventually caught her.

> Then the body gathered itself into furious and silent resistance
> which even then he might have discerned to be neither fright nor
> even outrage but merely surprise and annoyance. She was strong.
> He had expected that. He had wanted that, he had been waiting
> for it. They wrestled furiously. He was still smiling, even whispering.
> "That's it," he said. "Fight it. Fight it. That's what it is: a man
> and a woman fighting each other. The hating. To kill, only to do it
> in such a way that the other will have to know forever afterward he
> or she is dead...." He held her loosely, the better to feel the fierce
> resistance of bones and muscles, holding her just enough to keep her
> from actually reaching his face. She had made no sound, although
> her brother, who was never late in calling for her, must by now be
> just outside the building. Labove did not think of this. He would
> not have cared probably. He held her loosely, still smiling, whisper-
> ing his jumble of fragmentary Greek and Latin verse and American-
> Mississippi obscenity, when suddenly she managed to free one of her
> arms, the elbow coming up hard under his chin. It caught him
> off-balance; before he regained it her other hand struck him a full-
> armed blow in the face. He stumbled backward, struck a bench and
> went down with it and partly beneath it. She stood over him,
> breathing deep but not panting and not even dishevelled.
> "Stop pawing me," she said. "You old headless horseman Ichabod
> Crane" [pp. 121-122].

As precociously physically developed as Eula Varner is Claudine in Colette's *Claudine at School* (1900), for at fifteen, Claudine says, "... if my face looks younger than my age, my figure looks eighteen at least" (pp. 27-28). And far from being the intellectual clod that the former is or the sexual unsophisticate, Claudine is involved in a Lesbian relationship as well as a pedophilic one. Dr. Dutertre, the district school superintendent and local physician, is given to pawing the motherless Claudine. Her father is absorbed in the study of slugs and pays her little mind, so that Dutertre's attentions are not as severely and ludicrously repulsed as were Labove's toward Eula.

Dutertre had now arrived at the point he wanted to arrive at and I raised my head as Mademoiselle Sergent answered him.

'Claudine? Oh, she's still top. But it's not *her* fault. She's gifted for that and doesn't need to make any effort.'

He sat down on the table, and swinging one leg and addressing me as *tu* so as not to lose the habit of doing so.

'So you're lazy?'

'Of course. It's my only pleasure in the world.'

'You don't mean that seriously! You prefer reading, eh? What do you read? Everything you can lay hands on? Everything in your father's library?'

'No, Sir. Not books that bore me.'

'I bet you're teaching yourself some remarkable things. Give me your exercise-book.'

To read it more comfortably, he leant a hand on my shoulder and twisted a curl of my hair. This made the lanky Anaïs turn dangerously yellow; he had not asked for her exercise-book! I should pay for this favouritism by surreptitious pin-pricks, sly tale-telling to Mademoiselle Sergent, and being spied on whenever I talked to Mademoiselle Lanthenay. She was standing near the door of the small classroom, that charming Aimée, and she smiled at me so tenderly with her golden eyes that I was almost consoled for not having been able to talk to her today or yesterday except in front of my schoolmates. Dutertre laid down my exercise-book and stroked my shoulders in an absent-minded way. He was not thinking in the least about what he was doing, evidently ... oh, *very* evidently....

'How old are you?'

'Fifteen.'

'Funny little girl! If you didn't look so crazy, you'd seem older, you know. You'll sit for your certificate next October?'

'Yes, Sir, to please Papa.'

'Your father? What on earth does it matter to him? But you yourself, you're not particularly eager at the prospect?'

'Oh yes, I am. It'll amuse me to see all those people who question us. And besides there are concerts in the town then. It'll be fun.'

'You won't go on to the training-college?'

I leapt in my seat.

'Good heavens, no!'

'Why so emphatic, you excitable girl?'

'I don't want to go there any more than I wanted to go to boarding-school—because you're shut up.'

'Oho! Your liberty means as much as all that to you, does it? Your husband won't have things all his own way, poor fellow? Show me that face. Are you keeping well? A trifle anaemic, perhaps?'

This kindly doctor turned me towards the window, slipped his arm round me and gazed searchingly into my eyes with his wolfish stare. I made my own gaze frank and devoid of mystery. I always have dark circles under my eyes and he asked me if I suffered from palpitations and breathlessness.

'No, never.'

I lowered my lids because I felt I was blushing idiotically. Also he was staring at me too hard! And I was conscious of Mademoiselle Sergent behind us, her nerves tense.

'Do you sleep all night?'

I was furious at blushing more than ever as I answered:

'Oh, yes, Sir. All night long.'

He did not press the point but stood upright and let go my waist.

'Tcha! Fundamentally, you're as sound as a bell.'

A little caress on my cheek, then he went on to the lanky Anaïs who was withering on her bench [pp. 29-30].

*   *   *

When my cold was over, I observed that people at school were beginning to get very agitated about the approaching exams; we were now at the end of May and we 'went up' on the 5th of July! I was sorry not to be more moved, but the others made up for me, especially little Luce Lanthenay, who burst into floods of tears whenever she got a bad mark. As for Mademoiselle Sergent, she was busy with everything, but most of all, with the little thing with the beautiful eyes who kept her 'on a string'. She'd blossomed out, that Aimée, in an astonishing way! Her marvellous complexion, her velvety skin and her eyes, 'that you could strike medals out of', as

Anaïs says, make her into a spiteful and triumphant little creature. She is so much prettier than she was last year! No one would pay any more attention now to the slight crumpling of her face, to the little crease on the left of her lip when she smiles; and, anyhow, she has such white, pointed teeth! The amorous Redhead swoons at the mere sight of her and our presence no longer restrains her from yielding to her furious desire to kiss her darling every two minutes.

On this warm afternoon, the class was murmuring a *Selected Passage* that we had to recite at three o'clock. I was almost dozing, oppressed by a nervous lassitude. I was incapable of any more effort, when all of a sudden I felt I wanted to scratch somebody, to give a violent stretch and to crush somebody's hands; the somebody turned out to be Luce, my next-door neighbour. She found the nape of her neck being clutched and my nails digging into it. Luckily, she didn't say a word. I fell back into my irritated listlessness. . . .

The door opened without anyone having even knocked: it was Dutertre, in a light tie, his hair flying, looking rejuvenated and pugnacious. Mademoiselle Sergent sprang to her feet, barely said good afternoon to him and gazed at him with passionate admiration, her tapestry fallen unheeded on the floor. (Does she love him more than Aimée? or Aimée more than him? Curious woman!) The class had stood up. Out of wickedness, I remained seated, with the result that, when Dutertre turned towards us, he noticed me at once.

'Good afternoon, Mademoiselle. Good afternoon, little ones. *You* seem in a state of collapse!'

'I'm floppy. I haven't a bone left in me.'

'Are you ill?'

'No, I don't think so. It's the weather—general slackness.'

'Come over here and let's have a look at you.'

Was all that going to start over again . . . those medical pretexts for prolonged examinations? The Headmistress launched looks of blazing indignation at me for the way I was sitting and for the way I was talking to her beloved District Superintendent. I decided to put myself out and obey. Besides, he adores these impertinent manners. I dragged myself lazily over to the window.

'One can't see here because of that green shadow from the trees. Come out into the corridor, there's some sunlight there. You look wretched, my child.'

Triple-distilled lie! I looked extremely well. I know myself: if it was because I had rings round my eyes that he thought I was ill, he was mistaken. It's a good sign when I have dark circles under my eyes, it means I'm in excellent health. Luckily it was three in the afternoon, otherwise I should have been none too confident about going out, even into the glass-paned corridor, with this individual whom I mistrust like fire.

When he had shut the door behind us, I rounded on him and said:

'Now, look here, I *don't* look ill. Why did you say I did?'

'No? What about those eyes with dark circles right down to your lips?'

'Well, it's the colour of my skin, that's all.'

He had seated himself on the bench and was holding me in front of him, standing against his knees.

'Shut up, you're talking nonsense. Why do you always look as if you were cross with me?'

'. . . ?'

'Oh yes, you know quite well what I mean. You know, you've got a nice, funny little phiz that sticks in one's head once one's seen it!'

I gave an idiotic laugh. If only heaven would send me some wit, some smart repartee, for I felt terribly destitute of them!

'Is it true you always go for walks all by yourself in the woods?'

'Yes, it's true. Why?'

'Because, you little hussy, perhaps you go to meet a lover? You're so well chaperoned!'

I shrugged my shoulders.

'You know all the people round here as well as I do. Do you see any of *them* as a possible lover for me?'

'True. But you might be vicious enough. . . .'

He gripped my arms and flashed his eyes and his teeth. How hot it was here! I would have been only too pleased if he would have let me go back to the classroom.

'If you're ill, why don't you come and consult me at my house?'

I answered too hurriedly 'No! I won't go. . . .' And I tried to free my arms, but he held me firmly and raised burning, mischievous eyes to mine. They were handsome eyes too, it's true.

'Oh, you little thing, you charming little thing, why are you frightened? You're so wrong to be frightened of me! Do you think I'm a cad? You've absolutely nothing to fear . . . nothing. Oh, little Claudine, you're so frightfully attractive with your warm brown eyes and your wild curls! You're made like an adorable little statue, I'll swear you are. . . .'

He stood up suddenly, clasped me in his arms and kissed me; I hadn't time to escape, he was too strong and virile, and my head was in a whirl... What a situation! I no longer knew what I was saying, my brain was going round and round.... Yet I couldn't go back to the classroom, all red and shaken as I was, and I could hear him behind me.... I was certain he was going to want to kiss me again.... I opened the front door, rushed out into the playground and dashed up to the pump where I drank a mug of water. Ouf! ... I must go back.... But he must be ambushed in the passage. Ah! After all, who cares! I'd scream if he tried to do it again.... It was because he'd kissed me on the corner of the mouth, which was the best he could do, that beast!

No, he wasn't in the corridor. What luck! I went back into the classroom and there I saw him, standing by the desk and calmly chatting to Mademoiselle Sergent. I sat down in my place; he looked at me searchingly and inquired:

'You didn't drink too much water, I hope? These kids, they swallow mugfuls of cold water, it's shockingly bad for the health.'

I was bolder with everyone there.

'No, I only drank a mouthful. That was quite enough, I shan't take any more.'

He laughed and looked pleased:

'You're a funny girl. But you're not a complete idiot' [pp. 142-145].

Although the stereotype of the child molester is the old man, there is a wide age range among those who have sexual contact with children, from young men in their teens to senile old men (SIECUS, 1970). Most pedophilic behavior, however, is distributed among three distinct age groups, with peaks in puberty, the mid- to late thirties, and the mid- to late fifties. "There is a small minority of chronic agents who tend to remain pedophilic from childhood on. Thus, according to the three age groups in which pedophilia occurs, the deviations can be classified as adolescent pedophilia, middle-age pedophilia and senescent pedophilia ... The middle-age group consistently emerges as the largest one" (Mohr, Turner, and Jerry, 1964, p. 20). The median age for the child molester, according to the California Sexual Deviation Research Study, was 40.7 years (Magnus, 1953). Only ten per cent of the offenders were over sixty years of age. Thus the widely held idea that the "dirty old man" or men with senile or chronic organic brain syndrome are primarily responsible for this kind of sexual offense is statistically invalid. However, a pedophilic perversion may appear in the elderly or late middle-aged "whose defenses against their sexual drives have been altered by the multiple psychological and organic changes accompanying aging" (Socarides, 1959, p. 84). The vicissitudes of aging, with its gradually decreasing physiological capacities, prompt some of the unnatural acts older men commit. These are related in part to the struggle to maintain something which has been a valued part of their self-image for a number of years—their adult sexual capacities (Whiskin, 1967).

The question is frequently raised whether pedophilia is completely the fault of the offender or whether in many cases the child contributes to the situation. In large measure, the involvement of any specific child in a sex offense is accidental (SIECUS, 1970).

> It is only rarely that the needs of the child open him or her to interactions with persons who involve the child in sexual activity. And it is even more rare that the child is acting out any sexual need of his own in the process of, or in the origination of, the event. It is far more important to understand the nonsexual needs of the child than his purported sexual needs. The Freudian focus on the sexuality of children has led somewhat indirectly to the notion that some children serve to precipitate offense behavior and also to research that has examined the process by which children's acting out of their own needs may seduce adults ... If being sexual is recognizing the content of behavior and having a sense of its cognitive and emotional meaning during its performance, this is learned, by and large, after puberty. This notion leads to an important corrective of notions about the victimization-prone child or the child as seducer. Such children are in no sense seeking what adults would recognize as sexual gratification; they are looking for affection, means of control over adults, and the like. These children perform seductively to get many nonsexual gratifications, such as good grades in school, attention from daddy, candy from strangers ... Both boys and girls in the course of seductive behavior come across adults who interpret their actions as sexual and who consequently make advances to them. If the advances are made successfully, that is, if the adult supplies what the child wants in terms of affection or attention, the child tolerates the sexual activity. In some cases the sexual activity becomes a secondary gain for the child; if so, it is in the course of the victimization experience that the child learns to seek what are adult sexual goals... [pp. 91-92].

Investigators have found that the youngster may play a part in setting up the molestation by an adult and is not necessarily the victim of a "sex fiend" (Finch, 1973). There are instances when provocation by the child victim is real (Bowman, 1951). The victim selection may not occur by chance alone, for frequently the child is attractive, charming and possessed with a strong need for attention, often with a history of behavior difficulties, particularly restlessness and rebellion against parents (Gregory and Rosen, 1965). Most children can avoid being molested if they want to, according to Mohr (1968). "Two reasons children do become involved are (1) developmental and (2) emotional ... The majority of girl [victims] are between the ages of five and ten, with a peak at ages seven to eight ... The child's developmental stages, needs, and interests form a basis for molesting which from the children's side has to be seen as an extension of preadolescent sex play ... The second reason [reveals that] all studies conducted on victims agree that although there are accidental victims who become tangentially involved, in the main children tend to come from homes in which they do not get the care and affection they need. Early emotional deprivation made the children prone to seek satisfaction from an adult relationship to a point where the child might actually have been the seducer" (pp. 48-49). Finch (1967) describes youngsters who invite and even unconsciously welcome some type of sexual molestation by adults. They include hysterical girls whose rich fantasy life prompts them to behave in such a way that they seem to invite sexual assault. According to Anderson (1968), some girls who are lost in a world of books or fantasies have little ability to understand, much less to cope with the assault, and therefore become easy prey for molesters. Eaton and Vastbinder (1969) declare that many suspected cases of child molestation seen by physicians turn out to be the products of maternal anxiety or the child's fantasy rather than true molestation.

The errant nymph, Lolita, is fully aware of the role she is playing. Humbert fatuously tries to explain to her that while they travel they shall be thrown together a good deal. " 'Two people sharing one room, inevitably enter into a kind—how shall I say—a kind—' 'The word is incest,' said Lo—and walked into the closet, walked out again with a young golden giggle..." (Nabokov, p. 121). Lolita is an artful, sexually precocious girl who has already traded her virginity for some experiences at Camp Q. On their travels, Humbert "... had to keep a very sharp eye on Lo, little limp Lo! Owing perhaps to constant amorous exercise, she radiated, despite her very childish appearance, some special languorous glow which threw garage fellows, hotel pages, vacationists, goons in luxurious cars, maroon morons near blued pools, into fits of concupiscience which might have tickled my pride, had it not incensed my jealousy. For little Lo was aware of that glow of hers, and I would often catch her *coulant un regard* in the direction of some amiable male, some grease monkey, with a sinewy golden-brown forearm and watch-braceleted wrist, and hardly had I turned my back to go and buy this very Lo a lollipop, than I would hear her and the fair mechanic burst into a perfect love song of wisecracks" (p. 161). Bender and Blau (1937) examined sixteen unselected successive admissions of prepubescent children sent for observation to the psychiatric division at Bellevue Hospital following sexual relations with an adult. They noted that the children frequently had attractive, charming personalities, made personal contacts easily, showed an unusually strong need for affection, and were flirtatious with the male psychiatrist.

Fiedler (1958) has written that in the place of the sentimental dream of childhood, the pedophilic epilogues of writers such as Faulkner and Nabokov have been creating

a nightmare in which the child is no longer raped, strangled or seduced, but is himself (better herself!) rapist, murderer and seducer. Their books reflect a growing awareness on the part of us all that our society has tended (as least aspired) to become not the conspiracy against the child which our ancestors raged—but a conspiracy in his favor, against the adult. Certainly, in a permissive, family-oriented, servantless America, whose conscience is forged by popularizations of Freud, a new tyranny has become possible. If in the comics the baby-sitter cowers in terror before Junior and in Nabokov the grown man trembles in passion before the pre-pubescent coquette, the causes are the same. We begin to feel that we are the slaves of our anxieties about our children, guilt-ridden by our fear of rejecting them, not giving them enough security or love, robbing them of spontaneity or creativeness; and like slaves everywhere, we grow sullen and resentful. But the appeasement of the child is only one form of the appeasement of the id, a resolve to give the (former) devil his due. The child remains still what he has been since the beginnings of Romanticism, a surrogate of our unconscious, impulsive lives; and the pattern of the family (at least as we dream it) is a symbolic representation of the way in which we have chosen to resolve certain persistent conflicts of what used to be called the Heart and the Hand. The work of recent writers for whom tales of childhood are inevitably tales of terror, in which the child poses a threat, represents a literature blasphemous and revolutionary. Such writers have come to believe that the self can be portrayed by impulse as well as rigor; that an Age of Innocence can be a tyranny no less terrible than an Age of Reason; and that the gods of such an age, if not yet dead, must be killed, however snub-nosed, freckled-faced or golden-haired they may be [p. 29].

Almost as if to illustrate Fiedler's point, Alan Lelchuk's promiscuous college dean in *American Mischief* (1973) cites the

common predicament among young mothers with daughters, when there is no man around the house. The man naturally is going to be fought over vigorously, when he finally does show up and tries to play *father and husband.* Obviously Kate exaggerates the matter. But it's understandable. I do like Suzie, she is a charmer, as I've said, with her wild eyes and gypsy skin. But I like the mother too. Kate is a very different type, much longer and larger, less exotic but nevertheless lovely. Surely it would be senseless for me to try to explain to Kate that at age six her daughter is not at all that innocent; or that at times her pursuit of me reaches embarrassing proportions. Can I explain, for example, those afternoon phone calls that she makes to me while being baby-sat (on the pretense that she wants to tell me what school was like that day)? Or when she cons her mother into getting me to take her along to a Red Sox game, where she will sit only on my lap and continually play with my ears and hair? No, in certain situations, the wise man is he who keeps his wisdom secret, rather than blabbering it around. An embarrassing situation is an embarrassing situation [pp. 154-155].

Statistics indicate that some twenty-five per cent of women have had some sort of sexual experience in childhood, ranging from being fondled by a male adult to coitus (Herman, 1972): "The later effects on their sexual life are extremely variable, depending on the makeup of personality of the young girl and also the status of family interaction that exists at the particular time" (p. 60). Where violence and force are used, the likelihood of psychic damage increases. But the outcomes are as many as the variables. Finch (1973, p. 170) reminds us that "It has been traditional in psychiatry to believe that sexual seduction of the child by an adult must invariably cause serious emotional problems for the child. While this is often true, it is not inevitable. The variables are many and so are the outcomes. Among them are such things as age

of the child, the time span involved, the degree of threat and aggression, and the kind of adult involved. It should be remembered at the
outset that children are polymorphous perverse. This means they can
be 'taught' to enjoy a variety of sexual activities. They have not
achieved a genital primacy in the true sense and can find pleasure in
many kinds of sexual stimulation. At the time of seduction most
children have learned that sex is not an acceptable activity, so that
guilt usually follows any sexual involvement. The child's guilt is intensified by the seducing adult, who is usually secretive and warns or
threatens the child to keep the secret." Humbert Humbert
double-talks his way through the need for secrecy concerning his
activities with Lolita by terrorizing her. "Let us see what happens if
you, a minor, accused of having impaired the morals of an adult in a
respectable inn, what happens if you complain to the police of my
having kidnaped and raped you?" (Nabokov, p. 152). Although
Humbert admits he may go to jail for ten years, she would become a
ward of the Department of Public Welfare, placed in a correctional
school, a reformatory or a juvenile detention home under the close
supervision of hideous matrons. Humbert is successful in his efforts.
Lolita soon comes to realize she is his prisoner in their summer's trek
through the motels and movies of America, and Humbert would hear
her "sobs in the night—every night, every night—the moment he
feigned sleep" (p. 178).

While sexual molestation does not necessarily "ruin" a child's life, it
can create psychological problems of short or long-term duration. The
impact on the child fosters not only remorse and guilt but also pho-
bias, nightmares, and anxieties (Weiss et al., 1954). In Gagnon's
(1965) study the overwhelming majority of children who had been
subjected to sexual attack reported they reacted negatively. The most
common response was fright. In *The Adventurous History of Hsi Men
and His Six Wives* by Chin P'ing Mei (1609), the youngest servant of
Hsi Men's household, "pretty little" Hua Yung, is both frightened and
indignant by the importunings of Master Warm. He refuses to go on
an errand to the latter's house and because of this his employer
threatens him with dire punishment, the dreaded "finger press."
Caught between the two, the boy explains, "He wants to misuse me.
First he gets me over there, and gives me wine, and then . . . Today he
wanted to do it again, so I ran away. Now he's sent for me again, but
I'm not going" (p. 598). Anne, the surgeon's wife in Julius Horwitz's

(1973) *The Married Lovers,* is reminiscing about her childhood in New England. "The only person I remember being cruel to me as a little girl was my uncle from New York City. He once put my hand on his pants where I felt his bulge and I remember his eyeballs closing as though somebody had pulled a zipper across them. He was rather abrupt when he asked me to get him a Kleenex. Later he took the bulge out of his pants and made me stroke his flesh that looked like a chicken's neck with its feathers plucked off. After that I learned to avoid him" (p. 26).

In Gagnon's (1965) study, among the accidental victims of pedophilic abuse with a single experience,

> ... 84 per cent reported that the immediate reaction to the experience had been completely negative. Another 13 per cent reported some mixed reaction, while only three persons reported that the experience had been positive. Among the 34 cases where the response was reported as mixed there are 11 difficult cases. Within this category, but requiring special mention, were five subjects who reported that they were both frightened and sexually aroused by the experience. Also included here are females whose response to the event had been indifferent, but who in retrospect became horrified and upset because of the extreme character of the parental response to their report ... All of the events occurring to the five coerced victims were reported as negative, as might be expected. Among the collaborative victims, only one half of the events were reported as positive while the remainder had either negative or more alloyed responses ... There were three in which the child participated in the inception of the offense and in the sexual contact and then responded negatively. For most of the remainder of the cases, sexual and other gratifications on the part of the child were sufficient to maintain the mutual character of the encounter over long periods of time and for many more separate contacts. However, even these rewards were not able to prevent 19 per cent from reporting a mixture of reactions. Of course, it was far more difficult for these subjects to report adequately all of their reactions to long-term involvements than it was for the accidental victims to report their feelings about a single experience [p. 184].

Acute and long-term psychological sequelae of a sexual attack can be found in the Alexandria Quartet by Lawrence Durrell. The effect on adult adjustment, sexual and nonsexual, because of what Justine experienced as a street Arab at the hands of a relative, Da Capo, is traced in three of the four novels. Durrell describes his quartet as "a four-card trick in the form of a novel; passing a common axis through four stories . . . A continuum . . . embodying not a *temps retrouvé* but a *temps délivré"* (*Clea*, p. 135). The tetralogy, which serves as facets of a single novel, constitutes a multiplicity of interwoven themes, each one "true" when seen in relation to the rest but false when viewed in isolation. Like Henry Miller, whom he greatly admired, Durrell relates the theme of sex to the quest for self-realization. Connected with the compulsion of sex is the basic need to search for self-identity (Glicksberg, 1963). The three novels that concern the attack on Justine and her subsequent neurosis are *Justine* (1957), *Balthazar* (1958) and *Clea* (1960). The long-term impact of the sexual attack was influenced by a multiplicity of factors, as it is with all children.

> The form of attack is, of course, important. The form may range from mild sexual excitement to a brutal physical attack; it may seem to be an isolated event or part of a continuing attack; it may be carried out by a parent, a sibling, a friend or a stranger. Further, what seems to be equally important is the level of ego development, particularly in terms of the children's capacity to deal with anxiety, with or without support, and the closeness of the actual event to the prevailing fantasies . . . The relative imbalance . . . seems to be caused by two groups of factors. On the one hand, the ego itself is often immature and unprepared, and perhaps even predisposed to use fantasy excessively, or follow a regressive pathway . . . On the other hand, there may be too large an amount of anxiety aroused in too short a period of time, or too much strain over too long a period of time. Massive acute anxiety in the first instance may be aroused because of the closeness of the external event to the unconscious fantasy; chronic anxiety in the second instance may be experienced when there are repeated experiences of an associated nature, all tending to interfere with the resolution of developmental tasks and each making the child more vulnerable. A second feature is the external event. Besides being close to a fantasy, it is remarkable how the event is remembered, either in direct or disguised form. It seems as though the memory of the event is organized in such a way as to serve defensive and adaptive functions [Lewis and Sarrel, 1969, pp. 617-618].

In the first novel of Durrell's tetralogy, it is learned that Justine was raped as a child; in all her adulterous, nymphomaniac activities while married first to Arnauti and then to Nessim she is seeking to relive and to exorcize that experience. Justine is a sick woman, the prisoner of an imagination obsessed by a traumatic memory. "The progression of the companion novels of *Justine* ruthlessly diminish her mythical stature, expose her pretensions, and yet bring out in her unexpected qualities or capacities of a Stendhalian type. Sex is, after all, a secondary amusement for her" (Fraser, 1968, p. 136). Darley, the narrator in *Justine,* becomes her lover, one in a long line, and discovers he "was foolish enough to think that I could thaw her out and give her the physical peace upon which — I thought — mental peace must depend. I was wrong. There was some unresolved inner knot which she wished to untie and which was quite beyond my skill as a lover or a friend. Of course. Of course. I knew as much as could be known of the psychopathology of hysteria at that time. But there was some other quality which I thought I could detect behind all this. In a way she was not looking for life but for some integrating revelation which would give it a point" (p. 70). A bit later, Justine tells Darley what had happened to her as a child, and in the telling the impact it has had on her adult life becomes clear.

She told me one night as we lay in that ugly great bed in a rented room — a gaunt rectangular room of a vaguely French-Levantine shape and flavour: a stucco ceiling covered with decomposing cherubs and posies of vine-leaves. She told me and left me raging with a jealousy I struggled to hide — but a jealousy of an entirely novel sort. Its object was a man who though still alive, *no longer existed.* It is perhaps what the Freudians would call a screen-memory of incidents in her earliest youth. She had (and there was no mistaking the force of this confession for it was accompanied by floods of tears, and I have never seen her weep like that before or since): she had been raped by one of her relations. One cannot help smiling at the commonplaceness of the thought. It was impossible to judge at what age. Nevertheless — and here I thought I had penetrated to the heart of The Check: from this time forward she could obtain no satisfaction in love unless she mentally re-created these incidents and re-enacted them. For her we, her lovers, had become only mental substitutes for this first childish act — so that love, as a sort of masturbation, took on all the colours of neurasthenia; she was suffering from an imagination dying of anaemia, for she could possess no one thoroughly in the flesh. She could not appropriate to herself the love she felt she needed, for her satisfactions derived from the crepuscular corners of a life she was no longer living. This was passionately interesting. But what was even more amusing was that I felt this blow to my *amour propre* as a man exactly as if she had confessed to an act of deliberate unfaithfulness. What! Every time she lay in my arms she could find no satisfaction save through this memory? In a way, then, I could not possess her: had never done so. I was merely a dummy. Even now as I write I cannot help smiling to remember the strangled voice in which I asked who the man was, and where he was. (What did I hope to do? Challenge him to a duel?) Nevertheless there he was, standing squarely between Justine and me; between Justine and the light of the sun [pp. 78-79].

In an attempt to overcome this succubus, Justine and her first husband, Arnauti, took the grand tour of Europe. It was a heartbreaking predicament for Arnauti, who had had no intention of ever falling in love, and for Justine who only wished to be delivered of an obsession and set free to love. The obsession overtakes Arnauti, for Justine tells him, "You live now among my imaginary intimacies. I was a fool to tell you everything, to be so honest..." (p. 82). The couple sought help "in the book-lined cell of Czechnia, where the famous mandarin of psychology sat..." (p. 79), but to no avail. Speaking of their venture into psychoanalysis, Clea, who at one time had had a homosexual entente with Justine, told Darley, "She was not really clever, you know, but she had the cunning of a wild animal at bay. I'm not sure she really understood the object of these [psychoanalytic] investigations. Yet though she was evasive with the doctors she was perfectly frank with her friends. All that correspondence about the words 'Washington, D.C.,' for example, which they worked so hard on — remember? One night while we were lying together I asked her to give me her free associations from the phrase. Of course she trusted my discretion absolutely. She replied unerringly (it was clear she had already worked it out though she would not tell Arnauti) 'There is a town near Washington called Alexandria. My father always talked of going to visit some distant relations there. They had a daughter called Justine who was exactly my age. She went mad and was put away. She had been raped by a man.' I then asked her about D.C. and she said, 'Da Capo. Capodistria'" (p. 228). It was Da Capo who was the author of all Justine's misfortunes — a distant relative — and it was not until his announced death that Justine was released from the daemon of the pedophilic attack. "... In Justine's case, having become cured of the mental aberrations brought about by her dreams, her fears, she has been deflated like a bag. For so long the fantasy occupied the foreground of her life that now she is dispossessed of her entire stock-in-trade. It is not only that the death of Capodistria has removed the chief actor in this shadow-play, her chief gaoler. The illness itself had kept her on the move, and when it died it left in its place total exhaustion. She has, so to speak, extinguished with her sexuality her very claims on life, almost her reason" (p. 242).

In *Balthazar* (1958), the second novel of the Quartet, Justine is having an adulterous liaison with Pursewarden, who is telling her about his reactions to her first husband's autobiographical novel, *Moeurs,* which had had a popular success some years earlier. " 'Listen, Justine, you know what? I re-read *Moeurs* again last week for fun and I had an idea; I mean if all the song and dance about Freud and your so-called childhood rape and so on are true — are they? I don't know. You could easily make it all up. But since you knew who the man in the wretched eyepiece was and refused to reveal his name to the wretched army of amateur psychologists headed by Arnauti, you must have had a good reason for it. What was it? It puzzles me. I won't tell anyone, I promise. Or is it all a lie?' She shook her head, 'No' " (pp. 143-144). The narrative, as told by the physician Balthazar, continues with Justine reliving the tremendous effort she had made to rid herself of her obsession by going to Da Capo's residence and confronting him with a strange proposal. "I went in at last. He was there in his famous [pornographic] library! I was shaking like a leaf. You see, I didn't know what note to strike, something dramatic, something pathetic? It was like going to the dentist. Really, it was funny, Pursewarden. I said at last, 'Dear Da Capo, old friend, you have been my demon for so long that I have come to ask you to exorcise me once and for all. To take away the memory of a horrible childhood event. You must sleep with me!' . . . Poor Da Capo, he was so terribly shocked and alarmed to be told he had raped me when I was a street arab, a child. I have never seen a man more taken aback. He had completely forgotten, it is clear, and completely denied the whole thing from start to finish. In fact, he was outraged and began to protest . . . Do you know what slipped out in the course of his self-justifications? A marvellous phrase, 'Il y a quinze ans que je n'ai pas fait ca!' . . . I finished my whiskey at last and left, much to his relief. . ." (pp. 145-146).

In the third novel, *Clea* (1960), yet another version is presented, once more by Justine who is telling Darley, her lover, about her erstwhile lover Pursewarden, who himself had indulged in an incestuous relationship with his blind sister Liza and who subsequently committed suicide. Justine is reminiscing after his death. "It was he, too, who reconciled me to that whole business of rape, remember? All that nonsense of Arnauti's in *Moeurs*, all those psychologists! His single observation stuck like a thorn. He said: 'Clearly you enjoyed it, as any child would, and probably even invited it. You have wasted all this time trying to come to terms with an imaginary conception of damage done to you. Try dropping this invented guilt and telling yourself that the thing was both pleasurable and meaningless. Every neurosis is made to measure!' It was curious that a few words like this, and an ironic chuckle, could do what all the others could not do for me. Suddenly everything seemed to lift, get lighter, move about" (p. 59). Which fact was truth in this Rashomonlike tale? Regardless of fact or truth, the anxious, promiscuous, neurotic life of Justine may very well have been precipitated by the trauma of the childhood rape.

The possibility of far-reaching consequences of traumatic sexual experiences on the psychosexual development of children has been stressed by Rothchild (1967) and Finch (1967). Josselyn (1962) described the impact that even a routine genital examination on a developing girl might have. The more intensive and extensive the experience, the stronger the impact, a generalization that can be made whether the molestation is accidental, persistent, or a single encounter, coerced, passive, accepting, seductive or collaborative.

TECHNICAL REFERENCES

AMA Committee on Human Sexuality (1972), *Human Sexuality*. Chicago: American Medical Association.

Anderson, C. M. (1968), Molestation of children. *Journal of the American Medical Women's Association,* 23:204-206.

Ariès, P. (1960), *Centuries of Childhood. A Social History of Family Life*. New York: Vintage, 1965.

Bell, A. P. & Hall, C. S. (1971), *The Personality of a Child Offender. An Analysis of Dreams*. Chicago: Aldine-Atherton.

Bell, Q. (1972), *Virginia Woolf: A Biography*. New York: Harcourt Brace Jovanovich.

Bender, L. & Blau, A. (1937), The reaction of children to sexual relations with adults. *American Journal of Orthopsychiatry,* 7:500-518.

Bowman, K. M. (1951), The problems of the sex offender. *American Journal of Psychiatry,* 108:250-257.

Cassity, J. H. (1927), Psychological considerations of pedophilia. *Psychoanalytic Review,* 14:189-199.

de Mause, L. (1974), *The History of Childhood.* New York: Harper & Row.

Eaton, A. P. & Vastbinder, E. (1969), The sexually molested child. A plan of management. *Clinical Pediatrics,* 8:438-441.

Fenichel, O. (1945), *Psychoanalytic Theory of Neurosis.* New York: Norton.

Fiedler, L. A. (1958), The profanation of the child. *New Leader,* 41:26-29.

——— (1960), *Love and Death in the American Novel.* London: Paladin, 1970.

Finch, S. M. (1967), Sexual activity of children with other children and adults. *Clinical Pediatrics,* 6:1-2.

——— (1973), Adult seduction of the child: Effects on the child. *Medical Aspects of Human Sexuality,* 7(3):170-187.

Fraser, G. S. (1968), *Lawrence Durrell. A Critical Study.* New York: Dutton.

Freud, S. (1905), Three essays on the theory of sexuality. *Standard Edition,* 7:125-243. London: Hogarth Press, 1953.

Frosch, J. & Bromberg, W. (1939), The sex offender — A psychiatric study. *American Journal of Orthopsychiatry,* 9:761-771.

Gagnon, J. (1965), Female child victims of sex offenders. *Social Problems,* 13:176-192.

Glicksberg, C. I. (1963), *The Self in Modern Literature.* University Park, Pa.: Penn State University Press.

Gregory, I. & Rosen, E. (1965), *Abnormal Psychology.* Philadelphia: Saunders.

Gronicka, A. von (1956), Myth plus psychology. *Germanic Review,* 31:191-205.

Guttmacher, M. S. (1951), *Sex Offenses. The Problems, Causes and Prevention.* New York: Norton.

Hammer, E. G. (1954), A comparison of H.T.P.'s of rapists and pedophiliacs. *Journal of Projective Techniques,* 18:346-354.

Herman, M. (1972), Effects of child molestation. *Medical Aspects of Human Sexuality,* 6(2):60-61.

Hiatt, L. R. (1967), Nabokov's *Lolita:* A 'Freudian' cryptic crossword. *American Imago,* 24:360-370.

Hirning, L. C. (1947), The sex offender in custody. In: *Handbook of Correction Psychology,* ed. R. Lindner & R. V. Seliger. New York: Philosophical Library, pp. 233-256.

Josselyn, I. (1962), Psychological effect of the menarch. In: *Psychosomatic Obstetrics, Gynecology & Endocrinology,* ed. W. S. Kroger. Springfield, Ill.: Charles C Thomas, pp. 84-91.

Karpman, B. (1954), *The Sexual Offender and His Offenses.* New York: Julian Press.

Kingdon, F. (1961), Literature and sex. In: *Sex and Today's Society,* Vol. 5, ed. A. Ellis & A. Abarbanel. New York: Ace, 1967, pp. 174-191.

Kopp, S. B. (1962), The character structure of sex offenders. *American Journal of Psychotherapy,* 16:64-70.

Kozol, H. L. (1971), Myths about the sex offender. *Medical Aspects of Human Sexuality,* 5(6):50-62.

Kurland, M. L. (1960), Pedophilia erotica. *Journal of Nervous and Mental Disease,* 131:394-403.

Lewis, M. & Sarrel, P. M. (1969), Some psychological aspects of seduction, incest, and rape in childhood. *Journal of the American Academy of Child Psychiatry,* 8:606-619.

Lorand, S. & Schneer, H. I. (1967), Sexual deviations. In: *Comprehensive Textbook of Psychiatry,* ed. A. M. Freedman & H. I. Kaplan. Baltimore: Williams & Wilkins, p. 986.

Magnus, A. (1953), Sex crimes in California. In: *California Sexual Deviation Research.* Sacramento: California State Department of Mental Hygiene, pp. 38-40.

Massey, J. B., Garcia, C. R. & Emich, J. P., Jr. (1971), Management of sexually assaulted females. *Obstetrics and Gynecology*, 38:29-36.

Mayne, E. C. (1961), *Letters of Dostoevsky*. New York: Horizon.

McCaghy, C. H. (1967), Child molesters: A study of their causes as deviants. In: *Criminal Behavior Systems: A Typology*, ed. M. B. Clinard & R. Quinney. New York: Holt, Rinehart & Winston, pp. 75-88.

Messer, A. A. (1969), The Phaedra complex. *Archives of General Psychiatry*, 21: 213-218.

Mohr, J. W. (1968), A child has been molested. *Medical Aspects of Human Sexuality*, 2(11):43-50.

————, Turner, R. E. & Jerry, M. B. (1964), *Pedophilia and Exhibitionism: A Handbook*. Toronto: University of Toronto Press.

Pach, A. R., Halleck, S. L. & Ehomann, J. D. (1962), Diagnosis and treatment of the sexual offender. A nine year study. *American Journal of Psychiatry*, 118:802-808.

Peters, J. J. & Sadoff, R. L. (1970), Clinical observations on child molesters. *Medical Aspects of Human Sexuality*, 4(11):20-32.

Pratt, B. E. B. (1971), The role of the unconscious in *The Eternal Husband*. *Literature and Psychology*, 21:29-40.

Revitch, E. & Weiss, R. (1962), The pedophiliac offender. *Diseases of the Nervous System*, 23:73-78.

Rothchild, E. (1967), "Anatomy is destiny." Psychological implications of adolescent physical changes in girls. *Pediatrics*, 39:532-538.

Sex Information and Education Council of the United States (1970), *Sexuality and Man*. New York: Scribner's.

Slochower, H. (1969), Thomas Mann's *Death in Venice*. *American Imago*, 26:99-122.

Socarides, C. W. (1959), Meaning and content of pedophiliac perversion. *Journal of the American Psychoanalytic Association*, 7:84-94.

Stekel, W. (1952), *Patterns of Psychosexual Infantilism*. New York: Liveright.

Storr, A. (1964), *Sexual Deviation*. Baltimore: Penguin.

Swanson, D. W. (1971), Who violates children sexually? *Medical Aspects of Human Sexuality*, 5(2):184-197.

Traschen, I. (1965), The uses of myth in *Death in Venice*. *Modern Fiction Studies*, 11:165-179.

Vanggaard, T. (1969), *Phallòs, a Symbol and Its History in the Male World*. New York: International Universities Press, 1972.

Vilar, E. (1971), *The Manipulated Man*. New York: Farrar, Straus & Giroux, 1972.

Weiss, J., Rogers, E., Darwin, M. R. & Dutton, C. E. (1954), A study of girl sex victims. *Psychiatric Quarterly*, 29:1-27.

Whiskin, F. E. (1967), The geriatric sex offender. *Geriatrics*, 22(10):168-172.

LITERARY REFERENCES

Chin P'ing Mei (1609), *The Adventurous History of Hsi Men and His Six Wives*. New York: Putnam's, 1940.

Colette (1900), *Claudine at School*. London: Penguin, 1963.

de Maupassant, Guy (1903), Little Louise Roque. In: *The Complete Short Stories of Guy de Maupassant*. New York: Black, pp. 979-1003.

Durrell, Lawrence (1957), *Justine*. New York: Dutton.

———— (1958), *Balthazar*. New York: Dutton.

———— (1960), *Clea*. New York: Dutton.

Faulkner, William (1931), *The Hamlet*. New York: Random House.

Genet, Jean (1953), *Funeral Rites*. New York: Grove Press, 1969.

Gide, André (1902), *The Immoralist*. New York: Knopf, 1930.

Graves, Robert (1934), *I, Claudius*. New York: Vintage, 1961.

Horwitz, Julius (1973), *The Married Lovers*. New York: Dial Press.

Joyce, James (1918), *Ulysses*. New York: Random House, 1934.

Lelchuk, Alan (1973), *American Mischief*. New York: Farrar, Straus & Giroux.

Mann, Thomas (1913), *Death in Venice*. New York: Knopf, 1925.

Memmi, Albert (1955), *The Pillar of Salt*. New York: Orion Press, 1962.

Moravia, Alberto (1972), *Two: A Phallic Novel*. New York: Farrar, Straus & Giroux.

Nabokov, Vladimir (1955), *Lolita*. New York: Putnam's.

Petronius (c. 63 A.D.), I meet Eumolpus. In: *The Satyricon*. New York: New American Library, 1959, pp. 88-92.

Rechy, John (1956), *City of Night*. New York: Grove Press.

Salinger, J. D. (1948), A perfect day for bananafish. In: *Nine Stories*. Boston: Little, Brown, 1953, pp. 3-26.

Selby, Hubert, Jr. (1957), *Last Exit to Brooklyn*. New York: Grove Press.

Sulzberger, Cyrus L. (1973), *The Tooth Merchant*. New York: Quadrangle.

Trevanian (1972), *The Eiger Sanction*. New York: Crown.

Vidal, Gore (1962), *Julian*. New York: New American Library.

Wilson, Edmund (1942), *Memoirs of Hecate County*. New York: New American Library, 1961.

CHAPTER TWELVE

Exhibitionism and Voyeurism

Clinical material regarding the psychology of creative writers supports the conclusion that exhibitionism is indisputably one of the unconscious motives in artistic creation (Bergler, 1944). It is not a primary tendency, however, for the writer is also a voyeur who uses his exhibitionistic tendencies secondarily as a defense against repressed scoptophilic tendencies. In an analysis of forty writers, Bergler (1955) found them to be perpetually defensive against their regressive, oral masochistic and voyeuristic desires. The defenses consisted of attempts at autarchy, pseudo aggression, universalization of guilt feelings and exhibitionism. He concluded that difficulties in connection with scoptophilia may have given rise to difficulties in thinking up a plot (voyeurism) or writing it down (exhibitionism).

Every artist unconsciously is a voyeur who defends himself against this tendency by means of exhibitionism. "To perceive images, that means, to think up fantasies, is one of the most essential unconscious wishes of the creative artist. Since these desires are forbidden, because they are too immediately tied up with the infantile voyeuristic tendencies, he constitutes an inner alibi in the form of a defense reaction which says: 'I am not looking at something forbidden; on the contrary, I am permitting myself to be looked at'" (Bergler, 1947, pp. 270-271). Voyeuristic tendencies also have a sadistic undertone, such as pervades the artistic production of painters and photographers. It is not accidental that the photographer speaks of "shooting a picture" (Reik, 1960).

The twin subjects of exhibitionism and voyeurism have attracted innumerable novelists. Voyeurism is ubiquitous in Swift's *Gulliver's Travels* (1726) and Carroll's *Alice in Wonderland* (1865). Mark Twain had a predilection for naming his characters Tom, as Tom Sawyer, Tom Blankshift, Tom Nash, and Tom Driscoll, all of whom were associated with disaster, not only to themselves but also to relatives and friends. The association of Peeping Tom emerges (Barrett, 1955) with the scoptophilic and exhibitory implications. Twain himself was known to be an exhibitionist in his love of notoriety and his colorful appearance. He had, too, an exaggerated sense of responsibility and guilt for the welfare of his family, blaming himself for the accidental death of his brother Henry and for the deaths of two of his own children. His *Mysterious Stranger* served as an unconscious release from a long period of guilt, depression, and masochistic exhibitionism.

More recently, both Sutton and Robbe-Grillet even titled their novels *The Voyeur,* and Celine called his *Voyeur Voyant.* Sutton has written another, *The Exhibitionist,* in which the characters can be measured on a scale running from infantile to immature, so regressed or fixated are they—and so exemplary of the personality of the exhibitionist and voyeur. In Sutton's *The Voyeur* (1969), in response to a question how women benefit from his *Playboy*-type magazine, *Tomcat,* Irving Kane, the "mammary mogul" of the publication attempted this justification: ". . . the magazine provides for fantasy and voyeurism. Men are always looking for variety in their sexual lives, and as between actual and extramarital affairs and imaginary ones with the pictures in *Tomcat,* I think the majority of women would prefer the latter. Voyeurism—which is deriving sexual satisfaction, or at least sexual stimulation, from *looking*—is comparatively harmless, and yet it satisfies some of that sexual curiosity that all men have without threatening any of the real relationships upon which they have built their lives" (p. 38).

No one denies that seeing, which in voyeurism is the tool of perversion, plays a focal part in normal sexual and cultural development. As Freud (1905) put it, "Visual impressions remain the most frequent pathway along which libidinal excitation is aroused; indeed, natural selection counts upon the accessibility of this pathway—if such a teleological form of statement is permissible—when it encourages the development of beauty in the sexual object. The progressive concealment of the body which goes along with civilization keeps sexual curiosity awake. This curiosity seeks to complete the sexual object by revealing its hidden parts. It can, however, be diverted ('sublimated') in the direction of art, if its interest can be shifted away from the genitals on to the shape of the body as a whole" (p. 156).

In earlier centuries, the sublimation of exhibitionism and voyeurism in art took form in mythology and poetry. The legend of the wretched leper who found healing and transfiguration into Christ through contact with the naked body of a compassionate human being, or the healing of a leper by gazing upon the nude form of a pure virgin reveal a naïve need to justify exposure (Rank, 1913). The looking tendency in sagas and poetry has the identical motive found in dreams and neurotic symptoms and undergoes the same transfiguration. Exhibitionist behavior and myths often express the sensation of restraint, such as the naked dreamer experiences, but having no effect on the observers. The subject's apparent shame is interpreted as evidence of repression of the original pleasure in exposure. In neuroses as well as in myths, damage to the eyes bespeaks the idea of retribution as punishment for transgressing the normal functions of sight (Karpman, 1926). In myths punishment for voyeurism or exhibitionism takes the form of blindness, various abnormalities of the eyes, bodily disfigurements, the woman turning into a serpent, or the love object disappearing—that is, becoming invisible to the viewer.

Voyeurism almost inevitably has a sadistic element to it. Friedman (1959) interprets voyeurism as an attempt at reassurance against castration anxiety. Because such reassurance cannot be obtained, the voyeuristic tendencies usually become insatiable, sadistic, and displaced onto areas other than the genitals. In voyeurism, the original impulse to destroy is transformed into a milder one, to look: "I didn't do it, I only watched the other fellow do it." In Roman days, according to Masters (1962), bestiality as a spectator sport was part of the exhibitions staged at the arenas. For these games, "male animals of all sorts were trained from the earliest possible age to copulate with and even forcibly ravish girls and women. Bulls, giraffes, leopards, cheetahs, wild boars, zebras, stallions, jack-asses, huge dogs, various kinds of apes, and other animals were taught to perform these functions. On occasions, for a stirring climax . . . the beasts were permitted to kill and, if they wished, devour their human victims after assaulting them sexually. Such acts invariably brought down the house at the Games, and were even more popular than the often staged but never-wearied-of human sex orgies" (pp. 16-17).

In Ralph Ellison's (1947) *Invisible Man,* the bestial quality of the voyeuristic tendencies of the gentlemen of a Southern town is as apparent as the spectacular bestiality of the ancient Roman games. While the white gentlemen do not have to feed their Negroes to the lions, they can destroy them in a public, exhibitionistic display of calculated debasement. Caged like a burning bright tiger on exhibition in a long-forgotten basement room, with more than a thousand electric bulbs lighted in an abortive attempt to give the invisible man visibility, the nameless narrator relates past events which have led to his invisibility. He is no-man and everyman, the antithesis of the exhibition man; but his very anonymity gives way to an epic quest for identity. The first event occurs during his adolescence and is an ordeal, perhaps the initiation ceremony of a young black Ulysses about to be launched on his American odyssey. At the time of his graduation from high school, he is invited by the superintendent of schools to repeat his valedictory address to the town's white business and professional leaders. When the boy arrives at the hotel, he finds the affair is actually a stag smoker, which quickly exposes the voyeuristic and sadistic qualities of the white Southern world. Chairs are arranged around three sides of a portable boxing ring. The boy, along with nine other black youngsters, is put into the ring, blindfolded, and coerced into fighting in a battle royal. But before this happens, the boys are forced to watch a stark-naked, blonde belly dancer do her routine, which suggests the sadistic prurience underlying the victimizers' treatment of their victims. Held there against their will, wanting to see and not daring to see, sexual embarrassment becomes sexual torture.

Suddenly I heard the school superintendent, who had told me to come, yell, "Bring up the shines, gentlemen! Bring up the little shines!"

We were rushed up to the front of the ballroom, where it smelled even more strongly of tobacco and whiskey. Then we were pushed into place. I almost wet my pants. A sea of faces, some hostile, some amused, ringed around us, and in the center, facing us, stood a magnificent blonde — stark naked. There was dead silence. I felt a blast of cold air chill me. I tried to back away, but they were behind me and around me. Some of the boys stood with lowered heads, trembling. I felt a wave of irrational guilt and fear. My teeth chattered, my skin turned to goose flesh, my knees knocked. Yet I was strongly attracted and looked in spite of myself. Had the price of looking been blindness, I would have looked. The hair was yellow like that of a circus kewpie doll, the face heavily powdered and rouged, as though to form an abstract mask, the eyes hollow and smeared a cool blue, the color of a baboon's butt. I felt a desire to spit upon her as my eyes brushed slowly over her body. Her breasts were firm and round as the domes of East Indian temples, and I stood so close as to see the fine skin texture and beads of pearly perspiration glistening like dew around the pink and erected buds of her nipples. I wanted at one and the same time to run from the room, to sink through the floor, or go to her and cover her from my eyes and the eyes of the others with my body; to feel the soft thighs, to caress her and destroy her, to love her and murder her, to hide from her, and yet to stroke where below the small American flag tattooed upon her belly her thighs formed a capital V. I had a notion that of all in the room she saw only me with her impersonal eyes.

And then she began to dance, a slow sensuous movement; the smoke of a hundred cigars clinging to her like the thinnest of veils. She seemed like a fair bird-girl girdled in veils calling to me from the angry surface of some gray and threatening sea. I was transported. Then I became aware of the clarinet playing and the big shots yelling at us. Some threatened us if we looked and others if we did not. On my right I saw one boy faint. And now a man grabbed a silver pitcher from a table and stepped close as he dashed ice water upon him and stood him up and forced two of us to support him as his head hung and moans issued from his thick bluish lips. Another boy began to plead to go home. He was the largest of the group, wearing dark red fighting trunks much too small to conceal the erection which projected from him as though in answer to the insinuating low-registered moaning of the clarinet. He tried to hide himself with his boxing gloves.

And all the while the blonde continued dancing, smiling faintly at the big shots who watched her with fascination, and faintly smiling at our fear. I noticed a certain merchant who followed her hungrily, his lips loose and drooling. He was a large man who wore diamond studs in a shirtfront which swelled with the ample paunch underneath, and each time the blonde swayed her undulating hips he ran his hand through the thin hair of his bald head and, with his arms upheld, his posture clumsy like that of an intoxicated panda, wound his belly in a slow and obscene grind. This creature was completely hypnotized. The music had quickened. As the dancer flung herself about with a detached expression on her face, the men began reaching out to touch her. I could see their beefy fingers sink into the soft flesh. Some of the others tried to stop them and she began to move around the floor in graceful circles, as they gave chase, slipping and sliding over the polished floor. It was mad. Chairs went crashing, drinks were spilt, as they ran laughing and howling after her. They caught her just as she reached a door, raised her from the floor, and tossed her as college boys are tossed at a hazing, and above her red, fixed-smiling lips I saw the terror and disgust in her eyes, almost like my own terror and that which I saw in some of the other boys. As I watched, they tossed her twice and her soft breasts seemed to flatten against the air and her legs flung wildly as she spun. Some of the more sober ones helped her to escape. And I started off the floor, heading for the anteroom with the rest of the boys.

Some were still crying and in hysteria. But as we tried to leave we were stopped and ordered to get into the ring. There was nothing to do but what we were told. All ten of us climbed under the ropes and allowed ourselves to be blindfolded with broad bands of white cloth. One of the men seemed to feel a bit sympathetic and tried to cheer us up as we stood with our backs against the ropes. Some of us tried to grin. "See that boy over there?" one of the men said. "I want you to run across at the bell and give it to him right in the belly. If you don't get him, I'm going to get you. I don't like his looks." Each of us was told the same. The blindfolds were put on. Yet even then I had been going over my speech. In my mind each word was as bright as flame. I felt the cloth pressed into place, and frowned so that it would be loosened when I relaxed.

But now I felt a sudden fit of blind terror. I was unused to darkness. It was as though I had suddenly found myself in a dark room filled with poisonous cottonmouths. I could hear the bleary voices yelling insistently for the battle royal to begin.

"Get going in there!"

"Let me at that big nigger!"

I strained to pick up the school superintendent's voice, as though to squeeze some security out of that slightly more familiar sound.

"Let me at those black sonsabitches!" someone yelled.

"No, Jackson, no!" another voice yelled. "Here, somebody, help me hold Jack."

"I want to get at that ginger-colored nigger. Tear him limb from limb," the first voice yelled.

I stood against the ropes trembling. For in those days I was what they called ginger-colored, and he sounded as though he might crunch me between his teeth like a crisp ginger cookie.

Quite a struggle was going on. Chairs were being kicked about and I could hear voices grunting as with a terrific effort. I wanted to see, to see more desperately than ever before. But the blindfold was as tight as a thick skin-puckering scab and when I raised my gloved hands to push the layers of white aside a voice yelled, "Oh, no you don't, black bastard! Leave that alone!"

"Ring the bell before Jackson kills him a coon!" someone boomed in the sudden silence. And I heard the bell clang and the sound of the feet scuffling forward.

A glove smacked against my head. I pivoted, striking out stiffly as someone went past, and felt the jar ripple along the length of my arm to my shoulder. Then it seemed as though all nine of the boys had turned upon me at once. Blows pounded me from all sides while I struck out as best I could. So many blows landed upon me that I wondered if I were not the only blindfolded fighter in the ring, or if the man called Jackson hadn't succeeded in getting me after all.

Blindfolded, I could no longer control my motions. I had no dignity. I stumbled about like a baby or a drunken man. The smoke had become thicker and with each new blow it seemed to sear and further restrict my lungs. My saliva became like hot bitter glue. A glove connected with my head, filling my mouth with warm blood. It was everywhere. I could not tell if the moisture I felt upon my body was sweat or blood. A blow landed hard against the nape of my neck. I felt myself going over, my head hitting the floor. Streaks of blue light filled the black world behind the blindfold. I lay prone, pretending that I was knocked out, but felt myself seized by hands and yanked to my feet. "Get going, black boy! Mix it up!" My arms were like lead, my head smarting from blows. I managed to feel my way to the ropes and held on, trying to catch my breath. A glove landed in my mid-section and I went over again, feeling as though the smoke had become a knife jabbed into my guts. Pushed this way and that by the legs milling around me, I finally pulled erect and discovered that I could see the black, sweat-washed forms weaving in the smoky-blue atmosphere like drunken dancers weaving to the rapid drum-like thuds of blows.

Everyone fought hysterically. It was complete anarchy. Everybody fought everybody else. No group fought together for long. Two, three, four, fought one, then turned to fight each other, were themselves attacked. Blows landed below the belt and in the kidney, with the gloves open as well as closed, and with my eye partly opened now there was not so much terror. I moved carefully, avoiding blows, although not too many to attract attention, fighting from group to group. The boys groped about like blind, cautious crabs crouching to protect their mid-sections, their heads pulled in short against their shoulders, their arms stretched nervously before them, with their fists testing the smoke-filled air like the knobbed feelers of hypersensitive snails. In one corner I glimpsed a boy violently punching the air and heard him scream in pain as he smashed his hand against a ring post. For a second I saw him bent over holding his hand, then going down as a blow caught his unprotected head. I played one group against the other, slipping in and throwing a punch then stepping out of range while pushing the others into the melee to take the blows blindly aimed at me. The smoke was agonizing and there were no rounds, no bells at three minute intervals to relieve our exhaustion. The room spun round me, a swirl of lights, smoke, sweating bodies surrounded by tense white faces. I bled from nose and mouth, the blood spattering upon my chest.

The men kept yelling, "Slug him, black boy! Knock his guts out!"

"Uppercut him! Kill him! Kill that big boy!"

Taking a fake fall, I saw a boy going down heavily beside me as though we were felled by a single blow, saw a sneaker-clad foot shoot into his groin as the two who had knocked him down stumbled upon him. I rolled out of range, feeling a twinge of nausea.

The harder we fought the more threatening the men became. And yet, I had begun to worry about my speech again. How would it go? Would they recognize my ability? What would they give me? [pp. 16-19].

While the black youth is wondering what he will get, he discovers he is left alone with one other boy to slug it out. He is filled with panic, especially when the blindfolds are removed and he sees his opponent is the biggest of the lot. He tries to make a deal with him, "Fake like I knocked you out, you can have the prize," but he is rebuffed: "I'll break your behind," he whispers hoarsely. "For *them?*" "For *me,* sonofabitch!" (p. 20). Here, Ellison shows how the white powers make the blacks channel aggressive impulses inward instead of toward their true foes, who remain on the sidelines supervising the fray to make certain the violence is directed away from them (Kostelanetz, 1967). It is only after the boy is knocked out that the fight is halted. He is wringing wet and his mouth is filled with blood. He wonders if he will be able to give his speech, which incidentally is on the subject of humility. The attendants roll the portable ring away and place a small square rug in the vacant space surrounded by the chairs. He thinks, "Perhaps . . . I will stand on the rug to deliver my speech" (p. 21).

Then the M.C. called to us, "Come on up here boys and get your money."

We ran forward to where the men laughed and talked in their chairs, waiting. Everyone seemed friendly now.

"There it is on the rug," the man said. I saw the rug covered with coins of all dimensions and a few crumpled bills. But what excited me, scattered here and there, were the gold pieces.

"Boys, it's all yours," the man said. "You get all you grab."

"That's right, Sambo," a blond man said, winking at me confidentially.

I trembled with excitement, forgetting my pain. I would get the gold and the bills, I thought. I would use both hands. I would throw my body against the boys nearest me to block them from the gold.

"Get down around the rug now," the man commanded, "and don't anyone touch it until I give the signal."

"This ought to be good," I heard.

As told, we got around the square rug on our knees. Slowly the man raised his freckled hand as we followed it upward with our eyes.

I heard, "These niggers look like they're about to pray!"

Then, "Ready," the man said. "Go!"

I lunged for a yellow coin lying on the blue design of the carpet, touching it and sending a surprised shriek to join those rising around me. I tried frantically to remove my hand but could not let go. A hot, violent force tore through my body, shaking me like a wet rat. The rug was electrified. The hair bristled up on my head as I shook myself free. My muscles jumped, my nerves jangled, writhed. But I saw that this was not stopping the other boys. Laughing in fear and embarrassment, some were holding back and scooping up the coins knocked off by the painful contortions of the others. The men roared above us as we struggled.

"Pick it up, goddammit, pick it up!" someone called like a bass-voiced parrot. "Go on, get it!"

I crawled rapidly around the floor, picking up the coins, trying to avoid the coppers and to get greenbacks and the gold. Ignoring the shock by laughing, as I brushed the coins off quickly, I discovered that I could contain the electricity—a contradiction, but it works. Then the men began to push us onto the rug. Laughing embarrassedly, we struggled out of their hands and kept after the coins. We were all wet and slippery and hard to hold. Suddenly I saw a boy lifted into the air, glistening with sweat like a circus seal, and dropped, his wet back landing flush upon the charged rug, heard him yell and saw him literally dance upon his back, his elbows beating a frenzied tattoo upon the floor, his muscles twitching like the flesh of a horse stung by many flies. When he finally rolled off, his face was gray and no one stopped him when he ran from the floor amid booming laughter.

"Get the money," the M.C. called. "That's good hard American cash!"

And we snatched and grabbed, snatched and grabbed. I was careful not to come too close to the rug now, and when I felt the hot whiskey breath descend upon me like a cloud of foul air I reached out and grabbed the leg of a chair. It was occupied and I held on desperately.

"Leggo, nigger! Leggo!"

The huge face wavered down to mine as he tried to push me free. But my body was slippery and he was too drunk. It was Mr. Colcord, who owned a chain of movie houses and "entertainment palaces." Each time he grabbed me I slipped out of his hands. It became a real struggle. I feared the rug more than I did the drunk, so I held on, surprising myself for a moment by trying to topple *him* upon the rug. It was such an enormous idea that I found myself actually carrying it out. I tried not to be obvious, yet when I grabbed his leg, trying to tumble him out of the chair, he raised up roaring with laughter, and, looking at me with soberness dead in the eye, kicked me viciously in the chest. The chair leg flew out of my hand and I felt myself going and rolled. It was as though I had rolled through a bed of hot coals. It seemed a whole century would pass before I would roll free, a century in which I was seared through the deepest levels of my body to the fearful breath within me and the breath seared and heated to the point of explosion. It'll all be over in a flash, I thought as I rolled clear. It'll all be over in a flash.

But not yet, the men on the other side were waiting, red faces swollen as though from apoplexy as they bent forward in their chairs. Seeing their fingers coming toward me I rolled away as a fumbled football rolls off the receiver's fingertips, back into the coals. That time I luckily sent the rug sliding out of place and heard the coins ringing against the floor and the boys scuffling to pick them up and the M.C. calling, "All right, boys, that's all. Go get dressed and get your money."

I was limp as a dish rag. My back felt as though it had been beaten with wires.

When we had dressed the M.C. came in and gave us each five

dollars, except Tatlock, who got ten for being last in the ring. Then he told us to leave. I was not to get a chance to deliver my speech, I thought. I was going out into the dim alley in despair when I was stopped and told to go back. I returned to the ballroom, where the men were pushing back their chairs and gathering in groups to talk.

The M.C. knocked on a table for quiet. "Gentlemen," he said, "we almost forgot an important part of the program. A most serious part, gentlemen. This boy was brought here to deliver a speech which he made at his graduation yesterday ..." [pp. 21-23].

The forced viewing of the blonde belly dancer, the battle royal, and grabbing for the fake coins on all fours is evidence of the debasement and manipulation of the blacks' sexual potency. By such behavior, the white mutes the threat of the black and at the same time experiences it vicariously (Baumbach, 1963, p. 76). According to Klein (1964, p. 257), the blacks are "goaded, threatened, tantalized, promised money, beaten, degraded, and insulted, worked to the hysteria," which is that of the white folks. This crucial initiatory experience of the high-school boy is climaxed when, finally, he is permitted to give his graduation speech on humility. This, too, is received with howls of derisive laughter from the mob. When he uses the phrase, 'social responsibility,' he is made to repeat it several times, until, in a beautiful slip of the tongue, he says, 'equality,' whereupon he is humiliated into admitting his error. He completes the speech to mocking, thunderous applause. His reward is a scholarship to a Negro college and a new calfskin briefcase: "In a dream that closes the nightmarish episode, the boy opens the briefcase. Inside, he finds an official envelope stamped with the state seal; and inside the envelope he finds another and another, endlessly, until he thinks he will fall of weariness. Finally he comes to the document, engraved with the brief message, in letters of gold: 'To Whom It May Concern: Keep This Nigger-Boy Running'" (Bone, 1958, p. 204).

According to Fenichel (1945), the tendency to replace sadistic action by the more ego-syntonic form of looking or watching represents active sadistic castration tendencies, reduced from action to observation. The explicit portrayal on the stage and in films of sexual intercourse turns audiences into voyeurs. Exhibitionism is, in the male, characterized by repeated episodes wherein he displays his genitalia to a female, usually someone unknown to him. In the female, exhibitionism is characterized by the display of the entire nude body. A symbiotic relationship between exhibitionism and voyeurism is manifested in myriad socially acceptable ways: topless waitresses and diners; artists and models; the bikini-clad and the girl-watchers; the braless sinuous gyrations of the go-go dancers and their oglers; Candid Camera television productions and viewers, *ad infinitum*. Sublimation of exhibitionistic needs were manifested in the once fashionable phallic fins of long-bodied automobiles— "look at my penis"—tight sweaters, form-fitting jeans, miniskirts, décolletage, and a host of other devices that conform more or less to society's changing morality. The extent of exhibitionism in Chaucer's day is reflected in the following excerpt from the Parson's Tale (1388) in *The Canterbury Tales*.

Now there are two kinds of pride; one of them lies within the heart of man, and the other lies without. Whereof, truly, these aforesaid things, and more than I have named, appertain to that pride which is within the heart of man; for that other species of pride lies without. But notwithstanding, one of these species of pride is a sign of the existence of the other, just as the fresh bush at the tavern door is a sign of the wine that is in the cellar. And this second kind of pride shows itself in many ways: as in speech and bearing, and in extravagant array of clothing; for truly, if there had been no sin in clothing, Christ would not have noted and spoken of the clothing of that rich man in the gospel. And, as Saint Gregory says, that same precious clothing is culpable for the glory and beauty of it, and for its softness, and for its strange new modes, and its fantastic ornamentation, and for its superfluity, and for the inordinate scantiness of it. Alas! May not men see, in our days, the sinfully costly array of clothing, especially in the matter of superfluity, or else in inordinate scantiness?

As to the first sin, it lies in the superfluity of clothing, which makes cloth so dear, to the harm of the people; not only the cost of embroidering, the elaborate notching or barring, the waved lines, the stripes, the twists, the diagonal bars, and similar waste of cloth in vanity; but there is also the costly furring of gowns, so much perforating with scissors to make holes, so much slashing with shears; and then the superfluity in length of the aforesaid gowns, trailing in the dung and in the mire, a-horseback and afoot, as well of man's clothing as of woman's, until all this trailing verily, in its effect, wastes, consumes, makes threadbare and rotten with dung the superfluity that rather should be given unto the poor; to the great harm of the aforesaid poor. And that in sundry wise: this is to say, the more that cloth is wasted, the more it costs the people because of its scarcity; and furthermore, if they would give such perforated and slashed clothing to the poor folk, it would not be suitable for their wearing, what of their state, nor sufficient to help their necessity to keep themselves from the fury of the elements. On the other hand, to speak of the horrible inordinate scantiness of clothing, let us notice these short-cut smocks or jackets, which, because of their shortness, cover not the shameful members of man, to the wicked calling of them to attention. Alas! Some of them show the very boss of their penis and the horrible pushed-out testicles that look like the malady of hernia in the wrapping of their hose; and the buttocks of such persons look like the hinder parts of a she-ape in the full of the moon. And moreover, the hateful proud members that they show by the fantastic fashion of making one leg of their hose white and the other red, make it seem that half their shameful privy members are flayed. And if it be that they divide their hose in other colours, as white and black, or white and blue, or black and red, and so forth, then it seems, by variation of colour, that the half of their privy members are corrupted by the fire of Saint Anthony, or by cancer, or by other such misfortune. As to the hinder parts of their buttocks, the thing is horrible to see. For, indeed, in that part of their body where they purge their stinking ordure, that foul part they proudly show to the people in despite of decency, which decency Jesus Christ and His friends observed in their lives. Now, as to the extravagant array of women, God knows that though the faces of them seem chaste and gentle, yet do they advertise, by their attire, their lickerousness and pride. I say not that a moderate gaiety in clothing is unseemly, but certainly the superfluity or inordinate scantiness of clothing is reprehensible. Also, the sin of adornment or apparel lies in things that appertain to riding, as in too many fine horses that are kept for delight, that are so fair, fat and costly; in many a vicious knave who is kept because of them; in too curious harness, as saddles, cruppers, poitrels, and bridles covered with precious caparison and rich, and with bars and plates of gold and silver. As to which God says by Zechariah the prophet: "I will confound the riders of such horses." These folk have but little regard for the riding of God of Heaven's Son and of His trappings, when He rode upon the ass and had no other caparison than the poor cloaks of His disciples; nor do we read that ever He rode upon any other beast. I say this against the sin of superfluity, and not against reasonable display when the occasion requires it [pp. 512-513].

More than a thousand years before Chaucer penned this passage, Theophrastus (319 B.C.) described the exhibitionist in *The Characters*.

It is not hard to define Buffoonery; it is a naked and objectionable sportiveness; and the Buffoon is one that will lift his shirt in the presence of free-born women; and at the theatre will applaud when others cease, hiss actors whom the rest of the audience approves, and raise his head and hiccup when the house is silent, so that he may make the spectators look round. You will find him standing at the time of full-market where they sell nuts or apples or other fruits, and eating of them while he talks to the seller. He will call by name one of the company with whom he is not well acquainted; and should he see any man in a hurry, is sure to bid him wait. One that has lost a great suit he will accost on his way from court and give him his congratulations. He will do his own marketing and hire flute-players himself; he will show his friends the good things he has bought, and invite them then and there to 'come and eat this with me'; and will stand beside the shop of the barber or the perfumer, and tell the world that he is about to get drunk. He will use words of ill-omen when his mother returns from the diviner's; and while the company is at their prayers and libations, will drop the cup and laugh as if he had done something clever. When he is listening to the fluteplayer he will be the only man present to beat time, and will whistle the air, and chide the girl for stopping so soon. And when he would spit something out, he spits it across the table at the butler [pp. 69, 71].

Judeo-Christian tradition has it that the wish, the fantasy, the impulse, and the deed are equally sinful. The King James version of the Biblical story of David and Bath-Sheba relates, "And it came to pass in an eveningtide that David arose from off his bed, and walked upon the roof of the King's house: and from the roof he saw a woman washing herself; and the woman was very beautiful to look upon." The not-too-innocent voyeurism in this verse becomes deliberate in the tale of Daniel and Susanna found in *The Apocrypha*. The sadistic aspect of the voyeurs is not lost on the reader.

There once lived in Babylon a man named Joakim. He married Susanna daughter of Hilkiah, a very beautiful and devout woman. Her parents, religious people, had brought up their daughter according to the law of Moses. Joakim was very rich and his house had a fine garden adjoining it, which was a regular meeting-place for the Jews, because he was the man of greatest distinction among them.

Now two elders of the community were appointed that year as judges. It was of them that the Lord had said, 'Wickedness came forth from Babylon from elders who were judges and were supposed to govern my people.' These men were constantly at Joakim's house, and everyone who had a case to be tried came to them there.

When the people went away at noon, Susanna used to go and walk in her husband's garden. Every day the two elders saw her entering the garden and taking her walk, and they were obsessed with lust for her. They no longer prayed to God, but let their thoughts stray from him and forgot the claims of morality. They were both infatuated with her; but they did not tell each other what pangs they suffered, because they were ashamed to confess that they wanted to seduce her. Day after day they watched eagerly to see her.

One day they said, 'Let us go home; it is time for lunch.' So they went off in different directions, but soon retraced their steps and found themselves face to face. When they questioned one another, each confessed his passion. Then they agreed on a time when they might find her alone.

And while they were watching for an opportune day, she went into the garden as usual with only her two maids; it was very hot, and she wished to bathe there. No one else was in the garden except the two elders, who had hidden and were spying on her. She said to her maids, 'Bring me soap and olive oil, and shut the garden doors so that I can bathe.' They did as she told them: they closed the garden doors and went out by the side door to fetch the things they had been ordered to bring; they did not see the elders because they were hiding. As soon as the maids had gone, the two elders started up and ran to Susanna. 'Look!' they said, 'the garden doors are shut, and no one can see us. We are burning with desire for you, so consent and yield to us. If you refuse, we shall give evidence against you that there was a young man with you and that was why you sent your maids away.' Susanna groaned and said: 'I see no way out. If I do this thing, the penalty is death; if I do not, you will have me at your mercy. My choice is made: I will not do it. It is better to be at your mercy than to sin against the Lord.'

With that Susanna gave a loud shout, but the two elders shouted her down. One of them ran and opened the garden door. The household, hearing the uproar in the garden, rushed in through the side door to see what had happened to her. And when the elders had told their story, the servants were deeply shocked, for no such allegation had ever been made against Susanna.

Next day, when the people gathered at her husband Joakim's house, the two elders came, full of their criminal design to put Susanna to death. In the presence of the people they said, 'Send for Susanna daughter of Hilkiah, Joakim's wife.' So they sent for her, and she came with her parents and children and all her relatives. Now Susanna was a woman of great beauty and delicate feeling. She was closely veiled, but those scoundrels ordered her to be unveiled so that they might feast their eyes on her beauty. Her family and all who saw her were in tears. Then the two elders stood up before the people and put their hands on her head. She looked up to heaven through her tears, for she trusted in the Lord. The elders said: 'As we were walking alone in the garden, this woman came in with two maids. She shut the garden doors and dismissed her maids. Then a young man, who had been in hiding, came and lay down with her. We were in a corner of the garden, and when we saw this wickedness we ran up to them. Though we saw them in the act, we could not hold the man; he was too strong for us, and he opened the door and forced his way out. We seized the woman and asked who the young man was, but she would not tell us. That is our evidence.'

As they were elders of the people and judges, the assembly believed them and condemned her to death. Then Susanna cried out loudly: 'Eternal God, who dost know all secrets and foresee all things, thou knowest that their evidence against me was false. And now I am to die, guiltless though I am of all the wicked things these men have said against me.'

The Lord heard her cry. Just as she was being led off to execution, God inspired a devout young man named Daniel to protest, and he shouted out, 'I will not have this woman's blood on my head.' All the people turned and asked him, 'What do you mean by that?' He came forward and said: 'Are you such fools, you Israelites, as to condemn a woman of Israel, without making careful inquiry and finding out the truth? Re-open the trial; the evidence these men have brought against her is false.'

So the people all hurried back, and the rest of the elders said to him, 'Come, take your place among us and state your case, for God has given you the standing of an elder.' Daniel said to them, 'Separate these men and keep them at a distance from each other, and I will examine them.' When they had been separated Daniel summoned one of them. 'You hardened sinner,' he said, 'the sins of your past have now come home to you. You gave unjust decisions, condemning the innocent, and acquitting the guilty, although the Lord has said, "You shall not put to death an innocent and guiltless man." Now then, if you saw this woman, tell us, under what tree did you see them together?' He answered, 'Under a clove-tree.' Then Daniel retorted, 'Very good: this lie has cost you your life, for already God's angel has received your sentence from God, and he will cleave you in two.' And he told him to stand aside, and ordered them to bring in the other.

He said to him: 'Spawn of Canaan, no son of Judah, beauty has been your undoing, and lust has corrupted your heart! Now we know how you have been treating the women of Israel, frightening them into consorting with you; but here is a woman of Judah who would not submit to your villainy. Now then, tell me, under what tree did you surprise them together?' 'Under a yew-tree', he replied. Daniel said to him, 'Very good: this lie has cost you your life, for the angel of God is waiting with his sword to hew you down and destroy you both.'

Then the whole assembly gave a great shout and praised God, the saviour of those who trust in him. They turned on the two elders, for out of their own mouths Daniel had convicted them of giving false evidence; they dealt with them according to the law of Moses, and put them to death, as they in their wickedness had tried to do to their neighbour. And so an innocent life was saved that day. Then Hilkiah and his wife gave praise for their daughter Susanna, because she was found innocent of a shameful deed, and so did her husband Joakim and all her relatives. And from that day forward Daniel was a great man among his people [pp. 267-270].

The aim of the voyeur is active, the exhibitionist's essentially passive. But although the latter derives pleasure in being sexually "viewed," he most frequently takes the initiative in the act (Glover, 1960). Bowman (1951), Guttmann (1953), and Rickles (1955) observe that voyeuristic tendencies often accompany exhibitionism. The same observation emerged from the Forensic Clinic Study in Toronto (Mohr et al., 1964, p. 161) although true voyeurism occurred in only a few cases where it tended to alternate with exhibitionism. In *Cain '67* by Johannes Simmel (1971), Vanessa's need to exhibit her body in public display derives from narcissistic and masochistic elements. Vanessa's father married her unattractive mother, who was twenty years older than he, for money. Both his wife and Vanessa were aware of his adulterous indiscretions. At ten, the child was sent away to a private school in Switzerland, and as a result felt rejected and abandoned. At thirteen, she was seduced by a sixteen-year-old; by fifteen, she had had several experiences with older men. When her mother died, she blamed her aristocratic, rejecting father, and when he married his mistress, Vanessa turned to exhibitionism in an attempt to punish him. The unresolved oedipal feelings run their course through a compulsive, sexualized need to be looked at. In the exhibitionist and voyeur, there is continued heightened importance attached to the childish desire to look at and be looked at, which plays a primary role and frequently displaces adult heterosexual intercourse (English and Finch, 1954). An example of how closely intertwined are exhibitionism and voyeurism is seen in the following excerpt from Simmel's novel.

I switched on the stereo. As soon as the music — clarinet, piano and strings — of the record came through the loudspeakers, Vanessa began to work.

The first part of her appearance was a common enough act. The girl sheds garment after garment searching for an imaginary flea. The second part was sensational: "Vanessa's Famous Candle Act." The prices were high in the mirror-walled back room with its intimate red light, small black tables and black leather chairs, but our customers felt they got their money's worth.

While the first song was playing Vanessa, with much wriggling and twisting, managed to extricate herself from her black evening gown. In her search for the flea she slipped off her elbow-length black gloves to the music of the second record. Next followed a chemise, and circulating among the tables and with the help of several customers, she began to unhook her bodice.

She winced whenever the imaginary flea bit her; she sat on the laps of a few men and women while they tried to undo her bodice; she sighed, whimpered and moaned. Vanessa, twenty-two years old, a natural blonde, slim and full-bosomed, was our treasure. A first-rate training had made her a past master of chichi. She could affect an enchanting, vapid baby face, pout à la Bardot and wink her big blue eyes.

The Strip was situated in the inner city of Frankfurt am Main. The large club had two bars, many small tables, a dance floor illuminated from below and a small stage for artists and strippers.

They were all excellent, but Vanessa was sensational. Boris Minski, my partner, had signed her to an exclusive contract, its many clauses providing protection for us and penalties for Vanessa should she ever try to leave us.

"She won't leave us," I often said. "After all, you did help her that time and she is grateful to both of us."

"Once you've helped somebody who feels obliged to be grateful you've got to be goddam cautious," was Boris's invariable answer.

We usually engaged artists and strippers only for a few weeks since we frequently changed the program in the bar out front. The same applied to the combos, too. I say "out front" intentionally since for those with well-filled wallets there was also the other bar, this mirror-walled back room with its soft lighting where Vanessa appeared. We had pushed the small black-lacquered tables and leather chairs close together; the room could hold an unexpectedly large number of people. Friday and Saturday we were always filled to capacity. Today, Monday, the week's poorest day, the mirrored room was three-quarters full. If the country was experiencing an economic crisis it certainly was not evident here. But then Frankfurt with its banks, industry, tourists, fairs and expositions was the ideal location for a club such as ours. Our Strip made us a fortune.

In the back room, to which customers were admitted only by Boris or me, we served only champagne or high-priced drinks. Naturally, we had our regulars, among them a very wealthy lesbian, Petra Schalke. She came twice a week, usually escorted by a bleached-blond dress designer who had had his face lifted, wore gold bracelets on his wrists and affected an intellectual look by wearing black horn-rimmed glasses. Petra Schalke often came with friends, queers or heterosexuals. Most of our customers were quite ordinary and normal.

Another song had started up and Vanessa examined her brassiere and her voluptuous breasts, but the imaginary flea was now apparently in her panties and she began to search for it there.

During the next song a fat man in a tuxedo, sipping Veuve Clicquot 1952, helped to remove her bra and people close by were permitted to see if the flea perhaps could be found on her large white breasts with their pink nipples. She wiggled on the fat man's knees and blinked her big blue eyes. She was a very beautiful girl and she performed with expertise, I thought again as I watched her through the one-way mirror in my office.

We needed that mirror to anticipate any possible trouble during Vanessa's act and, if necessary, call in the bouncers. Since Vanessa's work began at 2 A.M., following the usual show, her audience, after drinking in the other bar, was by then more or less tipsy. We kept a close watch. In our line of work we rarely got to bed before 5 A.M., more often at 7.

"More than twenty-two percent in Neugablonz," said Minski. Then he began to laugh. He was sitting at his old-fashioned desk, before him a stack of morning newspapers which had been brought about midnight. We usually took care of the paperwork while Vanessa was performing; this night we were reading newspapers.

*   *   *

Our office was soundproof. A flick of the switch and, through an intercom, we could hear all that went on in the bar outside. Everything was all right. The record circled on the turntable. Vanessa had sat on the laps of Petra Schalke, the lesbian with a mannish haircut, and had slowly taken off her net stockings. This sapphist, a black mink coat draped over her shoulders, had pursued Vanessa for months now—in vain—and was grateful if Vanessa as much as sat on her knees. The silver-blond fashion designer with his frilled shirtcuffs and gold bracelets was studiously examining his fingernails while Vanessa stretched out her bare legs and carried on. Then she permitted her passionate admirer to undo her garter belt.

We had instructed Vanessa always to allow Petra Schalke something like this. She brought us many customers and drank only the most expensive champagne. We simply had to show some human kindness! The forty-five-year-old lesbian—her love unrequited— fussed over Vanessa's garter belt and in her excitement pinched her finger. It hurt. Her escort blew on it, stroking it tenderly. Petra Schalke, her face taut and hungry, whispered something in Vanessa's ear. Vanessa had to giggle and roll her big blue eyes.

*   *   *

Another record had started and Vanessa jumped and shook herself. It was obvious that the flea had to be in the one garment which she still had on—aside from her shoes. When we had started rehearsing this act I had told Vanessa that she had to be undressed by the end of the first record. After all, two records ran about thirty minutes.

Vanessa had protested. "I need those thirty minutes to get them in the mood for the candle act! Believe me, Richie. No one will be bored. If I can't do very much—*that* I know how to do."

"Yes, darling, yes, but . . ."

"Leave it to her," Boris had said. "I think she has something there."

She had been right. She managed both sides of the record and, during the first part of her act, drinks were still being served by very pretty girls in black miniskirts with tiny white aprons and caps.

The music came to an end. During the few seconds that passed before the next record began, Vanessa slithered snakelike through the room, passing between guests, brushing or touching as many as possible. A superb talent.

The music resumed. Vanessa rolled around on a small carpet in the center of the mirrored room, moaning and wailing because the flea in her panties plagued her. The fourth song had her crawling on all fours, her bottom up so high that men, and women too, could try to pull down her black bikini panties. But she was too elusive.

I had gone to Minski's desk. On it were newspapers, bank statements and a magazine. . . .

*   *   *

. . . Vanessa began slowly, ever so slowly, to take off the g-string which remained all she wore.

*   *   *

The red light grew dimmer. The music stopped. A well-rehearsed ceremony followed. Two especially pretty girls in their black, short costumes placed a tigerskin, complete with head, in the center of the room. The beast's glass eye glittered dark-green. The girls curtsied and escorted Vanessa to the tigerskin, curtsied again and disappeared. Vanessa slowly sank to her knees, rose slightly to a crouch and opened her thighs. There was no music during this last part of her performance. Always a hushed silence — if one discounted the strange sounds Vanessa uttered.

*   *   *

A black haired girl, dressed as a maid, tripped through the mirrored room to Vanessa, who was crouching on the tigerskin, curtsied and offered her a black, silken cushion, holding a candle. The girl curtsied again and slipped away. Vanessa deposited the cushion and candle alongside.

Through the one-way mirror in our office I watched our star performer half-close her eyes and begin to caress her nipples. I turned up the loudspeaker which brought in the sound from the bar and heard Vanessa softly sighing. In a little while her right hand moved down and the soft sighs became more audible moans.

"What's the matter with her? She sounds hoarse. Does she have another —"

"That's right," said Minski. "Another cold. Quite a bad one this time."

"It's really not surprising," I said. "In there it's hot while those damned corridors outside are cold and drafty enough to blow one down. Every day a girl runs around there half-naked. It's amazing she doesn't have a chronic cold. Or, with this crazy weather, pneumonia."

*   *   *

I saw that Vanessa's breathing had become irregular; her full breasts rose and sank. The audience sat spellbound. Petra Schalke of the mannish haircut held her hands pressed to her mouth, biting her knuckles. The two special-effects men were whispering excitedly.

The telephone on Minski's desk began to ring.

*   *   *

In the mirrored room Vanessa on her tigerskin became very restless. Her hips swayed, her fingers moved softly. Someone tipped over a glass. Minski was still talking . . . .

I looked through the mirror. Vanessa was grinding her teeth. She had rehearsed that thoroughly. It was most effective. I lowered the volume of the loudspeaker so that Boris could continue his telephone conversation undisturbed, then watched Vanessa reach for the red candle on the silk cushion, pull her hand back as though ashamed, reach out again, bite her lower lip, sigh and go on with her performance.

*   *   *

Vanessa, suddenly, with resolute determination, reached for the red candle, pushed it into herself and groaned loudly. Loudly and hoarsely. If only she didn't come down with the flu!

*   *   *

Through the loudspeaker, although I had turned it down, we could hear Vanessa. She acted so convincingly that one simply had to believe she was nearing climax. She uttered short, high screams. Her hand moved rapidly. I hope she doesn't have to sneeze now, I thought.

* * *

Vanessa on the tigerskin opened and closed her thighs; her head lowered, her blond hair cascaded over her face, she whimpered in a high monotone. Her body arched, her free hand alternately pounded the rug or drummed on her flat abdomen. The fan switched on again. I thought of our saving grace, the IIO.

The International Investors' Organization was one of the world's largest, representing almost two hundred investment funds...

Through the loudspeaker came sounds as international as the IIO, understood by people all over the globe: Vanessa acted out the climax. She cried out loud, her voice died down to a murmur, she gasped for air and sank down on the tigerskin, her body twitched.

"How do I look?" Minski asked and stepped before me.

"Great," I said.

"And I'm fifty-four," he remarked. "Eleven years older than you! You ought to look much better! But you don't take care of yourself."

"But you do."

"I have to—if I'm to think for all of you. Have to watch my health, eat a lot of fruit, mustn't smoke, no alcohol..."

Vanessa was still motionless. It was part of her act. At last she rose. The two girls dressed as ladies' maids brought a knee-length ermine cape which they draped about her shoulders and disappeared with candle, cushion and tigerskin. The light became brighter now and Vanessa walked from table to table, her big blue eyes opened wide. From time to time she played with herself and amorously displayed her fingers to the guests.

It was *ne plus ultra!*

Guests were speechless as always, except for the two special-effects men, who were whispering animatedly.

"Just look how happy we've made them again," Minski remarked.

"And when you consider—just an act."

"It's almost as easy to make people happy as it is to make them unhappy," said Minski, the man who once dreamed of devoting his life to butterfly research [pp. 39-75, *passim*].

Perhaps the apogee in fictional exhibitionism and voyeurism is to be found in the deadly, macabre satire of Virgilio Martini (1936), *The*

World Without Women. This fantasy evokes the world of 2,000 and after, in which a super-disease, "fallopitis," hoked up by homosexuals to destroy womankind nearly does so. By 2,029 only one female capable of bearing children is left. She had been put in a "cataleptic trance" nineteen years previously by her prescient father. At the propitious time, he offers Rebecca at public auction to a panic-stricken, male world. The successful bidder is the President of the Republic, Geo Maatschippij, who on the radio proudly announces:

... that that very night he would offer to the entire body of the citizenry a most exceptional television program: the defloration of Rebecca. The world was stricken with envy and admiration. That night the entire population of the earth watched the long broadcast, eyes glued to the television screen. Millions followed every detail of the two principals' encounter, naked and infinitely exciting in their faraway lust. Millions of ears caught every gasp of the male and each sigh of the female. Millions waited to admire a few spots of red, listened for a piercing cry, or a long marveling moan. But before fifteen minutes had passed in kisses and embraces, sighs and caresses, suddenly—horror of horrors!—the splendid energy of the fiery President of the Republic had ebbed away! The public gaped, transfixed with disbelief. A hundred times the athletic Geo tried desperately to reawaken his slumbering powers; a hundred times the lovely Rebecca, trembling with desire, lavished kisses and caresses upon him in an effort to assist him. But the vagrant spirit was not to be summoned up again. At dawn, after seven hours of vain effort, Geo Maatschippij threw himself in fury on the television camera, whose presence in the nuptial chamber had brought about his discomfiture and broadcast it to the four winds, and he shattered it to bits. All the screens went blank, and millions of mouths emitted monstrous guffaws. All that day the President of the Republic was at home to no one. By nightfall, as his nerves began to relax, with admirable vigor and spirit he accomplished his mission as a male [pp. 102-103].

Exhibitionism involves the intentional and usually compulsive exposure of the adult genitalia under inappropriate conditions (Mathis, 1969). The term was first coined by a French neurologist, Lasègue (1877) and subsequently defined by Krafft-Ebing (1912, p. 505) as

"men who ostentatiously expose their genitals to persons of the opposite sex ... without, however, becoming aggressive." Krafft-Ebing
described two major categories of the exhibitionist: patients in whom
genital exhibition may be a symptom of an organic psychosyndrome
and those in whom it is an outcome of an impulsive-compulsive drive.
The irresistibility of the urge is indicative of the weakness of the ego.
Unable to tolerate frustration, according to Sperling (1947), the exhibitionist attempts to work out his problems narcissistically through
reassuring denials. Instead of avoiding danger, he feels drawn to it. He
denies his castration anxiety by exhibiting his penis. "To display the
penis, or any of its surrogates, is to say, 'I am not afraid of you. I defy
you. I have a penis'" (Freud, 1922, p. 274). The vast majority of
exhibitionists are not dangerous and for the most part do not touch or
attack the "victim." They seek some response in the female, invariably
a stranger, in a search for reassurance that they will not be rejected.
The typical personality description is that of a quiet, shy, "nice guy,"
with severe feelings of inadequacy, inferiority, and insecurity in interpersonal and social relations (Reitz and Keil, 1971). Feelings of
strength and manhood are likely to result from exhibiting one's penis
in a fully erect state. The exhibitionist is filled with anxieties, tensions,
and restlessness; he struggles hopelessly with his compulsions (Guttmann, 1953), is held spellbound, unable to contain the impulse to
exhibit his genitalia. By overcompensating, he feels superior to everybody else.

The exhibitionist's shyness is at a minimum in the presence of young
girls, though he knows that exposure to children involves extra-heavy
penalties from the law. The interior monologue of the protagonist in
Such Good Friends by Lois Gould (1970) explores the effect on two
little girls who caught sight of an exhibitionist.

> ... I saw the erect male penis of a total stranger when I was ten
> (he was waving at me from the bottom of a hill in Central Park,
> where Pamela and I went sledding). Look, Pam, there's a man down
> there—look what he's doing. I think he's looking up our skirts.
> Maybe we better go down headfirst on the sled instead of sitting like
> this. Look at his thing—are they always red like that, or is his just
> cold? My brother's isn't red, but he's only twelve, said Pamela.
> Maybe we should move over to *that* hill, Pam; I'm getting scared.
> What're *you* scared for, I'm the one who started men-strew-ating.
> I'm the one who could get pregnant, you know. Anyway, he isn't

going to do anything; he just wants to see our underpants. I think it's funny [p. 70].

In one respect, Pamela is certainly correct: the exhibitionist will not make any contact; he wants no partnership, but needs female spectators to fan his narcissism at their expense. Thus, by a retreat from object libido, the male exhibitionist arrives at a feeling of hermaphroditic self-fulfillment, a sense of intoxication with his own power (Christoffel, 1956).

Isadora, in Erica Jong's (1973) novel, *Fear of Flying,* remembers how she had cowered at the age of thirteen "when exhibitionists started unzipping their pants at me on the deserted subway to high school. I actually used to be afraid they'd be *insulted* and take terrible revenge unless I remained rooted to my seat. So I stayed, looking away, pretending not to notice, pretending not to be terrified, pretending to be reading and hoping somehow that the book would protect me" (p. 298).

The exhibitionistic attacks Pamela and Isadora were subjected to are essentially regressive, a symbolic seeking of repetition of particular, vividly remembered acts and scenes of bygone days of childhood (Karpman, 1926). If the victim is a child, the exhibitionist may, by a process of identification and differentiation, identify with the victim, on the one hand, and with his mother, on the other hand. Exhibitionism is a recrudescence or persistence of infantile sexuality in an adult setting. In the earliest forms of his instinctual drives, the oral, the exhibitionist is tied to his mother; in later forms of polymorphous sexuality he is tied to childish and youthful, predominantly female, objects. There tends to be premature attainment of the phallic stage, followed by no further advance to the genital phase and it is this standstill, according to Christoffel (1956), that is the precondition of male genital exhibitionism. Thus, exhibitionism is a remainder and a surrogate of a polymorphous infantile sexuality.

There are different grades and conditions of the disorder. Mild forms of exhibitionism are probably of the same developmental level as mild hysterias or mild impotence, whereas the impulsive-compulsive form is of a deeper and more intractable and narcissistic nature (Glover, 1960), sometimes taking symbolic form. In Jonathan Swift's *Gulliver's Travels* (1726), active exhibitionism and passive voyeurism are found throughout the voyages. The first voyage may well express the primary narcissistic omnipotence of the infant. The second voyage expresses the helplessness of a child against giants when he is aware of his size. In general, the exhibitionism here is expressed in excretory rather than genital or reproductive terms. In the third voyage, the voyeurism is almost wholly active, shown largely in social terms (Greenacre, 1955). The strong exhibitionistic tendencies of Gulliver and his great desire that the Lilliputians admire him for the size of his genital are revealed in the following description of a parade held by the Lilliputian army in his honor.

> Two days after this adventure, the Emperor having ordered that part of his army which quarters in and about his metropolis to be in a readiness, took a fancy of diverting himself in a very singular manner. He desired I would stand like a colossus, with my legs as far asunder as I conveniently could. He then commanded his general (who was an old experienced leader, and a great patron of mine) to draw up the troops in close order, and march them under me, the foot by twenty-four in a breast, and the horse by sixteen, with drums beating, colours flying, and pikes advanced. This body consisted of three thousand foot, and a thousand horse. His Majesty gave orders, upon pain of death, that every soldier in his march should observe the strictest decency with regard to my person; which, however, could not prevent some of the younger officers from turning up their eyes as they passed under me. And, to confess the truth, my breeches were at that time in so ill a condition, that they afforded some opportunities for laughter and admiration [Swift, p. 34].

Swift drew a true picture of the exhibitionist who suffers from the idea that his penis is too small and impulsively has to display it for the admiration of others. Gulliver committed an offense that imperiled his life when he urinated before the Empress, who is a typical symbol of the mother. A fire broke out in her apartment, and the Lilliputians were unable to extinguish it.

> The case seemed wholly desperate and deplorable, and this magnificent palace would have infallibly been burnt down to the ground, if, by a presence of mind, unusual to me, I had not suddenly thought of an expedient [narrates Gulliver]. I had the evening before drank plentifully of a most delicious wine ... which is diuretic. By the luckiest chance in the world, I had not discharged myself of any part of it. The heat I had contracted by coming very near the flames, and by my labouring to quench them, made the wine begin

to operate by urine; which I voided in such a quantity, and applied so well to the proper places, that in three minutes the fire was wholly extinguished, and the rest of that noble pile, which had cost so many ages in erecting, preserved from destruction ... I could not tell how his Majesty might resent the manner by which I had performed [this service]: for, by the fundamental laws of the realm, it is capital in any person, of what quality soever, to make water within the precincts of the palace. But I was little comforted by a message from his Majesty, that he would give orders to the Grand Judiciary for passing my pardon in form; which, however, I could not obtain. And I was privately assured, that the Empress, conceiving the greatest abhorrence of what I had done, removed to the most distant side of the court, firmly resolved that those buildings should never be repaired for her use... [p. 45].

The extinguishing of a conflagration in a woman's house, especially when this is done by urinating into it, refers to the child's idea of sexual intercourse, the woman being symbolized by the house (Ferenczi, 1928). The heat mentioned by Gulliver, Ferenczi interpreted, is symbolic of the male's passionate desire. At the same time, fire stands for the dangers to which the genital is exposed. "In point of fact, with Gulliver the threat of punishment follows hard upon the misdeed and characteristically proceeds from the Emperor, the typical father-substitute ... The death penalty is revoked by the mercy of the Emperor, but Gulliver cannot escape punishment in another form ... the loss of his eyes.... The punishment ... is the same as that which King Oedipus inflicted upon himself for his sexual intercourse with his mother. Putting out the eyes may be a symbolic distortion of the punishment of castration" (Ferenczi, 1928, pp. 292-293). After blinding himself, Oedipus called attention to the connection between sight and sexual vitality, where blindness signifies punishment in the form of sexual weakening. Gulliver's tale continues:

When I was just preparing to pay my attendance on the Emperor of Blefuscu, a considerable person at court (to whom I had been very serviceable at a time when he lay under the highest displeasure of his Imperial Majesty) came to my house very privately at night in a close chair, and without sending his name, desired admittance: the chairmen were dismissed; I put the chair, with his Lordship in it, into my coat-pocket; and giving orders to a trusty servant to say I was indisposed and gone to sleep, I fastened the door of my house, placed the chair on the table, according to my usual custom, and sat down by it. After the common salutations were over, observing his Lordship's countenance full of concern, and enquiring into the reason, he desired I would hear him with patience in a matter that highly concerned my honour and my life. His speech was to the following effect, for I took notes of it as soon as he left me.

You are to know, said he, that several committees of council have been lately called in the most private manner on your account: and it is but two days since his Majesty came to a full resolution.

You are very sensible that Skyresh Bolgolam (*Galbet,* of High Admiral) hath been your mortal enemy almost ever since your arrival. His original reasons I know not, but his hatred is much encreased since your great success against Blefuscu, by which his glory, as Admiral, is obscured. This lord, in conjunction with Flimnap the High Treasurer, whose enmity against you is notorious on account of his lady, Limtoc the General, Lalcon the Chamberlain, and Balmuff the Grand Justiciary, have prepared articles of impeachment against you, for treason, and other capital crimes.

This preface made me so impatient, being conscious of my own merits and innocence, that I was going to interrupt; when he entreated me to be silent, and thus proceeded.

Out of gratitude for the favours you have done me, I procured information of the whole proceedings, and a copy of the articles, wherein I venture my head for your service.

Articles of Impeachment against Quinbus Flestrin
(*the* Man-Mountain).

ARTICLE I.

Whereas, by a statute made in the reign of his Imperial Majesty Calin Deffar Plune, it is enacted, that whoever shall make water within the precincts of the royal palace shall be liable to the pains and penalties of high treason: notwithstanding, the said Quinbus Flestrin, in open breach of the said law, under colour of extinguishing the fire kindled in the apartment of his Majesty's most dear imperial consort, did maliciously, traitorously, and devilishly, by discharge of his urine, put out the said fire kindled in the said apartment, lying and being within the precincts of the said royal palace, against the statute in that case provided, etc., against the duty, etc.

*   *   *

There are some other articles, but [this is] the most important, of which I have read you an abstract.

In the several debates upon this impeachment, it must be confessed that his Majesty gave many marks of his great lenity, often urging the services you had done him, and endeavouring to extenuate your crimes. The Treasurer and Admiral insisted that you should be put to the most painful and ignominious death, by setting fire on your house at night, and the General was to attend with twenty thousand men armed with poisoned arrows to shoot you on the face and hands. Some of your servants were to have private orders to strew a poisonous juice on your shirts and sheets, which would soon make you tear your own flesh, and die in the utmost torture. The General came into the same opinion, so that for a long time there was a majority against you. But his Majesty resolving, if possible, to spare your life, at last brought off the Chamberlain.

Upon this incident, Reldresal, Principal Secretary for Private Affairs, who always approved himself your true friend, was commanded by the Emperor to deliver his opinion, which he accordingly did; and therein justified the good thoughts you have of him. He allowed your crimes to be great, but that still there was room for mercy, the most commendable virtue in a prince, and for which his Majesty was so justly celebrated. He said the friendship between you and him was so well known to the world, that perhaps the most honourable board might think him partial: however, in obedience to the command he had received, he would freely offer his sentiments. That if his Majesty, in consideration of your services, and pursuant to his own merciful disposition, would please to spare your life, and only give order to put out both your eyes, he humbly conceived, that by this expedient justice might in some measure be satisfied, and all the world would applaud the lenity of the Emperor, as well as the fair and generous proceedings of those who have the honour to be his counsellors. That the loss of your eyes would be no impediment to your bodily strength, by which you might still be useful to his Majesty. That blindness is an addition to courage, by concealing dangers from us; that the fear you had for your eyes was the greatest difficulty in bringing over the enemy's fleet, and it would be sufficient for you to see by the eyes of the ministers, since the greatest princes do no more.

This proposal was received with the utmost disapprobation by the whole board. Bolgolam, the Admiral, could not preserve his temper; but rising up in fury, said, he wondered how the Secretary durst presume to give his opinion for preserving the life of a traitor: that the services you had performed were, by all true reasons of state, the great aggravation of your crimes; that you, who were able to extinguish the fire by discharge of urine in her Majesty's apartment (which he mentioned with horror), might, at another time, raise an inundation by the same means, to drown the whole palace; and the same strength which enabled you to bring over the enemy's fleet might serve, upon the first discontent, to carry it back: that he had good reasons to think you were a Big-Endian in your heart; and as treason begins in the heart before it appears in overt acts, so he accused you as a traitor on that account, and therefore insisted you should be put to death [Swift, 1726, pp. 53-57, *passim*].

Freud (1905, p. 169) made the point that the eye corresponds to an erotogenic zone in the looking and seeing mania. Clinical studies frequently reveal eye problems in relation to the voyeur. Abraham (1913) and Vasquez (1970), among others, treated patients with pronounced photophobia. Vasquez's patient was a forty-nine-year-old priest, a photophobic voyeur. Contributing to his condition were a domineering mother, an intense fear of committing sin, a sexual obsession to see a woman with a penis, and extreme anxiety leading to fear of light, the sun, blindness, sleep, and madness. He associated St. Thomas and St. Paul with voyeurism because they symbolized eternal happiness through beatific vision. In his paper on eye symbolism, Ferenczi (1913) stated:

The symbolic identification of external objects with bodily organs makes it possible to find again, on the one hand, all the wished-for objects of the world in the individual's body, on the other hand, the treasured organs of the individual's body in objects conceived in an animistic manner. The tooth and eye symbolism would be examples of the fact that bodily organs (principally the genital ones) can be represented not only by objects of the outer world, but also by other organs of the body. In all probability this is even the more primary kind of symbol-creation.
    ... this symbolic equating of genital organs with other organs and with external objects [is] secondarily made to serve repression, which seeks to weaken one member of the equation, while it symbolically over-emphasises the other, more harmless one by the amount of repressed affect. In this way, the upper half of the body, as the more harmless one, attains its sexual-symbolic significance,

and so comes about what Freud calls "Displacement from below upwards." In this work of repression the eyes have proved to be specially adapted to receive the affects displaced from the genital region, on account of their shape and changeable size, their movability, their high value, and their sensitiveness. It is to be supposed, however, that this displacement would not have succeeded so well, had not the eye already had from the beginning that significant libidinous value that Freud describes in his *Sexualtheorie* as a special component of the sexual instinct (the impulse of sexual visual curiosity) [pp. 275-276].

Ralph Ellison's *Invisible Man* is all about the black man who is unseen though obviously present. The novel is replete with puns that jump out everywhere — on eyes, vision, and visions, according to Klein (1964, p. 253): "The hero is troubled by a burning eye within. His one current friend, in the Prologue, is 'a junk man I know, a man of vision,' who has supplied him with wire and sockets [for a forgotten basement apartment in which he rigs up 1,369 electric lights, all eyes that shed light on his invisibility]. The double joke is that electricity is light and power and therefore vision, and that the 'junk man' is a narcotics peddler, one who has visions to sell. A moment later in a marijuana sleep the hero has his first, this time surreal, vision of the facts of Negro experience. And there is more around every corner. All the novel's purpose is reiterated constantly, in fact, as its basic metaphor is elaborated: the hero is invisible because no one sees him and it is the function of every episode to confirm the fact that this black man is condemned to a hopeless struggle to be seen." Most of the people the nameless narrator meets do not see him because of the inner eyes of racial traditions, barriers, and sexual jealousies, on the part of both whites and blacks. On the campus of the Negro college he attends, there is a statue of its founder in the act of holding a veil over the face of a kneeling slave; the man is described as having "empty eyes." "Miss Susie Gresham, the college's old matron . . . listens to a speech given in the chapel with her eyes closed . . . The Reverend Barbee [is eulogizing] the empty-eyed Founder. The climax of the speech comes . . . when Barbee drops the dark glasses he is wearing, revealing that he is blind . . . In contrast to their empty, closed, and blind eyes are the sharp, clear eyes of Dr. Bledsoe, the president of the college, who can terrorize students and faculty with a glance" (Bloch, 1966, p. 1019-1020). When the nine high-school boys in the stag scene are confronted with the naked blonde, they are threatened equally whether they look or they avert their eyes, and are then thrust blindfolded into a prize-fight ring and forced to battle one another. The voyeuristic degradation of the white observers forces the black boys into an innocent exhibitionistic spectacle. The battle of the black boys, blindly flailing away, becomes a demonstration of potency to titillate the impotent (Baumbach, 1963).

Later in the novel, the protagonist's first speech for the Brotherhood is delivered in an arena reminiscent of the smoker scene, and it deals with blindness. He is blinded by a white spotlight and sees the audience only as a black pit. He says: "They've dispossessed us each of one eye since the day we were born. So now we can see only in straight 'white' lines"; "I feel your eyes upon me"; "I feel that here, after a long and desperate and uncommonly blind journey, I have come home..." (pp. 260-262, *passim*). Under the Brotherhood's leadership, the one-eyed men will join together and the blind will lead the blind—but the protagonist himself cannot see and is invisible to the audience. He speaks of becoming "more human ... with your eyes upon me I have found my true family ... I am a citizen of the country of your vision" (p. 262). But he exists only in the eyes of the audience and coming off the platform, blinded by the light, he stumbles "as if in a game of blindman's buff" (p. 263). The next time, he decides, he will wear dark glasses; when he does so, he finally sees people as they are.

At a meeting of the Brotherhood, the narrator discovers that its leader, Brother Jack, has a glass eye. This occurs at a crucial moment: the hero learns that the words of brotherly love are only mouthings with which to dupe their fellow Harlemites. It is at this juncture that the eye pops out. Jack retrieves it and puts it in a glass of water where, magnified, it mocks the narrator, and he begs Jack to replace it so everything will again appear normal. "I stared at the glass, seeing how the light shone through, throwing a transparent, precisely fluted shadow against the dark grain of the table, and there on the bottom of the glass lay an eye. A glass eye. A buttermilk white eye distorted by the light rays. An eye staring fixedly at me as from the dark waters of a well" (p. 358). The theme of blindness is thus related to the notion of invisibility, the imagery of black and white, and the perversities of exhibitionism and voyeurism.

The novelist as voyeur is evident in Nathaniel Hawthorne's *The Blithedale Romance* (1852), in which the repressed sexuality is displaced to the eyes. Throughout the novel, as in *Invisible Man,* there is a preoccupation with the eye. In sixteen randomly selected pages, there are eight references to that organ. For instance: "... and you will look with a knowing eye at oxen" (p. 478). Three pages later, Miles Coverdale, the bachelor Peeping Tom of the book and its narrator, says, "Zenobia, I suspect, would be given her eyes, bright as they were, for such a look." "I could not turn away my own eyes," Miles says (p. 484). He comments on a stranger he has met: "... his manners, being so furtive, remind me of those of a rat, a rat without mischief, the fierce eyes" (p. 488). And "... there was in his eyes ... the naked exposure of something that ought not to be left prominent" (p. 493). And again, "... his eyes, too, were black and sparkling..." (p. 493). Finally, "... his eyes sparkled out at me, whether in fun or malice I knew not, but certainly as if the Devil were peeping out of them" (p. 494). Coverdale is constantly and covertly observing all the other characters in the book: the adolescent Priscilla, the mature Zenobia, the maddening Hollingsworth, the lumpish Silas Foster. He seems to know what each is doing in matters big and small. An elderly gentleman, for example, approaches Blithedale who offers a picture of him which is sheer projection: " 'I know this old gentleman,' said I to Hollingsworth, as we sat observing him; 'that is, I have met him a hundred times in town, and have often amused my fancy with wondering what he was before he came to be what he is. He haunts restaurants and such places, and has an odd way of lurking in the corners or getting behind a door whenever practicable, and holding out his hand with some little article in it which he wishes you to buy. The eye of the world seems to trouble him, although he necessarily lives so much in it...' " (p. 488).

The passive omnipotence of the voyeur is characteristic. Coverdale expresses it succinctly when he says, "My own part in these transactions was singularly subordinate. It resembled that of the Chorus in a classic play, which seems to be set aloof from the possibility of personal concernment, and bestows the whole measure of its hope or fear, its exultation or sorrow, or the fortunes of others, between whom and itself this sympathy is the only bond" (p. 496). And it is at this point that the open act of voyeurism in the narrative erupts. Coverdale's peeping amounts to an unconscious but omnivorous desire to take possession of the object by looking at it, and in describing his voyeurism he uses language that is highly symbolic sexually.

Long since, in this part of our circumjacent wood, I had found out for myself a little hermitage. It was a kind of leafy cave, high upward into the air, among the midmost branches of a white-pine tree. A wild grape-vine, of unusual size and luxuriance, had twined and twisted itself up into the tree, and, after wreathing the entanglement of its tendrils almost around every bough, had caught hold of three or four neighboring trees, and married the whole clump with a perfectly inextricable knot of polygamy. Once, while sheltering myself from a summer shower, the fancy had taken me to clamber up into this seemingly impervious mass of foliage. The branches yielded me a passage, and closed again beneath, as if only a squirrel or a bird had passed. Far aloft, around the stem of the central pine, behold a perfect nest for Robinson Crusoe or King Charles! A hollow chamber of rare seclusion had been formed by the decay of some of the pine branches, which the vine had lovingly strangled with its embrace, burying them from the light of day in an aerial sepulchre of its own leaves. It cost me but little ingenuity to enlarge the interior, and open loopholes through the verdant walls. Had it ever been my fortune to spend a honeymoon, I should have thought seriously of inviting my bride up thither, where our next neighbors would have been two orioles in another part of the clump.

It was an admirable place to make verses, tuning the rhythm to the breezy symphony that so often stirred among the vine-leaves; or to meditate an essay for "The Dial," in which the many tongues of Nature whispered mysteries, and seemed to ask only a little stronger puff of wind to speak out the solution of its riddle. Being so pervious to air-currents, it was just the nook, too, for the enjoyment of a cigar. This hermitage was my one exclusive possession while I counted myself a brother of the socialists. It symbolized my individuality, and aided me in keeping it inviolate. None ever found me out in it, except, once, a squirrel. I brought thither no guest, because, after Hollingsworth failed me, there was no longer the man alive with whom I could think of sharing all. So there I used to sit, owl-like, yet not without liberal and hospitable thoughts. I counted the innumerable clusters of my vine, and fore-reckoned the abundance of my vintage. It gladdened me to anticipate the surprise of the Community, when, like an allegorical figure of rich October, I should make my appearance, with shoulders bent beneath the burden of ripe grapes, and some of the crushed ones crimsoning my brow as with a blood-stain.

Ascending into this natural turret, I peeped in turn out of several of its small windows. The pine-tree, being ancient, rose high above the rest of the wood, which was of comparatively recent growth. Even where I sat, about midway between the root and the topmost bough, my position was lofty enough to serve as an observatory, not for starry investigations, but for those sublunary matters in which lay a lore as infinite as that of the planets. Through one loophole I saw the river lapsing calmly onward, while in the meadow, near its brink, a few of the brethren were digging peat for our winter's fuel. On the interior cart-road of our farm, I discerned Hollingsworth, with a yoke of oxen hitched to a drag of stones, that were to be piled into a fence, on which we employed ourselves at the odd intervals of other labor.

Turning towards the farm-house, I saw Priscilla (for, though a great way off, the eye of faith assured me that it was she) sitting at Zenobia's window, and making little purses, I suppose; or, perhaps, mending the Community's old linen. . . .

*   *   *

Voices were now approaching through the region of the wood which lay in the vicinity of my tree. Soon I caught glimpses of two figures — a woman and a man — Zenobia and the stranger — earnestly talking together as they advanced.

Zenobia had a rich, though varying color. It was, most of the while, a flame, and anon a sudden paleness. Her eyes glowed, so that their light sometimes flashed upward to me, as when the sun throws a dazzle from some bright object on the ground. Her gestures were free, and strikingly impressive. The whole woman was alive with a passionate intensity, which I now perceived to be the phase in which her beauty culminated. Any passion would have become her well; and passionate love, perhaps, the best of all. This was not love, but anger, largely intermixed with scorn. Yet the idea strangely forced itself upon me, that there was a sort of familiarity between these two companions, necessarily the result of an intimate love, — on Zenobia's part, at least, — in days gone by, but which had prolonged itself into as intimate a hatred, for all futurity. As they passed among the trees, reckless as her movement was, she took good heed that even the hem of her garment should not brush against the stranger's person. I wondered whether there had always been a chasm, guarded so religiously, betwixt these two.

As for Westervelt, he was not a whit more warmed by Zenobia's passion than a salamander by the heat of its native furnace. He would have been absolutely statuesque, save for a look of slight perplexity, tinctured strongly with derision. It was a crisis in which his intellectual perceptions could not altogether help him out. He failed to comprehend, and cared but little for comprehending, why Zenobia should put herself into such a fume; but satisfied his mind that it was all folly, and only another shape of a woman's manifold absurdity, which men can never understand. How many a woman's evil fate has yoked her with a man like this! Nature thrusts some of us into the world miserably incomplete on the emotional side, with hardly any sensibilities except what pertain to us as animals. No passion, save of the senses; no holy tenderness, nor the delicacy that results from this. Externally they bear a close resemblance to other men, and have perhaps all save the finest grace; but when a woman wrecks herself on such a being, she ultimately finds that the real womanhood within her has no corresponding part in him. Her deepest voice lacks a response; the deeper her cry, the more dead his silence. The fault may be none of his; he cannot give her what never lived within his soul. But the wretchedness on her side, and the moral deterioration attendant on a false and shallow life, without strength enough to keep itself sweet, are among the most pitiable wrongs that mortals suffer.

Now, as I looked down from my upper region at this man and woman—outwardly so fair a sight, and wandering like two lovers in the wood,—I imagined that Zenobia, at an earlier period of youth, might have fallen into the misfortune above indicated. And when her passionate womanhood, as was inevitable, had discovered its mistake, here had ensued the character of eccentricity and defiance which distinguished the more public portion of her life.

Seeing how aptly matters had chanced thus far, I began to think it the design of fate to let me into all Zenobia's secrets, and that therefore the couple would sit down beneath my tree, and carry on a conversation which would leave me nothing to inquire. No doubt, however, had it so happened, I should have deemed myself honorably bound to warn them of a listener's presence, by flinging down a handful of unripe grapes, or by sending an unearthly groan out of my hiding-place, as if this were one of the trees of Dante's ghostly forest. But real life never arranges itself exactly like a romance. In the first place, they did not sit down at all. Secondly, even while they passed beneath the tree, Zenobia's utterance was so hasty and broken, and Westervelt's so cool and low, that I hardly could make out an intelligible sentence on either side. What I seem to remember, I yet suspect, may have been patched together, by my fancy, in brooding over the matter afterwards [pp. 497-501].

Coverdale, the voyeur, is satisfied with his fantasies related to his visual stimulation. The exhibitionist looks for a significant reaction from the female to whom he exposes his genitals; he wishes to display his desire, but has no need to be desired in return. The voyeur, on the other hand, requires no recognition by his object at all (Nagel, 1971). The voyeur is fearful of frustration and disapproval; the activity, almost always secret, represents a stealthy yet defiant way of attaining a limited goal, for it frequently brings a feeling of power over those being looked at (Maslow and Mittelman, 1951), as it does Coverdale. In exhibitionism, the self-exposure represents an aggrandized "showing off."

The most common and harmless form of exhibitionism is exposure in the act of micturition (Stekel, 1952). Having urinated, the exhibitionist suddenly turns around, if and when he senses women or children are in the vicinity; in this way he can always plead inadvertence or absentmindedness if he is accused. A number of Abraham's (1971) patients reported to him that the physical sensation of premature seminal emission was identical with that of urinary incontinence that they connected with childhood memories of exhibitionistic pleasure in passing urine in the sight of another person. They derived infantile pleasure from the outflow of their bodily products. Springmann (1970) reports the case of a homosexual patient raised in an Israeli kibbutz whose incestuous dreams tapped a stream of memories about the pleasure of urinating in his mother's presence. Through adulthood, he liked to urinate with the lower half of his body completely exposed. George Mitchell, under the psychiatric care of Dr. Bernstein in Roderick Thorp's novel, *Slaves* (1972), writes of his doctor who had flown up to New Hampshire for his once-a-week session with him, "He went directly to the bathroom, as always. He is one of those morons who urinate in the middle of the water, just where it makes the most noise. You could have food on the table outside, and he'd do it anyway. If I were that stupid, and he had the sensitivity to feel the revulsion that I feel, he would label it infantile exhibitionism and base the next six months' sessions on it" (p. 41).

Exhibitionism is a way of conferring love and asking for it. In the second half of the third year and the first half of the fourth especially, according to Abraham (1917), small boys are very prone to exhibit themselves before their mother, particularly when micturating, for which function they no longer need their mother's help as they did before. "A boy of about four years of age whose urethral erotism was well within the normal limits often used to ask his mother if he should show her his penis. . . . When he had passed water he often used to ask if it was 'a lot.' His narcissism appears very clearly here—his desire to be admired for his performance" (p. 293-294). Such narcissism is seen in the novel, *Run Down,* by Robert Garrett (1972): "I . . . stood there listening to the sound of my own water tumbling into the bowl. I flushed the bowl, took a quick wash, and started to get dressed" (p. 45). Christoffel (1936) called attention to the Mannekin-Pis in Brussels, whose exhibition of urination has been celebrated since 1698.

An equally classical expression is exposing the buttocks as a measure of contempt, a gesture performed primarily by women. This was a common practice among certain groups in Albania and other Slavonic people (Karpman, 1926). In Emile Zola's *Germinal* (1885), the colliers of Montsou were on a two-month strike. Three thousand strong, with their women and hungry children, they marched along the narrow streets of the town in confused, serried ranks, singing the Marseillaise and crying "Bread! bread! bread!" The bourgeoisie were fearful:

> Was the old social order cracking this very evening? And what they saw immediately after completed their stupefaction. The band had nearly passed by, there were only a few stragglers left, when Mouquette came up. She was delaying, watching the bourgeois at their garden gates or the windows of their houses; and whenever she saw them, as she was not able to spit in their faces, she showed them what for her was the climax of contempt. Doubtless she perceived someone now, for suddenly she raised her skirts, bent her back, and showed her enormous buttocks, naked beneath the last rays of the sun. There was nothing obscene in those fierce buttocks, and nobody laughed [p. 268].

The conception of exhibitionism as a process of erotic symbolism is found in several fictional accounts. The impotent hero in Poe's *Some Passages in the Life of a Lion* (1835) prides himself on his huge phallic nose as the basis of his social success, even when at the end of the tale the Elector of Bluddennuff shoots it off in a duel. In Gogol's "The Nose" (1836), the exhibitionist's sensibilities are always inhibited or in abeyance, and he is unable to estimate accurately either the impression he produces or the general results of his action, or else he is moved by a strong obsessive impulse that overpowers his judgment (Ellis, 1906). Gogol himself was plagued by an unsightly nose, a nose of such length and mobility that he could perform parlor tricks with it, the favorite being to touch the tip of his nose with his underlip (Freedman, 1951). Thus his own nose was the hero of many of his stories. In "The Nose," Major Kovalyov wakes up one morning to discover that his familiar, pimpled appendage has disappeared. He is appalled, but there is a detachment to his feelings. The fundamental structure of the narrative resembles that of the nakedness dream in which the dreamer scurries about in embarrassment, seeking shelter while the spectators remain frighteningly indifferent; the exhibitor wrestles with castration anxiety to create in the end a compromise formula through which he is gratified by the very castration (Kanzer, 1955). And so Kovalyov's fetishistic nose is actually no more than a mask for the unconsciously exhibited phallic equivalent. He strolls along the boulevard and soon meets an intolerable sight: his own nose, brilliantly attired in a gold-braid uniform, wearing a stiff collar, leather breeches, plumed hat, and a sword hanging at its side. This is displacement downward, nose to phallus, a detached nose with human consciousness and feeling. Gogol makes the uncanny so habitual that the nose, arrayed as it is in uniform, may strut about like any ordinary mortal and even have an argument with the baffled man who has lost it. The dreamlike quality of the story persists when Kovalyov meets up with the indifference to his fate of the clerk in the classified advertising department of the newspaper, the policeman from whom he solicits help, his servant, and even his physician.

Major Kovalyov was in the habit of taking a stroll on Nevsky Avenue every day. The collar of his shirt front was always extremely clean and well starched. His whiskers were such as one can still see nowadays on provincial district surveyors, architects, and army doctors, as well as on police officers performing various duties and, in general, on all gallant gentlemen who have full, ruddy cheeks and are very good at a game of boston: these whiskers go right across the middle of the cheek and straight up to the nose. Major Kovalyov wore a great number of cornelian seals, some with crests and others which had engraved on them: Wednesday, Thursday, Monday, and so on. Major Kovalyov came to Petersburg on business, to wit, to look for a post befitting his rank: if he were lucky, the post of a vice-governor, if not, one of an administrative clerk in some important department. Major Kovalyov was not averse to matrimony, either, but only if he could find a girl with a fortune of two hundred thousand. The reader can, therefore, judge for himself the state in which the major was when he saw, instead of a fairly handsome nose of moderate size, a most idiotic, flat, smooth place.

As misfortune would have it, there was not a single cab to be seen in the street and he had to walk, wrapping himself in his cloak and covering his face with a handkerchief, as though his nose were bleeding. "But perhaps I imagined it all," he thought. "It's impossible that I could have lost my nose without noticing it!" He went into a pastry cook's for the sole purpose of having a look at himself in a mirror. Fortunately, there was no one in the shop: the boys were sweeping the rooms and arranging the chairs; some of them, sleepy-eyed, were bringing in hot cream puffs on trays; yesterday's papers, stained with coffee, were lying about on tables and chairs. "Well, thank God, there's nobody here," he said. "Now I can have a look." He went timidly up to the mirror and looked. "Damn it," he said, disgusted, "the whole thing is too ridiculous for words! If only there'd be something instead of a nose, but there's just nothing!"

Biting his lips with vexation, Kovalyov went out of the pastry cook's and made up his mind, contrary to his usual practice, not to look or smile at anyone. Suddenly he stopped dead in his tracks at the front doors of a house; a most inexplicable thing happened before his very eyes: a carriage drew up before the entrance, the carriage door opened, and a gentleman in uniform jumped out and, stooping, rushed up the steps. Imagine the horror and, at the same time, amazement of Kovalyov when he recognised that this was his own nose! At this extraordinary sight everything went swimming before his eyes. He felt that he could hardly stand on his feet; but he made up his mind that, come what may, he would wait for the gentleman's return to the carriage. He was trembling all over as though in a fever. Two minutes later the nose really did come out. He wore a gold-embroidered uniform with a large stand-up collar, chamois-leather breeches, and a sword at his side. From his plumed hat it could be inferred that he was a State Councillor, a civil servant of the fifth rank. Everything showed that he was going somewhere to pay a visit. He looked round to the right and to the left, shouted to his driver, who had driven off a short distance, to come back, got into the carriage, and drove off.

Poor Kovalyov nearly went out of his mind [pp. 208-209].

* * *

"Excuse me, sir," he said at last with impatience, "it's very urgent...."

"Presently, presently," said the grey-haired gentleman, flinging their notes back to the old women and the house porters. "Two roubles forty copecks! One moment, sir! One rouble sixty-four copecks! What can I do for you?" he said at last, turning to Kovalyov.

"Thank you, sir," said Kovalyov. "You see, I've been robbed or swindled, I can't so far say which, but I should like you to put in an advertisement that anyone who brings the scoundrel to me will receive a handsome reward."

"What is your name, sir?"

"What do you want my name for? I'm sorry I can't give it to you. I have a large circle of friends: Mrs. Chekhtaryov, the widow of a State Councillor, Pelageya Grigoryevna Podtochin, the widow of a first lieutenant. . . . God forbid that they should suddenly find out! You can simply say: a Collegiate Assessor or, better still, a gentleman of the rank of major."

"And is the runaway your house serf?"

"My house serf? Good Lord, no! That wouldn't have been so bad! You see, it's my—er—nose that has run away from me. . . ."

"Dear me, what a strange name! And has this Mr. Nosov robbed you of a large sum of money?"

"I said nose, sir, nose! You're thinking of something else! It is my nose, my own nose that has disappeared I don't know where. The devil himself must have played a joke on me!"

"But how did it disappear? I'm afraid I don't quite understand it."

"I can't tell you how it happened. The worst of it is that now it is driving about all over the town under the guise of a State Councillor. That's why I should like you to insert an advertisement that anyone who catches him should bring him at once to me. You can see for yourself, sir, that I cannot possibly carry on without such a conspicuous part of myself. It's not like some little toe which no one can see whether it is missing or not once I'm wearing my boots. I call on Thursdays on Mrs. Chekhtaryov, the widow of a State Councillor. Mrs. Podtochin, the widow of a first lieutenant, and her pretty daughter are also good friends of mine, and you can judge for yourself the position I am in now. I can't go and see them now, can I?"

The clerk pursed his lips tightly which meant that he was thinking hard.

"I'm sorry sir," he said at last, after a long pause, "but I can't possibly insert such an advertisement in the papers."

"What? Why not?"

"Well, you see, sir, the paper might lose its reputation. If every-one were to write that his nose had run away, why — — As it is, people are already saying that we are publishing a lot of absurd stories and false rumours."

*   *   *

Having said this, he walked out of the newspaper office, greatly vexed, and went to see the police inspector of his district, a man who had a great liking for sugar. At his home, the entire hall, which was also the dining room, was stacked with sugar loaves with which local tradesmen had presented him out of friendship. When Kovalyov arrived, the police inspector's cook was helping him off with his regulation top boots; his sabre and the rest of his martial armour were already hung peaceably in the corners of the room, and his three-year-old son was playing with his awe-inspiring three-cornered hat. He himself was getting ready to partake of the pleasures of peace after his gallant, warlike exploits.

Kovalyov walked in at the time when he stretched, cleared his throat, and said: "Oh, for a couple of hours of sleep!" It could, therefore, be foreseen that the Collegiate Assessor could have hardly chosen a worse time to arrive; indeed, I am not sure whether he would not have got a more cordial reception even if he had brought the police inspector several pounds of sugar or a piece of cloth. The inspector was a great patron of the arts and manufactures, but he preferred a bank note to everything else. "This is something," he used to say. "There is nothing better than that: it doesn't ask for food, it doesn't take up a lot of space, there's always room for it in the pocket, and when you drop it, it doesn't break."

The inspector received Kovalyov rather coldly and said that after dinner was not the time to carry out investigations and that nature herself had fixed it so that after a good meal a man had to take a nap (from which the Collegiate Assessor could deduce that the inspector was not unfamiliar with the sayings of the ancient sages), and that a respectable man would not have his nose pulled off.

A bull's eye!... It must be observed that Kovalyov was extremely quick to take offence. He could forgive anything people said about himself, but he could never forgive an insult to his rank or his calling. He was even of the opinion that any reference in plays to army officers or civil servants of low rank was admissible, but that the censorship ought not to pass any attack on persons of higher rank. The reception given him by the police inspector disconcerted him so much that he tossed his head and said with an air of dignity, with his hands slightly parted in a gesture of surprise: "I must say that after such offensive remarks, I have nothing more to say...." and went out.

He arrived home hardly able to stand on his feet. By now it was dusk. After all these unsuccessful quests his rooms looked melancholy or rather extremely disgusting to him. On entering the hall, he saw his valet Ivan lying on his back on the dirty leather sofa and spitting on the ceiling and rather successfully aiming at the same spot. Such an indifference on the part of his servant maddened him; he hit him on the forehead with his hat, saying: "You pig, you're always doing something stupid!"

Ivan jumped up and rushed to help him off with his cloak.

On entering his room, the major, tired and dejected, threw himself into an armchair and, at last, after several sighs, said:

"Lord, oh Lord, why should I have such bad luck? If I had lost an arm or a leg, it would not be so bad; if I had lost my ears, it would be bad enough, but still bearable; but without a nose a man is goodness knows what, neither fish, nor flesh, nor good red herring—he isn't a respectable citizen at all! He is simply something to take and chuck out of the window! If I had had it cut off in battle in a duel or had been the cause of its loss myself, but to loose it without any reason whatever, for nothing, for absolutely nothing!... But no," he added after a brief reflection, "it can't be. It's inconceivable that a nose should be lost, absolutely inconceivable. I must be simply dreaming or just imagining it all. Perhaps by some mistake I drank, instead of water, the spirits which I rub on my face after shaving. Ivan, the blithering fool, did not take it away and I must have swallowed it by mistake."

To convince himself that he was not drunk, the major pinched himself so painfully that he cried out. The pain completely convinced him that he was fully awake and that everything had actually happened to him. He went up slowly to the looking glass and at first screwed up his eyes with the idea that perhaps he would see his nose in its proper place; but almost at the same moment he jumped back, saying: "What a horrible sight!"

*　　　*　　　*

Meanwhile the rumours about this extraordinary affair spread all over town and, as usually happens, not without all sorts of embellishments. At that time people's minds were particularly susceptible to anything of an extraordinary nature: only a short time before everybody had shown a great interest in the experiments of magnetism. Besides, the story of the dancing chairs in Konyushennaya Street was still fresh in people's minds, and it is therefore not surprising that people soon began talking about the Collegiate Assessor Kovalyov's nose which, it was alleged, was taking a walk on Nevsky Avenue at precisely three o'clock in the afternoon. Thousands of curious people thronged Nevsky Avenue every day [pp. 215-227, *passim*].

Schnitzler's novella, *Fräulein Else* (1924), is one of the earliest examples of the stream of consciousness techniques in German. Schnitzler was a physician as well as a novelist and playwright, anticipating much of Freud's work in his artistic creations, as Freud (1906, 1922) himself acknowledged. In the novel, Else, a narcissistic, nineteen-year-old girl with unresolved oedipal feelings, is unequipped to adjust to any disturbance of her precarious equilibrium. Her lawyer father had embezzled a trust fund; he had been in similar difficulties before, when his relatives bailed him out, but this they refuse to do again. In desperation, the mother writes to ask Else to beg an art-dealer acquaintance, a Herr von Dorsday, for help in making restitution of the stolen 30,000 gulden, thus avoiding a scandalous trial and jail sentence for her father. Von Dorsday agrees—on one condition: Else is to let him see her in the nude for fifteen minutes either in his hotel room or in a starlit clearing in the nearby woods. "Why do I let him go on?" Else cries impatiently. She actually has to display herself to the repellent voyeur because although the act is consciously abhorrent to her, her latent, unconscious exhibitionism gets the better of her; further, Dorsday is the potential savior of Else and her family (Bareikis, 1969).

Her latent exhibitionism is demonstrated almost from the first page of the novel. In the interior monologue, Fräulein Else is a creature of the moment's grace. Everything takes place on a narrow stage where the inner life is revealed by the outward behavior, the suprapersonal by personal impulses, half-conscious states of feeling crystallized as strange consequences of fleeting events. "I think I'll turn around again and wave to them [Else says to herself]. Wave to them and smile. Now, don't I look gracious?" (p. 4). Her sexual fantasies are grandiose display fantasies: "I'd rather like to be married in America, but not to an American, or perhaps it would be pleasant to marry an American and then live in Europe. A villa on the Riviera with marble steps going into the sea" (p. 5). And, "I'll have a hundred lovers, a thousand; why not? Is the décolleté deep enough?" (p. 30). "Why do I smile at him so coquettishly? I don't mean it for him at all. Dorsday's leering at me" (p. 42). "Six o'clock in the morning, on the balcony, my proud Fräulein Else. Perhaps you didn't notice the two young people in a boat who were staring at you. Of course they couldn't identify my face at that distance, but they couldn't help noticing that I was in negligee. And it made me happy. Oh, more than happy. It was intoxicating. I drew my hands across my hips and acted as though I didn't know that anyone saw me — and the boat didn't move from that spot. Yes — I'm like that. Indeed I am. I'm a hussy" (p. 67).

Her display fantasies become imbued with a phallic, suicidal ideational martyrdom:

Who'll cry when I'm dead? Oh, how beautiful it would be to be dead! I lie on a bier in a salon, with candles burning. Long candles. Twelve long candles. The hearse is already downstairs. People are standing at the gate. How old was she? Only nineteen. Really only nineteen? — Think of it, her father in jail. Why did she kill herself? Because she loved a Filou [sheik] in vain. But what are you talking about? She was to have had a child. No; she fell from the Cimone. It's supposed to have been an accident. Good day, Herr von Dorsday. You too pay your last respects to little Else. Little Else, the old woman says. — Why? Certainly; I must pay my last respects. Wasn't I the first one to disgrace her? Oh, it was worth the trouble, Frau Winawer. I've never seen such a beautiful body. It cost me only thirty million. A Rubens costs three times as much. She poisoned herself with hashish. She merely longed for beautiful visions, but she took too much and never awoke. Why is Herr von Dorsday wearing a red monocle? At whom is he waving that handkerchief? Mother comes down the steps and kisses his hand. Terrible, terrible. Now they whisper to each other. I can't understand a word, because I'm on a bier. . . . Father'll be glad that I'm not buried. I'm not afraid of snakes. If only my foot isn't bitten by one. Oh, dear! [pp. 75-76, 78].

Her exhibitionist fantasies continue: "I must look very pretty in this wide landscape. Too bad there aren't more people in the clearing. Obviously I'm attractive to the gentleman out there near the edge of the wood. Oh, my dear sir, I'm even more beautiful naked..." (p. 65). "I'd like to lie alone by the sea on the marble steps and wait, and at last a man would come, or several men, and I'd choose one, and the others whom I'd reject would throw themselves despairingly into the sea. Or they'd have to be patient, until the next day. Oh, what a marvelous life that would be! Why have I my glorious shoulders and my beautiful slender legs, and for what reason, after all, do I exist?" (pp. 81-82). "He could do everything he wanted tonight. But not Dorsday. Not Dorsday! Not Dorsday! How his eyes will stab and drill their way into me. He'll stand there with his monocle and leer ... If only someone else were present. Why not? He didn't stipulate that he had to be alone with me. Oh, Herr von Dorsday, I'm so afraid of you. Won't you please do me the favor of bringing some mutual acquaintance with you? Oh, that's not at all contrary to our agreement, Herr von Dorsday. If I felt like it, I could invite the whole hotel and you'd still be bound to send the thirty thousand gulden..." (pp. 86-87). Soon afterward, her fragile equilibrium decompensates and Else acts out her fantasy.

> I can be over there where there are no aunts and no Dorsday and no father who embezzles trust funds....
> But I won't kill myself. That isn't at all necessary. And I won't visit Herr von Dorsday in his room. I wouldn't think of it. I'm blessed if for fifty thousand gulden I'll stand naked in front of an old roué just to save a good-for-nothing from jail. No, no—not in any case. How does Herr von Dorsday come into the picture? Must it be Herr von Dorsday? If one sees me, others shall see me. Yes! Wonderful idea! Everybody shall see me. The whole world shall see me—and then comes the veronal. No, not the veronal. What for? Next will come the villa with the marble steps and the handsome youths and freedom and the wide world. Good evening, Fräulein Else, I like you this way. Haha, down there you'll all think that I've gone mad. But I've never been sensible. For the first time in my life I'm really sensible. Everybody, all of them shall see me!—After that, there's no return. No return home to Father and Mother or uncles and aunts. Then I'll no longer be the Fräulein Else, who can be married off to any old Director Wilomitzer. I'll make fools of them all—especially that rotter Dorsday—and come into the world for a second time....
> Otherwise everything is useless—address remains Fiala. Haha!
> No more time to lose. Don't become cowardly again. Off with the dress. Who'll be the first? Will it be you, Cousin Paul? Your luck,

that the Roman head isn't here any more. Oh, how beautiful I am! Bertha has a black silk chemise. Refined. I'll be much more refined. Wonderful life. Off with the stockings. They'd be indecent. Naked, altogether naked. How Cissy will envy me. And others, too. But they don't dare. They'd all like to—so much. Take me as an example, all of you. I, the virgin, I dare. I'll laugh myself to death over Dorsday. Here I am, Herr Dorsday. Quick—to the post-office. Fifty thousand. Isn't it worth that much?

Beautiful, I'm beautiful! Look at me, Night! Mountains, look at me! Sky, look at me—how beautiful I am. But you are all blind. What are you to me? The people downstairs have eyes. Shall I loose my hair? No, I'd look like a madwoman. But you shan't think me mad. You're only to think me shameless. Canaille. Where's the telegram? For Heaven's sake, where have I left the telegram? There it is lying peacefully beside the veronal. "Repeat urgently—fifty thousand—otherwise everything useless. Address remains Fiala." Yes, that's the telegram. That's a piece of paper, and there are words on it. Despatched in Vienna at four-thirty. No; I'm not dreaming. It's all true, and at home they're all waiting for fifty thousand gulden, and Herr von Dorsday is waiting, too. Let him wait. There's plenty of time. Oh, how pleasant it is to walk up and down the room, naked. Am I really as beautiful as I look in that mirror? Oh, won't you come closer, pretty Fräulein? I want to kiss your blood-red lips. What a pity that the mirror comes between us. The cold mirror. How well we'd get on together. Isn't that so? We need nobody else. Perhaps there are no other people. There are telegrams and hotels and mountains and railroad stations and woods, but there are no people. We merely dream of them. Only Dr. Fiala exists—and his address. It always remains the same. Oh, I'm not at all mad. I'm only a little excited. That's quite natural when one is about to come into the world for a second time. For the Else that once existed is now dead. Yes, most certainly I'm dead. The veronal isn't necessary. Shouldn't I pour it out? The chambermaid might drink it by mistake. I'll leave a slip of paper there, and write on it: Poison: No—better: Medicine. So that nothing will happen to the chambermaid. I'm so noble! So.

*   *   *

What do you want, Herr von Dorsday? You look at me as though I were your slave. I'm not your slave. Fifty thousand! Does our agreement still hold, Herr von Dorsday? I'm ready. Here I am. I'm quite calm. I'm smiling. You understand my look? His eyes say to me: come! His eyes say: I want to see you naked. Well, you swine, I *am* naked. What more do you want? Send the message . . . immediately. Chills are running up and down my spine. She's playing on. How wonderful it is to be naked. Chills are running up and down my spine. She's playing on. She doesn't realize what's happening here. Nobody realizes it. No one sees me yet. Filou! Filou! Here I'm standing naked! Dorsday opens his eyes wide. At last he believes it. The Filou gets up. His eyes are glowing. You understand me, beautiful youth. "Ha, ha." The lady is playing no more. Father is saved. Fifty thousand! Address remains Fiala! "Ha, ha, ha!" Who's laughing there? Am I laughing? "Ha, ha, ha!" What are all those faces around me? "Ha, ha, ha!" How stupid of me to laugh. "Ha, ha, ha." I don't want to laugh — I don't want to. "Ha, ha!" — *"Else!"* — Who's calling Else? That's Paul. He must be behind me. I feel his breath on my bare back. My ears are ringing. Perhaps I'm already dead. What do you wish, Herr von Dorsday? Why are you so enormous, and why are you staggering towards me? "Ha, ha, ha!"

Now what have I done? What have I done? What have I done? I'm falling. All is over. Why has the music stopped? An arm is supporting my back. That's Paul. Where's the Filou? I'm lying here. "Ha, ha, ha!" The coat's thrown over me and I'm lying here. The people think me unconscious. No, I'm not unconscious. I'm in all my senses. I'm a hundred times awake, a thousand times awake. Only, I always have to laugh. "Ha, ha, ha!" Now you have your wish, Herr von Dorsday. You must send the money to Father, immediately. "Haaaaah!" I don't want to cry out and I always have to cry out. Why must I cry out? — My eyes are closed. No one can see me. Father is saved. — *"Else!"* [pp. 177-189, *passim*].

Else's exhibitionism, latent and overt, is inseparable from her narcissism, typical of the dynamics of exhibitionism which is "more narcissistic than any other partial instinct. Its erogenous pleasure is always connected with an increase in self-esteem, anticipated or actually gained through the fact that others look at the subject" (Fenichel, 1945, p. 72). Her death wishes are associated with unmistakable repressed libidinal desires that find expression in pleasurable sexual fantasies. "How would you like it, Father," (Else luridly fantasies), "if I auctioned myself off this evening just to save you from prison. It would make a sensation!" While her superego prevents any overt incestuous act, she can sublimate her need by exhibiting herself to Herr von Dorsday, "If one sees me, others shall see me. Yes. Wonderful idea. Everybody shall see me. The whole world shall see me — and then comes the veronal." Thus Else could satisfy both id and superego: her oedipal wish is resolved and she can then embrace death as a forfeit. For Dorsday is a father surrogate, and Else's hidden libidinal aim is conflated with the idea of death.

The fantasy of being seen naked by the "whole world" of men is a relatively common one. In Shelley List's *Did You Love Daddy When I Was Born?* (1972), Rachel, while in the throes of getting a divorce from her adulterous husband, was having an affair with John. "Another problem was that [Rachel] was absolutely in heat all the time. John had awakened in her a sensuality and sensitivity to her own sex that now permeated her days. She couldn't stand his having another woman. Even though whenever Rachel saw John she wanted to fly into bed with him, she retreated and became sullen because she was controlling her rage . . . He tired of her demands and berated her. She in turn became tired of watching her words in case she would be called spoiled or a brat or middle-class Jewish or selfish. She decided that she wanted hundreds of men leering at her rather than this one painful man" (p. 123).

Voyeuristic activity, like many other forms of sexual behavior, has significance in the sociocultural dimension as well as the psychological. Society designates voyeurism, as it does exhibitionism, illegal. The exposure of one's person or private parts to excite sexual interest in an otherwise uninterested person is a nuisance and violates the general taboo against flagrant or open sexual behavior (Wortis, 1939, p. 557): "By the same token, the occasional Peeping Tom is frequently regarded as no more than a distraction. Thus, normality in voyeurism is strongly colored by the acceptance of the individual, the interpersonal context of the act, and the culture in which the activity occurs. There is also a quantitative aspect of the normality of this mode of sexual behavior. If driven or compelled toward voyeurism as the only means of sexual gratification, the behavior is termed deviant."

The child is curious about sex, wondering especially about parental sexual activity. Various events, such as observing parental intercourse, seeing parents or siblings naked, or "playing doctor," serve as a starting point for voyeurism in some children. In the case of adolescents, arousal by perceptions of sexually related visual stimuli is common.

With the libidinal surge in adolescence, and with limited opportunities or know-how to release sexual drive, opportunities for voyeuristic activity are not to be missed.

Almost every novel dealing with adolescence, it would seem, has some passage in it relevant to peeping. In the Chinese novel, *The Adventurous History of Hsi Men and His Six Wives,* ascribed to Chin P'ing Mei (1609), the seventeen-year-old Pear Blossom spies on her mistress, Lady Hua, and her lover.

> Lady Hua had carefully shut the parchment-covered double window in order to elude any possible curious glances from outside. But she had not reckoned with the artfulness of her maid, Pear Blossom. This inquisitive, seventeen-year-old creature could not refrain from sneaking up under the windowsill, and, with a hairpin, boring a peephole through the twofold pane of parchment. And now she perceived, in the light of the lamp and the tapers, a something that outlined itself on the bed hangings like the shadow of a great, queerly-shaped, struggling fish. Then that queer being came to rest; it split into two halves... [p. 172].

Four hundred years later, novelists are still pursuing the theme of the adolescent as voyeur. Joyce did it in 1918 in his *Ulysses,* where Molly Bloom soliloquizes, ".... theres the mark of his teeth still where he tried to bite the nipple I had to scream out arent they fearful trying to hurt you I had a great breast of milk with Milly enough for two what was the reason of that he said I could get a pound a week as a wet nurse all swelled up in No 28 with the Citrons Penrose nearly caught me washing through the window only for I snapped up the towel to my face that was his studenting hurt me..." (p. 739). And demonstrating the complementary quality of exhibitionism and voyeurism, Molly says, "... standing at the fire with the little bit of a short shift I had up to heat myself I loved dancing about in it then make a race back into bed Im sure that fellow opposite used to be there the whole time watching with the lights out in the summer and I in my skin hopping around I used to love myself then stripped at the washstand dabbing and creaming only when it came to the chamber performance I put out the light too so then there were 2 of us..." (pp. 748-749).

An eighteen-year-old in Jim Harrison's *Wolf. A False Memoir* (1971) was full of fantasies of sex and grandeur. He lived in a small room in the Bronx spending "a lot of time with the lights out trying to get a peek at a naked woman across the alley but everyone's shades were drawn and most of the women I had seen on the streets I didn't want to see naked" (p. 182). One of the hilarious episodes of adolescent peeping tomism is found in Alan Friedman's *Hermaphrodeity* (1971, pp. 53-57), where the Rattlers would venture on long peeping-tomcat expeditions, skulking about for hours on the rooftops, scouting houses for the most promising lights. In order to achieve more satisfying rewards, the gang determined to put a hole through the wall of the girls' shower room in their high school, which they did, only to be frustrated anew because the angle of vision through their peephole never reached higher than the girl's shoulders and usually only to the navel. The protagonist lamented, "Dante, I later read, speaks of love first entering through the eyes. But that sex should enter through the eyes and from there pull the bodily strings and make that little naked unseen puppet rise and dance before its mistress seemed an unworthy image for poetry and a low image of life" (p. 56).

Another mode of "normal" voyeuristic activity has become legitimized and institutionalized in the image of the private detective of popular mystery stories—the "private eye." The hero detective in *The French Connection,* who drives wildly through Brooklyn streets in pursuit of an elevated train hijacked by a narcotics suspect, is called Popeye Doyle. Some self-indulgent fun on the theme of the private eye is found in this passage from the suggestively titled detective story, *The Lady Is Transparent* by Carter Brown (1962).

It was around four in the afternoon when I parked the Healey on the driveway of the Farrow house. All trace of the storm had long vanished, along with the witches, I guessed, and the sun shone fiercely from a cloudless blue sky. It was the kind of day that even the native Californians don't really believe in.

The Farrow estate—in contrast to the Harveys'—was kept in immaculate condition. Trim green lawns ran off in all directions, neatly dotted with carefully shaped flower-beds where all the flowers grew strictly to attention. The house itself was a rambling structure, maybe fifty years old, but it gleamed from the obvious, and lavish, application of care and money.

Instead of a barred peephole, there was a generous panel of clear plate glass cut into the front door, and I figured the Farrows must be open-minded people. With one finger poised on the buzzer, I suddenly had a startling firsthand confirmation of the Farrows' freewheeling approach to life.

Through the plate-glass panel I saw a girl appear at the far end of the hallway, then slowly saunter toward the front door. Either she was just out of the bath or the house was hot—I didn't care much either way. It's not very often a lieutenant, strictly in the line of duty, gets to see a stark-naked redhead walking toward him, idly trailing a robe from one hand. Like an idiot, I forgot to remove my finger from the buzzer and the next moment it squawked loudly.

The redhead reacted like it was the Doomsday Bell, going about a foot straight up into the air, then wrapping the robe around her body at the speed of light. By the time her feet touched down again, she was demurely swaddled from neck to knee in a thick toweling robe. I wondered bitterly if the curse of the Harveys had transferred itself into the curse of the Wheelers.

Then the door opened suddenly and I got the full arctic blast of her frigid glance. "I hate snoopers!" she said passionately. "Dirty, furtive little men who peer in through windows and doors, with their hot piggy eyes feeding the rotting garbage inside their minds!"

"I am not little," I said coldly.

"Whatever you're selling, we don't want any," she continued at full blast. "You can get off this estate before I have you thrown off! If there's anything I despise it's a foul-minded little—"

"Shut up!" I snarled.

Her eyes widened incredulously. "You can't—"

"Sure, I can!" I grated. "You should remember what they say about people who live in houses with plate-glass panels cut into their front doors—they should wear clothes when they walk down the hallway. I only got the merest glimpse, anyway, nothing beyond a swift guess of 37-23-38."

"38-23-37," she said slowly.

"And I think that little mole—right where it is—is real cute," I added warmly.

The flame-colored hair that was piled into a cone on top of her head teetered alarmingly. "Who are you?" she asked in a breathless voice. "I just changed my mind—I could buy some of whatever it is."

"Lieutenant Wheeler—from the sheriff's office." I told her. "I wanted to talk to George Farrow, but somehow it doesn't seem important any more."

"You—a police officer?" Her green eyes had a stunned look.

"It's not that wild a thought, is it?" I grunted.
"And I thought you were a peeper." She gurgled with laughter.
"I guess I was half right, you're a legal-peeper!" [pp. 52-53].

A deviant kind of voyeuristic activity is pictured in William Faulkner's *Sanctuary* (1931). Popeye, the impotent voyeur with the absurd and moronic stare his name implies, crouches at the foot of the bed in Madame Reba's whorehouse watching Temple and Red have intercourse. He is the avatar of the helpless and fascinated voyeur before the fact of genital love. In this episode, Temple Drake, the nineteen-year-old provocative virgin, raped by Popeye with a corncob, had been brought by him to the brothel to recover from hemorraghing. In an abortive attempt to escape, Temple phoned Red to rescue her, but Popeye had been spying on her and foiled the plan.

"He's a better man that you are!" Temple said shrilly. "You're not even a man. He knows it. Who does know it if he don't?" She began to shriek at him. "You, a man, a bold bad man, when you can't even—When you have to bring a real man in to—And you hanging over the bed, moaning and slobbering like a—You couldn't fool me once, could you? No wonder I bled and bhul—" his hand came over her mouth, hard, his nails going into her flesh. . . .
"You hurt my mouth," she said in a voice small and faint with self-pity. . . "You'll be sorry for this," she said in a muffled voice. "When I tell Red. Don't you wish you were Red? Don't you wish you could do what he can do? Don't you wish he was the one watching us instead of you?" [pp. 131-132].

Shortly thereafter, Popeye guns Red down in cold blood, ambushing him while he is climbing a drainpipe to Temple's room. At Red's wake, some of the prostitutes recount what happened, and Madame Reba Rivers declares:

". . . me trying to get word to [Popeye] to come and take her out of my house because I didn't want nothing like that going on in it. Yes, sir, Minnie said the two of them would be nekkid as snakes, and Popeye hanging over the foot of the bed without even his hat off, making a kind of whinnying sound."

"Maybe he was cheering for them," Miss Lorraine said. "The lousy son of a bitch" [p. 147].

In *The Tight White Collar* by Grace Metalious (1961), Mr. Justine would tell Doris, his Irish maid, to lie naked on the bed so that he could gloat over her. "She made her body curve, so that one hip was thrust higher than the other and when she looked at Theo, he had moved his hands from the door panels and was holding his groin. Doris sighed deeply and moved a little on the bed and with a gigantic breath that was almost a sob, Theo Justine reached his climax and it was over" (p. 84). In addition to their voyeuristic needs, men like Popeye, Theo Justine, and the protagonist in Junichirō Tanizaki's (1961) *The Key*, can unconsciously gratify other impulses. They may identify the other man as the father and find satisfaction in observing how he performs sexually. Intellectually they know "what daddy does," but anxiety about their own sexual competence compared to the father substitute forces them to repeat the experience again and again. Sometimes the husband unconsciously identifies with the female and can gratify his homosexual needs without recognizing their existence. The wife may accede through fear, coercion, or to appease the husband, or because it also gratifies some of her unconscious needs. "It may provide reassurance of her desirability to have two men seek her sexually. It may represent being in control of the situation or a masochistic need to be degraded. While a woman may engage in such [practices] once or twice as an expression of her curiosity and desire for new experiences or thrills, her continued participation indicates she has her own emotional problems" (Auerbach, 1970, p. 69). Whenever people engage in such unusual sexual activity compulsively, on a continuing basis, their behavior is not related to sexual needs but represents an attempt to solve deep-seated personal problems.

In Tanizaki's *The Key*, the husband and wife, Ikuko, each keep a secret diary. At fifty-five, with declining potency, he cannot satisfy Ikuko, although his sexual appetite is still strong. He finds his sexual impulses quickened by feasting his eyes on his wife's nakedness while she is in an alcohol-induced sleep and taking Polaroid photographs of her while in this state. He thrusts Kimura, a mutual friend, on his wife to become her lover so that he might watch them in congress. "These things are driving me beyond self-control, driving me to madness. Now

I am the unsatiable one. Night after night I immerse myself in un-dreamed ecstasies" (p. 67). Like many voyeurs, he develops double vision, slight amnesia, castration anxiety, and an assortment of so-matic symptoms.

A certain plan had been taking shape in my mind for a long time, and I needed privacy to carry it out . . . I went over and took Ikuko's pulse. It was normal: the Vitacamphor seemed to have worked. As far as I could tell, she was in a deep slumber. Of course she may have been only shamming. But that needn't hinder me, I thought.

I began by firing the stove up even hotter, till it was roaring. Then I slowly drew off the black cloth that I had draped over the shade of the floor lamp. Stealthily I moved the lamp to my wife's bedside, placing it so that she was lying within its circle of light. I felt my heart pound. I was excited to think that what I had so long dreamed of was about to be realized.

Next, I quietly went upstairs to get the fluorescent lamp from my study, brought it back, and put it on the night table. This was by no means a sudden whim. Last fall I replaced my old desk lamp with a fluorescent one, because I foresaw that I might sooner or later have a chance like this. Toshiko and my wife were opposed to it at the time, saying it would affect the radio; but I told them that my eyesight was weakening and the old lamp was hard to read by—which was quite true. However, my real reason was a desire to see Ikuko's naked body in that white radiance. That had been my fantasy ever since I had first heard of fluorescent lighting.

Everything went as I had hoped. I took away her covers, carefully slipped her thin nightgown off, and turned her on her back. She lay there completely naked, exposed to the daylight brilliance of the two lamps. Then I began to study her in detail, as if I were studying a map. For a while, as I gazed on that beautiful, milk-white body, I felt bewildered. It was the first time I had ever had an unimpeded view of her in the nude.

I suppose the average husband is familiar with all the details of his wife's body, down to the very wrinkles on the soles of her feet. But Ikuko has never let me examine her that way. Of course in love-making I have had certain opportunities—but never below the waist, never more than she had to let me see. Only by touch have I been able to picture to myself the beauty of her body, which is why I wanted so desperately to look at her under that brilliant light. And what I saw far exceeded my expectations.

For the first time I was able to enjoy a full view of her, able to explore all her long-hidden secrets.

*   *   *

What surpassed anything I had imagined was the utter purity of her skin. Most people have at least a minor flaw, some kind of dark spot, a birthmark, mole, or the like; but although I searched her body with the must scrupulous care, I could find no blemish. I turned her face down, and even peered into the hollow where the white flesh of her buttocks swelled up on either side. . . . How extraordinary for a woman to have reached the age of forty-four, and to have experienced childbirth, without suffering the slightest injury to her skin! Never before had I been allowed to gaze at this superb body, but perhaps that is just as well. To be startled, after more than twenty years together, by a first awareness of the physical beauty of one's own wife—that, surely, is to begin a new marriage. We have long since passed the stage of disillusionment, and now I can love her with twice the passion I used to have.

I turned her on her back once again. For a while I stood there, devouring her with my eyes. Suddenly it appeared to me that she was only pretending to be asleep. She had been asleep at first, but had awakened; then, shocked and horrified at what was going on, she had tried to conceal her embarrassment by shamming. . . . Perhaps it was merely my own fantasy, but I wanted to believe it. I was captivated by the idea that this exquisite, fair-skinned body, which I could manipulate as boldly as if it were lifeless, was very much alive, was conscious of everything I did. But suppose that she really *was* asleep—isn't it dangerous for me to write about how I indulged myself with her? I can scarcely doubt that she reads this diary, in which case my revelations may make her decide to stop drinking. . . . No, I don't think so; stopping would confirm that she *does* read it. Otherwise she wouldn't have known what went on while she was unconscious.

For over an hour, beginning at three o'clock, I steeped myself in the pleasure of looking at her. Of course that wasn't all I did. I wanted to find out how far she would let me go, if she were only pretending to be asleep. And I wanted to embarrass her to the point that she would have to continue her pretense to the very end. One by one I tried all the sexual vagaries that she so much loathes—all the tricks that she calls annoying, disgusting, shameful. At last I fulfilled my desire to lavish caresses with my tongue, as freely as I liked, on those beautiful feet. I tried everything I could imagine — things, to use her words, "too shameful to mention" [pp. 27-31].

TECHNICAL REFERENCES

Abraham, K. (1913), Restrictions and transformations of scoptophilia in psycho-neurotics. In: *Selected Papers*. New York: Basic Books, 1953, pp. 169-234.

—— (1917), Ejaculatio praecox. In: *Selected Papers*. New York: Basic Books, 1953, pp. 280-302.

Auerbach, A. (1970), Voyeuristic need. *Medical Aspects of Human Sexuality*, 4(2):69.

Bareikis, R. (1969), Arthur Schnitzler's *Fräulein Else:* A Freudian novella? *Literature and Psychology*, 19(1):19-32.

Barrett, W. G. (1955), On the naming of Tom Sawyer. *Psychoanalytic Quarterly*, 24:424-436.

Baumbach, J. (1963), Nightmare of a native son: *Invisible Man,* by Ralph Ellison. In: *Five Black Writers,* ed. D. B. Gibson. New York: New York University Press, 1970, pp. 73-87.

Bergler, E. (1944), On a clinical approach to the psychoanalysis of writers. *Psychoanalytic Review,* 31:40-70.

—— (1947), Psychoanalysis of writers and literary productivity. In: *Psychoanalysis and the Social Sciences,* 1, ed. G. Róheim. New York: International Universities Press, pp. 247-296.

—— (1955), Unconscious mechanisms in "writer's block." *Psychoanalytic Review,* 42:160-162.

Bloch, A. (1966), Sight imagery in *Invisible Man. English Journal,* 55:1019-1024.

Bone, R. (1958), *The Negro Novel in America.* New Haven: Yale University Press, 1968.

Bowman, K. M. (1951), The problem of the sex offender. *American Journal of Psychiatry,* 108:250-257.

Christoffel, H. (1936), Exhibitionism and exhibitionists. *International Journal of Psycho-Analysis,* 17:321-345.

—— (1956), Male genital exhibitionism. In: *Perversions: Psychodynamics and Therapy,* ed. S. Lorand & M. Balint. New York: Random House, pp. 243-264.

Ellis, H. (1906), *Studies in the Psychology of Sex,* 3. New York: Random House, 1942.

English, O. S. & Finch, S. M. (1942), *Introduction to Psychiatry.* New York: Norton, 1964.

Fenichel, O. (1945), *The Psychoanalytic Theory of Neurosis.* New York: Norton.

Ferenczi, S. (1913), On eye-symbolism. In: *Sex in Psycho-Analysis*. New York: Basic Books, 1950, pp. 270-276.

———— (1928), Gulliver phantasies. In: *Final Contributions to the Problems and Methods of Psychoanalysis*. New York: Basic Books, 1952, pp. 41-60.

Freedman, P. (1951), The nose. *American Imago*, 8:337-350.

Freud, S. (1905), Three essays on the theory of sexuality. *Standard Edition*, 7:125-243. London: Hogarth Press, 1953.

———— (1906, 1922), *Letters of Sigmund Freud*. New York: Basic Books, 1960, letters 123 and 197.

———— (1922), Medusa's head. *Standard Edition*, 18:273-274. London: Hogarth Press, 1955.

Friedman, P. (1959), Sexual deviations. In: *American Handbook of Psychiatry*, 1, ed. S. Arieti. New York: Basic Books, pp. 599-600.

Glover, E. (1960), *The Roots of Crime: Selected Papers on Psycho-Analysis*, 2. New York: International Universities Press.

Greenacre, P. (1955), *Swift and Carroll: A Psychoanalytic Study of Two Lives*. New York: International Universities Press.

Guttmann, O. (1953), Exhibitionism: A contribution to sexual psychopathology on twelve cases of exhibitionism. *Journal of Clinical and Experimental Psychopathology*, 14:13-51.

Horowitz, E. (1964), The rebirth of the artist. In: *On Contemporary Literature*, ed. R. Kostelanetz. New York: Avon, pp. 330-346.

Kanzer, M. (1955), Gogol—A study on wit and paranoia. *Journal of the American Psychoanalytic Association*, 3:110-125.

Karpman, B. (1926), The psychopathology of exhibitionism. *Psychoanalytic Review*, 13:63-97.

Klein, M. (1964), Ralph Ellison's *Invisible Man*. In: *Images of the Negro in American Literature*, ed. S. L. Gross & J. E. Hardy. Chicago: University of Chicago Press, 1966, pp. 249-264.

Kostelanetz, R. (1967), The politics of Ellison's Booker: *Invisible Man* as symbolic history. *Chicago Review*, 19(2):5-26.

Krafft-Ebing, R. von (1912), *Psychopathia Sexualis*. New York: Pioneer, 1947.

Lasègue, E. C. (1877), Les exhibitionistes. *L'Union Médicale*, 23:703.

Maslow, A. H. & Mittelman, B. (1951), *Principles of Abnormal Psychology*. New York: Harper.

Masters, R. E. L. (1962), *Forbidden Sexual Behavior and Morality*. New York: Julian Press.

Mathis, J. L. (1969), The exhibitionist. *Medical Aspects of Human Sexuality*, 3(6): 89-101.

Mohr, J. W., Turner, R. E. & Jerry, M. B. (1964), *Pedophilia and Exhibitionism: A Handbook*. Toronto: University of Toronto Press.

Nagel, T. (1971), Sexual perversion. In: *The New Eroticism*, ed. P. Nobile. New York: Random House, pp. 46-63.

Rank, O. (1913), Nakedness in saga and poetry. Abstracted in *Psychoanalytic Review*, 4:444, 1917.

Reitz, W. E. & Keil, W. E. (1971), Behavioral treatment of the exhibitionist. *Journal of Behavior Therapy and Experimental Psychiatry*, 2:67-69.

Rickles, N. K. (1955), Exhibitionism. *Journal of Social Therapy*, 1:168-181.

Sperling, M. (1947), The analysis of an exhibitionist. *International Journal of Psycho-Analysis*, 28:32-45.

Springmann, R. R. (1970), What he is or what he does. *International Journal of Psycho-Analysis*, 51:479-488.

Stekel, W. (1952), *Patterns of Psychosexual Infantilism*. New York: Liveright.

Theophrastus (319 B.C.), *The Characters*. New York: Putnam's, 1929.

Vasquez, J. (1970), Voyeurisme et photophobie: Un cas clinique. *Interprétation*, 4(1/2):165-186.

Wortis, J. (1939), Sex taboo, sex offenders and the law. *American Journal of Orthopsychiatry*, 9:554-564.

LITERARY REFERENCES

Apocrypha. Daniel and Susanna. New York: Oxford University Press, 1970.

Brown, Carter (1962), *The Lady Is Transparent*. New York: New American Library.

Carroll, Lewis (1865), *Alice in Wonderland*. New York: Norton, 1971.

Chin P'ing Mei (1609), *The Adventurous History of Hsi Men and His Six Wives*. New York: Putnam's, 1940.

Chaucer, Geoffrey (1388), The parson's tale. In: *The Canterbury Tales*. Chicago: Encyclopedia Britannica, 1952.

Ellison, Ralph (1947), *Invisible Man*. New York: Random House, 1952.

Faulkner, William (1931), *Sanctuary*. New York: Random House.

Friedman, Alan (1972), *Hermaphrodeity*. New York: Knopf.

Garrett, Robert, (1972), *Run Down. The World of Alan Brett*. New York: Atheneum.

Gogol, Nikolai (1836), The nose. In: *Tales of Good and Evil*. New York: Norton, 1965, pp. 208-221.

Gould, Lois (1970), *Such Good Friends*. New York: Random House.

Harrison, Jim (1971), *Wolf. A False Memoir*. New York: Simon & Schuster.

Hawthorne, Nathaniel (1852), *The Blithedale Romance*. New York: Modern Library, 1947.

Jong, Erica (1973), *Fear of Flying*. New York: Holt, Rinehart & Winston.

Joyce, James (1918), *Ulysses*. New York: Random House, 1934.

List, Shelley S. (1972), *Did You Love Daddy When I Was Born?* New York: Saturday Review Press.

Martini, Virgilio (1936), *The World Without Women*. New York: Dial.

Metalious, Grace (1961), *The Tight White Collar*. New York: Messner.

Poe, Edgar Allan (1835), Some passages in the life of a lion. In: *The Complete Works of Edgar Allan Poe*, Vol. II, ed. J. A. Harrison. New York: Ames Press, 1965, pp. 323-328.

Schnitzler, Arthur (1924), *Fräulein Else*. In: *Viennese Novelettes*. New York: Simon & Schuster, 1931.

Simmel, Johannes M. (1971), *Cain '67*. New York: McGraw-Hill.

Sutton, Henry (1969), *The Voyeur*. New York: Geis.

Swift, Jonathan (1726), *Gulliver's Travels*. Boston: Houghton Mifflin, 1960.

Tanizaki, Junichiro (1961), *The Key*. New York: Knopf.

Thorp, Roderick (1972), *Slaves*. New York: Evans.

Zola, Emile (1885), *Germinal*. New York: Dutton.

CHAPTER THIRTEEN

Group Sex

Group sex, mate swapping, orgies, *ménage à trois,* and similar variants of sexual expression have been present throughout much of human history. "Instances of such behavior can readily be found from Petronius's descriptions of ancient Rome to Gogol's portrayal of Russian peasants" (Walshok, 1971, p. 489). However, rigorous, sophisticated psychological studies in this area do not exist; what is available is unreplicable and unreliable, mostly devoted to the virtues of group sex or else moralizing against it. Walker and Walker (1968), in their investigation of the field, found it "inconsistent, self-contradictory, and filled with what were obviously inflated claims about the values to be gained by engaging in such activities. No solid piece of research had been done at the time" (p. 63), a statement still true today. Partisan accounts and secondary sources predominate, frequently written by married couples who have penetrated the swinging scene either by pretending to be swingers or forthrightly revealing themselves as sex researchers and then functioning as participant-observers. These factors, according to Walshok (p. 488), as well as society's prevailing puritanism, have contributed to the marginal legitimacy of the systematic study of group and co-marital sexual behavior.

Changes in the sexual climate of the United States appear to be profound, if the openness with which sex is discussed is taken as the measure of such changes, according to Simon (1969). While the actual changes in behavior are often less profound, there does appear to be a greater tolerance for deviation from traditional sexual patterns, partially as a result of a desire for more intense experience. And new directions in sexuality may be indicated by increasing emphasis on sexual competence. In earlier times, sexual deviance was generally limited to the aristocracy; other classes most frequently indulged in deviant sexual practices in the context of festivals (Walshok, 1971). What makes contemporary co-marital behavior sociologically interesting is its preponderance among basically middle-class and essentially conventional people, and its somewhat bureaucratized and decidedly unfestival-like quality.

"In this country there has been a tradition of great ideological commitment to the importance of confining sexual behavior in general, but sexual intercourse in particular, to the sanctity of the marital bed; concomitantly there has also been a rich history of institutionalized nonmarital sex, ranging from pornography to premarital intercourse to prostitution" (Denfield and Gordon, 1970, p. 88). The "immoral decade" of the 1960's was the scene of many movements and ideas whose time had come: the SDS, the Weathermen, the Southern sit-ins and marches, the bankruptcy of the Cold War, the immorality of the hot war in South East Asia, the academic-military complex— and group sex. It was during this decade that group sex became an established although minor feature of American urban and suburban life (Brecher, 1969). "At the present time, nonmonogamous indulgence appears to be increasing, especially on the part of educated and middle-class females; and the pronounced feelings of anxiety, guilt, and depression that once resulted from premarital and extramarital promiscuity are being considerably reduced. A recent development has been the advocacy and practice of ... group sex relations by certain segments of our population. Several important factors have encouraged American sexual promiscuity during the last decade— including technological advances, marital disillusionment, sociopolitical alienation, and increasing libertarianism" (Ellis, 1968, p. 58).

Although group sex is a highly explosive phenomenon, it arose from a long process of acculturation and is not really a radical departure from the American mode, but rather a modification of basic cultural patterns that only happen to be seeking outlet in this particular sexual form (Bartell, 1971, p. 46). For example, for thirty years during the nineteenth century, the Oneida Community, where both property and wives were held in common, flourished in upstate New York. Crucial to the understanding of the development of group and co-marital sex as an institutionalized form of extramarital sex is an appreciation of the shifts in attitudes toward female sexuality, premarital sex, and especially, marital sex. Another factor which has contributed to the development of mate swapping is the revolution in contraceptive techniques which allow intercourse with less apprehension and more pleasure. "The current conception of female sexuality as legitimate and gratifying, coupled with enlarged opportunities for women to pursue sex without unwanted pregnancies, is likely to have greatly increased the incentive for women to seek — as men have always done — sexual varieties outside marriage. Among the available ways for both husbands and wives to find such variety, mate swapping is the least threatening and the most compatible with monogamy" (Denfield and Gordon, 1970, p. 88). According to Vilar (1971, p. 81), "Wife-swapping parties and pluralist sex practices are favored by many women because they are means of controlling extramarital affairs and tend to neutralize the sexual fantasies of their husbands."

Mate swapping can be defined as the mutually agreed upon exchange of husband and wife with another cooperative couple. Brecher (1969) explains that "the term wife-swapping was objectionable because of its implication of sexual inequality and of male property rights in wives. Nor was 'husband-swapping' or 'mate-swapping' an adequate substitute. For much more was often involved than mere swapping — and unmarried men and women also participated. Hence the term 'swinging' came into general use in the 1960's, and the subculture engaged in such activities came to be known as 'the swinging set.' The ambiguity of the term swinging was no doubt one of the reasons for its popularity; one could 'feel out' prospective partners by launching a casual conversation about swinging . . . and then switch to the more innocent meaning of the term if the response was negative" (p. 250). According to Godwin (1973, p. 160), "Swinging in its specifically erotic connotation . . . denotes all forms of sexual promiscuity . . . To its organized adherents, it means copulation within a selected circle and under prearranged conditions of full equality." Swinging and co-marital sex embody two qualities, as described by Walshok (1971, p. 488): "One is the agreement between husband and wife to have sexual relations with other people, but in contexts in which they both engage in such behavior at the same time and usually in the same place. Such sexual involvement may be either in a group situation, such as an orgy, or where couples go into separate rooms for coition in private. The second quality is that the pursuit of these relationships [is] primarily by means of some organized or institutionalized pattern, that is, they are not spontaneous occurrences." Lewis (1969) concurs with this estimate, for he describes swinging as indiscriminate ultracasual copulation with relative or complete strangers in groups of two, three, four, and up. "As Pompeian frescoes testify, the multiple couplings that took place at Roman orgies are undistinguished from . . . contemporary parties. . . . What's new about swinging . . . is the fact that it's organized" (p. 36).

A champion of group sex, Bartell (1971) feels that the term group sex is more descriptive than swinging or spouse swapping because it does not restrict itself to married couples. Further, swinging "means a free, easy, venturesome, 'with it' life style and this reinforces the sexual swinger's own ego image" (p. 4). Symonds (1967) classifies two types of swingers, the recreational and the utopian. The former is defined as someone who uses swinging as a form of recreation and recognizes that he violates norms but accepts them as legitimate. The latter is non-comformist; he wants to change society and publicizes his opposition to the social norms. Swinging, for the utopian, is part of a new life style that emphasizes communal living. Smith and Smith (1970) refer to "co-marital sexual relations" as applying to married couples who are either involved together in establishing sexual relationships beyond the marital dyad or to couples who have knowledge of and consent to extramarital relations regardless of whether one or both partners are involved.

The research literature suggests that co-marital couples in the swinging subculture, while stemming from all socioeconomic classes, are predominantly middle-class, conservative in their political orientation, with traditional religious backgrounds and little premarital experience. They tend to marry young, and do not have varied sex lives in the early years of marriage. Bartell (1971) examines swinging in sociological and structural-functional terms, linking the phenomenon to its cultural origin. His sample consisted of 280 swinger couples from the metropolitan Chicago area and another sixty informants from Texas and Louisiana. All were white, middle-class suburbanites, with a median age of 29.3 years for women and 32 for men. The sample included teachers, physicians, pilots, factory workers, engineers, truck drivers, and small retail operators. Income began at $10,000, stretching to $70,000. The three major faiths were represented in proportion to the general population. Eighty-seven per cent of the couples interviewed had two or three children, with seventy-four per cent of them with children between the ages of seven and seventeen. Bartell's findings reveal that his swingers were adamant against the use of drugs and would not permit marijuana in their homes; however, the consumption of alcohol was perfectly permissible. Middle-class mores were imposed on most of their sexual attitudes. If, for example, swingers found out that men had been paying prostitutes to pose as swinging partners, males and females were equally outraged. The same sort of outrage was expressed toward couples who were not married, adulterers, hippies, and political radicals. Harris (1969), in her subjective findings, discovered that many mate swappers felt they had found "the only way of facing life honestly." They coveted their sexual liberation but distinguished sharply between co-marital exchanges and extramarital affairs, which were considered disreputable.

Recreational swingers, Denfield and Gordon (1970) discovered, occasionally drop out of swinging once the wife's pregnancy is known to the couple. "By not swinging, the couple can be assured that the husband is the father of the child; unknown or other parentage is considered taboo. This reflects a traditional, middle-class view about the conception and rearing of children. Swinging couples consider themselves to be sexually avant-garde, but many retain their puritan attitudes with respect to sex socialization. They hide their children from swinging publications. Swingers lock their childrens' bedrooms during parties or send them to relatives" (p. 94). Attitudes in Bartell's (1971, pp. 29-30) sample toward the matter of children and swinging "varied from panic, if any one even mentioned swinging in the children's presence, to the opposite extreme, i.e., ... that children should learn as soon as possible to cope with all situations concerning sex. Eleven per cent of our informants fell into each of these far extremes with the remaining 78 per cent somewhere in the middle ... Most parents take great care to keep youngsters out of the house on swinging nights, but not all couples bother to do so ... Many swinging parents feel that this knowledge will cause emotional problems for their children later in life ... [and thus] tend to go to considerable lengths to keep their children from listening in on telephone conversations on the extension, intercepting mail, and finding photographs of other couples engaging in sexual activity." In *A Die in the Country* by Tobias Wells (1972), two teen-age siblings, Delilah Farley, sixteen, and her seventeen-year-old brother, Gregg, discover their parents are swapping partners. The girl is explaining the situation to a neighbor, who is a newcomer to the suburb.

> "Any special reason why you and Gregg hate your folks so much?"
> An oblique glance, more lip licking, then, "Sure. Sure there is. Wouldn't you hate your folks, too, if they were lousy, dirty wife-swappers?"
> I felt my mouth drop. This, I hadn't expected. "Your mother? And father?"
> "Who else?" She put on that closed young mask that so many kids wear for self-protection. "You know that bunch of beauts that were over at the house the other night when you were there? Well, they all play the game. It's group therapy, or something, for them. Gregg and I found it out one night by accident and after that"—she shrugged—"nothing mattered."
> "Which was when Gregg dropped out of school?"
> "Yep. I would have, too, but damn it, I like school. And I want to go to college. I wouldn't give it up, not for them. I told Gregg he was a fink and he just said maybe one day he'd have the guts to kick the old man in the . . ." She stopped, decided to finish with, "In the tail and get the hell out" [p. 103].

A number of investigators (Bartell, 1971; Smith and Smith, 1970; Walker and Walker, 1968; Walshok, 1971) have remarked on the elaborate subculture, similar in form to the deviant subcultures associated with drugs and homosexuality, that has developed among swingers insofar as they picture themselves as part of a happy, private universe of "in" people complete with a secret language, symbols, communication techniques, and isolation and alienation from society as a whole. But swingers do not conform to the stereotyped image of the deviant; every study of swingers has emphasized the over-all normality, conventionality, and respectability of recreational swingers (Denfield and Gordon, 1970).

Nevertheless, Amir (1971) has applied the term "group perversion" to any sort of sexual activity involving participation of more than two persons. "The main explanation of group perversion appears to be psychoanalytically oriented. According to Freud [1921], group structure and group dynamics are developed from two elements; the first of these is the erotic factor which colors group relations and leadership. Group behavior ... is actually the behavior of individuals who are enmeshed in a certain kind of social and emotional interaction. However, through such interaction the group can be perceived as a psychological whole, as having dynamic properties, such as organization, structure, ideal and climate ... Freud's theory of group formation and dynamics deals exclusively with the emotions and attitudes, primarily unconscious, but sexual. People constitute a group if they have the same model object or ideals, or both, in their superego. Added to this is the idea of mechanics of identification through which the group forms when several individuals use the same object as a means of transferring internal conflicts (usually around sexuality). Since sexuality is inherent in the group, the expression of regressive elements with their homosexual, aggressive, and sado-masochistic correlates is facilitated ... Implicit in psychoanalytic theory is the assumption that all groups have similar characteristics ... The differences are in susceptibility to suggestion, and in the forces making for aggression and its correlates" (pp. 183-185, *passim*). The universality and applicability of this passage is rendered clear when it is understood that Amir included it in his work on gangs and forcible rape.

Couples who feel a need for sexual gratification through mate swapping may be fulfilling ungratified childhood sexual curiosity, latent homosexual urges, voyeuristic and exhibitionistic tendencies, and the recapitulation, in adulthood, of the repressed memory of witnessing parental intercourse. A risk inherent in an adult love relationship is the potential rejection by one partner and the ensuing insult to the other's narcissism. Some men feel the need of new sexual experiences to reassure themselves of their ability to be sexually attractive to women. Others feel neglected and possibly are neglected by their wives when children come into the marriage. According to Bartell (1972), the isolation of the nuclear family does not meet the needs of American society. As a result, many turn to group sex as an outlet for their need to belong, as well as the more pervasive factor of acting out sexual needs that are largely based on masturbation fantasies retained from adolescence (Bartell, 1971, p. 57).

A variety of unconscious motivations for spouse swapping is spelled out by Walker and Walker (1968, pp. 75-77). "Those who take part in group sexual activities ... are likely to derive a good deal of sensual satisfaction from watching others; the appeal to the voyeur is very striking. The reverse side of the coin is, of course, the very direct means for the switcher to express his exhibitionistic tendencies. While the vast majority of men who indulge in group sex practices do not acknowledge the existence of any overt homosexual contact in theiṛ swapping sessions, the wives were quite aware of a homosexual component in their own psychic makeup and readily acknowledged that they enjoyed the periodic opportunity to act on it . . . The word 'bisexual' [was preferred] to 'homosexual' in describing such relationships. The narcissistic component in homosexuality [is frequently present in the switching situation]. Bisexual all too often means that the wife is simply passively narcissistic, is perfectly willing to relax and let anyone of any sex make love to her. She is not interested, capable of, or concerned about reacting, responding, or making love with the other person." Sadism, too, is involved in the homosexual relationship into which the husband almost forces his wife. Kinsey et al. (1953) in their study of female sexuality, noted that in a few instances in their sample the husband had encouraged other men to have intercourse with the wife because of the sadistic satisfaction derived from forcing her into an essentially degrading relationship. In their interviews, the Walkers "found that Kinsey's observation was borne out. To the extent that the wife felt humiliated or degraded, the husband's ego was artificially enhanced. There apparently is the need on the part of some group sex participants to be degraded, to suffer first in fantasy and then in reality the full pain of breaking a strong taboo and paying for it. The relatively large number of ads in wife-swapping publications which express a desire for sado-masochistic activities indicate that at least some of the participants are fully conscious of their motivations . . . One factor which . . . is characteristic of all sado-masochistic relationships [and which] shows up frequently in co-marital relationships, sado-masochistic or otherwise, [is] the incapacity for forming and maintaining close relationships with others" (1968, p. 76). And finally, there is the Don Juan factor, where the male mate trader is "always looking for new conquests . . . and the female must prove her desirability by accepting and encouraging the advances of the males she meets" (p. 77).

If voyeurism and exhibitionism are among the attractions of swinging, it can also turn some off, as is seen in this passage from *Your Friendly Neighbourhood Death Pedlar* by Jimmy Sangster (1971), in which Shirleen says to Anthony:

". . . Couldn't we give the others the slip and go off on our own? I'm not honestly mad for mixed doubles, are you?"

"I've never tried them," admitted Anthony. "What happens?"

Oh, you know . . . variations and permutations and exhibitions and all that. It's very boring. I'm a one-man girl myself."

"That's funny," said Anthony. "I'm a one-girl man" [p. 71].

Probably the classic examples of sexual activity as a coping mechanism are the efforts to compensate for feelings of inadequacy or inferiority (Coley, 1973, p. 45). "In some ways, self-affirmation may be one of the great benefits from normal sexual activity; the feelings of acceptance and success as a man or woman, the realization of the capacity to give and receive pleasure, are certainly emotionally valuable, and can certainly be seen to help counterbalance the many self-doubts and disappointments inherent in living. Difficulties result, however, when the needs for reasurrance reach such great extremes as to exceed the capacity of even frenetic sexual activity to compensate." On the other hand, Smith and Smith (1970) say that swinging is not a fad, "or even an act of rebellion or frustration on the part of a neurotic minority. It may well be the sane, considered and totally healthy response of individuals in a certain sort of society" (p. 141). Grold (1970) ascribes widely varied motives to swingers: boredom with one another, a perfunctory sex relation, the need for adventurous sexual variety without emotional involvement, reassurance of masculinity or femininity, the mutual sanctioning of adultery, and the ceaseless search for virginal newness in sexual experience. Many of these factors are apparent in John Updike's (1968) *Couples.*

"Dear Janet," Marcia said. "Poor dear Janet. Tiptoeing in her Sunday-school dress down that long silent hall and pushing, pushing at that locked door."

"Shit," Janet said. "I never pushed at anything. Speak for yourself."

"Dear me," Marcia said. "I suppose that should hurt."

"Bad girl, Janet," Harold said. "You pushed me into the laundry."

"Because you looked so *mis*erable." Janet tried not to cry, which she knew would encourage them.

"Let Jan-Jan alone," Frank said. "She's a lovely broad and the mother of my heirs."

"There's Frank," Marcia said to her husband, "giving himself heirs again." Their intimacy had forced upon each a rôle, and Marcia had taken it upon herself to be dry and witty, when in fact, Janet knew, she was earnest and conscientious, with humorless keen emotions. Janet looked at her and saw a nervous child innocently malicious.

"You don't have to defend Janet to me," Harold told Frank. "I love her."

"You desire her," Marcia corrected. "You've cathected in her direction."

Harold continued, shinily drunk, his twin-tipped nose glinting, "She is the loveliest goddam p—"

"Piece," Marcia completed, and scrabbled in her bent pack of Newports for a cigarette.

"*Pièce de non-résistance* I've ever had," Harold finished. He added, "Out of wedlock."

"The horn, the horn, the lusty horn," Frank said, "is not a thing to laugh to scorn," and Janet saw that the conversation was depressing him also.

Harold went on with Janet, "Were your first experiences with boys under bushes interesting or disagreeable? *Intéressant ou désagréable?*"

"Buffalo boys didn't take me under bushes," Janet said. "I was too fat and rich."

Marcia said, "*We* were never really *rich*. Just respectable. I thought of my father as a holy man."

"Saint Couch," Harold said, and then repronounced it, "*San' Coosh!*"

"I thought of mine," Janet said, growing interested, beginning to hope they could teach her something, "as a kind of pushover. I thought my mother pushed him around. She had been very beautiful and never bothered to watch her weight and even after she got quite large still thought of herself as beautiful. She called me her ugly duckling. She used to say to me, 'I can't understand you. Your father's such a handsome man.' "

"You should tell it to a psychiatrist," Marcia said, unintended sympathy lighting up her face.

"No need, with us here," Harold said. "*Pas de besoin, avec nous ici.* Clearly she was never allowed to work through homosexual mother-love into normal heterosexuality. Our first love-object is the mother's breast. Our first gifts to the beloved are turds, a baby's turds. Her father manufactures laxatives. Oh Janet, it's so obvious why you won't sleep with us."

"She sleeps with me," Frank said.

"Don't brag," Marcia said, and her plain warm caring, beneath the dryness, improved Frank's value in Janet's eyes. She saw him, across the small round raft crowded with empty glasses and decanters, as a fellow survivor, scorched by the sun and crazed by drinking salt water.

"Why must you ruin everything?" he suddenly called to her. "Can't you understand, we all love you?"

"I don't like messy games," Janet said.

"As a child," Harold asked, "did they let you play in the buffalo mud or did you have an anal nanny?"

"Anal nanny," Marcia said. "It sounds like a musical comedy."

"What's the harm?" Frank asked Janet, and his boozy dishevelment, his blood-red eyes and ponderous head rather frightened her, though she had lulled him to sleep, her Minotaur, for ten years' worth of nights. He shouted to all of them, "Let's do it! Let's do it all in the same room! Tup my white ewe, I want to see her whinny!"

Harold sighed daintily through his nose. "See," he told Janet. "You've driven your husband mad with your frigidity. I'm getting a headache" [pp. 162-163].

Marriage, for many swingers it would seem, is hostage to boredom and dullness. The resolution of conflicts in the marriage may be sought through the mechanism of multiple, physically intimate contacts with the opposite sex. A number of reporters of the group sex scene certify to the salvaging of many marriages through swinging. A frequent comment by swingers, writes Walshok (1971, p. 493), is that "marital sex becomes more interesting, complex, and exciting as a result of co-marital encounters. The co-marital context provides an opportunity for sexual learning and experimentation in an affectively neutral setting. One can expand one's repertoire of behaviors, begin to feel comfortable with them, and then incorporate them into the emotionally involved marital relationship." One anonymous letter-writer to *Playboy* (1973) described his marriage relationship, after a group sex orgy with his wife, two single females, and another male, as better than ever. "My wife and I still love each other and I am a lot more tolerant of the differences in people's sexual tastes and appetites. While I wouldn't recommend orgies as a steady practice, I have found that an occasional repetition of that first experience with group sex adds excitement to our marriage and actually enhances our enjoyment of each other when we're alone" (p. 63). Most couples in Bartell's (1971) study reported that their sex life improved dramatically after swinging. Many of the respondents in the Smiths' (1970) study advised of a release from inhibitions and taboos through their group sexual encounters, experiencing a therapeutic effect and welcoming the release from their inhibitions as a primary benefit, to be valued for its own sake. In some instances, these couples claimed that "swinging repaired damaged egos by helping them to accept themselves for what they are. Body image and self esteem are enhanced by the release from sexual repression suffered" (p. 140). Acceptance by themselves and by others boosts self-image and emotional stability, resulting in reduced marital tension and improved social interaction. The findings of Godwin (1973) indicate that swappers feel their prime reason for swinging is to strengthen their marriage, "which might be a euphemism for rescuing it. They pictured the process as 'open-ended wedlock,' a kind of advanced form of togetherness" (p. 160). And Denfield and Gordon (1970) concluded from an analysis of the data available from studies on the subject, "Swinging may support rather than disrupt monogamous marriage as it exists in this society" (p. 98).

Polemicists for both sides are vigorous in the presentation of their case. Thus, the O'Neills (1972) state categorically, "Sexual fidelity is the false god of closed marriage, a god to whom partners submit or defy for all the wrong reasons" (p. 256). In their "open marriage" thesis, they affirm that "couples who insist upon exclusivity, who continue to believe that any husband or wife can be all to one another, are in fact only insuring that their relationship will eventually cease to be fulfilling in a mutual way" (p. 173). The Constantines (1973) flatly declare, "Sex is rarely a real problem . . . Respondents reported that their satisfaction with their sex life increased somewhat to greatly as the result of multilateral marriage. They were not just enjoying it more but also reported engaging in it more . . . In the long run sex is seldom a detriment to relationships; sometimes it facilitates growthful involvement, and at the very least it feels good" (p. 81). This may be considered a naïve approach to marriage, love, and sex. Little or no reference is made to the affective aspects of the marriage partnership, and the device of swinging is used as a strategy to revitalize marriage.

Swinging is dismissed by Avery and Avery (1964) because it is not typical of anything "except its own pathology . . . Two factors [are worthy of attention]: one is the almost overwhelming ordinariness — at least outwardly — of the people concerned. The other related fact is the misery which seems to motivate some of them. However insignificant the phenomenon may be in the general scheme of things, it is rather stunning to read that these couples resorted to 'wife swapping' in order to 'save' their marriages" (p. 254). Most people find the thought of spouse swapping repugnant, for it violates deeply ingrained feelings about decency and sexual privacy. Nonetheless, states Hunt (1969), "for those who are acutely bored by their marriages or are having sexual problems in them, but who are held back from extra-marital relations by conscience or by lack of self-confidence, it may prove quite functional: it minimizes guilt by making the act legitimate and freely condoned, and at the same time overcomes lack of confidence by guaranteeing each participant a willing partner" (p. 117). While swinging may stimulate general sexual excitement and increased sexual interest in the mate, there are drawbacks such as the inability to live up to one's psychosexual myth and self-illusions, jealousy, and the discovery of long-repressed unsavory aspects of the emotional self (Bartell, 1970). According to Lipton (1965), the practice of multiple mating is no panacea for the relations of the sexually neurotic, regardless of whether it is monogamic, extramarital, or premarital.

> Mate-switching, if it is conducted with intelligence by people who are capable of love and not just as a way of side-swapping the responsibilities and obligations of marriage, is beneficial to all concerned. But intelligent sexual selectivity and sexual health are much less common than mindless promiscuity and sexual sickness. For this reason . . . mate-swapping, for the most part, is carried on by people to whom it is little more than a more or less organized form of multiple adultery, with all the attendant guilt, remorse and mutual recrimination that is characteristic of people who have not succeeded in liberating themselves from their early upbringing and the values of society . . . Mate-switching can be regarded as a forward step to the New Morality when it succeeds in being a love-enhancing experience [pp. 83-84].

While Freud recognized that man is biologically polygamous, he also saw monogamy as an artifact of upbringing and social convention rather than part of instinctual human nature. Ellis (1958) stated, "One of the great myths of our society is that a stable, well-adjusted person can love only one member of the other sex at a time . . . Actually, practically all normal humans are capable of plural love . . . Wife-swapping, therefore, may sometimes greatly add romantic, tender, or companionship love to the lives of either or both mates who are doing the swapping. And in so doing, it may even enhance the existing emotional feelings between a husband and wife (although it may also, of course, distract and detract from such feelings)" (p. 134). Rachel and Fred, man and wife in List's (1972) *Did You Love Daddy When I Was Born?* are in the early throes of separation. Fred, on one unbearably hot and humid evening, suggests they go for a swim in the Teichers' pool. Rachel does not feel up to it, but rather than be considered a spoilsport agrees to go.

Fred brushed her shoulder with his hand. She noticed he had had the nails manicured.

"Look, I just don't like going—"

"Christ, you're a kill-joy. Look, if you don't want to go in the water, I won't mind, I promise. I just want to take a swim and cool off. I won't mind if you don't go in. God, all the girls do it and it means nothing, no funny business. It's just fun. Don't spoil it, come on."

About twenty people had already lined the pool, drinks in hand. The night was still stifling, but the end of the cove always had a breeze and the air was at least comfortable. Monique Teicher, the hostess, came down from the cabana, an engraved towel wrapped around her body. She had been a model for life classes years ago and her Italian bikinis and short tennis dresses still caused comment. Even the women admired the perfection of her body, the tilt of her breasts, the deep dimples before her buttocks, which rose large for a girl so small. It was her extraordinary pride in her body that disarmed everyone.

She descended into the water as they arrived, after slowly dropping the towel as a hush fell on the group. It was as though she was oblivious of every eye on her, as though the moment was only between her and her own nakedness.

Other couples broke the spell and peeled off their clothes. "Turn off the light," someone shouted. "Oh, God, I think I'm going to be sick." "No peeing in the pool!"

Rachel had watched Fred removing his clothes, folding each piece carefully and placing them on the rubber strips covering the deck chairs. She watched the familiar body emerge. The outside lights had been turned off so that only the bar and soft Japanese lanterns lit the scene. She could make out his silhouette; his bikini shorts bulging out his thighs, his small bottom barely filling them. She watched him dive into the pool and head for Monique, resting her head on the far side of the pool.

Ben Arrano, with full lips and heavily lidded eyes, moved toward her. He was naked under the towel wrapped loosely around him. "Coming in?"

"Not just yet," Rachel said.

"How about a drink?"

"I'd love one." She watched him, saw the bulge under his towel. She felt nauseous as she saw her husband swim toward Monique, place one arm on either side of her, heard her laughter. She wanted to vomit, all over her white silk dress.

"Scotch and water, I remembered from the last time." Ben was grinning as he sat down beside her. She remembered his pleading, whining voice at the last swimming party. Ben had forced his tongue deep into her mouth as she had emerged from the cabana that time, and, shaking, she almost had pushed him into the pool. Later, she had got very drunk, while out of the corner of her eye her husband had been smoothing someone's long, glistening braid.

There were now about six bodies in the pool and drinks were floating on rubberized coasters like miniature smoke-stacks. Like suburban water lilies.

Someone suggested water polo, and suddenly heavy-breasted, wide-hipped ladies grunted on hairy weaving shoulders. The moon caught glimpses of softened nipples, bristly pubic hair on nervous necks. The women wrestled one another, while the men tried to keep them afloat; the laughter split the night air, and the gulls competed with their own mating call. The women shook their breasts, lifted their arms high and straight to catch the beach ball someone had thrown in. It was a geyser of splashing and laughter and plump shaky thighs and arms uplifted pleading for the high breasts and firm bottoms of long ago. It wasn't Woodstock, but they were trying.

Tears were stinging Rachel's eyes and she felt the mascara irritate them. She downed the drink in several gulps. He refilled her glass.

"Where is Lorraine, Ben?" she had asked.

"Oh, she went home hours ago, it's only another month now, you know, and she gets tired early. It's been rough these last weeks, this no sex bit is for the birds. How did you ever manage?"

"Oh, I don't know, everyone gets through it."

"How about someone as sexual as you?"

"What?" Fred and Monique were doing the crawl, tandem style, arms gliding softly in and out of the water. Three speakers blared the Italian love song on the hi-fi.

"I said someone as sexual as you must have found it very difficult."

"Found what . . . oh, Ben, don't start that again. You know I'm a lost cause."

"No, I don't know that, no one is. Aren't you coming in the water?"

"Soon."

The beach ball hit her in the crotch. "Throw it back, throw it back."

Ben took it slowly from her, his fingers softly grazing the inside of her thigh.

Quickly, she said, "May I have a refill?"

"Coming right up."

Coming right up is right, she thought. She watched the montage of figures, some in beach robes, young for the moment, drenched hair combed back, blue-black night hiding care and puffy yellow lines. She watched the dancing, the humping, the squeaky forced laughter, the disappearances to the beach, into the cabana, sea shells she smelled, sea shells by the seashore. Rotten smell she had smelled, good smell, fish smell, oh summer lovely summer smell, coming back from the beach smell, after the waves, the high terrifying high frightening, rapacious waves that engulfed, swallowed, engulfed the little girl of her, the black fear of them, the dying of them swooping under disappearing into nothing for an instant and where was Daddy, oh, God, she had thought, Rachel is going to come up, she is dying, she will die at the bottom of the ocean. And the delicious fatigue, the exhaustion coming back from the beach, the enemy waves, always challenging, always conquered curled up in the back seat in the sun and sand and battle of the waves all part of a summer; "You are my princess," Daddy had said, my princess but even a princess could drown, even Daddy of shining bald pate and cow eyes and utter adoration could not protect her from the onslaught of the ocean waves . . . she had to dive into them fearing yet craving that split second of maybe never coming up. . . .

"Why do you watch Fred so?"

"Thanks for the drink."

"Why do you watch him so? Don't you know him by now?"

"You're getting loaded, Ben."

"I'd give anything to screw you."

"Oh, Christ, go away."

"Come on in swimming. Do you know that I have had just about every woman here?"

Husband help me, save me from the waves.

Fred and Monique were doing the back stroke now, her hard brown nipples skimming the water as she glided past. Rachel could not take her eyes off them.

"At this moment he doesn't know you're alive."

"Ben, fuck off." She felt Ben's deft hands unzipping the length of the dress in the back. She did not stir, but dropped her head back and stared into the moon as Ben slipped the top of the dress off her shoulders.

"You'll have to get up to get the rest off," he whispered. Slowly she stood, staring into the blackness of the pool. Only Fred and Monique remained. They were deep in conversation. Rachel trembled slightly as she unhooked her brassiere. She felt no embarrassment, nothing; her eyes riveted to the back of her husband's head. Ben dropped his towel and dove in.

Fred had looked up at the splash of Ben's body and stared at Rachel. She walked slowly to the shallow end, felt the cool water invade her . . . felt her thighs, hips, waist, breasts wet. She nestled against the wall of the pool, watching Fred at the other end. Ben swam over to her and she felt light, no weight, no substance. Ben smoothed her hair, put his arms around her. She saw her husband over Ben's shoulder past a hair growing out of a raised mole.

"Sure I stray," Ben had said, whispering into her ear. "You tell me how else to keep romance alive . . . impossible. It has nothing to do with love, you tell me what love is, just tell me. Who do you love? Him? Getting his kicks on the other side of the pool? Your kids, the dog?"

Weightless, no substance, wet and weightless. He had maneuvered her into a position in front of the filter, and the water rushed out hitting her buttocks.

"Lorraine's all right, she's a good mother," Ben had said, "we live together, but there's always someone else, wherever I go. Christ, there has to be, you know that . . . listen, don't put on the purity act. I can tell you're as anxious to get laid as I am."

Ben had entered her without her realizing it. People were around talking, flirting, shrill, soft swimming no one near her, he was watching, he was watching.

. He is gliding back and forth in me and I barely feel it, Rachel had thought, I am wet and weightless and Ben Arrano is inside me and my husband is across there watching at this moment. Can he see? Does it matter? Here we are in this giant Japanese bathtub fucking our lives away. . . .

The heavy coat of hair on Ben's chest tickled, crushed her breasts. She thought, and they nailed him to the cross and he never said a mumblin' word. That's it exactly, she thought, as Ben thrust and thrust and withdrew, pushing her rump into the heavy gushing water. He's dropping his foreign seed into me and I don't feel a thing. Across the pool Fred is watching, arms around a dimpled behind and Ellen is on the beach digging to China, and they nailed him — her to the cross and he never never never never never never never said a mumblin' word.

"Did you love Daddy when I was born?"
"Yes."
"Mommies should love daddies."
"I know" [pp. 126-131].

While group sex may seem to be an extension of emotional and sexual freedom, it is more likely an attempt to satisfy the hunger for variety in sex without imperiling the marriage. "The crux of group sex . . . lies in the dissociation it offers between tender love and sensuality, between varietism and commitment, thus tending to preserve the marriage and family ties while giving the partners a chance to act out their intense fantasy life which would otherwise be repressed, or indulged in with a sneaking sense of guilt" (Lerner, 1972, p. 101). But the need for variety, that is to say, the boredom of swingers, is a denial of life, and swapping partners is a stimulus to their boredom which is paid for in superego diminution. The despair of expressing what the person feels, even what he is — explains the trend to action therapies and nonverbal communication, and by extension, to impersonal group sex. Though one of the commonest symptoms of loneliness is a yearning for the solace of immediate intimacy, this, too, is hopeless, for intimacy requires a history; man is a symbol-making creature, and he needs a sustaining symbolism before he can experience love or intimacy (May, 1972).

Bartell (1971) found that while the basic motivation for swingers seemed to be the hope to improve their marriages, his respondents did not know how to form warm human relationships. The great hunger of people to relate to one another in groups, prompted in a measure, some claim, by the lack of nuclear family ties, leads them to hide behind their sexual openness. Meaningful intimacy becomes oppressive, incongruous, and unwelcome. Detachment is essential. "The bartering of sex for physical closeness and contact may appear similar to the attempt to obtain love but on closer study often has a somewhat different meaning . . . For certain persons contact and being held . . . appears to represent warmth, comfort, and security, a meaning possibly remaining from the associations of infancy. Because of this meaning, body contact then can be used to counteract feelings of loneliness and insecurity, with sexual activity being an available means of obtaining it" (Coley, 1973, p. 55). Swingers fear emotional involvement, and such involvement produces jealous reactions. "This is why the successful swinger must minimize total human interaction and reduce everything to sexual interaction. He can accomplish this by (1) swinging with a couple only once; (2) declaring dates outside the swinging scene to be taboo, which again minimizes interaction; (3) sanctioning females-with-females in sexual interaction, which does not threaten the dyadic or marital relationship" (Bartell, 1971, pp. 155-156). If two couples become too important to each other, a halt is called to the relationship and another co-marital affair is begun. Involvement and intimacy are, then, the great enemies; swapping is a safety valve that keeps intimacy at a tolerable level.

This form of casual sex is an attempt "to redefine marriage and fidelity in radically new terms that would make sexual intercourse as casual and unemotional as a handshake or eating a steak" (Francoeur, 1972, p. 137). Bartell (1971) found the female swingers were bored, often frustrated women who lacked inner resources and the ability to enjoy themselves; their conversations about nonsexual subjects rarely ranged beyond impersonal superficialities: "Even though they think of themselves as liberated sexually, they are terrified of the idea that involvement might take place. They take comfort from the fact that if they swing with a couple only once or twice, the chances of running into a marriage-threatening involvement are small" (p. 45). But it is a self-defeating process, for group sex activity may stem from prior inability of the individual to relate to others. The paradox about group sex, writes Lerner (1972) "is that it grows out of both the de-sexing and the depersonalizing of the marriage relationship; yet, in the effort to mend this, it focuses almost wholly on releasing sexual inhibitions, and does this through an added dose of depersonalization. The very people who have difficulty relating turn to an activity in which they can get the outward semblance of relating on a sensuous level, without having to relate ... on a deeper level" (p. 104).

In random interviews with American housewives, Gittelson (1972) found their major complaints to be about husbands who were dull lovers, with montonous and unvarying sexual techniques, neurotic and domineering. The wives had castrated their husbands and hated them for allowing it; the husbands felt castrated and hated their wives for it. *Proposition 31,* by Robert H. Rimmer (1968), depicts two middle-American couples, the Sheas and the Herndons, caught up in the humdrum routine of their lives. Horace Shea is a sociology professor and his wife Tanya an advertising director in a local department store. David Herndon owns a showcase-fixture business; Nancy is a house-wife. Each couple has a son and a daughter. At one point in the novel, David tells Nancy, "You are the salt of the earth. A dull husband, a dull wife, and two dull children. There's millions like us" (p. 38). Nancy sighs to herself and thinks, "David was right. My husband is a dull man. I'm a dull woman. We're well mated" (p. 45). Like a great many co-marital enthusiasts, the Sheas and the Herndons, next-door neighbors in sunny California, begin their activities independently of any subculture, but more as the consequence of a seemingly spontaneous happening. A high degree of intimacy builds up between them over the years and, as the Walkers (1968, p. 68), in their general description of swingers record, "for no discernible reason, two couples find themselves engaged in petting with each other's spouses. Later, perhaps on another evening, they trade spouses for the purpose of further sex play and intercourse. In time, they come to carry on their activities in the same room...." Something like this happens with the Herndons and the Sheas. In the following excerpt, the novelist traces the insidious development of co-marital sex between the two couples, with the initial inveighing against wife-swapping, and concluding with its practice. The boredom they have lived through in a decade and more of married life, the voyeuristic impulses, and the titillating conversations intended to arouse erotic sensations, are portrayed.

As they became closer friends Nancy had been somewhat concerned that their Saturday evenings, even while they were playing bridge, seemed to creep with increasing detail and hilarity into the subject of sex. Not just general sex and dirty stories, though David and Tanya seemed to pick up in their business contacts an endless fund of stories. Neither David nor Tanya seemed embarrassed to say any of the dirty words that made Nancy shudder when she heard them. But even worse, the stories often led to blushingly frank personal observations on the sexual idiosyncrasies of their respective partners.

"Horace doesn't waste time," Tanya chuckled. She patted Horace's cheek. "Each year it gets faster and faster. Pretty soon I guess all we'll do is talk about it."

Horace wasn't angry. "The trouble with Tanya is I have a feeling right at the crucial moment she's planning a new advertising campaign for Tom Bayberry." He stroked her arm. "Or maybe she is pretending I'm Tom Bayberry."

"Tom Bayberry is fifty-two years old," Tanya rolled her eyes. "He has grown such a belly I doubt if he has seen his instrument for several years."

"His wife must have to climb on him," David laughed. "It would be interesting to watch. Intercourse on a bowl of Jello. The trouble with Nancy is that she's a perfectionist. The kids must be asleep. The candles sputtering. The hi-fi playing Mantovani."

Nancy was angry, but she was careful to hide it. What would the Sheas think if she told them that many times she had waited for David, prayed that tonight was the night; had prepared herself for him. Then, more often than not he would simply kiss her, say, "I love you, Shea, but tonight I'm pooped," and calmly David would go to sleep. Maybe it was better fast than *not at all!*

But, while the Herndons and Sheas discussed the intimacies of sex, tried to evoke the true meaning of love and marriage, and inveighed against divorce and wife-swapping, they maintained a very proper relationship. Horace was always friendly with Nancy, but never so much as touched her. Often, it seemed to Nancy, he went to awkward extremes to avoid physical contact. David teased Tanya that she had a shape like a burlesque stripper. While occasionally Tanya might have wiggled her pelvis at him with what Nancy might have considered more than neighborly interest, yet on Christmas under the mistletoe and on New Year's Eve at midnight they kissed their respective spouses on the lips and each other's wives on the cheek.

*   *   *

Perhaps it might have continued that way if the Sheas hadn't decided to build a swimming pool into their rather crowded back-

yard. It wasn't really Horace's idea. Tanya had done the artwork
and illustrations for a construction company that installed the pools.
In payment she had the privilege of purchasing their best pool at
cost. As Tanya said, "While I'm not the mermaid type, it's such a
bargain that we can't afford not to buy one."

The Saturday after the pool was finished the Herndons were
invited to christen it. Nancy Herndon, wearing a discreet two-piece
flowered bathing suit, sat in a sun-chair beside the pool and sipped a
vodka collins which melted ice had reduced to a pale potency. She
watched David and Tanya, who were in the deep end of the pool.
They were playing water volleyball against the boisterous, combined
forces of the Herndon and Shea children.

"Come on in and help us, Nancy," Tanya yelled. She leaped out
of the water to return the ball across the net. "These kids are too
much for us."

Nancy shook her head. Your breasts, practically falling out of
your bikini, are too much for David, she thought. Nancy looked at
Horace. He was reclining in a beach chair, his face tilted to the late
afternoon sun; he didn't seem to give a damn. Nancy felt grim. She
wanted to poke him and say, Wake up, stupid! With that tiny bit of
cloth across her nipples, and that abbreviated diaper between her
legs that scarcely covers her cleft and leaves nothing to the imagination so far as her behind goes, your wife is seducing my husband!

When Tanya had sauntered toward the pool and David saw her
for the first time, hadn't Horace noticed the glazed look in David's
eye? Nancy did, and she would bet Tanya knew what she was doing.

"I wouldn't dare wear it to the beach," Tanya had confided.
Nancy complimented her but thought, like hell you wouldn't. "But
here in my own back yard," Tanya added, "among friends, it's
different."

Nancy was quite certain that it wasn't *that* different. She had
breasts and buttocks and a mound with hair on it too, but she wasn't
displaying them or wiggling them just to drive Horace crazy. Still,
Nancy knew she was being petty. Tanya was just Tanya; she was
much to ingenuous to tempt David. Subtlety and the femme fatale
approach were definitely not a part of her character. Really, after
three years of friendship, she should be used to Tanya's lack of
restraint. Last night when they were playing bridge was typical.
Tanya had asked David if, like Horace, he was inhibited in the
bathroom. Despite Horace's protest that bathroom habits weren't an
appetizing subject, Tanya rambled on.

"I'm not like Horace," she said calmly. "Traffic in the bathroom,
even if I am trying to shit, doesn't constipate me."

Shaking his head in dismay, Horace asked if it was necessary that Tanya be so vulgar; but he was too late. Tanya was already well into the details of the size of an amazing bowel movement she had had the day before. David, choking with hysterical laughter, encouraged her. Nancy told him later that she didn't think the subject was that funny.

"Oh, Nancy, for God's sakes, can't you relax? You're a big girl now. Thirty-six years old. You don't have to act the shy virgin any longer."

I don't have to act and talk like a prostitute either, Nancy thought.

*   *   *

David, sitting on the edge of the pool, dangling his feet in the water, ignored Nancy's attempt to have herself contradicted. "This is a very lovely pool," he remarked. "Back where I come from everybody knows in California they swim naked in their swimming pools and have orgies when the sun goes down." David's words sounded slurry to him. Without the cover of liquor he probably wouldn't have dared. Now, happily tipsy, he grinned at Tanya. "Come on, take off those handkerchiefs and swim in your skin."

Horace pointed at the reflection of the moon in the pool. "Let's be bare-assed astronauts," he agreed. "We can jump on the moon."

"A good idea," Tanya said brightly as she fumbled with the strings holding her bikini.

"The children!" Nancy wailed. "Besides, I can only swim dog paddle." She knew she just couldn't wiggle out of her bathing suit while everyone, especially Horace, watched her. "What if the kids are awake?" she asked. "What if they got up and discovered us all naked?"

Tanya agreed. First they should make certain the children were asleep. Conspiratorially, she led Nancy first to check Sue and Jimmy's bedroom. "I'm afraid I'll be embarrassed," Nancy whispered. Actually, she was both frightened and intrigued. She got Tanya to help turn out all the lights in both houses, so that the neighbors would think they had gone to bed. In Tanya's bedroom she slowly slipped out of her bathing suit as Tanya, already naked, urged her to hurry back to the pool. All four children were sound asleep; Nancy was sorry she couldn't use their presence to dampen the idea. Tiptoeing through the Sheas' kitchen, she was aware of her breasts swaying against her chest. Tanya opened the back door. They were both quite naked. Suddenly Nancy had to go to the john again.

"Silly!" Tanya said, and pushed her onto the patio. "You just leaked. Horace won't bite you, and after all these years David must have seen you in your birthday suit."

With the moon briefly behind a cloud, the pool was so shadowy that Nancy could see only the vague outlines of Horace and David placidly floating on the water. In hoarse whispers the men urged the women to hurry up, because the water was so erotically fine.

Horace soon discovered that Nancy's breasts were larger than Tanya's. With a large aureola framing each erect nipple, they seemed to be so friendly that they were extending an invitation to be caressed independently of what Nancy might want; she herself seemed rather shivery and grim, but at last she lowered herself into the water a respectable distance from Horace. Nancy noted that David and Tanya were diving and submerging together like playful porpoises. It was too dark to be sure, but she thought she saw Tanya clinging to David as they went under the water.

But Horace wasn't watching Tanya. Suddenly he dove for Nancy's legs and dragged her under with him. As she was pulled to the bottom, she struggled to escape Horace's quick, tingling embrace.

Nancy came to the surface gasping indignantly. "Horace," she whispered, frightened. "Don't do that again! I don't swim very well. You'll drown me. And I'm not *that* tight!" He watched the oval of her behind as she pulled herself onto the edge of the pool.

"I'm not tight," Horace muttered. "Just dangerously priapic." He hoisted himself out of the water and sat beside her. In spite of herself, Nancy grinned at him. "If the children woke and saw you like that, what would they think?"

"I'd tell them I'm practicing for the pole vault at a track meet." Horace smiled happily at her. "You obviously have unique powers, Nancy. You can raise the dead." He pulled on his bathing trunks and flopped in a chaise at a respectable distance from her.

Did David and Tanya, still heedlessly naked, join them somewhat reluctantly? Nancy was quite sure about one thing, David and Tanya both felt that Horace and Nancy were party-poopers. But they didn't voice the thought.

That was a month ago. Although there had been some very warm nights since, no one broached the subject of swimming in the Shea pool late at night — with or without clothes [pp. 27-34, *passim*].

The search for intimacy by members of the swinging set finds its closest realization in female homosexual relations which develop out of group sex activity. The frequency of ambisexual relations between women in a swinging situation is "possibly the most intriguing finding of our entire study . . . Sixty-five per cent of the informants admitted that they had had sexual relationships with other female swingers . . . The original initiative that leads to ambisexual activity between women most frequently comes from their men. It turns men on to watch two women together, and it conserves their own sexual energy . . . When girls get together it is almost always a male spectator sport . . . A swinger is never too jaded to enjoy voyeurism. . ." (Bartell, 1971, pp. 131-133). The recurrent theme of female bisexuality permeates the entire swap scene, according to Godwin (1973). "The near-taboo on male inversion . . . in part . . . is due to the fact that, while men find the spectacle of women making love to each other highly stimulating, women get no such charge from seeing men perform. This, however, is secondary. The prime factor lies in the traumatic attitude most men have toward homosexuality—an omnipresent threat to their masculine role, all the more potent because it just may strike a responsive chord in their own psyches. Their reaction is an instant— often hysterical—recoil . . . " (pp. 175-176).

Another way so-called isolation of the consanguineal family is being challenged is through group marriage. There is reason to believe that conventional marriage, as an institution, is undergoing change, for the problems, issues, and expectancies being dealt with by married people today are different from those of their parents. This is especially true of middle-class, college-educated people. At least one investigator (Gittelson, 1972) indicates that sexual happiness or any other form of happiness cannot be found in monogamy, and that many women are seriously disillusioned with it as a way of life. An increasing number are seeking alternative forms of relationships. In his book on marriage and its alternatives, Rogers (1972) states that many men and women are experimenting with new kinds of marriage and alternative ways of living together in an attempt to break free of the constricting roles assigned them by traditional society. Some of the experimentation includes couples giving complete sexual freedom to each other; a monagomous relationship varied to include female homosexuality; experimenting with lovers outside the marriage, in either a *ménage à trois* or with another married couple; and a variety of all shades of experiences.

Perhaps these are viable alternatives to what is traditionally available to couples, but the commonly held view is that marriage is the best and the worst of human relationships, which is why it will endure. In

1908, George Bernard Shaw wrote, "We may take it . . . that when a joint domestic establishment involving questions of children or property is contemplated, marriage is in effect compulsory upon all normal people; and until the law is altered there is nothing for us but to make the best of it as it stands. Even when no such establishment is desired, clandestine irregularities are negligible as an alternative to marriage. How common they are nobody knows; for in spite of the powerful protection afforded to the parties by the law of libel, and the readiness of society on various other grounds to be hoodwinked by the keeping up of the very thinnest appearances, most of them are probably never suspected. But they are neither dignified nor safe and comfortable, which at once rules them out for normal decent people. Marriage remains practically inevitable; and the sooner we acknowledge this, the sooner we shall set to work to make it decent and reasonable" (pp. 120-121).

While attitudes may have changed somewhat since this was written, "neither group marriage nor communes are recent innovations. Plato describes group marriage in *The Republic*, and communes have been a part of the American scene since 1680" (Allen and Martin, 1971, p. 128). Sororal polygyny was a recognized usage among ancient Jews, as related in the Biblical account of the marriage of Jacob. Solomon had 700 wives and 300 concubines, according to I *Kings*. In primitive societies, group marriage was regarded not only as a right and privilege, but as a moral obligation. "A community of wives was originally regarded as essential to the relationship of tribal brotherhood. There can be little doubt that the practice of exchanging wives temporarily, universal with all sections of the Eskimo race, is a survival of tribal sexual communism" (Briffault, 1927, p. 132). Polygamy was common among many primitive tribes of the world up to the end of the last century (Scrignar and Spiers, 1970). Westermarck (1921) said that polygamy was practiced among European Jews during the middle ages and it was not prohibited by rabbinical councils until the beginning of the eleventh century. Christianity developed its ideal of monogamy from Greece and Rome. However, the New Testament only once specifically proscribes polygyny, and this is directed just to bishops and deacons (I Timothy 3:2, 11).

Group marriage has been defined by the Constantines (1973) as a voluntary association into a family group of three or more members, based on a deep, affective bond, genuine intimacy, and interpersonal commitments among all members. The term "multilateral marriage" was coined as a substitute for group marriage because the latter traditionally involved two persons and thus the term would not accommodate a triad (Constantine and Constantine, 1971). The critical factor in group marriage, according to Ramey (1972a), is that the three or more participants consider themselves to be married to at least two other members of the group. These are pair-bonded instead of married, since the couples may not be legally married. There is cross-marital sexual involvement, and partners engage in sexual intercourse with people other than the legal spouse. Thus the signal, unique advantage of group marriage is that it provides sexual variety for both sexes within a stable marital configuration (Constantine and Constantine, 1973).

It should be understood that there is a difference between a person's desire for multiple sexual relations, as in group sex, and the desire to enter into the illegal and complex relations of multiple marriage (Scrignar and Spiers, 1970, p. 122). In *Proposition 31,* Rimmer differentiates swingers and group marriage participants: "Wife swappers flee from involvement while we love it." Ramey (1972b) reports the progressive increase in the degree of complexity in relationships as the individual moves from monogamous dyadic marriage through open marriage, intimate friendships, and communal living, to group marriage, marked by a willingness to take on ever-increasing responsibilities. Ramey's (1972a) study of three years' activity among a sample of eighty couples, almost all of whom were in the academic and professional world or in managerial positions, and who believed that group marriage might provide a framework in which they could do better what they were already doing well. Over two thirds had at least one child, and fifty per cent had at least two. The major motivation for the wives' involvement concerned "a sense of isolation with children, overdependence on the husband for adult contact, and underutilization of talents and training" (p. 649). For the men, their concern centered on "a means of freeing themselves from financial insecurity and the rat-race [of contemporary living. For both husbands and wives, the motivation involved] child-rearing practices, the freedom to include sexual intimacy among the joys of friendship when appropriate, and a shared concern about maximizing their potential, and opportunities and pleasure without the framework of current social strictures" (pp. 651-652). Most of the groups Ramey dealt with "were concerned about decision-making procedures, group goals, ground rules, prohibitions, intra- and extra-group sexual relations, privacy, division of labor, role relations, careers, relations with outsiders, degree of visibility, legal jeopardy, dissolution of the group, personal responsibility outside the group (such as parental support), geographic location, type of shelter, children, child-rearing practices, education of children, group member career education, taxes, pooling assets, income, legal structure, trial period, investment policy, sequential steps in establishing the group, and prerequisites for membership" (p. 653).

The concern about sexual relations in the group is an essential element of multilateral marriage. Among all such groups, the Constantines (1973) advise, "a three days-four days, four days-three days schedule has been reported most often where a fixed rotation scheme was in use. For groups not using a fixed rotation scheme, the decision-making process was either left unstructured or was undertaken by the group as a whole . . . Fixed rotation is an equalizer and leaves no one out, minimizing the potential for jealousy . . . [On the other hand] some form of free choice gives more freedom and permits spontaneity, its advocates argue" (p. 164).

Marriage in communes is yet another form that reaches very close to the central malaise of traditional marriage. Commune marriage and group marriage are not necessarily linked, but since the 1960's, several thousand communes have cropped up, most of them short-lived, but while they functioned, they experimented intensively with group sex practices (Lerner, 1972). "What sexual sharing has in common with the other sharings is the feeling that society has moved farther and farther away from the instinctual, that man has taken away from the soil and from its organic components. So, too, society has also taken man and woman away from the tenderness and from true sensuality and from fellow-feeling with others. The aim of the communes has been to overcome the overlaid sexual inhibitions by collective sex; to dynamite the nuclear family and to replace it by an organic extended family; to replace compulsory roles by voluntary and spontaneous roles (doing your thing); to find new mating patterns— triads, foursomes, three-couples, group marriage—that will not only add variety and spice to sexuality but will give the children a wider universe of parents, and will broaden and strengthen the basic human connection" (p. 105).

The common drive of all communes is utopian. As Bernard (1972) points out, most writers of utopias, virtually all of whom have been men, have not paid much attention to marriage. Those that have are male-oriented, as in Sir Thomas More's *Utopia*, where "the wives minister to their husbands; in Campanella's *City of the Sun*, the boys but not the girls learn the sciences, and there is a community of wives; in Etienne Cabet's *Voyage en Incarie*, women play a secondary role; in *Modern Utopia* by H. G. Wells, woman's role was primarily that of mother; in *Walden Two* by B. F. Skinner, men and women are equal and free, but marriage remains" (Bernard, p. 187). The feeling the reader gets from most utopias, Bernard concludes, is that even when the authors "had taken a determined stand on equality of the sexes, they could not really envision it; they betray themselves in one way or another. Women may enter the professions, but they must be professions appropriate for women. Their work is still women's work. The girls may be educated along with the boys, but they are not given adult male responsibilities. Women are still primarily mothers" (p. 187).

However, some recent novelists of utopias and science fiction have permitted a psychosocial and psychosexual latitude not hitherto displayed, whether it is the "orgy-porgy" of Aldous Huxley's *Brave New World* (1932), the Margaret Meadish sexual libertarianism in Irving Wallace's (1963) *The Three Sirens*, or the behavior of middle Americans in Rimmer's *Proposition 31*. The quest for sexual freedom can be regarded more as an accelerating movement toward the *Brave New World* presaged by Huxley than a liberation from Puritan shackles (Winthrop, 1970). In Huxley's novel, promiscuity is the norm. Fanny tells Lenina, " '. . . You *ought* to be a little more promiscuous.' Lenina shook her head. 'Somehow,' she mused, 'I hadn't been feeling very keen on promiscuity lately. There are times when one doesn't. Haven't you found that too, Fanny?' Fanny nodded her sympathy and understanding. 'But one's got to make the effort,' she said sententiously, 'one's got to play the game. After all, every one belongs to every one else.' 'Yes, every one belongs to every one else,' Lenina repeated slowly . . ." (pp. 49-50). Huxley had designed a standardized human product brought to fantastic extremes. In a foreword written in 1946, fourteen years after the original edition was published, Huxley stated that the sexual promiscuity in *Brave New World* did not seem so very distant; utopia was far closer than had been imagined, and the prototype Central London Hatchery and Conditioning Centre might be a reality within the time of living man.

In *The Three Sirens* by Irving Wallace (1963), a sexual utopia exists in that most romanticized of worlds, the South Sea islands. Wallace complains that after marriage "there's no extramarital freedom . . . Both sexes chafe along the same rails toward old age, scenery ignored, side trips not allowed. Church and state are kept happy. It is unrealistic, and if you stay on the rails, it's a strain, and if you don't, if you sneak in a few detours, it's always a strain" (p. 413). So Wallace constructs his utopian society, founded in the nineteenth century by a discontented Englishman named Wright and his family who flounder onto the island of Three Sirens and establish a new society with the natives. An anthropological team invades the island.

"You know how it is back home. Before you're married, you see a man who interests you, maybe in the street or in a store or across the room of a bar, but usually you never meet him. I mean, you simply don't. You meet only the people you're introduced to and get to know. And after you're married and become older—well, you wouldn't know that yet, Harriet, but take my word—it gets worse .it just does, it's gruesome, sad as hell. Lots of people have their cake and eat it. All kinds of furtive ratty cheating and infidelity goes on. I'm sure Cyrus has been unfaithful to me more than once, though I've never done that to him, I wouldn't consider it. I mean it's improper and dangerous and simply wrong. So you become older and older, a woman does, until you haven't got a chance, and you sort of die bit by bit on the vine."

She was lost in reflection a moment, and Harriet waited. Walking, Lisa stared at the turf, and then she looked up.

"I was just thinking—no, it's not like dying on the vine—it's like—well, you have only one life to live—and it lets out of you so gradually, like the air leaking out of a poorly tied balloon. There is nothing left. Do you understand, Harriet? All the while this is happening, you sometimes meet another man at a party or someplace and he thinks you're still something and you think he is charming and sweet. And you wonder, you wish—well, you think— maybe here is someone who could tie the balloon, stop life escaping. You would be new to him. He would be new to you. Everything would be taut and fresh again, not doughy and old. When you've been married as long as I have, Harriet, you collect a lot of bruises and bumps along the way. Every time you go to bed with your husband, you take beneath the blanket the scars of every disagreement, every unreasonableness, every lousy day. You also take all you know of his weaknesses, his failures as a person, his attitudes toward his mother, his father, his brother, his ineptness with his first business partner, his stupidity about his son, the way he couldn't hold liquor that night at the beach party, his childishness about getting into that club, his fears about colds and heights, his lack of grace at dancing and the way he can't swim and his awful taste in pattern neckties. And you take under the blanket yourself, your oldness and being taken for granted and neglected, and you know he thinks about you, if he thinks about you at all, the way you do about him, all the scars. You forget the good parts. So sometimes you long for someone else — not variety or sex alone — but only to be new to someone and be with someone new. You can't see their scars. They can't see yours. But what happens when you find a candidate? Nothing happens. At least not with women like myself. We're too conventional."

She seemed almost to have forgotten her companion, when suddenly she looked at Harriet. "I guess I got off the track a little," Lisa said, "but maybe not. Anyway, what I started to say is that right here on this island they've got it licked. The yearly festival is their safety valve. That's where you're recharged. According to this dance woman, in that one week any man or woman, married or unmarried, can approach any other person. For example, take a native married woman, maybe married ten or fifteen years. She is fascinated by someone else's husband. She simply hands him some kind of token — I think a shell necklace — and if he wears it, it means he reciprocates her feeling. They can meet openly. If they want to sleep together, they do. If they only want each other's company, fine, that's it. After the festival is over, the wife goes back to her husband and life goes on. No recriminations. It's tradition, perfectly healthy, acceptable to all. I think it's great."

"Are you sure about no recriminations?" asked Harriet. "I mean people are possessive, they get jealous."

"Not here," said Lisa. "They've grown up with this custom and it's with them all their lives. The dance woman, Oviri, said there were some adjustments sometimes, an appeal to the Hierarchy to shed one mate and take a new one, because of the festival, but rarely. I still think it's great. Imagine, doing whatever you want for a week with no one watching you or caring, and yourself not feeling guilty."

"It's fantastic. I've never heard anything like it" [pp. 289-290].

*   *   *

"Wright had seen too much sexual maladjustment in Great Britain. While he found matters improved on the Sirens, he wanted perfection. He wanted no one dissatisfied, ever. He has some eloquent passages on this point in his manuscript. He knew that his suggested innovations would not solve all marital problems, but he felt they laid a better foundation for happiness. So he introduced the idea of a second love partner, when a second one was required."

Courtney waited to see if Claire understood. She did not. "I may be slow," she said. "I still don't grasp what you mean."

Courtney sighed, and went on. "Wright found that, too often, after coitus, one partner was satisfied and the other was not. Usually, the man had enjoyed his orgasm, but his mate remained unfulfilled. Sometimes, it was the other way around. Under the new custom, if this occurred, the unfulfilled mate, let us say a married woman, could tell her husband she was going to the Social Aid Hut to finish her love. If he felt that she was not justified, was just being promiscuous, he had the right to challenge her and protest to the Hierarchy for a trial. If he felt that she was justified, and this was usually the case, he would let her go, and turn over and himself go to sleep. As for the unfulfilled one, she would make her way to the Social Aid Hut. Outside there were two bamboo shoots, each with a bell on the end, each tied down. If the visitor was a man, he would untie and release one bamboo, which jumped upwards and rang the bell. If visitor was a woman, she would release both bamboos. These would be heard inside. Having released two bells, she would proceed into a darkened room, unseen by anyone, and there would be a single man of sexual prowess waiting. What her husband had begun would now be finished by another. There you have it."

Claire had heard out the last with growing disbelief. "Incredible," she said. "Does it still go on?"

"Yes, but the practice has been modified since the turn of the century. The bells were torn down, thrown away. They were found to be too noisy—in fact, because of their sound, inhibiting. Today, the unfulfilled mate merely goes to the Social Aid Hut, quite openly selects a single man, bachelor or widower for her partner, and retires with him to a private room."

"And there is no embarrassment or humiliation in this?"

"None whatsoever. Don't forget, it is a revered and accepted practice. Everyone is told of it from childhood. Everyone participates, at one time or another" [pp. 309-310].

Utopian swingers, as contrasted with recreational swingers, are concerned in general with creating a better world. They see war, violence, possessiveness, jealousy, sexual exclusivity, and other common characteristics of society as evil (Symonds, 1967). But the sexual aspects of utopias, like group marriage and unlike group sex, doom it to failure because its "aim is not to dissociate sexuality from emotional involvement, and tender love from the sensual embrace. The result is a repetition, on another level, of the kind of rivalries, jealousies, infidelities, and emotional hang-ups from which the communards were fleeing" (Lerner, 1972, p. 106) originally.

Threesomes, which are on the borderline of communal sex, are most common among people who are involved in a group sexual encounter. Since it is nearly always a closed affair, it is really a variation on monogamy and subject to the same rules of exclusiveness and faithfulness as monogamic marriage, but where jealousy plays a more restrictive role (Lipton, 1965). The triad seems to work out better than other experimental forms, particularly if it consists of one man and two women. Taylor (1954) ascribes the success of the *ménage à trois* to "the desire to find within marriage both intellectual companionship and sexual passion. Heinrich F. Jacobi, who himself lived with two women, one whose task was to satisfy his body, the other his soul, described such an arrangement in his novel, *Woldemar*. Goethe recommended something similar in his *Stella*. This is the romantic conception attempting to incorporate the older tendency to separate Eros and Agape, and arriving at an echo of the Greek solution. Historically, however, the marriage *à trois* is not strictly a romantic conception but is a relic of the *Sturm und Drang* period" (p. 189). A threesome takes place in the Chinese classic, *Golden Lotus*, when Golden Lotus arranges for Chingchi to visit her and they play Turtle Chess with Plum Blossom. "In the Chinese code of love a turtle is a lover and sometimes a penis, and it appears likely that Turtle Chess is a threesome" (Atkins, 1970, p. 352).

At a symposium, reported by Socarides (1962), Rappaport presented clinical material dealing with orgy *à trois*, involving the wife, husband, and female companion simultaneously. In the ensuing discussion Socarides remarked, "in this and similar cases there is a compromise formation in the acting out of overt female homosexuality. The wife utilized the protective presence of the husband (father) while at the same time engaging in a fictive phallic coitus with the mother, thereby gratifying herself narcissistically. The presence of the husband also protected her against an unconscious sadistic attack protected her against an unconscious sadistic attack upon the mother's upon the mother's body. In addition, superego guilt was allayed as these women denied their homosexuality in this particular protective threesome" (p. 592). The *ménage à trois* is obviously oedipal on the surface, since the threesome equals parents plus child, but its deeper meaning is not sexual but rather a representation of the relation of self and other. This is particularly notable in pornographic fiction, such as the predilection of the narrator in *My Secret Life* for two women and as in Rousseau's fantasy for *Julie*. "The underlying model for such *affaires à trois* is not the triangle, which implies a return of the self and thus a sort of reciprocity . . . but is rather the infinite regress . . . in which there is no mutual stimulation, only unilateral voyeuristic pleasure . . . and this watching is a fantasy, a memory wrapped in sentiment" (Stoehr, 1967-1968, p. 54).

In the wryly titled chapter, "Family Talk," of Alan Lelchuk's (1973) novel, *American Mischief*, an orgy *à trois* is depicted. The protagonist, a brilliant, young Dean of a Boston area college, celebrates the second anniversary of his relationship with two women, Gwen and Angela, by wining and dining them in a local restaurant and then returning to his apartment for a nightcap and a near-midnight hubris. The passage reveals the dynamics of voyeurism, exhibitionism, sadomasochism, narcissism, and Lesbianism.

> Perfect little baroque dances of Praetorius and Gastoldi cheered the living room, while a round of vodka tonics came and went. Gwen, legs crossed demurely on the Morris chair, and Angela, sprawled languorously on the sofa, chatted about careers and roles for women. The circumstances turning the little boring talk into yet another charming, ironic episode! (Those circumstances! I couldn't stop enjoying them in my mind, like a boy crayoning all the pictures in his new coloring book the first day he receives it.) In the midst of the second drink, Gwen casually went to the record rack and bending low—that brown behind a pedestal of beauty—selected two records to replace the completed baroque. Listening to the infant prattle of Angie, I was taken by surprise by the full-throated sweetness of Aretha Franklin (a gift from Gwen). Which was nothing next to Gwen suddenly "moving" to the rhythms of Aretha, her hips and arms undulating, turning the room space into an aquarium, herself

into a fish. The talk stopped as Gwen began to hypnotize both of us. And when Aretha stopped, Gwen, smiling fully, gulping vodka tonic, unzipped her dress from her body and continued dancing in frilly black panties, floral black bra, stockings, and high heels. Now, to the rocking voice of Otis Redding, she swam about more lavishly, seductively. Well, it was breathtaking, the headiness of the atmosphere heated by the presence of a third party.

The evening expanded — blurred, diffuse, sensual. When the rock stopped, baby Angela rose, kicked off her shoes, and went to the records. While the Scott changer maneuvered, Angela unbuttoned her blouse, removed it, giggled, dropped her trousers to her ankles, and, like a little girl, sat on the floor and pulled them off. To the exotic Greek and Turkish music, in bare feet and brightly flowered bikini underwear, the slim boyish figure began her "thing," the belly dance. (During this unrobing process, Gwen had begun to tug at my shirt and more, so that I found myself watching the performance clothed in my Jockey briefs only.) Well, that whorish wop didn't embarrass me before the professional Gwen, not at all. Very suavely that belly gyrated round, pulsed in and out, teased up and down; that belly button eyeing us. Not bad at all — that amateur was giving the Brown Bomber a ride for the prize all right. And with that great sex instinct of hers — no amateur when it came to smelling *that odor* in the air — she edged to within a foot of myself and Gwen. Fixing our gaze, she rotated that white belly with slow expert provocativeness.

The next steps were both inevitable and surprising. As I leaned forward in a daze of sound and desire toward that pulsing body, a pair of brown hands reached out to rip away the bikini bottom. For four or five minutes, I was then tormented and tantalized, as that belly was joined by the naked mound of blond hair, to rub my nose and tongue, and then back off, rub, tantalize, and dance off. Meanwhile, hands were soothing my neck, urging me on. The three of us were then on the rug, caressing like calves. My briefs were slid away by brown hands, while black panties were removed by girlish hands. Certain things stood out amid that tangle of bodies. Immediately apparent was Angela's desire for Gwen; she was all over her, kissing her wildly, a thin white cub climbing upon the dark mature lioness. The passion was so devoted and total that I sat on my haunches and observed, like a wrestling referee on his knees, trying to assess a shoulder pinning. I was transfixed as that swooning Angela trailed her pink tongue down Gwen's luscious curves, Gwen taking her in and encouraging her and saying, of all things, "It's all right, baby, that's all right," before she started saying, "That's good, baby, that's good." To tell the truth, I could have stayed content in that spectator role, exulting in their lesbian lesson, except that Gwen lured me to her with her hands and engulfed my prick with her mouth. My thighs sandwiching Gwen's swollen upside-down face, I was able now from another view to watch the avid Angela sucking pleasure from and into Gwen's lower openings. Terrific stuff. I was dying to get hold of Angie, despite the other joys (watching and being swallowed). Finally I reached out, tugged Angie's hair, and managed to turn her around, so that I could go to work on her own bottom. With elbows, lips, and limbs mixing, and positions bizarre, it was like some European acrobatic team rehearsing for the Ed Sullivan show. Where were the CBS cameras?

The climax embarrassed me as much as it thrilled me. With moans and shrieks and body English growing more frenzied, I began finally coming into Gwen's mouth. But suddenly she maneuvered away so that I was lathering her face with the white sperm. Whereupon Angie, bellowing like a cow in heat, suddenly dove down upon that face and began lapping it up. Incredible. The denseness of appetites was so thick by then, the flow of juices and secretions and passions so rich, that it was like being at a feast of cannibals. I tell you, those girls would have eaten anything, anything!

We lay upon each other, three spent animals. Minutes followed of panting leisure, body odor, sated feeling, curious relief. We smoked and talked on the rug, Angela cupping a brown breast, Gwen covering my penis tenderly with her hand. Angie began asking us about our astrology charts, and gave a little spiel about the conjunction of my moon and Mercury. Was she demented? I wondered. And then we were going at it again, with Gwen and I fixing that wop's wagon — "You dirty little guinea!" I remember saying, picking up Gwen's hints — and glutting ourselves again. This time, thoroughly exhausted afterward, we simply lay in our perspiration and breathing: no talk, no touching, no anything. Glutted. Then we started to recoup and dress, the girls having to return home to release their baby-sitters.

I'm unsure how the fight started. I know the girls were three-quarters dressed, when some words were exchanged, looks grew harsh, and the atmosphere of sweet cordiality of ten minutes previous was suddenly shattered. Why do these girls do these things, tell me? Why must they always everywhere cause *some* trouble? (Angie says that Gwen suddenly grew jealous because she suddenly wanted to play more. Gwen says Angie just grew crazy and insulting.

Naturally I trust Gwen more — but in such circumstances, who could tell?) In any case, Angie was suddenly pulling upon Gwen (screaming her non sequitur, "Get away from him, you!"), who, half laughing, was trying to comfort her. But then they were going at it, full steam ahead. Pocketbooks swinging, hair pulled hard, crazy tumbling over. Gwen bitten on the side, screaming, and belting Angela in the jaw. After a futile attempt to separate them (getting scratched in the process), I stood aside and looked on. If the trio-sex was special, the fight was extra-special. What enormous joy in watching two women go at each other violently! How different from the fear when watching two men break each other's bones. Here there was perspiration, loose hair, girlish holds, bitching swearing, and no real damage. A pair of alley cats screeching and scratching. And over me! I restrained my laughter and joy.

It was over as suddenly as it had started. it simply ceased, the winner Gwen rising from the vanquished Angela. As soon as Angie was on her feet and I saw her crying lightly, I knew that she had gotten exactly what she had wanted from the evening: a split lip, ripped blouse and underwear, lots of sex and fighting, melodrama, whimpering tears, childish breakthroughs. What a whore! Delicious. Watching her phony feeble attempts to make herself presentable for the world again made me smile openly; even smirk, I'm afraid. Well, it was an error. Out of a sudden sympathy with her defeated enemy, Gwen walked toward me, saying, "Don't you laugh, buster!" And smacked me hard across my face. Me, an innocent bystander! Before I had time to recover, the two of them were upon me, clawing, wrestling, slapping. And cursing me: "You pervert!" cried the demented Angela, digging into my wrists with frantic fingernails. "You pervert! You brought us here to humiliate us! That's what you are, a pervert!" Weakened by drink, sex, laughter, I was no match for the pair of them. Tearing my robe from me, then ripping my Jockey briefs (a symbolical gesture, in place of castration?), they left me on the floor, naked, dazed, hurt. Her arm around her new pal's waist, Gwen led the whimpering Angela out of the room and the apartment. Lying there, near tears, I was in a state of shock from the turn of events and from the thought that I had messed up irreparably.

That's what hurt most, then, and in the next few days — that I had lost one or both of the girls. It was horrible. From greed, and overweening pride (that nightcap), I had bungled it all! I never knew how much I needed those girls until I was faced with the prospect of losing them. To do without Angela's sluttishness? Gwen's blackness? I would go crazy, absolutely crazy from my fantasies if I lost them! The jingle of Humpty Dumpty not being able to be put back together again kept running through my head. And apart from my need and desire, what about the *waste*? Two years of training, almost twenty-four months of work, down the drain! It killed me. After two or three days, I got up my perseverance and went around to beg and plead. What else could I do, suffer end-lessly? [pp. 137-141].

Orgiastic sex is by definition depersonalized and antithetical to any possible sharing beyond the physiological level; the emotional basis of an orgy is masturbatory and narcissistic (Hartogs, 1967). The orgy makes sex an end in itself because it presupposes the value and validity of intercourse without love, faithfulness, or the presumption of per-manence. The most intense excitement at an orgy comes less from what people are doing to one another than from the exhibitionism and voyeurism characteristic of children first discovering their bodies. And the group orgy protects the individual somewhat in that no one keeps close track of him (Grold, 1970).

The nude group encounter is of recent vintage, evidence perhaps of the hunger for sheer human contact, physical and emotional. "When people are naked you can really understand why human individuality is such a fragile thing," declares Kensuke Sugimoto, the cynical dilet-tante in *Thirst for Love* by Yukio Mishima (1969). "What's love? Nothing more than symbol falling for symbol. And when it comes to sex—that's anonymity falling for anonymity. Chaos and chaos, the unisexual mating of depersonalization with depersonalization. Mascu-linity? Femininity? You can't tell the difference" (pp. 111-112).

There are relatively few studies of nudism from a psychological point of view. "That this should be so cannot be without significance. That none of the more recent professional psychological publications contains any studies of an unusual social phenomenon of the propor-tion of the nudist movement indicates the extent to which irrational attitudes and unconscious motivations influence even workers in the fields of psychology, education, and sociology, to say nothing of psy-chiatry" (Hirning, 1961, p. 108). Otto and Otto (1972) state that despite the seemingly increasing acceptance of nudity there is tremen-dous ambivalence, fear, anxiety, and conflict attached to it.

Most people have been taught to feel disgust, shame, and guilt about their own and other people's nude bodies, at the same time recognizing the body as a source of pleasure. Symonds (1971) hypothesizes that much of normal sexual behavior is a desire for bodily contact with other people. The group she investigated was composed of middle-class professionals over thirty years of age and whose purpose it was to encourage skin contact and to learn about the body. Problems stemming from nudity in the group included uncomfortable sexual excitement, unfulfilled desire for verbal confrontation, and continued attendance after the group had fulfilled its usefulness. The advantages included the opportunity for body contact without commitment to sexual intercourse and the opportunity to become comfortable in the presence of, and to touch other people's bodies.

A nude marathon encounter group described by Gwen Davis (1971) in her novel, *Touching*, follows closely the procedure outlined by Bindrim (1969). His group, like Davis's, was in continuous session from Friday evening until Sunday afternoon, with six hours out each night for sleeping. After the first day their impressions included "a sense of pleasure from the freedom to look at the bodies of others and be looked at in return; a sense of personal comfort, exhilaration and freedom; the desire to touch and a sense of being inhibited in this desire; a sense of group closeness; relief and surprise among the men at not becoming unduly aroused sexually; a sense of guilty concern about one's body; and the experience of being high or at least unable to sleep for most of the night" (p. 103). Five weeks later fifteen of Bindrim's twenty participants reported beneficial changes in themselves and in their relations with their families and colleagues. The setting for Davis's *Touching* is the never-never land of California. Dr. Simon Herford is the grossly obese and vulgar therapist, "with something shamany about him." As the nude group encounter proceeds through progressively more intense stages, the characters and the incidents have a realism and candor which gives credence to the value of the procedure. As Bindrim testifies, "Self-acceptance is often associated with one's body image. Open exposure to group reaction in the nude state often remedies purely imaginary distortions, thereby increasing ego-strength and empowering men and women to make more honest and more salutary struggles with their core emotional problems. Since sensual body contact is often a primary way of expressing the self emotionally and of responding adequately to others, and since our culture defines sensuality and sexuality as bed-mates, perhaps we have blocked vital avenues of communication that might easily be reopened" (p. 106).

The emergence of a variety of sexually plural subcultures among middle Americans suggests that there is a recognizable minority that persists in stepping out of the restrictions of conventional sex roles into sexually polymorphous relationships. The majority of the population, on all socioeconomic levels, are chary of nonmonagomous patterns, feeling that swingers, in their nomadic affection, are pretending to a sexual liberation that is, in fact, a facade for a paucity of affect. The investment in sexuality as a safeguard for marriage, rather than a viable emotional compact, seems to be the benchmark of swingers. They present an interesting application of Babbitt values to what is considered to be a radical activity. Too much sex too soon leaves people at an adolescent stage of sexual development, incapable of achieving genuine intimacy with a person of the opposite sex. Such people may be acting out their childish impulses and fantasies under the guise of sexual liberation.

It is perhaps whimsical to conclude this chapter with two prophecies about the future of swinging, each diametrically opposed to the other. "Group sex," wrote Kellen (1972), "does not fit into the more sensitive and more genuinely liberated society foreseen for the 1980's. Despite its current great vogue, it will disappear before the decade is over, at least as a national phenomenon" (p. 152). Burke (1969), on the other hand, predicts, "within ten years we'll have the first (legal) group marriage ... By 1990, the old husband-and-wife unit will be nearly obsolete, too — in which, say, two guys and a girl live together and all groove on each other with no specific sexual roles. After that, group living. Group grooving. It's coming" (p. 315).

TECHNICAL REFERENCES

Allen, G. & Martin, C. G. (1971), *Intimacy. Sensitivity, Sex and the Art of Love.* Chicago: Cowles.

Amir, M. (1971), *Patterns in Forcible Rape.* Chicago: University of Chicago Press.

Anon. (1973), Letter. *Playboy,* 20(6):63.

Atkins, J. (1970), *Sex in Literature. The Erotic Impulse in Literature.* New York: Grove Press.

Avery, P. & Avery, E. (1964), Some notes on "wife-swapping." In: *Sex in America,* ed. H. A. Grunewald. New York: Bantam, pp. 248-254.

Bartell, G. D. (1970), Group sex among the mid-Americans. *Journal of Sex Relations,* 6:113-130.

——— (1971), *Group Sex: A Scientist's Eyewitness Report on the American Way of Swinging.* New York: Wyden.

———— (1972), In: *Marriage: For & Against,* ed. H. H. Hart. New York: Hart, pp. 210-220.

Bernard, J. (1972), *The Future of Marriage.* New York: World.

Bindrim, P. (1969), Naked therapy. In: *The New Eroticism,* ed. P. Nobile. New York: Random House, 1971, pp. 98-107.

Brecher, E. M. (1969), *The Sex Researchers.* Boston: Little, Brown.

Briffault, R. (1927), *The Mothers.* London: Allen, 1959.

Burke, T. (1969), The new homosexuality. *Esquire, 73:*315.

Coley, S. B. (1973), Sexual activity as a coping mechanism. *Medical Aspects of Human Sexuality,* 7(3):40-63.

Constantine, L. L. & Constantine, J. M. (1971), Multilateral marriage: Alternate family structure in practice. In: *You and I Searching for Tomorrow,* ed. R. H. Rimmer. New York: New American Library.

———— ———— (1973), *Group Marriage. A Study of Contemporary Multilateral Marriage.* New York: Macmillan.

Denfield, D. & Gordon, M. (1970), The sociology of mate swapping: Or the family that swings together clings together. *Journal of Sex Research,* 6:85-100.

Ellis, A. (1958), *Sex Without Guilt.* New York: Stuart.

———— (1968), Sexual promiscuity in America. *Annals of the American Academy of Political and Social Science,* 378:58-67.

Francoeur, R. T. (1972), *Eve's New Rib: Twenty Faces of Sex, Marriage, and Family.* New York: Harcourt Brace Jovanovich.

Freud, S. (1921), Group psychology and the analysis of the ego. *Standard Edition,* 18:67-143. London: Hogarth Press, 1955.

Gittelson, N. (1972), *The Erotic Life of the American Wife.* New York: Delacorte.

Godwin, J. (1973), *The Mating Trade.* Garden City, N.Y.: Doubleday.

Grold, J. L. (1970), Swinging: Sexual freedom or neurotic escapism? *American Journal of Psychiatry,* 127:521-523.

Harris, S. (1969), *The Puritan Jungle. America's Sexual Underground.* New York: Putnam's.

Hartogs, R. (1967), *Four-Letter Word Games: The Psychology of Obscenity.* New York: Evans.

Hirning, L. C. (1961), Clothing and nudism. In: *Sex and Today's Society,* ed. A. Ellis & A. Abarbanel. New York: Ace Books, pp. 86-115.

Hunt, M. (1969), *The Affair. A Portrait of Extra-Marital Love in Contemporary America.* New York: World.

Kellen, K. (1972), *The Coming Age of Woman Power.* New York: Wyden.

Kinsey, A. C., Pomeroy, W. B., Martin, C. E. & Gebhard, P. H. (1953), *Sexual Behavior in the Human Female.* Philadelphia: Saunders.

Lerner, M. (1972), In: *Marriage: For & Against,* ed. H. H. Hart. New York: Hart, pp. 92-100.

Lewis, R. W. (1969), The swingers. In: *Sex American Style,* ed. F. Robinson & N. Lehrman. Chicago: Playboy Press, 1971, pp. 30-69.

Lipton, L. (1965), *The Erotic Revolution.* Los Angeles: Sherbourne.

May, R. (1972), *Power and Innocence.* New York: Norton.

O'Neill, G. C. & O'Neill, N. (1970), Patterns in group sex activity. *Journal of Sex Research,* 6:101-112.

O'Neill, N. & O'Neill, G. (1972), *Open Marriage. A New Life Style for Couples.* New York: Evans.

Otto, H. A. & Otto, R. (1972), *Total Sex.* New York: Wyden.

Ramey, J. W. (1972a), Communes, group marriage, and the upper middle class. *Journal of Marriage and the Family*, 34:647-655.

———— (1972b), Emerging patterns of behavior in marriage: Deviations or innovations? *Journal of Sex Research*: 8:6-30.

Rogers, C. R. (1972), *Becoming Partners: Marriage and Its Alternatives*. New York: Delacorte.

Scrignar, C. B. & Spiers, D. (1970), Bigamy. *Medical Aspects of Human Sexuality*, 4(5):116-122.

Shaw, G. B. (1908), *Getting Married*. New York: Brentano's, 1909.

Simon, W. (1969), Sex. *Psychology Today*, 3(2):23-27.

Smith, J. R. & Smith, L. G. (1970), Co-marital sex and the sexual freedom movement. *Journal of Sex Research*, 6:131-142.

Socarides, C. W. (1962), Theoretical and clinical aspects of overt female homosexuality. *Journal of the American Psychoanalytic Association*. 10:579-592.

Stoehr, T. (1967-1968), Pornography, masturbation and the novel. *Salmagundi*, 2(2):28-56.

Symonds, C. (1967), *A Pilot Study of the Peripheral Behavior of Sexual Mate Swappers*. Unpublished Master's thesis. Riverside, Cal.: University of California.

———— (1971), A nude touchy-feely group. *Journal of Sex Research*, 7:126-133.

Taylor, G. R. (1954), *Sex in History*. New York: Ballantine.

Vilar, E. (1971), *The Manipulated Man*. New York: Farrar, Straus & Giroux, 1972.

Walker, B. R. & Walker, S. R. (1968), *The New Immorality*. Garden City, N.Y.: Doubleday.

Walshok, M. L. (1971), The emergence of a middle-class deviant subculture: The case of swingers. *Social Problems*, 18:488-495.

Westermarck, E. (1921), *The History of Human Marriage*, Vol. 3. New York: Allenton, 1922.

Winthrop, H. (1970), Focus on the human condition: Sexual revolution or inner emptiness: Portents of *Brave New World:* II. The skin trade versus holistic balance in sexuality. *Journal of Human Relations*, 18:924-938.

LITERARY REFERENCES

Davis, Gwen (1971), *Touching*. Garden City, N.Y.: Doubleday.

Huxley, Aldous (1932), *Brave New World*. New York: Harper & Row.

Lelchuk, Alan (1973), *American Mischief*. New York: Farrar, Straus & Giroux.

List, Shelley S. (1972), *Did You Love Daddy When I Was Born?* New York: Saturday Review Press.

Mishima, Yukio (1969), *Thirst for Love*. New York: Knopf.

Rimmer, Robert H. (1968), *Proposition 31*. New York: New American Library.

Sangster, Jimmy (1971), *Your Friendly Neighbourhood Death Pedlar*. New York: Dodd, Mead.

Skinner, Burrhus F. (1948), *Walden Two*. New York: Macmillan, 1964.

Updike, John (1968), *Couples*. New York: Knopf.

Wallace, Irving (1963), *The Three Sirens*. New York: Simon & Schuster.

Wells, Tobias (1972), *A Die in the Country*. Garden City, N.Y.: Doubleday.

CHAPTER FOURTEEN

Hallucinogenic Drugs and Sex

Marijuana and Hashish

One of the great literary legacies bequeathed on an all too gullible public that delighted in sensationalism was the work of the litterateurs of the nineteenth century which dealt with drugs and their intoxicating effects. A litany of lurid tales by some of the world's great poets—opium and hashish users all—was in very large measure responsible for perpetuating much of the misinformation about sex-crazed drug fiends and dangerous, murderous addicts. The evil representation of hashish was fanned by the embellished sagas of the Assassins, fortified for many years after by the effusions of celebrated literary hashish users. Among them were Baudelaire, Dumas, Gautier, de Nerval, Balzac, Charles Lamb and Fitzhugh Ludlow who painted extraordinary word pictures of their experiences under the influence of the drug. Some of their accounts were very accurate in terms of the characteristic features of intoxication with hashish, such as space and time distortion, increased motoric activity, ideational flights, euphoric exaltation and intensified sexual desire and performance dependent on the amount of hashish taken (Finch, 1960).

The accounts of these literary figures are important not only because they were so successful in putting into words the more subtle aspects of the experience, but because they have enormously influenced the general impression of the nature of acute cannabis intoxication (Grinspoon, 1971). Their effusive descriptions were often distorted and excessive because they were written under the influence of large amounts of ingested hashish and have little to do with moderate use of the drug. "Nonetheless, these writings, so influential in creating the Western impression of cannabis, deserve considerable study, just because they do illuminate some of the quantitative and qualitative differences between the intoxication produced by large amounts of ingested hashish and that of moderate doses of smoked marijuana. It is helpful to regard the French reports of hashish intoxication as offshoots of a literary revolution. Viewed in such a light, many excesses and exaggerations concerning the effects of hashish become less puzzling; in many cases it was not the hashish alone, but the excitement engendered by a new approach to literature, combined with the intoxication of the writers' already exceptional powers of imagination and narration, that caused the fantastic and unbelievable claims for the magical, supra-mundane effects of the drug. A fact that helps to establish this hypothesis of the direct relationship of the French literary revolt to the use of hashish is the absence of any subsequent writings concerning hashish that even approximates the extreme nature of the reports from Gautier, Baudelaire, and others" (Grinspoon, 1971, pp. 55-56).

The ecstasy Gautier (1846) felt in his hashish-intoxicated state is reflected in this sentence: "No terrestrial desire marred [the purity of my ecstasy]. Love itself . . . could not have increased it" (p. 173). In terms of the controversy concerning the aphrodisiac power of cannabis, Gautier wrote, "With a peaceful though fascinated eye, I watched a garland of ideally beautiful women, who diademed a frieze with their divine nudity; I saw a gleam of their satin shoulders, the sparkle of their silvery breasts, the overhead tripping of small pink feet, the undulation of opulent hips, without feeling the least temptation . . . By some bizarre prodigy, after several minutes of contemplation I would melt into the object looked at, and I myself became that object . . . A hashish-eater would not lift a finger for the most beautiful maiden in Verona" (p. 173). The sex-depressant effect, the depersonalization, the synesthesia, the sensitivity to sound and to touch, are indications that the amount of the drug Gautier took was considerable. Rabelais (1552) too sang the praises of *Cannabis sativa*, expatiating at length on its effect on the individual and society, and on sexual behavior.

Drugs have always been considered either sacred or diabolical. The background of drug use in history involves charms, magic potions, holy sacraments, and devil's orgies. In more advanced societies, the same cluster of ideas carries over into more modern distinctions between legal intoxicants, which are good, and illegal dope, which is bad. But that is purely a matter of social definition. In all sections of the Far East, hashish acted as a sexual stimulant. The favorite of the Hindustanis for provoking wild illusions and satyriasis was hemp, or bhang, according to Edwardes (1959). The hemp-eater would experience fantastic visions of Paradise, desirable nymphs and catamites; and such dreams were said to make men content who had psychologically become impotent. The chemical that opens the door to somatic and sensory experiences has been well known for centuries to cultures that stress delicate, sensitive registration for sensory stimulation: Arab, Indian, and Mogul cultures (Leary, 1968). It is marijuana.

In Western culture, the most popular cliché of the marijuana user is that he is unkempt, unemployed, footloose, politically radical or apathetic, sexually promiscuous, and under the influence of the drug all the time; but this image is gradually being replaced by one almost as absurd: the marijuana user is no different from the rest of us, who embrace all ages, professions, occupations and socioeconomic status (Goode, 1970). However, Goode does attempt a composite picture of the marijuana user. He is likely to be in his late teens or early twenties to be male rather than female, to live in or near an urban environment. The higher the education and income of the family, the more likely they are to smoke marijuana. More Jews smoke it than Gentiles, but the average pot smoker is highly unlikely to be religious in a traditional sense. He holds liberal or radical political views, generally does not have authoritarian attitudes, and tends to be liberal and permissive sexually. "Sexually permissive people are more likely to try and to use marijuana than those who are more restrictive, conservative, or conventional. The more liberal in sexual matters the individual is, the greater is his chance of using marijuana ... The more he rejects many of conventional society's sexual restrictions and prohibitions, the more acceptable marijuana will seem ... Relationships are not directly dependent on sex itself, but on more fundamental underlying attitudes and behavior. Both marijuana use and sexual permissiveness are dependent on the same basic factor, rather than one being dependent on the other" (p. 46).

Thus the drug revolution has combined with the sexual revolution to bring forth far-reaching results. "Chiefly what has happened, and is continuing to happen as more and more converts climb on the eroto-psychedelic bandwagon, can be described — paradoxically — as an upsurge of interest in the nonphysical side of sex. Even though the concept sounds like an oxymoron at first, we all know about the nonphysical or metaphysical aspects of our own eroticism. It is the emotional — or energetic — force that gives sex a flavor or a color quite independent of its physical spasms, albeit capable of enriching and even prolonging the physical aspect [p. xi].... If drugs can change the way in which the brain sees, hears, smells and assembles meaningful form out of the chaos of sensation, they can also radically transform the nature of sexual feeling ... [p. 61]. It stands to reason that a drug that will magnify sensation and externalize one's fantasies [as will hashish] will be a most powerful enhancer of the sex act if the experimenter's mind is open to its possibilities in advance" (Wilson, 1973, p. 117).

There are a number of ideas suggesting the origin of the word "marijuana," but it is still in doubt. Some authorities are of the opinion that it is derived from the Portuguese word "mariguano," meaning intoxicant, or, again from the Portuguese, "potiguaya," also meaning intoxicant, while others assert it has its derivation in the Mexican words for "Mary and Jane" (Solomon, 1966; Wilson, 1973). Cannabis is the Latin term for preparations made from the hemp plant, such as marijuana and hashish. The leaves and the flowering tops of the cannabis plant are dried, sometimes mixed with tobacco and then typically smoked in cigarette form. In the vernacular they are called "reefers," "joints," "pot," or "sticks" containing "hay," "grass," "weed," "tea," or "Acupulco gold." Hashish is the concentrated resin of the marijuana plant. Marijuana is considered to be a mild psychedelic, but since this class of drugs is rather loosely defined, it is difficult to ascertain whether it belongs to this group. Marijuana and hashish are drugs that expand consciousness and increase awareness of the surroundings and bodily processes. Yet, marijuana does not have the profound effects on cognition, perception, and personality characteristics of psychedelic drugs; cannabis can, at different stages, have an excitatory, as well as a depressant effect (Sinnett et al., 1972). Under the influence of cannabis, the subject is acutely aware of colors, sounds, and odors. The effects of the drug may be said to consist of the phenomenon of increased awareness, which may be pleasant or unpleasant depending on the content of the awareness (Burroughs, 1961).

Yorke (1970, p. 142) indicates the difficulty in defining addiction: "This is barely attempted by most writers, with the unhappy consequences that, when they speak of addiction, they are not all talking about the same thing. This appears to be an important source of confusion and contradiction in the literature." The true addiction syndrome, according to Stockings (1947), involves a physical craving, tolerance, abstention syndrome, and personality deterioration; it is peculiar to the cocaine and morphine group of drugs, whereas mescaline and cannabis do not induce comparable addiction. The drug addict is defined by Rosenberg (1969) as a person who, as a result of repeated administration, has become dependent on the effects of a drug, has an overpowering desire to continue taking the drug, and shows a marked tendency to increase the dose. Addiction, states Bejerot (1972), is a morbid condition in itself with its own dynamics of development.

The literature on the subject of marijuana abounds in contradictory statements. Praised by one researcher, dammed by another, it is astonishing how little is actually known. In particular, the data on sexual behavior under the impetus of drug usage are largely subjective and sparse. Although many papers are enlightened by clinical examples, in the main they repeat much of what has been said previously without contributing any appreciable clarification. Experimental studies of the sexual effects of marijuana and hashish are conspicuously few and even these have been conducted without scientific rigor. Attempts to be rational or objective about the use of marijuana and hashish seem doomed. The bias of the researcher, despite claims of neutrality, inevitably percolates through the evidence produced. Bloomquist (1971), for example, expresses the opinion that the adverse effects of marijuana outweigh its beneficial effects, and society should take a very firm stand to reduce or eliminate marijuana use before it is too late. But Bloomquist's review of the literature is highly biased and selective. Methodological criticisms of studies favorable to marijuana abound, while negative studies are hardly ever criticized.

Reports of subjective experiences are generally devalued in terms of their scientific merits, and findings from questionnaires have been largely disappointing. Yet multidimensional psychological scaling methods may have considerable potential worth for the measurement and classification of psychological phenomena. A number of studies tend to bear this out. The Sorensen (1973) probability sample of 2,042 households in the United States enumerated 839 adolescents from twelve to nineteen years of age, of whom 508 were eligible for interviews because parental consent was secured. A comparison of the sample frame (839) with the eligible roster (508) along a number of important sociocultural and demographic characteristics showed that the differences between the potential and eligible respondents were statistically insignificant. Eventually, 393 young people were interviewed. Again the differences between the eligible and actual participants were statistically insignificant. Thus the findings of Sorensen's study are statistically valid, reliable, and representative of the nation's young people. Sorensen found that a majority of adolescents interviewed agreed that marijuana increased sexual pleasure, that sexual beginners sample marijuana at the same rate as do the sexually experienced, and that marijuana use is significantly related to sexual behavior. Users are twice as likely to have had intercourse as are nonusers.

One hundred and fifty undergraduates selected at random from three Eastern universities were surveyed by Herz (1970) to determine attitudes and behavior with regard to sex and marijuana use. Her findings indicate at least some participation in the sex act by ninety-two per cent, drug experimentation at some time by twenty-six per cent, and more interest and enthusiasm shown for drugs than for sex. A survey correlating drug usage and sexual activity and enjoyment was taken of randomly selected patients at the Haight-Ashbury Free Medical Clinic of San Francisco (Gay and Sheppard, 1972). Over eighty per cent of the respondents reported that marijuana was the one drug that most enhanced their sexual pleasure. A sensory alteration consisting of a heightening of subjective inputs of taste, touch, sound, and color was generally reported. A "disinhibiting" effect was also noted, as was time distortion, which usually led to sensations of prolonged pleasure. Also reported were feelings of increased body warmth, brotherhood, empathy, and oneness with others, which were felt to contribute to more pleasurable sexual relations. The physiological sexual responses noted would appear to be of a mildly sedative hypnotic, cerebrally disinhibitory, and mildly psychedelic nature.

Subjects classified according to a conceptual systems theory as flexible, relativistic, and culturally independent were reported by Greaves (1971) to have significantly more experience with marijuana, LSD, premarital petting, premarital intercourse, and disposition to extramarital intercourse than subjects classified as rigid, rule-obeying, and authority- and culture-oriented. In interviews with 208 middle-class, adult users of pot, Lewis (1970) found them insisting that the drug was valuable to them because it enhanced their sexual lives, a response confirmed by seventy-three percent of a group of marijuana users in McGlothlin and West's (1968) sample.

A questionnaire survey by Tart (1971) attempted to determine what effects on sexuality are perceived by marijuana users. The responses ranged from an increase in sexual drive to no increase. Tart's population consisted of 150 people, primarily Californians, eighty-six per cent of whom were between seventeen and thirty, and thirteen per cent between thirty-one and fifty-one. Sixty-seven per cent were college students, eighteen per cent academics and mental health professionals, and fifteen per cent nonprofessionals. Thirty-five per cent used marijuana once a month or more; forty per cent once a week or more; and sixteen per cent almost every day. Most of the users smoked marijuana for one to two years, but some had used it for more than eleven years. Tart feels this is a fairly representative sample for a high-level educated group of frequent marijuana smokers. Most of the respondents commented that the sexual drive or need did not increase, but that intoxication increased their awareness of it. Sexual intercourse at very high levels of intoxication can be an ecstatic, overwhelming experience, but at these levels chances are that the user will be absorbed in his own inner experiences rather than become interested in having sexual relations with someone. A pattern that seemed to distinguish the college group with much drug experience from the professional group is that the former reported increased frequency of a variety of sensual enhancements and closeness to sexual partners, while the latter did not have as much sensual experience but had some at lower levels of intoxication. The professional group claimed to be better lovers at lower levels of intoxication and to experience increased closeness to their sexual partners less frequently.

Among the college-educated, there is a general pattern of having more experiences of sensory enhancement. This may reflect a generation gap, as the more educated professionals were generally older than the undergraduates in Tart's population, and may have had many more inhibitions about sensuality and sexuality.

This generational gap can be seen in Julius Horwitz's (1973) *The Married Lovers*. David, a surgeon, is in a hospital psychiatric wing after an abortive suicide attempt, evidently precipitated by his wife's clinically detailed description of her previous eight months of sexual experimentation with other men, including male prostitutes at orgies, in order to find out what he wanted from her in bed and why he found her so disappointing. Neither of them really knows what they wished for behind the closed door of their bedroom. While David is under observation, Anne spends her time surveying "the terrain of marriage," specifically the seventeen years of "emotional pollution" the two of them have undergone. What Anne says she wants is some recognition that she has feelings and a separate identity. David wants their marriage to come out of the closet, for everybody to learn not to be frightened of one another, and for their sixteen-year-old son, Martin, to stop smoking pot. "Is Martin still in his room smoking marijuana," David asks himself. "Inhaling, exhaling for a glimpse of the dream. In my time we masturbated." When his son replies, "I can handle it," David warns his own generation, "I would rather see you handling a paint brush or a hammer or a sailboat" (p. 40). The catechism follows.

> "Are you still smoking marijuana?" I asked my son.
> "Yes, Dad."
> "Do you enjoy it?"
> "It's all right."
> "Do you still fight with your mother over it?"
> "She yells once in a while."
> "When do you smoke it?"
> "Mostly in the evening."
> "Do you smoke it outside the house?"
> "Just once in a while."
> "Do you ever think about getting caught. You know they gave someone in Texas a fifty-year prison sentence for the possession of less than one ounce of marijuana."
> "That's in Texas, Dad, where they've got to preserve a morality they don't believe in. New York State is a little more liberal."

"Do you ever think about using heroin?"

"No. I find the heroin addicts a bore."

"Does the marijuana do anything special for you in the evening?"

"Nothing much, Dad. It's pleasant."

"But it's a ceremony, or has it become a habit."

"It's no habit, Dad, not the way heroin can be. It's nothing, Dad, really nothing."

"Where do you get the money for it now?"

"I seem to have it."

"You don't feel it's a habit?"

"Not more of a habit than watching TV or the way I tie my shoe laces."

"Does it still upset your mother?"

"I think she feels now that I'll grow out of it" [p. 39].

Perhaps one of the most significant sets of findings on cannabis published is the study by Rubin and Comitas (1975) in which Jamaican working-class subjects were used because of their high rate of pot smoking. Further, in this population marijuana is socially sanctioned, and it is the nonuser who is regarded as the nonconformist. Cannabis is used as an energizer in Jamaica. The study showed that workers performed better when they were using the drug than when they were not. Fear in the United States that marijuana use leads to lethargy is not borne out by the life histories of Jamaican working-class subjects or by objective measurements. While no threat to human genetics or reproduction by marijuana users was discovered, the report cautions against its use by pregnant women, since the drug easily crosses the placental barrier. Under certain conditions, which are not clearly defined, use of the herb reduces levels of testoserone, but the significance of this is unclear. In contrast to previous findings of subjective sensations reported by American users, few of the Jamaicans experienced a sharpening of taste, enhanced hearing and appreciation of music, or loss of a sense of elapsed time. This is also at considerable variance with what Baudelaire (1860) and Masters (1971), among others in the one-hundred-year interval, have written.

The medical controversy on the effects of long-term marijuana smoking persists, even as government reports reveal that more than half of the Americans in the eighteen to twenty-five age group have tried marijuana at least once. What was at one time clearly statistically deviant behavior has become the norm for this age group. New findings show that while in previous years use was correlated with level of education, the percentage now reporting marijuana use is virtually identical for high-school dropouts, high-school graduates, and college graduates in similar age ranges. Once a drug associated with the "counter-culture" and regarded as a symbol of opposition, marijuana has lost some of its anti-establishment symbolism.

Nevertheless, the fear of marijuana and hashish is one of the most pervasive of American bugaboos. Four faculty members of Columbia University's College of Physicians and Surgeons (Blanc, Frick, Manger and Nahas, 1975) associate long-term pot smoking with the following hazards: "hormonal imbalance, inhibition of spermatogenesis, lung damage, impairment of immunity, increased formation of chromo-some-deficient cells with possible damage to the offspring, interference with DNA formation, decreased cell division, apathy and lack of motivation, interference with memory and speech and impairment of driving performance" (p. 32). The four physicians point out that the marijuana controversy resembles that which occurred over tobacco: it took eighty years of scientific investigations to prove the damaging effect of tobacco cigarettes and to link smoking to cancer and heart disease. The moral is clear, they indicate.

Although there are no hard data on the issue, one of the most common informal topics at scientific conferences on drug use and abuse is just what happened in the 1960's to so vastly increase the use of marijuana and hashish. There are many possible answers, according to Kaplan (1970), but two involve a connection between sexual activity and drug use. "Both postulate an enormous increase in sexual activity and in sexually free attitudes on the part of the young—in part as a consequence of the pill. The first hinges on the additional assertion (also without present scientific support) that without the guilt which previous generations felt, sex becomes much more spiceless and bland. According to this theory, then, young people turn to drugs at least in part to provide the 'kick' that is now missing from their sex lives. The second of these two theories probably receives more support. It is that the increased access to sex has put upon many young people stress which, at their level of emotional maturity, they are not prepared to assume — especially since the boys tend to develop so much more slowly than their natural partners, the girls in their school classes. As a result of these strains, the need for something to reduce anxiety and to tranquilize becomes all the more acute—and since marijuana performs both these functions without inhibiting performance, it is a natural recourse" (p. 80).

It is not possible to make generalizations about the reasons for drug use because it appears that drugs meet different needs for different persons—a polemic which argues that the use of drugs among contemporary American youth is but one of many different behaviors and mystiques pervading their lives. Thus, a fascination with the encounter, with ethnicity, with expressive politics, with nomadism, with sexuality, as well as with drugs, suggests that youth are engaged in a frustrating dialectic between freedom and commitment (Miller, 1971). Marijuana use has become, according to Zinberg and Robertson (1972), a critical symbol between an emergent youth, "vociferously sacrilegious in their critique of social institutions," and "older and more traditionally American social groups," which explains the often irrational opposition to marijuana reform. Young people act out some of the repressed unconscious wishes of their parents. It is a well-known psychoanalytic axiom that parents may—not explicitly—communicate their own unconscious wishes to their progeny and achieve some measure of gratification through their offsprings' acting out of these wishes, while at the same time parents consciously condemn such behavior. "Accordingly, it is not surprising that one of the concerns uppermost in many parents' minds is that marijuana leads to antisocial behavior and sexual promiscuity" (Grinspoon, 1971, p. 182).

The desperation seen in the adolescent's need "to feel good" seems to be a response to an increasing incidence of chronic depression. "Depression is probably the most prominent symptom shown by these disaffected youths when they are not on drugs. This depression is usually long-lasting . . . If there is one thing which appears to be a constant in the heavy drug user as opposed to the occasional user, it is the presence of a fairly high degree of depression" (Dahlberg, 1971, p. 69). Many young people cannot communicate with their parents. They have all the pressures and expectations to achieve; they are confused about their role and their value system; they are expected to perform in ways for which they are not ready. There are no new frontiers. Jobs are difficult to find, and there are many more adolescents to compete with. Youngsters mature earlier than in previous generations. Despite this, they must endure a prolonged period of adolescence because society keeps them from performing as adults and provides limited employment, even for those with college degrees. The Vietnam war, Watergate and other political scandals involving corruption and venality on the highest Federal, state, and judicial levels of government has given many American young people a jaded outlook on society, justifying for them their own modest drug inclinations. The desperate lengths to which some of them go in their search for meaning in life leads them to marijuana or hashish in the hope that it will enable them to escape, however temporarily, from grimness and misery.

Traditional and children's stories are part of the folklore that gives insight into the cultures where the stories originate. Their symbols and imagery reflect the society's mores, ethics, and world view, as well as some of the realities of everyday life. When, at a rock festival taking place in Martin Smith's (1971) *Gypsy in Amber*, one hippie wishes another, "May hallucinations of sugarplums dance through your head," a picture of a definite generation comes to mind. In *Jack and the Beanstalk*, the reader is transported into a fantastic excursion which has many levels of reality. The story is deceptively simple, for on the superficial level it is an imaginative and exciting adventure story with vivid symbols of good and evil clearly stating an unambiguous moral position. But on the psychological level (Epstein, 1966) "a Freudian analyst has no difficulty in relating Jack, his mother and deceased father, the giant and his wife, and Jack's princesses as characters in a complex dream-like Oedipal situation. In this context the Freudian symbols are obvious: beanstalk—phallus; climbing beanstalk—sex act; hiding in oven—return to the womb; ogre who devours boys—reversal of original primal horde scene; chopping down of beanstalk—castration, etc. . . . The predominant image is one of a miraculous and powerful plant which provides the means to experience the truths, insights and perspectives attendant to a new level of reality or altered state of consciousness. *Jack and the Beanstalk* is thus a narrative of a psychedelic experience. The correspondence between the beanstalk and a plant such as marijuana is too close to be strictly fortuitous. One may argue that the magical seeds which Jack receives from the mysterious old woman are not hemp seeds but, for example, morning glory seeds; however this point is academic. What is of importance is the fact that the plant takes Jack to new heights of awareness and reality which enable him to live a richer and fuller life.

Upon 'awakening' in the morning Jack begins to climb to the 'other world' and is able to see his mother and past life from this new perspective. As he climbs 'higher and higher' he experiences aching limbs and fatigue, indications of the physical-somatic aspects of the psychedelic drug experience. Having reached the heights, he again meets the guru-like old woman who is of both worlds. Jack makes his way through the new reality-fantasy world and sees the extremes of horror and evil and truth and beauty with remarkable clarity. Jack visits this world three times, each time advancing to a greater level of awareness. At each successive level the horrors and encounters with the evil ogre are more dangerous but the rewards and treasures which he brings back are increasingly more beautiful. He is really not content until his third 'trip' when returning with the treasured singing harp he has his ultimate confrontation with the ogre. In slaying the pursuing ogre by chopping down the beanstalk Jack also destroys his means to the other world and thus accomplishes his final re-entry. In the context of the obvious conventional materialistic and capitalistic images of good and evil, he is able to function on a higher plane of reality by virtue of the experiences afforded by the magical plant" (pp. 178-179).

In marijuana literature, the famous Mayor's Committee on Marijuana (1944) reported, the action of the drug is usually described from retrospective observation of the effects on a single individual. "Relationships to varying dosage, to the subject's personality and background, to environmental conditions when the drug was taken, is given little if any attention. It is the lack of information concerning these and other factors involved in marijuana reaction which has given rise to the present confusion regarding its effects" (p. 35). But in the past thirty years, emphasis has begun to be placed on set and setting, expectation and surroundings, in determining the effect of a drug. Miller (1971) refers to marijuana as a magic drug because its users think of it in relation to its sacramental qualities, qualities that are reputed to liberate inherent sensation. "That the drug may be essentially a placebo is beside the point; the sacramental elements may exist in the expectations surrounding use as legitimately as in the molecular structure of the drug. The mystique of marijuana carries the message of sensory freedom" (p. 37). The set of the marijuana user is important, McGlothlin (1965) indicates, because cannabis is especially amenable to control and direction so that the desired effects can usually be obtained at will. "Cannabis is a dependable producer of the desired euphoria and sense of well-being. With the much stronger and longer lasting hallucinogens, LSD and mescaline, there is much less control and direction possible, and even the experienced user may find himself plunged into an agonizing hell, instead of experiencing Satori" (p. 373). The first law of psychopharmacology, states Wilson (1973), "is that the action of any drug depends partly on the drug itself and partly on the set and setting—the mental attitude of the user and the forces at work in his immediate environment. With these cautions carefully in mind, it is probably safe to say that the evidence to date indicates fairly conclusively that, for an overwhelming majority of users, marijuana is a decidedly safe and pleasant enhancer of sexual experience" (pp. 160-161).

Fräulein Else, the exhibitionistic sensualist in Arthur Schnitzler's (1924) novel of the same name, seeks desperately to express her sexuality in some fashion. In an interior monologue, she says, "I ought to try everything, even hashish. I think that Ensign Brandel brought some with him from China. Is hashish drunk or smoked? It's supposed to give you marvelous visions. Brandel invited me to drink—or smoke—hashish with him" (p. 12). Of Lionel Walker, an ordinary, overweight, uncharismatic and driven shoe manufacturing executive, Soralee, the protagonist in Gwen Davis's (1971) novel, *Touching*, says, "I've got to turn him on . . . He's such a dear man and he never has any fun. I've got to get him on grass so he'll find out what the moment is" (p. 47). That moment is discovered by Nina in another novel, Henry Sutton's (1969) *The Voyeur*. In it, Nina is introduced to cannabis by an experienced user, Bud, and in an appropriate, seductive atmosphere, the two indulge themselves.

She held the large glass ashtray under her chin. The cigarette flared in the semidarkness as she took a deep drag and passed it back to Bud. She kept her mouth closed in order to hold the smoke in as long as possible. By the time Bud had taken his drag on the cigarette and returned it to her, she had exhaled very slowly and was ready to puff again and to fill her lungs as deeply as possible with the dry, pungent smoke.

The glass ashtray felt cool against the flesh of her throat. She was peculiarly sensitive to the cool, smooth, brittle feel of it and she wondered whether her awareness of its weight and of its surface was an indication that the smoke had begun to take effect. But, no, it was too soon for that. They had only shared one cigarette, and were on their second. The only effect so far was a slight tingling sensation in her legs and in her fingertips. And their mutual silence.

The quality of the silence, though, was entirely different from what there had been, before, in the car. Now, sharing the marijuana, they were close again. That it was a pharmacological closeness did not matter. The end justified the means. Besides, it was more than a feeling of closeness. It was a way by which she could join him in that inner retreat he had constructed for himself, a bridge, a connection ...

In a sense the sharing of the marijuana defined their relationship, for with it they could lie together in bed, as they were doing now, naked and sharing the pot. And it was a beautifully sensual and yet strangely disembodied experience that they could not only share together but, more important, could share without pretense.

She took back the cigarette from Bud's fingers and, holding it upright so that the long coal would not fall and burn the sheet, took another drag.

"You high yet?" he asked, stroking the outside of her thigh with the tip of a speculative finger.

"Still climbing," she answered. She loved the dizzying sensation at the beginning of each high. Part of her mind was cold and analytical, watching the other part do strange things, as if it were performing an elaborate, courtly dance with the reasonable part, with her body as the ensemble providing the music for the dance. She became increasingly aware of the rhythms of her own heartbeat and respiration, which became more and more interesting. And the weight and density of her flesh and bones transformed themselves into acoustical resonators, enhancing the music of the dance.

Bud had introduced her to the marijuana a year before, late one night after a sticky ride back across the harbor. Tired from an extremely long day, relieved that the deadline had been met and all the copy and proof was off to the printers, and perhaps depressed, too, by the brusqueness that Irv could show when the pressure was on, he had invited her up for a nightcap. She had agreed, and had followed his car to his apartment house, and had come up for the first time to the rooms that she now knew so well.

*   *   *

At first she had returned the kiss, but then she had broken away from his embrace.

"What?" he had asked. "What's the matter?"

She had taken a sip of her drink before answering. It was all so difficult, so complicated. "It's not you," she had said, "but me."

"Oh?"

"I'm ... I'm just too tense."

"You don't have to be."

"It isn't that I *want* to be ..."

"Then relax."

"I would, if I could."

"Do you want some help?"

"What do you mean?"

"Have you ever tried pot?" he had asked.

"No," she had answered, truthfully.

"Try some. Here," he had said, and had reached for the silver cigarette box and offered her a marijuana cigarette.

She had held it in her fingers, had sniffed it, and then had tried to decide. The boldness, the simplicity, the suddenness of the suggestion were all too puzzling for her, too difficult for her to sort out. He had explained to her with clarity and frankness, what marijuana was like, how it often had a mild aphrodisiac effect, but how essentially it was relaxing and—interesting. They could do it, he had suggested, in a quietly experimental way, smoking a little together in the privacy and safety of his apartment. And she might find that it was helpful.

Nina had always thought that people who used drugs had turned to them to escape from the reality of their ugly or dreary or unsatisfying lives. And she had been surprised at Bud's offering it to her, and surprised by the fact that he obviously used it from time to time. After all, here was a man with a body of work, four novels, a fine job, culture, resources, success. He grumbled about his work, but he did the work with great competence and, his protestations to the contrary, even occasionally with relish and delight. He was hardly an unwashed dropout from society.

She had known people in college who had used marijuana or pep pills. Things like that. But she had had an instinctive aversion to anything that would cause her to lose control of herself. An aversion, and even fear. And for that reason, she had never been more than mildly high on alcohol.

But what did she have to show for all this care and restraint? A spectacularly successful life, a great marriage, a fine sense of fulfillment? None of these things. And the safety and reasonableness of the apartment and of Bud, himself, had been reassuring. And the frustration she had been living with for a year or so, having that absurd crush—which was what she had come to call it—on Irv Kane, had produced a kind of pressure that was enough to overcome her natural caution, her inertia, and make her want to experiment.

She could, she had told herself, try it just this once. Even if it was for people who had something wrong with them, didn't she qualify? And if it made her do dreadfully irresponsible things, weren't they the same things that she had been toying with the idea of doing anyway? She had come up for the drink with the idea that she might, after all, get seduced. With the marijuana, she would have an excuse for herself if it worked out badly.

So, she had accepted the proffered lighter, and had smoked the cigarette. She had been rather disappointed after the first cigarette, for nothing had happened. But Bud had reassured her that it took a little bit more than that, the first time. So she had smoked a second one with him, and the now familiar light-headed feeling had started to hit her. And then they had smoked a third, and he had begun to stroke her arm, and she had been puzzled by the preternatural clarity of the sensation. It was exactly what he had said it would be—interesting.

His fingertip on her arm was more absorbing, more intense a sensation than even the kiss had been, and yet she felt none of that tightening of nerves, no apprehension. Indeed, she could hardly connect it with anything else. Time seemed to stop under the influence of the marijuana smoke, and everything became so discrete, so detached, so beautifully isolated from everything else.

She watched his fingers as they traveled up and down her arm, and observed with a curiously remote eye as his hand wandered down from her arm to her breast. She had felt slightly dizzy and she could still hear a kind of singing in her head. It was a kind of choral singing, as if her heartbeat were somehow orchestrated.

"Lie down," he had instructed, and they had moved to the velvety gray rug. And it was on the rug that they had made love, but with a kind of lovemaking that she had never experienced before—not so much sexual as more generally sensual. She had been aware of him not simply in a genital way, but in a completely unfocused, dreamy manner. Her elbows had been as sensitive as her nipples, and her neck as responsive as the inside of her thighs. And it had been with a beautiful undersea languor that they had floated into the ultimate, intimate embrace.

And even then, there had been no urgent drive toward a climax, and therefore no possibility of fear lest she not arrive at one. In almost wavelike undulations, they had cruised around it, and practically without her noticing it they had arrived at a peak so intense that she had not been sure where her body stopped and his began. Neither had there been any sudden drop-off or withdrawal into post-coital tristesse. They were ineffably close, and her happiness was exhilarating. She remembered how strange it had been, not feeling close to him as an individual but as a glorious extension of herself. It had been a relationship of bodies, but neither gross nor crude. It had been a relationship, really, of idealized bodies, of improved bodies, as of two statues or paintings brought to life. She remembered how she had fallen asleep with him still in her and how they had awakened an hour or so later, not hung over, not at all depressed, but quite gay and ravenous.

And garrulous. She had been suddenly easy and talkative, and had told him about her marriage to Jon, and her discovery of his homosexuality and the shock that that had been to her, both as someone who loved him and also to herself as a woman, as a female. And she had told him about the brief, unsatisfactory liaisons she had attempted after the divorce. And she had even told him about her "fixation" — as she had called it — upon Irvin Kane. [pp. 61-67, *passim*].

Harry Haller, a man with two personality facades, one refined and clever, the other wolf, savage, untamable and dangerous, is led by the seductive musician Pablo to witness a peep show and to delude himself in acting out his repressed sexual desires in a magic theater. The scene occurs in Hermann Hesse's (1927) *Steppenwolf*, as Pablo insists Harry leave behind his personality which has imprisoned him all his life and enter a visionary world in order to learn how to laugh and develop unfeigned pleasure. Harry's dual self-image is, of course, a delusion. He has run through a series of vain attempts to conquer his despair, through alcohol, sex, music, and toying with suicide. Finally he enters the Magic Theater of his friend, Pablo, the price of admission for which is "your mind," which becomes for Harry a mind-loss experience. Leary (1968) considers this Hesse passage a psychedelic experience, "a drug-induced loss of self, a journey to the inner world. Each door in the Magic Theater has a sign on it, indicating the endless possibilities of the experience. A sign called 'Jolly Hunting. Great Automobile Hunt' initiates a fantastic orgy of mechanical destruction in which Harry becomes a lustful murderer ... Another sign reads: 'All Girls Are Yours,' and carries Harry into inexhaustible sexual fantasies. The crisis of the Steppenwolf, his inner conflicts, his despair, his morbidity and unsatisfied longing are dissolved in a whirling kaleidescope of hallucinations" (pp. 182-183).

'You're ready?' asked Hermine, and her smile fled away like the shadows on her breast. Far up in unknown space rang out that strange and eerie laughter.

I nodded. Oh, yes, I was ready.

At this moment Pablo appeared in the doorway and beamed on us out of his gay eyes that really were animal's eyes except that animal's eyes are always serious, while his always laughed, and this laughter turned them into human eyes. He beckoned to us with his usual friendly cordiality. He had on a gorgeous silk smoking-jacket. His limp collar and tired white face had a withered and pallid look above its red facings; but the impression was erased by his radiant black eyes. So was reality erased, for they too had the witchery.

We joined him when he beckoned and in the doorway he said to me in a low voice: 'Brother Harry, I invite you to a little entertainment. For madmen only, and one price only—your mind. Are you ready?'

Again I nodded.

The dear fellow gave us each an arm with kind solicitude, Hermine his right, me his left, and conducted us upstairs to a small room that was lit from the ceiling with a bluish light and nearly empty. There was nothing in it but a small round table and three easy chairs in which we sat down.

Where were we? Was I asleep? Was I at home? Was I driving in a car? No, I was sitting in a blue light in a round room and a rare atmosphere, in a stratum of reality that had become rarefied in the extreme.

Why then was Hermine so white? Why was Pablo talking so much? Was it not perhaps I who made him talk, spoke, indeed, with his voice? Was it not, too, my own soul that contemplated me out of his black eyes like a lost and frightened bird, just as it had out of Hermine's grey ones?

Pablo looked at us good-naturedly as ever and with something ceremonious in his friendliness; and he talked much and long. He whom I had never heard say two consecutive sentences, whom no discussion nor thesis could interest, whom I had scarcely credited with a single thought, discoursed now in his good-natured warm voice fluently and without a fault.

'My friends, I have invited you to an entertainment that Harry has long wished for and of which he has long dreamed. The hour is a little late and no doubt we are all slightly fatigued. So, first, we will rest and refresh ourselves a little.'

From a recess in the wall he took three glasses and a quaint little bottle, also a small oriental box inlaid with differently coloured woods. He filled the three glasses from the bottle and taking three long thin yellow cigarettes from the box and a box of matches from the pocket of his silk jacket he gave us a light. And now we all slowly smoked the cigarettes whose smoke was as thick as incense, leaning back in our chairs and slowly sipping the aromatic liquid whose strange taste was so utterly unfamiliar. Its effect was immeasurably enlivening and delightful—as though one were filled with gas and had no longer any gravity. Thus we sat peacefully exhaling small puffs and taking little sips at our glasses, while every moment we felt ourselves growing lighter and more serene.

From far away came Pablo's warm voice.

'It is a pleasure to me, my dear Harry, to have the privilege of being your host in a small way on this occasion. You have often been sorely weary of your life. You were striving, were you not, for escape? You have a longing to forsake this world and its reality and to penetrate to a reality more native to you, to a world beyond time. Now I invite you to do so. You know, of course, where this other world lies hidden. It is the world of your own soul that you seek. Only within yourself exists that other reality for which you long. I can give you nothing that has not already its being within yourself. I can throw open to you no picture-gallery but your own soul. All I can give you is the opportunity, the impulse, the key. I help you to make your own world visible. That is all.'

Again he put his hand into the pocket of his gorgeous jacket and drew out a round looking-glass.

'Look, it is thus that you have so far seen yourself.'

He held the little glass before my eyes (a children's verse came to my mind: 'Little glass, little glass in the hand') and I saw, though indistinctly and cloudily, the reflection of an uneasy, self-tormented, inwardly labouring and seething being—myself, Harry Haller. And within him again I saw the Steppenwolf, a shy, beautiful, dazed wolf with frightened eyes that smouldered now with anger, now with sadness. This shape of a wolf coursed through the other in ceaseless movement, as a tributary pours its cloudy turmoil into a river. In bitter strife, in unfulfilled longing each tried to devour the other so that his shape might prevail. How unutterably sad was the look this fluid inchoate figure of the wolf threw from his beautiful shy eyes.

'This is how you see yourself,' Pablo remarked and put the mirror away in his pocket. I was thankful to close my eyes and take a sip of the elixir.

'And now,' said Pablo, 'we have had our rest. We have had our refreshment and a little talk. If your fatigue has passed off I will conduct you to my peep-show and show you my little theatre. Will you come?'

We got up. With a smile Pablo led. He opened a door, and drew a curtain aside and we found ourselves in the horseshoe-shaped corridor of a theatre, and exactly in the middle. On either side, the curving passage led past a large number, indeed an incredible number, of narrow doors into the boxes.

'This,' explained Pablo, "is our theatre, an enjoyable theatre. I hope you'll find lots to laugh at.' He laughed aloud as he spoke, a short laugh, but it went through me like a shot. It was the same bright and peculiar laugh that I had heard before from below.

'This little theatre of mine has as many doors into as many boxes as you please, ten or a hundred or a thousand, and behind each door exactly what you seek awaits you. It is a pretty cabinet of pictures, my dear friend; but it would be quite useless for you to go through it as you are. You would be checked and blinded at every turn by what you are pleased to call your personality. You have no doubt guessed long since that the conquest of time and the escape from reality, or however else it may be that you choose to describe your longing, means simply the wish to be relieved of your so-called personality. That is the prison where you lie. And if you were to enter the theatre as you are, you would see everything through the eyes of Harry and the old spectacles of the Steppenwolf. You are therefore requested to lay these spectacles aside and to be so kind as to leave your highly esteemed personality here in the cloak-room where you will find it again when you wish. The pleasant dance from which you have just come, the treatise on the Steppenwolf, and the little stimulant that we have only this moment partaken of may have sufficiently prepared you. You, Harry, after having left behind your valuable personality, will have the left side of the theatre at your disposal, Hermine the right. Once inside, you can meet each other as you please. Hermine will be so kind as to go for a moment behind the curtain. I should like to introduce Harry first.'

Hermine disappeared to the right past a gigantic mirror that covered the rear wall from floor to vaulted ceiling

'Now, Harry, come along, be as jolly as you can. To make it so and to teach you to laugh is the whole aim of this entertainment — I hope you will make it easy for me. You feel quite well, I trust? Not afraid? That's good, excellent. You will now, without fear and with unfeigned pleasure, enter our visionary world. You will introduce yourself to it by means of a trifling suicide, since this is the custom.'

He took out the pocket-mirror again and held it in front of my face. Again I was confronted by the same indistinct and cloudy reflection, with the wolf's shape encircling it and coursing through it. I knew it too well and disliked it too sincerely for its destruction to cause me any sorrow.

'You will now extinguish this superfluous reflection, my dear friend. That is all that is necessary. To do so, it will suffice that you greet it, if your mood permits, with a hearty laugh. You are here in a school of humour. You are to learn to laugh. Now, true humour begins when a man ceases to take himself seriously.'

I fixed my eyes on the little mirror, where the man Harry and the wolf were going through their convulsions. For a moment there was a convulsion deep within me too, a faint but painful one like remembrance, or like homesickness, or like remorse. Then the slight oppression gave way to a new feeling like that a man feels when a tooth has been extracted with cocaine, a sense of relief and of letting out a deep breath, and of wonder, at the same time, that it has not hurt in the least. And this feeling was accompanied by a buoyant exhilaration and a desire to laugh so irresistible that I was compelled to give way to it.

The mournful image in the glass gave a final convulsion and vanished. The glass itself turned grey and charred and opaque, as though it had been burnt. With a laugh Pablo threw the thing away and it went rolling down the endless corridor and disappeared.

'Well laughed, Harry,' cried Pablo, 'You will learn to laugh like the immortals yet. You have done with the Steppenwolf at last. It's no good with a razor. Take care that he stays dead. You'll be able to leave the farce of reality behind you directly. At our next meeting we'll drink brotherhood, dear fellow. I never liked you better than I do today. And if you still think it worth your while we can philosophize together and argue and talk about music and Mozart and Gluck and Plato and Goethe to your heart's content. You will understand now why it was so impossible before. I wish you good riddance of the Steppenwolf for today at any rate. For naturally, your suicide is not a final one. We are in a magic theatre; a world of pictures, not realities. See that you pick out beautiful and cheerful ones and show that you really are not in love with your highly questionable personality any longer. Should you still, however, have a hankering after it, you need only have another look in the mirror that I will now show you. But you know the old proverb: "A mirror in the hand is worth two on the wall." Ha! ha!' (again that laugh, beautiful and frightful!) 'And now there only remains one little ceremony and quite a gay one. You have now cast aside the spectacles of your personality. So come here and look in a proper looking-glass. It will give you some fun.'

Laughingly, with a few droll caresses he turned me about so that I faced the gigantic mirror on the wall. There I saw myself.

I saw myself for a brief instant as my usual self, except that I looked unusually good-humoured, bright and laughing. But I had scarcely had time to recognize myself before the reflection fell to pieces. A second, a third, a tenth, a twentieth figure sprang from it till the whole gigantic mirror was full of nothing but Harrys or bits of him, each of which I saw only for the instant of recognition. Some of these multitudinous Harrys were as old as I, some older, some very old. Others were young. There were youths, boys, schoolboys, scamps, children. Fifty-year-olds and twenty-year-olds played leap frog. Thirty-year-olds and five-year-olds, solemn and merry, worthy and comic, well dressed and unpresentable, and even quite naked, longhaired, and hairless, all were I and all were seen for a flash, recognized and gone. They sprang from each other in all directions, left and right and into the recesses of the mirror and clean out of it. One, an elegant young fellow, leapt laughing into Pablo's arms, embraced him and they went off together. And one who particularly pleased me, a good looking and charming boy of sixteen or seventeen years, sprang like lightning into the corridor and began reading the notices on the doors. I went after him and found him in front of a door on which was inscribed:

ALL GIRLS ARE YOURS
ONE QUARTER IN THE SLOT

The dear boy hurled himself forward, made a leap and, falling head first into the plot himself, disappeared behind the door.

Pablo too had vanished. So apparently had the mirror and with it all the countless figures. I realized I was now left to myself and to the theatre, and I went with curiosity from door to door and read on each its alluring invitation [Hesse, pp. 197-205].

Baudelaire (1860) in *Artificial Paradise*, noted that hashish does not alter or add to the basic personality of the user, but only draws forth what is already latent. And so he summarized the ideal conditions under which hashish should be used. His message is reminiscent of Leary's and other recent writers' references to the importance of "set" and "setting" in taking any drug. The individual should be in a state of "perfect leisure," without any interfering "duties to accomplish that require punctuality, exactitude; no domestic cares, no love pangs" should be occupying his mind. Thus, there is a continuum of a number of authorities who have indicated that the effects of marijuana and psychedelic drugs are markedly affected by situational and personality factors (Ewing, 1972; Sinnett et al., 1972; Goode, 1970; Freeman, 1953).

While the effects of cannabis and hashish are different for each person, there are several general, common characteristics. The fantastic beauty of everything in the world is so great that the drug user becomes obsessed by the beauty of everything around him. He is in his own lovely world, creating thoughts, visions, sounds and sights—whatever he likes. Colors become increasingly bright and intense; sound and touch are full of beauty; the senses are heightened. Fantastic ideas thrown up by the imagination know no bounds. There is intense physical exhilaration as well, in which the user feels he is floating above reality or merging with another being. Afterwards, there is freedom from any serious aftereffects, but there is a difference: the person sees the world as it was when he was high, his life seems enriched, his imagination deeper, and his mind more active. Marijuana and hashish are not addictive sedatives or depressants, but agents that expand the consciousness of the user. William Burroughs (1961), the offbeat author and former addict, testifies that ". . . cannabis . . . which is certainly the safest of the hallucinogen drugs [is] unquestionably . . . very useful to the artist, activating trains of association that would otherwise be inaccessible, and I owe many of the scenes in *Naked Lunch* directly to the use of cannabis" (p. 445). *Lancet*, in 1963, editorialized that marijuana has no addictive properties, no harmful physiological effects, nor does it induce personality deterioration. The simplest summary of its action is that it induces an enhanced sense of delight and serenity.

Not all authorities, by any means, are as sanguine about marijuana use as this, but their posture is frequently a moral one and generally unprovable on the basis of scientific knowledge. The known physiological changes accompanying marijuana smoking at typical levels of American social usage are relatively few (Cox, 1973). "One of the most consistent is an increase in pulse rate. Another is a reddening of the eyes at the time of use. Dryness of the mouth and throat are uniformly reported. Although enlargement of the pupil was an earlier impression, more careful study has indicated that this does not occur. Blood pressure effects have been inconsistent ... Basal metabolic rate, temperature, respiration rate, lung vital capacity, and a wide range of other physiological measures are generally unchanged over a relatively wide dosage range of both marijuana and the synthetic form of the principal psychoactive agent, delta-9-THC. Neurological examinations consistently reveal no major abnormalities during marijuana intoxication ... Although users often report enhanced sensory awareness in the drugged state, objectively measurable improvements in visual acuity, brightness discrimination, touch discrimination, auditory acuity, olfactory threshold, or taste discrimination have not been found" (p. 432).

Yet, it is precisely these latter factors — the individual's perception of enhanced acuity of nearly all of the senses — that apparently accompanies marijuana and hashish intoxication. Innumerable subjects have been witness to the following sequence of events as described by Porot (1942): a transient euphoria; a rich, lively, internal experience, in which ideas rush through the mind; an enormous feeling of superiority, of superhuman clarity of insight; sensory hyperesthesia, and coenesthesias; sights and sounds become unusually vivid and meaningful; distortion of sense of time and space; loss of judgment; exaggerated affect; placid ecstasy; sleep. Not all people respond in this sequence or to all of these steps, for much depends on the personality of the user and the setting in which he finds himself. Penny, a college drop-out in Kingsley Amis's (1972) *Girl, 20*, who "can't stand being on my own, and I can't stand being with one person, and can't stand being with a lot of people," responds to the question her date puts to her, "Are you on drugs?" with "Not at the moment. You always think they're going to be good, but they're not really. Not for me, anyway. It gets like seeing everything in a lot of mirrors, or through funny glass like a migraine, or looking up from the floor, but it's the same thing really. Even when all the things look different, all covered with stuff or turned into lights and things, or even when you can't see or hear anything you're sort of used to, you know it's all there really. Not just it's going to be back when you're back, it's there all the time. Even when you can't just remember what it's like. . ." (p. 97).

The marked individual differences found in marijuana users'

reactions depends on a number of variables, ranging from the pharma-cological quality of the substance used, to, as has been stated, the personality of the user and the setting. Thus, the very unpredictability of the effect of marijuana on different people and on the same person at different times and under different circumstances increases the risk to the user (Clark and Nakashima, 1968). In *Another Country*, by James Baldwin (1962), Leona, a thirty-year-old Southern woman who is separated from her husband, wanders into a Harlem night club and is entranced by the jazz she hears, particularly by a black instrumentalist, Rufus Scott. After the last gig, she introduces herself to him and he brings her to a party which is in progress in a high-rise luxury apartment' building. Rufus is high on pot, Leona is getting there on alcohol. "He realized that he was high from the way his fingers seemed hung up in hers and from the way he was staring at her throat." The passage reveals some of the outrage that demeans the black man, the lack of inhibition which the drug user can display, as well as how time seems retarded.

"You never answered my question."
"What?"
He turned to face Leona, who held her drink cupped in both her hands and whose brow was quizzically lifted over her despairing eyes and her sweet smile.
"You never answered mine."
"Yes, I did." She sounded more plaintive than ever. "I said I wanted it all."
He took her drink from her and drank half of it, then gave the glass back, moving into the darkest part of the balcony.
"Well, then," he whispered, "come and get it."
She came toward him, holding her glass against her breasts. At the very last moment, standing directly before him, she whispered in bafflement and rage, "What are you trying to do to me?"
"Honey," he answered, "I'm doing it," and he pulled her to him as roughly as he could. He had expected her to resist and she did, holding the glass between them and frantically trying to pull her body away from his body's touch. He knocked the glass out of her hand and it fell dully to the balcony floor, rolling away from them. Go ahead, he thought humorously; if I was to let you go now you'd be so hung up you'd go flying over this balcony, most likely. He whispered, "Go ahead, fight. I like it. Is this the way they do down home?"
"Oh God," she murmured, and began to cry. At the same time, she ceased struggling. Her hands came up and touched his face as though

she were blind. Then she put her arms around his neck and clung to him, still shaking. His lips and his teeth touched her ears and her neck and he told her, "Honey, you ain't got nothing to cry about yet."

Yes, he was high; everything he did he watched himself doing, and he began to feel a tenderness for Leona which he had not expected to feel. He tried, with himself, to make amends for what he was doing — for what he was doing to her. Everything seemed to take a very long time. He got hung up on her breasts, standing out like mounds of yellow cream, and the tough, brown, tasty nipples, playing and nuzzling and nibbling while she moaned and whimpered and her knees sagged. He gently lowered them to the floor, pulling her on top of him. He held her tightly at the hip and the shoulder. Part of him was worried about the host and hostess and the other people in the room but another part of him could not stop the crazy thing which had begun. Her fingers opened his shirt to the navel, her tongue burned his neck and his chest; and his hands pushed up her skirt and caressed the inside of her thighs. Then, after a long, high time, while he shook beneath every accelerating tremor of her body, he forced her beneath him and he entered her. For a moment he thought she was going to scream, she was so tight and caught her breath so sharply, and stiffened so. But then she moaned, she moved beneath him. Then, from the center of his rising storm, very slowly and deliberately, he began the slow ride home [pp. 23-24].

Sexual love is a most complicated biological phenomenon, bringing into play psychological, neuronal, vascular and endocrine factors. The majority of users of marijuana and hashish indicate that this most intimate kind of interaction with another person is enhanced by the drug. Relevant characteristic sexual effects among Tart's (1971) sample were new qualities to touch and taste and smell — the intimate senses — and new pleasurable qualities to orgasm. "It was common for the user to feel more need and desire for sex, and particularly, to feel more sexual desire if the situation was appropriate. That is, marijuana is not an aphrodisiac in the sense of forcing sexual drive, but rather it makes sex more desirable if there is already an initial attraction. It was common for the users to feel that they were better lovers when intoxicated, to have much closer contact with their partner in making love, it being much more of a union of souls rather than just of bodies, and to be much more responsive to the sexual partner. Some users described making love at high levels of marijuana intoxication as so ecstatic as to be beyond words in many respects, a blending and fusing of essence and energy that took them beyond the bounds of time and space, and into one another. It should be noted, however, that one quarter of the users thought they were worse lovers when intoxicated than when straight, for, they reported, they became so immersed in their own intensified and pleasurable sensations that they paid little attention to their lovers" (p. 289).

That marijuana or hashish tends to diminish inhibitions and increase suggestibility is evident when it is used as an aphrodisiac. A socially communicated belief of this nature is likely to have psychological substantiation; the placebo effect is at its most powerful when supported by myth. That marijuana has the reputation of being an aphrodisiac is in itself enough to make it one in some cases (Masters, 1962; Ewing, 1972). In surveying effects of marijuana as described by volunteer users, Halikas et al. (1972) found thirty-three percent reported that they usually experienced increased sexual arousal and twenty-nine per cent mentioned better sexual performance than usual. A review of the marijuana literature by Schwartz (1969) revealed no evidence for any physical aphrodisiac effect, while a few studies alluded to a possible role for marijuana in the origin of some instances of impotence.

Wilson's (1973) examination of the effect of hashish on orgasm reveals that a hashish user might very well say "that his consciousness centered entirely in his penis; that he felt as if he were nothing but a penis, and one of gigantic dimensions. He might add that his girl friend seemed to be nothing other than a gigantic, very warm, delightfully moist vagina . . . At the moment of orgasm, ordinary consciousness was totally suspended, at least for a few seconds—quite in the manner described by D. H. Lawrence and Ernest Hemingway . . . even though 'realistic' sex manuals tell people not to expect such an apocalyptic cosmic storm at the sexual climax" (pp. xxi-xxii).

The extent to which a large amount of hashish can influence the sexual behavior is reflected in Alan Lelchuk's *American Mischief* (1973). Gwen Tresvant, a black teacher of acting and directing at Boston University, has taken up with the thirty-three-year-old boy dean of Cardozo College, Bernard Kovell. He plays "Moses the Lawgiver, David the King, Freud the Doctor" to his six mistresses, he who was "overwhelmed by the emphasis on eroticism; the need for carnal sex, the urges to fondle flesh, to pursue new secretions and odors." Kovell, a latter-day quasi Portnoy, treats his six mistresses initially as psychiatric patients until he works through some of their problems and enjoys them carnally. Sophie, one of his girls, describes him as "a regular little Goethe" in relation to himself and women, with the egotism of a seven-year-old boy; he is a boy-man, "with the urge to break rules, the inclination toward mischief, the passion for coming home with dirty clothes, bruised knees," and a copy of the Cardozo College bulletin to prove to her he is Dean/Professor. "And, of course, the curious boyish greed for the special love of a mother: totally protective and devoted, a universe of security." Kate suspects Kovell of pedophilic practices with her not-so-innocent six-year-old daughter. Melissa thinks he is obsessive-compulsive, punctilious, and occasionally impotent. Grace accuses him of being "the moodiest sonofabitch" she's ever met, the most impolite, as abrasive as sandpaper. Angela sees him as a pompous kook, insufferably superior, who looks upon women as sex machines. Gwen categorizes him as a timid, hypochondriacal neurasthenic. She is a masochist, with a desperate need to be sexually servile, abused, obedient and humiliated, even greater than the desperation of the Baron von Masoch himself. At one point, Gwen says to Bernard, "I want you for a master." She sleeps at the foot of his bed, like a dog might; she deliberately goads him by calling him a "Jew racist" and telling him he is "shitty in the sack" so that he will strike her. He rises to the bait and does, which makes Gwen smile beatifically. She seduces him into a reluctant sexual perversion by offering him some hashish one evening. Bernard, who rarely touched liquor, turns his "no" to acquiescence in the face of her diatribe about his infantile fears and her boredom at pampering him. He tells what happened that night.

Tricked again, I having no idea that the whole thing was yet another guerrilla ambush on my morals. In your bedroom I puffed against my will on the small silver pipe you handed me, passing it back and forth, back and forth. After some twenty minutes, you wavered as you came toward me, and when I reached out for the pipe and missed, the signal was clear for you. Without the deception of hashish, what happened next never would have happened. That goes without saying. And without a first time, there never would have been a second, a third. After all, there are certain limits beyond which even a driven man won't proceed, held in check — fortunately — by ancient codes and learned taboos. I don't remember all the sordid details. We were undressed, you were on your knees, I was being caressed, the odor was acrid, the walls were swimming . . . Can you imagine what it was like for me, Gwen, as you writhed and moaned with pleasure while that hot yellow stream poured upon those black papayas, the long neck, your lovely face? How I tried to turn away, do you recall, Gwen? Out of pain . . . humiliation . . . fear. Mostly fear. But you grabbed my hand and made such a love-sick call that I had to turn back. Half your pleasure, it was clear, was for me to view you in that position, basking in that unholy shower of thick yellow. Was I crazy in thinking that you were crying? (The fluids indistinguishable.) Who knew? But I was surely made crazy by your gesture of gratitude (kissing my hand). It was insane [pp. 108-109].

If hashish and marijuana are aphrodisiacs that create sexual desire in somebody one wishes to seduce, or that will create potency in the previously impotent, then Bernard Kovell is fictional proof which can be added to the data secured from the testimony of great numbers of respondents who have been positively affected sexually by these two substances. Marijuana and hashish have long had a reputation as powerful aphrodisiacs. Modern authorities, however, dispute the claim that either pot or any other drug is a true aphrodisiac, that any drug will provoke passion in an otherwise neutral situation (Wilson, 1973, p. 158). There can be little doubt, however, that they tend to enhance sex for many users when the situation is propitious. If one is sexually aroused, the judicious use of marijuana will stimulate the desire and heighten the pleasure immeasurably, "for it is perhaps the principal effect of marijuana to take one more intensely into whatever experience . . . It provokes a more sensual (or aesthetic) kind of concentration, a detailed articulation of minute areas, an ability to adopt play postures. What can be more relevant in the act of love?" (Trocchi, 1960, p. 123). While medical opinion as to the capacity of cannabis to act as an aphrodisiac is divided, Ausubel (1964) states, "The apparent erotic stimulator induced by marijuana in certain individuals . . . corresponds essentially to the release of inhibited personality traits. These persons prior to drug use tend to be excessively preoccupied with sexual gratification. Many also exhibit infantile and homosexual tendencies. In addition, the drug increases self-confidence and eliminates apprehension about the receptivity of the contemplated sex partner. Many users report that the sensual aspects of sexual enjoyment are prolonged as a consequence of the exaggerated perception of elapsed time" (p. 102). Virtually all investigators agree that whatever aphrodisiac qualities cannabis may possess, they are cerebral in nature and are due to reduced inhibition and increased suggestibility.

Among the more prominent subjective effects of cannabis are hilarity, often without apparent motivation; loquacious euphoria, with increased sociability as a result; distortion of sensation and perception, especially of space and time; impairment of memory and judgment; distortion of emotional responsiveness; and irritability and confusion (Eddy et al., 1970). Baudelaire (1860) wrote that the first observable effect of acute hashish intoxication is "a certain hilarity, irresistible, ludicrous, which takes possession of you." Gautier (1846), too, described a hashish session during which ". . . the awesome hilarity went ever increasing, the din grew in intensity, the floors and walls of the house heaved and palpitated like a human diaphram, shaken by the frenetic, irresistible, implacable laughter" (p. 170). In the novel, *Incident at Naha* by M. J. Bosse (1972), Virgil Jefferson, a Harlem-born black doctoral candidate at New York University is sharing his sublet apartment in Greenwich Village with Judy Benton, an Omaha-born blonde who is working for her Master's degree at the same institution and also working part-time as a waitress in a nightspot. Judy narrates her feelings one night while she is on cocktail duty.

> When he saw I was on a bummer that evening, the Feeler offered me a snort of Meth, but I never use Speed, so I compromised and accepted some authentic Lebanese hash. Was it groovy, and by the time Virgil arrived at Eros, I was off and *awaaaaaaaaaaaaaaay*. Virgil sat near the bandstand, cocking his ear to the music with that absolute intensity of his. I took him a rum Coke, his favorite drink. I saw him frowning from a hundred miles away, as I approached, but I kept giggling anyway. I couldn't stop because I was really stoned. He looked terribly square, eyeing me from the table like somebody's father. I bent over him, giggling, and told him so, and I told him I wanted to do all kinds of weird sexual things right then and there. Oh, I was funny, even though all I got out of Virgil was a thin-lipped stare. But thank God, he never stays angry very long, especially when there's music around to distract him. At closing time, when we left together, he took my arm with an unfatherly smile [p. 39].

A major problem for all disciplines concerned with human affairs, wrote J. Huxley (1965), whether biochemistry, psychology, psychiatry, or social anthropology, "is to investigate the extraordinary mechanisms underlying the organization and operation of awareness, so as to lay the foundation for and promote the realization of more meaningful and more effective possibilities in the psychosocial process of human evolution" (p. 140). The difficulty confronted by most writers and researchers is endemic to writing on the subject of heightened consciousness or mystical conscious states; it lies in the dilemma of rendering subjective or intuitive experiences in rational, objective terms. But medical men, biologists, physiologists, pharmacologists, and drug users have been unable to resolve this problem. It remains for the creative writer to describe these subjective experiences. Aldous Huxley (1966) wrote, "Through the use of harmless psychedelics, a course of chemically triggered conversion experiences or ecstasies ..., will provide all the sources of mental energy, all the solvents of conceptual sludge, that an individual requires. With their aid, he should be able to adapt himself selectively to his culture, rejecting its evils, stupidities and irrelevancies, gratefully accepting all its treasures of accumulated knowledge of rationality, human-heartedness and practical wisdom. If the number of such individuals is sufficiently great, if their quality is sufficiently high, they may be able to pass from discriminating acceptance of their culture to discriminating change and reform. Is this a hopefully utopian dream? Experiment can give us the answer, for the dream is pragmatic; the utopian hypothesis can be tested empirically. And in these oppressive times a little hope is surely no unwelcome visitant" (pp. 200-201). Burroughs (1961), another novelist who owed much to cannabis in his creative writing, eventually found that opiates hinder the artist because they act to diminish awareness of surroundings and bodily processes. "Cannabis serves as a guide to psychic areas which can then be re-entered without it. I have now discontinued the use of cannabis for some years and find that I am able to achieve the same results by non-chemical means: flicker, music through head phones ... It would seem to me that cannabis and other hallucinogens provide a key to the creative process, and that a systematic study of these drugs would open the way to non-chemical methods of expanding consciousness" (pp. 445-446). But anyone attempting research in an area as hotly immersed in controversy as marijuana use knows that he cannot expect his findings to be received with neutrality or scientific objectivity.

Mescaline and Peyote

Malcolm Lowry's *Under the Volcano*, a novel first published in 1947 and regarded by many as a masterpiece, describes the last twelve hours on earth of a brilliant dipsomaniac who is destroying himself through alcohol and mescaline hallucinations. Suffering from an acute paralysis of will, Geoffrey Firman, a minor British consul in Mexico, cuts himself off from those who want to help him — his wife Yvonne, his half-brother Hugh, and his boyhood friend Jacques Laruelle — and plunges deeper and deeper into a mescal-soaked hell that climaxes with his murder by profascist police. The story, which takes place shortly after the outbreak of World War II (on November 2, celebrated annually throughout Mexico as the Day of the Dead), is profoundly symbolic of man's fall from grace in a world whose natural laws of order and human interrelatedness he has chosen to ignore, defy, or transgress.

There are some who would read into the novel the penalty of drug abuse, but Aldous Huxley (1954), Burroughs (1961) and Masters (1962) deem such moralistic views as parochial and without foundation in fact. In the initial stages of mescaline intoxication, according to Huxley, the primordial vividness of visual impressions in perceiving commonplace objects is dominant. In the later stages, the feeling of superhuman insight into the nature of things, accompanied by a complete detachment from the self and from one's fellow man comes into play. Under the influence of mescaline, Burroughs had the experience of seeing a painting for the first time. Later he found that he could see it without using drugs, insights which carried over to music or a pedestrian object, so that one exposure to a powerful consciousness-expanding drug like mescaline often conveyed a permanent increase in the range of experience. "Mescaline transports the user to unexplored psychic areas, and he can often find the way back without a chemical guide" (p. 443).

Peyote belongs to the cactus family. It is a hallucinogenic agent, known to the Indians of Mexico since pre-Columbian days. Peyote looks like a button-shaped mushroom. After plucking, it is dried in the sun, and in its new form — known as a "mescal button" — is eaten. On being mundified, the crude peyotl plant yields more than ten alkaloids, among them mescaline (Ebin, 1961). Mescaline belongs to a group of chemicals known as amines that include the hormones adrenalin and nonadrenalin, and substances active in mind-body interaction. Mescalin is related also to the hallucinogenic and psychomimetic drug LSD-25, and has been synthesized.

Young Carl Swanson, the narrator vagabonding his way across America in Jim Harrison's *Wolf. A False Memoir* (1971), lived within a limited geometrical pattern: low-status jobs, alcohol, pot, hash, mescaline, promiscuity, periodic hunger, a life rich in fantasy, on the prowl to make his fame and fortune. Carol relates an incident that occurred in San Francisco: "We had split a hundred peyote buttons four ways, small cacti which after peeling remind one of gelatinous rotten green peppers. I chewed up an overdose of twenty buttons raw, one after another as if they were some sort of miraculous food, then vomited out of a window repeatedly for hours . . . [Later] in the peyote trance the naked chorus girls foolishly summoned up were peeled and beet red with snatches of inky and oily black, hard as basalt" (p. 23).

Masters (1962) states that probably the most discussed aspect of the mescaline experience is that of visual hallucinations — "pictures seen usually with the eyes closed, and which are intensely and richly colorful, seemingly drenched in a kind of preternatural light. These images may be, though they are customarily or even very often, sexual in content..." (p. 277). In a parody on mescal and Madison Avenue, Millie, the transsexual protagonist in *Hermaphrodeity* by Alan Friedman (1972) discovers what she thinks is a new aphrodisiac while she is on an archeological dig in Sardinia. "I knew perfectly well that after half an hour's chain smoking [of Fica], I could easily imagine myself a creature of nothing but erogenous zones all over — to my full height — cunnilingus without release" (p. 345). "Fica," it should be noted, is Italian for vagina. Millie would like to market her erotic cigarette in the United States with advertisements that "would visually suggest or show the mouth as an archetypical Vulva always holding in loving embrace a glowing Phallus." Millie's find is in effect an aphrodisiac giving a sensational, sensual, sensory stimulus — inhaling sex.

When sexual desire is present, mescaline, like marijuana and hashish, may contribute to the increased sexual potency of both male and female, probably by reducing anxiety. The drug seems to be a mild anesthetic that affects the genitals and so serves to facilitate the prolongation of the sex act. Since ejaculation and orgasm do not occur, the experience is likely to be so unusually psychologically satisfying that the absence of the physical climax seems of negligible importance. "The sex organs, and indeed all of the erogenous or sexually susceptible zones of the body, may seem to be unusually and very pleasurably engorged, turgid or tumescent, and may also be strangely 'rubbery' ... The feeling of control over one's sexuality, especially the absence of any worry on the part of the male about being able to sustain his erection indefinitely, is uniquely satisfying to a good many persons" (Masters, 1962, p. 276).

The effects of such intercourse over a period of time, without ejaculation or orgasm, is depicted by Gwen Davis (1969) in her novel, *The Pretenders*. Algernon "Ever-Reddy" Reddy, noted novelist, is the house guest and pet of two of the social leaders of Acapulco, the DeRevignys. They have installed a two-way mirror in the ceiling of the guest bedroom, unbeknownst to their guests, who perform "the floor show." "Ever-Reddy" is having a problem of relentless tumescence without ejaculation and is referred to Dr. Harry Krieger, a hypnoanalyst and psychiatrist, by one of his unsatisfied women. Narcosynthesis treatment proves fruitless since Algernon's resistance is very high. In the second month, Dr. Krieger tries mescaline, thinking hallucinogens might be the answer. Algernon is more than receptive since he had enjoyed marijuana and hashish.

> By the fourth mescaline session, Algernon was masturbating open-ly, and by the fifth, Krieger was happy to report, he had observed an emission. "As long as I'm helping you, Doctor," Algernon said. "Did you get a nice close look?"
> "I take no pleasure from this," Krieger said.
> "If you mean you didn't ejaculate I don't believe you."
> After the sixth session Krieger increased the dosage and Algernon's fantasies ceased to be sexual in nature. He was able to enter the heart of a rose, and he found inside the soft center petals the gentle naked-ness of his mother, her body still warm on the crucifix.
> "Oh my God," Algernon wept. "Oh my God."
> "Typical Catholic hallucination," Krieger said, once the chlorpro-mazine had taken effect. "The symbol of the rose, deeply religious in nature."
> "Not to mention socio-economic and political."
> "Don't try to couch your guilt in contempt. Not after you've re-vealed yourself so clearly."
> "Revealed what?"
> "The mother-martyr figure. Surely you can see it. You're angry be-cause you're coming so close."
> "You mean ejaculating in such proximity," Algernon said, got up. "You're up to your orifices in feces, Dr. Krieger," he said, and left the office for the last time.
> There was no doubt that Algernon was shaken. To have shared such intimacy with a quack like Krieger was inexcusable, and an in-sult to the memory of his mother. To screw or even masturbate with people watching was more than tolerable, it was amusing, because it

degraded the voyeurs as much as the participants, made them as contemptible as those who committed the vile act. But to have paraded the pale vision of her naked body before the depraved eyes of that pervert was a blasphemy. He could not be sure Krieger hadn't seen. Even as the drug was wearing off completely, he could not shake from his mind the conviction that the doctor had been inside his brain with him, and had seen what was in the center of the rose. He was deeply ashamed, not only for the iniquities visited on that saint in her lifetime, but for the indignity to which he had exposed her that day.

He did not intend to violate his inner privacy again. Mescaline could be had, and easily, without a fraud for a connection.

After a time, Acapulco ceased to amuse him. He had known about the two-way mirror for several months, every since he had become aware of light footfalls and distant subdued giggling, and explored the locked room above his own, bribing the maid for the master key. Even stopping his activities in medias res and turning over to stick out his tongue, or something more insulting, at the ceiling gave him little pleasure. For a while he tried fornicating while under the influence of mescaline, but he usually got sidetracked on a pleasanter, sadder fantasy if he used it alone, and if the partner of the moment were using it too, reactions were unpredictable. Either the women cried because they thought he despised them, or they became convinced that Algernon was not actually servicing them, or some other hallucination with which he could not deal, interfering as it did with his own fine time. Eventually he began receiving complaints from upstairs as to the quality of his performances. He told them they were all freaks and paranoids and they should take a flying jack off Dr. Krieger [pp. 114-115].

Mescaline is a much stronger and longer-lasting hallucinogen than cannabis; for example, less control and direction are possible "and even the experienced user may find himself plunged into an agonizing hell . . . The intake of . . . mescaline must usually be spaced over several days to be effective . . . The evidence of the use of mescaline indicates that, although the mild euphoria obtained from cannabis may be desirable daily, or even more frequently, the overwhelming impact of the peyote and LSD experience generally results in a psychological satiation that lasts much longer than the tolerance effect" (McGlothlin, 1965, p. 458). Mescalin and psilocybin were reported to Gay and Sheppard (1973) as "more of a body trip, less a mind-blower" than LSD, that is, the sensory bombardment was less extreme, although physical coordination was impaired, as was sexual performance. But here again there is contradictory testimony. Shepard (1972), a psychiatrist, reports his own experience while tripping with mescaline and having sexual intercourse as profoundly beautiful. "We lay there on the floor, which soon became a cloud. Then the cloud disappeared, leaving us floating in the vastness of the universe. With neither up nor down, top nor bottom, ceiling nor floor, we were lost in space, out in the heavens, knowing no *One* or no *thing* except one another. Wordlessly, peering deeply into each other's eyes, we entered each other from the inside out, she becoming me, I her, we becoming one. Every cell of my body had an intelligence of its own, a sensuality unto itself, and individual cellular orgasm. Time stood still. Now was forever. The merging was so complete, my flesh was so alive, that the coming was unnecessary. Snowflakes crystallizing out on water. Diamonds out of coal. And it was over" (p. 193).

What is known, positively and scientifically, about psychedelic chemicals is that they bring about certain alterations of sense perception, of emotional level and tone, of identity feeling, of the interpretation of sensory data, and of the perception of time and space. The nature of these alterations depends on three variables: the type and dosage of the chemical itself; the psychophysiological state of the individual, and the social and esthetic context of the situation. Watts (1967) states that the physiological side effects of cannabis and mescaline are minimal; they are not habit-forming as are alcohol and tobacco. Although some people may come to depend on them for neurotic reasons, their effects are not easily predictable since they depend largely upon such imponderables as the social situation and the attitudes and expectations of the users, and the majority of people who use them are pleasantly stimulated although some have unpleasant reactions.

For 2,000 years now, the controversy about the effects of marijuana and hashish has raged, and there is no sign of its abatement. Brunner (1973), in his paper on the literary evidence of marijuana use in ancient Greece and Rome, reveals that Greek and Roman authors show a considerable degree of ignorance about the properties of cannabis and its functions. But the descriptions by many of them of its effects parallel those of many modern-day observers. While Herodotus indicates the euphoric effect of the weed, its inhibition-reducing qualities, and its use as an intoxicant, others dwell on hemp for its value in textile manufacture and shipbuilding. Among medical authors, Dioscorides claims that when cannabis is eaten to excess it diminishes sexual potency. Galen echoes this; and Oribasius, personal physician to Julian, ascribes to the cannabis seed antiflatulent and weight-reducing properties. In a passage in *Natural History*, the Elder Pliny comments much in the manner of Dioscorides: "Its seed is said to make the genitals impotent." He inventories a wide range of domestic and medical applications of cannabis but appears unaware of its intoxicating potential. Pseudo-Theodorus repeats much of what Oribasius wrote earlier. Brunner concludes, "The evidence available from Greek and Latin literary sources—while establishing the fact that certain properties inherent in cannabis were known and used for medicinal purposes—does not permit us to postulate use of the plant as an intoxicant in Greece and Rome; claims to the contrary are no more supportable than the periodic attempts to prove marijuana use during Homer's time from the description of the Lotus Eaters, or Helen's drug nepenthe in the Odyssey" (p. 355). The mystery and the controversy continue.

TECHNICAL REFERENCES

Ausubel, D. P. (1964), *Drug Addiction: Physiological, Psychological and Sociological Aspects.* New York: Random House.

Baudelaire, C. (1860), *Artificial Paradise; On Hashish and Wine as Means of Expanding Individuality.* New York: Herder & Herder, 1971.

Bejerot, N. (1972), *Addiction.* Springfield, Ill.: Charles C Thomas.

Blanc, W., Frick, H. C., Manger, W. M. & Nahas, G. G. (1975), On the rush to legalize marijuana. *New York Times,* July 1, 1975, p. 32

Bloomquist, E. R. (1971), *Marijuana: The Second Trip.* Beverly Hills, Calif.: Glencoe.

Brunner, T. F. (1973), Marijuana in ancient Greece and Rome? The literary evidence. *Bulletin of the History of Medicine,* 47:344-355.

Burroughs, W. S. (1961), Points of distinction between sedative and consciousness-expanding drugs. In: *Marihuana Papers,* ed. D. Solomon. New York: Signet, 1966, pp. 440-446.

Clark, L. D. & Nakashima, E. N. (1968), Experimental studies of marijuana. *American Journal of Psychiatry,* 125:379-384.

Cox, F. (1973), *Psychology.* Dubuque, Ia.: Brown.

Dahlberg, C. C. (1971), Sexual behavior in the drug culture. *Medical Aspects of Human Sexuality,* 5(4):64, 69-71.

Ebin, D., ed. (1961), *The Drug Experience. First-Person Accounts of Addicts, Writers, Scientists, and Others.* New York: Grove.

Eddy, N. B., Halbach, H., Isbell, H. & Seevers, M. H. (1970), Drug dependence of cannabis (marijuana) type. In: *Drug Awareness,* ed. R. E. Horman & A. M. Fox. New York: Avon, pp. 224-226.

Edwardes, A. (1959), *The Jewel in the Lotus. A Historical Survey of the Sexual Culture of the East.* New York: Julian Press.

Epstein, P. S. (1966), A psychiatrist looks at "Jack and the Beanstalk." In: *The Book of Grass. An Anthology of Indian Hemp*, ed. G. Andrews & S. Vinkenoog. New York: Grove Press, pp. 177-179.

Ewing, J. A. (1972), Students, sex and marijuana. *Medical Aspects of Human Sexuality*, 6(2):101-103, 109, 113-115, 117.

Finch, B. (1960), The sexual power of drugs. In: *Passport to Paradise.* New York: Philosophical Library, pp. 25, 28-37, 55-56.

Freeman, H. (1953), *Report at New York Academy of Medicine, Conference on Drug Addiction among Adolescents.* New York: Blakiston.

Gautier, T. (1846), The Hashish Club. In: *The Marihuana Papers*, ed. D. Solomon. New York: Signet, 1966, pp. 163-178.

Gay, G. R. & Sheppard, C. W. (1973), "Sex-crazed dope fiends" — myth or reality? *Drug Forum*, 2:125-140.

Goode, E. (1970), *The Marijuana Smokers.* New York: Basic Books.

Greaves, G. (1971), Level of conceptual functioning in experience with sex and drugs. *Psychological Reports*, 28:130.

Grinspoon, L. (1971), *Marihuana Reconsidered.* Cambridge, Mass.: Harvard University Press.

Halikas, J. A., Goodwin, D. W. & Guze, S. B. (1972), Pattern of marijuana use: A survey of one hundred regular users. *Comprehensive Psychiatry*, 13:161-164.

Herz, S. (1970), Research study on behavioral patterns in sex and drug use on the college campus. *Adolescence*, 5:1-16.

Huxley, A. (1954), *The Doors of Perception, and Heaven and Hell.* New York: Harper & Row.

———— (1966), Culture and the individual. In: *The Book of Grass. An Anthology of Indian Hemp*, ed. G. Andrews & S. Vinkenoog. New York: Grove Press, pp. 192-201.

Huxley, J. (1965), Psychometabolism. In: *The Psychedelic Reader*, ed. G. M. Weil, R. Metzner, & T. Leary. New York: University Books, pp. 127-148.

Kaplan, J. (1970), *Marijuana—The New Prohibition.* New York: World.

Lancet (1963), Pop "pot" (editorial). *Lancet*, 2:989.

Leary, T. (1968), *The Politics of Ecstasy.* New York: Putnam's.

Lewis, B. (1970), *The Sexual Powers of Marijuana.* New York: Wyden.

McGlothlin, W. H. (1965), Hallucinogenic drugs: A perspective with special reference to peyote and cannabis. In: *The Marihuana Papers*, ed. D. Solomon. New York: Signet, 1966, pp. 455-472.

———— & West, L. L. (1968), The marijuana problem: An overview. *American Journal of Psychiatry*, 125:370-378.

Masters, R. E. L. (1962), *Forbidden Sexual Behavior and Morality.* New York: Lancer.

———— (1971), Sex, ecstasy and psychedelics. In: *Sex American Style*, ed. F. Robinson & N. Lehrman. Chicago: Playboy Press, pp. 144-180.

Mayor's Committee on Marihuana (1944), *The Marihuana Problem in the City of New York.* Lancaster, Pa.: Catell.

Miller, H. (1971), On hanging loose and loving: The dilemma of present youth. *Journal of Social Issues*, 27(3):35-46.

Porot, A. (1942), Le cannabisme (haschich — kif — chira — marihuana). *Annales Médicales-Psychologiques*, 101:1-24.

Rosenberg, C. M. (1969), Young drug addicts: Background and personality. *Journal of Nervous and Mental Disease,* 148:65-73.
Rubin, V. & Comitas, L. (1975), *Ganja in Jamaica.* A Study for the Center of Studies of Narcotic and Drug Abuse of the National Institute of Mental Health. Scotch Plains, N.J.: MacFarland Publications.
Schwartz, C. R. (1969), Toward a medical understanding of marijuana. *Canadian Psychiatric Association Journal,* 14:591.
Shepard, M. (1972), *A Psychiatrist's Head.* New York: Wyden.
Sinnett, E. R., Srole, L. A., Coles, G. & Washington, W. (1972), The subjective dimensions of the drug experience. *Journal of Psychedelic Drugs,* 5:37-44.
Solomon, D., Ed. (1966), *The Marihuana Papers.* New York: Signet, 1968.
Sorensen, R. C. (1973), *Adolescent Sexuality in Contemporary America.* New York: World.
Stockings, G. T. (1947), A new euphoriant for depressive mental states. *British Medical Journal,* 1:918-922.
Tart, C. T. (1971), *On Being Stoned. A Psychological Study of Marijuana Intoxication.* Palo Alto, Calif.: Science & Behavior Books.
Watts, A. (1967), A psychedelic experience. Fact or fantasy. In: *The Book of Grass. An Anthology of Indian Hemp,* ed. G. Andrews & S. Vinkenoog. New York: Grove Press, pp. 180-194.
Wilson, R. A. (1973), *Sex and Drugs. A Journey Beyond Limits.* Chicago: Playboy Press.
Yorke, C. (1970), A critical review of some psychoanalytic literature on drug addiction. *British Journal of Medical Psychology,* 43:141-159.
Zinberg, N. E. & Robertson, J. A. (1972), *Drugs and the Public.* New York: Simon & Schuster.

LITERARY REFERENCES

Amis, Kingsley (1972), *Girl, 20.* New York: Harcourt Brace Jovanovich.
Baldwin, James (1962), *Another Country.* New York: Dial.
Bosse, M. J. (1972), *The Incident at Naha.* New York: Simon & Schuster.
Davis, Gwen (1969), *The Pretenders.* New York: World.
———— (1971), *Touching.* Garden City, N.Y.: Doubleday.
Friedman, Alan (1972), *Hermaphrodeity.* New York: Knopf.
Harrison, Jim (1971), *Wolf. A False Memoir.* New York: Simon & Schuster.
Hesse, Hermann (1927), *Steppenwolf.* New York: Bantam Books.
Horwitz, Julius (1973), *The Married Lovers.* New York: Dial.
Lelchuk, Alan (1973), *American Mischief.* New York: Farrar, Straus & Giroux.
Lowry, Malcolm (1947), *Under the Volcano.* New York: Reynal & Hitchcock.
Rabelais, Francois (1552), *Gargantua and Pantagruel.* Chicago: Encyclopedia Britannica, 1952, Book III, Ch. 49-52.
Schnitzler, Arthur (1924), *Fräulein Else.* New York: Simon & Schuster.
Smith, Martin (1971), *Gypsy in Amber.* New York: Putnam's.
Sutton, Henry (1969), *The Voyeur.* New York: Fawcett, World, Crest.
Trocchi, Alexander (1960), *Cain's Book.* New York: Grove Press.

Narcotics and Sex

Narcotics includes opium, the opium alkaloid morphine, and its derivative, heroin, as well as codeine, percodan, demerol, and certain
cough syrups such as Cheracol and Hycodan. Their potential for
psychological and physical dependence is high, as is the potential for
tolerance and for over-all abuse. The narcotic drug fulfills the two
requirements for addiction: it creates a tolerance in the user so that his
body requires ever larger doses to produce the same effect, and it
causes a withdrawal sickness when its use is discontinued. Alcohol and
the barbituates also meet these criteria. Stimulants, such as cocaine
and the amphetamines, are characterized by only one of the qualities:
tolerance. Marijuana has neither. The craving for narcotics is the most
malignant of addictions for it presents the dynamics of the illness in its
purest form and best reveals the difficulties encountered in therapy.
The narcotic addictions are regarded as a symptom complex rather
than a disease entity, and as such may be part of a variety of psychic
disorders. Since the common trait of the addictive process is
impulsivity, it is generally included in the category of impulse
disorders of which it is a prime example (Savitt, 1963).

In attempting to evolve a general theory of the dependence on
narcotic drugs, using Freud's libido theory as his conceptual
framework, Rado (1957) regards drug dependence as a malignant
form of miscarried repair artificially induced by the individual
himself. Prodomal depression is a precipitating etiological factor,
because it sensitizes the patient to the psychodynamic action of the
narcotic drug. "By removing pain, relaxing inhibitory tensions,

inducing pleasure and facilitating performance, narcotic drugs produce a narcotic pleasure effect [in which the addict sees] fulfillment of his longing for miraculous help, and responds to it with a sense of personal triumph and a surge of overconfidence" (p. 165). Rado describes the course of events following these feelings. After the narcotic elation, sleep comes, but by the morning after, depression returns, deepened by fresh guilty fears and made more painful by contrast. "His situation is worse than before; he feels he must recapture yesterday's grandeur by taking another dose. Thus his craving for elation develops. Augmented by concomitant physiological changes, it builds up in him ever-increasing tensions which can be discharged only by means of a fresh elation. Henceforth, every phase of elation leads to a phase of narcotic craving for elation, thence to taking the drug, which brings forth another phase of elation, and so forth in a cyclic course. A narcotic system of self-government, founded on dependence on the intoxicating drug, is established" (p. 166).

The sexual effects of opium, and its derivatives, heroin and morphine, are radical since they render the addict totally impotent. There are some cases where, early in addiction, erection may be prolonged but orgasm usually does not occur; the individual becomes sterile and, inevitably, impotent (Masters, 1962). Rado concludes that the "ideal toxic inebriation" is essentially orgasmic. In genital orgasm, the sense of well-being that succeeds it is diffused throughout the organism, whereas satisfaction of component instincts retains its local character, and it is the diffusion that characterizes intoxication. In comparison with genital orgasm, Rado states the "pharmacogenic orgasm" is very protracted. In the latter, the drug user encounters a new kind of erotic experience which competes with his customary methods of gratification.

In such competition the artificial orgasm has a considerable advantage, which can only be increased whenever normal intercourse is threatened by neurosis or adverse circumstances. The moment intoxication becomes a principal sexual aim, addiction is established, and the subsequent course of the craving can rarely be arrested. For those who do succumb to addiction, the consequences are far-reaching. To begin with, libidinal satisfaction through drugs is a violent attack on the biological sexual organization. In the case of morphia administered by injection, the entire peripheral sexual organization is by-passed. The need for erotogenic zones, with all the complications which their use and interaction bring about, is done away with. The effect of the drug is immediate and central. Real genital potency progressively deteriorates as object relations are increasingly surrendered ... With the overthrow of genital primacy the erotic life of infancy and childhood is regressively reactivated. The precise part played by the erotogenic zones in fantasy may be concealed by the pharmacological shortcircuit, but the most imporant role will be played by the oral zone... [Yorke, 1970, p. 147].

Several of the short stories of Edgar Allan Poe tend to bear this out. Poe described his story, "Ligeia" (1838), as the best one he had ever written. It is a sophisticated structuring of an unconscious wish for the return of his lost mother, which surfaces through the narrator's recourse to opium. It also reveals Poe's sexual impotence, conditioned by a fixation on a dying mother and, later, a corpse. Poe was inhibited against all sexuality, since it could only mean to him both sadistic destruction and necrophilia. The narrator of "Ligeia" finds himself in a state of lost happiness and seeks to regain, recapture, or reproduce it. Over and over again, he refers to his compulsive desire to know Ligeia's secret, to penetrate her mystery, especially to discover the secret of her eyes, "those divine orbs." In describing the beauty of Ligeia, she "who was my friend and my betrothed, and who became the partner of my studies, and finally the wife of my bosom," Poe wrote, "in beauty of face no maiden ever equalled her. It was the radiance of an opium-dream—an airy and spirit lifting vision more wildly divine than the phantasies which hovered about the slumbering souls of the daughters of Delos" (p. 135).

That Poe was unconsciously identifying Ligeia with his mother is seen in this passage, wherein he describes his childhood amnesia: "There is no point, among the many incomprehensible anomalies of the science of the mind, more thrillingly exciting than the fact—never, I believe, noticed in the schools—that, in our endeavors to recall to memory something long forgotten, we often find ourselves upon the very verge of remembrance, without being able, in the end, to remember. And thus how frequent, in my intense scrutiny of Ligeia's eyes, have I felt approaching the full knowledge of their expression—felt it approaching—yet not quite be mine—and so at length entirely depart." Repression prohibited Poe from recovering the memory of his infantile incestuous wishes toward his dead mother, with their sadonecrophilic implications. The narrator's "Memory flew back, (oh, with what intensity of regret!) to Ligeia, the beloved, the august, the beautiful, the entombed. I revelled in recollections of her purity, of her wisdom, of her lofty, her ethereal nature, of her passionate, her idolatrous love ... In the excitement of my opium dreams (for I was habitually fettered in the shackles of the drug) I would call aloud her name, during the silence of the night, or among the sheltered recesses of the glens by day, as if, through the wild eagerness, the solemn passion, the consuming ardour of my longing for the departed, I could restore her to the pathway she had abandoned — ah, *could* it be forever? — upon the earth" (p. 146).

As Poe's narrator becomes more and more "a bounden slave in the trammels of opium, and my labours and my orders had taken a colouring from my dreams" (p. 143). The periodicity of Poe's use of the word "opium" is in direct proportion to the narrator's use of the drug and to his intoxicated state. The narrator continues: "... I was wild with the excitement of an immoderate dose of opium, and heeded these things but little, nor spoke to them to Rowena" (p. 147). And on the next page, two allusions to opium are made, one after the other: Rowena "swallowed the wine unhesitatingly, and I forbore to speak to her of a circumstance which must, after all, I considered, have been but the suggestion of a vivid imagination, rendered morbidly active by the terror of the lady, by the opium, and by the hour. Yet I cannot conceal it from my own perception that, immediately subsequent to the fall of the ruby-drops, a rapid change for the worse took place in the disorder of my wife; so that, on the third subsequent night, the hands of her menials prepared her for the tomb, and on the fourth, I sat alone, with her shrouded body, in that fantastic chamber which had received her as my bride. — Wild visions, opium-engendered, flitted, shadow-like, before me."

Opium, like all drugs, relaxes the control of the superego and so permits the infantile material buried in the unconscious to re-emerge. Thus, the narrator's unconscious incestuous wishes and sadonecrophilia are evident in "Ligeia" and perhaps even more in an earlier story, "Loss of Breath" (1835). In her study of Poe's major works, Bonaparte (1949) analyzes "Loss of Breath" as an illustration of sexual impotence brought about, in part, by opium addiction. In the story, a man loses his breath, the morning after his marriage, for trying to shout too loudly into his wife's ear. The lost breath is caught by his neighbor, Mr. Windenough, who happens to pass by. Mrs.

Lackobreath already loves the latter because of his mighty breath, and now he is doubly endowed. Nevertheless, Lackobreath, after various mishaps, such as being crushed in a coach by a huge fellow passenger, dissected by a surgeon, and hanged by the executioner, rediscovers his luckier rival in a tomb, harassed by his theft, and his double breath capacity. Lackobreath persuades Windenough to restore his stolen respiration.

"Breath is here the symbol of male potency, a confession of the truth, a wish fantasy that the potency stolen by his father be restored, as it is at the end of the tale, when he rediscovers the same father." Bonaparte traces the relation of male sexual potency to breath back to the Old Testament, where the concept of breath is a creative and fecundating force: "And the Lord God formed man of the dust of the ground, and breathed into his nostrils the breath of life; and man became a living soul." In Greek mythology, Hera is made pregnant by the wind. Freud (1910), in his study of Leonardo da Vinci, notes the ancient belief that all vultures are female and conceived by presenting the cloaca to the wind. Yet, Bonaparte asks rhetorically (p. 383), "How is it that in the unconscious, men came to substitute breath, or wind, for the generative fluid? The first and infantile prototype of an organ strikingly able to blow is the anus, whose functions are charged, for the child, with intense libidinal interest. The noises which accompany elimination greatly please the child. Yet the impressiveness of such noises is incalculably magnified when, like veritable thunderings, they issue from that dreaded, mighty being, the father ... To this a last fact must be added which gives wind, breath, and breathing such prime importance; namely, that the small child is often present at the sex acts of adults, too heedless of its sensitiveness to such impressions. What it then sees leaves indelible traces in the unconscious—traces which later analysis reveals ... Two senses in particular are concerned in the child's awareness of adult coitus ... sight and hearing; hearing above all, since the sex act commonly takes place in darkness. And what, to the ear, most characterizes coitus, if not its panting breath, its sighs and moans and—even, at times, gross as it seems—the sound of the woman breaking wind, as a result of abdominal compression in the coitus position. At such times ... the child habitually attributes such thunderings to the father; the omnipotent father he dreads and whom he imagines, in coitus, attacking the mother, since that is its earliest sadistic idea of the act" (p. 385).

"Loss of Breath" opens with the narrator's diatribe against his wife the morning after their wedding night. He is so aroused that he is about to attack her when he loses his breath and cannot "ejaculate" the more opprobrius epithet. Despite his consternation and despair at losing his breath, he makes a virtue of necessity, as the impotent so often do. He would be capable of pure love, of ardent and ethereal passion. The hero describes the impotent's plight: "I am serious in asserting that my breath was entirely gone. I could not have stirred with it a feather if my life had been at issue, or sullied even the delicacy of a mirror." His speechlessness is interpreted by Bonaparte as "an intestinal, pre-genital language, replacing the strictly genital type of speech symbolized by respiration, the gutteral sounds marking a regression to an earlier infantile, and hence, impotent, stage of libidinal development" (p. 375).

Lackobreath "hears his wife leave the house and thereupon begins a vigorous search for his lost breath—'it might even have a tangible form.' His exertions prove fruitless . . . although he discovers a packet of letters from his neighbor, Mr. Windenough, who is amply potent and who had found favor earlier with his wife. He takes flight from her, which is nothing less than a fugue from sex. The coach he boards is crammed and a man throws himself on top of Mr. Lackobreath, a crushing image of the father, depicted as this passenger whose mighty breath at once conjures up the most potent of all animal symbols, the bull" (p. 388). Multiple symbols of castration appear now in the story. The nine passengers on the coach "pulled my ear;" the surgeon "cut off my ears . . . made an incision in my stomach, and removed several of my viscera for private dissection."

The narrator's surrealist adventures lead him to the hangman's gallows and he hears a variety of noises—bells, drums, the sea. Simultaneously, his mental powers are strangely affected and permit him to analyze even his confused state with paradoxical clarity and precision. It sounds very much as if the narrator were intoxicated with some drug and that is just how he describes it: "A dreamy delight now took hold upon my spirit, and I imagined that I had been eating opium, or feasting upon the Hashish of the old Assassins." Thus Mr. Lackobreath's fantasies and sensations become clear. "This drug, by the fevered vision it inspires, and the utter immobility it imposes, is admirably fitted to conjure up the fantasies of Life in Death that haunted Poe's unconscious . . . The hanged man . . . has glimpses of 'pure unadulterated reason'" (Bonaparte, 1949, p. 391). In his drug-intoxicated state, he talks about Crabbe and Coleridge, two poets known to have taken opium. Though seemingly hung, drawn, and quartered, the narrator survives, but taken for dead, is laid out in a room preparatory for burial the next day. Corpselike, he relates the approach of death to the loss of the sense of time and space experienced in opium dreams for, despite having lost his breath and most of his viscera, he still, and with reason, refuses to believe he is dead.

Bonaparte explains (p. 393) that although one would expect Mr. Lackobreath to die of strangulation, Poe substitutes an opium dream. The basis for this is the unconscious association of the legend that hanging produces erection and ejaculation *in extremis.* "It is just when our hero has undergone his numerous visceral symbolic castrations at the surgeon's hands that Poe's unconscious, as it were, protests and avenges itself by thus attaching a new penis to our hero [p. 394] . . . Even the penis, so mock-heroically restored, with which he thus identifies himself with all his body, is itself no better than a man hanged, with its flaccidity and limpness. Here too, then, as with wind and breath, we find an impotency symbol symbolizing potency. The hanged man also reacts to his 'rephallization' in a similar manner. He feels voluptuous pleasure, it is true, but it is the 'chemotoxic orgasm' of opium, in which the libido short circuits itself inside the body, owing to inability to reach out to an external love object. The opium delirium, as that from all toxic substances, serves as a substitute for the masturbatory orgasm, a form of satisfaction derived from regression to the primal pregenital oral-erotic phase from which every trace of the child's penis-masturbation has vanished. Glimpses of this past activity, however, appear in our hero's opium dream when he hangs, and after he is cut down" (p. 395). Thus, the unconscious obsession with sexual impotence, with unrequited oedipal desires, and the phantasmagoria brought about by opium use, along with spatial and time distortions, are found in both "Ligeia" and "Loss of Breath." The original version of the latter follows, for in subsequent printings, Poe revised his story considerably.

The most notorious ill-fortune must, in the end, yield to the un-tiring courage of philosophy — as the most stubborn city to the ceaseless vigilance of an enemy. Shalmanezer, as we have it in the holy writings, lay three years before Samaria; yet it fell. Sardana-palus — see Diodorus — maintained himself seven in Nineveh; but to no purpose. Troy expired at the close of the second lustrum; and Azoth, as Aristaeus declares upon his honor as a gentleman, opened at last her gates to Psammenitus, after having barred them for the fifth part of a century.

"Thou wretch!—thou vixen!—thou shrew!" said I to my wife on the morning after our wedding, "thou witch!—thou hag!—thou whipper-snapper!—thou sink of iniquity!—thou fiery-faced quintessence of all that is abominable!—thou—thou" here standing upon tiptoe, seizing her by the throat, and placing my mouth close to her ear, I was preparing to launch forth a new and more decided epithet of opprobrium, which should not fail, if ejaculated, to convince her of her insignificance, when, to my extreme horror and astonishment, I discovered that *I had lost my breath.*

The phrases "I am out of breath," "I have lost my breath," etc., are often enough repeated in common conversation; but it had never occurred to me that the terrible accident of which I speak could *bona fide* and actually happen! Imagine—that is you have a fanciful turn—imagine, I say, my wonder—my consternation—my despair!

There is a good genius, however, which has never entirely deserted me. In my most ungovernable moods I still retain a sense of propriety, *et le chemin des passions me conduit*—as Lord Edouard in the "Julie" says it did him—*à la philosophie véritable.*

Although I could not at first precisely ascertain to what degree the occurrence had affected me, I determined at all events to conceal the matter from my wife, until further experience should discover to me the extent of this my unheard of calamity. Altering my countenance, therefore, in a moment, from its bepuffed and distorted appearance, to an expression of arch and coquettish benignity, I gave my lady a pat on the one cheek, and a kiss on the other, and without saying one syllable (Furies! I could not), left her astonished at my drollery, as I pirouetted out of the room in a *pas de zephyr.*

Behold me then safely ensconced in my private *boudoir*, a fearful instance of the ill consequences attending upon irascibility—alive, with the qualifications of the dead—dead, with the propensities of the living—an anomaly on the face of the earth—being very calm, yet breathless.

Yes! breathless. I am serious in asserting that my breath was entirely gone. I could not have stirred with it a feather if my life had been at issue, or sullied even the delicacy of a mirror. Hard fate!—yet there was some alleviation to the first overwhelming paroxysm of my sorrow. I found, upon trial, that the powers of utter-ance which, upon my inability to proceed in the conversation with my wife, I then concluded to be totally destroyed, were in fact only partially impeded, and I discovered that had I, at that interesting crisis, dropped my voice to a singularly deep gutteral, I might still have continued to her the communication of my sentiments; this pitch of voice (the gutteral) depending, I find, not upon the current of the breath, but upon a certain spasmodic action of the muscles of the throat.

Throwing myself upon a chair, I remained for some time ab-sorbed in meditation. My reflections, be sure, were of no consola-tory kind. A thousand vague and lachrymatory fancies took posses-sion of my soul—and even the idea of suicide flitted across my brain; but it is a trait in the perversity of human nature to reject the obvious and the ready, for the far-distant and equivocal. Thus I shuddered at self-murder as the most decided of atrocities while the tabby-cat purred strenuously upon the rug, and the very water-dog wheezed assiduously under the table; each taking to itself much merit for the strength of its lungs, and all obviously done in derision of my own pulmonary incapacity.

Oppressed with a tumult of vague hopes and fears, I at length heard the footsteps of my wife descending the staircase. Being now assured of her absence, I returned with a palpitating heart to the scene of my disaster.

Carefully locking the door on the inside, I commenced a vigorous search. It was possible, I thought, that concealed in some obscure corner, or lurking in some closet or drawer, might be found the lost object of my inquiry. It might have a vapory—it might even have a tangible form. Most philosophers, upon many points of philosophy, are still very unphilosophical. William Godwin, however, says in his "Mandeville," that "invisible things are the only realities," and this, all will allow, is a case in point. I would have the judicious reader pause before accusing such asseverations of an undue quantum of absurdity. Anaxagoras, it will be remembered, maintained that snow is black, and this I have since found to be the case.

Long and earnestly did I continue the investigation: but the con-temptible reward of my industry and perseverance proved to be only a set of false teeth, two pair of hips, an eye, and a number of billets-doux from Mr. Windenough to my wife. I might as well here observe that this confirmation of my lady's partiality for Mr. W. occasioned me little uneasiness. That Mrs. Lackobreath should ad-mire any thing so dissimilar to myself was a natural and necessary evil. I am, it is well known, of a robust and corpulent appearance, and at the same time somewhat diminutive in stature. What wonder, then, that the lath-like tenuity of my acquaintance, and his altitude, which has grown into a proverb, should have met with all due estimation in the eyes of Mrs. Lackobreath. But to return.

My exertions, as I have before said, proved fruitless. Closet after closet—drawer after drawer—corner after corner—were scrutinized to no purpose. At one time, however, I thought myself sure of my prize, having, in rummaging a dressing-case, accidentally demolished a bottle of Grandjean's Oil of Archangels—which, as an agreeable perfume, I here take the liberty of recommending.

With a heavy heart I returned to my *boudoir*—there to ponder upon some method of eluding my wife's penetration, until I could make arrangements prior to my leaving the country, for to this I had already made up my mind. In a foreign climate, being unknown, I might, with some probability of success, endeavor to conceal my unhappy calamity—a calamity calculated, even more than beggary, to estrange the affections of the multitude, and to draw down upon the wretch of the well-merited indignation of the virtuous and the happy. I was not long in hesitation. Being naturally quick, I committed to memory the entire tragedy of "Metamora." I had the good fortune to recollect that in the accentuation of this drama, or at least of such portion of it as is alloted to the hero, the tones of voice in which I found myself deficient were altogether unnecessary, and that the deep gutteral was expected to reign monotonously throughout.

I practised for some time by the borders of a well-frequented marsh;—herein, however, having no reference to a similar proceeding of Demosthenes, but from a design peculiarly and conscientiously my own. Thus armed at all points, I determined to make my wife believe that I was suddenly smitten with a passion for the stage. In this, I succeeded to a miracle; and to every question or suggestion found myself at liberty to reply in my most frog-like and sepulchral tones with some passage from the tragedy—any portion of which, as I soon took great pleasure in observing, would apply equally well to any particular subject. It is not to be supposed, however, that in the delivery of such passages I was found at all deficient in the looking asquint—the showing my teeth—the working my knees—the shuffling my feet—or in any of those unmentionable graces which are now justly considered the characteristics of a popular performer. To be sure they spoke of confining me in a strait-jacket—but, good God! they never suspected me of having lost my breath.

Having at length put my affairs in order, I took my seat very early one morning in the mail stage for ———, giving it to be understood, among my acquaintances, that business of the last importance required my immediate personal attendance in that city.

The coach was crammed to repletion; but in the uncertain twilight the features of my companions could not be distinguished. Without making any effectual resistance, I suffered myself to be placed between two gentlemen of colossal dimensions; while a third, of a size larger, requesting pardon for the liberty he was about to take, threw himself upon my body at full length, and falling asleep in an instant, drowned all my guttural ejaculations for relief, in a snore which would have put to blush the roarings of the bull of Phalaris. Happily the state of my respiratory faculties rendered suffocation an accident entirely out of the question.

As, however, the day broke more distinctly in our approach to the outskirts of the city, my tormentor, arising and adjusting his shirt-collar, thanked me in a very friendly manner for my civility. Seeing that I remained motionless (all my limbs were dislocated and my head twisted on one side), his apprehensions began to be excited; and arousing the rest of the passengers, he communicated, in a very decided manner, his opinion that a dead man had been palmed upon them during the night for a living and responsible fellow-traveller; here giving me a thump on the right eye, by way of demonstrating the truth of his suggestion.

Hereupon all, one after another (there were nine in company), believed it their duty to pull me by the ear. A young practising physician, too, having applied a pocket-mirror to my mouth, and found me without breath, the assertion of my persecutor was pronounced a true bill; and the whole party expressed a determination to endure tamely no such impositions for the future, and to proceed no farther with any such carcasses for the present.

I was here, accordingly, thrown out at the sign of the "Crow" (by which tavern the coach happened to be passing), without meeting with any further accident than the breaking of both my arms, under the left hind wheel of the vehicle. I must besides do the driver the justice to state that he did not forget to throw after me the largest of my trunks, which, unfortunately falling on my head, fractured my skull in a manner at once interesting and extraordinary.

The landlord of the "Crow," who is a hospitable man, finding that my trunk contained sufficient to indemnify him for any little trouble he might take in my behalf, sent forthwith for a surgeon of his acquaintance, and delivered me to his care with a bill and receipt for ten dollars.

The purchaser took me to his apartments and commenced operations immediately. Having cut off my ears, however, he discovered signs of animation. He now rang the bell, and sent for a neighboring apothecary with whom to consult in the emergency. In case of his suspicions with regard to my existence proving ultimately correct, he, in the meantime, made an incision in my stomach, and removed several of my viscera for private dissection.

The apothecary had an idea that I was actually dead. This idea I endeavored to confute, kicking and plunging with all my might, and making the most furious contortions — for the operations of the surgeon had, in a measure, restored me to the possession of my faculties. All, however, was attributed to the effects of a new galvanic battery, wherewith the apothecary, who is really a man of information, performed several curious experiments, in which, from my personal share in their fulfilment, I could not help feeling deeply interested. It was a source of mortification to me nevertheless, that although I made several attempts at conversation, my powers of speech were so entirely in abeyance, that I could not even open my mouth; much less, then, make reply to some ingenious but fanciful theories of which, under other circumstances, my minute acquaintance with the Hippocratian pathology would have afforded me a ready confuation.

Not being able to arrive at a conclusion, the practitioners remanded me for further examination. I was taken up into a garret; and the surgeon's lady having accommodated me with drawers and stockings, the surgeon himself fastened my hands, and tied up my jaws with a pocket-handkerchief — then bolted the door on the outside as he hurried to his dinner, leaving me alone to silence and to meditation.

I now discovered to my extreme delight that I could have spoken had not my mouth been tied up with the pocket-handkerchief. Consoling myself with this reflection, I was mentally repeating some passages of the "Omnipresence of the Deity," as is my custom before resigning myself to sleep, when two cats, of a greedy and vituperative turn, entering at a hole in the wall, leaped up with a flourish à la Catalani, and alighting opposite one another on my visage, betook themselves to indecorous contention for the paltry consideration of my nose.

But, as the loss of his ears proved the means of elevating to the throne of Cyrus, the Magian or Mige-Gush of Persia, and as the cutting off his nose gave Zopyrus possession of Babylon, so the loss of a few ounces of my countenance proved the salvation of my body. Aroused by the pain, and burning with indignation, I burst, at a single effort, the fastenings and the bandage. Stalking across the room I cast a glance of contempt at the belligerents, and throwing open the sash to their extreme horror and disappointment, precipitated myself, very dexterously, from the window.

The mail-robber W., to whom I bore a singular resemblance, was at this moment passing from the city jail to the scaffold erected for his execution in the suburbs. His extreme infirmity and long-continued ill-health had obtained him the privilege of remaining unmanacled; and habited in his gallows costume—one very similar to my own,—he lay at full length in the bottom of the hangman's cart (which happened to be under the windows of the surgeon at the moment of my precipitation) without any other guard than the driver, who was asleep, and two recruits of the sixth infantry, who were drunk.

As ill-luck would have it, I alit upon my feet within the vehicle. W——, who was an acute fellow, perceived his opportunity. Leaping up immediately, he bolted out behind, and turning down an alley, was out of sight in the twinkling of an eye. The recruits, aroused by the bustle, could not exactly comprehend the merits of the transaction. Seeing, however, a man, the precise counterpart of the felon, standing upright in the cart before their eyes, they were of the opinion that the rascal (meaning W——) was after making his escape (so they expressed themselves), and, having communicated this opinion to one another, they took each a dram, and then knocked me down with the butt-ends of their muskets.

It was not long ere we arrived at the place of destination. Of course nothing could be said in my defence. Hanging was my inevitable fate. I resigned myself thereto with a feeling half stupid, half acrimonious. Being little of a cynic, I had all the sentiments of a dog. The hangman, however, adjusted the noose about my neck. The drop fell.

Die I certainly did not. The sudden jerk given to my neck upon the falling of the drop, merely proved a corrective to the unfortunate twist afforded me by the gentleman in the coach. Although my body certainly *was*, I had, alas! no breath *to be* suspended; and but for the chafing of the rope, the pressure of the knot under my ear, and the rapid determination of blood to the brain, should, I dare say, have experienced very little inconvenience.

The latter feeling, however, grew momentarily more painful. I heard my heart beating with violence — the veins in my hands and wrists swelled nearly to bursting — my temples throbbed tempestuously — and I felt that my eyes were starting from their sockets. Yet when I say that in spite of all this my sensations were not absolutely intolerable, I will not be believed.

There were noises in my ears, first like the tolling of huge bells — then like the beathing of a thousand drums — then, lastly, like the low, sullen murmurs of the sea. But these noises were very far from disagreeable.

Although, too, the powers of my mind were confused and distorted, yet I was — strange to say! — well aware of such confusion and distortion. I could, with unerring promptitude determine at will in what particulars my sensations were correct — and in what particulars I wandered from the path. I could even feel with accuracy *how far — to what very point*, such wanderings had misguided me, but still without the power of correcting my deviations. I took besides, at the same time, a wild delight in analyzing my conceptions.

[The general reader will I dare say recognize, in these *sensations* of Mr. Lackobreath, much of the absurd *metaphysicianism* of the redoubted Schelling.]

Memory, which, of all other faculties, should have first taken its departure, seemed on the contrary to have been endowed with quadrupled power. Each incident of my past life flitted before me like a shadow. There was not a brick in the building where I was born — not a dogleaf in the primer I had thumbed over when a child — not a tree in the forest where I hunted when a boy — not a street in the cities I had traversed when a man — that I did not at that time most palpably behold. I could repeat to myself entire lines, passages, chapters, books, from the studies of my earliest days; and while, I dare say, the crowd around me were blind with horror, or aghast with awe, I was alternately with Aeschylus, a demi-god, or with Aristophanes, a frog.

For good reasons, however, I did my best to give the crowd the worth of their trouble. My convulsions were said to be extraordinary. My spasms it would have been difficult to beat. The populace *encored*. Several gentlemen swooned; and a multitude of ladies were carried home in hysterics. Pinxit availed himself the opportunity to retouch, from a sketch taken upon the spot, his admirable painting of the Marsyas flayed alive.

     .   .   .   .

A dreamy delight now took hold upon my spirit, and I imagined that I had been eating opium, or feasting upon the Hashish of the old Assassins. But glimpses of pure, unadulterated reason—during which I was still buoyed up by the hope of finally escaping that death which hovered, like a vulture above me—were still caught occasionally by my soul.

By some unusual pressure of the rope against my face, a portion of the cap was chafed away, and I found to my astonishment that my powers of reason were not altogether destroyed. A sea of waving heads rolled around me. In the intensity of my delight I eyed them with feelings of the deepest commiseration, and blessed, as I looked upon the haggard assembly, the superior benignity of *my* proper stars.

I now reasoned, rapidly I believe—profoundly I am sure—upon principles of common law—propriety of that law especially, for which I hung—absurdities in political economy which till then I had never been able to acknowledge—dogmas in the old Aristotelians now generally denied, but not the less intrinsically true—detestable school formulae in Bourdon, in Garnier, in Lacroix—synonymes in Crabbe—lunar-lunatic theories in St. Pierre—falsities in the Pelham novels—beauties in Vivian Grey—more than beauties in Vivian Grey—profundity in Vivian Grey—genius in Vivian Grey—every thing in Vivian Grey.

Then came, like a flood, Coleridge, Kant, Fichte, and Pantheism—then like a deluge, the Academie, Pergola, La Scala, San Carlo, Paul, Albert, Noblet, Ronzi, Vestris, Fanny Bias, and Taglion.

.   .   .   .

A rapid change was now taking place in my sensations. The last shadows of connection flitted away from my meditations. A storm—a tempest of ideas, vast, novel, and soul-stirring, bore my spirit like a feather afar off. Confusion crowded upon confusion like a wave upon a wave. In a very short time Schelling himself would have been satisfied with my entire loss of self-identity. The crowd became a mass of mere abstraction.

About this time I became aware of a heavy fall and shock—but, although the concussion jarred through my frame, I had not the slightest idea of its having been sustained in my own proper person, and thought of it as an incident peculiar to some other existence—an idiosyncrasy belonging to some other *Ens*. It was at this moment—as I afterwards discovered—that having been suspended for the full term of execution, it was thought proper to remove my body from the gallows—this the more especially as the real culprit had been retaken and recognized.

Much sympathy was now exercised in my behalf—and as no one

in the city appeared to identify my body, it was ordered that I should be interred in the public sepulchre in the following morning. I lay, in the meantime, without signs of life—although from the moment, I suppose, when the rope was loosened from my neck, a dim consciousness of my situation oppressed me like the nightmare.

I was laid out in a chamber sufficiently small, and very much encumbered with furniture—yet to me it appeared of a size to contain the universe. I have never before or since, in body or mind, suffered half so much agony as from that single idea. Strange! that the simple conception of abstract magnitude—of infinity—should have been accompanied with pain. Yet so it was. "With how vast a difference," said I, "in life as in death—in time and in eternity—here and hereafter, shall our merest sensations be imbodied!"

The day died away, and I was aware that it was growing dark—yet the same terrible conceit still overwhelmed me. Nor was it confined to the boundaries of the apartment—it extended, although in a more definite manner, to all objects, and perhaps, I will not be understood in saying that it extended also to all *sentiments*. My fingers as they lay cold, clammy, stiff, and pressing helplessly one against another, were, in my imagination, swelled to a size according with the proportions of the Antaeus. Every portion of my frame betook of their enormity. The pieces of money—I well remember—which, being placed upon my eyelids, failed to keep them effectually closed, seemed huge, interminable chariot-wheels of the Olympia, or of the Sun.

Yet it is very singular that I experienced no sense of weight—of gravity. On the contrary I was put to much inconvenience by the buoyancy—that tantalizing *difficulty of keeping down*, which is felt by the swimmer in deep water. Amid the tumult of my terrors I laughed with a hearty internal laugh to think of what incongruity there would be—could I arise and walk—between the elasticity of my motion, and the mountain of my form.

.   .   .   .

The night came—and with it a new crowd of horrors. The consciousness of my approaching interment, began to assume new distinctness, and consistency—yet never for one moment did I imagine *that I was actually dead.*

"This then"—I mentally speculated—"this darkness which is palpable, and oppresses with a sense of suffocation—this—this—is—indeed *death*. This is death—this is death the terrible—death the holy. This is the death undergone by Regulus—and equally by Seneca. Thus—thus, too, shall I always remain—always—always remain. Reason is folly, and Philosophy a lie. No one will know my sensations, my horror—my despair. Yet will men still persist in reasoning, and philosophizing, and making themselves fools. There is, I find, no hereafter but this. This—this—this—is the only Eternity!—and what, O Baalzebub!—*what* an Eternity!—to lie in this vast—this awful void—a hideous, vague, and unmeaning anomaly—motionless, yet wishing for motion—powerless, yet longing for power—forever, forever, and forever!"

But the morning broke at length, and with its misty and gloomy dawn arrived in triple horror the paraphernalia of the grave. Then—and not till then—was I fully sensible of the fearful fate hanging over me. The phantasms of the night had faded with its shadows, and the actual terrors of the yawning tomb left me no heart for the bugbear speculations of Transcendentalism.

I have before mentioned that my eyes were but imperfectly closed—yet I could not move them in any degree, those objects alone which crossed the direct line of vision were within the sphere of my comprehension. But across that line of vision spectral and stealthy figures were continually flitting, like the ghosts of Banquo. They were making hurried preparations for my interment. First came the coffin which they placed quietly by my side. Then the undertaker with attendants and a screw-driver. Then a stout man whom I could distinctly see and who took hold of my feet—while one whom I could only feel lifted me by the head and shoulders.

Together they placed me in the coffin, and drawing the shroud up over my face proceeded to fasten down the lid. One of the screws, missing its proper direction, was screwed by the carelessness of the undertaker deep—deep—down into my shoulder. A convulsive shudder ran throughout my frame. With what horror, with what sickening of heart did I reflect that one minute sooner, a similar manifestation of life would, in all probability, have prevented my inhumation. But alas! it was now too late, and hope died away within my bosom as I felt myself lifted upon the shoulders of men—carried down the stairway—and thrust within the hearse.

During the brief passage to the cemetery my sensations, which for sometime had been lethargic and dull, assumed, all at once, a degree of intense and unnatural vivacity for which I can in no manner account. I could distinctly hear the rustling of the plumes—the whispers of the attendants—the solemn breathings of the horses of death. Confused as I was in that narrow and strict embrace, I could feel the quicker or slower movement of the procession—the restlessness of the driver—the windings of the road as it led us to the right or to the left. I could distinguish the peculiar odor of the coffin—the sharp acid smell of the steel screws. I could see the texture of the shroud as it lay close against my face; and was even conscious of the rapid variations in light and shade which the flapping to and fro of the sable hangings occasioned within the body of the vehicle.

In a short time, however, we arrived at the place of sepulture, and I felt myself deposited within the tomb. The entrance was secured—they departed—and I was left alone. A line of Marston's "Malcontent,"

"Death's a good fellow and keeps open house,"

struck me at that moment as a palpable lie.

Sullenly I lay at length, the quick among the dead—*Anacharsis inter Scythas*.

From what I overheard early in the morning, I was led to believe that the occasions when the vault was made use of were of very rare occurrence. It was probable that many months might elapse before the doors of the tomb would be again unbarred—and even should I survive until that period, what means could I have more than at present, of making known my situation or of escaping from the coffin? I resigned myself, therefore, with much tranquility to my fate, and fell, after many hours, into a deep and deathlike sleep.

How long I remained thus is to me a mystery. When I awoke my limbs were no longer cramped with the cramp of death—I was no longer without the power of motion. A very slight exertion was suffi- cient to force the lid of my prison—for the dampness of the atmosphere had already occasioned decay in the wood-work around the screws.

My steps as I groped around the sides of my habitation were, however, feeble and uncertain, and I felt all the gnawings of hunger with the pains of intolerable thirst. Yet, as time passed away, it is strange that I experienced little uneasiness from these scourges of the earth, in comparison with the more terrible visitations of the fiend *Ennui*. Stranger still were the resources by which I endeavored to banish him from my presence.

The sepulchre was large and subdivided into many compart- ments, and I busied myself in examining the peculiarities of their construction. I determined the length and breadth of my abode. I counted and recounted the stones of the masonry. But there were other methods by which I endeavored to lighten the tedium of my hours. Feeling my way among the numerous coffins ranged in order around, I lifted them down one by one, and breaking open their lids, busied myself in speculations about the mortality within.

"This," I soliloquized, tumbling over a carcass, puffy, bloated, and rotund — "this has been, no doubt, in every sense of the word, an unhappy — an unfortunate man. It has been his terrible lot not to walk but to waddle — to pass through life not like a human being, but like an elephant — not like a man, but like a rhinoceros.

"His attempts at getting on have been mere abortions, and his circumgyratory proceedings a palpable failure. Taking a step forward, it has been his misfortune to take two toward the right, and three toward the left. His studies have been confined to the poetry of Crabbe. He can have no idea of the wonder of a *pirouette*. To him a *pas de papillon* has been an abstract conception. He has never ascended the summit of a hill. He has never viewed from any steeple the glories of a metropolis. Heat has been his mortal enemy. In the dog-days his days have been the days of a dog. Therein, he has dreamed of flames and suffocation — of mountains upon mountains — of Pelion upon Ossa. He was short of breath — to say all in a word, he was short of breath. He thought it extravagant to play upon wind-instruments. He was the inventor of self-moving fans, wind-sails, and ventilators. He patronized Du Pont the bellows-maker, and died miserably in attempting to smoke a cigar. His was a case in which I feel a deep interest — a lot in which I sincerely sympathize.

"But here," — said I — "here" — and I dragged spitefully from its receptacle a gaunt, tall, and peculiar-looking form, whose remarkable appearance struck me with a sense of unwelcome familiarity — "here is a wretch entitled to no earthly commiseration." Thus saying, in order to obtain a more distinct view of my subject, I applied my thumb and forefinger to its nose, and causing it to assume a sitting position upon the ground, held it thus, at the length of my arm, while I continued my soliloquy.

—"Entitled," I repeated, "to no earthly commiseration. Who indeed would think of compassionating a shadow? Besides, has he not had his full share of the blessings of mortality? He was the originator of tall monuments — shot-towers — lightning-rods — Lombardy poplars. His treatise upon "Shades and Shadows" has immortalized him. He edited with distinguished ability the last edition of "South on the Bones." He went early to college and studied pneumatics. He then came home, talked eternally, and played upon the French horn. He patronized the bagpipes. Captain Barclay, who walked against Time, would not walk against *him*. Windham and Allbreath were his favorite writers; his favorite artist, Phiz. He died gloriously while inhaling gas—*levique flatu corrupitur*, like the *fama pudicitiae* in Hieronymus. He was indubitably a————"

"How *can* you?—how—*can*—you?"—interrupted the object of my animadversions, gasping for breath, and tearing off, with a desperate exertion, the bandage around its jaws—"how *can* you, Mr. Lackobreath, be so infernally cruel as to pinch me in that manner by the nose? Did you not see how they fastened up my mouth—and you *must* know—if you know any thing—how vast a superfluity of breath I have to dispose of! If you do *not* know, however, sit down and you shall see. In my situation it is really a great relief to be able to open one's mouth—to be able to expatiate—to be able to communicate with a person like yourself, who do not think yourself called upon at every period to interrupt the thread of a gentleman's discourse. Interruptions are annoying and should undoubtedly be abolished—don't you think so?—no reply, I beg you,—one person is enough to be speaking at a time.—I shall be done by and by, and then you may begin.—How the devil, sir, did you get into this place?—not a word I beseech you—been here some time myself—terrible accident!—heard of it, I suppose?—awful calamity!—walking under your windows—some short while ago—about the time you were stage-struck—horrible occurrence!—heard of 'catching one's breath,' eh?—hold your tongue I tell you!—I caught somebody else's!—had always too much of my own—met Blab at the corner of the street—wouldn't give me a chance for a word—couldn't get in a syllable edgeways—attacked, consequently, with epilepsis—Blab made his escape—damn all fools!—they took me up for dead, and put me in this place—pretty doings all of them!—heard all you said about me—every word a lie—horrible!—wonderful!—outrageous!—hideous!—incomprehen sible!—et cetera—et cetera—et cetera—et cetera—"

It is impossible to conceive my astonishment at so unexpected a discourse; or the joy with which I became gradually convinced that the breath so fortunately caught by the gentleman (whom I soon* recognized as my neighbor Windenough) was, in fact, the identical expiration mislaid by myself in the conversation with my wife. Time, place, and circumstance rendered it a matter beyond question. I did not, however, immediately release my hold upon Mr. W.'s proboscis—not at least during the long period in which the inventor of Lombardy poplars continued to favor me with his explanations.

In this respect I was actuated by that habitual prudence which has ever been my predominating trait. I reflected that many difficulties might still lie in the path of my preservation which only extreme exertion on my part would be able to surmount. Many persons, I considered, are prone to estimate commodities in their possession—however valueless to the then proprietor—however troublesome, or distressing—in direct ratio with the advantages to be derived by others from their attainment, or by themselves from their abandonment. Might not this be the case with Mr. Windenough? In displaying anxiety for the breath of which he was at present so willing to get rid, might I not lay myself open to the exactions of his avarice? There are scoundrels in this world, I remembered with a sigh, who will not scruple to take unfair opportunities with even a next-door neighbor, and (this remark is from Epictetus) it is precisely at that time when men are most anxious to throw off the burden of their own calamities that they feel the least desirous of relieving them in others.

Upon considerations similar to these, and still retaining my grasp upon the nose of Mr. W., I accordingly thought proper to model my reply.

"Monster!" I began in a tone of the deepest indignation—"monster and double-winded idiot!—dost *thou*, whom for thine iniquities it has pleased heaven to accurse with a twofold respiration—dost *thou*, I say, presume to address me in the familiar language of an old acquaintaince?—'I lie,' forsooth! and 'hold my tongue,' to be sure!—pretty conversation, indeed, to a gentleman with a single breath!—all this, too, when I have it in my power to relieve the calamity under which thou dost so justly suffer—to curtail the superfluities of thine unhappy respiration."

Like Brutus, I paused for a reply—with which, like a tornado, Mr. Windenough immediately overwhelmed me. Protestation followed upon protestation, and apology upon apology. There were no terms with which he was unwilling to comply, and there were none of which I failed to take the fullest advantage.

Preliminaries being at length arranged, my acquaintance delivered me the respiration; for which (having carefully examined it) I gave him afterward a receipt.

I am aware that by many I shall be held to blame for speaking, in a manner so cursory, of a transaction so impalpable. It will be thought that I should have entered more minutely into the details of an occurrence by which—and this is very true—much new light might be thrown upon a highly interesting branch of physical philosophy.

To all this I am sorry that I cannot reply. A hint is the only answer which I am permitted to make. There were *circumstances*—but I think it much safer upon consideration to say as little as possible about an affair so delicate—*so delicate*, I repeat, and at the time involving the interests of a third party whose sulphurous resentment I have not the least desire, at this moment, of incurring.

We were not long after this necessary arrangement in effecting an escape from the dungeons of the sepulchre. The united strength of our resuscitated voices was soon sufficiently apparent. Scissors, the Whig editor, republished a treatise upon "the nature and origin of subterranean noises." A reply—rejoinder—confutation—and justification—followed in the columns of a Democratic gazette. It was not until the opening of the vault to decide the controversy, that the appearance of Mr. Windenough and myself proved both parties to have been decidedly in the wrong.

I cannot conclude these details of some very singular passages in a life at all times sufficiently eventful, without again recalling to the attention of the reader the merits of that indiscriminate philosophy which is sure and ready shield against those shafts of calamity which can neither be seen, felt, nor fully understood. It was in the spirit of this wisdom that, among the ancient Hebrews, it was believed the gates of Heaven would be inevitably opened to that sinner, or saint who, with good lungs and implicit confidence, should vociferate the word *"Amen!"* It was in the spirit of this wisdom that, when a great plague raged at Athens, and every means had been in vain attempted for its removal, Epimenides, as Laërtius relates, in his second book, of that philosopher, advised the erection of a shrine and temple "to the proper God."

Poe is one of the few American authors known to have taken opium, for it was not commonly used by Americans at the time. One must look to England to find literary luminaries who used the drug: George Crabbe, Coleridge, De Quincey, Francis Thompson, Elizabeth Barrett Browning, Rossetti, and Swinburne, among others. Many of them spoke of opium in terms singularly similar to the eulogies of today's LSD advocates. A measure of how drugs were accepted in England and America is provided by the most admired hero of Victorian literature—himself the creation of a physician—who relaxed at the Baker Street flat after his bouts with Professor Moriarity by summoning Dr. Watson to prepare him a needle (King, 1972, p. 17). De Quincey (1822) defended the user in his *Confessions of an English Opium Eater*: "The opium-eater loses none of his moral responsibilities or aspirations; he wishes and longs as earnestly as ever to realize what he believes possible, and feels to be exacted by duty" (p. 163). But Cohen (1968) suggests that opium was not the source of creativity of these poets, that they were gifted long before their drug encounter. Coleridge, after his experience with opium, bitterly called it "an accursed habit, a wretched vice, a species of madness, a derangement, an utter impotence of the volition." Long before the British poets found the drug, Homer (9th Century B.C.) mentioned it in the *Iliad*, where he described the effect of the cup of Helen as "inducing forgetfulness of pain and the sense of evil. . .''; and Virgil (70-19 B.C.) mentioned the sleep-bringing poppy in the *Georgics* and again in the *Anead* (Libre 4, Verse 486).

Scher (1966) points out that it is a gross exaggeration uniformly to classify all self-prescribing drug users as addicts. "So varied, complex, and changing is drug use, depending on shifting styles of use or abuse, altering availability, the introduction of new agents, changing group structure, membership, or mores in one location or different sections of the country, as well as police or legislative intensification, that the picture is one of kaleidescopic twists and turns at any particular moment" (p. 540). Thus in the England of the 1860's and 1870's, as depicted in John Fowles' (1969) novel, *The French Lieutenant's Woman*, Mrs. Poulteney, a rigidly devout woman, nicknamed the Abbess, is an opium addict. The author intervenes in the narrative in three ways: as a character, as a kind of Greek chorus commentator, and as *deus ex machina*. As commentator, he constantly relates his story and characters to history, physically, and in psychological and political terms. Thus, Mrs. Poulteney "was an opium-addict—but before you think I am wildly sacrificing plausibility to sensation, let me quickly add that she did not know it. What we call opium she called laudanum. A shrewd, if blasphemous, doctor of the time called it Our-Lordanum, since many a nineteenth century lady—and less, for the medicine was cheap enough (in the form of Godfrey's Cordial) to help all classes get through that black night of womankind—sipped it a good deal more frequently than Communion wine. It was, in short, a very near equivalent of our own age's sedative pills. Why Mrs. Poulteney should have been an inhabitant of the Victorian valley of the dolls we need not inquire, but it is to the point that laudanum, as Coleridge once discovered, gives vivid dreams. I cannot imagine what Bosch-like picture of Ware Commons Mrs. Poulteney had built up over the years; what satanic orgies she divined behind every tree, what French abominations under every leaf. But I think we may safely say that it has become the objective correlative of all that went on in her own subconscious" (p. 92).

Terry and Pellens (1928) stated that "no drug has been applied to so wide a variety of uses as has opium nor has any given rise to so much discussion and controversy as to qualities and therapeutic indications, the form of which it is best given, and the manifold advantages of its use; scarcely a disease exists for which it has not been advocated enthusiastically by some writer" (p. 59). And to moralize to an opium addict, wrote the French litterateur, Cocteau (1957), is like saying to Tristan, "Kill Iseult. You will feel much better afterwards. To say to an addict who is in a continual state of euphoria that he is degrading himself is like saying of marble that it is spoilt by Michelangelo, of canvas that it is stained by Raphael, of paper that it is soiled by Shakespeare, of silence that it is broken by Bach."

While opium increases sexual activity at first, accompanied by voluptuous fantasies and visions, continued indulgence produces impotence (Bloch, 1933). And although indulgence in opium is very frequently a group activity, it is also, in a very real sense, a solitary activity, for the "high" is an unsharable experience, unlike methamphetamine (Methedrine) or marijuana where the "high" may be socially or sexually shared (Scher, 1966). Physiologically, the reproductive organs present well-defined disturbances as a result of opium and opium derivative use. "Striking changes in both the physiologic and psychic functions of sex come about. Cessation of menstruation occurs in the female, with atrophy and cessation of the function of the mammae. Psychically, this is accompanied by more or less complete loss of all sexual desire, and of the emotions associated with sex. In the male, in advanced cases of morphinism, complete sexual impotence is frequently seen. Both sexes, in extreme addiction, are practically rendered emotionally asexual. On withdrawal of the drug the individual is often overwhelmed by tumultuous sex desire" (Wholey, 1924, p. 323). However, Terry and Pellins (1928) observed a number of cases where there was no diminution of sexual activity nor complete cessation of menstruation. Along with the exhaustion of sexual ability, impotence, and amenorrhea, the physical symptoms of prolonged use of opium may take the form of insomnia, anorexia, diarrhea alternating with constipation, gross muscular tremors, cardiac weakness, miosis, paresthesias, sensation of coldness, memory impairment, and inability to concentrate. Yet André Malraux (1933) ascribes to the sixty-year-old, opium addicted Gisors in *Man's Fate* quite other qualities: "For twenty years he has used his intelligence to win the affection of men by justifying them, and they were grateful to him for a kindness which they did not suspect had its roots in opium. People attributed to him the patience of a Buddhist: it was the patience of an addict" (p. 46).

Heroin addiction, it would seem, is as intractable a malady as heart disease or cancer. As has been noted, the complexity of the drug abuse problem usually leads to oversimplification. Very little controlled data exist concerning the sexuality of heroin addicts; most of the information comes from the addicts themselves, an obviously unreliable source. Knight (1937) states that addicts tend to be docile and passive, Bender (1963) that they are dependent and nonaggressive. Freeman's (1953) subjects were characterized by feelings of alienation and of being different. Isbell (1955) considers opiate taking as associated with an abnormal personality structure. Kolb (1962) suggests that neurotics use drugs to relieve their anxiety, psychopaths for the euphoriant effects, and psychotics to suppress their delusions. Fort (1954) finds that heroin addicts seek goals beyond their reach, particularly in the creative fields. Zimmering (1951) describes the heroin addict as nonaggressive, soft-spoken, verbally apt, unable to develop genuine human relationships, immature, easily moved to extreme emotional reactions, unable to tolerate frustration, frequently self-condemnatory and self-excusing, and marked by externalization and holding others, from the past and present, solely responsible for his plight.

A comparison was made by Gilbert and Lombardi (1967) of the personality characteristics, as measured by the MMPI, of forty-five young male narcotic addicts and forty-five nonaddicted males of similar socioeconomic levels. "Although some maladjustment existed in both groups, results suggest deep-seated and widespread pathology among the addicts. The most outstanding characteristics of the addict seem to be his psychopathic traits. He appears to be the kind of irresponsible, undependable, egocentric individual who disregards social mores, acts on impulse, and demands immediate gratification of his wants. He is impatient and irritable, lacks the persistence to achieve a goal, and will act out aggressively against authority ... [which] may then be followed by feelings of guilt and depression that can be alleviated only by more drugs. He tends to be hypersensitive, tense, apprehensive, insecure, and self-conscious, and he has trouble forming warm and lasting emotional relationships. He becomes depressed readily, lacks self-confidence, has poor morale, and finds it difficult to achieve a normal optimism with regard to the future; thus, the use of drugs may seem to him to be the only realistic solution to his problems" (p. 536).

There seems to be little for the addict to elevate his spirits more than the heroin he shoots up, the coke he snorts, or the tab he drops. They enable him to languish in a paradise of aphrodisiac dreams and debauch himself in lotus-land. For the drug user, libido is displaced onto the packet of heroin (Savitt, 1963). The heroin may be a substitute for and a defense against sexual feelings that provoke anxiety. It does not simply reduce inhibitions, as can marijuana and hashish, and allow the acting out of suppressed desires—it actually removes the desires. "It produces, in effect, nirvana. If nirvana is a place or state of oblivion to care, pain, or external reality, then the negative relationship of heroin to sex becomes clearer. Heroin . . . furnishes the ultimate in tranquilization. It leaves no anxieties to act upon—sexual or otherwise" (Mathis, 1970, p. 109). Thus it is the sexual desire, not necessarily the ability, that is totally destroyed by the psychophysiological function of heroin.

The needle junkie in William Burroughs' (1959) *Naked Lunch* says, "I am forgetting sex and all sharp pleasures of the body—a grey, junk-bound ghost" (p. 66). Old Doc Benway, the director of the heroin Reconditioning Center in the novel, expatiates on the junkies who are standing in groups in their quarters: "If all pleasure is relief from tension, junk affords relief from the whole life process, in disconnecting the hypothalamus, which is the center of psychic energy and libido. Some of my learned colleagues (nameless assholes) have suggested that junk derives its euphoric effect from direct stimulation of the orgasm center. It seems more probable that junk suspends the whole cycle of tension, discharge and rest. The orgasm has no function in the junky. Boredom, which always indicates an undischarged tension, never troubles the addict. He can look at his shoe for eight hours. He is only roused to action when the hourglass of junk runs out" (p. 35).

While heroin and morphine render the addict totally impotent during its use, Kinsey, Pomeroy, and Martin (1948) observed, "Among men who have suddenly been deprived of some drug to which they have been addicted, nocturnal emissions may occur several times in each of twenty-four hours, for two or three weeks or more" (p. 521). Heroin is more of an anaphrodisiac than even alcohol and barbituates, and the first sign of true addiction is permanent impotence and a total lack of interest in sex; a heroin diet seems to "solve" sexual problems by removing sex entirely (Wilson, 1973, pp. 19, 202). With the extinguished interest in love and sex, the heroin addict distorts his sexual life. "Many men feel like sexual giants under the influence of heroin [because they have been] reared in the tradition of the ideal . . . of the extended, rigid penis [and they] derive a special nobility in their own minds from their capacity to outlast any woman or even several women" (Fiddle, 1967, p. 84). The inability to ejaculate does not trouble the strongly addicted heroin user, but when he is on a maintenance dose and possibly suffering from premature ejaculation, this staying power is prized (Dahlberg, 1971).

Disturbances in sexual appetite and performance of fifty-three present and former heroin addicts were investigated by Cushman (1972, pp. 1262-1263). The interviews disclosed a high incidence of libido, potency, and ejaculation difficulties. The most common problem, reported by sixty-eight per cent, was a delay in ejaculation time beyond twenty-five minutes. Five patients were unable to ejaculate at all in at least fifty per cent of their attempts at sexual intercourse. Reduction in libido during heroin use in general was reported by sixty-five per cent of the population. The possible aphrodisiac effect of heroin was rare and seemed to be inconsistent in those subjects claiming it. Cushman comments that significant alterations in human sexual appetite and performance appear to accompany the process of heroin addiction. The admission of sexual difficulties by a group of heroin addicts, abstinent, and methadone-treated addicts during casual interviews confirmed his clinical impression. "Since the heroin addict is often unreliable in reporting an accurate history, and since males seldom easily volunteer information concerning their sexual inadequacies, it is not possible to estimate the true frequency of sexual disturbances in this series of hardcore heroin addicts. However, the prevalence of disturbed sexual performance must be rather high for only 24 per cent to claim fully normal sexual function. The disturbances reported most commonly are difficulty in achieving orgasm, loss of potency, and reduced libido. The roles of heroin, morphine, methadone or narcotic addiction in these sexual disturbances could not be defined. However, morphine itself may have been a contributory factor since (1) all patients said they were normal before narcotics use; (2) many patients reported that during sedation or euphoria induced by heroin, sexual performance and desire were reduced; (3) the patients in the narcotic-withdrawal syndrome usually disregarded sexual opportunities in favor of a more compelling drive to obtain narcotics; and (4) reversal of sexual problems rapidly occurred during enforced abstinence from narcotics. It should be emphasized that factors other than addicting drugs themselves may have been important in the sexual experiences of these patients" (Cushman, 1972, pp. 1264-1265).

One of the psychological factors seen in young heroin addicts is profound distortion of sexual identification. The family backgrounds of the population reviewed by Chein et al. (1964) appear to demonstrate the genesis of this confusion in sexual identity—a confusion by no means unique to the future heroin addict—but its role in the etiology of drug abuse is unclear. Many other social and individual factors coalesce to produce the narcotics addict. The male addict's "extremely ambivalent attitude toward the female, the confusion of sexual identity, the inability to relate sexually . . . all indicate an early and pervasive disturbance in the mother-child relationship. This is further evidenced by an unreal attitude toward the actual mother," according to Mathis (1970). "The addict is usually a staunch supporter of motherhood and very verbal in his concern for his own mother's welfare, while simultaneously making life miserable for her in every possible way. His ambivalence toward the mother figure is almost schizophrenic in nature" (p. 104). The ambivalent relationship between addict and mother is pointed up by Gerard and Kornetsky (1954) in a study in which they describe the regressive, manipulative, and seductive features of the relationship. Forty per cent of the mothers of the addicts were excessively controlling and strict; forty-eight per cent were excessively indulgent and nondisciplining; and twenty-four per cent were seductive. The findings of Mason (1958) validate these. Mothers he treated were controlling, overpowering, overprotective, guilt-ridden, unhappy and generally had profound hostile and aggressive feelings toward their children; but at the same time, they were unable to separate from them and grant them their independence. "The adjectives to describe them are numerous: narcissistic, inconsistent, rejecting, teasing, seductive, controlling, manipulative, and so on

... These mothers, because of their own problems, stimulate aggressive and sexual drives in their children and then proceed ... to deny and disapprove of them ... Their negative attitudes turn (their protective behavior) into controlling and domineering castrating behavior. This wavering back and forth between promise and fulfillment, on the one hand, and denial and punishment on the other, has ... a very definite place in the formation of a personality accustomed to accept pain and failure as an integral part of the promise of love. Such an extremely masochistic personality is represented by the addict, and the role of his own mother in the formation of his masochistic traits is clear" (p. 147). Savitt (1963) reports that in all of his patients "the immanence of incestuous wishes was at times an overwhelming threat which was seen as a motive for an increase in the addictive craving. There were instances of the defensive need to regress to primary narcissism where all sexual wishes, genital as well as pregenital, had to be denied. This seemed evident during the intervals of deep narcotic stupor in which libido was withdrawn from objects. During less regressed states pregenital wishes came to the fore in which the drug was equated with breast, food, warmth, and clinging" (p. 52).

While heroin might be an antidote for anxiety-producing sexual feelings, the concomitant low ego strength reduces the addict to helpless masochistic surrender. In Ed McBain's (1968) *Fuzz*, Mort Orecchio (a pun meaning, in Italian, "dead ear") is a psychotic assassin who has shot the Parks Commissioner with a telescopic lever-action carbine. In the course of investigating the site from which the shot was fired, Cotton Hawes, a detective, interrogates Polly Malloy.

He went into the apartment. She closed and locked the door behind him.

"I don't want trouble," she said. "I've had enough trouble."

"I won't give you any. I only want to know about the man down the hall."

"I know somebody got shot. Please don't get me involved in it."

They sat opposite each other, she on the bed, he on a straight-backed chair facing her. Something shimmered on the air between them, something as palpable as the tenement stink of garbage and piss surrounding them. They sat in easy informality, comfortably aware of each other's trade, Cotton Hawes detective, Polly Malloy addict. And perhaps they knew each other better than a great many people ever get to know each other. Perhaps Hawes had been inside too many shooting galleries not to understand what it was like to be this girl, perhaps he had arrested too many hookers who were screwing for the couple of bucks they needed for a bag of shit, perhaps he had watched the agonized writhings of too many cold turkey kickers, perhaps his knowledge of this junkie or any junkie was as intimate as a pusher's, perhaps he had seen too much and knew too much. And perhaps the girl had been collared too many times, had protested too many times that she was clean, had thrown too many decks of heroin under bar stools or down sewers at the approach of a cop, had been in too many different squadrooms and handled by too many different bulls, been offered the Lexington choice by too many different magistrates, perhaps her knowledge of the law as it applied to narcotics addicts was as intimate as any assistant district attorney's, perhaps she too had seen too much and knew too much. Their mutual knowledge was electric, it generated a heat lightning of its own, ascertaining the curious symbiosis of lawbreaker and enforcer, affirming the interlocking subtlety of crime and punishment. There was a secret bond in that room, an affinity—almost an empathy. They could talk to each other without any bullshit. They were like spent lovers whispering on the same pillow.

"Did you know Orecchio?" Hawes asked.

"Will you keep me clean?"

"Unless you had something to do with it."

"Nothing."

"You've got my word."

"A cop?" she asked, and smiled wanly.

"You've got my word, if you want it."

"I need it, it looks like."

"You need it, honey."

"I knew him."

"How?"

"I met him the night he moved in."

"When was that?"

"Two, three nights ago."

"Where'd you meet?"

"I was hung up real bad, I needed a fix. I just got out of Caramoor, *that* sweet hole, a week ago. I haven't had time to get really connected yet."

"What were you in for?"

"Oh, hooking."

"How old are you, Polly?"

"Nineteen. I look older, huh?"

"Yes, you look older."

"I got married when I was sixteen. To another junkie like myself. Some prize."

"What's he doing now?"

"Time at Castleview."

"For what?"

Polly shrugged. "He started pushing."

"Okay, what about Orecchio next door?"

"I asked him for a loan."

"When was this?"

"Day before yesterday."

"Did he give it to you?"

"I didn't actually ask him for a loan. I offered to turn a trick for him. He was right next door, you see, and I was pretty sick, I swear to God I don't think I coulda made it to the street."

"Did he accept?"

"He gave me ten bucks. He didn't take nothing from me for it."

"Sounds like a nice fellow."

Polly shrugged.

"Not a nice fellow?" Hawes asked.

"Let's say not my type," Polly said.

"Mm-huh."

"Let's say a son of a bitch," Polly said.

"What happened?"

"He came in here last night."

"When? What time?"

"Musta been about nine, nine-thirty."

"After the symphony started," Hawes said.

"Huh?"

"Nothing, I was just thinking out loud. Go on."

"He said he had something nice for me. He said if I came into his room, he would give me something nice."

"Did you go?"

"First I asked him what it was. He said it was something I wanted more than anything else in the world."

"But did you go into his room?"

"Yes."

"Did you seen anything out of the ordinary?"

"Like what?"

"Like a high-powered rifle with a telescopic sight."

"No, nothing like that."

"All right, what was this 'something nice' he promised you?"

"Hoss."

"He had heroin for you?"

"Yes."

"And that's why he asked you to come into his room? For the heroin?"

"That's what he said."

"He didn't attempt to sell it to you, did he?"

"No. But ..."

"Yes?"

"He made me beg for it."

"What do you mean?"

"He showed it to me, and he let me taste it to prove that it was real stuff, and then he refused to give it to me unless I ... begged for it."

"I see."

"He ... teased me for ... I guess for ... for almost two hours. He kept looking at his watch and making me ... do things."

"What kind of things?"

"Stupid things. He asked me to sing for him. He made me sing 'White Christmas,' that was supposed to be a big joke, you see, because the shit is white and he knew how bad I needed a fix, so he made me sing 'White Christmas' over and over again, I musta sung it for him six or seven times. And all the while he kept looking at his watch."

"Go ahead."

"Then he ... he asked me to strip, but ... I mean, not just take off my clothes, but ... you know, do a strip for him. And I did it. And he began ... he began making fun of me, of the way I looked, of my body. I ... he made me stand naked in front of him, and he just went on and on about how stupid and pathetic I looked, and he kept asking me if I really wanted the heroin, and then looked at his watch again, it was about eleven o'clock by then, I kept saying Yes, I want it, please let me have it, so he asked me to dance for him, he asked me to do the waltz, and then he asked me to do the shag, I didn't know what the hell he was talking about, I never even heard of the shag, have you ever heard of the shag?"

"Yes, I've heard of it," Hawes said.

"So I did all that for him, I would have done anything for him, and finally he told me to get on my knees and explain to him why I felt I really needed the bag of heroin. He said he expected me to talk for five minutes on the subject of the addict's need for narcotics, and he looked at his watch and began timing me, and I talked. I was shaking by this time, I had the chills, I needed a shot more than..."

Polly closed her eyes. "I began crying. I talked and cried, and at last he looked at his watch and said, 'Your five minutes are up. Here's your poison, now get the hell out of here.' And he threw the bag to me."

"What time was this?"

"It musta been about ten minutes after eleven. I don't have a watch, I hocked it long ago, but you can see the big electric numbers on top of the Mutual Building from my room, and when I was shooting up later it was 11:15, so this musta been about ten after or thereabouts."

"And he kept looking at his watch all through this, huh?"

"Yes. As if he had a date or something."

"He did," Hawes said.

"Huh?"

"He had a date to shoot a man from his window. He was just amusing himself until the concert broke. A nice fellow, Mr. Orecchio."

"I got to say one thing for him," Polly said.

"What's that?"

"It was good stuff." A wistful look came onto her face and into her eyes. "It was some of the best stuff I've had in years. I wouldn't have heard a *cannon* if it went off next door" [pp. 73-78].

Burroughs' knowledgeable junkie in *Naked Lunch* says, "It is doubtful if shame can exist in the absence of sexual libido . . . The junky's shame disappears with his non-sexual sociability which is also dependent on libido . . . The addict regards his body impersonally as an instrument to absorb the medium in which he lives, evaluates his tissue with the cold hands of a horse trader" (p. 67). Jilly, the poor-rich girl runaway whom Harry Angstrom takes in, in John Updike's (1971) *Rabbit Redux*, introduces Harry to the world of drugs. She tells him that the man she ran away with tried to get her into heavy drugs, acid, heroin and strange pills, but she was able to repulse him. "I would never let him break my skin. I figured, anything went in by the mouth, I could throw up, but anything went in my veins, I had no way to get rid of it, it could kill me. He said that was part of the kick. He was really freaked, but he had this, you know, power over me. I ran . . . Junkies . . . get to be bores. You think they're talking to you or making love or whatever, and then you realize they're looking over your shoulder for the next fix. You realize you're nothing . . ." (p. 145).

In a letter to Fliess in December 1897, Freud emphasized the link between addiction and masturbation. "It has dawned on me that masturbation is the one major habit, the 'primal addiction' and that it is only as a substitute and replacement for it that the other addictions—for alcohol, morphine, tobacco, etc.—come into existence..." (p. 272). The sexual implications of needle puncture as such and of needle sharing, go beyond any pure feelings of brotherhood and closeness. Time and again, heroin addicts describe the effects of their injection in sexual terms. "One addict said that after a fix he felt as if he were coming in every pore. Another said that he used to inject the solution in a rhythmic fashion until it was all used up, and said this was akin to masturbation albeit much better" (Hoffman, 1964, p. 268). Thirty-six intravenous drug users in Haight-Ashbury were questioned by Howard and Borges (1971) with regard to needle sharing. Sixty-four per cent reported there were sexual overtones related to needle use that either they or others involved had experienced. Seventeen per cent described the rush as orgasmic, and nineteen per cent drew the analogy between the penetration of the needle and the penetration of a penis. The needle was repeatedly described as a phallic symbol, and letting the blood in and out of the needle as like masturbating. "The initial rush derived from intravenously injected heroin is described as 'a warm, drifting sensation'" (Gay and Sheppard, 1973, p. 136). What becomes evident is that pharmacogenic attainment of pleasure initiates an artificial sexual organization which is autoerotic and modeled on infantile masturbation (Rado, 1933).

The interaction between pusher and addict, demonstrating the symbiotic relationship that can exist between them, as well as the intense sadism and sense of power of the former and the abject, dependent character of the latter, is manifest in Nelson Algren's (1949) *The Man with the Golden Arm*. Frankie Machine—all-around dealer, card sharp, dice man, and pool shooter—and Louie the Fixer are locked in a relationship which they do not begin to understand. Louie, the impotent fixer-voyeur, and Frankie, the morphine-masturbator, are both aroused by the injection of the needle and the orgasmic moment of the morphine hit. "Hit me, Fixer. Hit me," Frankie pleads but Louie likes to draw his pleasure out. "Louie waited ... Louie liked to see the stuff hit. It meant a lot to Louie, seeing it hit."

> ... By the time Frankie got inside the room he was so weak Louie had to help him onto the army cot beside the oil stove. He lay on his

back with one arm flung across his eyes as if in shame; and his lips were blue with cold. The pain had hit him with an icy fist in the groin's very pit, momentarily tapering off to a single probing finger touching the genitals to get the maximum of pain. He tried twisting to get away from the finger: the finger was worse than the fist. His throat was so dry that, though he spoke, the lips moved and made no sound. But Fomorowski read such lips well.

"Fix me. Make it stop. Fix me."

"I'll fix you, Dealer," Louie assured him softly.

Louie had his own bedside manner. He perched on the red leather and chrome bar stool borrowed from the Safari, with the amber toes of his two-tone shoes catching the light and the polo ponies galloping down his shirt. This was Nifty Louie's Hour. The time when he did the dealing and the dealer had to take what Louie chose to toss him in Louie's own good time.

He lit a match with his fingertip and held it away from the bottom of the tiny glass tube containing the fuzzy white cap of morphine, holding it just far enough away to keep the cap from being melted by the flame. There was time and time and lots of time for that. Let the dealer do a bit of melting first; the longer it took the higher the price. "You can pay me off when Zero pays you," he assured Frankie. There was no hurry. "You're good with me any time, Dealer."

Frankie moaned like an animal that cannot understand its own pain. His shirt had soaked through and the pain had frozen so deep in his bones nothing could make him warm again.

"Hit me, Fixer. Hit me."

A sievelike smile drained through Louie's teeth. This was his hour and this hour didn't come every day. He snuffed out the match's flame as it touched his fingers and snapped the head of another match into flame with his nail, letting its glow flicker one moment over that sievelike smile; then brought the tube down cautiously and watched it dissolve at the flame's fierce touch. When the stuff had melted he held both needle and tube in one hand, took the dealer's loose-hanging arm firmly with the other and pumped it in a long, loose arc. Frankie let him swing it as if it were attached to someone else. The cold was coming *up* from within now: a colorless cold spreading through stomach and liver and breathing across the heart like an odorless gas. To make the very brain tighten and congeal under its icy touch.

"Warm. Make me warm."

And still there was no rush, no hurry at all. Louie pressed the hypo down to the cotton; the stuff came too high these days to lose the fraction of a drop. "Don't vomit, student," he taunted Frankie to remind him of the first fix he'd had after his discharge — but it was too cold to answer. He was falling between glacial walls, he didn't know how anyone could fall so far away from everyone else in the world. So far to fall, so cold all the way, so steep and dark between those morphine-colored walls of Private McGantic's terrible pit.

He couldn't feel Louie probing into the dark red knot above his elbow at all. Nor see the way the first blood sprayed faintly up into the delicate hypo to tinge the melted morphine with blood as warm as the needle's heated point.

When Louie sensed the vein he pressed it down with the certainty of a good doctor's touch, let it linger a moment in the vein to give the heart what it needed and withdrew gently, daubed the blood with a piece of cotton, tenderly, and waited.

Louie waited. Waited to see it hit.

Louie liked to see the stuff hit. It meant a lot to Louie, seeing it hit.

"Sure I like to watch," he was ready to acknowledge any time. "Man, their *eyes* when that big drive hits 'n goes tinglin' down to the toes. They retch, they sweat, they itch — then the big drive hits 'n here they come out of it cryin' like a baby 'r laughin' like a loon. *Sure* I like to watch. *Sure* I like to see it hit. Heroin got the drive awright — but there's not a tingle to a ton — you got to get M to get that tingle-tingle."

It hit all right. It hit the heart like a runaway locomotive, it hit like a falling wall. Frankie's whole body lifted with that smashing surge, the very heart seemed to lift up-up-up then rolled over and he slipped into a long warm bath with one long orgasmic sigh of relief. Frankie opened his eyes.

He was in a room. Somebody's dust-colored wavy-walled room and he wasn't quite dead after all. He had died, had felt himself fall away and die but now he wasn't dead any more. Just sick. But not too sick. He wasn't going to be really sick, he wasn't a student any more. Maybe he wasn't going to be sick at all, he was beginning to feel just right.

Then it went over him like a dream where everything is love and he wasn't even sweating. All he had to do the rest of his life was to lie right here feeling better and better with every beat of his heart till he'd never felt so good in all his life.

"Wow," he grinned gratefully at Louie, "that was one good *whan*."

"I seen it," Louie boasted smugly. "I seen it was one good *whan*" — and lapsed into the sort of impromptu jargon which pleases junkies for no reason they can say — "vraza-s'vraza-s'vraza — it was one good *whan-whan-whan*." He dabbed a silk handkerchief at a blob of blood oozing where the needle had entered Frankie's arm.

"There's a silver buck and buck 'n a half in change in my jacket pocket," Frankie told him lazily. "I'm feelin' too good to get up 'n get it myself."

Louie reached in the pocket with the handkerchief bound about his palm and plucked the silver out. Two-fifty for a quarter grain wasn't too high. He gave Frankie the grin that drained through the teeth for a receipt. The dealer was coming along nicely these days, thank you.

The dealer didn't know that yet, of course. That first fix had only cost him a dollar, it had quieted the everlasting dull ache in his stomach and sent him coasting one whole week end. So what was the use of spending forty dollars in the bars when you could do better at home on one? That was how Frankie had it figured *that* week end. To Louie, listening close, he'd already talked like a twenty-dollar-a-day man.

Given a bit of time.

And wondered idly now where in the world the dealer would get that kind of money when the day came that he'd need half a C just to taper off. He'd get it all right. They always got it. He'd seen them coming in the rain, the unkjays with their peculiarly rigid, panicky walk, wearing some policeman's castoff rubbers, no socks at all, a pair of Salvation Army pants a size too small or a size too large and a pajama top for a shirt — but with twenty dollars clutched in the sweating palm for that big twenty-dollar fix.

"Nothing can take the place of junk — just junk" — the dealer would learn. As Louie himself had learned long ago.

Louie was the best fixer of them all because he knew what it was to need to get well. Louie had had a big habit — he was one man who could tell you you lied if you said no junkie could kick the habit once he was hooked. For Louie was the one junkie in ten thousand who'd kicked it and kicked it for keeps.

He'd taken the sweat cure in a little Milwaukee Avenue hotel room cutting himself down, as he put it, "from monkey to zero." From three full grains a day to one, then a half of that and a half of that straight down to zero, though he'd been half out of his mind with the pain two nights running and was so weak, for days after, that he could hardly tie his own shoelaces.

Back on the street at last, he'd gotten the chuck horrors: for two full days he'd eaten candy bars, sweet rolls and strawberrry malteds. It had seemed that there would be no end to his hunger for sweets.

Louie never had the sweet-roll horrors any more. Yet sometimes himself sensed that something had twisted in his brain in those nights when he'd gotten the monkey off his back on Milwaukee Avenue.

"*Habit? Man,*" he liked to remember, "I had a great *big* habit. One time I knocked out one of my own teet' to get the gold for a fix. You call that bein' hooked or not? *Hooked?* Man, I wasn't hooked, I was *crucified*. The monkey got so big he was carrying *me*. 'Cause the way it starts is like this, students: you let the habit feed you first 'n one morning you wake up 'n you're feedin' the habit.

"But don't tell *me* you can't kick it if you *want* to. When I hear a junkie tell me he wants to kick the habit but he just can't I know he lies even if *he* don't know he does. He *wants* to carry the monkey, he's punishin' hisself for somethin' 'n don't even know it. It's what I was doin' for six years, punishin' myself for things I'd done 'n thought I'd forgot. So I told myself how I wasn't to blame for what I done in the first place, I was only tryin' to live like everyone else 'n doin' them things was the only way I had of livin'. Then I got forty grains 'n went up to the room 'n went from monkey to nothin' in twenny-eight days 'n that's nine-ten years ago 'n the monkey's dead."

"The monkey's never dead, Fixer," Frankie told him knowingly.

Louie glanced at Frankie slyly. "You know that awready, Dealer? You know how he don't die? It's what they say awright, the monkey never dies. When you kick him off he just hops onto somebody else's back." Behind the film of glaze that always veiled Louie's eyes Frankie saw the twisted look. "*You* got my monkey, Dealer? You take my nice old monkey away from me? Is that my monkey ridin' your back these days, Dealer?"

The color had returned to Frankie's cheeks, he felt he could make it almost any minute now. "No more for me, Fixer," he assured Louie confidently. "Somebody else got to take your monkey. I had the Holy Jumped-up-Jesus Horrors for real this time — 'n I'm one guy knows when he got enough. I learned my lesson but *good*. Fixer — you just give the boy with the golden arm his very lastest fix" [pp. 56-60].

But Frankie was hooked. A short time later, the reader learns "... for the second time in the week he had his last, final and never-again fix. This time he was through and he meant it" (p. 152).

An authoritative account of the specific effects of the opiates—or other drugs—on sexual behavior and response cannot be given. Drugs may serve to release repressed behavior, thus permitting acting out of sexual fantasies, or drugs may serve as a replacement for sex, and the needle puncture may allude to phallic symbolism in terms of its vividly described orgasmic rush. Psychoactive drugs do not have uniform effects; they vary from person to person and from time to time in the same person. The effects change with the dose, with the expectations and desires of the user, and with the setting. Further, no study has been made of the sexual effects of drugs under controlled laboratory conditions. The only data available are anecdotal and derive from survey information. Addicts generally report a diminution of libido. Some of the drug users may have turned to narcotics in an attempt to defend against sexual desires. A number report enhanced sexual performance inasmuch as the opiate delays or blocks ejaculation entirely, thus prolonging coitus indefinitely. Whether the drug is a mind-expanding, mind-blowing, mind-bending and mind-transcending hallucinogen, or a desensitizing drug such as heroin or morphine, or a potion of Aphrodite, the use of any of them, whether to flee from the sexual self or to enhance sexual performance, is a measure of the individual's attempt to grapple with his sexual and personal problems.

TECHNICAL REFERENCES

Bender, L. (1963), Drug addiction in adolescence. *Comprehensive Psychiatry,* 4: 181-194.

Bloch, I. (1933), *Strange Sexual Practices.* New York: Falstaff.

Bonaparte, M. (1949), *The Life and Works of Edgar Allan Poe. A Psycho-Analytic Interpretation.* London: Imago.

Chein, I., Gerard, D., Lee, R. & Rosenfeld, E. (1964), *The Road to H. Narcotics, Delinquency, and Social Policy.* New York: Basic Books.

Cocteau, J. (1957), *Opium.* London: Owen.

Cohen, S. (1968), The cyclic psychedelics. *American Journal of Psychiatry,* 125: 393-394.

Cushman, P., Jr. (1972), Sexual behavior in heroin addiction and methadone maintenance. *New York State Journal of Medicine,* 72:1261-1265.

Dahlberg, C. C. (1971), Sexual behavior in the drug culture. *Medical Aspects of Human Sexuality,* 5(4):64-71.

De Quincey, T. (1822), *Confessions of an English Opium Eater.* New York: Mershon.

Fiddle, S. (1967), *Portraits from a Shooting Gallery. Life Styles from the Drug Addict World.* New York: Harper & Row.

Fort, J. P. (1954), Heroin addiction among young men. *Psychiatry,* 17:251-259.

Freeman, H. (1953), *Report at New York Academy of Medicine, Conference on Drug Addiction among Adolescents.* New York: Blakiston.

Freud, S. (1887-1902), Extracts from the Fliess papers. *Standard Edition,* 1:175-280. London: Hogarth Press, 1959, Letter 79.

——— (1910), Leonardo da Vinci and a memory of his childhood. *Standard Edition,* 11:59-137. London: Hogarth Press, 1957.

Gay, G. R. & Sheppard, C. W. (1973), "Sex-crazed dope fiends" — myth or reality? *Drug Forum,* 2:125-140.

Gerard, D. L. & Kornetsky, C. (1954), A social and psychiatric study of adolescent opiate addicts. *Psychiatric Quarterly,* 28:113-125.

Gilbert, J. B. & Lombardi, D. N. (1967), Personality characteristics of young male narcotic addicts. *Journal of Consulting Psychology,* 31:536-538.

Hoffman, M. (1964), Drug addiction and "hypersexuality": Related modes of mastery. *Comprehensive Psychiatry,* 5:262-270.

Howard, J. & Borges, P. (1971), Needle sharing in the Haight: Some social and psychological functions. *Journal of Psychedelic Drugs,* 4:71-80.

Isbell, H. (1955), Medical aspects of opiate addiction. *Bulletin of the New York Academy of Medicine,* 31:886-901.

King, R. (1972), *The Drug Hang-Up.* New York: Norton.

Kinsey, A. C., Pomeroy, W. B. & Martin, C. E. (1948), *Sexual Behavior in the Human Male.* Philadelphia: Saunders.

Knight, R. P. (1937), The psychodynamics of chronic alcoholism. *Journal of Nervous and Mental Disease,* 86:538-548.

Kolb, L. (1962), *Drug Addiction: A Medical Problem.* Springfield, Ill.: Charles C Thomas.

Mason, P. (1958), The mother of the addict. *Psychiatric Quarterly Supplement,* 32:189-199.

Masters, R. E. L. (1962), *Forbidden Sexual Behavior and Morality.* New York: Lancer.

Mathis, J. L. (1970), Sexual aspects of heroin addiction. *Medical Aspects of Human Sexuality,* 4(9):98-109.

Rado, S. (1933), The psychoanalysis of pharmacothymia (drug addiction). *Psychoanalytic Quarterly,* 2:1-23.

——— (1957), Narcotic bondage. *American Journal of Psychiatry,* 114:165-168.

Savitt, R. A. (1963), Psychoanalytic studies on addiction: Ego structure in narcotic addiction. *Psychoanalytic Quarterly,* 32:43-57.

Scher, J. (1966), Patterns and profiles of drug addiction and drug abuse. *Archives of General Psychiatry,* 15:539-551.

Terry, C. E. & Pellens, M. (1928), *The Opium Problem.* Montclair, N.J.: Patterson Smith, 1970.

Wholey, C. C. (1924), The mental and nervous side of addiction to narcotic drugs. *Journal of the American Medical Association,* 83:321-324.

Wilson, R. A. (1973), *Sex and Drugs. A Journey Beyond Limits.* Chicago: Playboy Press.

Yorke, C. (1970), A critical review of some psychoanalytic literature on drug addiction. *British Journal of Medical Psychology*, 43:141-159.

Zimmering, P. (1951), Heroin addiction in adolescent boys. *Journal of Nervous and Mental Disease*, 114:19-34.

LITERARY REFERENCES

Algren, Nelson (1949), *The Man with the Golden Arm*. Garden City, N.Y.: Doubleday.

Burroughs, William S. (1959), *Naked Lunch*. New York: Grove Press.

Fowles, John (1969), *The French Lieutenant's Woman*. Boston: Little, Brown.

Malrauz, André (1933), *Man's Fate*. New York: Modern Library, 1934.

McBain, Ed (1968), *Fuzz*. Garden City, N.Y.: Doubleday.

Poe, Edgar Allan (1835), Loss of breath. In: *The Complete Works of Edgar Allan Poe,* ed. N. H. Dole. Akron, Ohio: Werner, 1908, pp. 186-204.

_____ (1838), Ligeia. In: *The Best Tales of Edgar Allan Poe*. New York: Modern Library, 1924, pp. 134-152.

Updike, John (1971), *Rabbit Redux*. New York: Random House.

Credits

Index

I. TECHNICAL WRITERS

II. CREATIVE AUTHORS

III. LITERARY WORKS

IV. SUBJECT INDEX